MW00448686

The Company of the Preachers

A History of Biblical Preaching from the Old Testament to the Modern Era

Volume 1

The Company

of the

Preachers

A History of Biblical Preaching from the Old Testament to the Modern Era

Volume 1

David L. Larsen

Kregel
Academic & Professional

The Company of the Preachers: A History of Biblical Preaching from the Old Testament to the Modern Era, Vol. 1

Copyright © 1998 by David L. Larsen

Published by Kregel Publications, a division of Kregel, Inc., P.O. Box 2607, Grand Rapids, MI 49501. Kregel Publications provides trusted, biblical publications for Christian growth and service. Your comments and suggestions are valued.

All rights reserved. No part of this book may be reproduced, stored in a retrieval system, or transmitted in any form or by any means—electronic, mechanical, photocopy, recording, or otherwise—without written permission of the publisher, except for brief quotations in printed reviews.

Unless otherwise indicated, Scripture quotations are taken from the *Holy Bible: New International Version*®. Copyright © 1973, 1978, 1984 by International Bible Society. Used by permission of Zondervan Publishing House. All rights reserved.

Cover illustration: Patrick Kelley

ISBN 0-8254-3085-2

Printed in the United States of America

For the churches we have served
and the students we have taught.

*Because of the truth that lives in us
and will be with us forever.*
—2 John 2

Contents

	Preface	9
Introduction:	The Postulates of Preaching	11
Chapter One:	The Gestation Period of Biblical Preaching	19
Chapter Two:	The Glorious Birth of Christian Preaching	37
Chapter Three:	The Infancy and Childhood of Biblical Preaching (A.D. 70–450)	63
Chapter Four:	The Adolescence of Biblical Preaching (A.D. 450–1450)	95
Chapter Five:	The Reformation—Preaching Comes of Age	141
Chapter Six:	The Ripening Maturity of Biblical Preaching in the Seventeenth Century	199
Chapter Seven:	The Robust Days of the Puritan Pulpit	249
Chapter Eight:	Malaise and Revival: Preaching in the Eighteenth Century	327

Appendixes and indexes begin on page 853, volume 2

Preface

The Lord gives the command; great is the company of those who bore the tidings.

—Psalm 68:11 (NRSV)

To undertake a history of preaching in any form is to be aware of indebtedness to so many who have gone before on this journey of inquiry and evaluation. Broadus and Dargan (even as updated by Turnbull) are now out of print; Webber, while massive in its attention to the English-speaking world, does not go beyond it; Perry and Wiersbe have given us *The Wycliffe Handbook of Preaching and Preachers,* which is mainly skeletal and anecdotal; and numerous brief monographs by Brillioth, DeWitte T. Holland, and Paul Scott Wilson all whet our appetite for a contemporary work that is both descriptive and analytic. The forthcoming works of O. C. Edwards and Ronald E. Osborne have not been available to me as I have engaged in this study, but our perspectives are different.

Preaching in our time is in a dither. Questions and challenges and interest abound, and we are wrestling with so many issues about direction and thrust. This then is the hour in which we need the perspective of history and the sense of what preaching really is over against its biblical and historical roots. My focus has not been upon preaching in a generic sense but more narrowly upon biblical preaching, upon the endeavor to communicate the supernatural written Word of God. My viewpoint is unabashedly that of classical biblical Christianity.[1] Necessarily and often regrettably no living persons as of the date of this writing can be included in the history. The decisions regarding inclusion or exclusion of representative preachers in a given age have often been obvious and easy but, in other cases, tortuous and difficult.

My deepest thanks to the Regents of Trinity Evangelical Divinity School for sabbatical time to work on this project; to my colleagues and students for their interest and input; to my precious life-partner for over forty years, Jean, for her

understanding and encouragement; and to my son Dan, a history teacher himself, for his willingness to serve as my technical helper again and again. Preaching the Word of God has been my calling and my life. I have been preaching for
more than fifty years and still find indescribable fascination in the intricacies of
the craft. For many years in parish ministry and in pulpits around the world, my
hunger for greater effectiveness in expounding Scripture has led me to look at
the history of preaching over the centuries for such clues and insights as may be
afforded by a consideration of the able practitioners of the calling over time. What
have been the schools of preaching and how can we trace the evolution of sermonic form? The history of preaching has been one of my favorite courses in
my years of teaching preaching at Trinity. It is my prayer and desire that this
work will inflame and ignite interest and dedication for some of the preachers of
our time. *Ad Gloriam Dei.*

---

1. Cf. J. N. D. Kelly, *Early Christian Doctrines,* rev. ed. (New York: HarperCollins,
   1978). Kelly demonstrates that the early church held (as in Tertullian, for instance)
   to Scripture's "absolute authority"; "whatever it teaches is necessarily true and woe
   betide him who accepts doctrines not discoverable in it" (39); "Scripture is the doctrinal norm" (42); the primary task is "the exposition of the Bible" (46). Kelly shows
   their great reverence for the Old Testament (52) with a strong insistence on the unity
   of both Testaments (65). The full inspiration of Holy Scripture is assumed as their
   premise (64). What I have called classical biblical Christianity starts with these premises and then builds, and this is where I have also begun.

INTRODUCTION

The Postulates of Preaching

The goal of preaching is the glory of God in the glad submission of his people. . . .

—John Piper in *The Supremacy of God in Preaching*

"But let him who boasts boast about this: that he understands and knows me, that I am the LORD, who exercises kindness, justice and righteousness on earth, for in these I delight," declares the LORD.

—Jeremiah 9:24

The focus of this study is biblical preaching, the central concern of which is to communicate and apply what the Bible teaches. Thus, biblical preaching necessarily must be defined and developed in relationship to the nature and character of God.

The widespread focus on humanity's horizontal relationships and psychological experience in the preaching of our time reflects the increasingly pervasive banishment and exile of God from Western culture—even in the enclaves of conservative Christianity. The contemporary thinning and vivisection of evangelical theology make this study all the more imperative.[1] In spite of this growing aversion to normative theological constructs or the notion of orthodoxy itself, all human activity is to be doxological in nature, including preaching in and for the Christian church. Preaching, therefore, as an act which brings ultimate glory to God himself, should and must reflect both the objective truths of God's very nature and his character as expressed in the vertical relationships of Creator to creation and Redeemer to the redeemed.

The basic premises and essential presuppositions which will govern this study, therefore, need to be clearly stated at the outset.

The Importance of the Word of God

The voice of the LORD is powerful; the voice of the LORD is majestic.

—Psalm 29:4

You have exalted above all things your name and your word.

—Psalm 138:2b

Your word is truth.

—John 17:17b

The God of the Bible is a speaking God. The God of the Bible has revealed himself in nature and in the person of Jesus Christ. The Holy Scriptures give written and propositional interpretation to the mighty acts of God. What the Scriptures represent as fact and truth is indeed fact and truth. The words of Scripture are the words of God, and therefore the Scripture's assertions are totally trustworthy and reliable (John 10:34–36).

Moses declaimed "the word of the Lord" (Deut. 5:5). The speaking God is not silent (Ps. 50:1–3a). The Lord tells Isaiah, "I have put my words in your mouth" (Isa. 51:16). Again and again the servants of God announce, "Thus says the Lord!" Haggai is a case in point. Four times we read of the prophet's mediation of what God says and then the resultant positive response to "the voice of the LORD their God and the message of the prophet Haggai" (Hag. 1:12). To understand what a sunflower is, we need to make a primary induction—we need to look at a sunflower. To understand what the Bible is, we need to make a similar primary induction. We must examine the Bible's claim itself to be in truth the Word of God.

Christ and the apostles taught a *doctrine* of Scripture (cf. 2 Tim. 3:16–17). They submitted themselves to the text of Scripture. The Word of God was seen as "living and powerful" and confidently guaranteed to have an effect (Isa. 55:10–11). How this Word of God "spread rapidly and was honored" (2 Thess. 3:1) is chronicled in Acts and has been confirmed and corroborated down through the centuries. Our study of the history of preaching is grounded on the undying conviction of the absolute authority and total sufficiency of the Bible as the inerrantly and infallibly inspired Word of God.

The secularism of the Enlightenment mounted a relentless assault on the authority of Scripture. Every vestige of the supernatural was jettisoned. Other movements within Christendom have de-emphasized text in favor of experience. In the postmodern period, we now face a massive attack on the very notion of meaning itself and a denial of the fixity of any text. Today the interpreter is elevated over the author. The result has been a recession of the Bible in the church, indeed "a famine of hearing the words of the LORD" (Amos 8:11).[2] Our perspective here is the orthodox and received doctrine of the full inspiration of the Holy Scriptures.

The Importance of the Preaching of the Word of God

And we also thank God continually because, when you received the word of God, which you heard from us, you accepted it not as the word of men, but as it actually is, the word of God, which is at work in you who believe.

—1 Thessalonians 2:13

This conviction that the message comes from God is fundamental to effective preaching.

—Leon Morris

Preach the Word . . .

—2 Timothy 4:2

What we believe about the Bible shapes our view of what preaching is to be. The undercutting of authority and meaning generally in our culture and the undercutting of the authority and meaning of the biblical texts more specifically have had a marked impact upon preaching in our time. If, as many argue, "theology must begin not with revelation or an authoritative tradition but with ordinary human experience" enriched with some "signals of transcendence," then preaching is bound to be groping, hesitant and flat.[3] But if what the Bible says God says, then the preaching of the Word of God becomes an incredibly exciting enterprise.

So central and pivotal is preaching that it would not be overstatement to say that the history of the Christian church is the history of preaching. The day on which the church was born was a day of epochal preaching (Acts 2). When Jesus Christ drew upon the legacy of the seers and prophets of the Old Testament, he became the original preacher. Although beginning with the apostles and continuing down through successive historic periods, preaching has had its diverse styles and forms, its ups and downs, its traumas and its triumphs. Like the church itself which stands just one generation from extinction, so preaching has threatened to self-destruct with its own excesses or to be snuffed out by external foes and pressures. Yet preaching survives and underscores the abiding validity of P. T. Forsyth's classic aphorism, "With its preaching Christianity stands or falls."

The concentration of this study is not on preaching in a generic sense, however, but on biblical preaching as such. John Stott puts it with admirable succinctness: "To preach is to open up the inspired text with such faithfulness and sensitivity that God's voice is heard and God's people obey him."[4] A sermon is biblical when it says what the Scripture says. This may be done in topical, textual-topical, textual or expository form, to use the most basic nomenclature. The form employed, however, is no guarantee of biblical content (later in our study we shall examine the use and the abuse of all of these forms). Only exegetical conscience and the illumination of the Holy Spirit can keep the preacher from wandering away from the Word of God.

Yet the slant of this study cannot be disguised. An expository sermon uses a natural thought unit of biblical text (often in *lectio continua,* a series, as over against *lectio selecta,* not in a series) and seeks to make the sermon say what the specific text says in its actual context. The history of preaching bears out the acute dangers of preaching out of a text rather than preaching the text. Respect for authorial intention may be under siege currently, but it must be seen as the hermeneutical high ground which must not be surrendered. Finding truth in a text is quite different from finding the truth of the text. Given our understanding of what the biblical text in fact is—the very Word of God—what can be more honoring and pleasing to God than the communication of his truth in every possible setting, the resultant conversion of sinners, and the renewed commitment and worship of his people?

The Importance of the History of the Preaching of the Word of God

> In every age of Christianity, since John the Baptist drew crowds into the desert, there has been no great religious movement, no restoration of Scripture truth, and reanimation of genuine piety, without new power in preaching both as cause and effect.
>
> —John Broadus

> Decline of spiritual life activity in the churches is commonly accompanied by a lifeless, formal, unfruitful preaching, and this partly as cause, partly as effect. On the other hand, the great revivals of Christian history can most usually be traced to the work of the pulpit.
>
> —E. C. Dargan

Preaching has always been the life-blood of the Christian church. The average preacher spends countless hours in preparing messages and multiplies hundreds of thousands of words in conveying the everlasting gospel. Certainly exegesis of the scriptural text "is the central task of biblical exposition."[5] Technical homiletical concerns with form, structure, and delivery are essential. Warren Wiersbe has well said, "Homiletics is the science, of which preaching is the art, and the sermon is the product." It is a fascinating process by which the preacher moves from the then to the now, striking the preaching arc from the Word as written to the world in which the hearers live. We are not the first to walk on these trails of interpretation and application, and historical reflection provides a very significant and immensely rich perspective on how this has been done from the beginning until now.

Every discipline is well served by historical investigation and reflection. In contrast to industrialist Henry Ford who viewed history as "bunk," philosopher George Santayana well argued that "those who cannot remember the past are condemned to repeat it." Philosophy is enhanced by the history of philosophy. Art and sculpture are enhanced by appreciation of the schools and styles of the past. Theology and preaching need the history of doctrine. It is unimaginable that a preacher can practice his craft for a lifetime without historical references and context. Impatience or indifference to history is a regrettable oversight that will exact a loss in effectiveness and impact in preaching.

Reading the sermons of master preachers humbles us as we survey the high standards of many who have preceded us; realizing that even the best had their own weaknesses and were children of their times encourages us. While we should not read sermons in order to imitate them (or worse, appropriate them), we do find special friends and companions in our own pastoral journey and marvel at the diversity of the preaching which God has blessed. The history of preaching helps us understand the task with which we struggle and agonize every week. We are assisted in our quest for variety and enlightened to see contextualization in action. We garner new insights from familiar texts and glimpse into the wealth of unfamiliar texts. We are reminded of the importance of preaching and inspired by the lives and experiences of others who are part with us in "the royal order of the pulpit."

Some very effective practitioners are intuitive in their preaching and function well without a knowledge of preaching's history. More commonly, however, there are significant advantages to those who will reflect on the craft. They will examine issues of proper construction and the use of the various components of the sermon. They will familiarize themselves with the schools of preaching. A sense of such historical perspective develops caution as we trace wrong roads taken by others as well as provides consolation in our missteps. G. Ray Jordan sharpens the point when he observes, "The fact that many preachers do not diligently study the history of preaching is a major reason for so many failures in the pulpit."[6]

Laypersons as well need the history of preaching. There is no such thing as great preaching if there is not great listening, what Aaron Copeland called "talented listening." Laypersons need to know something of the history of biblical communication in order to reflect in an intelligent and spiritually insightful manner on the current crisis in the evangelical pulpit. Just as the crucial issues in contemporary missiology require reflection on the history of missions (as set forth, for instance, in Kenneth Scott Latourette's massive *A History of the Expansion of Christianity*), so we need broadened awareness of what the Holy Spirit has done in the two thousand years of Christian proclamation. If preaching is as important as we are arguing that it is, then the history of preaching assumes an importance rarely accorded it in our time.

The Importance of the History of the Preaching of the Word of God in Our Time

The fundamental issue is the issue of the truth.
—Carl F. H. Henry in *God, Revelation and Authority*

When the church gives to prayer and preaching their true biblical priority, she is able, under God, to meet the challenge of every generation.
—D. Martyn Lloyd-Jones

> I do not envy those who have to fight the battle in Christianity in the twentieth century.
>
> —Marcus Dods

This study advances, then, on the premise of the priority of the Word of God and its proclamation. Our times present some very special and perhaps some unique challenges for the preacher. The prevailing preference for the nonverbal is itself formidable. The average person in the United States receives twenty-eight hundred messages in advertising and general communication daily. The grand revolt against design in science and the runaway river of immorality and indecency in contemporary society make the preacher's task all the more difficult. Christians are enmeshed as well as non-Christians. J. I. Packer gives his opinion that at no time since the Reformation are so many Christians "unsure, tentative and confused."

The corroding doubts of twentieth-century thought have tended to undermine all structures of authority. Mounting biblical illiteracy and an increasingly acerbic struggle for attention confront us constantly as we seek to maintain that Christianity and the Bible are true. The all-too-common caricature of "the Bible totin' Scripture quotin' preacher" is unseemly to many. The pluralistic, multicultural venue of secularism introduces the need for further nuances. Ours is the era of political correctness, to the point of politically correct bedtime stories. The shift from the age of exposition to the age of entertainment injects new strains as the whole fate of reading in the Electronics Age seems up for grabs.[7]

How then has preaching fared in the recent past and how will it fare in the future? We are undeniably in another of those time periods when the basic idea of preaching is being challenged in some quarters, and the call for a minimalist approach comes ominously from many quarters. Some evangelical leaders disparage preaching as only the dessert of the meal. Others totally ignore preaching in the interest of small group experiences and the "meta-church." Some, in the wake of an upsurge of narrative and story, seem ready to toss out doctrine and direct application in total concession to the anti-propositional and anti-authority mood of modernity.[8] Clearly, some in the church are in an illicit affair with secular culture. The emphasis on marketing and management seems to hold sway over those who have not already been seduced by psycho-babble, and the result, as David Wells observes, has been "the virtual collapse of biblical preaching in the contemporary church."[9]

Evidence does exist of a paradigm shift underway in evangelical preaching from text-driven and text-dependent preaching to need-driven and market-driven preaching.[10] Some signs in homiletical training programs and recent homiletical publications reinforce the contention that serious attention and dialogue-in-depth are needed right now as we consider where we are and where we ought to go. There has never been a time when we had a greater need for the perspectives and patterns that can be drawn from the history of biblical preaching. In that interest and with that concern, we commence our journey into the fascinating and exciting terrain that looms before us.

1. N.B. the two thought-provoking volumes by David F. Wells: *No Place for Truth* (Grand Rapids: Eerdmans, 1989) and *God in the Wasteland: The Reality of Truth in a World of Fading Dreams* (Grand Rapids: Eerdmans, 1994).
2. James D. Smart, *The Strange Silence of the Bible in the Church* (Philadelphia: Westminster, 1970).
3. Peter L. Berger, *A Rumor of Angels: Modern Society and the Rediscovery of the Supernatural* (Garden City: Doubleday, 1969).
4. John R. W. Stott, *The Contemporary Christian: Applying God's Word to Today's World* (Downers Grove, Ill.: InterVarsity Press, 1992), 208.
5. Elliott E. Johnson, *Expository Hermeneutics: An Introduction* (Grand Rapids: Zondervan, 1990), 154.
6. G. Ray Jordan, *You Can Preach* (New York: Revell, 1951), 46.
7. Neil Postman, *Amusing Ourselves to Death: Public Discourse in the Age of Show Business* (New York: Penguin, 1985); and Sven Birkerts, *The Gutenberg Elegies: The Fate of Reading in an Electronic Age* (Boston: Faber and Faber, 1994).
8. Marsha G. Witten, *All Is Forgiven: The Secular Message in American Protestantism* (Princeton, N.J.: Princeton University Press, 1993) which states that based on a study of sermons by preachers in a number of denominations there is widespread cashiering of God's wrath and the need for repentance in preaching today and that God is in fact being refashioned and the message being made more palatable for complacent, comfortable hearers. Here is prima facie evidence of the ascendancy of the therapeutic gospel.
9. David F. Wells, *God in the Wasteland,* ibid., 196.
10. Gerald L. Nelson in a most significant Doctor of Ministry project for which I was mentor, shares the empirical data, cf. Preaching: A New Model for the Twenty-First Century (Deerfield, Ill.: Trinity Evangelical Divinity School, 1994).

CHAPTER ONE

The Gestation Period of Biblical Preaching

Your word, O LORD, is eternal; it stands firm in the heavens.
—Psalm 119:89

The LORD is faithful in all his words, and gracious in all his deeds.
—Psalm 145:13b (NRSV)

Every word of God is flawless; he is a shield to those who take refuge in him. Do not add to his words, or he will rebuke you and prove you a liar.
—Proverbs 30:5–6

The underlying metaphor in this study of the history of preaching is that, as several have suggested, preaching is more like birthing babies than it is like building buildings. A high view of Scripture requires a high view of preaching. The Second Helvetic Confession boldly says: *Praedicatio verbi dei est verbum dei* ("The preaching of the Word of God is the Word of God"). That is to say, to the degree that a sermon says what the Word of God says, that sermon is the Word of God. And thus, as the Word of God is "living and powerful," so the sermon should partake of that same vitality and liveliness through the Holy Spirit. There is order, structure, and architectonic balance to a sermon as there is to a building, but this form must be made alive through the life-giving Spirit.

In applying the metaphor of birth to the history of preaching, we may well ask a pregnant question: what is the genetic background of the preached word? What are the biblical genes and chromosomes that shape and determine the sermonic outcome? What is the spiritual DNA that makes the sermon what it is supposed to be?

Strangely, many treatments of the history of preaching succumb to a Marcionite attitude toward the Old Testament or at least ignore two thirds of the Bible. Christian proclamation has an Old Testament ancestry. The genealogy of preaching, like the genealogy of our Savior, can be traced through the Old Testament. Christ and the apostles were heirs to a legacy in communication. There is a primary tradition to which they and we are greatly indebted. A careful review of the Old Testament yields critical precedents and crucial preparation for the later development of preaching.

1.1 THE INITIATIVES OF THE SPEAKING GOD

My hand has made both earth and skies and they are mine. Yet I will look with pity on the man who has a humble and a contrite heart, who trembles at my word.

—Isaiah 66:2 (TLB)

I would have him take the best and most irrefragable of human theories, and let this be the raft on which he sails through life—not without risk, as I admit it, if he cannot find some word of God which will more surely and safely carry him . . .

—Plato's *Phaedo,* 85

In the past God spoke to our forefathers through the prophets at many times and in various ways.

—Hebrews 1:1a

Presume upon the veracity of God. . . .

—John Calvin

The God of the Bible is a speaking God. We read in Genesis 1 of the Creator of all that "God said," "God saw," "God called," and "God blessed." The triune God has from all eternity been in conversation within the mysterious counsels of the Godhead (Gen. 1:16; 11:7). Humankind as created in the image of God are likewise communicating beings. Everything in the history of preaching hinges on the univocal point of contact between God and humankind by virtue of the *imago dei.*

As God thinks, speaks, and acts so do we, although we exist on a finite and limited plane. God made our minds to work in an organized way according to thought patterns. After all, Greek philosophers did not invent the law of contradiction without which meaningful communication cannot take place. Thoughts consist of words. There cannot be thoughts without words anymore than there can be music without notes. Helen Keller, the deaf and blind woman who mastered so admirably the various aspects of discourse, maintained that a wordless thought is impossible.

That propositions may be true or false is a critical foundation for civilization and civil discourse. Truth is ultimately correspondence to the mind of God. J. G. Hamann, the German philosopher who was converted to pietistic Christianity (1730–88), vehemently argued that "Where there is no word, there is no reason—and no world."[1] For Hamann, if there is no text, there is nihilism. The three pounds of gray matter we call the brain are like a computer with experience, making new synapses to appear. Professor Pinker is certainly right at this point when he urges that "the language instinct is innate and universal, and that all human beings can, from a very early age, express themselves with more or less equal skill, unless they incur brain damage."[2] Indeed Professor Shevoroshkin of the University of Michigan is leading many linguists in search of the original "mother tongue" out of which all five thousand human languages have sprung.[3] The divine origin of speech steadies us gyroscopically in a time of the depreciation of words when images seem more attractive than ideas. The French social critic and philosopher Jacques Ellul characterized our times as the age of "the humiliation of the word."[4]

Preaching can then be called a "word-event." The common Hebrew term for "word" is *dabar* which is used three hundred and ninety-four times in the Old Testament for the revelation of God, and is translated "the word of God" in that familiar phrase. *Dabar* is both word and deed.[5] Words were seen as actions and God's word as powerful and proactive (Isa. 55:10–11). God's power attaches to the word. Indeed, from the Hebrew *amar* derives the Aramaic *memra* or "word" which is substituted for the name of the Lord one hundred and seventy times in the Targum of Onkelos alone as in Genesis 3:8, 10, and 24 and Deuteronomy 33:27, among other references.

The inscripturation of God's speech can then rightly be called "God's written voice" or "God's voice put to print."[6] Notwithstanding the culturally conditioned nature of language and the noetic effects of sin upon the human mind, language is sufficient to bear clear meaning. This is the assumption of all concourse and commerce. Words cause things to happen. William Safire reminds us of the pragmatic reality, "with words we govern men." Words have limitation even for God. There is, after all, that which can only be described as the "ineffable" and the "unspeakable."

While from the biblical perspective words are an event, we must strenuously hold that divine events and deeds necessitate an interpretive word. As J. I. Packer well argues: "The biblical position is that the mighty acts of God are not revelation to man at all, except in so far as they are accompanied by words of God to explain them."[7] God not only acts but God also speaks. This is the prolegomena to preaching. Preaching is in its essence sharing this word God has spoken.

Clearly, we recognize the primary nature of oral speech and then its complement, the written form of the spoken word. No scholar has been more helpful in showing how we need both the written word and the spoken word than Walter Ong. The word is first the impinging of sound. Ong is correct in insisting on "the strongly oral cast of the Hebrew and Christian Scriptures."[8] "Faith comes from hearing" (Rom. 10:17) is still the fact of the matter. "The air was full of the word of God" is normative.[9] The word needs to be preserved and propagated and hence must be written. But that word needs to be proclaimed and preached. The assertion of primitive orality can only reassure and comfort the preacher.

God, then, is the original proclaimer, and preaching from the beginning is listening to God speak, responding to God speaking, and then sharing what God has spoken. In a time like ours when the notion of a "sermon" often seems suspect and the very idea of preaching passé, we need to be reminded of the roots of the calling. Richard Weaver, the gifted rhetorician, defines rhetoric as "persuasively presenting choices." The title of his lead essay and the volume containing it is suggestively titled *Language Is Sermonic*.[10] The foundation stones of preaching are seen in the nature and character of God and in the reality of words and language as God has graciously given them to his creatures.

1. Isaiah Berlin, *The Magus of the North: J. G. Hamann and the Origins of Modern Irrationalism* (New York: Farrar, Strauss and Giroux, 1994).
2. Stephen Pinker, *The Language Instinct: How the Mind Creates Language* (New York: Morrow, 1994).
3. Harvey Hagman, "Tracking Mother of 5000 Tongues," in *Insight* (February 5, 1990): 54–55.
4. Jacques Ellul, *The Humiliation of the Word* (Grand Rapids: Eerdmans, 1986).
5. James G. S. S. Thompson, *The Old Testament View of Revelation* (Grand Rapids: Eerdmans, 1960), 57ff.
6. Charles Fuller, "Preaching and Education" in ed. Michael Diduit, *Handbook of Contemporary Preaching* (Nashville: Broadman Press, 1992), 470.
7. J. I. Packer, *Fundamentalism and the Word of God* (Grand Rapids: Eerdmans, 1952), 92.
8. Walter Ong, *The Presence of the Word* (Minneapolis: University of Minnesota, 1967, 1981), 317.
9. Ibid., 268. Another splendid title by Ong is *Orality and Literacy* (New York: Routledge, 1982).
10. Richard M. Weaver, *Language Is Sermonic: Richard M. Weaver on the Nature of Rhetoric* (Baton Rouge: Louisiana State University Press, 1970), 201.

1.2 THE INITIATION OF PEOPLE WHO SPEAK FOR GOD

My heart grew hot within me, and as I meditated, the fire burned; then I spoke with my tongue.

—Psalm 39:3

They took copies of *The Book of the Law of the Lord* to all the cities of Judah, to teach the Scriptures to the people.

—2 Chronicles 17:9 (TLB)

Hilkiah said to Shaphan the secretary, "I have found the Book of the Law in the temple of the LORD." . . . Hilkiah and those the king had sent with him went to speak to the prophetess Huldah . . . She said to them; "This is what the LORD, the God of Israel, says . . ."

—2 Chronicles 34:15, 22–23

Who speaks for God? The question seems almost too audacious and presumptuous were it not that God obviously calls and employs human beings in the process of communicating his truth. God wants to convey sentences and propositions, and he both speaks and writes (cf. Exod. 20:1; 31:18). Human beings in complicity with God both speak and write (cf. Exod. 34:27–28). Thus from the very beginning, it is clear that what we call preaching is God's word to humankind, not humankind's word about God.

Even prior to the deluge, two figures are identified from primal history as spokesmen for God. In each case the delivery of the message was highly confrontational. Of Enoch, who walked with God, Jude tells us (quoting from the ancient but noncanonical book of Enoch—a practice utilized by others in Scripture), "Enoch, the seventh from Adam, prophesied about these men: 'See, the Lord is coming with thousands upon thousands of his holy ones to judge everyone, and to convict all the ungodly of all the ungodly acts they have done in the ungodly way, and of all the harsh words ungodly sinners have spoken against him'" (Jude 14–15). The four occurrences of *ungodly* reflect the collision course that this godly man faced with his generation (Gen. 4:21–24; Heb. 11:5). Enoch did not so much speak words about God as indeed the words that God gave to him.

Noah, who lived in the same antediluvian decadence, was likewise a person who knew God personally and intimately (Gen. 6:9). For one hundred and twenty years he testified to his contemporaries as he built the ark, and is called consequently "a preacher of righteousness" (2 Peter 2:5). Noah's work is not evaluated numerically but in terms of his faithfulness and the practicality of his obedient construction of the ark. "The days of Noah" according to the words of the Lord Jesus are seen as typical of the apostasy of the end-time (Luke 17:26–27), but in all of this Noah preached righteousness and practiced what he preached.

Both Enoch and Noah were exercising the prophetic office, although Abraham is the first person called "a prophet" (Gen. 20:7; Ps. 105:15). A prophet is one who authoritatively represents God and speaks God's word. The much-discussed Hebrew word *nabhi* means "one who tells forth, announces, proclaims."[1] The prophet is God's messenger or God's herald. The prophet both foretells and "forthtells." Prophetic utterance is always predicated on the call of God and communion with God (Gen. 18:17ff.). The prophet or prophetess (which are also numerous in the Scriptures) stands before people because he or she has stood before God.

Moses must be seen as the model for the whole line of prophetic succession which includes Jesus Christ (Deut. 18:15, 18; Acts 3:25–26; 7:37). Moses is the trailblazer in challenging an idolatrous culture (Isa. 45:20–22). John Calvin discerned that the human mind is an idol factory, and this means that from the very beginning prophetic preaching is conducted in a hostile environment. Moses' exposition of the divine law laid bare what Richard Mouw has called "a divine-command morality" which has had rough sledding in modern ethical theory.[2] With regard to the idols of our culture, the prophet-preacher has the ministry of spiritual interpretation. The promise to the prophet is ever the same: "I will put my words in his mouth, and he will tell them everything I command him" (Deut. 18:18b).

In the Balaam cycle we see, among many interesting phenomena, a donkey to which speech is given (Num. 22:28ff.). Our inadequacies do not stymie our great enabling and empowering God. Balaam himself becomes the prototype of the false prophet who is mostly interested in profit, who sells out (cf. Num. 31:8, 16). Balaam is presented as both poet and orator, the master of blessing and cursing (Num. 22–24). Balaam spoke under divine endowment but ultimately would not pay the price for acting as God's prophet (2 Peter 2:15–16; Jude 11b). Undeniably the purpose of those who share the "oracles of God" (the *oi logoi*), is not primarily to help people with their problems, it is to speak for God who is ultimately the only help. Human beings "have been entrusted with the very words of God" (Rom. 3:2).

Early on Moses was very uneasy about his speaking role (Exod. 6:12; 7:1ff.).[3] Was this the result of immense discouragement with the children of Israel or an unrealistic feeling of inferiority? It is hard to say, but certainly Moses developed and grew in his communicative skills as one of whom it was later said, "Moses was educated in all the wisdom of the Egyptians and was powerful in speech and action" (Acts 7:22). Nowhere do we see this more strikingly than in Moses' valedictory address, which we know as Deuteronomy. The book of Deuteronomy is in point of fact a series of sermons. In his superb commentary on Deuteronomy, J. Ridderbos shows how "the reminiscences and the exhortations give the book the character of a sermon."[4] Here we have a series of discourses calling the people of God back to covenant renewal.

The rediscovery of this lost book in the days of young King Josiah and its reading and interpretation by the prophetess Huldah led to one of the most remarkable spiritual awakenings in the history of God's ancient people (cf. 2 Chron. 34:14ff.). To be sure, the Bible gives us many examples of effective speaking such as Judah pleading for Benjamin before Joseph (Gen. 44) or Jotham's brief speech which is essentially secular in content (Judg. 9). When we read Joshua's two farewells, ponder Nathan's dramatic appeal to David, marvel at David's eloquence in the Psalter, or consider Solomon's address at the Dedication of the Temple, we are standing again in the tradition of the God-intoxicated discourse of Moses as he bid the children of Israel farewell.

Although we shall deal extensively with the New Rhetoric in succeeding chapters, it is necessary to call attention to more recent trends in Old Testament study which have emphasized the rhetorical tenor of much of the Old Testament materials. In his work *The Great Code,* Northrop Frye demonstrates that the essential idiom of the Bible is oratorical. That is to say that the Bible has an oral and linear quality.[5] The resurgence of interest in literary criticism and rhetorical criticism has reinforced the declamatory and suasive aspects of the biblical material.[6]

In his epochal work, *The Pentateuch as Narrative,* John Sailhamer calls us boldly to the text of Scripture.[7] His work shows the striking literary and verbal parallelisms; the word plays; the numerical symbolism; the mixture of narrative and instruction; and the chiastic coordination—all of which buttress the essential unity of the five books and support the literary and rhetorical nature of the basic materials. In his similar argument for the evidence of the skilled storyteller in 1 and 2 Chronicles, Sailhamer shows how, for instance, 2 Chronicles 36:14–21 is a sermon, emphasizing how "the LORD, the God of their fathers, sent word to them through his messengers" (2 Chron. 36:15).[8]

These earliest preachers, in whose succession preachers of today truly stand, were mostly occasional preachers or messengers of God. Before the coming of the canonical or writing prophets, we see prophetic mountain peaks when Elijah or Elisha spoke for God with great drama and the corroboration of mighty signs. Spurgeon was right in saying that good preaching is always controversial; it must always face up to our accommodationist habits. Then there are undulating valleys as in the times described in 1 Samuel 3:1, "In those days the word of the LORD was rare; there were not many visions."

The persons who speak for God are in the category of witness. Indeed the Lord Jesus is called "the faithful witness" (Rev. 1:5; 3:14). Scripture warns about the false witness (Deut. 19:16; Prov. 6:14; 19:5, 28; 21:28, etc.). We are to bear witness and "a truthful witness does not deceive" (Prov. 14:5). Indeed "a truthful witness gives honest testimony" (Prov. 12:17). We are accountable in our witness to the Lord who ponders the heart and who weighs the spirits.

At the conclusion of his masterful survey of the pursuit of happiness, the teacher or preacher *(Koheleth)* in the book of Ecclesiastes describes his procedure. He writes, "Not only was the Teacher wise, but also he imparted knowledge to the people. He pondered and searched out and set in order many proverbs. The Teacher searched to find just the right words, and what he wrote was upright and true. The words of the wise are like goads, their collected sayings like firmly embedded nails—given by one Shepherd. Be warned, my son, of anything in addition to them" (Eccl. 12:9–12a).

The angel Gabriel spoke the good news as one who stood in the presence of God and was sent to speak (Luke 1:19). The angel in Revelation was "flying in midair, and he had the eternal gospel to proclaim to those who live on the earth" (Rev. 14:6).

This is the familiar track of preachers down through the centuries, even for these, the very earliest messengers of a holy God—an awesome pursuit and a high calling. All of those who to this hour stand in this succession are not so much entitled to their position as they have been entrusted with a legacy.

1. Walter Conrad Klein, "Prophecy, Prophets" in Hastings, *Dictionary of the Bible*, rev. ed. (New York: Scribner's, 1962), 802.
2. Richard J. Mouw, *The God Who Commands* (South Bend, Ind.: University of Notre Dame Press, 1990).
3. For a truly rich study of Moses' call, see James Hardee Kennedy, *The Commission of Moses and the Christian Calling* (Grand Rapids: Eerdmans, 1964).
4. J. Ridderbos, *Deuteronomy* in the *Bible Student's Commentary* (Grand Rapids: Regency/Zondervan, 1984), 3.
5. Northrop Frye, *The Great Code; The Bible and Literature* (New York: Harvest/HBJ, 1982), chap. 1.
6. David M. Howard Jr., "Rhetorical Criticism in Old Testament Studies," in *Bulletin for Biblical Research* 4 (1994), 87–104.

7. John Sailhamer, *The Pentateuch as Narrative* (Grand Rapids: Zondervan, 1992); see also my *Telling the Old, Old Story: The Art of Narrative Preaching* (Wheaton, Ill.: Crossway, 1995).
8. John Sailhamer, *I and II Chronicles* (Chicago: Moody Press, 1983).

1.3 THE EXTRAORDINARY INSPIRATION OF THE ANCIENT PROPHETS OF GOD

The Lord said to me, "I knew you before you were formed within your mother's womb; before you were born I sanctified you and appointed you as my spokesman to the world."

—Jeremiah 1:4–5 (TLB)

But who will listen when I warn them? Their ears are closed and they refuse to hear. The word of God has angered them; they don't want it at all.

—Jeremiah 6:10 (TLB)

And I can't quit! For if I say I'll never again mention the Lord—never more speak in his name—then his word in my heart is like fire that burns in my bones, and I can't hold it in any longer.

—Jeremiah 20:9 (TLB)

"Whatever happened to prophetic preaching?" was the doleful lament of an ecumenical preacher nostalgic for the days of preaching on social issues, "debatable, arguable, oppositional, global, national or local societal problems. Nobody gets hanged for talking about pastoral care. But prophetic sermons get preachers into hot water."[1] The tragedy of this kind of "prophetic preaching" in its heyday was not that the preachers did not find a kind of inspiration in the fiery counter-cultural passion of the canonical prophets, but rather that their confrontation was so often devoid of the supernaturally authoritative revealed word from God. One such beacon light apologized to a conference on solidarity with the Liberation Struggle for possibly offending anyone by referring to God in his invocation.

The spiritual Olympians we call the canonical prophets flourished in Israel and Judah during a period of four hundred years of abysmal moral and spiritual disintegration. Of course they are unique and unrepeatable as part of that once-for-all, segmented strand of history in which God revealed himself and his will as miraculously preserved in Holy Scripture. These prophets preached (as John Broadus exclaims, "The prophets were preachers!") under an amazing sense of God's call and authority. They were God's messengers and the "messenger formulas" abound in their recorded utterance—"thus says the Lord" and "the burden of the Lord." We do not replicate this role, but we likewise have no word of our own to share but are totally dependent on the biblical repository of supernaturally revealed truth. Thus prophetic preaching is to proclaim God's word as given by the inspiration of God canonically as in their case or to proclaim God's

	ethos ηθος—The Speaker	pathos παθος—The hearers	logos λογος—The message
Before the End Pre-exhilic: to Nineveh– **Jonah**	A super-patriot who defied God, then broke contritely under God's chastening hand. Mightily used in preaching (Matt. 12:41), he was out-of-sorts with a compassionate God.	The cruel and rapacious Assyrians and their powerful capitol, Nineveh, were simultaneously the objects of the goodness and the severity of God. God in mercy sends a preacher to warn them.	A real historical situation (as Jesus established, cf. Matt. 12:40f.; Luke 11:30). The rustic, bleached prophet comes striding through the city with his brief message (8 words in English, 5 in Hebrew) of impending doom. The result of this epochal day of preaching was radical repentance.
to Israel– **Joel**	As is not infrequent, we know little or nothing about the messenger, we have but the message. The dating is uncertain. The preacher uses bold and descriptive imagery and makes strong appeal.	An horrendous horde of locusts invades the land and devastates agriculture (chap. 1). "The word of the Lord" through the prophet sees this scenario as symbol of foreign invasion and the Day of the Lord.	An impassioned call for repentance ensues (2:12–17, a genuine and authentic repentance). Promise is given of an outpouring of the Spirit (fulfilled on Pentecost) and description of eschatological judgments and a final invasion of the land at the end of the Tribulation with the assurance of ultimate victory for God's people.
Hosea	A husband and a father in a marriage commanded by God (1:2), but Gomer his wife (like Israel) was unfaithful. He is instructed to buy her back from slavery. His marriage becomes the symbolic illustration of his message.	For sixty to seventy years Hosea addresses the deplorable spiritual and moral decline of Israel. "Israel has forgotten his maker" (8:14). Spiritual infidelity is analyzed and addressed. Baalism is choking the modern church—the gods of the land.	Using powerful figures of speech (especially the agricultural) and lyrical style (along with rhetorical repetitions and chiasms). Hosea preaches chesed (God's loyal covenant love), of a piece with the N.T. disclosure of love. The summons is to repentance (14:1–3) and the promise is restoration (14:4–8). God's love is triumphant over sin—both Paul and Peter pick up on this poignant preaching.
Amos	"The Lord has spoken—who can but prophesy?" (3:8). Amos, from Tekoah near Jerusalem, cared for sheep and had to do with sycamore-figs. The Lord took him and pressed him into prophetic ministry to Judah (7:10–17).	In a time of social and economic transition and upheaval, the rich were getting richer and the exploited poor were becoming poorer. The thirst for luxury, mounting injustice, and spiritual idolatry were objects of Amos' excoriating preaching.	The sermons of Amos (from within the perspective of God's ancient covenant) were a blistering challenge to the festive mood and frothy religiosity of the time. He used sarcasm, irony, and many rhetorical stratagems, "The lion has roared!" The final positive promise of the rehabilitation of the house of David (9:11–14) projects the pattern of a future and permanent reoccupation of the Land of Promise.
Nearing the Abyss to Edom– **Obadiah**	The name *Obadiah* (meaning "the servant of the Lord") was a common name—there being a dozen other Obadiahs in the O.T. We know virtually nothing about this prophet from Jerusalem who has given us this very slender but provocative piece.	This message of judgment is directed to the Edomites, descendants of Esau, who lived in Mt. Seir, south of the Dead Sea, and whose chief fortified city was Sela (later called Petra). Dated in relationship to some sack of Jerusalem earlier or later.	Snug and proud in their impregnable fortress, Edom watched Judah's discomfiture with glee. Using a typical messenger formula (v. 1) the prophet launches a scathing exposé of Edom's pride and arrogant self-sufficiency. The doom of Edom presages the eschatological Day of the Lord. The prophecy about the coming messianic kingdom is embedded in the text (v. 17) and is consistent with the general representation in all the prophets.

to Judah–

	ethos—The Speaker ηθος	pathos—The hearers παθος	logos—The message λογος
Isaiah	Isaiah, the prince of the prophets, lived in and around Jerusalem. When King Uzziah died after 52 years of rule, Isaiah had a transforming vision and call (chap. 6). His wife was a prophetess (8:3) and his children had symbolic names. He is called "the evangelical prophet."	Isaiah's sermons were addressed to kings and the common people. There is much political and diplomatic intrigue. The themes of holiness, the remnant, and Immanuel—the child King, virgin-born, who will save and rule—are oratorically directed to the hearers.	The prophet's theme is "salvation is of the Lord," which is the meaning of his name. Chapters 1–39 are heavy with indictment of Judah's neighbors and of Judah herself for spiritual declension in a time of great prosperity. Chapters 40–66 contain the messianic servant songs and speak with great specificity of Messiah's substitutionary death. The sermons conclude with a magnificent vignette of the perfected kingdom of God.
Micah	While Isaiah impacted the Jerusalem area, Micah reached a rural area in the same time-frame. "The word of the LORD came to him" (1:1). He spoke in the Spirit—"I am full of power by the spirit of the LORD" (3:8). A sensitive and feeling person (1:8–9), he knew loneliness and desolation for God.	Ministering during the tenure of three kings (one strong, two weak), he spoke of Jerusalem's destruction (2:6–7) and diagnosed the injustice, oppression of the poor, and spiritual apostasy that made it inevitable. Assyria besieges Jerusalem as a foreshadowing of what is coming.	His style is exquisitely ordered and compact. His sermons included judgment oracles and a great prophetic oracle that envisioned the coming of the child from Bethlehem who would shepherd the remnant and the nations (5:2–4). Exposition of what God requires (6:8) is coupled with a magnificent cameo of God's forgiving mercy (7:19). God spoke, yet Judah would not hear. This is always the preacher's grief.
Nahum	Nahum ("full of comfort"), a "village prophet" from Elkosh (1:1), probably in Judah. His work may date about 654 B.C. Bishop Lowth spoke of Nahum's "sublimity, ardor, and daring style." Some of the best poetry in the O.T.—used vivid language and "photographic description." Both assonance and alliteration.	Written to encourage God's people about the fate of Nineveh, "the bloody city," which did fall in 612 B.C. Insisting on the unswerving justice of God, Nahum's objective is to focus on God and foster faith in him (1:7). This is ever the source of comfort and consolation for the people of God.	The prophecy commences with a victorious ode celebrating the Lord's mighty power. The last two chapters describe the destruction of Nineveh. Dr. Walter Maier's peerless study identifies 22 specific prophetic predictions made by Nahum, everyone of which was literally and historically fulfilled. Elaborate archaeological evidence is cited to demonstrate the extraordinary accuracy and precision with which the prophet wrote and spoke.
On the Edge			
Habakkuk	Habakkuk has been called "the man with honest questions." He lived at "wit's end corner," and sought out God i "the watchtower (2:1). The posture must be "the just living by faith" (2:4)—a jewel picked up both by Paul in Romans and Galatians and in Hebrews. The principle is age-abiding.	Not sermons to others—"the private journal of a confused preacher." His problem is the "problem of history." How can a Holy God (1:13) tolerate and countenance such a wicked world power as Babylon? The taunt song of five "woes" directed shows the ultimate outcome of judgment for the oppressors.	As is always the case, an understanding and compassionate God speaks to the doubting and despairing prophet. God seeks to help him to understand the situation. The consequence is the outpouring of prayer (3:1–19) climaxing in a triumphant and confidence-exuding song of praise! Habakkuk 3:16–19 was John Newton's sermon text for his wife's funeral. The emergence of confidence and poise is a most beautiful and bracing example of the Lord's address to our needs.

Zephaniah	Probably the first prophet to speak after the wicked reign of Manasseh (before the renewal in the days of Josiah in 621 B.C.). Seemed to be a resident of Jerusalem from a respected old family (1:1). Possibly a religious official, he draws on Psalms, Amos, and Isaiah. One of the most neglected of the prophets in the O.T.	Manasseh and his son Amon were so desperately depraved. Then most unexpectedly King Josiah sought after God. And with the recovery of the Word of God (Deuteronomy) there was a great turning to God and the celebration of the greatest Passover since the days of Samuel (2 Chron. 35:18).	As a contemporary of Jeremiah, Zephaniah is facing impending judgment. He shares judgment speeches ever with an eye toward the ultimate Day of the Lord, in the light of which he calls to repentance. He closes with an upbeat projection of the perfected kingdom of God and its great joy: "He will rejoice over you with singing" (3:17). Ellison well argues: "Judgment on Israel is always linked, explicitly or implicitly, with ultimate restoration and blessing."
Jeremiah	Called "the prophet who wouldn't quit," from a family of priests living at Anathoth; for fifty years lived out his divine call (chap. 1). His "confessions" show his deep struggles (chap. 20). Aspects of his life and ministry have resemblance to Jesus (Matt. 16).	Jeremiah preached a series of sermons (as in the temple gate in chap. 7) that warned Judah of her spiritual decline and danger. He was imprisoned as a traitor and was a witness to the destruction of Jerusalem (cf. Lamentations). He was kidnapped and taken to Egypt where he died.	Contending with false prophets and faithless kings (to say nothing of a fickle populace), Jeremiah spoke of the perpetuity of God's ancient people and the glories of the new covenant (chap. 31). Biography and prophecy blend beautifully. His figures are poignant—"breakup your fallow ground," "circumcise your hearts," "broken cisterns," etc. He has given our language the word "jeremiad," which refers to a doleful and passionate lament.

Out of the Depths

Exilic:

Ezekiel	Ezekiel, from an old priestly family, was taken into exile in 597 B.C. (when he was 25, cf. 1:1). He was called to be God's spokesman to the captives in Chebar in the context of a visit by the throne-chariot of the Lord (chaps. 1–3). He spent the balance of his life and ministry with the exiles. He lived and spoke God's message.	Ezekiel showed the exiles why God judged Judah (chap. 8). He pressed their responsibility for their plight (chap. 18). Six months after the destruction of Jerusalem, the news came to Chebar (586 B.C.), but he had previously disclosed it in connection with his wife's death (25:15–24). Ezekiel used many visuals and symbolic acts in his communication.	Along with indictments of the nations and of the false shepherds of Judah (chap. 34). Ezekiel shares concerning the ultimate restoration to the land (chaps. 35–36), the physical and spiritual resurrection of God's people (chap. 37), various enemies and battles of the end-time (chaps. 38–39), and the millennial temple in a radically reconfigured Holy Land (chaps. 40–48). The visions of this "mystic" among the prophets are dazzling. He speaks of Job, Noah, and Daniel—among others.
Daniel	Daniel as a youth went into Babylonian captivity where he took a principled stand (1:8); interpreted the king's dream (chap. 2). He outlasted the Babylonians and persisted in a leadership role into Persian hegemony. He was a man of unflinching prayer (chaps. 6, 9–10). As far as we know he never returned home to eretz Israel.	Objectionable to critics because of his true prophecy and apocalyptic material, Daniel is endorsed by Jesus (Matt. 24) and by Hebrews (chap. 11). While not directly addressing his people, his testimony is to the glorious victory and rule of the sovereign God—the wild beasts are overcome in the coming of the Son o~"Man (chap. 7).	Chapters 1–6 give narratives from Daniel's life and times; chapters 7–12 share prophetic vistas of near-range (chaps. 8, 11—Antiochus Epiphanes) and far-range (chap. 7—the coming of the kingdom, chap. 9—a great chronological prophecy of the Messiah, chap. 12—the final events of space-time history). The N.T. (particularly Revelation) draws heavily on Daniel. The seven-year time interval, in two 3 1/2 year periods (corresponding to 42 months and 1,260 days), is the backbone of both books. The last chapter is replete with a magnificent promise of resurrection and an ominous warning.

Prisoners of Hope Post-exilic:	ethos ηθος—The Speaker	pathos παθος—The hearers	logos λογος—The message
Haggai	Called simply "the prophet" in 1:1 and in Ezra 5:1; 6:14. Among the remnant in 520 B.C. who had to face the unfinished temple. Publicly proclaimed God's Word—four of his sermons preserved (chap. 1; 2:1–9; 2:10–19; 2:20–23). God stirred the hearts of his people—the temple was rebuilt.	Conditions for the remnant were at low-ebb—returning home in 538 B.C. and laying the foundation of the new house—but distracted by a poor economic situation, their own selfish pursuits, and paralyzed by despair, the temple project languished. Some verses have poetic form.	Only two chapters and thirty-eight verses, Haggai preaches to the issue of priorities. Baldwin cites his favorite imperatives: consider (1:5, 7; 2:15, 18); take courage (2:4). Referred to earlier prophets and an apt metaphor (1:6e) as well as a dialogical illustration (2:10–12). The temple was rebuilt and dedicated in 516 B.C. a momentous little fragment. An eschatological overlay looks forward to the time when the Lord shakes heaven and earth, sea and dry land (2:6).
Zechariah	A book of visions from Zechariah, grandson of Iddo, a priest (1:1). Seems to have had a longer ministry than Haggai. The people needed to repent (1:1–6), needed to fast for God, not themselves (7:6). In the early section (chaps. 1–8), we have eight visions. The prophet is instructed to "cry out" (1:14). He does so.	Like Haggai he seeks to encourage the builders to the temple and looks forward to the Day of the Lord. There were tensions in the vassal province, external and internal. Both the high priest Joshua and the civil leader Zerubbabel faced challenge (chaps. 3–4). Haggai was practical—the man of action; Zechariah was the visionary. He shares his burdens for the future (chaps. 9–14).	Jerome wrote: "The most obscure and the longest of the Twelve . . ." Quoted most in the passion narratives and with 9–14 apocalyptic, very influential on Revelation. Seventy quotes or allusions in N.T. Some scholars see chiastic structure in 9–14. He depicts the coming of God's King in contrast to Alexander the Great (9:1–10). But God's Shepherd is rejected (11:4–17). The prophet describes how the enemy will besiege Jerusalem in the end, how God's people will repent when they confront the One who is pierced (12:10), and how the Lord will come in power and glory to the Mt. of Olives (14:1–15).
Malachi	Malachi ("my messenger" or "my angel") is probably a title for the anonymous prophet, not a proper name. The last of the canonical prophets moved in temple circles during or just after Nehemiah's time. His prophecy is termed an oracle or burden for Israel (1:1; as Zech. 9:1; 12:1). Short sentences and direct style.	The post-exilic community was disillusioned. High expectations were not realized; religion was a dull routine. The people were adrift in uneventful times. "Generations were dying without receiving the promises—Hebrews 11:13—many were losing their faith" (Baldwin). Uses disputation—quoting his antagonists and giving answers. Gives 47 first-person addresses from the Lord to Israel.	The over-arching theme is "God's unchanging love" (Kaiser). The sermonic sections treat their relationship to God, the quality of their worship, matters of marriage and divorce, the issue of justice, the practice of tithing, honoring God, and serving him. In all of this he summons the people to truly seek God in a context of God's love ("I have loved you"). Malachi emphasizes divine protection for God's people in a day of judgment (3:13–4:3). God's day is coming. The final plea for repentance comes in the setting of the prophecy of Elijah's coming prior to the final spasm of the time-space history.

word as given through the illumination of the word written through the agency
of the Holy Spirit. (Some too facilely equate the prophetic office with the preaching office of today. We shall address that question when we consider the relationship of the prophetic gift in the primitive church to preaching.)

Very clearly the vitality of this prophetic tradition is virtually without parallel
and without analogy as Leon Wood argues in his substantive work on the prophets.[2] Micah, Isaiah's country contemporary, laid bare the spiritual dynamic of
prophetism: "But as for me, I am filled with power, with the Spirit of the Lord,
and with justice and might, to declare to Jacob his transgression, to Israel his
sin" (Mic. 3:8). The fundamental reliance of all who speak for God is reiterated
again and again in the Old Testament (cf. 1 Sam. 10:10; 19:23; 2 Chron. 15:1ff.;
20:14; Ezek. 2:2; 3:12, 14; 37:1ff.; Neh. 9:30; Zech. 4:12; 7:1).

The prophets in faithfully representing God's message of judgment and grace
used rational discourse. If they were among us today, they would not join those
who denigrate rational consistency, empirical verification as a test of truth, or
the valid if limited benefits of general or natural revelation. Even so, the prophets were not image poor but used symbolic acts and object lessons, that is to say
"visuals."[3] They were not only concerned to communicate the insights God gave
them but to make them clear, compelling, and convincing. Rhetorical criticism
has assisted us in appreciating the attention given to form in discourse. What James
Muilenberg, the father of rhetorical criticism, termed "structural patterns," are to
be seen in remarkable diversity. Thus from the very outset of the history of preaching, we see precedent for attention to effective form as being an important and
necessary ally of right content.

Just as the Psalter contains seven alphabetical psalms and two partially alpha-
betic psalms (for communicative and mnemonic reasons), so we see such devices as inclusio and clusters used extensively in Isaiah. We discern chiasms in
Jeremiah.[4] Rhetorical components shape the parts and the whole of discourse.
Concern for form can become obsessive (as subsequent chapters will examine),
but as in worship, having no form is bad form. The challenge is always to find
the optimally beneficial and appropriate form. We are facing the rhetorical nature of biblical theology.

We know very little of "the company of the prophets" and the schools of the
prophets that apparently had their inauguration in Samuel's time (cf. 1 Sam.
10:5–10; 19:10). They came more prominently to the fore in Gilgal, Jericho, and
Bethel, "the very seats of idolatry" in the time of steepest decline in the northern
kingdom (cf. 2 Kings 2:3–7, 15–18; 4:38; 6:1–2). The courageous loneliness of
the prophetic role, particularly as the prophets stood against the false prophets—
the hirelings, the time-servers, the servile bootlickers—is quite impressive.
Micaiah, the son of Imlah, seems to be the first to square off against the false
prophets in his courageous stand. "As surely as the LORD lives, I can tell him
only what the LORD tells me" (1 Kings 22:14).[5] The free-wheeling, far-ranging
address of these venerable pioneers of preaching is remarkable as they addressed
the whole nation, the religious establishment, and the civil leaders as a "sinful
nation," "rebels," "oppressors," "godless," "drunkards," "faithless," "stupid children," "lusty stallions," and "lying sons."[6]

A recent study of the prophets which is of inestimable value for this endeavor is aptly titled *The Prophets as Preachers*. Author Gary V. Smith effectively analyzes how this ancient preaching transformed people and what it involved theologically, communicationally, and sociologically.[7] Each of these servants of God has a distinctive style and allows us to see his own life's anguish in the process of communication. Isaiah, the prince of prophets, has such a rich series of messianic vignettes and is on the whole quite personally recessive.[8] Jeremiah is psychological and confessional, and Ezekiel is mystical and visionary. Daniel is godly and apocalyptic. Reflect on Hosea's gripping figures of speech, Joel's use of the locust plague, and the oratory of Amos—"The lion has roared—who will not fear? The Sovereign LORD has spoken—who can but prophesy?" (3:8).

Jesus spoke of the preaching of Jonah (Matt. 12:41). God's servant Obadiah launched a scathing indictment against the pride and self-sufficiency of the Edomites. We marvel at the relevancy of Habakkuk's theodicy in his "wit's end corner," and the practical poignancy of Haggai's sermons delivered to the remnant which returned to build the second temple. Each one is uniquely appropriate and effective. These are the forebears and genetic roots of those who now seek to preach messages from God's Word that will be transforming and proactive in the face of our own cultural collapse. Long and loving personal reflection on God's servants, the prophets, will be amply repaid.

Studying Jeremiah is a case in point. His forty years in prophetic ministry spanned some indescribably trying times for Judah, including her capture and destruction. His skilled use of the question and answer pattern, his ability to reach a diverse audience (note the three audiences of Jeremiah 27), his sensuous imagery are all so instructive for us as his message is potent for us. Whether we look specifically at the sermon delivered at the Benjamin Gate, the sermon on the potsherd, or the sermon in the court of the Lord's house, we marvel. His third sermon preached on the subject of "The Temple of the Lord" (Jer. 7) is a classic in communication.[9] But along with his "jeremiads" of denunciation, there was also a broken and compassionate spirit. No wonder that some thought our Lord Jesus Christ was Jeremiah come back to life (Matt. 16:14).[10]

---

1. Richard C. Devor, "Whatever Happened to Prophetic Preaching?" in *Christian Ministry* (July–August 1990), 9; cf. also ed. Earl Shelp and Ronald Sunderland, *The Pastor as Prophet* (New York: Pilgrim Press, 1985).

2. Leon J. Wood, *The Prophets of Israel* (Grand Rapids: Baker, 1979), 674.

3. Elouise Renich Fraser, "Symbolic Acts of the Prophets," in *Studia Biblica et Theologica* (October 1974), 45–53.

4. Jack R. Lundbom, *Jeremiah: A Study in Ancient Hebrew Rhetoric* (Missoula, Mont.: Society of Biblical Literature and Scholars Press, 1975).

5. Several helpful studies of the false prophets include Dwight Stevenson, *The False Prophets* (Nashville: Abingdon, 1960); James Stalker's fourth lecture on "The Preacher as a False Prophet" in his Yale Lectures of 1891 titled *The Preacher and His Models;* and a very poignant address by G. Campbell Morgan on God's rebuke of Hananiah, a false prophet, "The Lord has not sent you; but you make this people

to trust in a lie" (Jer. 28:15) in his *Searchlights from the Word* (Old Tappan, N.J.: Revell, 1977), 247.

6. Otto J. Baab, *Prophetic Preaching: A New Approach* (Nashville: Abingdon, 1948), 24.

7. Gary V. Smith, *The Prophets as Preachers: An Introduction to the Hebrew Prophets* (Nashville: Broadman and Holman, 1994). The whole treatment is superb. Note also "The Prophets as Great Preachers" in Andrew W. Blackwood, *Preaching from Prophetic Books* (Nashville: Abingdon, 1951), 11–23.

8. An example of the positive value of rhetorical criticism is Robert B. Chisholm Jr., "Structure, Style and the Prophetic Message: An Analysis of Isaiah 5:8–30" in *Bibliotheca Sacra* 143 (January–March 1986): 46–60.

9. Especially tantalizing here is John Guest's commentary on Jeremiah in the *Communicator's Commentary Series;* see also on the third sermon, G. Ernest Wright, *The Rule of God* (New York: Doubleday, 1960), 77–92, which he entitles *Security and Faith.*

10. Still my favorite on the prophets as a whole is Edward J. Young, *My Servants the Prophets* (Grand Rapids: Eerdmans, 1952).

1.4 *THE INCEPTION OF INSTITUTIONAL STRUCTURES FOR PREACHING*

For Ezra had devoted himself to the study and observance of the Law of the LORD, and to teaching its decrees and laws in Israel.

—Ezra 7:10

And all the people listened attentively to the Book of the Law. Ezra the scribe stood on a high wooden platform built for the occasion. . . . Ezra opened the book. All the people could see him because he was standing above them; and as he opened it, the people all stood up. . . . The Levites . . . instructed the people in the Law while the people were standing there. They read from the Book of the Law of God, making it clear and giving the meaning so that the people could understand what was being read.

—Nehemiah 8:3b–5, 7–8

(The Jews) are taught, so to speak, from their swaddling clothes by their parents, teachers and those who bring them up, even before instruction in the sacred laws and unwritten customs, to believe in God the one Father and the Creator of the world. . . .

—Philo

Worship and didactic instruction are always central to the spiritual journey of the people of God. In all time periods, the people of God are to be both doxological and pedagogical. Worship fulfills preaching, and preaching fuels worship. While biblical fact and faith are fundamental to each, the actual structures employed in worship and preaching are historically contingent and relative. With the destruction of Solomon's temple in 586 B.C., the worship cultus had to decentralize.

Although there was a return after captivity by some and the rebuilding of a new temple, many Jews never lived in proximity to the Holy House again, and its destruction in 70 A.D. completed the temple era to this day. Significantly, the prophets in their exposure of the emptiness and hollowness of external ritual by itself seem to anticipate Christ's words about the locus of worship (John 4:21–24), the argument of Stephen in Acts 7, and the Epistle to the Hebrews in regards to the danger of absolutizing time-bound structures.

What is more, the four hundred years between the Testaments were a very turbulent and troubled time for those in the land of Israel as successive invasions upended the familiar stabilities. The Persians yielded to Alexander and the Greeks and ultimately the Roman colossus held power. After Malachi, the last of the writing prophets, the virtual disappearance of prophetism either in the land or in the diaspora occasion produced grave anxiety (cf. 1 Macc. 4:46; 9:27; 14:41).

The advancing waves of Hellenistic influence particularly threatened at times to inundate the frail surviving spiritual fabric. From within and from without, God's ancient people faced what seemed to be insuperable odds and obstacles. In this time-frame, some new structures came into being that more adequately addressed the crisis of decentralized worship and the need for strong teaching. The synagogue is a very strategic test-case, the first in a series, that helps us see stylistic and structural adaptations as necessary but potentially perilous. Since many of us stand liturgically and ecclesiastically in the synagogue-prophet-pulpit tradition rather than in the temple-priest-altar tradition, the rise of the synagogue is critical.

Such examples demonstrate that the authoritative message as given must be contextualized, that is, translated into the idiom and understanding of a given people and situation. Inspired Scripture is translatable and every serious preacher is involved in the process although no two communicators will pursue the process in identically the same way. The Oxford method of translation seeks to give the full idiom, while the Cambridge method of translation stresses great verbal accuracy at the expense of some literary attractiveness. We shall argue in this study that there is not a single informing rhetoric for biblical preaching, but in fact, there are many rhetorical models. There may be and indeed must be adaptations and shifts in many of the culturally conditioned aspects of biblical application (distinguishing between the normative pole which is the Bible and its theology and the relative pole which is culture or context).

Sources on the origin of the synagogue (literally, the "gathering together place") are sparse. The synagogue as such is not in the Old Testament but probably did strike its roots in the experience of the Babylonian exile. Without access to a central sanctuary, the Jews gathered in little clusters for worship and instruction. Had not the Lord promised to be their sanctuary in the nations to which they were scattered? (Ezek. 11:16). Perhaps early antecedents are to be seen in meetings conducted by the prophets for prayer (2 Kings 4:23) and the emphasis in Solomon's dedication prayer on the House of Prayer (cf. 1 Kings 8:27–30, also Ps. 99:6).[1] Ezekiel met with elders from among the exiles while at Babylon (cf. Ezek. 8:1; 14:1; 20:1). What is described so movingly in Nehemiah 8 in the public reading and interpretation of the Word of God reflects the serious intent of the people to hear God's Word.

Synagogue buildings began to proliferate throughout the diaspora. The two essential features were an ark or closet for the scrolls and a raised platform with a lectern for the reader of Scripture and for the leader of prayers. The service consisted of an invitation to prayer and then prayers, the lesson from the Torah (in a three-and-a-half-year cycle with an Aramaic interpretation since few knew Hebrew), a reading from the Prophets, after which someone present would give "an exposition of one or both of the passages,"[2] and then the service closed with the benediction. Actually the synagogue in the dispersion became not only the worship center, but the communal center and the school house for the instruction of children.

The rise of the synagogue has been pivotal for Christianity. When we come to the New Testament, we find thirty-four references to synagogues. The diaspora was far larger in the first century than the resident Jewish population in the land. There were apparently hundreds of synagogues in Alexandria, Egypt, a great Jewish center. By the first century A.D. synagogues were established throughout Palestine with thirteen in Tiberias, and according to the rabbis, four hundred and thirty-eight in Jerusalem.

The centrality of the reading of Scripture and its subsequent exposition are critical since demonstrably, the early Christian believers organized themselves for worship, prayer, and benevolence after the synagogue pattern. Most significantly, the sermon was also for Christ and the apostles very much in the tradition of the synagogue sermon.[3] Those who read the Scripture stood, and those who expounded it sat (cf. Luke 4:16–20). This address or discourse *(Deresha)* was given by a rabbi, visiting dignitary, or some qualified person in the congregation. Edersheim does not overstate the matter when he says, "Jewish tradition uses the most extravagant terms to extol the institution of preaching."[4] Usually at the end of the sermon the preacher would refer to the messianic hope. Fairweather concludes that this "homiletical discourse"[5] could be either thematic or, strictly speaking, expository, the latter being more analytical and didactic.[6]

The words *homiletics* and *homily* are from the Greek and have to do with speaking, discussing, and conversing (for which the Latin is *sermo, sermonis*) although Lloyd Perry has argued a derivation from *homo/laleo* meaning to speak the same thing as (the text). A sermon has always properly been talk about a text just as we see in the synagogue. Sandmel has maintained that even before the first century A.D. the structured homily emerged from random *halakic* (exegetical data) or *haggadic* (applicable data) inquiry connected with the reading of Scripture.[7] In fact *haggadic* material—the folk tales, narratives, and parables used by the rabbi for a text—really represent the "earliest extant synagogue homilies."

A case can be made for some influence of the Greek and Roman rhetorical diatribe on synagogue preaching. J. B. Lightfoot, in his notable essay on "St. Paul and Seneca," argued that since the principal Stoic teachers came from the East, this philosophical perspective had certain affinities with Judaism and Christianity.[8] The Stoic diatribe was a rhetorical genre, a "stylistic convention—an extension of moral sentiment so that the ethos of the speaker may abide in the mind of the hearer."[9] This was in a time when "public preaching was a prominent phenomenon in Greco-Roman society."[10] Cicero used the diatribe as did Philo and Paul. It was deeply embedded in Hellenistic communication. Romans and James reflect diatribal style, and certainly many who used it were not self-consciously aware of their usage. Many have equated the sermon or homily as being equivalent in some senses to diatribe. Certainly the moral sermons of Epictetus were called diatribes.

Surely in this time of immense flux and ferment, we see a virtual explosion of new forms and structures usable by the Spirit of God for the dissemination of the truth of God. The synagogue itself was a revolutionary development, and the synagogue sermon represented the institutionalization of "prophetism." But there were fresh and forceful formative influences that helped propel the Christian gospel out into the Greco-Roman world. When we come to the early pages of the New Testament, we find the synagogue in place and throughout the empire as the launching pad for the tremendous spiritual detonation described in Acts. At the heart of the synagogue worship and liturgy is the sermon, the opening and expounding of the text of Holy Scripture as read.

---

1. Louis Finkelstein, "The Origin of the Synagogue," in ed. Joseph Gutman, *The Synagogue: Studies in Origin, Archaeology and Architecture* (New York: Ktav, 1975), 49.
2. Bruce M. Metzger, *The New Testament: Its Background, Growth and Content* (Nashville: Abingdon, 1965), 59.
3. The general course and nature of Jewish preaching through the ages is beyond the purview of this study, but a very helpful survey of the subject is to be found in Raphael Levine, "Preaching in the Jewish Tradition," in ed. Ralph G. Turnbull, *Baker's Dictionary of Practical Theology* (Grand Rapids: Baker, 1967), 31–33; a representative Jewish work in homiletics can be seen in Henry Adler Sosland, *A Guide for Preachers on Composing and Delivering Sermons* (New York: Jewish Theological Seminary in America, 1988). Another ancillary thread of more than ordinary interest is the teaching and preaching in the Qumran Community as reflected in the Dead Sea Scrolls, cf. F. F. Bruce, William S. LaSor, and other perceptive writers on this theme.
4. Alfred Edersheim, *The Life and Times of Jesus the Messiah, Volume I* (Grand Rapids: Eerdmans, reprint, 1953), 446.
5. William Fairweather, *The Background of the Gospels: Judaism in the Period between the Old and New Testaments* (Edinburgh: T & T Clark, 1908), 26.
6. Bo Reicke, *The New Testament Era: The World of the Bible from 500 B.C. to 100 A.D.* (Philadelphia: Fortress, 1964), 123.
7. Samuel Sandmel, *The First Christian Century in Judaism and Christianity* (New York: Oxford University Press, 1969), 73.
8. J. B. Lightfoot, "St. Paul and Seneca," in *St. Paul's Epistle to the Philippians* (Grand Rapids: Zondervan, reprint 1953), 299.
9. George L. Kustra, *Diatribe in Ancient Rhetorical Theory*, No. 22 (Berkeley: The Center for Hermeneutical Studies, Graduate Theological Union/University of California, 25 April 1976): 7.
10. Ibid., 38.

CHAPTER TWO

The Glorious Birth of Christian Preaching

Preaching is the supreme work of the Christian minister.
—G. Campbell Morgan

Church history is the history of the exposition of Scripture.
—Gerhard Ebeling

The most urgent need in the church today is true preaching.
—D. Martyn Lloyd-Jones

Old Testament believers who eagerly awaited the coming of the Messiah found fulfillment in the advent of Jesus Christ the God-man. Christianity is Christ. The redemption he accomplished and announced is the moral and spiritual epicenter of history.

The downplaying of the accuracy of the New Testament documents and the historicity of Jesus Christ threaten to become the death knell of biblical Christianity. P. T. Forsyth was on target in his Yale Lectures on Preaching in 1907 when he argued for the historic Redeemer:

All the amateur philosophandering of the hour is fumbling to escape from a historic, positive, evangelical Christianity, and to preserve before God a remnant of self-respect, self-possession, and self-will. But the prime content both of Christian and human experience is the Savior, triumphant, not merely after the Cross, but upon it. This cross is the message that makes the preacher.[1]

Apart from the historic events of Christ's incarnation, atonement, and bodily resurrection there is nothing to preach and no gospel! (cf. 1 John 1:1–3).

Immediately we are struck by the prominence and importance of preaching in the New Testament. Careful studies of the documents indicate 221 references to preaching in the New Testament. The Greek vocabulary to describe preaching extends to thirty-seven different verbs. The Savior himself was a preacher, but he came so that there would a gospel to be preached. His coming into the world and the birth of Christian preaching to communicate his splendor and excellency now become the focus of our inquiry.

---

1. P. T. Forsyth, *Positive Preaching and the Modern Mind* (New York: Hodder and Stoughton, 1907), 71.

2.1 THE PREPARATORY PREACHING OF JOHN THE BAPTIST, THE FORERUNNER

A voice of one calling: "In the desert prepare the way for the LORD; make straight in the wilderness a highway for our God."
—Isaiah 40:3

"See, I send my messenger, who will prepare the way before me. Then suddenly the Lord you are seeking will come to his temple; the messenger of the covenant, whom you desire, will come," says the LORD Almighty.
—Malachi 3:1

In those days John the Baptist came, preaching in the Desert of Judea.
—Matthew 3:1

He must become greater; I must become less.
—John 3:30

What prepares the way for the manifesting of the glory of the Savior is preaching. The prolonged prophetic silence of the intertestamental period is suddenly shattered as angels from heaven articulate messages of climactic fulfillment and as the daring and dramatic preaching of John the Baptizer captivates and enthralls the nation.

2.1.1 THE ESSENTIAL CONTINUITIES IN THE PREACHING

And he will go on before the Lord, in the spirit and power of Elijah, to turn the hearts of the fathers to their children and the disobedient to the wisdom of the righteous.
—Luke 1:17

John the Baptist has been called the clasp of the two Testaments. He is the link and bridge between them. Like the fearless prophets of the Old Testament, John comes to declare the Word of God. His methodology, his distinctive dress and diet were doubtless shocking to the stiff and staid, but he broke the "grand and awful silence" with a ministry of proclamation from the edge of the sacred Jordan river to the villages and even possibly to Jerusalem itself.[1] His message, like that of the prophets before him, is explained in that "the word of God came to John son of Zechariah in the desert" (Luke 3:2). His mission was "to call Israel to submit to the reign of God, about to be manifested in Christ."[2] A. T. Robertson says: "The Spirit of God put a live coal upon his lip. The fire burned in his heart. He felt the woe of the true preacher upon him if he did not speak. He had to speak even if no one heard."[3]

1. Carl H. Kraehling, *John the Baptist* (New York: Scribner's, 1951), 64.
2. Alfred Edersheim, *The Life and Times of Jesus the Messiah* (Grand Rapids: Eerdmans, 1953), 1:270.
3. A. T. Robertson, *John the Loyal: Studies in the Life of John the Baptist* (New York: Scribner's, 1915), 34.

2.1.2 THE EXCITING DISCOVERIES IN THE PREACHING

The next day John saw Jesus coming toward him and said: "Look, the Lamb of God who takes away the sins of the world!"

—John 1:29

John stands in the succession of the prophets who went before him, but his was the joyful privilege of announcing, "He is here!" John spoke as "a friend of the bridegroom," and thus he spoke with overpowering joy (John 3:29), but without accompanying miracles (10:41). He proposed genuine repentance as the remedy for the nation and offered baptism to all Jews as an external expression of the heart's contrition (Luke 3:3). Their response was like Nineveh's repentance (Matt. 3:5–6). His simple, direct language and his practical application for religious leaders and others who interacted with him were critical in understanding his impact (Luke 3:10–14). Robertson correctly judges, "His sermons hit the center."[1] Marcus Loane's assessment is also accurate: "The vehemence and violence of his mighty preaching had set the land afire" (cf. Matt. 11:7–15).[2]

1. A. T. Robertson, *John the Loyal: Studies in the Life of John the Baptist* (New York: Scribner's, 1915), 92.
2. Marcus L. Loane, *John the Baptist as Witness and Martyr* (London: Marshall, Morgan, and Scott, 1968), 106.

2.1.3 THE EMBLEMATIC LEGACIES OF THE PREACHING

To this John replied, "A man can receive only what is given him from heaven."

—John 3:27

John's clarion call for decision stood in stark contrast with the endless disputes of contemporary Judaism. One critical scholar has strongly affirmed that "John's ministry was essentially a preaching one. . . . The primacy of preaching was thus one of the most marked features of John's ministry."[1] John's was a kerygmatic role, to use Walter Wink's phrase. Even Josephus characterizes John's call for virtue, justice, and piety as given with "great persuasiveness."[2]

John's ministry was not long; we possess less than two pages of the message he proclaimed. Yet the commendation of Christ and the lingering echoes of John's ministry (cf. Acts 19:4) require our underscoring the importance of the character of those who speak for God. We are told that "Herod feared John and protected him, knowing him to be a righteous and holy man. When Herod heard John, he was greatly puzzled; yet he liked to listen to him" (Mark 6:20). John had his dark valleys (cf. Matt. 11:2ff.). Yet he saw Christ as above all (John 3:31), as the coming One "mightier than I," whose ministry is both of judgment and restoration.[3] Who then is the preacher? The preacher is "a voice crying in the desert."

----

1. Charles H. H. Scobbie, *John the Baptist* (Philadelphia: Fortress, 1964), 209–10.
2. Josephus, *Antiquities of the Jews* 18.116–19.
3. Robert L. Webb, *John the Baptizer and Prophet: A Socio-Historical Study* (Sheffield: JSOT Press, 1991), 263.

2.2 THE POWERFUL PREACHING OF JESUS CHRIST THE SAVIOR

In principio erat sermo. ("In the beginning was the Word.")
—John 1:1, Latin translation by Erasmus

No one ever spoke the way this man does.
—the guards in John 7:46

For I gave them the words you gave me and they accepted them. . . . I have given them your word and the world has hated them. . . . I pray also for those who will believe in me through their message.
—John 17:8, 14, 20

Increasing recognition has been given in recent years to the oratorical style of Scripture.[1] The homiletical qualities of the gospel narratives are of special interest to us. But more central is the fact that Jesus Christ, God's only Son, must be seen as a preacher *par excellence*. Teaching and preaching were basic components of Christ's ministry. That "the good news is preached to the poor" is one of the proofs of his authenticity (Matt. 11:5). The apostle Paul summarizes Christ's ministry like this: "He [Jesus Christ] came and preached peace to you who were far away and peace to those who were near" (Eph. 2:17). The apostle Peter speaks of what may have been a ministry of Jesus immediately after his death in his descent into hades: "He went and preached to the spirits in prison who disobeyed long ago when God waited patiently in the days of Noah while the ark was being built" (1 Peter 3:19b–20a).

In what sense is Jesus our model and paradigm in preaching? No one will ever reproduce his ministry because of the uniqueness of who he is and what he came to do. Questions about format and structure of worship services and sermons cannot be answered from the New Testament documents. But what basic principles and patterns may we establish from the pages of Scripture that will serve as a reasonable model for Christlike ministry?

---

1. Northrop Frye, *The Great Code: The Bible as Literature* (New York: Harvest/HJB, 1982), 216.

2.2.1 Preaching as a Methodology of Jesus

From that time on Jesus began to preach, "Repent, for the kingdom of heaven is near."

—Matthew 4:17

Jesus Christ came into the world "to seek and to save what was lost" (Luke 19:10) and "to serve, and to give his life as a ransom for many" (Mark 10:45). In support of these objectives Jesus utilized the ministry of communication (he preached and taught), the ministry of compassion (he healed), and the ministry of companionship (he made disciples). It is difficult to rank these in importance and impossible to assign appropriate allocations of time. They all are complementary and crucial.

Just as the Gospels all speak of the preaching ministry of John the Baptist, so do they record the preaching aspect of Jesus' public ministry. Christ came preaching and teaching. (The words are used interchangeably, although we shall note the distinctions between *kerygma* and *didache* in the next section; N.B. Matt. 9:35). He used a variety of communicative forms and strategies, but his constant mission was to preach the kingdom of God.

Perhaps the best example of that preaching is the Sermon on the Mount (Matt. 5–7). This may be a collection of the sayings of Jesus, given when he sat down and taught as the second and greater Moses. The Sermon on the Mount might well be called the constitution of the kingdom, and ends with Jesus' exhortations to respond appropriately to his message (Matt. 7:24–27). The crowds were amazed by the authority evident in his teaching (Matt. 7:29).

Jesus deputized the Twelve to perpetuate the pattern. "As you go, preach this message: 'The kingdom of heaven is near'" (Matt. 10:7). The task is clear: "What I tell you in the dark, speak in the daylight; what is whispered in your ear, proclaim from the roofs" (Matt. 10:27). Indeed, to receive those whom Christ has commissioned is to receive Christ himself, and those who speak will obtain a prophet's reward (Matt. 10:40–41).

The discourses of Jesus are interspersed throughout the Gospels. Jesus' preaching in the synagogue in Nazareth (Luke 4:14–30) shows us another venue he utilized for proclamation. Both the "law and the prophets" were read in the synagogue. Our Lord's reading from Isaiah 61 is the earliest historical instance of a *haftarah* reading (a reading from the prophets).[1] Jesus had apparently announced a most exceptional Year of Jubilee ("the year of the Lord's favor"). The sermon seems brief, but the clause *he began to say* is in the Greek imperfect, "which could simply mean that 'he was talking to them.'"[2] The engaging move to contemporary application is clear when Jesus says, "Today this scripture is fulfilled in your hearing" (Luke 4:21). The pattern seems to be that Jesus the preacher takes a text of Scripture, reads it, explains it, and applies it. This is biblical preaching, and it was a central methodology employed by the Savior in his earthly ministry.

---

1. Michael Hilton with Gordian Marshall, *The Gospels and Rabbinic Judaism* (Hoboken, N.J.: Ktav, 1988), 45.
2. Ibid., 46. This section from Isaiah is omitted in the cycle of synagogue readings "probably because of its association with Jesus."

2.2.2 PREACHING AND THE MESSAGE OF JESUS

> The Spirit gives life; the flesh counts for nothing. The words I have spoken to you are spirit and they are life.
>
> —John 6:63

Everywhere Jesus went, people crowded around him "listening to the word of God" (Luke 5:1). Again we note a marked characteristic of the discourses of Jesus: "They were amazed at his teaching, because his message had authority" (Luke 4:32). This teaching was always rooted firmly in the Old Testament.

A key premise for Christ was "the Scripture cannot be broken" (John 10:35). John Wenham has masterfully shown that "belief in the Bible comes from faith in Christ," that is, "to Christ, what Scripture says, God says."[1] Jesus constantly quotes from the Old Testament and uses Old Testament narrative as straightforward records of fact. Jesus does not nullify the Old Testament in the "but I say to you" passages of Matthew 5, he deepens and enlarges the message and application because he has supernatural knowledge. Wenham is on target when he asserts, "When the moment came for his ministry to begin, he knew who he was, what his task was and what were the limitations of his human nature. With this authority he summoned his hearers to obedience to his word; with this authority he authenticated the Old Testament."[2]

This base of revealed knowledge in the Old Testament Scriptures helps us to understand why our Lord and the apostles kept underscoring the fulfillment of the Old Testament promises (Matt. 5:17–18). Repeatedly we see passages in the Gospels that make use of the "that it might be fulfilled" formula (Matt. 1:22; 2:15; 4:14; 8:17 and others). The kingdom of God depicted by the inspired prophets of the Old Testament (in both its material and spiritual dimensions)[3] was at hand, and both John the Baptist and Jesus took that prophetic definition as valid and built upon it without negating it. The time of fulfillment has come in Christ (Matt. 11:4–6); the powers of the age to come are breaking into this present evil age (Matt. 12:28; Heb. 6:5).

Jesus warned against the teaching of the Pharisees and Sadducees (Matt. 16:12). In contrast, Christ's teaching was new, and his listeners found it astonishing (Matt. 22:33; Mark 1:27; 11:18). Jesus developed a body of teaching (Mark 4:2) that was essentially the fulfillment of the Old Testament in his own person, life, deeds, sacrificial death, and resurrection.

Jesus speaks of this developing corpus when he says, "My teaching is not my own. . . . If anyone chooses to do God's will, he will find out whether my teaching comes from God or whether I speak on my own" (John 7:16–17). The content of this teaching was the subject of inquiry by the enemies of Jesus (John 18:19).

By the time we come to Acts, the gospel is called "the apostles' teaching" or "the apostles' doctrine" (Acts 2:42). In the writings of Paul it becomes "the faith" and "sound doctrine." This is the message Jesus preached. It has been called the *kerygma* or message of salvation (from "to proclaim," used sixty-one times in the New Testament). C. H. Dodd delineated the content of this heralded message (although he overstated the distinction between *kerygma* and *didache,* as we shall later discuss).[4] A. H. Hunter has instructively demonstrated that the content of the *kerygma* is essentially "Jesus Christ" (Rom. 16:25).[5] So Jesus explained to the disciples on the road to Emmaus, "And beginning with Moses and all the Prophets, he explained to them what was said in all the Scriptures concerning himself" (Luke 24:27).

The *kerygma,* or the gospel (virtually synonymous), is thus "a proclamation containing good news, the good news of an event, the event, the saving Act of God in Jesus Christ whereby 'He has visited and redeemed his people.'"[6] This body of teaching, this received tradition of fact, was first lodged in preaching. The good news is Jesus in his life, death, resurrection, and exaltation as fulfilling the Scriptures and summoning all of humankind to repentance and faith for the forgiveness of sin. This was the foundational message taking shape in the preaching of Jesus and reflected more fully in the preaching of the apostles.

So from the beginning, preaching has never been mere human words about God so much as God's words to humanity. We begin to see the relationship between the living Word (Christ Jesus), the written Word (the Scriptures), and the preached Word. Jesus Christ is himself the preacher above all other preachers, and in his majestic and powerful message we have the prototype of what all preaching is to be.

1. John W. Wenham, *Christ and the Bible* (Downers Grove, Ill.: InterVarsity Press, 1972), 6, 12.

2. Ibid., 60.

3. David L. Larsen, *Jews, Gentiles, and the Church: A New Perspective on History and Prophecy* (Grand Rapids: Discovery House, 1995), 11–27.

4. C. H. Dodd, *The Apostolic Preaching and Its Development* (London: Nisbet, 1936).

5. A. H. Hunter, *The Message of the New Testament* (Philadelphia: Westminster, 1954), 25.

6. Ibid., 25.

2.2.3   PREACHING AS THE MEDIUM OF JESUS

> The large crowd listened to him with delight.
>
> —Mark 12:37b

Jesus went into Galilee," we read in the gospel narrative, "proclaiming the good news of God" (Mark 1:14); for indeed as our Lord said, "Let us go somewhere else—to the nearby villages—so I can preach there also. That is why I have come" (Mark 1:38).

Even some evangelicals seem surprisingly skeptical about the trustworthiness of the representations made by the Evangelists. For example, some critics question if our Lord himself used the Trinitarian baptismal formula in the Great Commission of Matthew 28:18–20, or was it added later by a redactor? The verbal variations in the reporting of Christ's utterance in relation to the *ipssima verba* of Christ may be variously explained, but we must insist that the gospel report is reliable and true. We may be confident, as Carl F. H. Henry expresses it, "There is to be sure, no reason to question that the writers preserve the thought and teaching of Jesus with singular precision and accuracy."[1] Professor Linnemann rightly laments that "the authority of God's Word is undermined by the systematic exercise of a critical predisposition to reduce the Word of God to literary-theological construction, instead of seeing it as the revelation of our creator and redeemer."[2]

The parable of the sower and the seed in Matthew 13 shows us the importance of the Word of God (Luke 8:11). Here we wrestle with responses to the declaration and dissemination of the message of the Word. The sower and the four kinds of soul-soil show that Jesus carefully considered his audience. The audience criticism of J. Arthur Baird impressively establishes the fact that both Jesus and the Evangelists are concerned about who is being addressed. Several identifiable audiences must be considered: the twelve disciples, the crowd of disciples, the opponent crowd, and the opponents. Fascinatingly, "the Evangelists identify the audience in 98 percent of all the Synoptic logia and in 94 percent of all the Huck-Lietzmann units."[3] The nature of multilayered audiences is carefully spelled out.

The skill and acumen of the teaching approach of Jesus confronts us on every side.[4] Raymond Bailey is right when he says, "Jesus used every figure of speech and literary device imaginable."[5] He used metaphor (Matt. 5:13); simile (Matt. 10:16); hyperbole (Matt. 7:3–5; 19:24; 23:24); rhetorical questions (Luke 6:32; Matt. 6:27; 11:7; 18:12). He asked a total of 168 questions. And what shall we say about the incomparable parables of Jesus? And the double parables? And the allegories? And the visual object lessons? And the epigrams? Conversely, in the Gospel of Thomas we find 114 sayings but not a single story. The pattern of assertion, argument, illustration, and application is persistent in the discourses of Jesus.

Our Lord's view of the authority of Scripture—"You are in error because you do not know the Scriptures or the power of God" (Matt. 22:29)—assumes universals and principles. Biblical preaching is always a blend of inductive and deductive elements, but Christ's lead-in was generally inductive. He moved from the familiar to the unfamiliar, typically using an inductive pattern that began where the listeners were and led them to the principle and universal.

But Christ's preaching is supremely noteworthy not primarily because of his utilization of model technique. "The preaching of Jesus was distinctive for its great themes."[6] For centuries the sublime themes and powerful imagery of the discourses of Jesus have engaged the minds and hearts of young and old, rich and poor, educated and unlettered.

---

1. Carl F. H. Henry, *God, Revelation, and Authority* (Waco, Tex.: Word, 1979), 3:90. For an exceedingly competent treatment of these issues, see Ned B. Stonehouse, *Origins of the Synoptic Gospels: Some Basic Questions* (Grand Rapids: Eerdmans, 1963).

2. Eta Linnemann, *Is There a Synoptic Problem?* (Grand Rapids: Baker, 1992), 15.

3. J. Arthur Baird, *Audience Criticism and the Historical Jesus* (Philadelphia: Westminster, 1969), 33ff.

4. Herman Harrell Horne, *Jesus: The Master Teacher* (Grand Rapids: Kregel, 1964). On the content of Jesus' teaching, see G. Campbell Morgan, *The Teaching of Jesus* (New York: Revell, 1913).

5. Raymond Bailey, *Jesus the Preacher* (Nashville: Broadman, 1990). Analysis of Jesus' style in terms of adaptation, clarity, and impressiveness is revealing and positive; see Samuel S. Pan, "A Stylistic Analysis of Jesus' Teaching as Presented in the Canonical Gospels for Application to Contemporary Preaching" (Ph.D. dissertation, Penn State University, August 1990).

6. Francis J. Handy, *Jesus the Preacher* (Nashville: Abingdon-Cokesbury, 1949), 118. Other classic pieces in this area are Albert Richmond Bond, *The Master Preacher: A Study of the Homiletics of Jesus* (New York: American Tract Society, 1910); T. Alexander Hyde, *Christ the Orator* (Boston: Arena, 1893).

2.2.4 PREACHING AND THE MIGHTINESS OF JESUS

> "Where did this man get these things?" they asked. "What's this wisdom that has been given him, that he even does miracles!"
>
> —Mark 6:2b

The Christ we encounter in the gospel record is a supernatural Christ.[1] It is "the genius of the gospels," to use Merrill Tenney's apt phrase, to present in four matchless portraits the Lord of Glory, the God-man. There can be no accounting for his preaching and teaching apart from supernatural endowment. Thus in what we may call "the Bethlehem of preaching," essential foundations are laid for all subsequent preaching. Jesus notes these foundations when he speaks to the crowd about John (Matt. 11:7–19), excoriating the unrepentant cities of Galilee (vv. 20–24). As he is about to extend a tender invitation to the weary and burdened multitude (vv. 28–30), he consults with his Father and refers directly to their unique relationship:

All things have been committed to me by my Father. No one knows the Son except the Father, and no one knows the Father except the Son and those to whom the Son chooses to reveal him.

—Matthew 11:27

The total reliance of the Son upon the Father must be viewed as a model and a paradigm. This principle is apparent in John's gospel:

The one who comes from above is above all; the one who is from the earth belongs to the earth, and speaks as one from the earth. . . . For the one whom God has sent speaks the words of God, for God gives the Spirit without limit.

—John 3:31, 34

Jesus gave them this answer: "I tell you the truth, the Son can do nothing by himself; he can do only what he sees his Father doing, because whatever the Father does the Son also does. For the Father loves the Son and shows him all he does."

—John 5:19–20

Just as the living Father sent me and I live because of the Father, so the one who feeds on me will live because of me.

—John 6:57

I am one who testifies for myself; my other witness is the Father, who sent me.

—John 8:18

I have much to say in judgment of you. But he who sent me is reliable, and what I have heard from him I tell the world.

—John 8:26

I do nothing on my own but speak just what the Father has taught me.

—John 8:28b

Though you do not know him, I know him. If I said I did not, I would be a liar like you, but I do know him and keep his word.

—John 8:55

He who does not love me will not obey my teaching. These words you hear are not my own; they belong to the Father who sent me.

—John 14:24

If you obey my commands, you will remain in my love, just as I have obeyed my Father's commands and remain in his love.

—John 15:10

> I have called you friends, for everything that I learned from my Father I
> have made known to you.
>
> —John 15:15b

> All that belongs to the Father is mine. That is why I said the Spirit will
> take from what is mine and make it known to you.
>
> —John 16:15

The pattern of dependency is clear. While Christ is unique in his economic
subordination to the Father in the days of his flesh, he has marked out the way
that the preacher in every age must walk. We shall examine further the anointing
of the Spirit in relation to preaching, but surely if the Son of God needed to learn
of his Father, how much more do we?[2] Of the majestic discourse of Jesus, no
one ever said it more effectively than did John Broadus: "We know that preaching
deserves the highest excellence since it is the chosen instrument of the Savior
of the world, who himself came preaching."[3]

---

1. Wilbur M. Smith, *The Supernaturalness of Christ: Can We Still Believe in It?* (Boston: W. A. Wilde, 1940).
2. A salutary reawakening of interest in this subject is reflected in Dennis Kinlaw, *Preaching in the Spirit* (Grand Rapids: Frances Asbury, 1985); James Forbes, *The Holy Spirit and Preaching* (Nashville: Abingdon, 1989); Tony Sargent, *The Sacred Anointing: The Preaching of Dr. Martyn Lloyd-Jones* (Wheaton, Ill.: Crossway, 1994).
3. John Broadus, *On the Preparation and Delivery of Sermons* (New York: Harper, 1870), 5.

2.3 THE PROPULSIVE PREACHING OF THE FOLLOWERS OF JESUS

> I have revealed you to those whom you gave me out of the world. They
> were yours; you gave them to me and they have obeyed your word.
>
> —John 17:6

> We will . . . give our attention to prayer and the ministry of the word.
>
> —Acts 6:3–4

> Those who had been scattered preached the word wherever they went.
>
> —Acts 8:4

The bridal church that Jesus Christ promised to build (Matt. 16:18) was founded
on Christ himself, the Son of the living God, and upon the testimony of "the
apostles and prophets" (Eph. 2:20). The church came into being through the death
and resurrection of Christ and was born on Pentecost in a great outpouring of the
Holy Spirit. A vast spiritual explosion occurred, and led to exponential growth
that multiplied the members of Christ's body from a mere handful to about one
million believers by the end of the first century. Acts 1:8 maps the course of this

extraordinary phenomenon.

Energizing this expansion was the Holy Spirit of God (mentioned one hundred times in Acts). Also prominent was the preaching of the Word of God in the power of the Spirit. Roland Allen captures the reality: "The Holy Spirit was given: forthwith the apostles began to preach Christ. They began to preach Christ to those who did not believe."[1]

Many scholars who write about the sermons in Acts are skeptical about the historicity of Luke's report, but our analysis advances on the premise that we have accurate reporting of what was said.[2] Curiously, many secular writers have given greater support to the historical worth of Acts than have many religious writers. But what does Acts tell us about the preaching?

---

1. Roland Allen, *The Ministry of the Spirit* (Grand Rapids: Eerdmans, 1960), 22.
2. Everett F. Harrison, *Interpreting Acts: The Expanding Church* (Grand Rapids: Zondervan, 1986), 24ff. N. B. W. Ward Gasque, *Sir William Ramsay* (Grand Rapids: Baker, 1966) and the whole collection of Ramsay's books and research, which while older, strongly buttress the case for the historicity of the Book of Acts.

2.3.1 THE DIVERSE THREADS IN THE TAPESTRY

So the word of God spread. The number of disciples in Jerusalem increased rapidly, and a large number of priests became obedient to the faith.

—Acts 6:7

Those who "from the first were eyewitnesses" were also "servants of the word," Dr. Luke states (Luke 1:2). Jesus the great proclaimer becomes the proclaimed. C. K. Barrett is right when he insists that "New Testament Christianity was a proclaimed faith."[1] Acts is full of many kinds and genres of preaching. The Greco-Roman rhetoricians stressed adaptability in discourse. This is noticeable in Acts, where we detect "the necessity of presenting the Gospel in a form which will appeal to each particular audience."[2] Preaching is so prominent in Acts that Bailey goes so far as to say that "one of the purposes of the writer of Acts was to instruct readers in the art of preaching."[3]

In Acts we see instructions to leadership from both Peter and Paul. We have preaching in the precincts of the temple and in synagogues to Hellenistic Jews. We have messages to heathen in the provinces and on the Areopagus to the intellectual upper crust. Paul's speeches at the trial afford us glimpses into proclamation under exceedingly difficult circumstances. So we shall focus on some very different personalities in a variety of situations but all under the unction of the Holy Spirit.[4] Nowhere do we see the need and promise of Christian preaching any clearer than in the narratives of the Book of Acts. Let us examine some of these strands.

Peter as a Preacher

1. Acts 1:16–22. Peter addresses the followers of Jesus before Pentecost.
2. Acts 2:14–36. Keyed to the audience, saturated with Scripture, definite arrangement.
3. Acts 3:12–26. On the occasion of the healing of the lame man; the mission of Christ.
4. Acts 4:8–12, 19–20. To the Jewish leadership. Moves strongly to the person of Christ.
5. Acts 5:29–32. Another response to pressure that moves clearly to Jesus' death.
6. Acts 10:34–43. The great kerygmatic sermon on the house of Cornelius.
7. Acts 11:5–17. Peter's effective message in Jerusalem explaining Caesarea.
8. Acts 15:7–11. Peter's statement at the Jerusalem Council on Gentile salvation.

Stephen as a Preacher

Acts 7:2–53. A new kind of preacher (out of Hellenistic culture). Long historical survey from the Old Testament. Climaxes in salvation. Anticipates the argument of Hebrews.

Philip as a Preacher

Acts 8:4–8, 26–40. Philip preaches Christ to a city and to a solitary listener.

James as a Preacher

Acts 15:13–21. Powerful use of Amos 9 as authority. He speaks of how Moses "is preached in every city from the earliest times." Others besides Christians also preach.

Paul as a Preacher

1. Acts 9:20, "At once he began to preach in the synagogues that Jesus is the Son of God."
2. Acts 13:13–47. To Hellenistic Jews—Jesus is Savior (v. 23); Jesus is King (v. 22); Jesus is the Son (v. 33).
3. Acts 14:8–18. To pagan Gentiles—spoke of general revelation and ended with stoning.
4. Acts 17:15–34. To the Greek intellectuals; cites philosophers and poets; begins with the inscription on the statue. God is Creator. God is Sustainer. God is Judge.
5. Acts 20:15–38. To the elders of the assembly in Ephesus, "I have not hesitated to preach anything that would be helpful to you" (v. 20).
6. Acts 21–26, Paul's speeches at the trial;[5]
    a. on the steps of the castle, 21:27–22:29;
    b. before the council, 22:30–23:10;
    c. before Felix, 24:1–27. Paul shares vivid knowledge of the events.
    d. the appeal to Caesar, 25:1–12;
    e. before Agrippa, 25:13–26:32. The conversion testimony of Paul repeated three times. The messages here "more personal in tone and character."[6]

In the light of this data, Dibelius does not overstate the facts when he observes about Paul, "Preaching was in fact his calling, and with a fine single-mindedness he made it his life's work, everything else being subordinated to it."[7] We turn now to assay the message of the preaching in Acts.

---

1. C. K. Barrett, in Joseph A. Fitzmyer, "Preaching in the Apostolic and Subapostolic Age," in *Preaching in the Patristic Age,* ed. David G. Hunter (New York: Paulist, 1989), 24ff.
2. Maurice Jones, *St. Paul the Orator* (London: Hodder and Stoughton, 1910), 28.
3. Raymond Bailey, *Paul the Preacher* (Nashville: Broadman, 1991), 11.
4. F. Dale Bruner, *A Theology of the Holy Spirit* (Grand Rapids: Eerdmans, 1970). This is one of the richest and most satisfying treatments of this theme in the last half of the twentieth century.
5. Jones, *St. Paul the Orator.* Another important and solid study of this data is found in John Eadie, *Paul the Preacher* (London: Richard Griffin, 1859).
6. Jones, *St. Paul the Orator,* 164.
7. Martin Dibelius, *Paul,* as quoted in Bailey, *Paul the Preacher,* 87.

2.3.2 THE DYNAMIC THEMES OF THE STORY

But the word of God continued to increase and spread.

—Acts 12:24

The object of the apostles was to preach the Word of God everywhere (Acts 16:6). After all, there is no good news unless it is told. They varied their approach to suit their audience.[1] Lake and Cadbury have demonstrated Paul's distinctive style before the Areopagus (his use of neuters, particles, alliteration, repetitions, and various idiomatic expressions).[2] If this is so, the issue yet remains: Was there a common and shared message that, although adapted, did not change?

We have already argued our agreement with C. H. Dodd that there was a defined and identified core of preaching material used by all of the apostles in their proclamation. While there is a distinction between preaching and teaching *(kerygma and didache),* it is generally felt that Dodd overstated the distinction.[3] The essence of the message is Jesus Christ (cf. 1 Cor. 15:1–3). In what seems to be a curious disparagement of doctrinal assertion, Michael Green inveighs against "a fixed *kerygma.*"[4] Granted the variations to which we have already alluded, we are assisted by Mounce's observation that the *kerygma* is "not the outline of a particular sermon" or "a ready-made proclamation that was delivered on every occasion."[5] The *kerygma* is rather "a survey of primitive Christology arranged as such." It is "the theology of the primitive church."[6] Mounce argues well for a pre-Pauline *kerygma* and effectively speaks to Green's concerns. Mounce well concludes that preaching involves the miraculous contemporizing of the Christ-events "and moves the individual to respond in faith."[7]

The unchanging theme of Christian preaching then is Jesus Christ. The Old Testament is seen as promising Christ; the preacher heralds the fulfillment. Building on Wilhelm Vischer's *Christological Exegesis of the Old Testament,* G. C.

Berkouwer concludes: "Either the Old Testament is full of Christ or the writers of the New Testament have simply, on the basis of their Christian faith, read Christ into the Old Testament—an undeniable falsification of history."[8]

The discourses of Acts are studded with reference to Christ. Even in the supposedly atypical sermon in Athens, Paul preaches Jesus and the Resurrection. If the Christian were to preach a sermon from an Old Testament text that a Jewish rabbi could preach, then that sermon is not Christian proclamation. The theme of the ministry of the Holy Spirit is ever our Lord, and the theme of Christian preaching under the tutelage of the Holy Spirit is Jesus Christ (cf. John 15:26–27; 16:13–15). If Christ is the only way to the Father, then we are not surprised he is the subject and focus of apostolic preaching (Acts 4:12).

Jesus anticipated the worldwide proclamation of the good news (Matt. 26:13), which we watch take place in Acts. The early believers could not be silenced in their testimony, insisting "we cannot help speaking about what we have seen and heard" (Acts 4:20). Even the remembrance of the Lord in Communion was a proclamation of his death (1 Cor. 11:26, *katangello*). All believers properly shared in the proclamation (1 Cor. 14:26; 1 Peter 2:9). The themes are "the wonders of God," the work of God in Christ, the death and resurrection of Jesus, and the necessity of faith and repentance. The pattern is first vertical—what God has done; then horizontal—what God expects us to do. This is the pattern found in the Epistles, as we shall see in the next section. In the light of these building blocks, we can underscore the contention of John Bright: "The strength of the church lies in the gospel it proclaims—thus in its preaching today. . . . The church lives, let it be repeated, in her preaching—always has and always will."[9]

---

1. F. F. Bruce, *The Defense of the Gospel in the New Testament* (Grand Rapids: Eerdmans, 1959); Abraham J. Malherbe, *Paul and the Thessalonians* (Philadelphia: Fortress, 1987). Both afford splendid insights.
2. K. Lake and H. J. Cadbury, *The Beginnings of Christianity* (London: Macmillan, 1933), 1:209.
3. Supplying appropriate critique and correction for C. H. Dodd are Robert H. Mounce, *The Essential Nature of New Testament Preaching* (Grand Rapids: Eerdmans, 1960); Jesse Burton Weatherspoon, *Sent Forth to Preach: Studies in Apostolic Preaching* (New York: Harper, 1954); Robert C. Worley, *Preaching and Teaching in the Earliest Church* (Philadelphia: Westminster, 1969). A very helpful study is Everett F. Harrison, "Some Patterns of the New Testament Didache," *Bibliotheca Sacra* 119, no. 474 (April 1962): 118–28.
4. Michael Green, *Evangelism in the Early Church* (Grand Rapids: Eerdmans, 1970), 60.
5. Mounce, *Essential Nature of New Testament Preaching,* 64.
6. Ibid.
7. Ibid., 153.
8. G. C. Berkouwer, *The Person of Christ* (Grand Rapids: Eerdmans, 1954), 129.
9. John Bright, *The Authority of the Old Testament* (Nashville: Abingdon, 1967), 162, 164.

Table 2: Greek Words Used in the New Testament for Preaching and Communication

1. LEGŌ	preaching as "face-to-face direct-personal speech"	John's gospel uses LEGŌ 266 times—emphasizing the spontaneous character of Jesus' discourse
2. LALEŌ	outward utterance, speech, talk	John's gospel uses LALEŌ 60 times, not so much the substance of discourse
3. ERŌ, EIPOV	to say, speak, use language, command	often used in reporting what the Old Testament prophets said, now being fulfilled
4. EUANGELIZŌ	to announce and emblazon the good news	Matt. 11:5; Luke 4:18; 7:22; Acts 8:25; Rom. 1:15; 10:15; 15:20; 1 Cor. 1:17; 9:16
5. KĒRUSSŌ	to herald, proclaim, publish, announce	1 Cor. 1:21, 23; 2 Cor. 4:5. "No appeal without proclamation; No proclamation without appeal."[1]
6. ANANGELIZŌ	to announce, make known, report, rehearse	Acts 14:27; John 16:13–15; 1 John 1:5; Rom. 15:21; Acts 16:38; 2 Cor. 7:7
7. APANGELLŌ	to bring word, to report, proclaim	1 Thess. 1:9; 1 John 1:2; Acts 26:20; Heb. 2:12; Luke 8:34
8. HOMILEŌ	to converse with, to talk with	Luke 24:14, 17; Acts 20:11; 24:26
9. MARTUREŌ	witness, preaching as born of experience	John 1:7–8, 15, 32, 34; 3:26; 5:33; Acts 10:43; 23:11; 1 Cor. 15:15
10. KATANGELLŌ	to announce, to proclaim publicly, publish	Acts 13:5; 17:13; 1 Cor. 2:1 (with the idea of celebrating, commending)
11. DIDASKŌ	to teach, instruct, to give instruction	Matt. 4:23; 9:35; Rom. 12:7; 1 Cor. 4:17; 1 Tim. 2:12; 4:11
12. PROPHETEUŌ	to prophesy, to be a prophet, to foretell	1 Cor. 11:4–5; 13:9; 14:1, 3–5, 24, 31, 39; Rev. 11:3; 1 Peter 1:10; Jude 14
13. PARAKALEŌ	to beg, beseech, console, comfort	Acts 20:2; Rom. 12:8; 2 Tim. 4:2; Acts 25:2; 1 Cor. 16:12; Acts 21:12
14. PRO-EVANGELIZŌ	to announce good news beforehand	Gal. 3:8 (before the event by which the promise is made good)
15. DIANGELLŌ	to tell or announce thoroughly	Luke 9:60; Acts 21:26; Rom. 9:17 (to carry a message through)
16. PROKĒRRUSŌ	to cry or proclaim beforehand	Acts 3:20, 24; 13:24 (to proclaim by herald. cf. kērussō)
17. PARRĒSIAZOMAI	to be free in speaking, to have boldness	Acts 9:27, 29; 18:26; 19:8 (n.b. also Acts 13:46; 26:26; Eph. 6:20)

1. Cf. John Stott, *The Preacher's Portrait* (Grand Rapids: Eerdmans, 1961). A marvelous chapter on "The Herald," pp. 33–59.

#	Term	Definition	References
18.	PARAMUTHEOMAI	to address, calm, encourage, console	John 11:31 (also 16:19); 1 Thess. 2:12 (for the purpose of arousing)
19.	NOUTHETEŌ	to admonish, warn, exhort, put in mind	Acts 20:31; Rom. 15:14; 1 Cor. 4:14; Col. 1:28; 3:16; 1 Thess. 5:12, 14
20.	DIALOGIZOMAI	to bring together reasons, deliberate	Acts 20:7 (Luke 1:29; 5:21; Heb. 12:5), a more conversational word
21.	PHĀME	to make known one's thoughts, to say	2 Cor. 10:10; Luke 7:44; Acts 26:32; Acts 10:28; 16:1; 1 Cor. 10:15, 19
22.	PROLEGŌ	to say beforehand, to predict	2 Cor. 13:2; Gal. 5:21; 1 Thess. 3:4 (PRO may have the sense of plainly)
23.	PLĒROŌ	to fulfill, to fully preach	Rom. 15:19; Col. 1:25 (to cause to be everywhere known)
24.	AKOĒ	the word of hearing	Heb. 4:2, what is heard by the ear
25.	PEITHŌ	to persuade, to convince, to win over	often used of Paul's preaching in Acts (13:43; 17:2–4; 18:4; 19:8, 26; 26:28)
26.	DIALEGOMAI	to discourse, argue, discuss	Acts 17:2, 17; 24:12; Heb. 12:5 (preached in Acts 20:7, 9 AV)
27.	SUZĒTEŌ	to discuss, dispute, reason with	Acts 28:29 (Luke 24:15; Mark 8:11); Acts 11:29 (examine together)
28.	PARAINEŌ	to exhort, admonish, recommend	Acts 27:9, 22 (with the addition of LEGŌ + direct discourse)
29.	PROTREPŌ	to urge forward, exhort, encourage	Acts 28:27. From Homer down, but only once in the N.T.
30.	GNORIZŌ	to make known, to cause to be recognized	Luke 2:15; John 15:15; 17:26; Rom. 9:22; 2 Cor. 8:8; Eph. 3:5, 10; 6:21
31.	DĒLOŌ	to make manifest by relating, declare	1 Cor. 1:11; 3:13; Col. 1:8; Heb. 12:27; 1 Peter 1:11; 2 Peter 1:14
32.	DIĒGEOMAI	to recount, to relate in full, set forth	Acts 8:33; 9:27; 12:17; Heb. 11:32 (cf. Mark 5:16; Luke 8:39; 9:10)
33.	EKDIĒGEOMAI	to narrate in full or wholly, tell, declare	Acts 13:41; 15:3 (cf. Hab. 1:5 LXX), used in Aristotle's *Rhetoric*
34.	EXĒGEOMAI	to recount, rehearse, to lead out	Acts 10:8; 15:12; 21:19 (cf. Luke 24:35). To unfold—John 1:18.
35.	PHRAZŌ	to indicate plainly, make known, declare	Matt. 13:36; 15:15. To explain—as the thought in a parable.
36.	PROSLALEŌ	to speak to or with someone	Acts 13:43; 28:20. Preaching is certainly acoustical as Luther said.
37.	PLĒROPHOREŌ	to fulfill, accomplish, to fully proclaim	2 Tim. 4:17, with kerygma (mg. proclamation)

2.3.3 THE DRIVING THRUSTS OF SPIRITUAL URGENCY

> In this way the word of the Lord spread rapidly and grew in power.
> —Acts 19:20

Before us then is the high-density mass of apostolic preaching in Acts, a corpus of sentences and propositions about Jesus the Messiah and his redemptive works.[1] Though they are varied and often contrasting in format and nuance, a common core of fixed truth is evident. The purpose of this proclamation was not simply to inform minds of truth but to transform lives by the power of God. The ministry of the Holy Spirit who is ever "in, with and under the Word" is highlighted.

Peter's preaching on Pentecost is most instructive. Surely one of the most gripping miracles of Pentecost was the boldness and scriptural competence of Peter, who so recently had quailed in cowardice before a servant girl and seemed to be in a fog regarding the crucifixion and resurrection of the Lord. Now he is filled with the Holy Spirit. The narrative describes what happened: "Then Peter stood up with the Eleven, raised his voice and addressed the crowd" (Acts 2:14). In this sermon, as is evident again and again in Acts, the preacher is preaching for a verdict.

Powerful preaching is accompanied by response, both positive and negative. The aftermath is as supernatural as is the utterance itself. F. F. Bruce reminds us, "The worthlessness of the vessels is evidence of the transcendent power which attends the preaching of the gospel, the change which it effects in human lives is God's and not the apostles'."[2] In a most impressive climactic conclusion, Peter affirms the crucified one as both "Lord and Christ" (Acts 2:36). The result is stated: "When the people heard this, they were cut to the heart" (v. 37). The verb (katanusso) is strong, meaning to prick or pierce, to sting to the quick, to pain the mind sharply, to agitate it vehemently. This is a fulfillment of Jesus' prediction of the convicting work of the Holy Spirit (John 16:8–11).

We see joined in this sermon and its consequences the total sovereignty of God and the complete responsibility of humans in response. In the call to repentance (in the plural) and in the call for baptism to make the commitment visual and public (in the singular) we see clearly what is involved in obtaining the forgiveness of sins and the gift of the Holy Spirit (Acts 2:38–39). Peter warns and pleads "with many other words" (v. 40). The consequence of his urgent plea, "Save yourselves from this corrupt generation," was the baptism of three thousand persons. The pattern here is with regard not only to the truth conveyed but also to the power energizing the communication and its follow-up. The sermon Peter preached in Solomon's Colonnade after the healing of the beggar closes with the accent on conversion—"turning each of you from your wicked ways" (3:26)—and not surprisingly results in the further swelling of the ranks of those who believed (4:4).

Apostolic discourse is always disruptive and disturbing. It raises questions (Acts 4:15–17). The status quo is interrupted and the messengers become the objects of resentment and anger. "When they heard this, they were furious and wanted to put them to death" (5:33). To proclaim Christ is to enter the spiritual battle. It is warfare. But of the apostles we read, "Day after day, in the temple courts and from house to house, they never stopped teaching and proclaiming the good news that Jesus is the Christ" (v. 42).

Stephen's preaching elicited an even more drastic response. Of his efforts it is recorded, "They could not stand up against his wisdom or the Spirit by whom he spoke" (Acts 6:10). The radiance of his demeanor (v. 15) and the steadfastness of his vision of the living Christ (7:55–56) were part of his impression even on the uncircumcised hearts and ears. If indeed preaching is an extension of the ministry of Jesus, we see a marked resemblance of the servant to his Master in his martyrdom (see vv. 59–60). Jesus himself knew so painfully the agony of rejection and negative response even as Isaiah described it (cf. John 12:37–41).

The preaching of Paul corroborates these findings. Each of the apostle's sermons centers around a single thought, and that thought is invariably Jesus Christ and the redemption he purchased for us. Paul did not preach *like* Jesus, he preached *Jesus*. Like all of the apostolic preachers, Paul sought a faith-hearing and faith-response. (The word *faith* occurs two hundred times in Paul's writings.) The mood of the sermon corresponds to the situation. In this he and John, although so contrastive, are in accord. Paul's theology is a conversion theology.[3] His preaching was part of the eternal call of God to errant humankind (cf. 2 Thess. 2:13–14). Reception and refusal bring us to the drama of the proposal, and in this process we see hearing, acceptance, rejection, learning, obedience.[4]

Paul's preaching again and again rises out of the Old Testament but focuses on the Good News (Acts 14:21). After Paul ministered for three consecutive Sabbaths in Thessalonica ("reasoned . . . explaining . . . proving" [17:1–3]), the house was divided. Some were persuaded. Eadie is right in observing of this effort: "His argument lay in his exposition."[5] In Athens similarly, some hearers sneered, some equivocated, and some believed (17:32–34). We see the same in Corinth, Ephesus, and wherever Paul ministered. The same is true down to this present preaching hour.

Fascinatingly, at the conclusion of Acts (28:30–31), we again have the Isaiah oracle about the hardening of hearts in response to the truth. (It also occurs in Matthew 13 and in John 12.) Human resistance to the truth comes to a point where preaching itself hardens and makes the hearer impervious. But all of this is in the context of the relentless wooing and striving of the Holy Spirit (Gen. 6:3). God will not break down the door to the human heart, but will eternally accommodate those who choose not to welcome him into their lives. And so the Acts concludes with the apostle Paul preaching the gospel in Rome itself. We now turn to study the apostolic understanding and theology of the preaching event.

---

1. One cannot help being impressed with the sheer bulk of this material when examining this data in the pages of Rudolf Stier's massive work, *The Words of the Apostles* (Edinburgh: T & T Clark, 1860).
2. F. F. Bruce, *1 and 2 Corinthians* in the *Century Bible* (London: Oliphant, 1971), 197.
3. See my book *The Evangelism Mandate: Recovering the Centrality of Gospel*

Preaching (Wheaton, Ill.: Crossway, 1992) for a discussion of Paul's own conversion and a conversion theology.

4. Jerome Murphy-O'Connor, *Paul on Preaching* (New York: Sheed and Ward, 1963).
5. John Eadie, *Paul the Preacher* (London: Richard Griffen, 1859), 163.

2.4 THE PROFOUND PREACHING OF THE NEW TESTAMENT WRITERS

"Everyone who calls on the name of the Lord will be saved." How, then, can they call on the one they have not believed in? And how can they believe in the one of whom they have not heard? And how can they hear without someone preaching to them? And how can they preach unless they are sent? . . . Faith comes from hearing the message, and the message is heard through the word of Christ.

—Romans 10:13–14, 17

The Bible is truly the treasury of preaching. It is the document that establishes what preaching is and what it is intended to be. The Scriptures overflow with instructive narratives that describe various kinds of communication used by God. Preaching and testimony persist throughout the Canon all the way to the end of God's great plan as revealed in the Book of Revelation.[1]

Yet narrative does not yield doctrine or theology. Theology is reflection and rigorous rumination on the meaning of deeds and behavior, both divine and human. The Gospels give us the facts of Jesus' suffering and death with a body of predictive prophecy and a few glimmers of interpretive comment (such as Mark 10:45). But it is in the Epistles that inspired interpretation is shared, establishing the vicarious, substitutionary nature of Christ's redemptive death.

We turn now to the wealth of teaching by the apostles as stored up in their Epistles. Here we shall discern the critical understanding of preaching and its place as set forth by the apostolic preachers themselves. The awesome nature of the preaching task is described strikingly by Peter, who says, "If anyone speaks, he should do it as one speaking the very words of God" (1 Peter 4:11).

---

1. A valuable study of one aspect of preaching in Revelation can be seen in Rodney L. Petersen, *Preaching in the Last Days: The Theme of "Two Witnesses" in the Sixteenth and Seventeenth Centuries* (New York: Oxford University Press, 1993).

2.4.1 CATCHING THE IMPERATIVE OF PREACHING

To the New Testament writers, preaching stands as the event through which God works.

—Haddon Robinson

The apostle Paul's preaching came before his writing. Personal and private reading of the Scripture is not enough. That word must be spoken. Selwyn argued that much of the New Testament material was catechetical in nature.[1] Beyond that it may be asserted that many of the Epistles are written sermons or notes of sermons. The epistle of James is a prime example of this. Hebrews with all of its exhortations is surely a sermon-epistle, a blending of exposition and admonition that can be called a homily (Heb. 13:22).

Preaching was absolutely central to Paul. Karl Barth is perceptive when he sees preaching as a language event that is "God's activity, his address to each of us personally."[2] Preaching is the true translation of the text. "The task of the sermon is to make space for the Word of God."[3] This is why Barth argues so strenuously that preaching must be exposition of Scripture, not something lifted out of the Bible, but what the Bible says.[4]

In writing to the Galatians, Paul traces his conversion and call: "But when God, who set me apart from birth and called me by his grace, was pleased to reveal his Son in me so that I might preach him among the Gentiles, I did not consult any man" (Gal. 1:15–16). The gospel is at the core of ministry (1:11). That is why "another gospel is a contradiction in terms."[5] The standard for preaching is the gospel. So we understand that the obligation of the preacher rises out of "the essential authoritative nature of the gospel."[6] Paul solemnly intones, "If anybody is preaching to you a gospel other than what you accepted, let him be eternally condemned!" (1:9).

Similarly in the Corinthian correspondence, Paul makes his prioritization clear: "Christ did not send me to baptize, but to preach the gospel" (1 Cor. 1:17). The great themes are the preaching of the cross (vv. 17–25), the resurrection (15:1–12), and the lordship of Christ (2 Cor. 4:1–6).[7] Consistent with this sense is what A. T. Robertson called "the glory of the ministry—Paul's exultation in preaching." Paul stoutly insists, "Woe to me if I do not preach the gospel!" (1 Cor. 9:16). This necessity and compulsion were supernaturally laid upon the apostle.

In this light a helpful definition of preaching emerges. "Preaching is an act which fulfills the will of the sovereign in a public proclamation."[8] This explains Paul's passion to preach in Rome, Spain, and the regions beyond. He says, "I am so eager to preach the gospel also to you who are at Rome" (Rom. 1:15). He is not embarrassed by the gospel because of its power to save (vv. 16–17).

The Epistle to the Romans is the classic exposition of that gospel. Thus we understand why it is that "the gospel requires the immediacy of the oral voice" of the preacher.[9] Here we face the incomparable privilege, the agony and the ecstasy, of being entrusted with "the ministry of reconciliation" (2 Cor. 5:18). "And he has committed to us the message of reconciliation. We are therefore Christ's ambassadors, as though God were making his appeal through us. We implore you on Christ's behalf: Be reconciled to God" (vv. 19b–20).

In a time that F. F. Bruce describes as "a landslide away from apostolic teaching," the apostle John, writing in 1 John with "conscious authority," summons his hearers back to the "apostolic tradition," and in so doing puts the function of preaching in bold relief.[10] Some have maintained that the theme of 1 John is "the apostolic proclamation of the Word of Life."[11] In the first paragraph of the epistle we see the pattern:

What we have heard . . . we proclaim to you (1:1–2).
What we have heard . . . we proclaim to you (1:3).
The message we have heard . . . we announce to you (1:5).[12]

Thus the message that is eternal life in Christ and its communication are at the front of John's thinking and sense of purpose, as was the case with Paul and should be with all who follow in their calling.

---

1. E. G. Selwyn, *The First Epistle of Peter* (London: Macmillan, 1946), essay 2, 363ff.
2. Karl Barth in John William Beaudean Jr., *Paul's Theology of Preaching* (Macon, Ga.: Mercer University Press, 1988), 3.
3. Karl Barth, *Homiletics* (Louisville: Westminster/John Knox, 1991), 122.
4. Ibid., 49.
5. Beaudean, *Paul's Theology of Preaching,* 69.
6. Ibid., 86.
7. Ibid., 88.
8. Ibid., 153.
9. Ibid., 208.
10. F. F. Bruce, *The Epistles of John* (Grand Rapids: Eerdmans, 1970), 14, 17.
11. Gary Derickson, "What Is the Message of 1 John?" *Bibliotheca Sacra* 150, no. 597 (January 1993): 99.
12. Charles P. Baylis, "The Meaning of Walking in Darkness," *Bibliotheca Sacra* 149, no. 594 (April 1992): 219.

2.4.2 CONSIDERING THE IMPRESSIVENESS OF PREACHING

For what I received I passed on to you.

—1 Corinthians 15:3

The city of Corinth was an intimidating field of ministry for the apostle Paul (Acts 18:9–10). A notoriously wicked seaport (which has given the expression "to Corinthianize" to our language, a synonym for debauchery and licentiousness), Corinth was the milieu for an eighteen-month ministry in which "Paul devoted himself exclusively to preaching" (Acts 18:5). The response led to baptisms and a congregation of notable import. The soundness and legitimacy of Paul's gospel was never at issue in Corinth, but there were those in the assembly who criticized his appearance and his speaking style ("In person he is unimpressive and his speaking amounts to nothing" [2 Cor. 10:10]). This scathing and biting criticism set the stage for an informative and significant discussion by Paul of the relationship between preaching and rhetoric or style.

Rhetoric according to Aristotle is "giving effectiveness to speech." We shall have occasion to speak at greater length about Aristotle's influential book *Rhetoric* and the thinking of other Greco-Roman rhetoricians. Rhetoric is essentially how ideas are packaged for communication, and as such the word does not bear the generally pejorative sense in which the word is used today (e.g., "That is mere rhetoric!"). Aristotle's axiom is "For it is not enough to know what we ought to say; we must also say it as we ought."

We have already traced varying rhetorical styles in the prophets. We have seen diverse influences shaping synagogal rhetoric (i.e., how the truth of Scripture was conveyed or communicated). George A. Kennedy speaks of the *kerygma* as "a mode of rhetoric" and shows examples of deliberative rhetoric (Sermon on the Mount); epideictic rhetoric, the oratory of praise or blame (John 13–17); and judicial rhetoric (2 Corinthians). A variety of forms is used in the New Testament documents and proclamation.[1]

Rhetoric had to be important in Greco-Roman society. Duane Litfin has shown that there were two kinds of rhetoric: primary or functional and secondary or decorative. Unfortunately "the decorative or showcase declamation" seemed to be winning in the struggle between the two kinds of rhetoric.[2] The Corinthians tended to judge Paul by the standards of secondary or decorative rhetoric. They were prone to overdo just about everything. The Corinthian arch with its rows of leaves and its pairs of scrolls meeting at the corner in spiral volutes was the most elaborate and ornate of all the arches. Paul in his classic argument in 1 Corinthians 1–2 thus readily concedes that he did not come to Corinth with an impressively ornate rhetoric—"I did not come with eloquence or superior wisdom as I proclaimed to you the testimony about God" (2:1).

But what to the Corinthians seemed unimpressive and plain matched "the foolishness" of the cross which was "a stumbling block . . . and foolishness" but indeed "the power of God and the wisdom of God" (1 Cor. 1:21, 23–24). The Corinthians were not contesting the content of his preaching, but were finding fault with his form. Apollos, the Greek orator, was more to their liking. Paul wanted to avoid words of human wisdom and preach that bloody cross "with a demonstration of the Spirit's power" (2:4). The Corinthians were of the opinion that the only way to be wise was to be eloquent.[3] Paul did not repudiate rhetoric or proper concern for form. Rather, he warned against placing undue emphasis on form, which would make the gospel herald vulnerable to distortion and distraction.

Some have argued, in error I believe, that Paul is repenting of his Areopagus address in Athens as he writes these words to the Corinthians. As we have already noted, the content is correct at Athens and the rhetorical flexibility commendable. Both in his use of sources and quotations and in his style and strategy, we have a model to emulate in Paul on the Areopagus.[4] There is no inconsistency with 1 Corinthians 1–4, where Paul is essentially countering the lionization of secondary rhetoric.

Also consistent in 1 Corinthians is the apostle's preference for the gift of prophecy over the more flamboyant gift of glossalalia or speaking in tongues (1 Cor. 14:5). Paul lays stress on the communication of content and intelligibility. Thomas Gillespie has recently argued that prophecy is preaching, basically the interpretation of the apostolic *kerygma*.[5] It would seem closer to the facts not to equate prophecy with preaching but rather to emphasize that the charism of prophecy is a gift of special illumination of a truth of Scripture and its application. With the canon of Holy Scripture closed, we deny continuing revelation in the root sense. Yet the Spirit affords insight and wisdom in the Scripture. This is a gift that some preachers manifest but it is a gift that all Christians may exercise (cf. 14:31ff.; 11:4–5). To equate prophesying with "exhortatory preaching" is to ignore the more unstructured kinds of sharing insights from the Word in the life of a normal Christian assembly (14:26ff.). Such insights ought to appear in the content of preaching but in every case "the others should weigh carefully what is said" (v. 29). Obviously the gift of prophecy as discussed in 1 Corinthians has both continuity and discontinuity with the canonical prophets of the Old Testament and prophetic utterance found in other places in the New Testament. An immense literature has arisen in recent years on thorny aspects of the use and misuse of this charism of the Spirit.[6] The inclusion of 1 Corinthians 13 in the discussion of these gifts which speak the Word further buttresses Paul's earlier argument that the truth and its inward grasp and our motivation and spirit are more critical than outward appearance and impression (13:1–3).

---

1. George A. Kennedy, *New Testament Interpretation Through Rhetorical Criticism* (Chapel Hill: University of North Carolina Press, 1984). Another important treatise is Amos N. Wilder, *Early Christian Rhetoric: The Language of the Gospel* (London: SCM Press, 1964).
2. Duane Litfin, *St. Paul's Theology of Proclamation: 1 Corinthians 1–4 and Graeco-Roman Rhetoric* (Cambridge, Mass.: Cambridge University Press, 1994), 110.
3. Ibid., 245.
4. For useful treatments of the Areopagus address see Ned B. Stonehouse, *The Areopagus Address* (London: Tyndale, 1949); Kenneth O. Gangel, "Paul's Areopagus Speech," *Bibliotheca Sacra* 127, no. 508 (October 1970): 308ff.; John R. W. Stott, "The Paroxysm of Paul: Summary of a Sermon," *The Pulpit* (July–August 1964): 21–22.
5. Thomas W. Gillespie, *The First Theologians: A Study in Early Christian Prophecy* (Grand Rapids: Eerdmans, 1994), 165.
6. Wayne A. Grudem, *The Gift of Prophecy in 1 Corinthians* (Lanham, Md.: University Press of America, 1982). For a thoughtful response to Grudem, see Robert L. Thomas, "Prophecy Rediscovered?" *Bibliotheca Sacra* 149, no. 593 (January–March 1992). It is difficult for me to see an exegetical case for cessationism.

2.4.3 CONFIRMING THE IMPACT OF PREACHING

. . . in truthful speech and in the power of God.
—2 Corinthians 6:7

The scene is the pagan world of the first century with all of its sights, sounds, and sins.[1] The Book of Acts concludes with an open-ended picture of Paul at Rome. "For two whole years Paul stayed there in his own rented house and welcomed all who came to see him. Boldly and without hindrance he preached the kingdom of God and taught about the Lord Jesus Christ" (Acts 28:30). The gospel was spreading and the church was growing explosively and exponentially.

The dynamics of this growth are clear, and Michael Bullmore's nuanced study of Paul's theology of preaching in 1 Corinthians 2:1–5 contrasts "the traveling orators in which the power lay in the speaker and his stylistic virtuosity"[2] with Paul's dedication to the plain style (as over against the grand style preferred by the Corinthians). Paul was not rhetorically unaware. Like other writers in the New Testament he would occasionally indulge in beautiful Greek prose (cf. Eph. 1 or the writer to the Hebrews' magnificent period sentence in Heb. 1:1ff.), yet he diligently sought to avoid any stylistic artifice that might obstruct the proclamation of the crucified One.

Paul had preached to the Corinthians and they had received the message (1 Cor. 15:1–2). Preaching was the instrument used by the Holy Spirit to reach the lost. Ernst Fuchs insists that in this sense preaching "participates in God's omnipotence."[3] The impact of preaching is unequivocally clear when Paul states, "Our Gospel came to you not simply with words, but also with power, with the Holy Spirit and with deep conviction" (1 Thess. 1:5). In the following chapter the pattern is clear:

> The gospel is spoken—"We dared to tell you his gospel" (2:2).
> The gospel is shared—"Delighted to share the gospel" (2:8).
> The gospel is preached—"We preached the gospel of God" (2:9).
> The gospel is recognized as the Word of God—"You received the word of God" (2:13).[4]

In summary, "There is a divine, creative energy released in the act of listening to the orally proclaimed gospel,"[5] for "we speak not in words taught us by human wisdom but in words taught by the Spirit, expressing spiritual truths in spiritual words" (1 Cor. 2:13).

The whole "proclamatory interaction" must be seen as taking place in a fierce spiritual battle (2 Cor. 4:3–4). The assured ultimate triumph (2:14) cannot eclipse the reality of the division between "those who are being saved and those who are perishing" (2:15). In our preaching, "To the one we are the smell of death; to the other, the fragrance of life" (2:16). In all of this "our competence comes from God" (3:5b). The stakes are so high and the issue of eternity so weighty that Paul warns, "Do not peddle the word of God for profit" (2:17), and "do not use deception, nor . . . distort the word of God" (4:2). We are called as preachers to "speak before God with sincerity, like men sent from God" (2:17). Also, "by setting forth the truth plainly we commend ourselves to every man's conscience in the sight of God" (4:2). We are not to "preach ourselves, but Jesus Christ as Lord, and ourselves as your servants for Jesus' sake" (4:5). The Word of God will then illuminate and transform (4:6). We must not get in the way of or impede the work of the Holy Spirit in blessing the word of God. Preaching is ever "I, yet not I."

This section in the Corinthian correspondence (2 Cor. 2:12–4:6) is like a capstone to all that Paul shares with us about what preaching is and should be. G. Campbell Morgan says of this portion, "Perhaps nowhere in the New Testament is the subject of the ministry set forth in its sublimity as it is here."[6] On the basis of these steady and enduring foundations, Ralph Turnbull asserted a generation ago, "In spite of the ferment and the new forms of ministry devised by the church, the heart of the ministry of the past half century was, as it ever has been, the proclamation of the good news, the gospel, and its claim upon the whole life as taught by our Lord."[7]

---

1. E. M. Blaiklock, *The Christian in Pagan Society* (London: Tyndale Press, 1951).
2. Michael A. Bullmore, *St. Paul's Theology of Rhetorical Style: An Examination of 1 Corinthians 2:1–5 in the Light of First Century Graeco-Roman Rhetorical Culture* (San Francisco: International Scholars publications, 1995), 169f., 205–222.
3. Ernst Fuchs in John William Beaudean Jr., *Paul's Theology of Preaching* (Macon, Ga.: Mercer University Press, 1988), 17. Fuchs insists, "Proclamation requires the text, because it only continues what was revealed through Jesus, the event of God's word."
4. Ibid., 54.
5. Ibid., 56.
6. G. Campbell Morgan, *The Corinthian Letters of Paul* (New York: Revell, 1956), 234.
7. Ralph Turnbull, *A History of Preaching,* vol. 3 of Dargan (Grand Rapids: Baker, 1974), 14.

CHAPTER THREE

The Infancy and Childhood of Biblical Preaching (A.D. 70–450)

> The law of the LORD is perfect, reviving the soul. The statutes of the LORD are trustworthy, making wise the simple. The precepts of the LORD are right, giving joy to the heart. The commands of the LORD are radiant, giving light to the eyes. The fear of the LORD is pure, enduring forever. The ordinances of the LORD are sure and altogether righteous. They are more precious than gold, than much pure gold; they are sweeter than honey, than honey from the comb. By them is your servant warned; in keeping them there is great reward.
>
> —Psalm 19:7–11

We often hear nostalgic sighs for the worship practices of the early church. Doubtless there are some worship principles that are always relevant. But we must recognize the absence of evidence for a uniform liturgy in the early church.

Certainly there was no wedge between Jesus and Paul. The apostles enjoyed doctrinal harmony, and a rich diversity of expression existed among them as well. Yet there were differences and tensions. Recall the discussion in Galatians 2.

As we move beyond the apostolic age into the patristic period, material evidence is somewhat sparse, but we can see a common heritage preserved while variation in expression continues. The preaching Fathers are still deeply indebted to the Old Testament and are indeed *Benai-Tanakh* (children of the Scriptures).[1] They are the legatees of the developing New Testament canon, consisting of accounts of Jesus (Luke 1:1–4) and the expanding collection of apostolic correspondence among other items.

Just as God's revealed truth was expressed variously during the Exile, the return, and the intertestamental period, so the Fathers adapted to an ever-shifting kaleidoscope of circumstances. Just as the synagogue sermon that accompanied the reading of Scripture could be topical or expository, so we shall discern a similar variation among the preaching Fathers.[2] But whatever the environment for proclamation, Scripture was highly regarded. In the first-century synagogue, the reading could not be too long lest the expositor get away from the text, nor could the exposition be given more loudly than the reading of the text lest greater prominence be given to the interpretation.[3] The emphasis remained on the text. We now move to a more detailed examination of preaching among the Fathers.

---

1. A lovely expression coined by Bernard and Sue Bell.
2. Everett Ferguson, *Backgrounds for Early Christianity* (Grand Rapids: Eerdmans, 1987), 461.
3. Isaac Levy, *The Synagogue: Its History and Function* (London: Vallentine Press, 1963), 102.

3.1 THE UNEVEN LANDSCAPE OF PREACHING IN THE EARLY CHURCH

Much of our preaching in church at the present day would not have been recognized by the early Christians as *kerygma*.

—C. H. Dodd

Then the disciples went out and preached everywhere, and the Lord worked with them and confirmed his word by the signs that accompanied it.

—Mark 16:20

We can discern a continuity in preaching from New Testament times to the fifth century.[1] Three principal settings are in view in the postapostolic period: (1) kerygmatical or missionary preaching; (2) catechetical or instructional preaching; and (3) liturgical or preaching for the worshiping community. While A. T. Robertson in his *Types of Preachers in the New Testament* and others have underscored the rich variety of spokesmen for the gospel from the very beginning, early preaching was cut from the same piece of cloth. It is text-dependent.[2]

The preparations for the coming of Christ into the world are also to be seen as preparations for the promulgation of the gospel message Christ made possible. Speaking of the first-century world, Paul Johnson is graphic: "The world was intellectually ready for Christianity . . . it was waiting for God."[3] The early Christian proclaimers confronted a Greco-Roman world in decline and which was moving toward its demise before the barbarian hordes. Her divisions and debaucheries rendered her increasingly helpless and hopeless. The gospel message was vibrant with hope and power and made an immediate and revolutionary impact. Johnson aptly characterized the early church as "a loosely organized revivalistic movement awaiting the *parousia* (the second coming of Christ)." The place of preaching in this expansion is now before us.

---

1. Robert D. Sider, *The Gospel and Its Proclamation* (Wilmington, Del.: Michael Glazier, 1983), 14.
2. John Ker, *Lectures on the History of Preaching* (New York: Armstrong, 1889), 54.
3. Paul Johnson, *A History of Christianity* (New York: Atheneum, 1976), 7.

3.1.1 PREACHING AND THE ENLARGEMENT OF VISIBILITY

Preaching carries the church.

—Elizabeth Achtemeier

Organizational patterns began to shift with the death of the apostles. Volz concludes, "It is certain that by the end of the first century the Pauline multiplicity of ministries given by the Spirit has developed into the threefold offices of bishop, presbyter (or elder), and deacon. Yet there was considerable overlap between the two triads and within them."[1] There is a sense of order and proper authority (1 Clement 44:1–6, c. A.D. 96).

Without church buildings and with the synagogues less available, many meetings were held in homes, the discourse informal. We have fragments of the preaching but little extant preaching from before the middle of the third century. Laypersons, bishops, and itinerant evangelists preached. Howden characterizes it all: "Early Christian preaching was biblical preaching," in which Scripture was cited as authority and Scripture was applied, usually explicitly.[2]

The geographical extension of Christianity through North Africa and up into the Rhone Valley in Europe made the increase in visibility and influence a vexing problem for Imperial Rome.[3] Serious inroads were being made into all classes in society. Sporadic local outbursts of persecution and a series of empire-wide persecutions followed.

Amid all this tumult, preaching continued. Wayne Meeks, who has concentrated on the early urban Christians, concedes the point: "Beside exposition of Scripture, preaching in the assemblies must have included other things, preeminently statements about Jesus Christ, and inferences, appeals, warnings, and the like, connected logically or rhetorically with these statements."[4] Michael Smith likewise concludes: "From what we can tell, Bible reading and preaching composed much of the programme of the public meetings of the Christian congregations."[5]

Eusebius, the first church historian, describes the action in the province of Asia around the turn of the first century: "Many, who amplified the Message, planting the saving seed of the heavenly kingdom far and wide in the world . . . evangelizing with God's help and favor . . . [relying] not on plausible, clever argument but on manifestations of the Holy Spirit and of supernatural power."[6] With cascading numbers of conversions, enemies of Christianity from within and without were hard at work.[7]

The believers needed to be alert to false prophets and false teachers. The *Didache* (c. A.D. 100) warns against false prophets and contrasts them with genuine prophets (11:3). The Shepherd of Hermas (c. A.D. 100–150) speaks of "apostles and teachers who preached unto the whole world" (15:1) and focuses on purity in the church. Polycarp to the Philippians (c. A.D. 108 or 116) is full of scriptural allusions. The Epistles of Ignatius (c. A.D. 107 or 115) center on the unity of the church and pastoral holiness.

Generally considered the oldest surviving sermon manuscript from this period is the anonymous homily called Second Clement (c. A.D. 120–140). Based on Isaiah 54:1, the homily is described by Hatch as "inspired by a genuine enthusiasm, it is rather more artistic in its form than a purely prophetic utterance is likely to have been."[8] Somewhat Pauline in tone, it ends with a splendid ascription. The writer calls his hearers to "pay attention while we are being exhorted by the Elders, but also when we have gone home let us remember the commandments of the Lord" (17:3–5).[9]

What leaves us uneasy in our survey of this foundational time is a perceptible weakening of the gospel message itself. We listen in vain to hear the kerygmatic proclamation of the death, burial, and resurrection of Christ. In his doctoral work, T. F. Torrance surveyed *The Doctrine of Grace in the Apostolic Fathers* and found that the doctrine of grace which was absolutely pivotal in the New Testament "did not have that radical character" in this expression.[10] A teaching of salvation by works or hypersacramentalism seeps in insidiously. We have seen the shape of what is to come.

---

1. Carl A. Volz, *Pastoral Life and Practice in the Early Church* (Minneapolis: Augsburg, 1990), 19.
2. William D. Howden, "Preaching," in *Encyclopedia of Early Christianity,* ed. Everett Ferguson (New York: Garland, 1990), 748.
3. Kenneth Scott Latourette, *The First Five Centuries* (Grand Rapids: Zondervan, 1970), 65–113.
4. Wayne A. Meeks, *The First Urban Christians: The Social World of the Apostle Paul* (New Haven, Conn.: Yale University Press, 1983), 146.
5. Michael Smith, *From Christ to Constantine* (Downers Grove, Ill.: InterVarsity Press, 1971), 39.
6. Eusebius *Ecclesiastical History* 3.37, quoted in Ramsay MacMullen, *Christianizing the Roman Empire* (New Haven, Conn.: Yale University Press, 1984), 25.
7. Robert L. Wilken, *The Christians As the Romans Saw Them* (New Haven, Conn.: Yale University Press, 1984). A thoughtful study of the early Christians.
8. Edwin Hatch, *The Influence of Greek Ideas and Usages Upon the Christian Church* (London: Williams and Norgate, 1901), 106.
9. In *Twenty Centuries of Great Preaching,* ed. Clyde Fant Jr. and William M. Pinson Jr. (Waco, Tex.: Word, 1971), contains the entire sermon, 1:19–25, and characterizes it as the "oldest surviving sermon manuscript." The next sermon in this fine collection is from Origen.
10. Thomas F. Torrance, *The Doctrine of Grace in the Apostolic Fathers* (Grand Rapids: Eerdmans, 1959), 133ff.

3.1.2 PREACHING AND THE EXPLORATION OF IDENTITY

> On the day called Sunday, there is a meeting for "all in one place," according to the city or the countryside where one lives . . . the Memoirs of the Apostles or the Writings of the Prophets are read as long as there is time, and when the reader has ceased, the president in an address gives a reminder and a challenge to imitation of these good things.
>
> —Justin Martyr *Apology I* 67

As the gospel message moved powerfully into the Greco-Roman world, the church faced the pressures of Greek influence and thought. Western civilization is built both on a Christian and a classical legacy. Cultural conflict provided the backdrop against which the church sought to forge a sense of her identity in Christ. Already in 1 Clement to the Corinthians (A.D. 80–100), a pastoral concern for staying with the Holy Scriptures appears. "You have studied the Holy Scriptures, which are true, and given by the Holy Spirit. You know that nothing unjust or counterfeit is written in them" (45:2–3).[1]

Evidence of Greek rhetorical influence can be seen in Melito of Sardis (c. A.D. 150) in his *On the Pascha:* "For born Son-like, and led forth lamb-like, and slaughtered sheep-like, and buried man-like, he has risen God-like, being by nature God and man." Thomas Carroll discerns new elements of Greek influence here, but rhetoric is still servant and not master.[2]

An important early defender of the purity of the message was Justin Martyr (d. about A.D. 166). Justin was born in Palestine and converted in Ephesus. He shows significant Greek influence but defended Christianity from both Jewish and Greek attack. A layman himself, he yet pleaded, "Everyone who can preach the truth and does not preach it, incurs the judgment of God."

Justin must also be seen as an important interpreter of Christian worship, especially baptism and communion and their relationship to preaching. Also critical is his rejection of Marcionism (that is, the rejection of the Old Testament) and his insistence that "all Scripture came through the Logos, centered on the Logos, and led back to the Logos," the Logos being Jesus Christ.[3] He is apparently responsible for the well-known gloss on Psalm 96:10, "The Lord has reigned from the tree." The final paragraph of his *Dialogue with Trypho* (142) discloses the heart of the communicator:

> And I in turn prayed for them, saying, "I can wish you no greater blessing than this, gentlemen, that, realizing that wisdom is given to every man through this Way, you also may one day come to believe entirely as we do that Jesus is the Christ of God."

Another key leader who labored to coalesce Christian and classical components was Clement of Alexandria (A.D. 150–215). Clement is at the vortex of the mingling of Greek gnostic thinking, Philonic Jewish exegesis, and emerging Christian theology. With his student, Origen, Clement is responsible for a school of biblical interpretation with immense implication for preaching.

Clement was active in the worshiping communities of cosmopolitan Alexandria. He may have been the first thinker to speak of the written Old Testament and written New Testament as such.

He has left us only one sermon, a message titled "Who Is the Rich Man Who Can Be Saved?" based on Mark 10:17–31. Some of the wealthy were being drawn to Christianity, and Clement warns them but argues that money is essentially value-neutral.

Clement was quite possibly influenced in his sermon by *The Epistle to Diognetus,* which is addressed to an inquirer after the truth (possibly the Diognetus who was tutor to Marcus Aurelius). The preaching here begins with the prologue of John's gospel and moves quickly to John 3:16. He holds forth Christ the eternal One as the Savior.[4]

While *The Epistle of Barnabas* reflects early feuds between Christians and Jews, some fragments of the life of Bishop Papias of Hierapolis also survive and contribute to our grasp of the developing situation. Irenaeus attributes to him the authorship of *Expositions of the Oracles of the Lord.* Eusebius notes how Papias used *Gospel* and *Epistle* and related the story of Jesus before the woman accused of many sins. Papias wishes to purge Christianity of gnosticism.[5] But another factor must be considered.

---

1. The source of most of these quotations is J. B. Lightfoot, *The Apostolic Fathers* (Grand Rapids: Baker, 1980) or *The Apostolic Fathers,* ed. Kirsopp Lake, in the Loeb Classical Library (Cambridge, Mass.: Harvard University Press, 1952) in two volumes.

2. Thomas K. Carroll, *Preaching the Word: Messages of the Fathers of the Church* (Wilmington, Del.: Michael Glazier, 1984), 37.

3. Walter H. Wagner, *After the Apostles: Christianity in the Second Century* (Philadelphia: Fortress, 1994), 164.

4. John Foster, *After the Apostles: Missionary Preaching of the First Three Centuries* (London: SCM Press, 1951), 82.

5. Edward H. Hall, *Papias and His Contemporaries* (Boston: Houghton Mifflin, 1899).

3.1.3 PREACHING AND THE EXPERIENCE OF AGONY

The blood of the martyrs is the seed of the church.

—Tertullian

The ministry and outreach we have described is set in intense conflict. In his classic work, H. E. W. Turner shows how the early church sought to keep the teachings of the Lord Jesus and the traditions of the apostles undefiled. He argues that the development of Christian theology is "the interaction of fixed and flexible elements, both of which are necessary."[1]

Equally as bruising for the life of the church organism was its persecution. There were those who cowered and quailed before pressure, but the example and nobility of so many sufferers made a deep and indelible impression upon the world. Their testimony became a sermon for their generation.

Christianity was a destabilizing force in its challenge to emperor worship and its leveling of social stratification. The relentless evangelism seemed only to be fueled by persecution (cf. "On that day a great persecution broke out against the church at Jerusalem, and all except the apostles were scattered throughout Judea and Samaria. . . . Those who had been scattered preached the word wherever they went," [Acts 8:1, 4]).

Such oppression prevented the church from becoming "at ease in Zion." As Clement of Alexandria put it in the dialogue between Rusticus the Prefect and Justin: "We would rather suffer now and please the Lord, than please you and suffer on that day."[2]

Workman observes that the suffering foundations of the Christian church were laid "deep in Calvary."[3] A theology of suffering has always been a necessity for the church. Christian proclamation of the gospel inevitably brought the early church on a collision course with constituted authority and culture. Seneca said of both slaves and Christians that anything was lawful against them. Tacitus described some of the scenes of suffering:

> Mockery of every sort was added to their deaths. Covered with the skins of beasts, they were torn by dogs and perished, or were nailed to crosses, or were doomed to the flames and burnt, to serve as a nightly illumination when daylight had expired. Nero offered his gardens for the spectacle, and was exhibiting a show in the circus, while he mingled with the people in the dress of a charioteer or stood aloft in a car.
>
> —*Annals* 15.44

And in all of this the preaching of the Word continued under the outpoured blessing of the Spirit of God.

---

1. H. E. W. Turner, *The Pattern of Christian Truth* (London: Mowbrays, 1954). Another key volume is the superb treatment by Harold O. J. Brown, *Heresies* (Grand Rapids: Baker, 1984).
2. David Winte, *100 Days in the Arena* (Wheaton, Ill.: Shaw, 1977), day 80.
3. Herbert B. Workman, *Persecution in the Early Church* (Nashville: Abingdon, 1906, 1960), 11.

3.2 SOME SHINING LIGHTS AMONG THE PREACHERS

The preaching of the truth shines everywhere and enlightens all men that are willing to come to a knowledge of the truth. This preaching, as cited, and this Faith, as forementioned, the Church although scattered in the whole world, diligently guards as if it lived in one house, and believes, like the above, as if it had but one mind and the same heart, and preaches and teaches and hands on these things harmoniously, as if it had but one mouth. And although there are different languages in the world, the force of the tradition is one and the same.

—Irenaeus *Adversus Haereses* 1.10

Christianity was born into the matrix of Greco-Roman and Jewish tension. Mediterranean culture helped create an uneven fusion between the classical heritage and the Judeo-Christian heritage. In intellectual centers like Alexandria, there is an almost overmastering Greek influence, as we can trace in a Jewish thinker like Philo. In other areas the authentic message of historic Christianity is distinctively preserved.

When after 250 years of persecution the church came under imperial favor, even more pressure was brought to bear upon her to conform to the prevailing culture as a whole. This tension affects preaching in two particular areas: (1) hermeneutically, that is, in terms of understanding and interpreting the Scripture; and (2) homiletically, that is, in terms of preaching and communication of the truth. We shall examine some leading preachers of the time and how they demonstrate diverse approaches in the developing synthesis.

3.2.1 TERTULLIAN—THE CHAMPION OF TRUTH

> We assemble to read our sacred writings, if any peculiarity of the times makes either fore-warning or reminiscence needful. However it be in that respect with the sacred words, we nourish our faith, we animate our hope, we make our confidence more steadfast; and no less by inculcations of God's precepts we confirm good habits.
> —Tertullian *Apologeticus* 1.118

Although we have no extant sermons from Tertullian, he is apparently the first to give the name *sermon* to the Christian address. He was born about 150 in Carthage in North Africa, the son of a Roman centurion. He studied law in Rome and was attracted to Stoicism, which may have led him to study Christianity. He was converted in 193 and ultimately came under the influence of Montanus, who began to prophesy against the formalism and sinfulness of the church in Asia about 170.[1]

Tertullian was a doughty defender of orthodox Christology and Trinitarian theology. He addressed contemporary issues like divorce and remarriage and Christian participation in the shows with fiery discourse. He criticized the academy and asked, "What has Athens to do with Jerusalem?" He contrasted knowledge in general (such as philosophical knowledge) with divine revelation. Jerome called him a man of "sharp and vehement temper."

Danielou characterizes the Latin Christianity Tertullian influenced as having "a realism which knows nothing of the Platonic devaluation of matter; a subjectivity which gives special prominence to inner experiences; and a pessimism which lays more stress on the experience of sin than on transfiguration."[2] Obviously Tertullian is a forerunner of Augustine.

Robert Payne speaks of Tertullian as "the thunderer." He is witty and eloquent. He hates deeply and feels keenly. "In that overheated world where Tertullian explores his own anger, there are occasional moments of coolness, of an unexpected tenderness. At such moments the lawyer's tricks fall away."[3] In his puritanism and Montanism he took a firm stand against strangulating sacramentalism and vapid intellectualism.

1. Timothy David Barnes, *Tertullian: A History and Literary Study* (Oxford: Clarendon, 1971) is the best overall study of Tertullian and his times that I have seen.
2. Quoted in Thomas K. Carroll, *Preaching the Word: Messages of the Fathers of the Church* (Wilmington, Del.: Michael Glazier, 1984), 138. Also, Robert Dick Sider, *Ancient Rhetoric and the Art of Tertullian* (New York: Oxford, 1971).
3. Robert Payne, *The Fathers of the Western Church* (New York: Viking, 1951), 47.

3.2.2 Irenaeus—The Churchman Always

This, beloved, is the preaching of the truth, and this is the manner of our salvation, and this is the way of life, announced by the prophets and ratified by Christ and handed over to the apostles and handed down by the church in the whole world to her children. This must be kept in all security, with good will and by being well-pleasing to God through good works and sound moral character.

—Irenaeus, *Proofs*, 98

The worthy bishop at Lyon in the Rhone Valley, Irenaeus (135–202?) ministered in the administrative center of all Gaul. He was born in Smyrna and heard the sermons of the great leader and martyr Polycarp. He speaks of the New Testament as a gathered collection and refers to the preaching of both Paul and Peter in Rome as well as the character of the four gospels (*Adversus Haereses* 3.1.1). His ecclesiology reflects great pastoral concern and traces four dispensations from Adam and Eve until Christ. His doctrine of Christ and his *Christus Victor* have enjoyed new popularity in our own time. He insisted that the God of the Old Testament and the God of the New Testament are the same.

Irenaeus fought the gnostics who made inroads on his own congregation and seduced away the wife of one of his deacons. He conceded that his preaching was not eloquent, but he maintained that it was without distortion. He preached in the outdoor markets of Lyons as well as in the villages in the general area (preface to *Adversus Haereses* 1.1). He preached to the Celts in their own language and apologized because his Greek had become rusty. His absorbing concern was for the unity of the church, and he sought to clarify the implications of Montanism. God used his ministry and message to establish the church in southern France.[1]

1. For an important study of Irenaeus, see J. Barton Payne, "The Biblical Interpretation of Irenaeus," in *Inspiration and Interpretation* (Grand Rapids: Eerdmans, 1957). For Irenaeus, the words of Scripture are the words of God.

3.2.3 Hippolytus—The Charge Against Heresy

Feed the holy flock.
    —Hippolytus *Apostolic Tradition*, the first duty of the ordained

Hippolytus (c. 150–235) was apparently a disciple of Irenaeus who served in the church of Rome. He was inspired by Irenaeus to engage in lifelong combat with the gnostics and other heretical groups. He is considered one of the four ranking theologians of his time, along with Tertullian, Clement of Alexandria, and Origen. His description of a worship service in Rome makes mention of the reading of Scripture and the exposition of the lessons. Also among his legacies are examples of eucharistic prayers, catechetical forms, discussions on baptism (even to such practical matters as not wearing jewelry during baptism), the role of deacons in assisting the bishop, and even a baptismal liturgy from which the Apostles' Creed may have developed.[1]

A controversialist, Hippolytus even wrote a defense of apostolic authorship of the Fourth Gospel and the Book of Revelation. We have his sermon "In Sanctam Theophaniam," based on Matthew 3:13–17. Garvie observes that this preaching justifies the title Eusebius gave him, "man of the word."[2] The sermon artfully uses analogy and is highly rhetorical in form. Thus Hippolytus takes his stand in the enlarging circle of witnesses to the nature of the early preaching.

---

1. F. F. Bruce, *The Spreading Flame* (Grand Rapids: Eerdmans, 1958), 254.
2. Alfred Ernest Garvie, *The Christian Preacher* (New York: Scribner's, 1923), 68ff.

3.2.4 CYPRIAN—CUSTODIAN OF THE MIDDLE

> Thus the Church, filled with the light of the Lord, sends forth her beams over the whole earth; the light which is diffused over all places, being one, and the unity of the body unbroken. So the Church expands her boughs over the whole world in the rich results of her exuberance, and scatters, with beneficent hand, onward-flowing streams; yet is there one head, one source, one mother, whose abundance springs from her own fruitfulness.
>
> —Cyprian, *Treatises,* 5

Cyprian (c. 200–258) was born to an upper-class family near Carthage in North Africa. He was well educated and served for years as a teacher of rhetoric. He was converted in 246 and made bishop of Carthage, where he served from 248 until his martyrdom in 258. With Tertullian, after whom he modeled himself, he presents us with examples of the earliest Latin exegesis and preaching.

Greatly concerned about the unity of the church, he fled from persecution in the early Decian massacres. The persecution was followed by a devastating plague. Cyprian ultimately died a martyr's death, the first North African bishop to be slain for the gospel.

While lacking the fire of Tertullian, Cyprian was a generous and self-giving leader, notwithstanding his social origin and the apparent fact that he was a senator. We do not have any of his sermons but do possess fourteen treatises, eighty-one epistles, and a short memoir by his deacon. These all reflect the flavor of his often ornate but effective discourse. He dealt with the critical issues in polity and church life, insisting strongly, for instance, that presbyters "be well-informed in the Word and exemplary in life."[1] While he held to a high view of the power of the episcopate, he was merciful and generous to the "lapsed."

Cyprian describes his missionary preaching in the marketplaces during the time of persecution. His writings have the sound of sermons, such as his address to "insincere repentance" (Treatise 6), or "The Christian's Native Land" on heaven (Treatise 9 on Mortality).[2] In the face of schism and imminent death, Cyprian preached faithfully and finally laid down his life for Christ.[3]

---

1. Edward P. Echlin, *The Priest As Preacher: Past and Future* (Notre Dame, Ind.: Fides, 1973), 42.
2. William Wilson, *Popular Preachers of the Ancient Church* (London: James Hogg and Sons, n.d.), 40ff.
3. Kurt Aland, *A History of Christianity* (Philadelphia: Fortress, 1985), 1:156–61.

3.2.5 ORIGEN—THE CRAFTSMAN OF THE TEXT

All in whom Christ speaks, that is to say every upright man and preacher who speaks the word of God to bring men to salvation—and not merely the apostles and prophets—can be called an arrow of God. But what is sad, I see very few arrows of God. There are so few who so speak as to inflame the heart of the hearer, drag him away from his sin, and convert him to repentance. Few so speak that the heart of their hearers is deeply convicted and his eyes weep for contrition. There are so few who unveil the light of the future hope, the wonder and glory of God's Kingdom to such effect that by their earnest preaching they succeed in persuading men to despise the visible and seek the invisible, to spurn the temporal and seek the eternal. There are all too few preachers of this calibre.

—Origen *Commentary on Psalm 36*

Born in a Christian home in Alexandria (his father was martyred in 202), Origen (185–254) may be viewed as the father of Greek preaching and a figure of significance for theology. Matriculating in Clement's academy, Origen became a teacher and a lay preacher. From childhood he was severely ascetic, owning but one coat and no shoes, drinking no wine, and sleeping on the bare floor.[1] Thomas Carroll points out that Origen wrestled with the whole Bible and with the Bible as a whole.[2]

To Origen the preaching of the Word was emphasized over the sacraments. He was the first to speak of taking a text and explaining it. Justin Martyr described the use of a text, but Origen speaks of it by name. He traveled widely, mastered Hebrew, and was finally ordained, moving to Caesarea in 233. He wrote a number of commentaries and left many homilies (mainly from the Old Testament). Jerome asked, "Has anyone read everything that Origen has written?"

According to his biographer, Origen preached virtually every day. He spoke to the eucharistic assembly on Sunday, for the Wednesday and Friday eucharist at 3 P.M., and every day but Sunday for early morning services in which the Scripture was read in a three-year cycle and preached in series.[3] He preached without notes and often ended abruptly with a doxology. He attempted to "explain the Bible with the Bible." F. W. Farrar claimed, "He was by general admission the greatest, in almost every respect, of all the great Christian teachers of the first three Christian centuries." His recorded sermons were widely circulated.

Origen must be seen as both debit and credit theologically and exegetically. He was the first to formulate clearly the doctrine of the eternal generation of the Son, and yet his unblushing optimism led him to foresee a totally Christian world (*Contra Celsum* 8.68–72) and the ultimate salvation of all persons. Unduly influenced by Greek ideas, he denied the bodily resurrection and taught the Platonic preexistence of the soul. He never expressed concern for authorial intentions.[4]

Like Justin, Origen accused the Jews of an opaque literalism in interpreting the Old Testament, for instance, failing to see that reference to "God's hands" is anthropocentric language. This legitimate concern, however, led him to espouse Philo's overly allegorical approach to Scripture.

Origen was by no means the first Christian expositor to emphasize allegorization. As early as The Epistle of Barnabas (c. 130) we see allegorical explication of the Old Testament. Certainly there is allegorization in the interpretative efforts of the Qumran community, and in Justin and Hippolytus on Daniel, or Heracleon on the Fourth Gospel. Our Lord himself uses allegory in his discourse on the vine and the branches in John 15 and in his words shortly before the cross in Matthew 21:33–41. Paul makes use of carefully controlled allegory in Galatians 4:21–31.

Origen's Greek-influenced hermeneutic must be seen as part of an apologetical strategy. But it was also his conviction that the literal involves insoluble contradictions. He sees Scripture as verbally inspired,[5] indicating that "The wisdom of God has penetrated to all the inspired Scripture even as far as the slightest letter." Origen saw three levels of meaning in Scripture:

1. the literal, earthly, sensual, carnal—of minimal significance—the body;
2. the moral, religious, doctrinal, practical—more important—the soul;
3. the spiritual, heavenly, allegorical, mystical, speculative—the greatest—the spirit.

Allegorical preaching loses control in the interpretation of the text when it disregards the author's purpose. The conflict between the Alexandrian allegorists and the Antiochian advocates of historico-grammatico exegesis is one of the key watersheds in the history of interpretation.[6]

Gregory, the "wonder worker," was led to Christ and discipled by Origen. In his *Panegyric,* he reflects on Origen's teaching:

Like some spark it came dropping into my inmost soul. And there, being kindled and catching fire, was love: Love toward the Word (Logos) Himself, most alluring to all by reason of beauty unspeakable, the holy, the most lovely. And love toward this man, His friend and representative. By this love sore wounded, I was induced to give up all the aims which I was proposing to myself, for my affairs and education, among other things, even my law-studies of which I was proud; yes, fatherland and family, both relatives in Caesarea and those left behind at home. I had one regard, one passion—theology, and this godlike man, master therein.

Origen encouraged itinerant preaching and the opening of Scripture. Yet his overly-allegorical approach still yields a negative effect today. Any sermon may be striking. Yet the important question to ask is, Does the text really say what the sermon claims? Put more colorfully, if the text had a contagious disease, would the sermon catch it?

---

1. A. H. Newman, *A Manual of Church History* (Philadelphia: Judson, 1899), 28.
2. Thomas K. Carroll, *Preaching the Word: Message of the Fathers of the Church* (Wilmington, Del.: Michael Glazier, 1984), 49.
3. Joseph T. Lienhard, "Origen as Homilist," in *Preaching in the Patristic Age*, ed. David G. Hunter (New York: Paulist, 1989), 40.
4. Eugene de Faye, *Origen and His Work, The Olaus Petri Lectures for 1925* (New York: Columbia University, 1929), 37.
5. R. P. C. Hanson, *Allegory and Event: A Study of the Sources and Significance of Origen's Interpretation of Scripture* (Richmond: John Knox, 1959), 187.
6. Milton S. Terry, *Biblical Hermeneutics* (Grand Rapids: Zondervan, n.d.), 639–41.

3.2.6 THE CAPPADOCIAN CLOVERLEAF—CONNOISSEURS OF COMMUNICATION

My only affection was eloquence, and long did I apply myself to it with all my might; but I have laid it down at the feet of Christ, and subjugated it to the great word of God.

—Gregory of Nazianzen

With the aging of Hellenism, increasing syncretism, the weakening of Imperial Rome, and the growing dominance of Greek rhetoric, Christian preachers faced new challenges in keeping Scripture and sermon in sync. Three noteworthy preachers bear analysis in this context. They are often called the Cappadocian cloverleaf because they all came from that region of modern Turkey and have striking natural and spiritual linkages.

Basil the Great (329–379), a rigorous ascetic and skilled rhetorician, became the bishop of Caesarea (370). He lived in the waning days of Constantine and saw the bizarre reign of Julian the Apostate (361–363). His grandmother was known for her great love for Scripture and had been a follower of Gregory of Thaumaturgus. A devotee of Origen, Basil shows profound influence by Greek philosophy and rhetoric. His sermons are based on biblical texts and show orderly arrangement and simple ideas. Rhetorically, he is the least extravagant of the three. His sermons are strong in application and practical import. He inveighs against profiteers and the indifferent rich in a time of famine.[1] In a well-known passage, Basil speaks to the affluent:

> The bread that you hold back belongs to the hungry; the coat that you hoard in your cupboard belongs to the naked. The shoe that is gathering mildew in your home belongs to the unshod; the money you have hoarded belongs to the poverty-stricken. Thus you are oppressing as many people as you could have helped with your possessions.

His nine sermons on the six days of creation (Hexaemeron) are classic, showing careful adherence to the text but a commanding commitment to the unity of the sermon. Other memorable sermons include "Spiritual Work and Warfare" and "The Peril of Procrastination."[2]

Gregory of Nazianzen (329–389), a friend of Basil, was a leader of whom it was said, "His words were thunder; his life lightning." He was a true rhetorician and a poet. He has been described as having a "nervous rhetorical nature." His emphasis on style has prompted some critics to say that his lectures were "more oratorical masterpieces than sermons on Bible texts."[3]

Gregory of Nyssa (335–395) was the brother of Basil and himself a philosopher and rhetorician. He was Platonic in his philosophy and Origenistic in his interpretation. We see this particularly in his fifteen notable *Homilies on the Song of Songs*. He had great admiration for the pagan rhetorician Libanius. In a great passage on pride, Gregory takes a tour of a cemetery and asks, "Where in these bones are all these things about which you are now so greatly puffed up?"[4] He has left us beautiful homilies on the Beatitudes of Jesus and the Lord's Prayer. He also wrote passionately of yearning for God *(epiktasis)*, and said, "The true sight of God consists in this, that the one who looks up to God never ceases in that desire."

Other respected preachers in the Greek tradition were Cyril of Jerusalem, who has left us twenty-four sermons preached to the catechumens of Jerusalem, and Athanasius, bishop of Alexandria (328–375), whose took a strong stand for orthodox Christology. His homilies focus on the incarnation of Christ.

With the growing dominance of Greek rhetorical form, the church would soon face a more balanced and judicious blending. Content and form are both essential and inescapable.

But the most powerful preaching of the period is yet to be surveyed. We see the hardening of a kind of Byzantine scholasticism at this juncture in which "Greek theology gradually suffocated by its own traditionalism."[5] It was left powerless to face Islam.

---

1. Hans von Campenhausen, *The Fathers of the Greek Church* (London: Adam and Charles Black, 1963), 91.
2. William Wilson, *The Popular Preachers of the Ancient Church* (London: James Hogg, n.d.), 196.
3. von Campenhausen, *The Fathers of the Greek Church*, 103.

4. Carl A. Volz, *Pastoral Life and Practice in the Early Church* (Minneapolis: Augsburg, 1990), 127.
5. von Campenhausen, *The Fathers of the Greek Church,* 175.

3.2.7   JEROME—THE ICONOCLAST OF THE COMPANY

When teaching in church, seek to call forth not plaudits but groans. Don't be a ranter, one who gabbles without rhyme or reason. Show yourself versed in the mysteries of God. To astonish an unlettered crowd with oratorical skill is a sign of ignorance. Season your speech with frequent reading of Scripture.

—St. Jerome to a young preacher

Jerome (345–420) is considered one of the Four Doctors of the Latin Church. Born in Dalmatia, Jerome studied in Rome and traveled widely. When he was in Antioch he had a vision and fell ill. The experience led him to spend six years as a hermit in the desert. He returned to Antioch and was ordained in 379. He studied later under Gregory of Nazianzus and was commissioned by Pope Damascus to translate the Scriptures. This translation, the Vulgate, became widely used. In 385 he went to Bethlehem, where he labored in translation and commentary writing for thirty-five years. His friend Sulpicius Severus said of him, "He is always reading books . . . he is always either reading something or writing something."[1]

Jerome was outspoken, prickly in disposition, and extremely opinionated, but he was a scholar of the Word. He wrote poems and letters and preached against "the purple-clad harlot" of Rome."[2] He detested Ambrose of Milan because of his patrician background, cursed the rhetoricians, and shuddered at the news of distant invasions and wars. He carried on a contentious correspondence with Augustine, although they stood together against Pelagius. We possess ninety-six of his sermons. His chief significance in the history of preaching beyond his work in translation is his concern about Greek rhetorical influence on preaching. His advice to Nepotian is typical: "Let the presbyter's preaching be based on his reading of the Scriptures. I do not want you to be a declaimer, or argumentative, or longwinded."[3]

1. Robert Payne, *The Fathers of the Western Church* (New York: Viking, 1951), 87.
2. Ibid., 114.
3. Carl A. Volz, *Pastoral Life and Practice in the Early Church* (Minneapolis: Augsburg, 1990), 120ff.

3.2.8   AMBROSE—THE COUNSELOR OF THE CONFRATERNITY

We have given a daily sermon on morals, when the deeds of the Patriarchs or the precepts of the Proverbs were read, in order that, being informed and instructed by them, you might become accustomed to enter upon the ways of our forefathers and to pursue their road, and to obey

the divine commands, whereby, renewed by baptism, you might hold to
that manner of life which befits those who are washed.

—Ambrose in *De Mysteriis*

With the Latin fathers we sense at once that style becomes more direct and
concise. Ambrose (340–397) is a case in point. His role as the preacher who
gripped and moved Augustine guaranteed him a lofty niche in the company of
the preachers.

Born to the ruling class, at the age of twenty-nine Ambrose was appointed
governor of the province of which Milan was the chief city. When he was not
yet baptized, he was appointed bishop of Milan in a time of crisis and confusion.
Orthodox in his theology, he clashed repeatedly with the emperor and empress.
He loved music and wrote hymns, several of which are still part of the western
liturgy ("O Splendor of God's Glory Bright" and "O Trinity Most Blessed Light").

Ambrose was influenced by Platonic ideas and was thoroughly allegorical in
his approach to the text.[1] Often deep in his books or involved in discussion and
debate with others, he was not easily accessible. Yet Augustine testifies: "I first
began to love him . . . as a man who showed me kindness."[2] Peter Brown describes the man who so touched Augustine as "a passionate little man . . . a frail
figure . . . clasping the codex of the Scriptures, with a high forehead, a long melancholy face, and great eyes."[3]

His sermons on the six days of creation in Genesis particularly moved Augustine, who up to this time had a distinct aversion to the Old Testament. His
treatment of the sacraments and his two volumes on repentance in relation to
Novatian practice reflect his preaching style. His address about drunkenness *(De
Elia et Jeiunio)* illustrates his appealing discourse:

> Strong drink alters the senses and the forms of men. By it they are turned
> from men into neighing horses. A drunken man loses voice, he changes
> color, he flashes fire from his eyes, he pants, he snorts, he goes stark
> mad, he falls into a foaming pit. . . . Hence come also vain imaginings,
> uncertain vision, uncertain steps: often he hops over shadows, thinking
> them to be pits. The earth acquires a facial expression and nods to him;
> of a sudden it seems to rise and bend and twist. Fearful, he falls on his
> face and grasps the ground with his hands or thinks that the mountains
> close in on him. There is a murmur in his ears as of the surging seas; he
> hears the surf booming on the beach. If he spies a dog he imagines it a
> lion and takes to his heels.

Thus Ambrose preached and steeped himself in Scripture with the end that
his hearers would confront Christ, for indeed it is Jesus Christ "to whom no price
or ornament can be compared. Take as your counselors Moses, Isaiah, Jeremiah,
Peter, Paul, John and the greatest counselor of all, Jesus the Son of God, that you
may gain the Father."

Gibbon in his classic history of the Roman Empire observes that "The custom
of preaching, which seems to constitute a considerable part of Christian devotion"

was to be found everywhere in the Roman Empire. Indeed, "The pulpits of the empire were now filled with sacred orators who possessed the advantage of not being questioned without danger of interruption or reply."[4] And the two most powerful and significant preachers of this age are now before us.

---

1. For helpful discussion of typology in relation to allegory, see F. F. Bruce, *Hebrews* (Grand Rapids: Eerdmans, 1990), 96–97; Leonard Goppelt on "tupos" in *Theological Dictionary of the New Testament,* ed. G. Kittel and Gerhard Friedrich (Grand Rapids: Eerdmans, 1972), 246–59.
2. Augustine *Confessions* 5.13.23. Cf. also Neil B. McLynn, *Ambrose of Milan: Church and State in a Christian Capital* (Berkeley: University of California Press, 1995).
3. Peter Brown, *Augustine of Hippo* (Berkeley: University of California, 1967), 83.
4. Edward Gibbon, *The Decline and Fall of the Roman Empire* (J. B. Bury Edition of 1909) 20:6.

3.3 THE EXPLOSIVE LUSTER OF CHRYSOSTOM, JOHN OF ANTIOCH

> Preaching makes me well; as soon as I open my mouth to speak, my weariness is forgotten.
>
> —Chrysostom

Before us now is unquestionably the greatest preacher of the early church. John of Antioch, or Chrysostom (meaning the "golden-mouthed," a name given him 150 years after his death), lived from 343 to 407. At the pinnacle of his ministry, he was the archbishop of Constantinople. He suffered greatly at the hands of the rulers of the eastern empire. Chrysostom was preeminently a biblical preacher whose approach to Scripture was Antiochene rather than Alexandrian.

Mediterranean society was in a state of drift and division in the fourth century. Constantine's Edict of Milan of 313 legalized Christianity. With Constantine's death in 337, however, a new period of disorder ensued. The empire was under severe strain, and the church was torn by doctrinal controversies. Now patronized rather than persecuted, the church tasted of power and sought more, prompting Chrysostom to write, "The desire to rule is the mother of heresies." With the death of Theodosius, the empire grew unwieldy and split into two segments in 395. Yet the preaching of Chrysostom rises above the chaotic times.

3.3.1 CHRYSOSTOM—THE PILGRIM

> You praise what I have said, and receive my exhortations with tumults of applause; but show your approbation by obedience; this is the only praise I seek.
>
> —Chrysostom

John was born in Antioch into a devout home. His father, Secundus, died when

John was young, and his mother, Anathusa, dedicated herself to rearing her gifted son. R. A. Krupp reminds us that John was "a chauvinist raised by a woman."[1] When he was twenty years of age he began to study law under the famous pagan rhetorician Libanius, who highly regarded John and considered him a prospect as his successor.

While in his youth John had "plunged into the whirlpool of the world." But he came to Christ and was baptized. He served as a reader in the church in Antioch but was soon inclined to go to the mountains as a hermit. When his mother pleaded with him not to leave her, he changed their home into a monastery where he stayed until her death. A strong ascetic streak is apparent in his life and teaching.[2]

John then spent four years as a monk in company with an aged hermit and another two years alone in a cave. A slight man whose health was permanently affected by his extreme asceticism, he returned to Antioch where he was ordained as a deacon at the age of thirty-seven and began to preach two or three times weekly to increasing audiences. Steeped in the classics, polished as an orator, but fashioned as a disciple of Christ, he was ready for one of the most remarkable ministries the world has ever seen. He had virtually memorized the Scriptures and preached systematically and consecutively through book after book of the Bible. He condemned empty oratory but used the finest skills of his age in opening the Word of God.

After twelve years as chief presbyter in Antioch, John was coerced into becoming archbishop of Constantinople, where he served for six years in running controversy with the empress Eudoxia, but with a resoundingly effective pulpit ministry in St. Sophia's. Twice banished because of his unwillingness to compromise on principle, Chrysostom died in exile. Because of Chrysostom's commitment to biblical preaching and his fiery zeal, Bishop Kallistos Ware has recently written of him, "He can be truly called an evangelical."[3] We shall trace the significance of his attachment to "the literal and historical meaning of the text."

---

1. R. A. Krupp, *Shepherding the Flock of God: The Pastoral Theology of John Chrysostom* (New York: Peter Lang, 1991), 1. This is an exceedingly valuable and helpful treatment by my former colleague at Trinity Divinity School. Vying for this niche is J. N. D. Kelly's new *Golden Mouth: The Story of John Chrysostom, Ascetic, Preacher, Bishop* (New York: Cornell University Press, 1995).

2. For a superb work of historical fiction, nothing is better than F. W. Farrar, *Gathering Clouds: A Tale of the Days of St. Chrysostom* (New York: Longmans, Green, 1895). The classic work on the life of Chrysostom remains F. Chrysostomos Baur, *John Chrysostom and His Time* (Westminster, Md.: Newman, 1960), translated from German in two volumes.

3. Bishop Kallistos Ware of the Antiochene Orthodox Church in the splendid issue on Chrysostom in *Christian History* 44:13 (November 1994), 36.

3.3.2 CHRYSOSTOM—THE PERSONALITY

> Or do you not know what a passion for oratory has nowadays infatuated Christians? Do you not know that its exponents are respected above everyone else, not just by outsiders, but by those of the household of the faith? How, then, can anyone endure the deep disgrace of having his sermon received with blank silence and feelings of boredom, and his listeners waiting for the end of the sermon as if it were a relief after fatigue; whereas they listen to someone else's sermon, however long, with eagerness, and are annoyed when he is about to finish and quite exasperated when he decides to say no more?
>
> —Chrysostom on Priesthood

Although both Syrian Antioch and Constantinople were about half Christian, they were cesspools of depravity. This in part explains John's ascetic bent.[1] The church was hideously corrupt. Such a deeply feeling person as John recoiled from the sinful scenes and inclined to monastic seclusion. Just forty miles east of Antioch was the pillar on which Simon Stylites lived for thirty-seven years in protest of the wickedness of his day.

But this kind of monastic severity spawns the intense individualism we see again and again in John. Described by one scholar as a "choleric ascetic," his enemies thought him hard, arrogant, morose, overly passionate. He heaped up illustrations and metaphors, and his vocabulary was undisciplined. His first sermon is described as "embroidered rhetoric gone wild."[2]

Despite a possible touch of Pelagianism, he is on the whole steadfastly orthodox. In preaching on Hebrews 10:9, he insists, "We do not offer another sacrifice, but we make a commemoration of a sacrifice." He confronts the drift of his times as "the dementation before doom." Krupp shows how he preached against excesses at wedding celebrations, spoke against abortion, critiqued aspects of slavery,[3] protested the abuses of wealth and power, and opposed gluttony, drunkenness, and class distinctions. His occasionally irritable nature showed itself in unfortunate anti-Semitic outbursts.[4]

John wrestled with why people did not come to church, especially in the summer months. "I hear them saying, 'The heat is excessive; the scorching sun is intolerable; we cannot bear to be crushed in the crowd and to be oppressed by the heat and confined space.'"

Chrysostom essentially wrote the eastern liturgy, which even in this century has inspired the great Russian composer Sergei Rachmaninoff ("Liturgy for the Holy Communion: Liturgy of John Chrysostom, Patriarch of Constantinople," written 1910–11). Many Christians are familiar with his invocation: "Almighty God, unto whom all hearts are open, all desires known, and from whom no secrets are hid; cleanse the thoughts of our hearts by the inspiration of your Holy Spirit, that we may perfectly love you, and worthily magnify your holy name, through Christ our Lord."[5]

1. John Heston Willey, *Chrysostom: The Orator* (Cincinnati: Jennings and Graham, 1906), 45.
2. Ibid., 62.
3. R. A. Krupp, *Shepherding the Flock of God: The Pastoral Theology of John Chrysostom* (New York: Peter Lang, 1991), 188.
4. Robert L. Wilken, *John Chrysostom and the Jews: Rhetoric and Reality in the Late Fourth Century* (Berkeley: University of California, 1983).
5. Quoted in Carl A. Volz, *Pastoral Life and Practice in the Early Church* (Minneapolis: Augsburg, 1990), 127.

3.3.3 CHRYSOSTOM—THE PREACHER

I cannot let a day pass, without feeding you with the treasures of the Scripture.

—Chrysostom *Homilies from Genesis* 1.82.2

Chrysostom stands tall among preachers as one whose sermons took the text of Scripture with utmost seriousness. His question was never, Is this a suitable occasion for preaching? but rather, Why should not this be a suitable occasion for preaching?[1]

We have more than seven hundred of Chrysostom's sermons, including twenty-one given during the infamous tax revolt in Antioch in A.D. 387. His address on the nature of homiletics in *On the Priesthood* focused on the fact that "Preaching is a work for God and its object must never be forgotten." His devotion to the text led him to produce running commentary, and he systematically expounded whole books of the Bible, among them Genesis (75 sermons), the Psalms (144), Matthew (90), John (88) and a number of Paul's epistles (244). His fifty-four messages on the Acts constitute what may be the first real commentary on that book. He generally preached for an hour.

Chrysostom did not divide the text for preaching but typically added an applicatory section to his exegetical address. No wonder that John Calvin chose to write a preface to an early edition of Chrysostom's sermons in which he lauds Chrysostom for excelling the other Fathers in seeking the true sense of the scriptural text.[2]

Personally wed to careful Bible study, Chrysostom urged personal and family study and application of the Word. In his preaching, he "works steadily through the chosen passage . . . he tries to let it speak to himself, and hopes that in this way it will speak to his hearers . . . the sermon is a real exposition of the Word of God."[3] T. Harwood Pattison quotes Macgilvray's description of Chrysostom in action:

As he advanced from exposition to practical appeals, his delivery became gradually more rapid, his countenance more animated, his voice more vivid and intense. The people began to hold in their breath. The joints of their loins were loosened. A creeping sensation like that produced by a series of electric waves passed over them. They felt as if drawn toward the pulpit by a sort of magnetic influence. Some of those who were sitting rose from their seats; others were overcome with a kind of faintness as if the preacher's mental forces were sucking the life out of their bodies, and by the time the discourse came to an end the great mass of that spellbound audience could only hold their heads and give vent to their emotions in tears.[4]

The style of the preaching was direct and homely. The preacher did not have an extraordinary voice. He used rhetorical and linguistic skills in shaping discourse.[5] Often he carried on what seems to be a dialogue with his congregation, with question and response. He preferred his ambo, or pulpit, rather than the bishop's throne because it was closer to the people. He was sometimes criticized for being too dramatic.

John Chrysostom's sermons were quoted by preachers up to the Reformation. His influence can be traced clearly in Fénelon's *Dialogue on Eloquence*. Themes he developed included the truthfulness of the Holy Scripture (with a pronounced harmonistic tendency[6]); Christ dying for all, even those who reject him; the free will of man; male headship. He saw homosexuality as a detestable perversion and took exception to certain Mariological trends.[7]

The quest for holiness was uppermost for Chrysostom. Little wonder that Dante in *Paradisio* puts him between Nathan, who rebuked sin in King David's court, and St. Anselm of Canterbury.

In his own time he was known as the golden lyre of the Holy Spirit. As Thomas Carroll describes it, "For Chrysostom preaching was essentially the interpretation of a text from Scripture and its application to a particular congregation. Exegesis is, therefore, the starting point of his preaching as exhortation is its conclusion."[8]

He could be especially sharp in his denunciations. He spoke of the empress: "Again Herodias raves; again she rages; again she dances; again she asks for the head of John [Chrysostom] upon a charger." This spelled the end for the preacher. But in his final sermon, which meant exile and death, he preached:

> The waters are raging and the winds are blowing but I have no fear for I stand firmly upon a rock. What am I to fear? Is it death? Life to me means Christ and death is gain. Is it exile? The earth and everything it holds belongs to the Lord. Is it loss of property? I brought nothing into this world and I will bring nothing out of it. I have only contempt for the world and its ways and I scorn its honors.[9]

---

1. As quoted in E. M. Blaiklock, *The Pastoral Epistles* (Grand Rapids: Zondervan, 1972), 119.
2. R. A. Krupp, *Shepherding the Flock of God: The Pastoral Theology of John Chrysostom* (New York: Peter Lang, 1991), 234.
3. Stephen Neill, *Chrysostom and His Message* (London: Lutterworth, 1962), 17.

4. T. Harwood Pattison, *The History of Christian Preaching* (Philadelphia: American Baptist Publication Society, 1903), 71.
5. Paul Scott Wilson, *A Concise History of Preaching* (Nashville: Abingdon, 1992), 46.
6. Krupp, *Shepherding the Flock of God,* 73.
7. Ibid., 169.
8. Thomas K. Carroll, *Preaching the Word: Message of the Fathers of the Church* (Wilmington, Del.: Michael Glazier. 1984), 114.
9. Ibid., 126–27.

3.3.4   CHRYSOSTOM—THE INTERPRETER

> When a king made his entrance into a city, certain ones among the dignitaries, the chief officials and those who were in the good graces of the sovereign would go forth from the city in order to meet him, while the guilty and the criminals are kept within the city where they await the sentence which the king will pronounce. In the same manner, when the Lord will come, the first group will go forth to meet him with assurance in the midst of the air, while the guilty and those who are conscious of having committed many sins will await below their judge.
>
> —Chrysostom on the *parousia* in a sermon from 1 Thessalonians 4:17

The importance of Chrysostom for preaching derives not only from his devotion to the exegesis of the text and its forceful proclamation but also from his careful and exemplary hermeneutical principle. Hermeneutics (not an exact science) is our method of interpreting the Scripture. The word comes from the name of Hermes, who in the pantheon of Greek gods was the messenger. We may have the highest view of scriptural authority, but if we cannot get at the meaning of the text, our esteem for it is in vain. If the author's intent is inaccessible, we are left with the reader-response approach to meaning so rife today, which says in effect that the meaning of a text is in our own imaginations.

The spiritualization of a text can be useful in avoiding apologetical discussion of a historical Garden of Eden or ark of Noah. But if Scripture has hidden spiritual meanings, we have reserved its interpretation for the elite and torn it from average believers—and we have done so contrary to apostolic representation (cf. 2 Peter 1:19–21; 1 John 2:26–27).

Allegory is extended metaphor. Indeed, modest allegory is found in Scripture, but it is clearly identified as such (Matt. 21:33–46, labeled as parable; John 15:1ff.; Gal. 4:21–31, in which Sarah and Hagar are seen as figurative in a careful and restrained contrast). But the influence of the Alexandrian hermeneutic was widespread and devastating. The heirs of the allegorists let imagination run rampant, and allowed Job's three thousand camels to represent the depraved Gentiles. Ruth's lunch in the field of Boaz came to symbolize the Lord's Supper. The three baskets on the baker's head in Joseph's interpretation of the dream were said to represent the Trinity; the twopence given by the Good Samaritan represented baptism and the Lord's Supper; Elijah's four barrels of water symbolized the four gospels; the ship in which Jesus crossed Galilee described the Church of England and the "other ships" the nonconformist groups. We shall see vestiges of this overallegorization in Augustine and through the Middle Ages. Such a fine witness and careful commentator as Ephrem the Syrian (306–373) was misled by Origen's views and arrived at some outlandish interpretations.[1]

In our own day the hypertypologists (who see Abraham's servant's seeking a wife for Isaac as setting forth forty characteristics of the ministry of the Holy Spirit) and the allegorists have surrendered up the text. We can lose scriptural authority in adopting a wrong hermeneutic.[2]

Staunchly poised against the Alexandrian allegorists was the Antiochene school, originating in the very city where believers were first called Christians (Acts 11:26). This school emphasized a literal, simple meaning of the text. This is not, as some have alleged, "A wooden-headed literalism," but rather a dedication to finding the author's purpose in the text and its literal meaning wherever possible. The interpretation of a text must take into account its literary genre. Precursors to the Antiochene approach abound in individuals such as Theodorus of Antioch, who championed the historical sense in the Genesis account, Julius Africanus in Palestine, Dorotheus in Antioch, and Lucian in Edessa and later of Antioch. All of these were known as strong biblical expositors.[3] Also in this lineage was Eusebius of Emesa, known for his adherence to "the historical sense of Scripture."

The prime mover in the Antiochene school was Diodorus (d. 394), who later became bishop of Tarsus. He argued that the prophetic predictions of the Old Testament "were at the same time both historical and Christocentric,"[4] the phenomenon of prophetic perspective. Diodorus was the teacher of both Theodore of Mopsuestia (350–428) and John Chrysostom. Both of these influential leaders learned historical exegesis from their mentor.

Chrysostom recognized types and figures in the biblical text, but Origen rejected any reference to physical bread in the petition "Give us this day our daily bread" and argued that this was a reference to Christ himself. Chrysostom urged that we understand the text as being a plain and natural reference to daily nutriment.

Influenced more by the empiricism of Aristotle than the rational idealism of Plato, Chrysostom and the Antiochene school stressed the historical, grammatical, and literal meaning of a text. What is called the Antiochene *theoria,* or idea of a supernatural insight given the inspired writers by the Holy Spirit and the illuminating ministry of the Holy Spirit for biblical exegetes and readers, is clearly based on a commitment to the plenary and verbal inspiration of the autographs.[5] Nassif speaks of the *theoria* in exegesis as "that prophetic vision whereby the prophet saw and recorded both the present historical and future Messianic meanings under one literal and hyperbolic mode of expression without division."[6] This asserts that texts may have a double meaning (as the Gospel of John is built on a series of double meanings), and there may be a mild *sensus plenior* in a text (see 1 Peter 1:10–12). Yet the base and control are always historical, literal, and grammatical in a text. This is where Chrysostom stood, and this became the launching pad for his public proclamation of the Word of God. The contrast with the contemporary "new hermeneutics" is clear and painful. The difference is demonstrated in a comment made by Chrysostom interpreting Isaiah 2:5–6:

We are not the lords over the rules of interpretation, but must pursue Scripture's interpretation of itself and in that way make use of the allegorical method. . . . This is everywhere a rule in Scripture: when it wants to allegorize, it tells the interpretation of the allegory, so that the passage will not be interpreted superficially or be met by the undisciplined desire of those who enjoy allegorization to wander about and be carried in every direction.[7]

Clearly, Chrysostom's hermeneutical framework is critical to the whole proclamatory enterprise.[8] A final word from him seems relevant to our times: "The church is not a theater, that we should listen for amusement. With profit ought we to depart hence, and some fresh and great gain should we acquire before we leave."

---

1. Frederic W. Farrar, *History of Interpretation, The Bampton Lectures of 1885* (Grand Rapids: Baker, 1961), 209ff.
2. For a superb study, see David S. Dockery, *Biblical Interpretation: Then and Now* (Grand Rapids: Baker, 1992). Also worthwhile in this area is Karlfried Froehlich, *Biblical Interpretation in the Early Church* (Minneapolis: Fortress, 1984).
3. Milton S. Terry, *Biblical Hermeneutics* (Grand Rapids: Zondervan, n.d.), 644.
4. Dockery, *Biblical Interpretation*, 107.
5. Bradley L. Nassif, *Antiochene Theoria in John Chrysostom's Exegesis* (Ann Arbor: UMI Dissertation Services, 1991), 157.
6. Ibid., 158.
7. Dockery, *Biblical Interpretation*, 117.
8. For a fascinating comparison of the exegesis of Chrysostom, Augustine, and Origen on Romans 1–11, see Peter Gorday, *Principles of Patristic Exegesis* (Lewiston, N.Y.: Edwin Mellen Press, 1983).

3.4 AUGUSTINE—THE STELLAR LUMINARY AMONG HOMILETICIANS

To have to preach, to inveigh, to admonish, to edify, to feel responsible for every one of you—this is a great burden, a heavy weight upon me, a hard labor.

—Augustine

Preaching never enjoyed great prominence in the Eastern church. Worthy of note, however, is an eighth century movement in Isauria, in the western part of what we know today as Turkey. In the so-called Isaurian Dynasty there arose an iconoclastic move against elaborate liturgy and in favor of bringing the Word to the people.[1] But by and large, preaching has not been strongly highlighted in Orthodoxy. To find out why, we must turn to the Western church and the preacher who had such influence in shaping it theologically and homiletically. These facts merit our review:

1. Alexandrian allegorization carried the day in the East. Its triumph was adverse to biblical preaching.
2. From early on, the church in the West was more institutional and consistent with characteristically Roman efficiency and organization. Thinkers like Novatian and Cyprian tilted the Western church toward an order that esteemed preaching. In contrast, a standard history of the Eastern church did not include a single reference to preaching.[2]
3. The Eastern church's theology of glory put the liturgy essentially out of sight of the congregation with an emphasis on "a continuum reaching into eternity."[3] The stress was on the incarnation of Christ; in the West the atonement of Christ was accented. Tertullian in *De Resurrectione* stresses "order and simplicity in theology," going "hand in hand with the concern for the institutional life of the church."[4] The Western emphasis was more pastoral; hence, preaching loomed larger.
4. Tertullian's reservations about Greek philosophy were part of his crusade against all paganism, Greek or Latin. While he is more indebted to Stoicism than he acknowledges, he is critical of Platonism.[5] The Eastern church was Platonic and mystical while the Western church was Aristotelian and empirical. The monasticism of the East seemed sharper and more severe than in the West. All this shaped the place of preaching.
5. While Chrysostom is virtually unexcelled as a preacher, what promised to be a reflection on preaching in *On the Priesthood* actually focused more on purity and the morality of the clergy. The West had Augustine, who gave us our first textbook on homiletics.

It is our contention that Augustine's contextualizing synthesis of biblical truth and classical rhetoric is a defining hour for preaching. We shall trace how Augustine's contribution helps explain the prominence of preaching in the West.

---

1. Research on these aspects of the Isaurian Dynasty by Walter Persson of Stockholm and Thonos Karbonis of Athens is slated to take book form in the future.
2. Aziz S. Atiya, *History of Eastern Christianity* (Notre Dame, Ind: University of Notre Dame Press, 1968).
3. Danielou, *The Origins of Latin Christianity,* 471.
4. Ibid., 474.
5. Ibid., 224.

3.4.1 THE SPIRITUAL JOURNEY OF AUGUSTINE

I do not care whether you expect some well-turned phrases today. It is my duty to give you due warning in citing the Scripture.

—Aurelius Augustine

Aurelius Augustine was born November 13, 354 in Tagaste in Roman Numidia (modern Souk Ahras in Algeria), North Africa. His parents were poor, but his father, Patricius (a pagan until shortly before his death in 372), and his mother, the saintly Monica, shared a driving aspiration for their son. His early years of study in Madaura and Carthage were years of sin and license. His unnamed concubine bore him a son, Adeodatus, who died at the age of seventeen. For eleven years he was a traditional school teacher who increasingly longed to go to Rome.

As her son moved successively from dualistic Manichaeism and its austerities to a more philosophical neo-Platonism, Monica lived in agony. She would stay for days in a chapel to fast and pray for her wayward son.[1] To her dismay, in 383 Augustine sailed for Rome and then on to Milan, where he was appointed professor of rhetoric in the fall of 384. The following spring Monica pursued him to Milan.

Augustine was "a master of the spoken word" and had the ability and the training to produce what Brown calls "verbal fireworks . . . with sudden meteorites."[2] He soon came under the influence of the sermons and exhortations of Ambrose in Milan. In 386 he was converted and then baptized by Ambrose in 387, abandoning his career as a rhetorician and professor.

After the death of his mother, Augustine went back to North Africa where he was ordained in Hippo in 391. His powerful preaching and prolific writing gave him a special place in the doctrinally divided and politically imperiled area. He was consecrated as a bishop in 395 and established what was in effect a theological seminary. For thirty-five years he labored as a spiritual leader, finally dying in 430.

The conversion of Augustine, so powerfully chronicled in his famous *Confessions,* must be seen as the outcome of his dear mother's ceaseless intercession, the preaching of the Word by Ambrose, the influence of friends, and his own reading of Romans 13:13–14. On the day of his conversion he heard the famous words *tolle, lege,* or "Take up and read." He never got away from the grip of Holy Scripture, as is clear from the *Confessions.*[3]

Augustine supplied us with works still profitably read today, including *On Free Will* (in which he defends free moral agency against Manichaean determinism) or *On the Trinity* (one of the choicest expositions of the triune nature of God ever written) or *The City of God* (his magnificent philosophy of history as the Roman Empire disintegrates). He can justly be called the father of systematic theology. As Rudolph Eucken described him, "The single greatest philosopher on the basis of Christianity proper the world has had." Harnack termed him "the incomparably greatest man in the Church between St. Paul and Luther," and Souter called him "the greatest man who wrote in Latin." But no less impressively, we see Augustine as an outstanding preacher and exegete who shaped aspects of preaching both in his own time and yet in ours.

---

1. Peter Brown's rich and magnificent treatise *Augustine of Hippo* (Berkeley: University of California Press, 1967).
2. Ibid., 22–23.
3. R. L. Ottley, *Studies in the Confessions of St. Augustine* (London: Robert Scott, 1919). Another superb anthology is *St. Augustine: His Age, Life and Thought* (New York: Meridian, 1957). An old landmark is B. B. Warfield, *Calvin and Augustine*

(Philadelphia: Presbyterian and Reformed, 1956), especially 305–477. The entire issue of *Christian History* 6:3 is devoted to Augustine.

3.4.2 THE PREACHING STORY OF AUGUSTINE

My preaching almost always displeases me. For I am eager after something better, of which I often have an inward enjoyment before I set about expressing my thoughts in audible words. Then, when I have failed to utter my meaning as clearly as I conceived it, I am disappointed that my tongue is incapable of doing justice to that which is in my heart. What I myself understand I wish my hearers to understand as fully; and I feel I am not so speaking as to effect this. The chief reason is that the conception lights up the mind in a kind of rapid flash; whereas the utterance is slow, lagging and far unlike what it would convey.
—Augustine in *De Catechizandis Rudibus* (chapter 2)

Augustine's ministry took root amid widespread cultural decay. An inner rottenness had gutted the once proud empire, and even though the emperor Theodosius declared Christianity the state religion, the church was unresponsive to the events swirling about her. Even as Augustine lay dying at the age of seventy-six, the Vandals surrounded Hippo and were in the process of torching the city. Rome was sacked in 410.

Augustine had battled the Manicheans, the Donatists, and the Pelagians in the interest of biblical integrity. He had written 230 books. He was to be the fountainhead from which Luther, Calvin, and Jansenius drank. But he was most of all a consummate preacher. The focus of his life and ministry was the Word of God. He held stoutly to verbal inspiration.[1] In a letter to Jerome, Augustine wrote, "For I confess to your charity that I have learned to defer this respect and honor to those scriptural books only which are now called canonical, that I believe most firmly that no one of these authors has erred in any respect of writing."[2] We are not surprised then to hear him say (again to Jerome, who claimed Paul might have used a white lie in Galatians):

It seems to me that most disastrous consequences must follow upon our believing that anything false is found in the sacred books: that is to say that the men by whom the Scripture has been given to us and committed to writing, did put down in these books anything false. If you once admit into such a high sanctuary of authority one false statement, there will not be left a single sentence of those books, which, if appearing to any one difficult in practice or hard to believe, may not by the same fatal rule be explained away as a statement, in which, intentionally the author declared what was not true.[3]

Further influencing Augustine's preaching was his early vocation as a schoolmaster and his high regard for teaching. In the New Testament, preaching and teaching are used virtually interchangeably. Yet there is a useful distinction when we recognize that a good preacher will use much teaching and a good teacher will at some point preach. Teaching is absorbed primarily with a subject; preaching tilts toward obsession with an object.

Augustine argued for the significance of verbal signs in achieving understanding. He reasoned that since Christ is prophet and teacher, the believer is in union with him and is to share in that office. Not only the bishop is to preach; Christ speaks through his messengers.[4]

Thus we see the man who as a youth had loved to steal pears, who early on prayed "Give me chastity but not yet," whose sexuality was sublimated in his disputations, who saw the world "as a sea in which men devour one another like fish." In appearance Augustine was a brother of the Berbers of the North African desert, "tall and long limbed, thin chested, with sloping shoulders . . . long nose, high forehead, thick lips, tremendous black eyes . . . his skin a kind of dark bronze."[5] This was the preacher.

Dressed in street clothes, he preached without manuscript or notes. We have 685 of his sermons, some of which consumed an hour and some of which were very brief. He was sparse with illustration but fond of pithy aphoristic sayings, loved rough Punic words, and was noted for his logic and rhetorical devices such as alliteration and rhyme. He explained and repeated the text, although he was guilty of horrendous misinterpretation on occasion. His delivery had striking beauty and effect.

Augustine was highly doctrinal in his preaching. He used spacious themes and spoke of the mysteries without being patronizing or condescending. He could weep in the pulpit. Occasionally he indulged in gross allegorization, yet he held to the literality of Genesis 1 but not creation in seven literal days of twenty-four hours. Typical discourse is from a sermon on Proverbs 10:

> Thus our summer is the advent of Christ, our winter his concealment in heaven. Our summer is the revelation of Christ. In a word, to good and faithful trees, the Apostle addresses these words: "You are dead, and your life is hid with Christ in God." Certainly dead, but dead in appearance, living at the root. Fix your eye on the season of summer that is to come; mark how it follows: "When Christ, who is your life, shall appear, then shall you also appear with Him in glory."[6]

Peter Brown emphasizes that Augustine seldom preached from "without" to his beleaguered congregants but rather from "within" the flock. As he puts it, "This is the secret of Augustine's enormous power as a preacher. He will make it his first concern to place himself in the midst of the congregation, to appeal to their feelings for him to react with immense sensitivity to their emotions, and so, as the sermon progressed, to sweep them up into his own way of feeling."[7] Eye to eye with those who stood in the front rows, "For Augustine and his hearers, the Bible was literally the 'word' of God."[8]

"Let me try to winkle out the hidden secrets of this Psalm we have just sung; and chip a sermon out of them, to satisfy your ears and minds,"[9] he would seductively say in tones resonating with excitement and thrill. His sermons on the

Psalms are especially impressive. Apparently his voice became even richer and more dulcet in his late middle age (when he preached *The City of God*). Little wonder that Spurgeon called Augustine "the quarry from which nearly every preacher of note has dug." The old proverb stands apropos, "A sermon without Augustine is as a stew without bacon."[10]

---

1. David W. Kerr, "Augustine of Hippo," in *Inspiration and Interpretation,* ed. John Walvoord (Grand Rapids: Eerdmans, 1957), 73.

2. *Epistolae* 82.3.

3. *Epistolae* 28.3. For an very important study see A. D. Polman, *The Word of God According to St. Augustine* (Grand Rapids: Eerdmans, 1961), especially "The Word of God as Holy Scripture," 39–122.

4. Edward J. Hughes, *The Participation of the Faithful in the Regal and Prophetic Mission of Christ According to Saint Augustine* (Mundelein, Ill.: St. Mary of the Lake, 1956), 52.

5. Robert Payne, *The Fathers of the Western Church* (New York: Viking, 1951), 139.

6. Sermon 212 on Proverbs 10.

7. Peter Brown, *Augustine of Hippo* (Berkeley: University of California, 1967), 251. Also of relevance is Brown's more recent *Power and Persuasion in Late Antiquity* (Madison: University of Wisconsin, 1994).

8. Ibid., 253.

9. Ibid., 254.

10. T. Harwood Pattison, *The History of Christian Preaching* (Philadelphia: American Baptist Publication Society, 1903), 63.

3.4.3 THE RHETORICAL ODYSSEY OF AUGUSTINE

> It is better that we should use these barbarisms and be understood by you than be artists in speech and talk past you.
> —Augustine in *De Doctrina Christiana*

Augustine's hermeneutic was somewhat eclectic. Although he did lapse into the allegorical mode, we must still view him as the dean of preachers in the Western church, standing head and shoulders above his noteworthy contemporaries. These included Hilary, bishop of Poitiers (d. 368), whose reverent use of Scripture can be traced in his sermons on Matthew and in his twelve volumes on the Trinity; Zeno of Verona (d. 380), from whom we have ninety-three well-illustrated tractates; and Pacianus, bishop of Barcelona (d. 392), who is favorably mentioned by Jerome; and Gaudentius of Brescia (d. 410), who corresponded with Chrysostom.[1]

In every age communicators must grapple with the culturally appropriate and conditioned form that will most effectively transmit the "everlasting gospel." The question of form is the question of rhetoric. Today, rhetoric bears the largely negative connotation of meaning "empty talk." A rhetorical question requires no answer. "That is just so much rhetoric," is dismissive. Against that reductionism,

Lischer is correct in asserting that "Rhetoric is the theory and practice of purposive discourse."[2] Aristotle proposed five divisions of rhetoric:

1. Invention—the composition of content
2. Arrangement—"beauty is a kind of order"
3. Style—elocution, selection of words, grammar
4. Delivery—the actual communication of content
5. Memory—freedom from dependence on written material

The Romans learned from Greek rhetorical style and in turn produced Cicero (d. 43 B.C.), whose *De Oratore* so shaped Augustine. Like Aristotle, Cicero valued *ethos* (or the character of the speaker) more than *logos* or *pathos*.[3] Augustine was the Ciceronian man as set forth in Cicero's *Brutus*, well rounded and inspiring.

Also very influential in this field was Quintilian (d. 120), whose twelve-volume manual *Institutes of Oratory* is even more finished than Aristotle. In *The Schoolmaster,* Quintilian argues typically: "I dare affirm that even a mediocre speech will be more effective, if delivered well, than the best speech, if poorly delivered."[4] We have already detected the influence of the Athenian School of Rhetoric on Chrysostom through his teacher Libanius, but other schools in Constantinople and in Gaza exerted extensive influence. Their counterparts were in the West.[5]

Edwin Hatch argues that Greek rhetoric created the Christian sermon and in the process effectively killed it.[6] Others have claimed that Greek philosophy exerted only a deleterious influence on Christian thought. But it is inaccurate to issue a wholesale condemnation of Greek rhetorical influence on the sermon. Cicero's contention that style should always be adapted to purpose is sound and was strongly commended to Augustine and by Augustine.

Thus we must concur with an approach to preaching that speaks of "The Preacher as Rhetorician"[7] or a treatment of preaching style that probes rhetorical and traditional sources.[8] The significance of Augustine here is his clear thinking on the relationship between the cultural significance of contemporary rhetorical categories and the Word of God he was committed to proclaim. In the next section we shall examine his *De Doctrina Christiana,* in which he advances a balanced solution to the dilemmas of the Christian communicator. In essence, Augustine baptized Aristotle's rhetorical approach through Cicero into the Christian church. The gospel of Christ made oratory Christian.

---

1. E. C. Dargan, *A History of Preaching* (Grand Rapids: Baker, 1954), 93ff.
2. Richard Lischer, *Theories of Preaching* (Durham, N.C.: Labyrinth, 1987), 209.
3. James M. May, *Trials of Character: The Eloquence of Ciceronian Ethos* (Chapel Hill: University of North Carolina Press, 1989).
4. Marcus Fabius Quintillianus, *The Schoolmaster* (Nashville: George Peabody University Press, 1951), 1:294. This is the book title used for *Institutio Oratorio.* I am indebted to my former student, Dr. Don Whitney, for the reference.
5. George A. Kennedy, *Greek Rhetoric Under Christian Emperors* (Princeton, N.J.: Princeton University Press, 1983).

6. Edwin Hatch, *The Influence of Greek Ideas and Usages on the Christian Church* (London: Williams and Norgate, 1901), 113ff.
7. Lester De Koster, "The Preacher as Rhetorician," in *The Preacher and Preaching: Reviving the Art in the Twentieth Century,* ed. Samuel T. Lorgan Jr. (Phillipsburg, N.J.: Presbyterian and Reformed, 1986), 303–30.
8. William H. Kooienga, *Elements of Style for Preaching* (Grand Rapids: Zondervan, 1989), 19ff.

3.4.4 THE HOMILETICAL THEORY OF AUGUSTINE

> We must beware of the man who abounds in eloquent nonsense, and so much the more if the hearer is pleased with what is not worth listening to, and thinks that because the speaker is eloquent, what he says must be true . . . A man speaks with more or less wisdom to the extent he has made more or less progress in the knowledge of the Scripture, not just in knowing them but especially in understanding them correctly . . . It is more important to speak wisely than eloquently.
>
> —Augustine in *De Doctrina Christiana*

Some have called Chrysostom's *On the Priesthood* the first book on homiletics, but this tome really addresses the character of the preacher rather than the craft of preaching. It is Augustine's *On Christian Doctrine* that can legitimately claim to that title. Books 1–3 of his treatise, written in 397, address the Scriptures and a proper hermeneutic. His final section, written thirty years later, concerns the methodology of preaching. Britannica's *Great Books* (volume 18, 621–98) contains this work in an able translation by J. F. Shaw.

Augustine sets forth the necessity of an inquiring spirit: "What says the Scripture?" He seeks an environment in which people can "feed on the good bread of the Lord." While Scripture is veiled to the non-Christian, Augustine sees it as a river in which an elephant can swim and a little child can wade. He maintained that a lifetime of studying the Bible would leave him "still making progress in discovering their treasures."[1]

In what Peter Brown maintains is "one of the most original [books] that Augustine ever wrote,"[2] we mark a strong emphasis on "the words of Scripture." Augustine sees words as signs, and grapples with the inadequacy of language. He underscores what he calls "the primary principle" on interpretation, seeing every part in relation to the teaching of Scripture as a whole as relating to God's redeeming love for humanity and humanity's response to God.

In Book 4 Augustine turns to effective rhetoric. Classical rhetoric can enhance preaching, he argues, but rhetorical skill can be gained from the careful study of Scripture itself.

Content is more than form, maintains Augustine. Content is the foundation, but the Christian expositor is to combine wisdom with eloquence.[3] Drawing upon his Ciceronian roots, Augustine agrees that the purpose of the speaker is "to teach, to delight and to move . . . of these teaching is the most essential."[4] He strongly reinforces the necessity of prayer[5] and underscores the importance of a consistent life.[6]

In the closing movement of this landmark, Augustine urges, "But whether a man is going to address the people or to dictate what others will deliver or read to the people, he ought to pray God to put into his mouth a suitable discourse."[7]

Augustine thus stakes out a position that effectively models a prudent use of stylistic forms in the interest of valid communication of the changeless gospel. Erich Auerbach describes Augustine's approach as generally using *sermo humilis* (or down-to-earth speech) but on occasion using when appropriate a more elevated style.[8] Above all, Augustine maintained his determination to stay close to the text. Was this not the practice of the apostle Paul?

"More heavily than all rhetorical brilliance on the one hand, or the displeasure of the grammarians because of unpolished diction on the other hand, there weighed on Augustine the duty of explaining the Word of God in so plain a manner that the less gifted could also grasp it."[9]

---

1. Augustine, *Epistolae* 137.3.
2. Peter Brown, *Augustine of Hippo* (Berkeley: University of California, 1967), 264.
3. Augustine, *De Doctrina Christiana* 4.5.8.
4. Ibid., 12.27.
5. Ibid., 15.32.
6. Ibid., 27.59.
7. Ibid., 30.63.
8. Erich Auerbach, *Literary Language and Its Public*, quoted in William H. Kooienga, *Elements of Style for Preaching* (Grand Rapids: Zondervan, 1989), 28–29.
9. Thomas K. Carroll, *Preaching the Word: Message of the Fathers of the Church* (Wilmington, Del.: Michael Glazier, 1984), 196.

CHAPTER FOUR

The Adolescence of Biblical Preaching (A.D. 450–1450)

Jesus of Nazareth . . . a prophet, powerful in word and deed before God
and all the people.   —Luke 24:19

He said to them, "How foolish you are, and how slow of heart to believe
all that the prophets have spoken! Did not the Christ have to suffer these
things and then enter his glory?" And beginning with Moses and all the
Prophets, he explained to them what was said in all the Scriptures concerning himself.

—Luke 24:25–27

They asked each other, "Were not our hearts burning within us while he
talked with us on the road and opened the Scriptures to us?"
—Luke 24:32

He told them, "This is what is written: The Christ will suffer and rise
from the dead on the third day, and repentance and forgiveness of sins
will be preached in his name to all nations, beginning at Jerusalem."
—Luke 24:46–47

The important thing is that in every way . . . Christ is preached.
—Philippians 1:18

After Augustine, preaching entered its adolescence. Civilization settled uneasily into the Middle, or Dark Ages, and feudalism took root. It was a time of violence and disorder, of introversion and gloom. And yet it was not a period of unrelieved darkness. The preaching of the Word retained certain vital qualities. As Professor Bark argued, "Nothing better attests to the creative genius, the capacity both to learn and to originate, of western civilization, *even in the period of its youth,* than the mighty product of its religious art, which combined spiritual aspiration, warm human feeling and artistic excellence, in a way unknown to pagan, classical antiquity."[1]

After the death of Constantine in 337, the Roman Empire gradually disintegrated. In 395, the empire split in half, and a process of barbarization began. Cicero saw the empire as "a picture fading because of old age." Ambrose preached that "we are indeed in the twilight of the world."[2] Eusebius had been optimistic about the ultimate victory of the empire, but Augustine in *De civitate dei* delineated the need for the separation of the church from the state.[3] Augustine proved prophetic. Sin and corruption within and the barbarian hordes without eroded the structures of government. In 476, the last emperor, the boy Romulus Augustulus, had the crown taken from him and placed on the head of Odovacar.

The irreversible decline of the Roman Empire has been explained by Professor Trevor-Roper:[4]

1. The ruralization of Europe, the decline of the cities, exhaustion of the soil, economic depression, the prolonged effects of slavery, insufficient numbers of soldiers for defense in the face of hired mercenary barbarians, the loss of promise and hope.
2. The incursions of new religions from the East, including Christianity, which "stabilized on a rural base." Religious syncretism undercut vitality. Clovis of the Franks (466?–511) provides us with a colorful example. Clovis promised God he would become a Christian if he won a great battle. He was subsequently baptized with three thousand of his warriors but tellingly held his battle ax out of the water.
3. The invasion of the barbarians, who did not destroy the empire but continued many aspects of it. First were the Arians, followed by the Arabs, and ultimately the Vikings, who swept across Europe amid a vacuum of governmental institutions, violence, and chaos.[5]

For an example of sermons from this tumultuous era, we turn to Quodvultdeus, bishop of Carthage, who faced the Vandal conquest. He was a mighty preacher of repentance, and saw God as punishing Rome and the Christians for their sins. He urged his hearers not to put their hope in this world but to look forward to the joys of heaven.[6]

The sense of devastation and defeat was profound, but the resultant power vacuum presented an opportunity for the Christian church. Thus Professor Bark sees a "frontier quality" in the early Middle Ages, the emergence of something new in place of shattered antiquity. Professor von Campenhausen, in a memorable post-World War II address titled "Augustine and the Fall of Rome," called for theology to maintain its historic and God-given role to assert divine truth to all of its pagan opponents, no matter how tragic history may have become.[7] We now survey preaching in the Middle Ages.

---

1. William Carroll Bark, *Origins of the Medieval World* (Palo Alto, Calif.: Stanford University Press, 1958), 70ff. The italics are mine.
2. Santo Nazzarino, *The End of the Ancient World* (New York: Knopf, 1966).
3. Bark, *Origins of the Medieval World,* 109.
4. Hugh Trevor-Roper, *The Rise of Christian Europe* (New York: Harcourt Brace, 1965).
5. Richard E. Sullivan, *Heirs of the Roman Empire* (Ithaca, N.Y.: Cornell University Press, 1960), 45.
6. Robert B. Eno, "Christian Reaction to the Barbarian Invasions and the Sermons of Quodvultdeus," in *Preaching in the Patristic Age,* ed. David G. Hunter (New York: Paulist, 1989), 153.
7. Bob Patterson, ed., *Makers of the Modern Theological Mind: Pannenberg* (Waco, Tex.: Word, 1973).

4.1 THE LOWERING OF THE LIGHTS AND THE GATHERING OF THE GLOOM

See what has befallen Rome, once mistress of the world. She is worn down by great sorrows, by the disappearance of her citizens, by the attacks of her enemies, by numerous ruins. Thus we see brought to fulfillment what the prophet [Ezekiel] long ago pronounced on the city of Samaria.
—Gregory I (593 or 594)

With the catastrophic collapse of the effective structures of governance in the empire, the world braced for three developments:

1. The rise of the Byzantine Empire, in which preaching was virtually nonexistent. Some spiritual leaders fled to the west, such as Maximus the Confessor, whose labors in Carthage (614–638) were exegetically and hermeneutically important. His anti-Origenistic bent gives him special significance.[1]
2. The birth of Islam and the new civilization it brought, as well as the strange absence of a vigorous evangelistic effort to win Muslims to Christ.
3. The stirrings of Western European civilization as the church became the preserver and guarantor of the revealed truth of Scripture through a dismal time.

At first the church seemed paralyzed by what has been termed "despondent passivity." A marked decay in the arts and letters took place. The middle class was hounded out of existence and the growing peasantry was "reduced to total dependency."[2] The sacerdotalism of the clergy removed them from preaching and the people were increasingly ignorant and illiterate. Dean Milman characterized the situation: "Actual preaching had fallen into disuse."[3] The peasant class might see a priest once a year in order to receive the sacraments.

Education and the reading arts were confined to the monasteries. One conservative estimate indicates 90 percent of the literate men in the Middle Ages received their instruction in a monastic school.[4] The effective loss of the Bible and its truth with the related demise of biblical preaching spelled curtains for Christian vitality. Who and what kept the light shining in this darkness? We sense in our own time "a famine of hearing the words of the LORD" (Amos 8:11) and a growing biblical illiteracy among churched people. Some beacon lights of resistance to the drift of the period require consideration.[5]

---

1. Paul M. Blowers, *Exegesis and Spiritual Pedagogy in Maximus the Confessor* (Notre Dame, Ind.: Notre Dame University Press, 1991). Maximus was Christocentric in his interpretation of Scripture with an emphasis on the indwelling of Christ in the believer's life. He was concerned about both the *theoria* and *praxis* of scriptural truth.
2. William Carroll Bark, *Origins of the Medieval World* (Palo Alto, Calif.: Stanford University Press, 1958), 64.
3. Quoted in Arthur H. Smith, *Preachers and Preaching* (Philadelphia: United Lutheran Publication House, 1925), 12.
4. Norman F. Cantor, *The Civilization of the Middle Ages* (New York: HarperCollins, 1993), 153.
5. We seem to be facing a similar move from the Scriptures and text-driven preaching in our time, and it will have identical ramifications. One prominent pulpiteer recently explained to a Christian media convention: "You'll notice that I don't have a Bible. I've stopped using a Bible in the pulpit. People don't want sermons; they want to hear what God means to us in our own hearts." This retreat from Scripture will be as disastrous now as it was long ago.

4.1.1 LEO THE GREAT—PREACHER OF COURAGE

Love your Bible and you will not fulfill the lusts of the flesh.

—Jerome

He who knows his Bible, as men ought to know it, is offended at nothing that befalls him, but bears all things with noble endurance.

—Chrysostom

The church fathers placed considerable focus on the Scriptures, both in study and proclamation. For Augustine, "Bible study is the highest kind of Christian learning."[1] It was also a time of writing many commentaries. Such leaders as Cyril of Alexandria (d. 444), Theodore of Mopsuestia (d. 428), and Theodoret of Cyrus in Syria (d. 460) wrote significant commentaries. (Interestingly, the cults have never been much interested in writing Bible commentaries.)

A great drawback of the era was that it was left to bishops and prelates to do the preaching. As late as 692 the Council of Quinisext advised that the bishop had the responsibility of preaching to both clergy and laity as follows:

It behooves those who preside over the churches, every day but especially on the Lord's Day, to teach all the clergy and people words of piety and right religion, gathering out of Holy Scripture meditations and determinations of the truth, and not going beyond the limits now fixed, nor varying from the tradition of the God-bearing fathers.[2]

Bishops then were critical in preserving and promulgating biblical truth. Among the early bishops who did this commendably was Leo the Great (390–461). Born south of Pisa, he was a true Etruscan aristocrat. While on a mission in Gaul, he was was informed that he had been chosen bishop of Rome (440). Leo was a doughty defender of the faith, both against Manichaeism and Pelagianism, but also against a Paulinianism "formulated in the context of the ancient liturgy."[3] Paulinianism was a kind of adoptionist Christology. Leo also took vigorous leadership on behalf of the full deity and humanity of Christ, the victory of the Cross, the Resurrection, and the Ascension, and the principles of the new life in the believer. He had great courage and withstood both Attila the Hun and Genseric the Vandal to spare Rome from destruction. He exerted strong influence on the Council of Chalcedon to abide by his position on the fully divine and fully human natures of Christ without debate (451).

Leo the Great was dedicated to preaching. He was saturated in the Scriptures and preached sermons from the whole liturgical cycle. He held to "the unyielding truth of the gospels,"[4] emphasizing that what the apostles preached the prophets had previously announced. Murphy stresses the depth of his theological perception, his unmistakable social consciousness, and his "homiletical omnicompetence."[5] We have a fair sample of extant sermons.[6]

Examination of the sermons indicates they are more homilies than full-blown expositions. Leo quoted much Scripture. The sermons were Christocentric and he did not hesitate to engage falsehood and heresy. He emphasized personal union with Christ as the wellspring of the sanctified life. His passiontide sermons strongly underscored God's strict justice in redemption along with God's mercy.[7] While his claims for the Petrine priority of the Roman bishopric are exaggerated, we must see his energetic pursuit of sound doctrine, liturgical purity, and biblical preaching as pivotal in a time of drastic transition.

---

1. Beryl Smalley, *The Study of the Bible in the Middle Ages* (Notre Dame, Ind.: University of Notre Dame Press, 1964), 26.
2. James J. Murphy, *Rhetoric in the Middle Ages: A History of Rhetorical Theory from St. Augustine to the Renaissance* (Berkeley: University of California, 1974), 284.
3. Louis Bouyer, *A History of Christian Spirituality: The Spirituality of the New Testament and the Fathers* (Minneapolis: Seabury, 1960), 529.
4. Francis X. Murphy, "The Sermons of Pope Leo the Great: Context and Style," in *Preaching in the Patristic Age,* ed. David G. Hunter (New York: Paulist, 1989), 186.
5. Ibid., 195.
6. Trevor Jalland, *The Life and Times of St. Leo the Great* (New York: Macmillan, 1941), 495–514, 525.

7. William Bright, *Select Sermons of St. Leo the Great* (London: J. Masters and Co., 1886).

4.1.2   GREGORY THE FIRST—PREACHER OF CONVICTION

> The martyrs preached, till their bodies were dissolved in death; their bodies were dissolved in death, that they might shine forth with miracles; they shone forth with miracles, that they might overthrow their enemies with divine light; so that they might no longer stand up and resist God, but submit to, and be afraid of, Him.
>
> —Gregory *Moralia* 30.76

Born in a turbulent time to patrician parents, Gregory I, or Gregory the Great (540–604), rose quickly to Roman preferment. At age thirty-three he was made prefect or mayor of Rome and rode in a chariot pulled by four snow-white horses. Coming into contact with some of the disciples of the monastic St. Benedict, he dedicated his life to Christ and subsequently had a monastic tinge to his yearning to have "the odor of all flowers" pervading his life.[1] Dispositionally he tended to be bipolar ("I am all honey and stings"), and he served a stint as Roman representative in Constantinople. Gregory never learned Greek, and his Latin grammar was atrocious, yet he was made bishop of Rome in 590.

Gregory was a key figure in defining the evolving role of the papacy. He regarded the Western church as a ship which "creaked shipwreck." He founded monasteries and sent out missionaries while establishing strong ties with emerging monarchies.[2]

Gregory saw himself as "servant of the servants of God" and gave himself to the improvement and development of the clergy. His extended sermon on the Book of Job, the *Moralia,* runs to two thousand pages. The treatise has a powerful section on the resurrection of the flesh. His simple Latin writing style made this a classic. John Milton read this work deeply and drew upon it when he formed *Samson Agonistes.*

Gregory called preachers to the Scripture. In his own preaching he took a text step-by-step. In the *De cura pastorali,* he gave practical pointers to preachers. He wrote, "It is indeed difficult for a preacher who is not loved, however well he may preach, to be willingly listened to. He then that is over others, ought to study to be loved, to the end that he be listened to."

Yet at the heart of his commitment to preaching was a deathless conviction of the centrality of Scripture. Walker says that Gregory's attitude toward Scripture "is completely fundamentalist" (i.e., he believed of the Book of Job that "It is very pointless to ask who composed this volume, since we believe loyally that its author was the Holy Ghost").[3] He was concerned "to erect on the foundation of history a spiritual edifice." He summoned those called to the cure of souls to daily meditate, to feed on the Word of God, and to obey it. "We hear the Words of God if we act upon them," he argued. Of the preacher he says:

For it is true that whosoever enters on the priesthood undertakes the office of herald, so as to walk, himself crying aloud, before the coming of the judge who follows terribly. Wherefore, if the priest knows not how to preach, what voice of a loud cry shall the mute herald utter? For hence it is that the Holy Spirit sat upon the first pastors under the appearances of tongues (Acts 2:3); because whomsoever He has filled, He himself at once makes eloquent.[4]

The exact status of the Second Dialogue of Gregory the Great (with Benedict) is highly controverted, but here we have representations consistent with what we have been ascribing to the man some call "the father of the medieval papacy."[5]

Gregory broke new ground in his extensive audience analysis. A master storyteller, he may have been the first to introduce a sequential story for illustrative purposes in his sermons. He recommended that officiants read a patristic sermon, which may have tended to further fossilize preaching for many. His own preaching was often thunder and lightning and frequently reflected his conviction that the end of human history was near. The recession of the Parousia was not in evidence in his discourse (*Homillae in Ezechielem* 2.8):

Fiery swords, which reddened with the blood of mankind, and soon after flowed in streams were seen in the heavens before Italy became the prey of the Lombards. Be watchful and alert! Those who love God should shout for joy at the end of the world. Those who mourn are they whose hearts are rooted in love for the world, and who neither long for the future life, nor have any foretaste of it within themselves. Every day the earth is visited by fresh calamities. You see how few remain of the ancient population: each day sees us chastened by new afflictions, and unforeseen blows strike us to the ground. The world grows old and hoary, and through a sea of troubles hastens to approaching death.

Other preachers of the day, like the oratorical Peter Chrysologus of Ravenna (d. 451), tended to be moralistic. Maximus of Turin (d. 465) was known as a gifted extempore preacher who used word pictures skillfully. Caesarius of Arles (d. 542) argued that "the Word should not be honored less than the Body of the Lord" but tended to borrow heavily from Augustine. Others make us appreciate all the more the gifts and convictions of Gregory, who was often called "the last of the Romans."[6] Bible preaching was slipping away.

---

1. Robert Payne, *The Fathers of the Western Church* (New York: Viking, 1951), 201. For a vivid description of Gregory in action, see 199.
2. Norman F. Cantor, *The Civilization of the Middle Ages,* rev. ed. (New York: HarperCollins, 1963, 1993), 153.
3. G. S. M. Walker, *The Growing Storm: Sketches of Church History from A.D. 600 to A.D. 1350* (Grand Rapids: Eerdmans, 1961), 13.
4. James J. Murphy, *Rhetoric in the Middle Ages: A History of Rhetorical Theory from*

St. Augustine to the Renaissance (Berkeley: University of California Press, 1974), 292.

5. Pearse Cusack, *An Interpretation of the Second Dialogue of Gregory the Great* (Lewiston, N.Y.: Edwin Mellen Press, 1993). This is volume 31 in the series Studies in the Bible and Early Christianity.

6. Thomas K. Carroll, *Preaching the Word: Message of the Fathers of the Church* (Wilmington, Del.: Michael Glazier, 1984), 206ff.

4.1.3 SAINT PATRICK—PREACHER OF CONVERSION

That is why I am now ashamed and am seriously afraid of revealing my unskilfulness, the fact that I cannot hold forth in speech to cultivated people in exact language.

—Confessions 10

Who am I, Lord, and what is my calling since you have worked with me with such divine power?

—Confessions 34

But I see that I have been promoted beyond measure by the Lord in this present age and I was not worthy nor the kind of person to whom he might grant this.

—Confessions 55

Even without embellishment, Patrick (389–461) stands as a spiritual giant. He may never have driven the snakes out of Ireland or proved the doctrine of the triune nature of God with a shamrock, but he is the first British churchman whose writings have come to us. We are just now learning of the animistic and totemistic worship of the Druids. Pre-Christian religion in the British Isles was gross and dismal.

Christianity arrived in Roman Britain sometime after A.D. 100. Britons soon were making significant contributions. Alban (c. 208) was martyred when he refused to denounce Christ. Athanasius reported that British bishops stood with him in Nicea (325). Pelagius (354–418) was a Welshman whose teachings troubled the British scene, although his controversies with Augustine followed his departure from Britain. Christian churches were also springing up across the stormy Irish Sea in Ireland (Hibernia to the Romans).

Patrick was born on the west coast of England or Wales and reared in an aristocratic home. His father, Calpurnius, seems to have been a municipal officer and a deacon in the church. At the age of sixteen (405) Patrick was kidnapped by Irish pirates and worked six years in County Mayo as a slave caring for sheep. He escaped across country to Wexford or Wicklow and returned to England. In 430 he returned as bishop and poured the balance of his life into vigorous evangelization. It was this role that ensured his place in the history of biblical preaching.

Patrick traveled widely, planting about 365 churches and winning some 120,000 converts to Christ.[1] He also won the man whose slave he had been, as well as many Irish kings.[2]

In conjunction with prayer, the Scripture was primary for Patrick and Celtic Christianity. He was said to have prayed one hundred times a day. Hanson describes his constant quoting from the Latin Bible, which "impregnated his mind and dominated his thought."[3] He loved the promises of the Old Testament but most frequently quoted from Romans. He had a good grasp of justification by faith alone,[4] and his interpretation was generally balanced and sound. He experienced the Holy Spirit praying in him.[5] Patrick's conviction with regard to Scripture was clear: "That which I have set out in Latin is not my words but the words of God and of his apostles and prophets who of course have never lied."[6]

In his Letter to Coroticus he indicates his conviction that the last days of history are upon the church. He wrote that toward this end the gospel must be preached "as a testimony to all nations"[7] (Matt. 24:14). The flavor of Patrick's preaching may be tasted in a piece from his famous *Hymn Before Tara* (Tara being the High King of Ireland), called St. Patrick's Breastplate, or the Deer's Cry:

> At Tara today
> May God be my stay.
> May the strength of God now nerve me!
> May the power of God preserve me!
> May God the Almighty be near me!
> May God the Almighty espy me!
> May God the Almighty hear me!
> May God give me eloquent speech!
> May the arm of God protect me!
> May the wisdom of God direct me!
> May God give me the power to teach and to preach!
> May the shield of God defend me!
> May the host of God attend me,
> And ward me.[8]

---

1. For the overall picture of this period, see V. Raymond Edman, *The Light in Dark Ages* (Wheaton, Ill.: Van Kampen, 1949), 97–103; Kenneth Scott Latourette, *The First Five Centuries*, volume 1 in *A History of the Expansion of Christianity* (Grand Rapids: Zondervan, 1937, 1970), 216–23; F. F. Bruce, "The Apostle of Ireland," in *The Spreading Flame* (Grand Rapids: Eerdmans, 1958), 371–83. A very choice study: Thomas Cahill, *How the Irish Saved Civilization* (New York: Doubleday, 1995). Shows "The Untold Story of Ireland's Heroic Role from the Fall of Rome to the Rise of Medieval Europe."

2. James Bulloch, *The Life of the Celtic Church* (Edinburgh: Saint Andrew Press, 1963); Kathleen Hughes, *Early Christian Ireland* (Ithaca, N.Y.: Cornell University Press, 1972); Donald E. Meek, "Modern Celtic Christianity: The Contemporary 'Revival' and Its Roots," *Scottish Bulletin of Evangelical Theology* 10 (spring 1992), 6–31. I am indebted to my former teaching fellow Jeffrey Sickles for introducing me to these titles.

3. R. P. C. Hanson, *The Life and Writings of the Historical Saint Patrick* (New York: Seabury, 1983), 45.

4. Ibid., 39.
5. Ibid., 48.
6. Ibid., 46.
7. Ibid., 68.
8. Saint Patrick: Apostle of Ireland in *Notre Dame Lives of the Saints* (London: Sands, 1911), 252. We still have the sermon as more of a homily than oratio. This is contrary to Edwin Hatch's frequently cited lament that Christian preaching was handicapped early on by adopting Greek and Roman rhetorical forms such as introduction, division of the matter, and conclusion; see Edwin Hatch, *The Influence of Greek Ideas and Usages upon the Christian Church* (London: Williams and Norgate, 1901), 107ff. Hatch actually argues most curiously that the tragic development was the replacement of prophesying by preaching. D. Martyn Lloyd-Jones endorses this notion in his *Knowing the Times* (Edinburgh: Banner of Truth, 1989), 270. We must be wary of a knee-jerk reaction against the influence of Greek rhetoric which is not historically discerning and careful with the facts.

4.2 PRESERVING POINTS OF LIGHT—PREACHING IN THE GLOOM

He who realizes the living place which preaching in its most vital forms has ever taken in the spiritual life of the Church will need no further assurance of its great importance. He will not fail to note that the preacher's message and the Church's spiritual condition have risen or fallen together. When life has gone out of the preacher it is not long before it has gone out of the church also. On the other hand, when there has been a revival message of life on the preacher's lips there comes as a consequence a revived condition of the Church itself. The connection between these two things has been close, uniform and constant.

—John Brown, *Puritan Preaching in England*

The interrelationship of the health of the church, the health of biblical awareness, and the health of preaching is nowhere more striking than in the Middle Ages. All three were at an abysmally low ebb. The role of preaching was explicitly clear in the Gallican Rite (sixth century French Ecclesiastical Rule) and in Gregory's *Moralia*. Yet in practice preaching was nonexistent for most, and where it did exist it was gravely defective.

But God had not abandoned his beleaguered people. A multiplicity of movements reflected his faithfulness. The Bible was yet preserved, and in fascinating and fruitful ways it was yet proclaimed.

A wealth of research in recent years has taken issue with the long-prevailing view that the Bible was of little consequence during these one thousand years. This reversal is largely due to the studies of Beryl Smalley and her mentor, F. M. Powicke. In Professor Powicke's tenure at Manchester and Oxford and in his lectures on Stephen Langton at Oxford in 1927, he argued for the influence of the theology of the schools on medieval life. Smalley gave a lifetime to the study of the biblical commentaries of the Middle Ages and to the identification of the *Glossa Ordinaria*, a compilation of biblical text commentary begun by Walafrid

Strabo, a ninth-century German monk, and continued by such luminaries as Stephen Langton in Paris, Anselm of Laon, Andrew of St. Victor, and Herbert of Bosham. Several of these scholars were eminent Hebraists, and the work was generally based on a literal exegesis of Scripture.[1]

The *locus classicus* embodying this research may be seen in Smalley's incomparable *Study of the Bible in the Middle Ages*.[2] Here is evidence indicating how the Bible was preserved in a decadent period and how the light of the Scripture glimmered out of the monasteries in an ever-increasing brilliance until the dawn of the Reformation in the sixteenth century. What a debt of gratitude we owe to those who nourished and fed that flame. Our analysis must touch a variety of movements and influences.

---

1. R. W. Southern, "Beryl Smalley and the Place of the Bible in Medieval Studies, 1927–84" in *The Bible in the Medieval World* (Ecclesiastical History Society, Oxford: Blackwell, 1985), 1–16.
2. Beryl Smalley, *The Study of the Bible in the Middle Ages* (Notre Dame, Ind.: University of Notre Dame Press, 1964).

4.2.1 POINTS OF LIGHT—THE PREACHING OF THE MONASTICS

Let us pray that what is hidden may be revealed to us, and let us by no means desist from our studies.

—Cassiodorus

The instinct to withdraw in time of peril to seek purity is a two-sided coin. There *is* a biblical summons to separation (Rom. 12:2; 2 Cor. 6:17–18), but this must not entail isolation (John 17:15). We withdraw so that we may reenter refreshed and renewed. The Sabbath principle enshrines the soundness of going in and going out.

The earliest monastics, the so-called Desert Fathers, were responding to a situation of external decline and internal desire. **Anthony of Egypt** (d. 356) began as a solitary hermit in order to battle the Devil and later founded a community of hermits. He took literally Christ's command, "Go sell all that you have." Athanasius' great treatise on *The Life of St. Anthony* gave a significant boost to the monastic way of life.

Pachomius (290–346) brought together thousands of Egyptian Christians in communities of work and obedience. Helen Waddell's memorable observation is to the point, "These men [the North African ascetics] stamped infinity on the imagination of the West." All of this has immense implication for preaching.

Athanasius (328–373), the stalwart defender of orthodox Christology and bishop of Alexandria, brought the monastic ideal to the West in his Italian exile (c. 340).

Two early planters of monasteries in Gaul, **Martin of Tours** (316–397) and **St. John Cassian** (360–432), were not only contemplative but also evangelistic, in contrast to the Egyptian ascetics. Preaching was important to Martin of Tours, though it was not his strength. Cassian had sought admission to the Cave of the Nativity in Bethlehem, knew Chrysostom personally during his several years in Constantinople, and after a sojourn in Rome planted two monasteries in Marseilles (c. 410).[1]

Cassian's *Institutes and Conferences* give insight into the life of the community. The sacrament was shared daily. Scripture was basic. "The mind, in its course of growth, is to be filled and conditioned by meditations upon Scripture."[2] Wrestling with the meaning of texts, understanding the Scripture first in its literal or historical sense, pursuing moral application—these encapsulate the rhythm of monastic life. The copying of manuscripts was crucial. The Irish monks from the sixth century on preserved western culture in a very real sense as the world was overrun by barbarians. Cassian's monks copied and recopied the manuscripts.

Basil of Caesarea (330–379) struck a balance between biblical and theological study and the necessity of outreach by exposition and hospice work.

Benedict of Nursia (480–547), author of the influential Benedictine Rule, renounced the world in his fourteenth year. Born in Rome (and very much a Roman in his approach to all things), Benedict eventually established the great monastery at Monte Cassino.[3] His Rule not only governed the Benedictines but by the ninth century dominated all other rules and was the basis for the establishment of the Cluniacs and Cistercians. The Rule was hard law, and set forth twelve rungs of humility and seventy-two spiritual tools to be used in monastic ritual.

"The art of the Benedictine scribe" was instrumental in saving civilization through its copying of manuscripts. In the daily vigils there was great emphasis on Scripture, on "holy reading," on the library with its scrolls.[4] "St. Benedict's doctrine was based upon the Holy Scripture, so profoundly meditated upon and assimilated that his quotations enter easily and naturally into his text."[5] He was a prayerful man who practiced the praying of Scripture.[6] Benedict's emphasis on Scripture and the life of devotion, as well as his blend of preaching, education, and the arts for maximum cultural impact, became paradigmatic for centuries to come.

Cassiodorus in the mid-sixth century and **Boethius** (480–524) were significant because of their formative influence on the shaping of the monastic schools. Cassiodorus' volume on *Divine and Secular Learning* was critical in keeping education and literacy alive.

Another stellar figure reflecting the virility of Anglo-Saxon preaching was the monk known as **The Venerable Bede** (673–735). This worthy lived, preached, and died in the north of England, at the Church of Ceolfrith, in Jarrow, almost in the shadow of Hadrian's Wall. Fluent in Latin and an author of Anglo-Saxon poetry, his *Ecclesiastical History of the English Nation* remains an invaluable guide to understanding the advance of Christianity. *Liber de schematibus et tropis* is considered the first book of rhetoric written in England, and Bede's *De arte metrica* deals with grammatical lore. **Alcuin** (735–804) extended Bede's concerns on the Continent.[7]

Bede's chief distinctiveness, however, resided in his great love for Scripture and his dedication to preaching. Cloistral preaching (i.e., preaching within a monastery), like cloistral learning, was central to the survival of biblical communication. But Bede also preached to the people. His homilies were not long and frequently indulged in painful allegorization, but they were based on Scripture. G. F. Browne describes his method: "He took a passage of some considerable length, one of the lessons for the day, for example, and went through it, verse by verse, expounding rather than preaching."[8] He may have been the first preacher to use the church year in projecting his sermons.

The better preaching of this period has great resemblance to the popular Bible reading or running commentary which came into such vogue in the nineteenth century and continues on into our own time. Yet Jenkins observes correctly, "No reader of Bede can fail to observe his insistence, repeated and manifold, on the blessing which attends preaching . . . a blessing not only for the hearers but also for the preacher himself."[9]

Tradition has it that when Bede was dying, he was translating John's gospel into Anglo-Saxon and urged his amanuensis to "write quickly." He wanted "one more sentence" and was given the next verse from John 19, "It is finished," to which he replied, "Aye, it is finished." And he died.

Amid the deplorable moral and spiritual collapse, some of the monastics began to reach out in preaching missions into the cities and countryside, such as **Leander** and **Isidore** in Spain. The preaching was generally in Latin, but interpreters were beginning to be employed. In 762 **Chrodegang**, archbishop of Metz, in his *Regula Canonicorum* stipulated that there must be preaching at least twice every month in every parish, hopefully on every feast day and on every Lord's Day, and "that the preaching must be such as the people can understand."[10] Similarly in Charlemagne's *Capitularia,* as early as 769 priests are "forbidden to feign and preach to the people out of their own understanding and not according to the Sacred Scriptures, new or uncanonical things."[11]

One of the foremost examples of monastic preaching must be that of **St. Bernard of Clairvaux** (1091–1153), called "the last of the Fathers," and "the mellifluous doctor" by Pius XII at the eighth centenary of his death in 1953. Luther regarded him as "the most pious of all the monks," and said of him, "He preached Christ most charmingly. I follow him wherever he preached Christ, and I pray to Christ in the faith in which he prayed to Christ."[12] Erasmus paid tribute to Bernard's fiery eloquence in his *Art of Preaching,* saying, "Bernard is an eloquent preacher, much more by nature than by art; full of charm and vivacity, and knows how to reach and move the affections."

Brought up near Dijon in an aristocratic family, Bernard early in life entered the Cistercian abbey at Citeaux, where at the end of his first year he could not recall whether the ceiling was vaulted or if there were two or three windows in his cell. He was a man of singular discipline. In time he established Clairvaux in the Burgundian hills. His organizational genius, his writing and preaching, his involvement in the Second Crusade (Christendom's highly flawed military effort to combat Muslim expansionism, described by Professor Trevor-Roper as "a deplorable outburst of fanaticism and folly"), and his rescue of the papacy from the Great Schism are all most remarkable. His conflict with Peter Abelard is the stuff of fiction.[13] We would love him if only for "O Sacred Head Now Wounded" and "Jesus the Very Thought of Thee."

Yet here we note particularly his strong biblical preaching. Two daily sermons were given to "the white monks" in this tradition. Bernard's preaching was influential through the written transcripts circulated far and wide. The eighty-six sermons he preached from the Song of Solomon are of special significance, as are his preaching on the love of God and his extraordinary sermons on conversion.

The sermons of Bernard are the first to divide discourse into sections. He typically took a text and then studded his message with Scripture.[14] Clear throughout is his high view of biblical inspiration. Like a skilled physician, he analyzes the "hidden sores of mankind," but then he insists that "[we] must rely upon grace and not upon nature, nor even upon sincere efforts. [We] must turn toward the Word, because the affinity which links [our] soul to Him is not illusory. The proof of this kinship is the likeness which remains."[15] Even his sermons on "Various Meanings of the Kiss" and "The Breasts and Their Perfume" from the Canticles, while a bit of a stretch, are yet full of devotion to Christ. "To know Jesus and Him crucified is the sum of my philosophy," he would argue. His preaching on conversion is aggressive and clear and he would often ask for a response after the message.[16]

Bernard's life and testimony exerted a profound influence on his own and subsequent times. He inveighed against the doctrine of papal infallibility, monastic corruption, the doctrine of the immaculate conception of Mary, and atrocities against the Jews. Conservative and controversial, he was a servant of Christ.

We must consider one more monastic, the Cistercian from southern Italy, **Joachim of Fiore** (1135–1202). He was the abbot of the monastery of Curazzo in Calabria. Joachim loved the exposition of Scripture and emphasized the essential agreement of the Old Testament and the New Testament in his widely read *Liber concordie*. He advanced the idea of the future conversion of the Jews and advocated the establishment of preaching orders.

With a strong following up into the sixteenth century, Joachim has bequeathed us "his great lyrical outbursts on the glories of the Age of the Spirit."[17] Unlike Thomas Aquinas, who taught that hope is a transcendent virtue and that the fulfillment of promise would not be in time/space history, Joachim taught the overlap of the two ages and a chiliastic age in which all of the Old Testament promises will be fulfilled. Moltmann argues that Joachim is more alive and relevant today than Aquinas.[18] Wycliffe quoted him often, and his influence on the Franciscans has been traced. His preaching rhythms move right into the Renaissance. The biblical and spiritual resources preserved and promulgated through the monastic system are a resounding testimony to God's gracious providence.

---

1. Owen Chadwick, *John Cassian* (Cambridge, Mass.: Cambridge University Press, 1968), 10, 19, 23.
2. Ibid., 101.
3. For a superbly researched historical novel about St. Benedict, see Louis de Wohl, *Citadel of God* (San Francisco: Ignatius, 1959).
4. T. F. Lindsay, *Saint Benedict: His Life and Work* (London: Burns and Oates, 1949), 119.

5. Ibid., 149.

6. Ibid., 163.

7. James J. Murphy, *Rhetoric in the Middle Ages: A History of Rhetorical Theory from St. Augustine to the Renaissance* (Berkeley: University of California Press, 1974), 76ff.

8. G. F. Browne, *The Venerable Bede: His Life and Writings* (London: SPCF, 1930), 232.

9. Claude Jenkins, *Bede As Exegete and Theologian,* ed. A. H. Thompson (New York: Atheneum, 1966). For a fascinating probe of Bede's exegesis for preaching, see Judith McClure, "Bede's Notes on Genesis and the Training of the Anglo-Saxon Clergy," in *The Bible in the Medieval World,* essays in memory of Beryl Smalley (Oxford: Blackwell, 1985), 17–30. He also plumbed deeply into Ezra and Nehemiah to parallel his own times.

10. E. C. Dargan, *A History of Preaching* (New York: Hodder and Stoughton, 1905), 1:134.

11. Ibid.

12. James M. Houston, ed., *The Love of God by Bernard of Clairvaux* (Portland, Oreg.: Multnomah, 1983), 19–20.

13. Denis Meadows, *A Saint and a Half: The Remarkable Lives of Abelard and St. Bernard of Clairvaux* (New York: Devin-Adair, 1963). Meadows sees Bernard as a joyous mystic.

14. Jean Leclercq, *Bernard of Clairvaux and the Cistercian Spirit* (Kalamazoo, Mich.: Cistercian Publications, 1976), 129ff., on "Bernard the Biblical Preacher"; M. Basil Pennington, ed., *Saint Bernard of Clairvaux: Studies Commemorating the 8th Century of His Canonization* (Kalamazoo, Mich.: Cistercian Publications, 1977), 101ff.

15. Bernard of Clairvaux, *On the Song of Songs,* 3 vols. (Spencer, Mass.: Cistercian Publications, 1971).

16. Bernard of Clairvaux, *Sermons on Conversion* (Kalamazoo, Mich.: Cistercian Publications, 1981).

17. Marjorie Reeves, *The Influence of Prophecy in the Later Middle Ages* (London: Oxford, 1969); also Marjorie Reeves, *Joachim of Fiore and the Prophetic Future* (New York: Harper, 1976).

18. Jurgen Moltmann, *History and the Triune God: Contributions to Trinitarian Theology* (New York: Crossroad, 1992), 92ff.

4.2.2 POINTS OF LIGHT—THE PREACHING OF THE MISSIONARIES

But you will receive power when the Holy Spirit comes on you; and you will be my witnesses in Jerusalem, and in all Judea and Samaria, and to the ends of the earth. . . . One of these must become a witness with us of his resurrection.

—Acts 1:8, 22b

In analyzing the place of preaching in the essentially chaotic period of the Dark Ages we are pursuing subjects of more than antiquarian interest. In our time we hear Charles Colson and Alasdair MacIntyre saying that "the new dark ages are already engulfing us." Leslie Newbigin opines, "It is hard to see any future except collapse." Carl Henry tells us, "The barbarians are coming." How relevant, then, is it for us to understand what took place in the Dark Ages! The preservation and preaching of Scripture are the significant actions of the Middle Ages. We want also to note what forces and forms tended to impede scriptural advance.[1]

Preaching could not be limited to the daily *collatio,* where the abbot preached to the monks and the monks asked questions. Such was the tradition of Augustine in *De Doctrina Christiana.* Teaching and preaching are exegesis, and exegesis is teaching and preaching.[2] Here we are viewing the high regard for Scripture reflected in Gregory the Great's attitude toward the Bible, the *lectio divina,* the *sacra pagina.* But the monks were thrust out of seclusion (which was an essential denial of the gospel, cf. Matthew 5:12–14) into the highways and byways of public concourse, as evidenced in the ministry of St. Bernard, who become a public preacher of considerable distinction.

The early Middle Ages were a time of population migration and dislocation. In 596 Gregory the Great dispatched Augustine, prior of the monastery of St. Andrew on the Caelian Hill in Rome, to lead a party in the evangelization of England. His interest in the Britons had been kindled when he saw some fair-haired youth in the Forum and learned they were "Angles." He is supposed to have said, "A good name, too, for they look like angels and they ought to be joint-heirs with the angels of heaven."[3]

In all of this, we see a remarkable spread of the gospel, with preaching at the forefront. This expansion of the faith is doubly impressive in light of the fact that Christianity was a diminishing presence in large parts of the Near East and the Mediterranean right up to 732, when Charles the Hammer halted the Saracen advance at the Pyrenees.[4]

While evangelistic efforts did emanate from Rome, the most potent thrusts for renewal came from the outposts of Celtic Christianity, where Scripture was cherished (e.g., the illuminated manuscripts such as *The Book of Kells,* which can still be seen at Trinity College, Dublin). The missionary breakthroughs of this period were led by preaching.

The role of preaching in Christianity is unique, as Dargan points out: "There was nothing in ancient oratory corresponding to our lecture platform or pulpit."[5] A preaching ministry was an indispensable aspect of the remarkable growth of Christianity "in a crumbling world."[6] Pointing out how Christianity utilized many viable rhetorical forms familiar within the culture, Professor Latourette argues: "In the fourth and fifth centuries eloquent preaching which conformed to these models won loud acclaim from huge audiences."[7]

With the Frankish church in decline, the fire came from Ireland (largely because of its bibliocentric tradition). According to Bede, **St. Ninian** brought the gospel to the Picts of Southern Scotland in the fifth century and **St. David** to Wales in the sixth century. But it was the brave Irishman **Columba,** who with twelve others landed on the island of Iona in 563 and declared their resolution to stay by burning their boats. A bit of the flavor of his preaching can be sensed in his hymn "Altus Prosator," written to describe the day of doom:

The Day of God's provings, King over kings,
The Day of His anger loud, darkness and cloud,
The Day of the thunder's sound, heard in the heavens around,
The Day in mourning clad, bitter and sour and sad.
When women's love lies dead, and men now have fled
All lust and petition of this world's ambition.

Then stand we shall trembling before the Lord's judging
To account for our actions, our sins, laws infractions;
Then shall we see nearby our wickedness clearly,
The book of our conscience shall look in our face.
Into weeping we break forth, all hope we forsake,
Gone now is the hour once held in our power.[8]

In 633–34 King Oswald of Northumbria sent to Ireland for a bishop who would come to preach. Ultimately the godly **Aidan** was sent. He entered into evangelization on horseback, "Preaching, baptizing, doing all a mission bishop's work."[9] Still another Irish missionary monk of impact was **Columban** from Bangor, who in the sixth and seventh centuries exerted himself in frenetic preaching in France, Italy, and Switzerland. Following forays of monks to the Orkney Islands, the Shetlands, and Iceland, evangelization soon moved to the European continent. Bede (1.26) described how missionary work began in a part of England:

There was on the east side of the city, a church dedicated to the honour of St. Martin, built whilst the Romans were still on the island, wherein the Queen, who, as has been said before, was a Christian, used to pray. In this they first began to meet, to sing, to pray, to say mass, to preach, and to baptize, till the king, being converted to the faith, allowed them to preach openly, and build or repair churches in all places.

We must remember that while all of this was going on in the West, missionary advance in the East was limited due to doctrinal conflict, the Muslim explosion, and what Dargan characterizes as "continuous decline in preaching."[10] Ker is undoubtedly correct in alleging, "A great torpor has benumbed the preaching of this church for centuries. No great name stirring the hearts of the masses and shining out to lands beyond has appeared for more than a thousand years."[11]

Still another luminous herald of the gospel, **Wilfrid of Northumbria,** started out for the continent in 678 and evangelized Friesland. Bede records: "He was honorably received by that barbarous people and their King Aldgist, to whom he preached Christ, and instructed many thousands of them in the word of truth, washing them from their abominations in the laver of salvation. Thus he there began the work of the gospel which was afterwards finished by Willibrord" (5.19).

Willibrord was trained by Wilfrid and left in 692 to do evangelism along the southern shores of the North Sea. The devastating raids by the pirates of Scandinavia pointed to the urgent need to bring the gospel to those farther east.

Willibrord succeeded in enlisting thirty Danish boys to be trained as future missionaries in their homeland and to the north.

Born in Devon in England in 675 and influenced by Wilfrid and Willibrord, **Winfrid** (later called **Boniface**) spearheaded the gospel advance to the pagan Germans. He courageously challenged the pagan gods, felling the notorious pagan symbol of the Oak of Thor and building a monastery at Fritzlar out of its timbers.[12] He was used mightily to spread the church in Bavaria, Thuringia, and Hesse. Winfrid's sermons were rich with Scripture, his appeals were seethed with earnestness:

> Apply yourselves to learn the Lord's Prayer and the Creed, and teach them to your children. Fast, love righteousness, resist the devil, receive communion at the appointed seasons. Believe that Christ will come again, that there will be a bodily resurrection, and a general judgment of all men. Then the evil will be divided from the good, and the one will go to eternal burning, the other to eternal bliss, to enjoy life everlasting in God with no more death, light without darkness, health without suffering, joy without fear, happiness without sorrow; peace there shall be forevermore, and the righteous shall shine like the sun, for eye hath not seen, nor ear heard, neither hath it entered into the heart of man to conceive what things God has prepared for them that love Him.[13]

Known as the apostle of the north, **Anskar** or **Ansgar** (known to the Scandinavians as Oscar) was born in 801 in northern France. He was first master and preacher at a monastic school in Westphalia. Anskar went to Denmark as a missionary and established a mission in Schleswig in 827. Appointed bishop of Hamburg and all of the north, he survived the destruction of Hamburg by the king of Denmark, then regrouped and advanced into Denmark and Sweden with the preaching of the Word of God. Facing an opportunity to preach in the court of King Harald of Sweden, he and his party were set upon by bandits en route and robbed of all of their possessions. They persevered and won converts in their preaching mission. Again and again there were setbacks and discouragements. But Anskar was a man of God. He loved the Psalms especially and sang them day and night. The great spiritual tide would not reach Scandinavia as a whole until 1000, but the seeds had been sown in his faithful preaching labors. In the next section we shall consider the revitalization of the Frankish church and its outreach into Bohemia and Jugoslavia.

Some of the most powerful sermons in all of history have been preached by dedicated missionaries. Often unnoted in the annals of homiletics and frequently performed in the face of grave danger, the torch of divine truth has been lifted high again and again by Christ's special servants, the foreign emissaries of the gospel.

---

1. For further background of the Middle Ages one can read the historical novels of Sir Walter Scott, such as *Ivanhoe* or *The Talisman*. A diary from the Middle Ages such

as Louise Collis, *Memoirs of a Medieval Woman: The Life and Times of Margery Kempe* (New York: Harper Colophon, 1964) is also helpful. One can also learn from well-researched novels of suspense like those by Ellis Peters depicting Brother Cadfael or the splendid works of Edward Marston, P. C. Doherty, or (by the latter's pen name) C. L. Grace. The finest collection of the art and architecture of the Middle Ages in the US is at the Cloisters, a branch museum of the Metropolitan Museum of Art, located in Fort Tryon Park, New York.

2. Beryl Smalley, *The Study of the Bible in the Middle Ages* (Notre Dame, Ind.: University of Notre Dame Press, 1964), 35.

3. F. F. Bruce, *The Spreading Flame* (Grand Rapids: Eerdmans, 1958), 397.

4. For a delightful survey of this theme, see Eleanor Duckett, *The Wandering Saints of the Early Middle Ages* (New York: W. W. Norton, 1959).

5. For a discussion of this point, see my "Does Preaching Have a Future?" in *The Anatomy of Preaching* (Grand Rapids: Baker, 1989), 11–21.

6. Kenneth Scott Latourette, *A History of the Expansion of Christianity: The Thousand Years of Uncertainty* (Grand Rapids: Eerdmans, 1938), 2:252.

7. Ibid., 2:328.

8. Duckett, *The Wandering Saints*, 86.

9. Ibid., 101.

10. E. C. Dargan, *A History of Preaching* (New York: Hodder and Stoughton, 1905), 1:157.

11. John Ker, *Lectures on the History of Preaching* (New York: Armstrong, 1889), 79.

12. G. M. S. Walker, *The Growing Storm: Sketches of Church History from A.D. 600–A.D. 1350* (Grand Rapids: Eerdmans, 1961), 30.

13. Ibid., 32.

4.2.3 POINTS OF LIGHT—THE PREACHING OF THE SCHOOLMEN

The Holy Spirit makes use of the human tongue as an instrument, but it is He who perfects the work within us.
—Thomas Aquinas in *Summa Theologica* 2a, 2ae, 177, 1

In tracing the epochal expansion of Christianity across these centuries, Professor Latourette characterizes the pattern as one of advance and recession.[1] We have seen that even in the Dark Ages there was considerable light both in the monasteries as well as on the frontier of missionary proclamation, in both cases evidencing quite a commitment to exegetical preaching. Yet there was an appallingly widespread ignorance and superstition, as we see when Gregory I sent a little filing dust from the alleged chains of the apostle Paul to the Eastern empress to help her face a crisis!

Public worship centered on "the doctrinally undefined sacrifice of the mass" in the Latin language, meaning that "missionary preaching, the marriage ceremony and confession were the only rites of Christianity performed in the language of the people."[2] Worshipers attended church weekly and received the sacrament three times a year. In the East the sacrament totally overpowered preaching; there was little emphasis on evangelism or missions. Yet at this very dire time, we see a movement of renewal known as the Carolingian Renaissance (756–882) under **Charles the Great** (or Charlemagne) and its counterpart, the Revival in Britain (871–899) under **King Alfred,** the greatest of the Anglo-Saxon kings.

The catalytic influence on Charlemagne was an Englishman, **Alcuin of York,** a spiritual heir of Bede (735–804), who had headed the Cathedral School in York. Alcuin went to work for Charlemagne as his personal tutor and advisor, and had spearheaded the revival of learning. This revival brought needed discipline for the clergy, helped establish schools, and sparked a renewal in preaching. The vast Frankish kingdom[3] thus saw marked change under the aegis of a spiritual leader who saw all of Scripture as "divinely inspired."

Under the Decree of 789 every local parish was to operate a school open to all children. If people were to read the Bible, they needed to know how to read. Alcuin set himself to purge all corruption from the Vulgate, and presented the revision to Charlemagne at his coronation in 800. He insisted that new converts be instructed in the Christian faith before being baptized.

Following Augustine's essential prescription from *De Doctrina Christiana* and the method of the Venerable Bede, Carolingian scholars collated Scripture with extracts of patristic interpretation. The result is called the Gloss, and did not take final shape until the twelfth century.

Two of the most prominent commentators in the ninth century were **Paschasius Radbertus** (c. 830) and **John Scotus Erigena** (born in Ireland about 810). John insisted, "The authority of Scripture in all things is to be followed," and spoke of "the unshakable authority of Holy Scripture."[4] Though an unconventional genius, John the Scot introduced theological discussion that shaped the preaching of the time.[5] Theological discussion was becoming part of exegesis. This is proper since we must proceed with a sense of theological construct. Yet it is dangerous if our theological presuppositions alter and determine our exegetical outcomes. John the Scot urged that "the Fathers stood below the divine authority of Scripture."[6]

Another theologian who was influential in the movement toward and within the monastic and cathedral schools was **Haimo,** who wrote commentaries (840–860) and gathered a rough concordance of texts. **Heiric of Auxerre** was a strong exponent of literal exegesis. **Remigius'** comments were crisp and concise. Like Jerome, he made important comparisons with the Hebrew. **Theodulf,** bishop of Orleans, was another proponent of linguistic studies. Although the preaching of the day often consisted of reading these extracts in relation to a text, they had the strength of being strongly biblical and highly exegetical.

After 908 this process was interrupted. Not a single commentary emerged for a century and a half. Smalley rightly argues that this regrettable hiatus cannot be explained simply in terms of wars and Viking invasions.[7] Liturgy preempted textual study and proclamation (a recurrent danger for the church). So much creative energy went into liturgical poetry and drama that there was precious little left for preaching. Smalley shows how the Cluniac abbots "in their sermons and meditations concentrate on the dramatic and emotional aspects of Scripture."[8] Thus, in our survey of the undulating story of medieval preaching, we have come to another trough.

In England at this time, we do have superb examples of more exegetical preaching from **Aelfric,** Abbot of Eynsham near Oxford (appointed in 1005), and **Wulfstan,** bishop of Worcester and archbishop of York (appointed in 1002). They flourish as part of the ripple effect of the Carolingian renewal experienced in Britain. But the lights were again dimming as the Danish King Canute established himself in their domains. Aelfric's homilies, or postils (since each homily began with the words *Post illa verba textus,* "after these words of the texts"), generally adhered to the literal and historical text. The preaching of both of these expositors was heavily eschatological.[9]

Also in this time, called the Ottonian period in Germany, we have **Liudprand of Cremona,** whose notable Easter sermon (delivered c. 960) on central tenets of the Christian faith is found in Bishop Abraham's collection and brings us into the central drama of the Christian faith.[10] He includes imaginary dialogue and persuasive argument.

In the eleventh and twelfth centuries we witness another resurgence of exegetical productivity in the schools. By this time the cathedral schools, forerunners to the universities in Paris and at Oxford, were more prominent than the monastic schools. An honor roll of outstanding teachers and exegetes must include **Fulbert of Chartres,** so concise in his literal exposition; his pupil **Berengar of Tours,** whose exegetical labors in Paul's epistles have been described as demonstrating "strenuous vigilance in understanding and expounding Scripture";[11] and Archbishop **Lanfranc,** the teacher of Anselm of Canterbury. By now, scholarly work was being centralized in Paris. The marginal and extralinear notes which would comprise the Gloss were nearly complete.

The central figure among these glosatores is **Anselm of Laon.** Along with others, he sought to merge the various glosses which had developed into Magna Glosatura to be used as a supplement for preachers.[12] But a problem arose, blunting the move back to the text. Smalley concedes that the tendency toward endless theological dialectic and philosophical hair-splitting led the cathedral schools away from "old-fashioned Bible study."[13]

The consequences for preaching were lamentable. The promise of the eighth and ninth centuries was the identification of theology with exegesis; now we find exegesis identified with theology and a diminishing exegetical scholarship.[14] Smalley lists the rediscovery of Aristotle, canon law interest, reason, speculation, and endless discussion of abstruse issues (all good in themselves) combining to discourage and reduce concentration on the Scriptures. But then came a renewal of biblical scholarship, a "back to Scripture framework" in the twelfth century.

The Bible was in fact the textbook of the Middle Ages. It was an Age of Faith, in which the biblical worldview informed cultural and societal thought. The authority of the Bible was final. Sir Maurice Powicke of Oxford saw the twelfth-century renaissance as significant as the later Italian renaissance. The scriptural body of truth informed all of life and presented a *preparatio evangelica,* a preparation and presentation of the Good News, in terms of which a medieval preacher observed: "Many throughout all the world have eagerly received faith in the Savior and His teaching, and so they shall do continually until the end of the world."[15]

The loss of focus on Scripture in the schools and in preaching is a downturn; the recovery of exegetical focus is an upswing.

The center of this crucial recovery was the Abbey of St. Victor in Paris, founded by **William of Champeaux** in 1110. Here **Hugh of St. Victor** (the second Augustine, d. 1141), his thought saturated with Scripture, called the church back to *De Doctrina Christiana.* He was a champion of the literal, historical sense and urged interpreters not to take the text "as an excuse for preferring our own ideas to those of the divine authors."[16]

Another stalwart in this school was **Andrew of St. Victor** (d. 1175). He combined vigorous study of the text of Scripture with "cataracts of eloquence" in expressing its truth. He was called "the second Jerome," but quoted secular sources such as Horace, Ovid, Virgil, Juvenal, Lucan, and Josephus. Andrew had interest in the geography and chronology of the Old Testament and exerted much influence on the Cistercians, Roger Bacon, and the English monastics. He was quoted often by Stephen Langton of Paris, who divided the Bible into chapters. Andrew's work is requisite background for understanding the biblical scholarship of the later preaching orders of friars. He insisted:

> The whole context must be carefully considered and expounded, lest we who rebut the errors of others, if it be done more carelessly, be ourselves rebutted.[17]

We shall meet later his famous student in another connection, **Herbert of Bosham,** secretary and biographer of Thomas Becket.

In a moving chapter titled "Masters of the Sacred Page," Professor Smalley shows how the Victorines fostered "new devotion to the letter of Scripture." Signal contributors here were the Paris masters: **Peter the Comestor** (d. 1169),[18] **Peter the Chanter** (d. 1197), and **Stephen Langton** (d. 1228). All stressed literal exposition in *lectio* (lectures), *disputatio* (debates), and *predicatio* (sermons). They stressed also the spiritual sense or application of the text. Their sermons were recorded by stenographers *(reportatio),* which meant some distinct reportorial differences in the style such as St. Bonaventure's "University Sermons at Paris between Easter and Whitsuntide, 1273."[19]

Langton urged his students to preach to the people where they are and not just as they would to their fellow students. He himself was a popular preacher. An excerpt from a sermon on Shamgar's ploughshare out of Judges 3 illustrates several points:

> See! This makes clear that a preacher should not always use polished, subtle preaching, like Aod's sword, but sometimes a plough-share, that is, rude and rustic exhortation. Very often a popular story *(exemplum vulgare)* is more effective than a polished, subtle phrase. Aod killed one man only with a two-edged sword, Shamgar six hundred with a plough-share; so, whereas the laity are easily converted by rude, unpolished preaching, a sermon to clerks will draw scarcely one of them from his error.[20]

We wince at aspects of this thrust but identify with the point being made. Langton's motivation was ever, "The Word of the Lord must be turned into deed, we must act on what we have heard or read."

These preachers also developed another homiletical tool replicated frequently in the twelfth century and afterward. This new method involved building a sermonic skeleton by collecting all references through Scripture to a given theme or image. This was called a *distinctio*.[21]

Clearly we are in a fertile and fruitful time for biblical preaching and will not be surprised to discover some fascinating homiletical implications. The core of the issue is the thesis of Professor Powicke, who writes, "The legacy of medieval Christianity to later ages was the problem of authority," that is, what is to be the basis of life and trust.[22] Thus the critique of the prolific medieval historian G. G. Coulton is to the issue when he faults the medievals for their bibliolatry, although he concedes they received it from the Jews. He rejects God as the author of Scripture and the noncontradictory nature of the biblical text.[23] But the answer to the question of biblical authority shaped the approach to preaching as here described. Our answer shapes our preaching. The belief in the literal and historical truth of Scripture led further to the founding of two great preaching orders in the medieval church. That is our next area of inquiry.

---

1. We are immensely in the debt of Professor Latourette's magnificent study, but we should not be oblivious to certain regrettable premises in his work; see John D. Hannah, "Kenneth Scott Latourette—A Trailblazer," *Grace Theological Journal* 2:1 (spring 1981): 3–32.
2. William Ragsdale Cannon, *History of Christianity in the Middle Ages* (New York: Abingdon, 1960), 50.
3. An invaluable tool in these studies is Charles S. Anderson, *Augsburg Historical Atlas of Christianity in the Middle Ages and Reformation* (Minneapolis: Augsburg, 1967). For a readable and reliable overview of this complex period, see Brian Tierney and Sidney Painter, *Western Europe in the Middle Ages, 300–1475* (New York: Knopf, 1970).
4. G. S. M. Walker, *The Growing Storm: Sketches of Church History from A.D. 600 to A.D. 1350* (Grand Rapids: Eerdmans, 1961), 53.
5. Bernard McGinn and Willemien Otten, eds., *Eriugena: East and West, Papers of the Eighth International Colloquium of the Society for the Promotion of Eriugenian Studies, 1991* (Notre Dame, Ind.: University of Notre Dame, 1994).
6. Beryl Smalley, *The Study of the Bible in the Middle Ages* (Notre Dame, Ind.: University of Notre Dame, 1964), 39.
7. Ibid., 44.
8. Ibid., 45.
9. Milton McC. Gatch, *Preaching and Theology in Anglo-Saxon England: Aelfric and Wulstan* (Toronto: University of Toronto, 1977).
10. Karl Leyser, "Liudprand of Cremona, Preacher and Homilist," in *The Bible and the Medieval World* (Oxford: Blackwell, 1985), 43.
11. Drogo in Smalley, *The Study of the Bible*, 47.
12. Ibid., 63.

13. Ibid., 76.

14. Ibid., 77.

15. Maurice Powicke, *The Christian Life in the Middle Ages* (Oxford: Oxford University Press, 1935), 83.

16. Smalley, *The Study of the Bible,* 94. The five senses of Scripture are (1) literal and historical; (2) allegorical; (3) tropological, holds the mirror up to us, satirical; (4) anagogical or mystical; (5) moral.

17. Ibid., 128.

18. David Luscombe, "Peter Comestor," in *The Bible in the Medieval World,* 109–29.

19. Smalley, *The Study of the Bible,* 208.

20. Ibid., 253–54.

21. Ibid., 248. This technique is used by all preachers on occasion but was particularly popular among the Brethren preachers and was widely published in the works of F. E. Marsh, in many volumes such as *Illustrated Bible Studies* (New York: Revell, n.d.). In a sermon outline on "whatsoever you shall ask" (Matt. 21:22):

    1. Asking in prayer, Matthew 7:7–11
    2. Asking for help, Luke 6:30
    3. Asking for water, John 4:9–10
    4. Asking for light, Acts 26:29
    5. Asking for wisdom, James 1:5
    6. Asking for filling, Colossians 1:9
    7. Asking for a murderer, Matthew 27:20; Acts 3:14 (cf. 186–87)

22. Powicke, *Christian Life in the Middle Ages,* 1.

23. G. C. Coulton, "Medieval Panorama," in *The Twelfth-Century Renaissance,* ed. C. Warren Hollister (New York: Wiley, 1969), 154.

4.2.4   POINTS OF LIGHT—THE PREACHING OF THE MENDICANTS

> Masters, I could have told you, said this friar . . . after the texts of Christ and Paul and John . . . such torments that your hearts would shake with dread, albeit by no tongue can half be said, although I might a thousand winters tell, of pains in that same cursed house of Hell. But all to keep us from that horrid place, watch, and pray Jesus for His holy grace.
>
> —Chaucer, "The Friar's Tale" from
> *Canterbury Tales in Modern English*[1]

Some of the sunshine and deep shadows of this time are reflected in Chaucer's characters, such as the Monk, the Friar, the Pardoner, and the Nun's Priest. Chaucer (1340–1400) pictured those who journeyed to Canterbury in unforgettable vignettes of medieval life. The preaching friars were part of the preaching effort before all the people and were recognized for their preaching, but they were not all exemplary:

> Oh, how the friar behaves himself / Full wisely can they preach and say / When he comes to the house of a poor man! / But as they preach nothing do they.[2]
>
> Oh, well he knows how to preach![3]

This realism, as Pattison pointed out, was the theme of Henry Wadsworth Longfellow's "Golden Legend," in that "through the darkness and corruption of the Middle Ages ran a bright deep stream of faith strong enough for all of the exigencies of life."[4]

The setting for the revival of preaching through the friars was a great ferment and flux which must take into account:

1. The depletion of the Crusades (although the Crusades stimulated the growth and renewal of the cities). **Urban II** launched the first crusade with a mighty sermon at the Council of Clairmont in southern France in 1095. One historian calls it "one of the most skillful and effective examples of rhetoric in European history." **Bernard of Clairvaux** preached the second crusade in 1144. **Peter the Hermit** enlisted a great following. This huge popular response reflects "the millennial and apocalyptic outlook of the lower and middle classes of European cities" at this time.[5]
2. The Great Schism between the Eastern and Western churches in 1054.
3. The rapid growth of the cathedral schools as such leaders as **Anselm of Canterbury, Abelard,** and **Peter Lombard** press toward the emergence of the universities which become the centers for the friars and their revival of preaching in Paris, Lyons, Cologne, Florence, and Bologna.
4. The reforms of **Hildebrand,** or Gregory VII (1073–1085) emphasized the mission of the church. In 1074 he wrote to Herman of Metz, "We have a mission to evangelize mankind—woe be to us if we preach not the gospel." This is an important phase in the development of the power of the papacy.
5. The conversion of Russia and the fruit of Anskar's ministry in the conversion of the Scandinavian countries, with the baptism of King Olof Skotkonung near Skara in 1008.
6. The intensification of church-state tensions as the papacy seeks to be all-encompassing in its power, as when **Henry II** and **Thomas Becket** faced off in England. The institution of the Inquisition in this period was a significant step.
7. The twelfth-century scholastics and their controversies with the rediscovery of Aristotle, in which discussions no one seemed to take a more balanced view than **John of Salisbury** (1125–1180), an Englishman who was to become prominent in the School of Chartres.[6]

In this period a portentous revival of preaching providentially took place. The need for more and better preaching was apparent. Preaching aids had become a business.

Two-tiered sermons were seen in embryonic form (in which there is first a basic and elementary statement supplemented by deeper and more technical material). Since the days of **Paul the Deacon** (eighth century), we have an annual cycle for the church year in which the passage for the day is called the pericope. We are beginning to see "macaronic preaching," in which Latin and the vernacular were blended. **Albertano of Brescia** (1250) numbered his points. The *florilegium,* or collections of sermons, are seen early.[7] Under the driving influence of

Innocent III (1198–1218) the Fourth Lateran Council ordered more frequent preaching and more popular preaching. Preaching was beginning to be seen as part of the *vita apostolica* (apostolic life of the church).

Innocent was genuinely concerned about preaching. In 1213 he deposed a bishop because he was too aged and infirm to preach. Innocent's own preaching has been characterized as "dignified and scriptural, but brilliant rather than profound."[8] Out of this matrix came the two powerful preaching orders, the Dominicans and the Franciscans. Moving out from their university bases, they traveled through the countryside, towns, and cities preaching, sometimes with the approval and sometimes with the opposition of the regular clergy.[9]

The Dominicans were founded by the Spanish-born **Domingo de Guzman (Dominic)**, born in 1170 and died in 1221. The order he established was called by the pope "the brethren preachers," or Friar Preachers. The Dominicans were more intellectual in a time when the systematizing of knowledge was popular. We can see this emphasis in two great schoolmen of this order, **St. Albert the Great** and **St. Thomas Aquinas**. The Rule of St. Augustine was adopted by the order. The purpose was "for the sake of preaching and the salvation of souls." The foundation was *missio a Deo*. Great stress was placed on contemplation and proclamation (*infusio* and *effusio*). An insightful theme was ever before these preachers: *sine periculo non praedicatur* (preaching is a dangerous occupation). Emphasis was placed on both the grace of preaching (*gratia praedicantionis*) and the preaching of grace. **Hugh of St. Cher** (d. 1264) argued that the commission of John 20:21–23 was to preach, and **Humbert** (1200–1277) contended that "preachers are the mouth of God. No human activity is so noble as talking, because it is in this especially that man excels the animals. So preaching, being an activity of the mouth, is a noble task."[10] For the Dominicans, the contemplative basis for preaching was foundational.

Among the outstanding members of this "order of the prophets" were such gifted preachers as **John Bromyard**, **Meister Eckhart** (1260–1327), **Henri Dominique Lacordaire** (1802–1861), **Peter Martyr** (1200–1252), whose preaching led to the conversion of so many Catharists, **Johannes Tauler** (1300–1361), and **Vincent Ferrer** (1350–1419). Ferrer was a fiery preacher described as "a heavy-built old man with a bad leg, wearing an old green hat or a bonnet of black wool armed with a crucifix and perched on the back of a little ass. Yet the moment he spoke it seemed as if an angel entered into him."[11] He loved to preach to the Jews in Spain. The order also had units for women among which was the celebrated mystic and lay preacher, **Catherine of Sienna** (d. 1380). Catherine was one of only two women named Doctor of the Church. Her testimony was "Jesus died for me. This is the true science."[12] **Humbert of Romanis**, later General of the Order, argued in *De Eruditione Praedictaorum* that the sermon is of a higher order than is the mass. The unknown author of a thirteenth-century work titled *Tractatus de Arte Praedicandi* (A Treatise on the Art of Preaching) differentiates three kinds of preaching: topical, textual, and expository.

The greatest influence to emanate from the Dominicans was certainly **Thomas Aquinas** (1225–1274), of whom his mentor Albert said "It is a grace of preaching that enables a dumb ox to fill the whole world with his bellowing."[13] Like

Albert, Thomas took Scripture in a literal and historical sense. He believed canonical Scripture to be God-authored and inerrant. Besides his extraordinary theological treatises, he wrote an extensive series of solid Bible commentaries.[14] He said, "Holy Scripture sets up no confusion, since all meanings are based on one, namely, the literal sense. From this alone can arguments be drawn . . . nor is anything lost from Sacred Scripture on this account, for nothing that is necessary for faith is contained under the spiritual sense which is not openly conveyed by the literal sense elsewhere."[15]

The Angelic Doctor, as he was called, was a gifted preacher. He was also a poet and hymn writer. "He preached plain, powerful sermons, always in the vernacular of the people, keeping his eyes shut and his mind directed toward heaven while he spoke."[16]

If preaching is now aimed at winning souls as Gilson so well insists, then he is right in asserting that the move from fine-lined reasoning and disputation to preaching must take place. In the new method seen within these orders, reasoning was far less formal. Divisions were being made in the discourse (*primo, secundo, tertis, quarto*, etc.) to help hearers to fix in their minds easily what is being presented.[17] Such categorizations did not derive from Aristotle or Cicero but from the scholastic penchant for division and subdivision. Only one authority should be quoted in each division, as **Richard of Thetford** maintained, "lest it should appear that in dividing he has invented the members" (i.e., that what the text itself says should be obscured by imposition of external ideas). Interestingly, Dante was a student of the Dominicans and held to the highest doctrine of biblical inspiration himself.

The founder of the Franciscans, **Francis of Assisi** (1182–1226), was born the son of a cloth merchant. He has become exceedingly appealing in his austere wedding to poverty and preaching. He renounced all for Christ and urged his followers to possess nothing and to beware of learning. The Franciscans were more emotional than were the Dominicans. Of the life and legend of St. Francis and his preaching we have beautiful *residuum*.[18] He emphasized living the life one preaches. He was so unconventional as on one occasion after severe illness he was led before the people naked to preach to them.[19] He led the bandits to Christ who came to waylay him. He stressed the prayers and tears of those who would win others to Christ. He set the example by doing the humblest of tasks. He faced the most vexed opposition to his preaching. "Let every friar make his own life a sermon to others," he urged. His advice to the preachers was succinct:

> I warn and remind friars that whenever they preach, their words are to be well chosen and pure, so as to help and edify the people, and to define virtues and vices, punishment and glory. And let them be brief, for the Lord Himself while on earth was brief.[20]

The word of the Franciscan to the leper and to the sultan was "repent." Evangelical preaching was the way to win all people everywhere to Christ.

We have little that remains of Franciscan preaching because it was ad hoc in nature. We do have "The Sunday Sermons" *(Sermones Dominicales)* of

Bonaventure (1221–1274), successor to Francis as governor general of the order. The man called Good Fortune (his actual name was John Fidanza) was somewhat mystical. He studied with **Alexander Hales** in Paris and was a close friend to Thomas Aquinas. When Thomas visited and asked to see his library, Bonaventure pointed to the cross on the wall and said: "This is where I learned everything I know." He felt that too many preachers put learning before holiness. The Franciscans widely employed *exempla,* or illustrative stories and anecdotes, mixing in popular proverbs as "spice for the exegesis." Bonaventure wrote a small but useful volume on *The Art of Preaching.*

Up until the time of the great plague and the Black Death, there were upwards of two thousand Franciscans in Britain alone. While they had houses at Oxford and Cambridge and elsewhere, they wandered and evangelized over the countryside.[21] They would preach in churches, or in the fields and squares if they were denied access to the churches. Their preaching was forceful and popular.

A superb example of Franciscan roving was **Anthony of Padua** (1195–1231), born in Lisbon. He joined the Franciscans after seeing the remains of two Franciscans who were martyred in Morocco. Anthony ministered in Africa and throughout Italy. Up to thirty thousand people would listen to him preach outdoors. He divided the sermons under headings and used extensive illustration. He lit huge bonfires after the messages to burn up playing cards and similar items. He was known everywhere as "the friend of the poor." Another outstanding Franciscan was **Berthold of Regensburg** (1220–1272), whose lively and imaginative style was heard throughout Germany and Switzerland. The axiom of Jean de Verdi catches the heart of this resurgence in popular and effective preaching: "Lectures are to instruct the intellect, but preaching is to educate the heart."

A modern listener can scarcely imagine the impact of the preaching of an itinerant friar upon ignorant and isolated people. Huizinga describes the impression made by the Franciscan friar Richard, who preached in Paris in 1429 for ten consecutive days. "He began at five in the morning and spoke without break till ten or eleven, for the most part in the Cemetery of the Innocents. When, at the close of his tenth sermon, he announced that it was to be his last, because he had no permission to preach more, 'great and small wept as touchingly and as bitterly as if they were watching their best friends being buried; and so did he.' Thinking that he would preach once more at Saint Denis on the Sunday, the people flocked thither on Saturday evening, and passed the night in the open, to secure good seats."[22]

Reportedly, Francis received the stigmata after forty days of fasting. He then wrote his famous "Hymn to the Sun," so full of joy and praise to God. His sense of mission is reflected in his famous dedication:

> Lord, make me an instrument of Thy peace;
> Where there is hatred, let me sow love;
> Where there is injury, pardon;
> Where there is doubt, faith;
> Where there is despair, hope;
> Where there is darkness, light;
> Where there is sadness, joy.

O Divine Master, grant that I may not so much seek
To be consoled as to console,
To be understood as to understand,
To be loved as to love;
For it is in giving that we receive;
It is in pardoning that we are pardoned;
It is in dying that we are born to eternal life!

The same passion that typified the Franciscan preachers was also true of the Dominicans. Note this response to the Dominican Vincent Ferrer: "When he spoke of the Last Judgment, of Hell, or of the Passion, both he and his hearers wept so copiously that he had to suspend his sermon till the sobbing had ceased. Malefactors threw themselves at his feet, before everyone, confessing their great sins."[23] One friar put decaying corpses about the pulpit as he preached on death; another drew a human skull from within the folds of his robe to make a particularly dramatic point. With all of its spurts and spasms, this was a time of glorious promise for preaching.

---

1. Geoffrey Chaucer, *Canterbury Tales in Modern English* (New York: Garden City Publishing Co., 1934), 355. Chaucer (1340–1400) was a genius in the portrayal of daily medieval experience.
2. Edith Rickert, *Chaucer's World* (New York: Columbia University Press, 1948), 373.
3. Ibid., 378.
4. Henry Wadsworth Longfellow, *The Complete Poetical Works* (Boston: Houghton Mifflin, 1899), 516. Longfellow also has a striking poem on "The Abbot Joachim" of Flora (or Fiore) which closes with the trenchant lines,

   Love is the Holy Ghost within;
   Hate the unpardonable sin!
   Who preaches otherwise than this
   Betrays his Master with a kiss! (514–15).

5. Norman F. Cantor, *The Civilization of the Middle Ages* (New York: HarperCollins, 1993), 293.
6. Michael Wilks, ed., *The World of John of Salisbury* (Oxford: Blackwell, 1984).
7. R. H. Rouse and M. A. Rouse, *Preachers, Florilegia and Sermons: Studies on the Manipulus Florum of Thomas of Ireland* (Toronto: University of Toronto Press, 1979).
8. G. S. M. Walker, *The Growing Storm: Sketches of Church History from A.D. 600 to A.D. 1350* (Grand Rapids: Eerdmans, 1961), 163.
9. D. L. d'Avray, *The Preaching of the Friars* (Oxford: Clarendon, 1985). A choice treatment.
10. Simon Tugwell, O.P., *The Way of the Preacher* (Springfield, Ill.: Templegate, 1979), 27, 30.
11. Ibid., 75.
12. A. T. Pierson, *Catherine of Sienna* (New York: Funk and Wagnalls, 1898).

13. G. K. Chesterton, *Saint Thomas: The Dumb Ox* (Garden City, N.Y.: Doubleday/Image, 1956).

14. Thomas Aquinas, *St. Paul's Epistle to the Ephesians* (Albany, N.Y.: Magi, 1966).

15. Ibid., quote from *Summa Theologiae,* 15.

16. Walker, *The Gathering Storm,* 203.

17. d'Avray, *The Preaching of the Friars,* 177.

18. G. K. Chesterton, *Saint Francis of Assisi* (Garden City, N.Y.: Doubleday/Image, 1957); for a recent important title, see Duane W. H. Arnold and C. George Fry, *Francis: A Call to Conversion* (Grand Rapids: Zondervan, 1988).

19. Leo Sherley-Price, trans., *St. Francis of Assisi: His Life and Writings As Recorded by His Contemporaries* (New York: Harper, 1959), 74.

20. Ibid., 233. An intriguing book and film about the Franciscan William Baskerville's visit to the abbey of Melk in Italy may be found in Umberto Eco's *The Name of the Rose.*

21. John R. H. Moorman, *The Grey Friars in Cambridge, 1225–1538* (Cambridge, Mass.: Cambridge University Press, 1952).

22. J. Huizinga, *The Waning of the Middle Ages* (London: Edward Arnold, 1924), 4.

23. Ibid., 5. Concerning the itinerant ministry of Peter Waldo and his followers, a contemporary, Friar Steven de Borbonne, wrote: "A rich man in Waldensis, hearing the Gospels, and having a little learning, desirous to know their contents, made a bargain with these priests, that one should translate the Gospels into the vernacular language, and the other should write under the dictation of the first. . . . Now the same citizen, after reading those writings and learning them by heart, resolved to keep evangelical perfection as the Apostles did. He sold everything he had . . . and preaching the Gospels . . . succeeded in gathering together men and women; and teaching them the Gospels induced them to do the same. They were called to account by the bishop of Lyons who commanded them not to dare to explain the Scriptures nor to preach any more. They defended themselves with the answer of the Apostles from Acts 5." From T. J. Bach, *Vision and Valor* (Grand Rapids: Baker, 1963), 28.

4.2.5 POINTS OF LIGHT—THE PREACHING OF THE PARISH MINISTERS

The preacher of the Gospel, who, like the Apostle, ought not to be ashamed of the Gospel . . . ought every Sunday to set before the faithful peoples specified sections of the Gospel . . . like the specified measures of wheat.

—Bertrand de la Tour (a fourteenth-century Franciscan)

It should be considered that everything which ought to be put over successfully will be introduced into the mind of the hearer much better through similitudes, than through the simple naked truths.

—Thomas of Cobham
(probably identical with Thomas of Salisbury, c. 1238)

The status of biblical preaching in local parishes was uneven and spotty. Archbishop Pecham of Canterbury made a stipulation in 1281 ordering parish ministers to expound fourteen articles of faith, the ten commandments, the gospel, seven works of mercy, seven deadly sins, seven chief virtues, and the seven sacraments in the vernacular four times a year.[1] The archbishop of York duplicated the expectation. In many quarters there was gross ignorance among both clergy and laity. As late as 1551 one bishop found that nine of his priests did not know how many commandments there were; thirty-three did not know where they occurred in the Bible (Matthew was the primary guess); thirty-four did not know who wrote the Lord's Prayer and ten were not able to recite it.

Yet preaching was now more generally practiced than previously. Alexander Carpenter in the fifteenth century wrote, "Now, in many places, there is greater abundance of preaching of the Word of God than was customary before our time."[2] Berthold of Regensburg in the thirteenth century advised his listeners, "Although you lay folks cannot read as we priests can, yet God has given you two books to read . . . one is the heavens, and the other the earth."[3] The confidence of the preacher is seen in the words of a twelfth-century homilist: "Many throughout all the earth have eagerly received faith in the Saviour and his teaching, and so they shall do continually until the end of the world."[4]

Listening to preaching in a vast Gothic cathedral did inculcate a sense of religious exaltation. Winchester Cathedral can only be described as "ordered, magnificent stability" in a time when people genuinely felt upended and insecure.

The sermon was evolving from the rambling, ad hoc homily to something more cohesive and structured. Anthony of Padua carefully divided his sermons under *mains* (as in Revelation 14: the debt of nature; the merit of grace; and the reward of glory).[5] Thematic preaching made its appearance in the thirteenth century, the same century that produced hundreds of manuals on theoretical preaching.

The influence of the roving preaching orders had a salutary effect upon many local clergy. St. Francis scored heavily in his insistence on personal piety and a walk with the Lord. "No purse—no scrip—as you go, preach!" was his watchword. When he penetrated a camp of Saracens, he announced fearlessly: "I am not sent of man, but of God to show you the way of salvation."[6]

No one has served us better in our analysis of thirteenth-century parish preaching in England than has G. R. Owst of Cambridge in his two classic volumes, *Preaching in Medieval England* (1926) and *Literature and Pulpit in Medieval England* (1933). Owst contends that the local preacher was the chief mediating cultural influence in the Middle Ages. The prototypes of John Bunyan lived. Yet there was always a struggle to preserve the sacred page from the abuse of allegorization, bizarre numerology, and extensive moralization.[7]

Parish preaching demonstrated a growing interest in biblical characters, a highly developed demonology, and elaborate and vivid teaching about hell. Hagiography also hung heavily over the preaching scene. The use of *exempla*, or sermon illustrations, was typical. Even *narratio jocosa* (witticisms) were used, along with riddles and plays on words. **Robert of Holyard** used the properties of a magnet to illustrate his point on sin and salvation. Satire was common. Anglo-Norman verse-making was in evidence in local preaching. Miracle and morality plays would serve as the antecedents of Elizabethan drama.

Under the influence of the preaching orders, application of the Word to the political and social mind-set of the time was strong. The English Dominican **John Bromyard** (thirteenth into the fourteenth century) castigated the rich and oppressive nobility. "They provide for their dogs better than for the poor," he protested.[8] He flayed the aristocracy and criticized the jousting tournaments. He rebuked the vices of the clergy as well. Bromyard called for justice and denounced all its corrupters.[9]

The literature of the clergy helped lead the way as well. "Piers Ploughman" was a poem likely written by a peasant priest named **William Langland,** who created a Dickensian clergyman called Parson Sloth. Langland denounced high fashion, the use of oaths in conversation, and the follies of the inebriate. The drunkard's homecoming is seen as "a peep into hell" and the tavern as "the devil's church."

Owst maintains that "the medieval pulpit was a creative center,"[10] with the Shepherd's Plays depicting the Last Judgment and the terrors of death. Shakespeare's "seven ages of man" clearly built on the common pulpit discourse of the prior century. In Langland, it was the angelic figure of the preacher who dared to speak out, but what we see is preaching that is stronger in application but weak in Scripture. The brighter lights on the local parish scene addressed the pressing needs, as they well ought to, but if their prescription for the problems is denatured Scripture, what would save them from vapid moralism and mere good advice?

In a most remarkable survey of preaching on the continent in this period, Larissa Taylor shows that in France also "the pulpit was the mass medium of the era."[11] Although printed sermons were not always as preached, five thousand volumes of sermons were published in the period 1460 to 1500. Twenty-five percent of all religious books were sermonic. Earlier in the Middle Ages preaching had almost disappeared in the Mass; now there was an extraordinary upsurge of preaching. The bishop of Meaux "urged preaching in a more biblical manner."[12] Large towns would sometimes employ a preacher. "When a great preacher came to town, representatives of all classes and occupations would turn out to greet him at the city gates."[13] Styles ranged from the colloquial and racy, to the plain, to the ornate. Open-air preaching was not uncommon.

Jean Vitrier, who preached up to seven times daily, usually for an hour at a time, was a typically popular preacher. His homilies were "filled with Scripture, for he knew how to preach nothing else." His sermons were more thematic and unified than the earlier medieval preaching had been. He used illustrations and stories as parables with a decided entertainment value. His style embraced histories and legends, contemporary events and recollections, fables, and descriptions of animals.[14]

Illyricus was another noted preacher who preached literally hours every day. He claimed, "I preach to you for the health of your souls. Whoever wants to hear philosophy preached will have to seek from someone else." **Guillaume Pepin** preached amid considerable eschatological ferment. The Black Death and a poor quality of life contributed to a profound sense of dislocation. Pepin spoke of the three provinces of the afterlife: heaven, hell, and the present world.[15]

The quality of preaching was lacking, however, as Heath shows in his analysis of John Myrc's work in his *Festial,* a collection of sermons for feast days.[16] Myrc cautioned, "For little of worth is the preaching if you be of evil living," but we must express disappointment that his own preaching on the high holy days is so lacking in clear proclamation of the gospel of Christ. There is a massive dose of sacramentalism, too many fables, too little exegesis, too much Mariolatry, too much bizarre spiritualization. A major recovery of Scripture was needed.

Yet there were in fact local clergy like the Parson of Chaucer's depiction:

> There was a good man of religion, too,
> A country parson, poor, I warrant you;
> But rich he was in holy thought and work . . .
> Who Christ's own gospel truly sought to preach;
> Devoutly his parishioners would he teach.
> He had no thirst for pomp or reverence,
> Nor made himself a special, spiced conscience,
> But in Christ's own lore, and His apostles' twelve
> He taught, but first he followed it himself.[17]

1. Peter Heath, *The English Parish Clergy on the Eve of the Reformation* (Toronto: University of Toronto Press, 1969), 93.
2. Ibid., 94.
3. Maurice Powicke, *The Christian Life in the Middle Ages* (Oxford: Clarendon, 1935), 78.
4. Ibid., 83.
5. Robert D. Sider, *The Gospel and Its Proclamation* (Wilmington, Del.: Michael Glazier, 1983), 102ff. The most trenchant analysis of this shift is found in the new and massive study of H. Leith Spencer's *English Preaching in the Late Middle Ages* (Oxford: Clarendon, 1993), 228–268.
6. T. Harwood Pattison, *The History of Christian Preaching* (Philadelphia: American Baptist Publication Society, 1903), 105.
7. G. R. Owst, *Literature and Pulpit in Medieval England: A Neglected Chapter in the History of English Letters and of the English People* (Cambridge, Mass.: Cambridge University Press, 1933), 76.
8. Ibid., 327.
9. Ibid., 345.
10. Ibid., 469.
11. Larissa Taylor, *Soldiers of Christ: Preaching in Late Medieval and Reformation France* (Oxford: Oxford University Press, 1992), 4. Exploring a parallel in Italy cf., Augustine Thompson, *Revival Preachers and Politics in Thirteenth Century Italy: The Grand Devotion of 1233* (Oxford: Oxford University Press, 1992).
12. Ibid., 16ff.
13. Ibid., 28. Note the classic study: Allan Temko, *Notre Dame de Paris* (New York: Viking, 1952).
14. Ibid., 68.

15. Ibid., 96. This powerful book concludes with an invaluable series of brief biographical sketches of a number of the more noteworthy of these preachers, 235–42.
16. Heath, *The English Parish Clergy,* 94ff.
17. Geoffrey Chaucer, *Canterbury Tales in Modern English* (New York: Garden City Publishing Co., 1934), 15–16.

4.3 PUNCHING HOLES IN THE DARKNESS

Do your best to present yourself to God as one approved, a workman who does not need to be ashamed and who correctly handles the word of truth.

—2 Timothy 2:15

The unifying structure of Scripture is the structure of redemptive history. The Bible does not have the form of a textbook, and the witness to Christ unfolds with the progressive epochs of revelation which in turn are grounded in the successive periods of redemption.

—Edmund Clowney

After 1270 we begin to see the decline of the medieval papacy. The Great Schism and the Babylonian Captivity discredited the ecclesiastical behemoth of the Middle Ages.[1] The papacy of the Borgias had ceased to be a spiritual power by 1500. Protests by heretical movements like the Albigensians, who dominated southern France, and the Cathari, along with the Bogomils in the Balkans, sapped further strength. Many orthodox critics of the papacy such as Bernard of Clairvaux became a growing chorus of dissent. The corruption of certain of the monastic orders and the greed and cruelty of the Templars ate away at the heart of piety.

Peter Waldo of Lyon, a wealthy merchant, was moved to rise up in protest, reflecting the anticlericalism and the antisacerdotalism of the time. Securing a translation of the Bible in French, Waldo defied prohibitions to preach. The Waldensians were condemned and excommunicated. Still they went out two by two to preach the gospel of Christ. Something of the apocalypticism of Joachin of Fiore, who had disapproved of the Crusades and urged Christians "not to fight but to preach,"[2] can be seen among the Waldensians. John Milton's beautiful "Sonnet 15" is a fitting tribute to these champions of the faith who fled into the mountains of northern Italy.

Historians trace the dissolution concluding the Catholic Middle Ages, a dissolution that was fomented by economic depression, the Hundred Years' War, the plague and pestilence of the Black Death, and "the little ice age"—the unusually heavy winters of the fourteenth century. Yet a great change was taking place. Cantor quotes Johan Huizinga's great dictum: "A high and strong culture is declining, but at the same time and in the same sphere new things are being born. The tide is turning, the tone of life is about to change."[3]

It was, of course, the Renaissance. Many factors brought about the end of medieval winter. One cannot draw a sharp line between the Middle Ages and the Renaissance, but the new classical learning took root. The power vacuum in the empire and in the papacy opened up new opportunities. Italianization was more Platonic than Aristotelian.[4] Travel, exploration and discovery, mail service, and the invention of printing with the circulation of books were all part of it. The gothic was supplanted by the baroque. We see the rebirth of all the arts, as art again became realistic. The merchant class rose with power. It was an age of "more."[5] We see renewed interest in the natural sciences, philology, and aesthetics. Hale talks about a "genius for the use of words."

Developments in preaching were an integral part of this rebirth. We shall trace the impact of the Reformation, the greatest recovery of the power of biblical preaching in the history of Christianity. Faithful practitioners of the craft of preaching had been hard at work. They were instrumental in the recovery from the panic of the Black Death in the middle of the fourteenth century "by making the Gospel story as real as possible to them." This "was achieved chiefly through anecdotal and story-telling sermons and homilies."[6]

Yet, as Francis Schaeffer has pointed out, the seeds of serious spiritual sedition were also sprouting. The parity of divine revelation and human reason had been given to Western civilization largely by the scholastics, who placed humankind at the center. Hence, the Renaissance was the birth of a new humanism. The concept of autonomous man took root. The Copernican revolution no longer saw the earth as the center of the universe, but man became the new center of the universe of thought.[7] It was a time of great horizontalization, as in our own time.

The "man at the center" would later be enshrined and ensconced in the Enlightenment. He is man as Thomas Aquinas understood him, only "partly affected by the fall." As Schaeffer observes, "The intellect was not affected."[8] Bishop Cannon makes the same observation: "Yet the total depravity of man, stressed so vigorously by Augustine, got weak and half-hearted support from the scholastics. Human nature, they felt, is not totally corrupted by sin."[9] The Reformers and their forerunners had their work cut out for them. Rapid societal change and positive progress on the whole do not always make the task of the Christian proclaimer any easier.

1. C. Warren Hollister, *Medieval Europe: A Short History,* 5th ed. (New York: John Wiley, 1982), 326–27.

2. G. S. M. Walker, *The Growing Storm: Sketches of Church History from A.D. 600 to A.D. 1350* (Grand Rapids: Eerdmans, 1962), 146.

3. Norman F. Cantor, *The Civilization of the Middle Ages* (New York: HarperCollins, 1993), 562.

4. Jacob Burkhart, *The Civilization of the Renaissance in Italy,* 2 vols. (New York: HarperColophon, 1958).

5. John Hale, *The Civilization of Europe in the Renaissance* (New York: Athenaeum, 1994).

6. Ibid., 226.

7. Francis A. Schaeffer, *How Should We Then Live? The Rise and Decline of Western Thought and Culture* (Old Tappan, N.J.: Revell, 1976). The seminal volume is Schaeffer's *Escape from Reason* (Downers Grove, Ill.: InterVarsity Press, 1968) particularly 9–19.

8. Ibid., 52.
9. William Ragsdale Cannon, *History of Christianity in the Middle Ages: From the Fall of Rome to the Fall of Constantinople* (New York: Abingdon, 1960), 266.

4.3.1 THE RETOOLING OF THE PATTERN

> The Bible is an eloquent preacher, much more by nature than by art; full of charm and vivacity, and it knows how to reach and move the affections . . .
> —Erasmus in his *Art of Preaching*

During the approximately one thousand years of medieval Christianity, preaching had been conducted for the most part on the Augustinian definition. At its best, medieval preaching used patristic exposition as its model, Augustine's eclectic heremeneutic as its guide, and the Augustinian modus operandi with classical rhetoric as its standard. **Michael Psellus** (1018–1072) illustrates this accommodation well:

> I soon mastered the rhetoric enough to be able to distinguish the central theme of an argument and logically connect it with my main and second points. I also learned not to stand in complete awe of the art, nor to follow its precepts in everything like a child . . . I acquainted myself sufficiently with the art of reasoning, both deductive and inductive.

While there were abundant examples of the egregious abandonment of the text and much outlandish interpretation, there were conspicuous examples of powerful biblical preaching. The German bishop **Rabanus Maurus** (776–856) reiterated Augustine's analysis (quoting him seventy-eight times) in his widely used work *On the Institution of the Clergy*. But Perry is right that little attention was given to homiletical theory.[1] **Guibert's** (1053–1124) *Book on How a Sermon Is to Be Given* was more on scriptural interpretation than on preaching itself.

Faithful and loyal Christian proclamation took place here and there, as is demonstrated in the missionary passion and gifts of **Raymond Lull**. Born on the island of Majorca in 1232, his life was transformed by a vision of the crucified Christ. He followed after the Dominicans. After mastering Arabic, Lull became an apologist and missionary to the Muslim world. He used visuals skillfully, and wrote *On the One Hundred Names of God,* showing that Christianity exceeded Islam by one. He wrote 250 books, and urged the church to set aside 10 percent of its funds for missions.[2]

The outburst of preaching in the thirteenth century through the Dominican and Franciscan orders required new attention to the theory and form of the sermon. We are not caught unawares, then, that with all of the preparations for the strong recovery of the Scriptures for preaching in the Reformation, we have at this time the first formal consideration of preaching and its cultural forms since the time of Augustine nearly one thousand years earlier. The leading figure here was **Alan of Lille** (d. 1202), a Cistercian, influenced greatly by Gilbert of Poitiers and

William Thierry of Chartres. His *Art of Preaching* and his *Sermons* were defining for medieval preaching to follow. Here we see the scholastic desire for order and exactness. The legacy of Alan long survived him in the history of preaching, and its echoes are heard even in our own century.

Alan crystallized the method of taking a theme and text and dividing it. In the introduction, or protheme, the preacher sought the good will of the listeners and invited them to join him in prayer. The narrative usually was divided into three parts, with a rhyming scheme to help preacher and listener remember. The dilation of the argument utilized such techniques as *digressio, correspondentia, circulatio, unitio,* and *convolutio.* Conceding that "little has been said of this,"[3] he argued that the amplification of the proposition can be achieved by the constant reintroduction of the theme.

The definition of preaching given by Alan was clear: "Preaching is an open and public instruction in faith and behavior, whose purpose is the forming of men; it derives from the path of reason and from the fountainhead of the 'authorities'" *(Scripture and the Patristics).*[4] He differentiated between preaching and teaching. He also urged "weight in the thought of a good sermon," not to be dissipated by too much childish jesting.

> Preaching should not glitter with verbal trappings, with purple patches, nor should it be too much enervated by the use of colorless words: the blessed keep to a middle way.[5]

Concerned about the variegated congregations to be addressed, Alan tenaciously insisted that the object of the preaching was true repentance. "So the preacher should come to the exposition of the proposed text, and bend everything he says to the edification of the listener . . . let him not begin with a text which is too obscure or too difficult . . . nor in the expounding of his authority should he move too quickly away from his text."[6] He advocated the careful selection of a good blend of illustration. Alan emphasized the importance of a right life and godly example on the part of the preacher. Much good can be discerned in his conceptualization. The torrent of writers who followed him on this subject expose a totally new genre by 1220: books on preaching, the influence of which has continued down through the centuries.

Alexander of Ashby (c. 1200) allowed for only the briefest recap in the conclusion and insisted urgently that the Scripture must furnish the material of the sermon. **Thomas Chabham** or **Thomas of Salibury** (c. 1219) argued for the "artistic sermon," with preachers more like poets. A clear theme was essential, and division was necessary. **Richard of Thetford** (c. 1245) wrote about the art of amplifying thought in sermons using a triplex *divisio.* **Robert Basevorn** (c. 1322) wrote on *The Form of Preaching,* and **Thomas Tode** (c. 1380) wrote about its rhythms.

The French General of the Dominicans, **Humbert de Romanis** (d. 1277), spoke of preaching as an extension of the dialogue of heaven. He contended that preaching was superior to the mass and all liturgical expression. He urged the Dominicans to preach the gospel of Christ as the fundamental responsibility of the clergy. As Paul urged in 1 Corinthians 14:9, "Unless you speak intelligible words with your tongue, how will anyone know what you are saying? You will just be speaking into the air." Humbert asserted that the dish (the form) is far less important than the food (the Word). The renewed interest in preaching must be seen as preparatory for the Reformers and their forebears.

Why do we not see more full-blown expository preaching of natural thought units from the Scripture in *lectio continua*? The reasons at this point would seem to be that

1. preaching was frequently in a liturgical straight-jacket, subordinated to sacraments;
2. tradition often undermined *sola Scriptura;*
3. the persistence of the allegorical method in interpretation (still with us);
4. the historico-grammatico approach to exegesis was not tuned up;
5. preaching tended to be quite moralistic, not sufficiently God-centered;
6. the widespread ignorance of the clergy.

These issues all cried for attention. The Reformation would address them shortly.

---

1. Warren W. Wiersbe and Lloyd M. Perry, *The Wycliffe Handbook of Preaching and Preachers* (Chicago: Moody, 1984), 31.
2. G. S. M. Walker, *The Growing Storm: Sketches of Church History from A.D. 600 to A.D. 1350* (Grand Rapids: Eerdmans, 1962), 227. A priceless new study of Lull's preaching: Mark D. Johnston, *The Evangelical Rhetoric of Roman Lull: Lay Learning and Piety in the Christian West Around 1300* (Oxford: Oxford University Press, 1996). Professor Johnston shows Lull's commitment to preaching as "the paramount exercise of eloquence." The division of the text and the arrangement of the sermon are critical for him.
3. Alan of Lille, *The Art of Preaching* (Kalamazoo, Mich.: Cistercian Publications, 1981), 16. It is interesting that Dargan does not mention Alan of Lille, nor is he descriptive or analytic with respect to this transition.
4. Ibid., 16–17.
5. Ibid., 18.
6. Ibid., 21–22.

4.3.2 THE RENEWAL IN DEVOTION

We improve the preaching by improving the preachers.
—Warren Wiersbe and Howard Sugden

A minister of Christ is often in highest honor with men for the performance of one half of his work, while God is regarding him with displeasure for the neglect of the other half . . .
—Richard Cecil

Take heed to the ministry which thou hast received in the Lord, that thou fulfil it.

—Colossians 4:17 (KJV)

The quality of preaching is directly correlated with the godly character and compassion of the preacher. The Reformation touched not only technical aspects of sermonic form but also the well-springs of the inner life of devotion and intimacy with Christ. We have seen how vital Francis of Assisi's vision of the crucified Christ was for his subsequent ministry. Now we turn to a crucial movement of spiritual renewal. William Blake observed, "The inner world is all-important." Dag Hammarskjold believed, "The longest journey is the journey inward." George Herbert opined, "The greatest and hardest preparation is within."

The spiritual movement that made such dynamic impact on northern Europe and on the Reformers was known as The Brethren of the Common Life, or *devotio moderna* (the new devotion). The movement had its roots in the concern for clerical reform by **Jan van Ruysbroeck** (1293–1381) from Brussels. Taking the Rule of St. Augustine, he and several friends established a priory to which both Tauler and Groote came.

The founder of the Brethren of the Common Life was **Gerard Groote** (1340–1384), a Carthusian who was born in Deventer in the Netherlands and trained at the University of Paris. He was gloriously converted and began to preach against decadent scholasticism. Not a solitary like van Ruysbroeck, Groote established schools and houses even after he was forbidden to preach. By the middle of the next century there were more than one hundred such houses in the Low Countries and Germany. The fruit of this movement included **Thomas à Kempis, Wessel Gansfort** (who had a profound influence on Martin Luther), and **Erasmus** (who studied with the Brethren of the Common Life for twelve years).

In his definitive study, Professor Hyma describes Groote's ministry: "He preached the gospel of repentance . . . like John the Baptist 'laying the axe to the root of the tree.' His magnetic personality, burning zeal to win souls, and power of conviction carried their message straight to the heart."[1] He would preach in Latin to the clergy but in the vernacular to the people, who came from miles around. He would sometimes preach outdoors because the churches could not contain the crowd. Groote emphasized the intensely personal nature of Christian experience.

Originating in the beautiful Yssel Valley in the Netherlands, this movement spurred what is called the Christian Renaissance, something unrelated to the Italian Renaissance. The life and preaching of it were focused on the Cross of Christ,[2] the centrality of the Word, which laymen were encouraged to read,[3] the nonsacramental confession of sins,[4] and the true church of the little flock as compared with the organizational outer court.[5]

The essential message of the movement can be seen in Thomas à Kempis' *Imitatio Christi*, undoubtedly the most widely read book of Christian devotion in the world. It has gone into six thousand editions. Thomas, born Thomas Hammerken in Kempen (1379–1471), called people to the way of the Cross. He joined the Augustinian order, and preserved and published many of Groote's works. Another leader in the movement was **John Cele,** whose school at Zwolle was the model for the gymnasia of John Sturm at Strasbourg and John Calvin at Geneva. **Wessel Gansfort** (1419–1489) gave the Scripture authoritative standing above the pope and preached powerfully against indulgences in the church. In this he blazed the trail for Luther, who spoke of him as "that most Christian author." Luther also said, "If I had read his works earlier, my enemies might think that Luther had absorbed everything from Wessel: his spirit is so in accord with mine."[6]

Luther paid immense tribute to the Brethren of the Common Life. The influence of this positive "Christ-mysticism" (as contrasted with the often pantheistic metaphysical mysticism of a Jacob Boehme, for instance) had a long and powerful impact on French believers, even up to Port Royal and the Jansenists. Others who benefited from Wessel's work included Nicholas of Cusa, Ignatius of Loyola, John Calvin, and Zwingli. It was a defining movement in terms of the Word, salvation, the Cross in justification, and sanctification.

The roots of *devotio moderna* were solidly in the biblical preaching of Groote. Hyma contends, "The Christian Renaissance may be said to have had its birth in Groote's first sermons, preached early in 1380."[7] And indeed Luther quotes Groote in his seminal lectures on Romans.[8] "We do not believe the Gospel for the Church's sake,"[9] Gansfort argued. Many reforming insights abound in this movement. The worship style of the Brethren of the Common Life beyond question influenced Bucer, Calvin, and Zwingli. Calvin declared his desire "to follow Bucer, man of holy memory,"[10] and Bucer was an intimate of *devotio moderna*. The influence on Zwingli was through Erasmus, who visited him in 1516, two years before he heard of Luther.[11] The flame of this fervent fellowship also spread to England through the Brownists and the Barrowists, who had a colony at Kampen on the Yssel. In summation, we can accurately represent a most significant visit of the Holy Spirit through a bibliocentric movement of piety and devotion prior to the Reformation. God was at work. The pieces of the mosaic are fitting into place.

1. Albert Hyma, *The Christian Renaissance* (New York: Century, 1924), 13. A longtime professor at the University of Michigan, Hyma also wrote *The Brethren of the Common Life* (Grand Rapids: Eerdmans, 1950).
2. Ibid., 54, 58.
3. Ibid., 69, 93ff.
4. Ibid., 78.
5. Ibid., 107.
6. Ibid., 191.
7. Ibid., 303.
8. Ibid., 309, 318.
9. Ibid., 323.
10. Ibid., 337.
11. Ibid., 342.

4.3.3   THE REKINDLING OF PASSION

> Preaching is Christian only when it is passionately, uncompromisingly biblical, that is, when it sets forth faithfully what the Bible teaches on a given topic.
>
> —Richard Allen Bodey

> "Is not my word like fire," declares the LORD, "and like a hammer that breaks a rock in pieces?"
>
> —Jeremiah 23:29

In any time of spiritual decay we can mark a tendency to turn toward the cultivation of the inner life, as in the case of monastic spirituality early in the Middle Ages. In the deepening shadows of dissolution we see the same countercultural phenomenon in mystical spirituality. Church history is replete with instances of undue subjectivity in some mystics in which the Creator/creature distinction is in danger of being obliterated. Yet a solid "Christ-mysticism" (to use Deissman's expression) is certainly consistent with Galatians 2:20 and a host of other passages.

Several medieval English mystics began to exert an inordinately positive influence. Among these are **Richard Rolle** (1300–1349), given to excessive alliteration and misogyny, yet whose *Incendium* argues against the overcerebralization of the Christian faith. Then there was the unknown author of *The Cloud of Unknowing,* who so profoundly explores the treasures in the dark clouds of human anguish. **Walter Hilton** (d. 1396), an Oxford don and an Augustinian, testified to an experience of the Holy Spirit and likened the Christian life to a pilgrimage toward maturity. **Dame Julian of Norwich** (1342–1420) had a sense of the great love of God that was overpowering.[1] But here we want to focus on **Johannes Tauler** (1300–1361), whose ministry in Strasbourg, Cologne, and Basle was mightily owned of God and who must be considered one of the premier preachers among the mystics.

Tauler was born into a family of means (his father was a senator) in a time that the historian Barbara Tuchman describes as disaster—plague, war, taxes, brigandage, bad government, insurrection, and schism in the church.[2] He became a Dominican, renouncing the world, and matriculated at the University of Paris. Dissatisfied with the subtleties of the dialecticians, he began to identify with the movement known as The Friends of God, who under the influence of Ruysbroeck sought spiritual rather than formalistic piety.[3] Tauler was also much influenced by **Meister Eckhart** (1260–1328), the noted Dominican mystic, who twice served stints at the University of Paris.

We have about one hundred of Eckhart's sermons, preached in Latin to the clergy and in the vernacular to the laity. Often quite abstract, his burden in preaching was on target:

> When I preach, I am careful to speak about detachment and that a person should become free of self and of all things. Secondly, that one should

be re-formed in the simple good that is God. Thirdly, that one should think of the great nobility which God has placed in the soul, so that a person may thereby come to God in a wonderful way. Fourthly, concerning the purity of divine nature—there is such brilliance in it that it is inexpressible.[4]

Eckhart preached in Strasbourg, and his searing sense of sin along with his tendency to speculate always seemed to land him in ecclesiastical hot water. The contemporary apostate Roman Catholic thinker, Matthew Fox, has latched onto something of the creation spirituality in Eckhart and run it into the ditch. Contemporary New Age spirituality deifies nature and worships Mother-Earth *(Gaia)*, often within a pantheistic framework.

Tauler enjoyed considerable success in preaching to the Rhenish states before his remarkable conversion in 1338. Then a mysterious layman confronted him with the ultimatum: "You must die, Dr. Tauler! Before you can do your greatest work for God, the world, and this city, you must die to yourself, your gifts, your popularity, and even your own goodness, and when you have learned the full meaning of the Cross, you will have new power with God and man."[5] Consequently, his preaching evidenced more searching application and trembled with much greater sorrow over sin.[6] When the Black Death visited Strasbourg in 1348, all saw Tauler's great zeal for discipline and self-denial. He was walking the way of the Cross.

Possessing about eighty of his sermons, we can well appreciate the impression made upon Christina Ebner, a contemporary: "His fiery tongue kindled the entire world."[7]

This preacher rocked a nation with reverberations that would reach to the time of Martin Luther, who read and annotated his sermons. Tauler blended the two main forms of preaching popular at time—the exegetical homily and the more thematic sermon based on the university sermon model. In the thema, the topic and text were announced in Latin and then immediately rendered into the vernacular. This was frequently followed by the prothema with an amplification of the biblical theme. In "Sermon I for Christmas," based on Isaiah 9:6, we see a threefold division of the text. Tauler did not give equal treatment to the three mains, and the third main did not relate in clear fashion. Yet he stayed close to the biblical images and evinced a sense of close relationship to the congregation.[8]

A computer-aided analysis of syntactic patterns and idiosyncrasies has been made on the styles of Eckhart, Tauler, and Suso. Tauler is shown to plough his own furrow, using short sentences in an oral pattern, and stressing logical disposition amid reflective units and application.[9] Clearly Tauler must be recognized as one of the most gifted and influential preachers of this time. His sermons had a profound impact upon the Reformers.

An impressive example of the effect of impassioned preaching upon a city may be seen in the utterance of **Girolamo Savonarola** (1452–1498). To the great disappointment of his physician father, Savonarola entered a Dominican monastery in Bologna in 1475 after writing an essay, "The Contempt of the World." As a child he had loved the Bible. Disappointed in love and in his studies in philosophy at the university, he heard the call of the Nazarene (Matt. 11:28). Savonarola followed, joining the Dominicans, the *Domini cani,* the hounds of the Lord.

Savonarola was born to preach—"he was enlightened in order to illuminate."[10] Still his initial efforts in preaching were dismal. He struggled at San Marco and failed again at San Lorenzo. One professor worked with him to add an oratorical dimension to his discourse, but the struggle was too painful. Discouraged, Savonarola determined to leave the pulpit forever. Then the Count of Mirandola took an interest in him. His preaching was transformed. Soon he was preaching from a strong and deathless conviction deep with in him. He itinerated for about three years before returning to San Marco in Florence. One biographer describes his preaching:

> A new man . . . dominated by an overpowering personal emotion that inspired him with daemonic energy. He preached like a man fighting for life; he struck, exhorted, appealed, menaced; the words poured forth in a rhapsodic stream; he leaned over the pulpit, as if to seize the dense inimical mass at his feet and breathe into it his passion, to hypnotize it with his emotion, and to force it to feel with him. Like a castaway, gesticulating, exclaiming, struggling to rejoice humanity, he struggled for communion and response; and only when it came, only when he felt at last the hostile mass moving to his dictating emotion, he paused and drew breath—a long breath of victorious relief. For it was a triumph—the response came in a tide of exclamations and sighs; he had sprung the secret of the revivalist; he had tapped a great undertow of popular emotion; and henceforth he was to be its master and its creature.[11]

Savonarola was drawn to the wrathful and the apocalytpic, chiefly enjoying the Old Testament. He particularly loved preaching from Genesis and Haggai, and in the New Testament from the Book of Revelation. He was given to *lectio continua* (consecutive book exposition). He saw himself as a "reviver of scripturalism,"[12] and called Florence back to the Word of God. He stood in contrast to the popular humanistic orators of his time. Summoned to "quicken the sluggish conscience of the age,"[13] he found his former doubts vanishing when he stood in the pulpit. Boldness became his stock in trade.

In the fall of 1494, Charles VIII of France drew near to Florence with forty thousand soldiers and one hundred siege guns. Savonarola picked up his accustomed Advent theme of the coming fifth age when the Antichrist would appear, Christ would conquer, and the Turks and pagans would be baptized. This was a variation of the Christian apocalypticism of Joachine of Fiore (Joachite prophecy). Savonarola blended both the optimism of Augustinian eschatology (the final victory of God and his own) with a realistic pessimism about the human prospect (influenced by the Joachites). Throughout the crisis, Savonarola preached daily in the cathedral "to swollen and frightened crowds."[14] He was a patriot and a peacemaker, because it was he who confronted the French king and ordered him to depart. He did.

Savonarola was supreme for three and a half years. He was the most articulate theorist and spokesman of republican liberty in Florence. His early-morning audiences outgrew the Duomo, and a wooden amphitheater was put up against the walls. He gave a famous ultimatum to Lorenzo the Magnificent on the latter's deathbed. He relentlessly attacked Rome and its abuses and corruption. With his vigilantes, he launched moral crusades against sodomy, gambling, insufficient apparel for women, and certain kinds of art. And yet the foremost artists of the time read his sermons and painted his versions of doomsday. Michelangelo's "The Last Judgment" carries Savonarola's theme right into the Vatican.[15] Of course many, like Machiavelli, dismissed him as a "windbag," but others saw him as God's special preacher of repentance and divine wrath upon a decadent civilization. Bartolomeo Redditi testified, "I believed and I believe, because his preaching made Florence a paradise on earth."[16]

The conflicts deepened, and finally Savonarola was excommunicated. The following day, the pope died. The new pope put the city under interdict, and the people turned against him. Savonarola defied the ban and was brought to trial. He was tortured and hung on May 23, 1498, his body burned and his ashes flung into the river. Savonarola spent his last nights poring over the prophecy of Jeremiah, the man of God whose last days in Egypt were with those who rejected the Lord and his counsel. In his last sermon, Savonarola spoke to himself, as it were:

> O Father, we are little scandalized that you should submit your decision to men. If your preaching or not preaching depends on God, it does not seem proper that you should yield to men, and we believe no longer . . . I told you that God recommended my preaching and perseverance; but I told you also that it was not His purpose to grant you salvation against your will; and there I consented to your councils and agreed to observe their decisions, because the Lord will not force your welfare upon you . . . but when I mounted the pulpit, I could not contain myself, I could not do otherwise. The Word of the Lord became, in this place, like a consuming fire devouring my heart and my marrow; I could not gainsay it, I must needs utter it, for I burn with it utterly, I feel myself inflamed with the Spirit of the Lord.[17]

Certainly critical questions must be raised about Savonarola's message and methods. Did he too uncritically identify the kingdom of God with the republic of Florence? Did he see the Florentines as "God's chosen" in too cavalier a fashion? If so, he was not the first nor the last to do so of a beloved country or society. Did this fiery preacher become too embroiled in the political process of the republic? Did he curtail his spiritual ministry by too much involvement in the machinations of power? Every preacher who would significantly address the issues of the times faces this dilemma.

Savonarola's end-time scenario for his powerful preaching reconfigured daily life and experience in Florence. Professor Weinstein, who is not given to careless overstatement, is right that the Savonarola movement must be seen in relation to the Protestant Reformation ready to break out over Europe as "a harbinger of things to come."[18]

1. For what is in my opinion the best overview of Christian spirituality and spiritual formation over the centuries, see Cheslyn Jones, Geoffrey Wainwright, Edward Yarnold, eds., *The Study of Spirituality* (Oxford: Oxford University Press, 1986). This runs to more than six hundred pages and is a gem!

2. Cited in Josef Schmidt, "Introduction," Johannes Tauler, *Sermons* (New York: Paulist, 1985), 3. This is in The Classics of Western Spirituality series.

3. Susanna Winkworth, *The History and Life of Doctor John Tauler* (London: Allennson, 1905), 131. This volume is our sentimental favorite on Tauler and is replete with John Greenleaf Whittier's great poem on Tauler and an introductory preface by Charles Kingsley, the eminent preacher and novelist.

4. Jill Raitt, ed., *Christian Spirituality: High Middle Ages and Reformation* (New York: Crossroad, 1987), 147.

5. F. B. Meyer, *Five Musts of the Christian Life* (Chicago: Moody, 1927), 41.

6. Winkworth, *Doctor John Tauler,* 142–43.

7. Schmidt, "Introduction," xi.

8. Ibid., 17.

9. Ibid., 17ff.

10. Ralph Roeder, *Savonarola: A Study in Conscience* (New York: Brentano's, 1930), 26.

11. Ibid., 46. George Eliot has a striking description of Savonarola's preaching in *Romola,* 2:xxiv, "Inside the Duomo."

12. Donald Weinstein, *Savonarola and Florence: Prophecy and Patriotism in the Renaissance* (Princeton, N.J.: Princeton University Press, 1970), 183. A recent and very important study is Lorenzo Polizzotto's *The Elect Nation: The Savonarolan Movement in Florence* (Oxford: Oxford University Press, 1995).

13. Roeder, *Savonarola,* 96.

14. Weinstein, *Savonarola and Florence,* 114.

15. Roeder, *Savonarola,* 181.

16. Weinstein, *Savonarola and Florence,* 239.

17. Roeder, *Savonarola,* 266ff.

18. Weinstein, *Savonarola and Florence,* 377; and Augustine Thompson, *Revival Preachers and Politics in Thirteenth-Century Italy: The Great Devotion of 1233* (Oxford: Oxford University Press, 1993). Savonarola picked up the cues left by the "alleluia preachers" of 1233.

CHAPTER FIVE

The Reformation—
Preaching Comes of Age

How can a young man keep his way pure? By living according to your word.

—Psalm 119:9

I have hidden your word in my heart that I might not sin against you.

—Psalm 119:11

Open my eyes that I may see wonderful things written in your law.

—Psalm 119:18

My soul is weary with sorrow; strengthen me according to your word.

—Psalm 119:28

Then I will answer the one who taunts me, for I trust in your word.

—Psalm 119:42

How sweet are your words to my taste, sweeter than honey to my mouth!

—Psalm 119:103

Your word is a lamp to my feet and a light for my path.

—Psalm 119:105

All your words are true; all your righteous laws are eternal.

—Psalm 119:160

Of all the actions of the Christian ministry, preaching is the highest, and the test of our reverence for our profession is our performance of the preacher's duty.

—Bishop Hensley Henson

Baring Gould characterized the preaching of the Middle Ages: "We find that preaching consisted chiefly in scriptural exposition, the only order being observed being the sacred text."[1] Whether the simpler homilies or the more complex university sermons, solid scriptural preaching did manage to bubble to the surface. But it is the Protestant Reformation that must be seen as one of the most fertile and forceful times of biblical preaching.

Some preachers fixated on form, as St. Victor of Paris observed: "There are many who, when they come to the sermon—do not care what the preacher says; but only how he says it."[2] This was in part due to the dominance of the medieval papacy. The Scripture fairly suffocated under the dead weight of ecclesiastical structures and politics. The sacramental system held Scripture at bay. Tradition was choking and stifling the Word of God.

The "flying wedge" we call the Reformation was the insight and doctrine of the Reformers, who restored preaching to its proper place in the church and its life.[3] The centrality accorded to the Word and its proclamation ignited an unparalleled revival of preaching. Preachers long "wearied of conventional restraints" began to preach the Word with freedom and fire. They "spoke from their hearts" the marvelous Word of God.[4] The Reformers insisted that the Word always be expounded in the administration of the sacraments but also held that the Word of God could be proclaimed without the sacraments. This is a key insight.

Certainly the spiritual turnaround did not take place in a vacuum. We shall examine three persons out of the fourteenth century who are direct antecedents of the Reformers. We will see how the growth of national consciousness prepared the way for the German princes' support of Luther.[5] With the papacy seemingly bent on self-destruction, England, France, Bohemia, and even Italy pulled away from subordination to the pope.

Yet Aland is right when he points to something altogether new at the heart of the Reformation—the universal priesthood of all believers.[6] This emphasis on access to the Scriptures, along with the invention of the printing press, opened new doors of opportunity and obligation. What McLuhan and Postman speak of as a "print culture" made "the age of exposition" possible.[7]

The Reformers subscribed to a view of scriptural authority which made biblical preaching a necessity. As Schaeffer characterizes them: "They refused to accept the autonomy of human reason."[8] Thus, "At its core, therefore, the Reformation was the removing of the humanistic distortions which had entered the church."[9] While far from perfect, the Reformers have bequeathed us a legacy which we dare not squander.

---

1. S. Baring Gould, *Post-Medieval Preachers* (London: Riverton's, 1865), 7.

2. Charles Smyth, *The Art of Preaching: A Practical Survey of Preaching in the Church of England 747–1939* (London: SPCK, 1940), 41.
3. D. Martyn Lloyd-Jones, *Knowing the Times* (Edinburgh: Banner of Truth, 1989), 102.
4. Gould, *Post-Medieval Preachers,* 22.
5. Kurt Aland, *A History of Christianity* (Minneapolis: Fortress, 1985), 1:352.
6. Ibid., 357.
7. Neil Postman, *Amusing Ourselves to Death: Public Discourse in the Age of Show Business* (New York: Viking Penguin, 1985), 63.
8. Francis A. Schaeffer, *How Should We Then Live?* (Old Tappan, N.J.: Revell, 1976), 81.
9. Ibid., 82.

5.1 THE QUICKENING OF EXPECTATION

> The reason for the great weight that the Reformers laid on preaching was not educational or social but theological.
>
> —T. H. L. Parker

Preaching is a theological act. Karl Barth says, "Theology is the conscience of preaching." But homiletical theology means more than that. If the Bible is supremely authoritative, the translation of Scripture into the language of the people must follow. Then, given the accessibility of Scripture, the necessity for the preaching and dissemination of the truth of the Word of God must follow that. Preaching then is not chiefly rhetorical or communicational but theological.

The growing respect for the authority of the Word over ecclesiastical structures would culminate in the Reformation. Somewhat ahead of his time, University of Paris chancellor **John Gerson** (1363–1429) protested corruption and abuses in the church and called for biblical preaching:

> Many believe that sermons should be delivered only that the people may learn and know something they did not know before. Hence their scornful saying, "What is preaching to me? I already know more good than I am willing to do!" But these people are in error; for sermons are not delivered for this reason only, that one may learn something, but also for this reason, to move the heart and inclination so that they shall love, desire, and accomplish that which is good. Therefore the apostle desires not so much that one should learn what is in Christ, as that he should be like-minded with him. They, however, who attend sermons only to learn something new are like those of whom the apostle writes, that they are ever learning and yet know nothing.[1]

Others who would shape the coming Reformation included **Richard Grosseteste** (1175–1253), bishop of Lincoln and an eminent preacher who taught homiletics at Oxford. He influenced Wycliffe with his urgent appeal to the authority of Scripture. In his last illness, Grosseteste castigated the papacy with these words frequently quoted by the Reformers.[2] "But what is the cause of this hopeless fall of the Church? Unquestionably the diminution in the number of good shepherds . . . no wonder, for they preach not the Gospel of Christ with that living word which comes forth from living zeal for the salvation of souls, and is confirmed by an example worthy of Jesus Christ."[3]

William of Occam (1285–1347), a philosopher and theologian, taught at Oxford and influenced all of the Reformers. He argued that popes and church councils may err but Scripture may not err, for the Scripture alone has universal validity. William maintained that the pope was a heretic and that even the lowest peasant may be guided by the truth of the Bible. He saw that the propositions of theology cannot be established by reason but are derived from special revelation. Not surprisingly, William was excommunicated.

These were the ideas that filled the air when Wycliffe was at Oxford. Like subsequent Reformers, he found them congenial. Also shaping Wyclifffe's Augustinian bent was **Thomas of Brandwardine** (1290–1349). Appointed archbishop of Canterbury shortly before his death, Thomas was initially Pelagian in his inclinations but came to see "God's free and unmerited grace in the conversion and salvation of man."[4] Here was a herald of grace a full century before the Reformation! And now to the three towering figures of the time.

----

1. Alfredo E. Garvie, *The Christian Preacher* (New York: Scribner's, 1923), 123ff.
2. F. R. Webber, *A History of Preaching in Britain and America* (Milwaukee: Northwestern, 1952), 1:144–45. Webber's two volumes are an invaluable and exceedingly sound study, though they are limited to the English-speaking world.
3. W. L. Watkinson, *John Wycliffe* (Mobile, Ala.: R E Publications, n.d.), 10–11.
4. Ibid., 30.

5.1.1 THE GOLDEN FINGERS OF THE DAWN—JOHN WYCLIFFE

The highest service that men may attain to on earth is to preach the Word of God . . . hereby should they produce children to God, and that is the end for which God has wedded the Church. And for this cause Jesus Christ left other works, and occupied Himself mostly in preaching; and thus did His Apostles, and for this God loved them. Jesus Christ, when He ascended into heaven, commanded it especially to all His Apostles, to preach the Gospel freely to every man. In this stands the office of the spiritual shepherd.

—John Wycliffe

John Wycliffe (1320 or 1325–1384) has a special niche among those who preceded the Reformation. John Milton said of him, "He was honored of God to be the first preacher of a general revelation to all Europe."[1] We know little of his life; we do know that he earned his B.A. at Oxford in 1356 and became a Doctor of Theology in 1372. He had a distinguished academic career at Oxford[2] and wrote several learned philosophic tomes which gave him considerable academic prestige. In one of his books, *On the Truth of Holy Scripture,* he defended the doctrine of the literal inspiration of Scripture. Here he writes: "Holy Scripture is the faultless, most true, most perfect, and most holy law of God, which it is the duty of every man to learn, to know, to defend, and to observe, inasmuch as they are bound to serve the Lord in accordance with it, under the promise of an eternal reward."

Wycliffe's view of Scripture led him to translate the Bible from the Latin Vulgate into the English language, "the very first to give the whole of Revelation to his countrymen."[3] He regarded the Bible as the Christian's Magna Carta and gave his life to making that Word so filled with Christ available to the rank and file. In this we see striking parallels with Luther, who did much to shape the German language with his translation. Workman says he was "irresistibly driven into translation."[4]

Out of this great reverence for Scripture came his compunction to preach it. Innis puts Wycliffe's dedication in context: "Preaching the Word was the efficient means of extending the Kingdom in Apostolic times—every awakening has seen the marked increase and amount and intensity of the public exposition of Scripture."[5]

Wycliffe began to preach during his student days in 1361. He longed for the purity of the church and treasured the message of salvation by grace. He repeatedly reiterated that the first duty of the clergy is to preach.[6] The Scripture was the living seed and was to be preached openly to the people, and Wycliffe insisted on serious exposition for himself and those whom he trained to preach.[7] His sermons were revolutionary in that he drew back from the popular overuse of *exempla,* or fables, which had begun to consume discourse. Yet he did make use of illustrations, often from the science of optics.

Wycliffe's eloquent and moving sermons against the corruption and worldliness of the church and its clergy quickly got him into trouble. He opposed the worship of the Virgin, the invocation of the saints, the veneration of relics, the infallibility of the pope and the church. Ultimately he did come to see the error of transubstantiation, but he never renounced the doctrine of purgatory. He sent his Lollard missionaries out through the countryside, and congregations were established for his preachers.

When the peasants rebelled, national leaders turned against Wycliffe (cf. Luther and the Peasant's Rebellion). He was summoned to St. Paul's Cathedral for trial in 1377. He refused to go to Rome but returned to his beloved parish in Lutterworth, where a granite pillar in his honor now bears the words *Search the Scriptures.*

Wycliffe parted company with the mendicants of Oxford because they invariably served the cause of papal absolutism. He was the object of five papal bulls. In his latter years he was in constant peril and danger. He died of a violent stroke on December 31, 1384. Let us remember Wycliffe in his prime, preaching the gospel as he loved to do it:

> A tall thin figure, covered with a long light gown of black cloth, with a girdle about his body, the head adorned with a full flowing beard, exhibiting features clean and sharply cut, the eyes clear and penetrating, the lips firm closed in token of resolution, the whole man wearing an aspect of lofty earnestness, and replete with dignity and character.[8]

Preaching was soon to have seismic repercussions on the Continent, even to central Europe. In the decades after Wycliffe's death his teaching found "widespread acceptance."[9] Eventually he was condemned posthumously by the Council of Constance in 1415. His body was disinterred and burned, and his ashes scattered on the River Swift. When the converts of Wycliffe were burned at the stake, Wycliffe's Bible was put around their necks and burned with them. Luther wrote a hymn with obvious reference to Wycliffe's life and ministry:

> Fling to the heedless winds,
> On the water cast,
> Their ashes shall be watched,
> And gathered at the last.
>
> And from the scattered dust
> Around us and abroad,
> Shall spring a plenteous seed,
> Of witnesses for God.
>
> Jesus hath now received
> Their latest, dying breath.
> Yet vain is Satan's boast
> Of victory in their death.
>
> Still, still, though dead, they speak,
> And triumph-tongued proclaim,
> To many a waking land
> The one availing name.[10]

1. George S. Innis, *Wycliffe: The Morning Star* (Cincinnati: Jennings and Graham, 1907), 15.
2. K. B. McFarland, *John Wycliffe and the Beginnings of English Nonconformity* (London: English University Press, 1952), 5.
3. W. L. Watkinson, *John Wycliffe* (Mobile, Ala.: R E Publications, n.d.), 151.
4. Herbert B. Workman, *John Wycliffe* (Oxford: Clarendon, 1926), 2:155, 185. Two classic volumes.
5. Innis, *Wycliffe*, 143.
6. Douglas C. Wood, *The Evangelical Doctor: John Wycliffe and the Lollards* (Welwyn Herts, England: Evangelical Press, 1984), 88.
7. Workman, *John Wycliffe*, 213.
8. Innis, *Wycliffe*, 212.
9. McFarland, *John Wycliffe*, 129.
10. Quoted in W. A. Criswell, *Expository Sermons on Revelation* (Grand Rapids: Zondervan, 1962), 1:134.

5.1.2 GRACIOUS FOREGLEAMS OF THE COMING DAY—JOHN HUSS

But I hope that God will send after me champions stronger than I, who will better bare the sin of Anti-christ, and who will expose themselves to death for the truth of the Lord Jesus Christ, who will give to you and to me eternal glory.... I hope that the life of Christ, that I painted through His Word at Bethlehem in the hearts of men, and that His enemies have tried to destroy by forbidding all preaching at the chapel and wishing to raze it to the ground; I hope, I say, that this same life will be better drawn in the future by preachers more eloquent than I, to the great joy of the people who cling with all their hearts to Christ.

—John Huss

In my opinion, John Huss bought with his own blood the gospel which we now possess.

—Martin Luther

At Worms in Germany, there stands an imposing statue paying tribute to the Reformation. The forerunners of the Reformation are represented and they are three: John Wycliffe, John Huss, and Savonarola. **John Huss** (1369–1415) must have a place in this chronicle as a Reformation statesman and as a great and gifted preacher. Despite being born of peasant stock, he matriculated at the University of Prague, which by 1400 had thirty thousand students, many from outside Bohemia. Here he successively took his B.A. in 1393, his Th.B. in 1394 and his M.A. in 1396. He became a public teacher at the university. Even with his Wycliffian ideas, Huss was so popular he was named dean of the philosophy faculty in 1401 and rector of the university in 1402.

Students in Prague frequently debated with students from Oxford. (**Jerome of Prague,** the young, brilliant contemporary of John Huss, studied at Oxford for a time.) Huss became an avid student of Wycliffe, saying, "I confess before you here that I have read and studied the works of the Master, John Wycliffe, and I have learnt from them much that is good."[1]

"Wycliffe was the original and bolder mind—the pathfinder."[2] As early as 1399, Huss publicly defended the propositions of Wycliffe at the university. He became an articulate part of that crescendo of criticism protesting the oppressive hierarchy of the papacy and the unsound teachings emanating from the papal chair.

Even in tiny Bohemia there were fiery preachers who roused the populace to concern and commitment. **Conrad of Waldhausen** (d. 1369) preached on the true nature of sin and its overbearing pride, insisting that outward religious ritual and form could not insure salvation.[3] **Militz of Kremsier** (named by Neander as the first Reformation preacher in Bohemia) was a millennial type who attracted a huge following. **Matthias of Janow** was influential through his writings, such as *Studies on True and False Christianity.* He delineated the signs of the approaching antichrist. These preachers pioneered the impetus to protest in Bohemia.

Also assisting the ferment in favor of Wycliffite teaching was Anna, the sister of the Bohemian King Wenzel, who married Richard II of England and personally encouraged Wycliffe in his immense task of Bible translation.

Like Wycliffe, Huss and his followers ascribed ultimate and absolute authority to the Scriptures alone. David Schaff says, "He followed Wycliffe in demanding that the Scriptures should be in the hands of the people and that the priest's first duty is to expound their teachings to all men alike."[4] The Bible, the incontrovertible authority, is the Book of Life *(liber vitae).* Like Wycliffe and Luther, Huss also translated Scripture, revising an old Bohemian version. In the face of scrutiny and hatred, Huss was a man of "irreproachable personal conduct" and was never faulted by his critics.

The locus of Huss's powerful preaching ministry was the famous Bethlehem Chapel (meaning "House of Bread" in Hebrew) in Prague. This vast structure was built in 1391 largely through the influence of Militz of Kremsier and Matthias of Janow in Prague's old town. Gregory XII indicated that its purpose was "for the preaching of the Word of God" in the Czech language. It was not a parish church but featured worship services and preaching on the Lord's Day, during the week, and on holy days. It was destroyed by the Jesuits in 1786.

Huss's early preaching was done in St. Michael's parish church in Prague. We possess none of these early sermons but can deduce that they were eminently biblical and full of Christ. He was called to be the fourth person to fill the office of preacher at Bethlehem in which he functioned simultaneously with his work at the university. He lived in a dwelling room in the chapel, with a staircase directly to the pulpit.[5] In his preparation he steeped himself in Scripture and laced all discourse with the Word. Overflow crowds jammed the chapel to hear him. The fawning discourses of the friars *(blandis sermonibus)* had little appeal now.[6] Sometimes Huss enjoyed audiences of close to ten thousand. He wrote to England of what was happening in Bohemia:

> The people will hear nothing but the Scriptures, especially the gospels and epistles. And wherever, in town, village, house or castle, a preacher of the sacred truth appears, there the people flock together in crowds. Lo, I have but touched the tail of Anti-christ, and it has opened its mouth that it may swallow me up with my brothers . . . Our Lord the king and his whole court, queen, barons, and common people are all for the word of Jesus Christ . . .[7]

Yet clearly Huss was on a collision course. The first lesions with the hierarchy surfaced when Huss was appointed to be part of an official commission of inquiry. He was adverse to the miracle of Wilsnack, one of a series of superstitions. His identification with Wycliffe incurred the wrath of Pope John XXIII, who determined to close all private chapels and forbade Huss to preach. Needless to say he continued to preach. The tension was exacerbated when Huss and his compatriots took a stand against the sale of indulgences by Wenzel Tiem in 1412. Huss went briefly into exile at Austi, which later on became a center of Taborite life.

Even though he believed the tribunal of Christ was higher than the tribunal of the church, Huss traveled to the Council of Constance with a promise of safe conduct, but this was broken. Huss was imprisoned and finally burned at the stake in 1415, as was Jerome of Prague. The same council deposed John XXIII.

The shadow of the life and death of John Huss was very much over Martin Luther. Luther found a volume of the sermons of Huss at Erfurt and observed, "On reading, I was overwhelmed with astonishment. I could not understand for what cause they had burnt so great a man, who explained the Scriptures with so much gravity and skill."[8] At Leipzig, Eck accused Luther of being a Hussite.

After the martyrdom of Huss, his followers broke into two groups: the Calixtines, or Utraquists; and the Taborites, or radicals, who were very much like the Puritans of England. Much influenced by Joachim of Fiore, they were distinctly millennial. The tragic Bohemian wars and the Thirty Years' War decimated the population of Bohemia from about four million to seven or eight hundred thousand. Still the *Unitas Fratrum,* or Brethren group (out of which Jan Amos Comenius [1592–1640] came; he was once invited to become president of Harvard[9]), and the Moravian church survive as a tribute and evidence of the faithful testimony and witness of God's servant, John Huss.

---

1. Herbert B. Workman, *The Age of Huss* (London: Charles H. Kelly, 1902), 130.
2. David S. Schaff, *John Huss: His Life, Teaching and Death* (New York: Scribner's, 1915), 44.
3. Oscar Kuhns, *John Huss: The Witness* (Cincinnati: Jennings and Graham, 1907), 31ff.
4. Schaff, *John Huss,* 282.
5. Workman, *The Age of Hus,* 120.
6. Schaff, *John Huss,* 35.
7. Workman, *The Age of Hus,* 148.
8. Ibid., 117.
9. An entire issue of *Christian History* 6:1 is devoted to Comenius, great leader and Christian educator.

5.1.3 MR. FACING BOTH WAYS—ERASMUS

I have tried to call back theology, sunk too far in sophistical subtleties, to the sources and to ancient simplicity.
— Erasmus to Jean Gachi, October 1527

So keep on believing what you have been taught from the beginning. If you do you will always be in close fellowship with both God the Father and his Son.
—1 John 2:24 LB

His name is virtually a synonym for the Renaissance. He was "an enormous celebrity" in his time but a tragic figure. **Desiderius Erasmus** (1467–1536) was born in Rotterdam in the Netherlands in the difficult circumstance of illegitimacy. Early cast adrift, he was educated at Gouda and by the Brethren of the Common Life in Deventer. In 1486 he entered the Augustinian monastery at Steyn and was ordained in 1492. He traveled as secretary to the bishop of Cambrai, but soon began his study of Scripture at the University of Paris. He spent time in England where he came under the influence of **John Colet,** the New Testament lecturer of Oxford, and **Thomas More,** the author of *Utopia.* Erasmus spent two years in More's home while he wrote *In Praise of Folly,* a debunking of the pretensions of the medieval church. Often in dire poverty, he traveled extensively and spent his last years in Basle.

Erasmus was a genius whose thoughts lent themselves to the kind of circulation now made possible through the printer's art. His *Enchiridion* is a manual for spiritual warfare and a lusty call back to the Scripture.[1] He was revulsed by the methods of scholasticism, yet he was no systematic theologian and could be unguarded in his expression. He adulated the philosophy of Christ (i.e., the basics of Christian belief and loving conduct). Who he really was and where he really stood are matters of great controversy and difference. As Huizinga says of his first pamphlet, Erasmus was not "fervent" and took an "ambiguous position."[2] Yet this teacher of teachers is germane to our narrative for three reasons.

One, Erasmus was a linguist whose Latin was impressive and who learned Greek for the sake of reading the Greek New Testament. He was committed to the text of Scripture. He suffered under some six hundred mistranslations in the Vulgate, and set himself to identifying the true text of the New Testament through what we would call today the science of lower criticism. While greatly limited in his tools from our standpoint, his *Novum Instrumentum* in 1516 has been strikingly influential. Some of his "caustic notes stirred the ire of the priests,"[3] but this publication was the standard for three hundred years.

While the debates between John William Burgon and Westcott and Hort about the *textus receptus* are beyond the scope of our present discussion, we who hold to the inerrancy of the original autographs treasure the laborious work of textual critics who have collated and compared the thousands of extant manuscripts and vouchsafed to us the substantial accuracy of our present text. In this tedious but important work Erasmus must be seen as a pioneer. He had profound knowledge of Scripture and believed that the Bible is "divinely inspired and perfected by God its Author."[4] He wrestled with seeming contradictions, as did Luther after him, with reference to the Book of James,[5] and was keenly interested in text.[6]

Two, Erasmus influenced the Reformers, though it is exaggeration to say that "Erasmus laid the egg of the Reformation and Luthered hatched it." He was a very inward man, a believer who never had a Damascus Road experience like St. Paul. He wanted to get back through the medieval accretions to the Fathers and the simplicity of the gospel.

Many have pointed to the influence of Erasmus on the young Luther. Indeed, Erasmus criticized indulgences fifteen years before Luther did.[7] He also had ties with Zwingli, who wrote in 1516, "The Swiss account it a great glory to have seen Erasmus."[8] He was not at all confrontational and hated dissension, coming to the conclusion that Luther was using "extreme remedies." He and Luther broke sharply over the issue of the freedom of the will, prompting Erasmus to speak of "the Lutheran tragedy."

Erasmus found it hard to champion any cause.[9] Preserved Smith faults him for not really supporting the Reformation. His language was always qualified; he certainly was not the stuff of which martyrs are made. He was too perceptive to support Catholicism and too evasive to support Protestantism. Erasmus tended to shade his yes until it was no, and then burnish his no until it became yes, as someone has put it. Yet Bainton argues that the whole English Reformation was in its early stages Erasmian.

Three, Erasmus is also relevant because he skillfully used the art of rhetoric in Christian communication. He said of the training of preachers, "If elephants can be trained to dance and lions to play and leopards to hunt, surely preachers can be taught to preach." *On Preaching* (1535) urges that the introduction be close to the theme and that the sermons be divided. The basic outline of his treatment is

I. The dignity of the preaching office;
II. Doctrines and precepts on the art of preaching;
III. Particular subjects for pulpit treatment (to awaken feeling, one must feel).[10]

Like many scholastics, Erasmus was lost in allegorism early on. Yet as he turned more to Jerome as his pattern, he made a radical shift to "go to the sources themselves to deduce from that which precedes and from that which follows, the natural sense of the Scriptures."[11] Luther followed suit. He wrote to John Lang in 1517 that he was reading Erasmus, "And it pleases me that he constantly condemns both monks and priests for their inveterate ways and stupid ignorance."[12] Although he was to show considerable disdain for Erasmus later on (as he did to Karlstadt and Zwingli), Luther acknowledged his debt to him:

There has never been a great revelation of the word of God unless He has first prepared the way by the resurgence and prospering of languages and letters, as though they were John the Baptists.

To Oecolampadius, Luther wrote, "Erasmus has recalled the world from godless studies and reinstated the ancient languages, though, like Moses, he could not himself enter the promised land."[13]

In his declining years Erasmus became increasingly conservative. In many ways he disappoints us. Nonetheless, his work was essential.

---

1. Johan Huizinga, *Erasmus and the Age of Reformation* (Princeton, N.J.: Princeton University Press, 1924, 1984), 51.
2. Ibid., 31.
3. A. T. Robertson, *An Introduction to the Textual Criticism of the New Testament* (Nashville: Broadman, 1925), 18.
4. John C. Olin, *Six Essays on Erasmus* (New York: Fordham University Press, 1979), 6.
5. Bruce Ellis Benson, "Erasmus and the Correspondence with Johann Eck: A Sixteenth-Century Debate over Scriptural Authority," *Trinity Journal* 6 n.s. (1985): 157–65.
6. Marjorie O'Rourke Boyle, *Erasmus on Language and Method in Theology* (Toronto: University of Toronto Press, 1977); also Marjorie O'Rourke Boyle, *Rhetoric and Reform: Erasmus' Civil Dispute with Luther* (Cambridge, Mass.: Harvard University Press, 1983). These are both worthwhile studies.
7. James McConica, *Erasmus* (Oxford: Oxford University Press, 1991).

8. Huizinga, *Erasmus and the Age of Reformation*, 96.

9. Olin, *Six Essays on Erasmus*, 62.

10. Roland H. Bainton, *Erasmus of Christendom* (New York: Scribner's, 1969), 268ff.

11. John William Aldridge, *The Hermeneutic of Erasmus* (Richmond: John Knox, 1966), 30.

12. Ibid., 35.

13. Ibid., 37.

5.2 MARTIN LUTHER—THE EXPONENT OF THE GOSPEL OF GRACE

The Lord God is the real preacher.

When one for the first time mounts the pulpit, no one would believe how very afraid one is! One sees so many heads down there! Even now when I am in the pulpit I look at no one but tell myself they are merely blocks of wood which stand there before me, and I speak the word of my God to them.
—Martin Luther

We have seen that Erasmus felt the truth-unity tension but unwisely veered toward unity. We now consider a company of preachers who opted strongly for truth. Their stand would become the Protestant Reformation of the sixteenth century.

Luther, Calvin, and Zwingli loom large in this company. Professor Aland helpfully underscores how different each was:

1. Luther, the prophet and interpreter of Scripture; German profundity;
2. Calvin, the scholar and church leader; French clarity;
3. Zwingli, the Christian humanist and preacher; Swiss practicality.[1]

Yet they hold historic orthodoxy with one voice. Most particularly, "They develop their common understanding of the primacy of the newly discovered and newly understood Scriptures."[2]

The outgrowth of this common view of Scripture was the high view of preaching, which was an inevitable concomitant of a high view of Scripture. The primacy of the preaching of the Word would become one of the identifying marks of the Reformation.

The German theologian Christlieb points out the Roman Catholic devaluation of preaching historically and the contrasting Reformation emphasis on didactic preaching "built on the basis of the text alone."[3] Standing squarely in the Reformation tradition, he critiques Schleiermacher's "devotional-aesthetic" conception of preaching and pleads for active and passionate preaching for a decision, which has as its objective conversion, "fruit for the Kingdom of God."[4] As one the Reformers recognized "the supreme and ultimate act to be exposition of the Word of God."[5] The result was painful, but led to some improvements in Roman Catholic preaching.

---

1. Kurt Aland, *A History of Christianity* (Philadelphia: Fortress, 1986), 2:17.

2. Ibid., 18. I am using Aland chiefly among others as the check on the complex historiography of this period.

3. Theodor Christlieb, *Homiletic: Lectures on Preaching,* trans. C. H. Irwin (Edinburgh: T & T Clark, 1897), 93–94, 101.

4. Ibid., 111.

5. Edward P. Echlin, *The Priest As Preacher: Past and Future* (Notre Dame, Ind.: Fides, 1973), 60. This Roman Catholic lecturer at Durham makes the case for preaching as the priest's primary mission (p. 72) and calls for a renewed dedication to the ministry of preaching.

5.2.1 LUTHER AND SALVATION

I am not good and righteous, but Christ is.

When I became a Doctor I did not know we cannot expiate our sins.

The Cross is the safest of all things. Blessed is the man who understands this.

—Martin Luther

God's man in God's hour for the Reformation was the earthy, courageous, and gifted **Martin Luther** (1483–1546). A child of his turbulent times, Luther was truly a medieval, but the great step for him was his break with medieval soteriology. Luther saw all of humanity "locked in a profound conflict between God and the Devil while the Last Judgment rapidly approached."[1]

This millennial cast is not new to us, but it is the context in which Luther's personal struggles and battles must be seen. He has learned of no gracious God in his parental home or in his schooling. His resort to the monastery came out of fear. The fear of God's wrath upon him eternally drove him desperately. Education as such (he received his Th.D. in 1512) did not ameliorate his anguish. Involvement in the church and in its ministry could not palliate his agony (he was ordained in 1507). All of the frenetic works of supererogation could not bring peace to his troubled soul. He visited Rome as part of a delegation from the Augustinian Hermits but found no solace there. In fact, the shallowness and supercilious mood there depressed him all the more, and he exclaimed, "If there is a hell, Rome is standing on it."[2]

When he stood at the altar as an officiant, "a deep fear dismayed him."[3] A series of significant appointments as professor of Bible at Wittenberg, as monastery preacher, and as successor to **Johann von Staupitz** as head of the Augustinian Hermits did nothing to placate his sense of spiritual estrangement and alienation. His early sermons and lectures were very much in the pattern of the medieval scholastics. He was very probing of the biblical text. And this is what brought him to his Damascus Road.

Luther was very conscious of his sin, and spoke of the plague of his own heart. He saw sin as man *incurvatus en se,* or turning in upon oneself. Setting himself to study the Scriptures for his lectures and sermons, he was in his tower-study.[4]

No one tells of Luther's evangelical experience as does Roland Bainton, who describes his attention to the Psalms, Romans, and Galatians. Staupitz had directed him "to the wounds of the sweet Savior." Luther saw the cross of Christ in Psalm 22.[5] Then in Romans and Galatians he saw how wrath and love fuse on the cross. "The All Terrible Is the All Merciful." He wrote to his mother that the Word of God teaches us to trust only in Christ. To use Luther's own words:

> I greatly longed to understand Paul's Epistle to the Romans and nothing stood in the way but that one expression, "the justice of God" . . . . Night and day I pondered until I saw the connection between the justice of God and the statement that "the just shall live by faith." Then I grasped that the justice of God is that righteousness by which through grace and sheer mercy God justifies us through faith. Thereupon I felt myself to be reborn and to have gone through open doors into paradise. The whole of Scripture took on a new meaning.[6]

The relationship of his liberating experience of grace to his exegetical insight and his theological understanding of the meaning of the Cross is clear. Indeed he had formerly hated God and was angry with God, but now he was convulsed with love for God and his Word. His writings from 1518 have a new tone and dimension.

Luther's new forensic understanding of "justification by faith apart from the works of the law" was for him "the summary of all Christian doctrine." The traditional Lutheran preaching pattern of beginning with law and moving to grace has its genesis in Luther's own spiritual journey (although perhaps the real order is grace-law-grace). Luther described the transactual nature of Christ's work on the cross—in which Christ takes our sins and we take his righteousness by faith—as that "sweet exchange." So thus the believer in Christ is "at once righteous and a sinner" *(simul iustus et peccator)*.[7] This message was a total breach with the semi-Pelagianism endemic in the medieval world which threatens the message of grace and salvation in all ages.

Luther's discovery of the righteousness of God led to the formulation of a *theologia crucis*. Alister McGrath brilliantly demonstrates the scope of Luther's theological breakthrough. On justification he was a true Augustinian, and "the cruciality of the Cross embedded itself more and more deeply" into the man and into his message.[8] "The Cross alone is our theology" *(Crux sola est nostra theologia)* was his confession (Wa. 5.176.32–33). The whole medieval notion of accumulating merit before God was destroyed.[9] Out of this radical revolution in his thinking come deep and deathless convictions about his sources and authority and the proclamation which must be made. Spurgeon quotes Luther as to why he preached justification constantly: "Because the people would forget it; so that I was obliged almost to knock my Bible against their heads, to send it into their hearts."[10]

---

1. Heiko A. Oberman, *Luther: Man Between God and the Devil* (New Haven, Conn.: Yale University Press, 1989), 61ff.

2. Kurt Aland, *A History of Christianity* (Philadelphia: Fortress, 1986), 2:38.

3. Ibid., 35.

4. Some have been influenced by psychoanalytic theorists like Erik Erikson in *The Young Man Luther* (1958) to see Luther's tower experience as his moving from anal retentive to anal explosive (incorrectly translating *cloaca* as "privy" rather than the study in the tower above the privy). This is another example of extreme psychobiography.

5. Roland H. Bainton, *Here I Stand* (New York: Mentor, 1950, 1977), 47.

6. Ibid., 49.

7. Timothy George, *Theology of the Reformers* (Nashville: Broadman, 1988), 71.

8. Alister E. McGrath, *Luther's Theology of the Cross* (London: Blackwell, 1985), 26.

9. Alister E. McGrath, *Iustitia Dei: A History of the Christian Doctrine of Justification* (Cambridge, Mass.: Cambridge University Press, 1986).

10. Charles H. Spurgeon, "The Carnal Mind Enmity Against God," in *Spurgeon's Sermons* (New York: Funk and Wagnalls, n.d.), 1:248.

5.2.2 LUTHER AND THE SCRIPTURES

I simply taught, preached, wrote God's Word . . . otherwise I did nothing . . . the Word did it all.

Now let me and everyone who speaks of the word of Christ freely boast that our mouths are the mouths of Christ. I am certain indeed that my word is not mine, but the word of Christ. So must my mouth be the mouth of him who utters it.

—Martin Luther

Our doctrine of the Scripture determines the direction and nature of our theology and ministry. Up to age twenty, Luther had apparently not even seen a Bible. While he was a student at Erfurt he discovered the Bible and was given his own copy when he entered his novitiate. He began studying Hebrew in 1507 (Reuchlin's Hebrew text was published in 1506) and made considerable progress, followed then by his study of Greek.[1] Vivian Green helpfully observes, "The Sacred Scriptures in which his mind became so saturated formed the central feature of his study."[2] As he read the Scriptures the light began to dawn. Everything soon changed. He concurred with Augustine, "Everything written in Scripture must be believed absolutely."[3] Subsequently, everything for Luther hinged on his conviction, *sola Scriptura*. He rested his entire argument on Scripture. His indictment of his frequent adversary Eck lays out the issue:

I regret that the holy doctor penetrates the Scriptures as deeply as a spider does the water: in fact, he runs away from them as the devil from the cross. Therefore, with all my regard for the fathers, I prefer the authority of the Scriptures, which I commend to those who will judge me."[4]

We marvel at what has been called the kerygmatic exegesis of Luther the commentator on Scripture. His work is voluminous, extending to about one hundred volumes. He broke loose from the medieval "four senses of Scripture" to reinstate the original text and its literal sense.[5] As with Wycliffe and Huss, he saw the necessity of translating the Scripture into the language of the people, and his German Bible became the "keystone of the Reformation." The Bible became the people's book. Luther did not see the Scripture as a "waxen nose" to be twisted this way and that, and he warned against the "spiritualizers" among his own followers.

Professor Prenter's classic study of Luther's concept of the Holy Spirit shows that he did not regard the Holy Spirit as a warm feeling but as the one on whom we rely for understanding and preaching of the Word of God. "The Word is the means of the Holy Spirit."[6] The sacraments are seen as visible words.

All sides in the modern theological debate about Scripture have tried to claim Luther, but Pelikan is surely right that for Luther the Bible is the Word of God and does not become the Word when we believe. It has ontic status as the Word of God whether or not we believe it.[7] Worthies such as Reinhold Seeberg and Philip Watson espoused the more subjective idea of biblical inspiration. J. Theodore Mueller,[8] A. Skevington Wood, J. Michael Reu, Herman Sasse, and Klaas Runia all take seriously Luther's words when he argues for the objective nature of biblical revelation.[9] Listen to Luther:

So then the entire Scriptures are assigned to the Holy Ghost (St.L. 3, 1890);

The Holy Scriptures have been spoken by the Holy Ghost (St.L. 3, 1895);

In the Book of the Holy Ghost, that is Holy Scripture, we must seek and find Christ (St.L. 9, 1775);

In the Scripture you are reading not the word of man, but the Word of the most exalted God (St.L. 9, 1818);

The Scriptures have never erred (St.L. 9, 356).[10]

Luther's radical Christocentrism simply recognized the mediatorial office of Christ in its rich, full sense and took seriously the teaching of Scripture itself (cf. Luke 24:27; John 5:39). The difficulty Luther had with several portions of Scripture was not in relation to inerrancy but rather in relation to canonicity. His view of the inerrant and infallible nature of scriptural authority led him to some issues with respect to the canon. Since Scripture cannot be contradictory, and wondering if James did not contradict Paul on "justification by faith apart from the works of the law," he called James "a right strawy epistle." Rather than creating a problem about a noncontradictory Scripture, Luther's position supported the view that Scripture is noncontradictory. "The Scriptures cannot lie," remained his stand.

Holy Scripture was thus his sword and his light. At the Diet of Worms in 1521 he declared to the emperor and five thousand people: "Unless I am convicted of error by the Holy Scriptures, I neither can or dare retract anything; for my conscience is held captive by God's Word. Here I stand, I can do no other. God help me. Amen." The Word always afforded him the most amazing confidence and courage, as he later wrote:

> That word above all earthly powers, no thanks to them, abideth:
> The Spirit and the gifts are ours Thro' Him who with us sideth.
> Let goods and kindred go, this mortal life also; The body they may kill:
> God's truth abideth still, His kingdom is forever.

Such a view of Scripture inescapably gives rise to a perception and practice of preaching.

---

1. Luther was always strong for the mastery of the biblical languages, as when he insisted: "Languages are the sheath in which hides the Sword of the Spirit—so although the faith of the gospel may be proclaimed by a preacher without the knowledge of the languages, the preaching will be feeble and ineffective. But where the languages are studied, the proclamation will be fresh and powerful, the Scripture will be searched, and a faith will be constantly rediscovered through ever new words and deeds" (cited from Peter Meinhold in Fred W. Meuser, *Luther the Preacher* [Minneapolis: Augsburg, 1983], 42ff.).
2. A. Skevington Wood, *Captive to the Word: Martin Luther: Doctor of Sacred Scripture* (London: Paternoster, 1969), 42. This choice volume is Wood's Ph.D. dissertation at the University of Edinburgh.
3. Ibid., 39.
4. Ibid., 70.
5. Ibid., 78.
6. Regin Prenter, *Spiritus Creator: Luther's Concept of the Holy Spirit* (Philadelphia: Muhlenberg, 1953). One must beware of a severe Barthian tinge throughout the work.
7. Jaroslav Pelikan, *From Luther to Kierkegaard* (St. Louis: Concordia, 1950), 18.
8. J. Theodore Mueller, "Luther and the Bible," in *Inspiration and Interpretation*, ed. John Walvoord (Grand Rapids: Eerdmans, 1957).
9. Wood, *Captive to the Word*; James Atkinson in *The Great Light: Luther and the Reformation* (Grand Rapids: Eerdmans, 1968) holds that "Luther's soul was saved by an unyielding and uncompromising faith in the Bible" (20).
10. Mueller, "Luther and the Bible," 97ff.

5.2.3 LUTHER AND THE SERMON

Always preach in such a way that if the people listening do not come to hate their sin, they will instead hate you.

It is disgraceful for the lawyer to desert his brief; it is even more disgraceful for the preacher to desert his text.

To preach simply is a great art . . . Christ understood it and practiced it
. . . He speaks only of the ploughed field, of the mustard seed, and uses
only common comparisons from the countryside.

My best craft is to give the Scripture with its plain meaning; for the plain
meaning is learning and life.

—Martin Luther

"Luther's influence was due to the wide-ranging character of his evangelical
preaching"[1] claims one Luther scholar. The data suggest this is not an overstatement. At the Leipzig debate with Eck in 1519, Luther contended that the true
church exists where the Bible is preached, the sacraments are administered, and
faith, hope, and love exist. His insights into the Scripture were embedded in his
sermons, such as his crucial "Treatise on Good Works." His direct, Spirit-anointed
preaching touched the hearts of the masses. John Ker depicts the scenario:

On the way to Worms to meet the Diet, he could not escape from the
crowds. At Erfurt the church was so crowded they feared it would fall.
At Zwickau, the marketplace was thronged by 2,500 eager listeners and
Luther had to preach from a window. He continued to preach to the end
of his life though so broken in health that he often fainted from exhaustion. To the end he retained his wonderful power. The last time he entered the pulpit was February 14, 1546, a few days before he died.[2]

Protestantism was a movement in which the pulpit was literally higher than
the altar. In the Wittenberg church where Luther often preached, the schedule
was 5–6 A.M., exposition of the Pauline Epistles; 9–10 A.M., exposition of the
Gospels; afternoon, the morning theme continued or the catechism, and then
preaching every day. He would often preach four times on Sunday. We possess
about 2,300 of his sermons, delivered in German but transcribed by his friends
in Latin.[3] As in his famous *Table Talk,* his preaching abounds with German sayings and peasant crudities. He would speak of how Mary took baby Jesus "and
wiped his bottom before putting him to her breasts."

Preaching the church year was important to Luther. Though his was a "theology of the cross," the resurrection of Christ was prominent among his themes.
On one occasion, when things seemed very bleak, he was seen tracing on a table
with his finger the words *Vivit, vivit,* "He lives, he lives!"[4] Preaching for Luther
was an outcropping of the eschatological battle. The pulpit was a battlefield.

Luther would take his concept or his basic schema with him into the pulpit
but would sometimes move entirely away from it. He strongly emphasized the
spiritual preparation of the preacher, urging that to pray well is to study well. As
with all of the Reformers, he believed that the text should control the sermon—
the main point or *hertzpunkt* to which the preacher is to come back again and
again. Structure as such was not strong in Luther's preaching, but his running
commentary was directed by the central thought. As he put it, "In my sermons I
bury myself to take just one passage and there I stay so the hearers may be able

to say 'That was the sermon.'"[5] He held to the real presence of Christ in preaching and that the preaching of Christ is Christ preaching. There can be no higher view of preaching than this.

Luther said he would rather be a preacher than a king, but when he was wrung out he would become discouraged and weary. He saw the preacher as both soldier and shepherd. "He must nourish, defend and teach; he must have teeth in his mouth and be able to bite and fight." Sometimes the drained and depleted Luther wanted to quit, and told his congregation he was going to do so.

Yet he loved the tension of dialectic in preaching. "When I preach a sermon, I take an antithesis."[6] And that he did in pressing law/gospel; God/Satan; sin/grace. He always aimed at both the heart and mind of his hearers.[7] Although he confessed timidity (always appropriate for the preacher in dependence on the Lord), his delivery was forceful and sometimes bombastic. He frequently offended by language and action. He spoke of "stink" and "manure" from the pulpit. At Eisenach on one occasion he hammered away at a text while preaching so that he split a three-inch board.[8]

As we have pointed out there was what Meuser calls a kind of "heroic disorder"[9] in Luther's preaching, which is only to say that he exalted the Word and generally disdained the form. Still well worth reading, the sermons of Luther have great mood swings and sudden surges. He was immensely pictorial in his preaching.[10] But in all of this the Word of God dominated and directed and determined. Luther was not in comparison with Calvin a systematic thinker. He was far more a feeling preacher but under the text. As he put it, "A little word of God makes the whole world too narrow for me."

While always in reaction against that which was too fine or too ornate, Luther defined the preacher as "a logician and a rhetorician."[11] In his *Table Talk* he indicates that a preacher should have these qualities: (1) to teach systematically; (2) to have a ready wit; (3) to be eloquent; (4) to have a good voice; (5) to have a good memory; (6) to know when to make an end (Luther could be very brief as well as extended); (7) to be sure of his doctrine; (8) to venture and engage body and blood, wealth and honor in the Word; (9) to suffer himself to be mocked and jeered of everyone.[12]

Luther's famous sacristy prayer lays bare his own soul as he prepared to preach:

> O Lord God, dear Father in heaven, I am indeed unworthy of the office and ministry in which I am to make thy glory and to nurture and to serve this congregation. But since thou hast appointed me to be a pastor and teacher, and the people are in need of the teaching and the instruction, O be thou my helper and let thy holy angels attend me. Then if thou art pleased to accomplish anything through me, to thy glory and not to mine or to the praise of men, grant me, out of thy pure grace and mercy, a right understanding of thy Word and that I may also diligently perform it. O Lord Jesus Christ, Son of the living God, thou shepherd and bishop of our souls, sent thy Holy Spirit that he may work with me, yea, that he may work in to will and to do through thy divine strength according to thy good pleasure. Amen.[13]

1. D. Olivier, *Luther's Faith: The Cause of the Gospel in the Church* (St. Louis: Concordia, 1982), 110.
2. John Ker, *Lectures on the History of Preaching* (New York: Armstrong, 1889), 152ff.
3. Roland H. Bainton, *Here I Stand: A Life of Martin Luther* (New York: Mentor, 1950, 1977), 272–81.
4. Cortland Myers, *Making a Life* (New York: Revell, 1900), 142.
5. Fred W. Meuser, *Luther the Preacher* (Minneapolis: Augsburg, 1983), 47. Meuser points out that the Franciscans and Dominicans gave up the cruciform church building and took the huge hall churches with the pulpit on one of the middle pillars, thus sparing the Reformers the necessity of developing their own architectural style. He also shows how Tauler influenced Luther on the need for the sermon to be "centered." This influence on Luther was more telling than even Augustine's homiletical form (cf. 91).
6. A. Skevington Wood, *Captive to the Word: Martin Luther: Doctor of Sacred Scripture* (London: Paternoster, 1969), 91.
7. Meuser, *Luther the Preacher*, 38.
8. Charles H. Spurgeon, *Lectures to My Students* (Grand Rapids: Zondervan, 1954, 1979), 282.
9. Meuser, *Luther the Preacher,* 57.
10. Ibid., 78.
11. Thomas S. Kepler, ed., *The Table Talk of Martin Luther* (New York: World, 1952), 251.
12. Ibid., 238.
13. Meuser, *Luther the Preacher,* 51. For a delightful sampling of Luther's sermonic material in all of its vigor, see *Martin Luther, Day by Day We Magnify Thee: Daily Readings for the Entire Year* (Philadelphia: Fortress, 1982).

5.3 JOHN CALVIN–THE EXEGETE OF GOD'S WORD

When the Word of God is rightly expounded, the faithful are not only edified, but if an unbeliever come into the church and hear the doctrine of God he is reproved and judged.

When the gospel is preached in the name of God, it is as if God spoke in person.

The office of the Spirit promised to us is not to form new and unheard of revelations . . . but to seal on our minds the very doctrine which the gospel recommends.

—John Calvin

Two sharply different traditions in preaching vie for adherents in our time and through the last several hundred years. Preaching in the tradition of the Reformation is God-centered with vertical dominance; preaching in the tradition of the Enlightenment is anthropocentric with horizontal dominance. F. W. Boreham relates a comment of a parishioner to his departing pastor: "I never had but one objection to you—your preaching was always too horizontal."[1] At the aorta of the Reformation, that was seldom the problem.

Ulrich Luz has observed that "until the Enlightenment, the scholarly and the homiletical interpretation of the Bible were closely related—witness, for example, the influence of the homilies of Chrysostom or the relationship between the lectures and sermons of Luther—but since the Enlightenment they have been diverging more and more, leading to a far-reaching divorce between text and sermon, as becomes apparent very often in homileticial practice and sometimes even in homiletical theory."[2]

The result is "the empty pulpit," as Nigel Watson describes it, and urges on us a definition of preaching to counteract it. Preaching is "an act of worship which seeks, in dependence on the presence of God, to bring this passage of Scripture, or this aspect of Christian doctrine, to life as a word of importance for the members of this congregation."[3] The preacher must be an exegete of the text. We now turn to John Calvin, whose genius as an exegetically savvy preacher has set the standard since Reformation days.

---

1. F. W. Boreham, *The Luggage of Life* (London: Charles H. Kelly, 1912), 183.
2. Ulrich Luz as cited in Nigel Watson, *Striking Home: Interpreting and Proclaiming the New Testament* (London: Epworth, 1987), 15ff.
3. Ibid., 120.

5.3.1 CALVIN—IN HIS SAVIOR

> Grant, Almighty God, that as Thou hast been pleased to set before us an example of every perfection in Thine only-begotten Son, we may study to form ourselves in imitation of Him, and so to follow not only what He has prescribed, but also what He really performed.
> —Calvin's prayer after a lecture on Jeremiah

Many would agree that **John Calvin** (1509–1564) "gave the ablest, soundest, clearest expositions of Scripture that had been seen in one thousand years, and most of the Reformers worked in the same direction."[1] Luther excelled at grasping the one great central truth of a text and pounding it home. But Calvin, fragile in contrast to the emotionally volatile "wild boar" of Saxony, was like a skilled surgeon with the text of Scripture, cool and lucid in his analysis of revealed truth.

In both Luther and Calvin, "the force of their character gave great force to their utterance."[2] Our challenge is to probe what made John Calvin so utterly God-centered in his preaching and so committed in his exegesis. William J. Bouwsma's recent well-received study of Calvin is amazingly destitute of reference to his theology.[3] Bouwsma sees Calvin as a troubled and anxious man in a troubled and anxious age, caught between his medieval scholasticism and his Renaissance humanism. But this distinguished scholar does not allow for the reality of the supernatural in Calvin's life, apart from which his ministry is indeed inexplicable.

John Calvin was born in Noyon in beautiful Picardy, France, the son of a lay diocesan official. Both Calvin's father and brother died as excommunicates because of their questioning of church practices. John was sent to Paris by his father in 1523 to study law (an intriguing parallel with Luther) and then to Orleans, where he earned his doctorate in 1533.

By training he was a skilled rhetorician. His first publication was on the rhetoric of Seneca.

In 1533 he fled Paris because he had written an oration sympathetic to Reformation ideas, which was given by the rector of the University of Paris, Nicolas Cop.

In 1534 he experienced the crisis of "conversion." Later he described it, "At last, God turned my course in a different direction by the hidden bridle of his providence . . . by a sudden conversion *(subita conversione)* to docility, he tamed a mind too stubborn for its years."[4] Bouwsma denigrates real significance in Calvin's conversion,[5] but soon thereafter Calvin resigned his benefices in the church to take a dramatically different course.

At the age of twenty-six, he wrote his famous *Institutes* in Basel in 1535, revising and expanding these throughout his life. (We must note that Calvin and Calvinism are not the same, as McGrath and R. T. Kendall remind us with regard to the doctrine of limited atonement, which they assert is the product of Beza, for example.) Regardless of our own particular theological perspective, the *Institutes* are a beautiful, precise, and focused work. Kenneth Scott Latourette calls the work "the most influential single book of the Protestant Reformation." Book 1 is *The Knowledge of God the Creator;* Book 2 is *The Knowledge of God the Redeemer;* and Book 3 is *The Mode of Obtaining the Grace of Christ.* Sections on our knowledge of God in creation and on the illuminating work of the Holy Spirit are classic.[6] Calvin was a God-intoxicated man!

Calvin fed deeply on the writings of Martin Luther. Our argument is that because the Reformers had such a strong vertical theology, they readily yielded to the supremacy of the Word. Their preaching arose out of their theology. In the *Institutes* we see how Calvin has imbibed Luther, as is demonstrated by his eloquence on justification by faith alone.

Calvin's personal preference would have been to live a scholar's life in Basel, but the God he knew through Christ had called him to preach, to teach, and to lead. His two stints in Geneva and the four intervening years in Strasbourg give proof of his obedience to that call.

Bucer urged him to find a wife, and in 1540 he married a widow, Idelette de Bure. She bore him three children, all of whom died. She herself died nine years later. Calvin also knew oppressive illness and physical weakness, but these did not impede his prodigious labors in preaching, writing, and administration. We see him at a disputation in Lausanne in 1536, where Farel and Viret are the protagonists. When the Romanists accuse the Protestants of neglecting the church fathers, it is Calvin who rises to his feet.

He suggested that the Romanists might read the Fathers before they mentioned them, and quoting one Father after another in exact content, he argued his case with unerring certainty. Men realized that there stood in their midst not a man who had memorized catenae of the Fathers but one who had read them, understood them and set them forth in their proper relation to true catholicism.[7]

Certainly John Calvin was a child of his times, but what is ignored by those who rail against him in caustic caricature and crass condemnation is the unmistakable evidence of the reality of God in his life and his dogged insistence on "the utter gratuity of grace." Apart from this, nothing that he said or did finds explanation. As he himself stressed: God selects vile and worthless persons to instruct and warn us, in order to subdue our pride. Indeed, God employs many in the publishing of His Word "who are not quite so agreeable to the human mind."[8]

---

1. Leroy Nixon, *John Calvin, Expository Preacher* (Grand Rapids: Eerdmans, 1950), 29.
2. Ibid., 31.
3. William J. Bouwsma, *John Calvin: A Sixteenth-Century Portrait* (Oxford: Oxford University Press, 1988).
4. Alister E. McGrath, *A Life of John Calvin* (Oxford: Blackwell, 1990), 70.
5. Bouwsma, *John Calvin,* 10–12.
6. John Calvin, *Institutes* (Grand Rapids: Eerdmans, 1953), 43–45, for instance, where Calvin graphically pictures the "audacious despiser of God" as in fact "most easily disturbed, trembling at the sound of a falling leaf."
7. James Atkinson, *The Great Light: Luther and the Reformation* (Grand Rapids: Eerdmans, 1968), 162.
8. As cited from commentaries and sermons in Ronald S. Wallace, *Calvin's Doctrine of the Word and Sacrament* (Grand Rapids: Eerdmans, 1957), 117.

5.3.2 CALVIN—IN HIS STUDY

Christ hath therefore been appointed by the Father, not to rule after the manner of princes, by the force of arms and by surrounding Himself with other external defenses, to make Himself an object of terror to His people; but His whole authority consists in doctrine, in the preaching of which He wishes to be sought and acknowledged.

The Scriptures are thus sufficient in themselves to furnish the people of God with all the inspiration and knowledge they require apart from any other source. Through them the Spirit leads us into all truth, and to imagine that this needs supplementing is "to do grievous injury to the Holy Spirit."

—John Calvin

Vadian's famous evaluation of Erasmus—that "he was strong in expression but weak in substance"—could never be offered concerning Calvin because of his total sense of call to be an interpreter of Scripture. Calvin lived and breathed the inspired text, and his commentaries, treatises, and sermons show it. When he first went to Geneva in 1536 under pressure from **William Farel,** he went not in any pastoral capacity but as a "reader in Holy Scripture." He led Bible studies. Although he was never ordained, Calvin's gifts and leadership were soon recognized. He wrote *Ordinances of the Church in Geneva,* in which he saw the pastoral office as "proclaiming the Word of God and instructing believers in wholesome doctrine."

In his first stay in Geneva, a burgeoning republic of about ten thousand people, Calvin was constantly embroiled in controversy. Yet he gave himself wholly to the study of Scripture. He would sleep little, and begin his day of study about 5 or 6 A.M. His sermons were built out of the commentaries and his commentaries are sermonic. His magnificent commentary on Romans came in 1539.

Underlying Calvin's herculean labors was his conviction that "the Bible is true."[1] In his invaluable treatment of Calvin and the Bible, Kenneth Kantzer shows that "Calvin's loyalty to the written Scriptures knows no bounds."[2] While indebted to general or natural revelation, Calvin saw special revelation as "a surer and more direct means" to the knowledge of God as Creator and the only means of knowledge of God as Redeemer. He was convinced of the "divine authority" of the self-authenticating Scripture, and made it clear that this view is the universal view. As a foundation for the Westminster divines and others who followed, Calvin stressed the witness of the Holy Spirit to the authority, accuracy, and sufficiency of Scripture as decisive.[3] Kantzer adds, "According to [Calvin] the human authors of Scripture were controlled by God in every detail of what they wrote."[4] The Scriptures are like spectacles to give us "a clear view of the true God." He saw the sacraments as seals of the divine Word, bringing into the senses what has been thought in the mind. They are extensions of the preached Word and in this respect are to be considered a form of preaching (cf. 1 Cor. 11:26).

When Calvin returned to Geneva in 1541, he spent a great part of his time exegeting and writing commentaries. He delivered Bible readings on the basis of his commentary work several afternoons each week. In his epochal volumes on the commentaries, T. H. L. Parker pays tribute to Calvin's scholarly work.[5] The commentaries demonstrate the application of Calvin's inerrancy to exegesis.[6] Even Jacob Arminius praised Calvin's commentaries, saying that his work was "incomparable in the interpretation of the Scripture."[7] Arminius recommended Calvin's commentaries next to the Bible itself.

Calvin was always concerned about the question of canonicity (again reflecting Luther), and held to the perspicacity (clarity and wisdom) of Scripture. He saw the doctrine of salvation as clear in the Scripture even for the unconverted, but maintained that comprehending the full meaning of the text always relied on the collaboration of the Holy Spirit.[8] He advocated what he called "the natural" meaning of the text. Like Luther, Calvin abandoned the medieval hermeneutic, and pleaded, "Don't use fanciful allegories."[9]

Using Greek and Hebrew with ease, Calvin has given us commentaries on almost all of the New Testament books and many Old Testament books. He had a great love for the Old Testament and emphasized preaching Christ from it (as did Luther). Calvin saw Christ foreshadowed everywhere in the Old Testament, especially in the sacrifices, priesthood, and ritual of the tabernacle and temple. Of the Old Covenant people, Calvin wrote, "The manifestation of Christ was the goal of the race which God's ancient people were running."[10] The inscripturated Word and the preached Word give meaning to the signs which God has given. Commenting on 2 Timothy 2:15, Calvin remarks:

> This is a beautiful metaphor. Since we ought to be satisfied with the Word of God alone, what purpose is served by hearing sermons every day, or even the office of pastors? Has not every person the opportunity of reading the Bible? But Paul assigns to teachers the duty of dividing or cutting, as if a father in giving food to his children were dividing the bread and cutting it in small pieces.[11]

Thus Calvin observed that it was Philip, not an angel, who opened the Word to the Ethiopian on the Gaza road.

In four happy years in Strasbourg, Calvin served as chair of exegesis. Only reluctantly did he go back to Geneva to battle for the integrity of the Word of God. When he did return to Geneva in 1541, he was made head pastor and gave much to his people. From 1550–1559 he performed 270 weddings and 50 baptisms out of St. Pierre's Church. Still, in a one typical year during his second tenure in Geneva, he preached 286 sermons and gave 186 lectures. In his last years he ate a single meal daily and on some days would walk only in his room. "The feeble-looking Frenchman," as he was called, suffered from asthma, weak digestion, and numerous other complaints. Ironically, his wheezing made it easier for those who transcribed his discourses because his pace was necessarily slower. Of his preaching Beza said: "Every word weighed a pound."

---

1. Kenneth S. Kantzer, "Calvin and the Holy Scriptures," in *Inspiration and Interpretation,* ed. John F. Walvoord (Grand Rapids: Eerdmans, 1957), 145.

2. Ibid., 155.

3. Bernard Ramm, *The Witness of the Spirit: An Essay on the Contemporary Relevance of the Internal Witness of the Holy Spirit* (Grand Rapids: Eerdmans, 1959). Ramm wrestles with the origin of Calvin's doctrine, opining that it may derive from his personal study of Scripture along with his own experience in conversion. The Word of God is objective revelation in Scripture for Calvin, but because of the noetic effects of sin the ministry of the Holy Spirit is necessary and essential.

4. Kantzer, "Calvin and the Holy Scriptures," 140. Another Genevan professor of some years later argues the same case; see L. Gaussen, *Theopnuestia: The Inspiration of the Holy Scriptures* (Chicago: Moody, 1949).

5. T. H. L. Parker, *Calvin's Old Testament Commentaries* (Louisville: Westminster/John Knox, 1986); *Calvin's New Testament Commentaries* (London: T & T Clark, 1971). Parker shares Karl Barth's praise of Calvin's exegesis to Eduard Thurneysen: "Calvin is a cataract, a primeval forest, a demonic power, something directly down from Himalaya, absolutely Chinese, strange, mythological; I lack completely the means, the suction cups, even to assimilate this phenomenon, not to speak of presenting it

adequately. What I receive is only a thin little stream and what I can then give out again is only a yet thinner extract of this little stream. I could gladly and profitably set myself down and spend all the rest of my life just with Calvin" in *Calvin's Old Testament Commentaries,* frontispiece.

6. Kantzer, "Calvin and the Holy Scriptures," 140.
7. Timothy George, *Theology of the Reformers* (Nashville: Broadman, 1988), 187.
8. Kantzer, "Calvin and the Holy Scriptures," 152. That even the unregenerate can understand clear language and its meaning can be seen in E. D. Burton's great commentary on Galatians in the old ICC. Burton pointed out that the apostle Paul clearly believed in the substitutionary atonement and taught it in Galatians, but Burton himself held another view.
9. Ibid., 152.
10. Ronald S. Wallace, *Calvin's Doctrine of the Word and Sacrament* (Grand Rapids: Eerdmans, 1957), 59.
11. Ibid., 115.

5.3.3 CALVIN—IN HIS PULPIT

Let the preachers attempt nothing by their own brains; let them bring forth, as coming from God, all that they proclaim.

Therefore lest, like giants, we make war against God, let us learn to hearken to the ministers by whose mouth He teaches us.

The office of a good and faithful shepherd is not barely to expound the Scripture, but he must use earnestness and sharpness, to give force and virtue to the Word of God.

God sometimes connects Himself with His servants and sometimes separates Himself from them . . . He never resigns to them His own office. . . . When God separates Himself from His ministers, nothing remains in them.

—John Calvin

Scholarship in this century has tended to emphasize Calvin as pastor and preacher. His conviction about Scripture and his indefatigable labors in exegesis climaxed in the pulpit communication of Scripture. He exalted preaching because "this incomparable treasure set in our midst by the grace of God . . . the Word which is able to save the human soul."[1] Calvin spoke of "my beloved Holy Scriptures." As early as his stay in Paris he was exposed to powerful preaching by the evangelical **Gerard Roussel,** who drew "large crowds with his preaching during Lent 1533."[2] The sermons of Roussel commanded the attention of the nation, including the king.

During Calvin's four years in Strasbourg when he pastored the French church, he preached nearly every day and twice on Sundays. Until he died, the pulpit was the heart of his ministry. When summoned back to Geneva in 1541, he resumed his exposition on the next verse from the place where he had stopped. The pattern of preaching twice on Sundays and in alternate weeks at a daily evening service continued in Geneva. He preached extempore, that is, without a manuscript. (Calvin faulted the English for using manuscripts.) A paid stenographer recorded his sermons.

He moved consecutively through book after book. We possess about a thousand of his sermons, many of which have not been translated. Yet this signal preaching ministry was always conducted in the face of strong opposing forces. In Geneva, "He was insulted in the streets, and fireworks were put in his door, while lewd louts sang obscene songs in his window at night."[3]

He was encouraged by an influx of French immigrants who fled religious tensions in France. He appealed to them to come and help him, and the population of Geneva swelled to upwards of 19,000. The presence of so many émigrés complicated the already tense political situation for Calvin's implementation of his dream of a Christian commonwealth.

Building on his magisterial analysis of Calvin's commentaries, Parker has recast his brilliant *The Oracles of God: An Introduction to the Preaching of John Calvin* (1947) in the magnificent successor volume, *Calvin's Preaching* (1992). He shows how Calvin moved away from the "pick and choose" approach to scriptural truth by systematic verse by verse exposition.[4] Calvin's sermons then are more like the homilies of Augustine than the structured university sermons of Alan of Lille in the High Middle Ages. The price Calvin paid for this is frequently a lack of unity in the sermon. Division implies unity. Here, perhaps, the commentator has overpowered the preacher. Then too, there is a danger "to exalt the expounding above what is expounded."[5] Yet the strength of Calvin's content and his application tended to compensate.

Each of Calvin's sermons was about an hour long. He used language simply and directly, and had a remarkably retentive mind, but he was utterly destitute of imagination and humor.[6] He employed no introduction to the sermon, and would invariably launch into the text by saying, "We saw yesterday" or "We have seen this morning." His conclusion amounted to "Therefore we see now" or "We will have to save the rest until tomorrow."[7]

The context was critical for Calvin. He delighted in word studies but never quoted the Hebrew or Greek in the sermon. He insisted, "I do not willingly accept interpretations which can only be fitted to the words by twisting the words to them."[8] He used virtually no anecdotes and had little sense of climax or crescendo, and was weak in image and metaphor. From Sermon XVI in the 2 Samuel series we glean his viewpoint:

> When we have access to the preached Word, God speaks to us in a common and ordinary fashion. It is an illustration of his condescension. Hence the preaching of the Gospel is like a descent which God makes in order to seek us. We must not abuse this simplicity of the Word of God by disdaining it. Rather we must receive it all the more, recognizing that he indeed deigns to transfigure himself, so to speak, that we might approach him. He is not content with giving us his word, but adds baptism to it . . . the point is of course that since God has come down to us, we must go up to him.[9]

Many were irresistibly drawn to the teaching and preaching ministry of Calvin—John Knox from Scotland sat entranced with many other clergy and political figures in St. Pierre's. He said that Calvin's Geneva was "the most perfect school of Christ that ever was in the earth since the days of the Apostles."[10] This remarkable appeal may be found in the biblical richness and substance which Calvin set as a feast for his hearers. It was this content, carefully and skillfully applied, that drove the biblical truth into the heart of the hearers. The movement in the sermon was from the exegesis to the application to the exhortation, from the "then" of biblical revelation to the "now" of present daily life.[11] John Leith frames the issue succinctly:

> First of all, Calvin understood preaching to be the explication of Scripture. The words of Scripture are the source and content of preaching. As an expositor, Calvin brought to the task of preaching all the skills of a humanist scholar. As an interpreter, Calvin explicated the text, seeking its natural, its true, its scriptural meaning . . . Preaching is not only the explication of Scripture, it is also the application of Scripture. Just as Calvin explicated Scripture word by word, so he applied the Scripture sentence by sentence to the life and experience of the congregation.[12]

Calvin used words artfully. He used the expressions of the people. He read them well and knew how to get them to listen. He was well schooled in Quintilian and he quoted Cicero. But he insisted that this by itself is not enough. Calvin used an intensely personal conversational style he called *familiere*. He did not use long sentences. He employed question and answer and objection and reply as bridges in his communication.

Parker helpfully catalogues the course of his preaching.[13] The consistency and clarity of Calvin's expositions, along with the gravity and earnestness of his delivery, make him one of the sterling models of biblical preaching in the history of the Christian church. In what Dargan called "the mighty wave of reformatory preaching," John Calvin was the master preacher.

---

1. Ronald S. Wallace, *Calvin's Doctrine of the Word and Sacrament* (Grand Rapids: Eerdmans, 1957), 89.
2. Alister E. McGrath, *A Life of John Calvin* (Oxford: Blackwell, 1990), 63.
3. James Atkinson, *The Great Light: Luther and Reformation* (Grand Rapids: Eerdmans, 1968), 164.
4. T. H. L. Parker, *Calvin's Preaching* (Louisville: Westminster/John Knox, 1992), v.
5. Ibid., 20.
6. Leroy Nixon, *John Calvin: Expository Preaching* (Grand Rapids: Eerdmans, 1950), 31ff.
7. John Bishop, "John Calvin: Character in Preaching," *Preaching* (January–February 1993), 60–61.
8. Douglas F. Kelly, "Some Aspects of the Preaching of John Calvin," *Evangel* (autumn 1987), 11.
9. Ibid., 13.

10. Timothy George, *Theology of the Reformers* (Nashville: Broadman, 1988), 167.
11. As so classically articulated in John R. W. Stott, *Between Two Worlds: The Art of Preaching in the Twentieth Century* (Grand Rapids: Eerdmans, 1982). McGrath incisively demonstrates how Calvin addressed "real and specific situations—social, political, and economic—with all the risks that such precision entails" (*Life of John Calvin*, 220ff). He explains Calvin's appeal but also the vicious antagonisms he confronted.
12. John H. Leith in "Calvin's Doctrine of the Proclamation of the Word and Its Significance for Today in the Light of Recent Research," *Review and Expositor* 86 (winter 1989), 33, quoted in Harold T. Bryson, *Expository Preaching: The Art of Preaching Through a Book in the Bible* (Nashville: Broadman and Holman, 1995), 17.
13. Parker, *Calvin's Preaching*, 150ff.

5.4 HULDRYCH ZWINGLI—THE EXPOSITOR OF SCRIPTURE

No matter who a man may be, if he teaches you in according with his own thought and mind his teaching is false. But if he teaches you in accordance with the word of God, it is not he that teaches you, but God who teaches him. For as Paul says, who are we but ministers of Christ and dispensers or stewards of the mysteries of God? Again, I know for certain that God teaches me, because I have experienced the fact of it: and to prevent misunderstanding this is what I mean when I say that I know for certain that God teaches me. When I was younger, I gave myself overmuch to human teaching, like others of my day, and when about seven or eight years ago I undertook to devote myself entirely to the scriptures I was always prevented by philosophy and theology. But eventually I came to the point where led by scripture and the word of God I saw the need to set aside all these things and to learn the doctrine of God direct from his own word. Then I began to ask God for light and the scriptures became far clearer to me—even though I read nothing else—than if I had studied many commentators and expositors. Note that is always a sure sign of God's leading, for I could never have reached that point by my own feeble understanding. You may see then that my interpretation does not derive from the overestimation of myself, but the subjection.

—Huldrych Zwingli

The rallying cry in the Reformation from Luther on was to preach God, not man. Yet one lingering vestige of medieval preaching continued to be problematic. Both Calvin and Zwingli tended to moralizing preaching on occasion.[1] Moralism is a heavy dose of exhortation; it is attaching branches to an umbrella stand rather than seeing branches grafted into a living organism. It is preaching from the circumference of duty without sufficient attention to the dynamic center. The apostle Paul's practical admonitions followed his doctrinal delineation of who God is and what He has done (as in Romans and Ephesians). The thirteen hortatory "let us" references in the Epistle to the Hebrews always build upon doctrine. Much hortatory preaching tends to moralism. How growth in the sense of God-centered reality and discourse altered Zwingli's preaching is now before us.

1. Ulrich Gabler, *Huldrych Zwingli: His Life and Work* (Philadelphia: Fortress, 1986), 33, for the early preaching of Zwingli as consisting chiefly of "moral admonitions." Cf. T. H. L. Parker, *Calvin's Preaching* (Louisville: Westminster/John Knox, 1992), 20.

5.4.1 ZWINGLI'S PERSONAL PILGRIMAGE

But we, to whom God himself has spoken through his Son and through the Holy Spirit, are to seek these things not from those who are puffed up with human wisdom, and consequently corrupted what they received pure, but from the divine oracles.

For as often as by the use of clear passages of scripture they are driven to the point of having to say, I yield, straightway they talk about "the Spirit" and deny scripture . . . As if indeed the heavenly Spirit were ignorant of the senses of scripture which is written under his guidance or were anywhere inconsistent with himself.

The word of God is so sure and strong that if God wills all things are done the moment that he speaks his word. For it is so living and powerful that . . . things both rational and irrational are fashioned and despatched and constrained in conformity with its purpose.

—Huldrych Zwingli

Although he was not of the stature of Luther and Calvin, **Huldrych Zwingli** (1484–1531) was the leader of the Swiss German Reformation and a pivotal figure in the unfolding drama we call the Protestant Reformation. He was born the oldest of nine children to a rural chief magistrate and his wife in the Toggenburg Valley in the Swiss Confederation. He studied at the University of Vienna and learned his Aristotelian texts at the University of Basel, where he took his M.A. His first pastorate was in Glarus (1510–1516), where he wrote a political tractate against alliance with the French in the form of a poetic fable about an ox. He felt unsettled about his early more moralistic preaching, and began to move from absorption in the commentaries themselves to the text of Scripture. In 1516 he was one of the first to get the new Greek text from his friend Erasmus. The influence of the biblical text and Augustine's writings on the Fourth Gospel moved him to begin preaching Christ and the gospel.

Zwingli's next pastorate was in Einsiedeln (1516–1518), which was also the site of "an image of the Black Virgin" and a place to which many pilgrims came. As Potter reports, "Many visitors came home to report that the preacher was saying new things and introducing passages from the Bible, and particularly of the New Testament, into his discourses . . . he made a passionate appeal for a direct approach to God the Father through God the Son."[1]

Zwingli was more Erasmian than any of the other Reformers. His personal library of some 350 volumes contained many classics and patristic works. When the position of people's priest opened at the Great Minster in Zurich in 1518,

Zwingli was at the apex of his power, and desirable in the political complexity of the time because of his hostility to France. One impediment loomed, and it was that he had yielded to the advances of a common prostitute. Gabler speaks of the resolution of this problem: "In an unreservedly candid letter to Henrich Utinger, dated December 5, 1518, Zwingli confessed to the errors of youth, stressed the secrecy of his actions, spoke of his repentance and vowed never again to touch a woman."[2]

Thus at age thirty-five, on January 1, 1519, he began his preaching ministry in the famous collegiate church in Zurich, a church that dated back to the eighth century. Zwingli announced that on the following Sunday he would start an extended series of expositions from Matthew's gospel, the pattern throughout his ministry in Zurich.

Potter asserts, "Even more than Luther, Zwingli valued preaching very highly and was indefatigable in the pulpit."[3] He practiced and urged the simple exposition of Scripture in the pulpit. About this time, Zwingli experienced a spiritual crisis in which, influenced by Lutheranism, he turned from Erasmian humanism to a new commitment to the Bible as "the direct Word of God." It is possible that nearly dying of the plague in 1519, when two thousand of Zurich's seven thousand people died, may have motivated his about-face. Or perhaps it was his own revitalized experience in the Word. Bullinger, his successor, related that Zwingli had memorized the entire Greek New Testament.

Throughout these years Zwingli also served as a chaplain in the Swiss army, which was valued everywhere for its mercenaries. (It survives to this day as the Swiss Guard in the Vatican.) He both ministered to the troops and fought in military engagement himself.

Described as a "cheerful, sanguine, short-sighted priest," Zwingli found his stride as a preacher who was "fast becoming Scripture-dominated"[4] and who preached Christ and the cross as the essence of the gospel. He loved to speak of "the reborn Christ" in every believer. Needless to say, he was on a collision course with Rome. His first rift with Rome came over the issue of fasting during Lent and indulgences. Even though a cardinal's hat was dangled before him, he soon became an ardent Reformer. Under the influence of his new view of Scripture and its priority, Zwingli renounced his papal pension, ate sausages during Lent,[5] and got married. He argued in *The Clarity and Certainty of the Bible* for the need of positive scriptural evidence for church practice, and hence he challenged images, prayers to the saints, the mass as performed, purgatory, and distinctive clergy dress.

No longer were popes or councils to steer the church—it must be Christ and the Bible alone. In his Sixty-seven Articles of 1523 he advances the convictions *sola Scriptura, sola Christus.* He did not question the canon, and held that "the very words directly inspired by the Holy Spirit were those for them to read."[6]

He engaged in many public disputations at this time and urged that only the gospel be preached. The Zurich council ordered that all preachers were to follow Zwingli's example. Monasteries and nunneries were emptying. He reorganized the minster and set up a Latin school in order to institutionalize sound exegesis. As Professor Aland concludes: "The means by which the Reformation took hold among the populace was the reading and exposition of the Bible—the 'reading' or the Prophezei."[7]

The Marburg Colloquy in 1529 was the opportunity for Luther and Zwingli to unite in common cause. Disagreement over the Lord's Supper made the desired convergence impossible. Philip of Hesse had catalyzed the conference, but Luther came "overconfident and abusive" and Zwingli did not get the recognition he craved.[8] Luther quickly categorized Zwingli as being like Karlstadt and the "spiritualists." Throughout their discussions Luther kept calling him "Zwingel" and angrily denounced him and his "rabble." He described Zwingli as a heathen,[9] even though Zwingli's good friend and Luther's cohort Melancthon seemed to indicate that Augustine favored Zwingli's position.[10] Zwingli understood the phrase "this is my body" to mean "this *signifies* my body." That was unacceptable to Luther, whose doctrine of consubstantiation is a curious stopoff on the way from transubstantiation. Luther felt the commemorative view of the Supper involved a denial of the full deity of Christ and the Trinity. This was the death knell of any hope for unity. Luther summed up his contentions with Zwingli by saying: "You have a different spirit than we."

Zwingli was an effective shepherd of souls, and spoke of the pastoral office as that of shepherd or watchman. He wrote copiously on many subjects theological and practical, including a splendid analysis of pastoral work in 1525 titled *The Shepherd*. He detested what he called "noisy hymns" in the worship service.

Serfdom was a widespread grievance that led to the great Peasants' War in 1525. According to the scholar Peter Blickle, the impact of Zwingli's ministry may be seen in the conflict. Many Roman Catholic thinkers have blamed Luther for this tragic uprising which led to the slaughter of more than one hundred thousand peasants. In his general aversion to chaos of any kind, Luther took the side of the nobility.

But Blickle argues that Zwingli and other Reformers must bear some responsibility for the war. Zwingli's preaching of the Word of God presented a mandate for freedom. Blickle points out, "What united the peasants and the townspeople was the Gospel."[11] Some of the key leaders in the movement were disciples of Zwingli. Indeed, Zwingli had categorically stated, "The most peaceful and God-fearing regime will be found where the Word of God is preached most purely."[12] The Revolution of 1525 must then be seen as part of the unfolding of the Reformation and its message. The desire for freedom is the fruit of the gospel. Serfdom was abolished in Zurich and Bern, and the free election of pastors became the practice.

In the Second Kappel War between Catholics and Protestants, Zwingli was killed on the battlefield on October 11, 1531. The issue in the conflict for Zwingli was "the free preaching of the word of God."

Even at this time, Calvin was experiencing his conversion in Paris and Orleans and would soon inherit the leadership of the Swiss French Reformation.

---

1. G. R. Potter, *Zwingli* (Cambridge, Mass.: Cambridge University Press, 1976), 42. A rewardingly rich study.

2. Ulrich Gabler, *Huldrych Zwingli: His Life and Work* (Philadelphia: Fortress, 1986), 44.

3. Potter, *Zwingli,* 61.

4. Ibid., 62.

5. Kurt Aland, *A History of Christianity* (Philadelphia: Fortress, 1986), 2:167.

6. Potter, *Zwingli,* 64.

7. Aland, *A History of Christianity,* 171.

8. Potter, *Zwingli,* 329.

9. E. J. Furcha and H. Wayne Pipkin, eds., *Prophet, Pastor, Protestant: The Work of Huldrych Zwingli after Five Hundred Years* (Allison Park, Pa.: Pickwick, 1984), 77ff.

10. W. P. Stephens, *The Theology of Huldrych Zwingli* (Oxford: Clarendon, 1986), 21n.

11. Peter Blickle, *The Revolution of 1525: The German Peasants' War from a New Perspective* (Baltimore: Johns Hopkins University Press, 1977), 115.

12. Ibid., 159.

5.4.2 ZWINGLI'S PROWESS IN PREACHING

This is the seed I have sown. Matthew, Luke, Paul and Peter have watered it, and God has given it splendid increase, but this I will not trumpet forth, lest I seem to be canvassing my own glory and not Christ's.

Whithersoever, then, prophets or preachers of the word are sent, it is a sign of God's grace that he wishes to manifest the knowledge of himself to his elect; and where they are denied, it is a sign of impending wrath.

The work of prophecy or preaching I believe to be most holy, so that above any other duty it is in the highest degree necessary. For in speaking canonically or regularly we see that among all nations the outward preaching of apostles and evangelists or bishops has preceded faith, which we nevertheless say is received by the Spirit alone. For alas! we see very many who hear the outward preaching of the gospel, but believe not, because a dearth of the Spirit has occurred.

—Huldrych Zwingli

The vacuum of vapid moralism in the early preaching of Zwingli and the Reformers was soon filled with the wonder of Scripture and an expansive sense of the greatness and majesty of a holy and merciful God. Zwingli preached from the Gospels with the Greek text of the New Testament before him. One listener in Zurich named Thomas Platter was so euphoric in hearing the bracing exposition of the text that he felt he was "being pulled by the hair on his head." Zwingli's determination was clear from the outset:

The life of Christ has been too long hidden from the people. I shall preach upon the whole of Matthew's gospel, chapter by chapter, according to the inspiration of the Holy Ghost, without human commentaries, drawing solely from the fountain of Scripture, according to its depths, comparing one passage with another and seeking for understanding by constant and earnest prayer. It is to God's glory, to the praise of His holy Son, to the real salvation of souls, and to their edification in the true faith that I shall consecrate my ministry.[1]

Typical of the Reformers, Zwingli had a great love for the Old Testament. Both Zwingli and Calvin would abandon the prescribed pericope texts in favor of book exposition *lectio continua*. Zwingli preached more from the Old Testament than from the New. He preached 134 sermons on the Book of Deuteronomy alone. Professor Reu's deft analysis of the Reformers' use of the Old Testament shows the refreshing balance and soundness of their approach.[2] God's people in all times need the older and larger Testament as well as the New.

"Preaching is the sign of the true pastor" Zwingli maintained, and a veritable epidemic of evangelical and biblical preaching followed his example.[3] This was so because he had submitted to "the tyranny of the Book."

Unfortunately, we do not possess many of Zwingli's sermons, because they were delivered extempore and no stenographers took them down. Occasionally he would transcribe a sermon from memory, but these tended to be unduly long. He filled himself with the truth through careful preparation and prayer and then burst into the pulpit.

His exegetical works give us the substance of his preaching,[4] and a careful and thorough inventory of his scriptural citations fully discloses his real biblicality.[5] Close examination of his pulpit ministry during the critical year 1522 shows how adroitly he used the biblical text to relevantly address the controversial questions and practical issues of the time.[6]

Zwingli's sermons would begin with the reading of the biblical text, then a wrestling with its meaning with adaptation to the hearers and their situation. He used homely illustrations and borrowed from the classics. He loved farm illustrations we might consider crude, and made artful use of humor as a bridge to reach his audience. He preached with little gesture in an unadorned style. His voice was on the weak side. When he preached in Strasbourg many complained they could not hear him. He had none of the bombast of Luther, nor did he have the extraordinary brilliance of Calvin, but he preached the Word with power for the changing of human hearts.

Zwingli never divided the text for purposes of exposition as in the homilies that were common among the Reformers. James McGraw points out the vulnerability of this approach:

> The principal criticism of Zwingli's sermons is that they are somewhat formless in their composition. The scriptural examples are unnecessarily numerous, and in them there are many exegeses of passages which are not directly related to the main theme. In spite of these homiletical weaknesses, there is a fine power and freedom in his development of the subject.[7]

This is only to say that high-density exegesis without sufficient attention to form and communication can be detrimental. It is most striking, however, that as different as the three great continental Reformers were, they shared an avid dedication to biblical exposition. Zwingli, like his compatriots, saw grave danger in elevating tradition over Scripture or being too subjectivistic and individualistic in interpretation. He argued for a kind of *analogia fidei* in the expression of his pastoral concern:

> How dare you introduce innovations into the church simply on your own authority and without consulting the church? I speak only of those churches in which the word of God is publicly and faithfully preached. For if every blockhead who had a novel or strange opinion were allowed to gather a sect around him, divisions and sects would become so numerous that the Christian body which we now build up with such difficulty would be broken to pieces in every individual congregation. Therefore no innovations ought to be made except with the common consent of the church and not merely of a single person. For the judgment of scripture is not mine or yours, but the church's.[8]

1. Quoted in John Bishop, "Ulrich Swingli: the Swiss Reformer," *Preaching* (January–February 1994), 61.
2. M. Reu, *Homiletics* (Grand Rapids: Baker, 1924), 279ff.
3. G. R. Potter, *Zwingli* (Cambridge, Mass.: Cambridge University Press, 1976), 135.
4. Ulrich Gabler, *Huldrych Zwingli: His Life and Work* (Philadelphia: Fortress, 1986), 161.
5. E. J. Furcha and H. Wayne Pipkin, eds., *Prophet, Pastor, Protestant: The Work of Huldrych Zwingli after 500 Years* (Allison Park, Pa.: Pickwick, 1984), 57–58.
6. Ibid., 59–61.
7. Bishop, "Ulrich Swingli," 61.
8. W. P. Stephens, *The Theology of Huldrych Zwingli* (Oxford: Clarendon, 1986), 266.

5.5 BIBLICAL PREACHING AMONG THE ENGLISH REFORMERS

> The visible Church of Christ is a congregation of faithful men, in which the pure Word of God is preached, and the Sacraments be duly ministered according to Christ's ordinance.
> —Nineteenth Article of the Thirty-nine Articles

> By the preaching of God's Word the glory of God is enlarged, faith is nourished, and charity increased. By it the ignorant is instructed, the negligent exhorted and incited, the stubborn rebuked, the weak conscience comforted . . . by preaching also due obedience to Christian princes and magistrates is planted in the hearts of subjects.
> —Archbishop Edmund Grindal

The Reformation in England is such an integral part of this narrative, and yet it baffles us with its complicated and intricate turns. Here we see almost without parallel how preaching shaped the life of a nation.

Wales had furnished England with the ruling house of the Tudors, out of which came **Henry VII,** a shrewd and irenic statesman. In 1509, his ambitious son **Henry VIII** ascended the throne. Henry's divorce was the precipitating factor of the English Reformation but it was not the cause. The papacy had lost the respect of Christendom as a whole but nowhere more obviously than in England.[1] Much antipapal feeling and deep anticlericalism were felt in England, where by the sixteenth century there was clearly "long-standing aloofness to Rome."[2] Lollardism (the preaching movement initiated by John Wycliffe, cf. 5.1.1) had never really died on the island nation.

Thus while there was much political machination on the part of Henry VIII and his early cohort Cardinal **Thomas Wolsey,**[3] as well as his powerful secretary, **Thomas Cromwell,** we sense the genuine spiritual aspirations of Cranmer, Latimer, and Ridley. Henry wanted a Roman Catholic Church, but without the authority of the pope to challenge him. Social and economic variables must be also be factored in, as well as a huge dollop of nationalism.

Cranmer, Hooker, and Ridley were Wycliffite in their sympathies and were subsequently exposed to Luther's writings. Preaching was at low ebb in the kingdom, but as the spiritual movement quickened so did theological reconstruction and the call for biblical preaching. By 1536 Archbishop Cranmer successfully petitioned for a Bible in the vernacular. Thus during all of the intrigue of the king's six marriages, significant reformatory progress was being made. When Henry died in 1547, it was Cranmer he called to his deathbed.

Under the impetus of Cranmer and company, we see the Protestant movement flourishing during the reign of young **Edward VI** (1547–1553). Cranmer preached Edward's coronation sermon, in which he acclaimed the boy as "a new Josiah who was to reform the worship of God, destroy idolatry, banish the bishop of Rome, and remove images."[4] Many refugees from the Continent assisted Cranmer in publishing and preaching ventures which laid firm foundations for Protestantism.

But the reaction under **Queen Mary** (1553–1558) saw the reimposition of all the medieval ceremonies and rites in detail. The Protestant bishops were imprisoned and martyred. Some four hundred gave their lives for Christ at this time.

Upon Mary's death her half-sister **Elizabeth I** (1558–1603) came to the throne. Elizabeth had lived all her life "under the shadow of the block," and while she was not personally devout, she was politically shrewd. She perceived that England would increasingly become Protestant. Out of the conflict between the Romanists on the one hand—whom Elizabeth detested—and the Puritans on the other hand—who always displeased her—the Church of England emerged. The "Anglican Compromise"[5] in a sense did not please anyone fully, but it was a *modus vivendi* in which all sides conceded the primacy of preaching. After all, preaching was "the tap-root" of the Reformation. Not only were crosses, images, and altars removed from St. Paul's and other London churches, but biblical preaching began to thrive in England once again. [6]

---

1. L. Elliott-Binns, *The Reformation in England* (London: Duckworth, 1937), 16.

2. James Atkinson, *The Great Light: Luther and the Reformation* (Grand Rapids: Eerdmans, 1968), 194.

3. See the invaluable two volumes on Wolsey by Charles W. Ferguson, *Naked to Mine Enemies* (New York: Little, Brown 1958).

4. Elliott-Binns, *The Reformation in England*, 97.

5. Atkinson, *The Great Light*, 258.

6. My favorite treatment of Elizabeth and her times is Elizabeth Jenkins, *Elizabeth the Great* (New York: Coward-McCann, 1958). The queen did not require thirteen thousand learned preachers for England but "honest, sober and wise men and such as can read the Scriptures and the Homilies well unto the people" (289).

5.5.1 THOMAS BILNEY, THE PRELUDE

Thomas Bilney (1495–1531) is significant to the Protestant preaching that followed him. Born near Norwich, he studied at Trinity Hall, Cambridge, and came under the influence of Luther's writings and was considered a disciple of Erasmus. Tormented by lack of the assurance of salvation, he found deliverance in 1 Timothy 1:15 out of the Greek New Testament. Justification by faith alone became his song. He preached with growing popularity and often attacked Romish practice. Imprisoned in the Tower by Wolsey in 1526, he was released to preach again. God used Bilney to bring Hugh Latimer to Christ at Cambridge. Bilney often preached to great crowds in the open fields. He was burned at the stake in the Lollards' Pit near his hometown of Norwich, saying to Dr. Warner, who accompanied him, "Feed your flock, so that when the Lord cometh he may find you so doing."[1]

1. F. R. Webber, *A History of Preaching in Britain and America* (Milwaukee: Northwestern, 1952), 1:176–79.

5.5.2 JOHN ROGERS, THE PIONEER

John Rogers, otherwise known as Thomas Matthew from Matthew's Bible (1500–1555), was born near Birmingham and took his degree from Cambridge. He served Holy Trinity Church in London before becoming chaplain to the Merchant Adventurers in Antwerp. There he met William Tyndale and gave his life to Christ. Upon the arrest of Tyndale in 1535, Rogers finished Tyndale's translation under the pseudonym of Thomas Matthew.[1] He served a congregation in Wittenberg for eleven years and returned to England during the reign of Edward VI but got in trouble because of his vehement preaching in Mary's years. He was the first to be martyred under Mary. He served as prebendary (salaried preacher) at St. Paul's, and was burned at the stake in February of 1555.

Although we do not possess any of Rogers' sermons, we understand from his contemporaries something of the quality of his biblical and controversial preaching. His wife and children urged him to remain courageous as he walked to the place of execution. The French ambassador who witnessed the martyrdom wondered about the man because he went to his death as one might go to his or her wedding.[2]

---

1. David Daniell, *William Tyndale: A Biography* (New Haven, Conn.: Yale University Press, 1995). This extraordinary new work underscores the need for the Scriptures in England.
2. E. C. Dargan, *A History of Preaching* (New York: Hodder and Stoughton, 1905), 1:484–86.

5.5.3 THOMAS CRANMER, THE PRIME MOVER

The doctrinal heavyweight in the English Reformation was **Thomas Cranmer** (1489–1556), who was born near Nottingham and matriculated at Cambridge. After his ordination, he was appointed university preacher and a teaching fellow. He traveled to Germany and there married the niece of Osiander, the German reformer. Always influenced by Lutheran thinking, Cranmer favored continental connections for the English Reformation. He recommended that Henry VIII seek the counsel of university faculties rather than the pope in his marital dilemmas and as a result was appointed archbishop of Canterbury in 1532.[1] He was forthright in his opposition to Rome, on one occasion preaching for two hours out-of-doors at Paul's Cross with a bad cold and cough. He called the pope the Antichrist, and anathematized images, adoration of the saints, purgatory, and monasteries.[2]

In 1547, Cranmer issued *The Book of Homilies,* consisting of a series of topical homilies. Of these he authored several himself, including the first, titled "A Faithful Exhortation to the Reading and Knowledge of Holy Scripture." Ultimately there were two such volumes.[3] Illustrations and classical allusions abounded in them. Cranmer was also responsible for "The Order of Communion in English" and the Prayer Books of 1549 and 1552. Both show his "unrivaled skill in composing collects."[4] The 1552 volume known as *The Book of Common Prayer* was written with the collaboration of Bucer and Peter Martyr, and was more acceptable to the Reformation party.[5] He also authored the Forty-two Articles (later to become the Thirty-nine Articles). Commendably, he promoted the publication and reading of the Bible by the laity.

Bromiley has shown the Reformation orthodoxy of Cranmer's views, demonstrated in his writing and preaching.[6] During the Marian restoration, Cranmer stood adamantly against the reinstitution of the Mass. He did not agree with Luther on the Lord's Supper, but they were in accord on justification by faith alone. He conducted the funeral of the deceased young king Edward VI in Westminster Abbey according to the Reformed ritual.[7] Meanwhile, Mary celebrated a requiem for her brother in the Tower. The following month, Cranmer and Ridley stood against eleven Romanists at Oxford in a debate over eucharistic doctrine. They were afterward remanded to custody. Although he recanted, Cranmer publicly renounced his recantation and was martyred in March of 1556. His theology and leadership were critically formative in the English Reformation, even if he disappointed at times with inconsistent leadership.

1. Jasper Ridley, *Thomas Cranmer* (Oxford: Clarendon, 1962), 50ff.
2. Ibid., 98.
3. J. W. Blench, *Preaching in England in the Late Fifteenth and Sixteenth Centuries* (New York: Barnes and Noble, 1964), 87.
4. L. Elliott-Binns, *The Reformation in England* (London: Duckworth, 1937), 105.
5. Samuel Leuenberger, *Archbishop Cranmer's Immortal Bequest* (Grand Rapids: Eerdmans, 1990). The Swiss scholar argues that *The Book of Common Prayer* of 1552 is a model of soundness on the Scriptures and is indeed an evangelistic and revivalistic liturgy. He contrasts it with the Oxford Group's later abandonment of *sola Scriptura.*
6. G. W. Bromiley, *Thomas Cranmer Theologian* (New York: Oxford University Press, 1956).
7. Elliott-Binns, *The Reformation in England,* 120.

5.5.4   HUGH LATIMER: THE PREACHER'S PREACHER

Take away preaching and take away salvation . . . Preaching is the thing the devil hath wrestled most against . . . This office of preaching is the only ordinary way that God hath appointed to save us all.

—Hugh Latimer

Born in Leicestershire and receiving his B.D. from Cambridge, **Hugh Latimer** (1485–1555) was the most able all-round preacher of this time. After defending his dissertation, which was a full-press assault against Melancthon's teachings, Latimer was visited by Thomas Bilney, who led him to see Luther's doctrine of justification and brought him to conversion. As Latimer describes it:

Master Bilney, or rather Saint Bilney, that suffered death for God's word sake—the same Bilney was the instrument whereby God called me to knowledge; for I may thank him, next to God, for that knowledge I have in the Word of God. For I was as obstinate a papist as any was in England . . . he came to me afterwards in my study and desired me to hear his confession. I did so; and to say the truth, by his confession I learned more than before in many years. So that from that time forward I began to smell the Word of God and forsook the school doctors and such fooleries.[1]

His preaching began to draw quite a following, and he was successively expert on canon law, chaplain to the queen, and bishop of Worcester. His faithful servant, Augustine Bernher, recorded many of his sermons, and these have been preserved for us. Latimer often preached before King Henry and on one reported occasion began augustly: "Latimer, Latimer, King Henry is listening." Then after a pregnant pause he continued: "Latimer, Latimer, Almighty God is listening!" Then he preached boldly against marital infidelity. He was fearless but exceedingly shrewd and adaptive to the audience and the immediate situation.

Latimer has been called the father of English preaching. His effectiveness grew out of his scriptural soundness combined with a likableness and an encouraging manner that endeared him to his listeners. Children even followed him through the streets.[2] Organization of discourse was not his forte, but he displayed good variety. On occasion he would use visual aids. Blench lauds him as "the greatest pulpit exponent of the colloquial style in the century."[3] He used humorous stories, proverbs, and exempla.

Latimer was relentless in his condemnation of abuses and superstitions in the church. He referred to "strawberry prelates" who preached only seasonally. In and out of favor, he began to preach again with the accession of Edward. His legendary Sermon on the Plough was especially timely. Here he spoke of the Devil as the most diligent preacher in England, always at his plough. His series of sermons on The Card are creative and compelling. Since the people played so many card games at Christmas, he wanted to show them how to play with Christ's cards and come out winners.[4] He tended to implement long introductions, running applications, and brief, direct conclusions. John Brown says of him, "Other preachers have excelled him in rhetoric, refinement and accuracy; but few have proved his equals in broad, forceful influence over all classes of people, and his sermons remain prose classics to this day."[5]

When he preached at St. Margaret's, Westminster, the crowds were so great that they broke the benches. He was often heard in St. Paul's Cross, "the most celebrated pulpit in England." In his final imprisonment, Latimer read his New Testament through seven times. When he and Ridley were burned at the stake on October 16, 1555, he made his famous statement and testament: "Be of good comfort, master Ridley, and play the man. We shall this day light such a candle by God's grace in England, as I trust shall never be put out."[6]

---

1. E. C. Dargan, *A History of Preaching* (New York: Hodder and Stoughton, 1905), 1:488.
2. Jay E. Adams, *Sermon Analysis* (Denver: Accent, 1986), 97. A fine workbook with model sermons.
3. J. W. Blench, *Preaching in England in the Late Fifteenth and Sixteenth Centuries* (New York: Barnes and Noble, 1964), 142.
4. T. Harwood Pattison, *The History of Christian Preaching* (Philadelphia: American Baptist Publication Society, 1903), 152.
5. F. R. Webber, *A History of Preaching in Britain and America* (Milwaukee: Northwestern, 1952), 1:167.
6. For a satisfying biography of Latimer, see Harold S. Darby, *Hugh Latimer* (London: Epworth, 1953).

5.5.5   NICHOLAS RIDLEY, THE PEDAGOGUE

The man who died beside Latimer was his colleague and friend **Nicholas Ridley** (1500–1555). From Northumbria, Ridley was trained at Cambridge, often the center of the English Reformation. Cambridge may have produced Cranmer, Latimer, and Ridley, but they burned at Oxford.[1]

Ridley was an effective preacher, perhaps second only to Latimer, but he was preeminently a theologian and teacher. He studied at both the Sorbonne and at Louvain. In 1533 he became senior proctor and university chaplain at Cambridge.[2] Eventually he aspired to master of Pembroke Hall, then chaplain to the king, bishop of Rochester, and ultimately bishop of London. His was the sermon at St. Paul's Cross announcing the death of the young Edward VI. It was in this sermon that Ridley declared both Mary and Elizabeth illegitimate, in the hope of the succession of Lady Jane Gray and the Protestant succession.[3]

He had once preached such a forceful sermon before young Edward VI about the poor of London that a subsequent interview with the king led to the establishment of three new London hospitals.[4] Ridley had significant influence on Cranmer and *The Book of Common Prayer* and was beyond doubt the intellectual genius of Reformation theology in England. He spent long hours memorizing the New Testament Epistles as he walked his "famous orchard walk" at his college.[5] A leading ecclesiastic observed, "Latimer leaneth to Cranmer, Cranmer leaneth to Ridley, and Ridley to the singularity of his own wit." John Foxe of martyrs' fame described Ridley's preaching:

> Every holiday and Sunday he preached in some place or other, unless hindered by weighty business. The people resorted to his sermons, swarming about him like bees, and coveting the sweet flowers and wholesome juice of the fruitful doctrine which he did not only preach, but showed the same by his life.[6]

Such was a tribute and testimony every preacher might cherish.[7]

---

1. L. Elliott-Binns, *The Reformation in England* (London: Duckworth, 1937), 47.
2. F. R. Webber, *A History of Preaching in Britain and America* (Milwaukee: Northwestern, 1952), 1:183.
3. J. W. Blench, *Preaching in England in the Late Fifteenth and Sixteenth Centuries* (New York: Barnes and Noble, 1964), 277.
4. E. C. Dargan, *A History of Preaching* (New York: Hodder and Stoughton, 1905), 1:495.
5. Elliott-Binns, *The Reformation in England,* 47.
6. Dargan, *A History of Preaching,* 495ff.
7. An excellent biographical survey is J. G. Ridley's, *Nicholas Ridley: A Biography* (London: Longmans, Green, 1957).

5.5.6 JOHN BRADFORD, THE PROCLAIMER

It was **John Bradford** (1510–1555) who first uttered the immortal words when seeing someone being led off to execution, "There but for the grace of God goes John Bradford." Reared in Manchester, he served with the British forces in France. Later in London he came under deep conviction through the preaching of Hugh Latimer. While an older student at Cambridge, he wrestled with the call to preach. Among the many foreign scholars at Cambridge at this time was Martin Bucer, the Reformation leader in Strasbourg. He urged Bradford to enter the ministry because he saw his preaching gifts. Bucer told him, "If you don't have fine manchet bread, then give the people barley bread."[1] Ridley appointed Bradford a prebendary at St. Paul's in London, and he also served as one of six traveling preachers during the reign of Edward VI who gave themselves to evangelistic labor throughout the kingdom.

A contemporary description of Bradford's preaching gives the following sketch:

> A master of speech, his eloquence native, masculine, modest, in one word, heavenly, for if you mark him he favors and breathes nothing but heaven; yea, he sparkles, thunders, lightens; pierces the soft, breaks only the stony heart.[2]

Two volumes of his sermons have been preserved, including stellar efforts on "The Lord's Supper," with three careful divisions, and "Repentance," likewise deftly divided into three parts. In a style influenced by Melancthon and Erasmus,[3] Bradford was highly doctrinal in his preaching. He made artful use of humor, alliteration, word lists, and agricultural metaphors.[4] His messages abounded with scriptural quotation and allusion. Ridley said of him, "He was a man by whom God hath and doth work wonders in setting forth his word."[5]

Bradford had a tremendous passion to preach even during his long imprisonment in the Tower. He was so trustworthy that he was occasionally permitted to leave the Tower to perform good deeds. He was burned at the stake in Smithfield Market in 1555 in the Marian persecution (cf. 5.5). At these martyrdoms, formal sermons were preached by direction of the Crown.

John Brown said of Bradford:

> A man of bold and daring energy who had great power of command over an audience. Filled with the Spirit of God and with a passionate love for Christ and the souls of men, wherever he was announced to preach the people crowded around him, their beating hearts responding to his burning words.[6]

---

1. E. C. Dargan, *A History of Preaching* (New York: Hodder and Stoughton, 1905), 1:499.
2. T. Harwood Pattison, *The History of Christian Preaching* (Philadelphia: American Baptist Publication Society, 1903), 148.
3. While Melancthon, Luther's systematician, did not feel called to preach, he pressed for biblical preaching in his famous *Loci communes*. N.B. Joseph Stump, *A Life of Philip Melancthon* (Reading: Pilger, 1897).
4. J. W. Blench, *Preaching in England in the Late Fifteenth and Sixteenth Centuries* (New York: Barnes and Noble, 1964), 155.
5. Dargan, *A History of Preaching,* 502.
6. F. R. Webber, *A History of Preaching in Britain and America* (Milwaukee: Northwestern, 1952), 1:192.

5.5.7 JOHN HOOPER, THE PURITAN

Different in many ways but one with the illustrious champions of the Reformation in England is **John Hooper** (1495–1555), who came from comfortable circumstances in Somersetshire and took his degree at Oxford in 1519. He apparently became a Cistercian monk. When his abbey was closed he went to London. Through the influence of the writings of Zwingli and Bullinger, Hooper began to study the Pauline Epistles and became committed to the Reformation position. He visited Strasbourg, Basel, and Geneva.[1] He came back to England tilted not only toward the Reformation view but toward an even more drastic position on vestments, foreshadowing the convictions of those who would be called Puritans. He quickly became spokesman for the Reformers on the right, and had running encounters with the more conciliatory Cranmer and Ridley.

Hooper's preaching was somewhat gruff and austere, but he preached with marked effect. He gained considerable favor when he presented a series of expositions on the Book of Jonah before young King Edward VI. Although he was embroiled in controversy, he was consecrated as bishop of Gloucester in 1550. Hooper was proactive in his approach to every aspect of the life of the diocese. His wife complained to Bullinger that her husband "preached four or at least three times every day and I am afraid lest these over-abundant exertions should cause a premature decay."[2]

At times his theological burdens intruded unnaturally into his exposition. He used extensive Scripture quotation, very short sentences, and few illustrations. We see in Hooper the embryonic development of what would increasingly be the Puritan sermon form with two main sections: doctrine and its uses.

Hooper was imprisoned in 1553 and brought to trial two years later. He was burned at the stake in front of the cathedral in Gloucester. The execution was handled clumsily and he suffered unspeakably.

---

1. F. R. Webber, *A History of Preaching in Britain and America* (Milwaukee: Northwestern, 1952), 1:179.
2. E. C. Dargan, *A History of Preaching* (New York: Hodder and Stoughton, 1905), 1:497.

5.5.8 MILES COVERDALE, THE PUBLISHER

A significant contribution to the cause of the English Reformation was made by **Miles Coverdale** (1488–1568). The Coverdale Bible was well known and widely disseminated, furthering the cause of biblical preaching by putting the Scriptures in the language of the people.

Coverdale came from Yorkshire and graduated from Cambridge, becoming first an Augustinian friar. He traveled as an itinerant and then surfaced in 1535 with his translation of the first complete Bible in English.[1] He also worked on the Great Bible while he was in Paris in 1538, and he edited Cranmer's Bible in 1540. Coverdale served as a Lutheran pastor in Germany, returning to England in 1551 to become chaplain to the king. In 1551 he was appointed bishop of Exeter but was imprisoned by the queen. The king of Denmark persuaded the queen to release Coverdale, who traveled to Denmark and later Germany.[2] He did return to England in the Elizabethan settlement but turned down bishoprics because of his growing Puritan convictions. Coverdale was pastor of St. Magnus Martyr near London Bridge until his seventy-eighth year.[3] Regarded as a strong biblical preacher, for Coverdale conviction always took precedence over ecclesiastical preferment.

---

1. F. R. Webber, *A History of Preaching in Britain and America* (Milwaukee: Northwestern, 1952), 1:168.
2. James Atkinson, *The Great Light: Luther and the Reformation* (Grand Rapids: Eerdmans, 1968), 224n.
3. Webber, *A History of Preaching,* 1:169. Among the memorable translations is Coverdale's rendition of Genesis 39:2, "And the Lorde was with Joseph in so moch that he became a luckye man" or Isaiah 24:9, "The beer shall be bitter."

5.5.9 MATTHEW PARKER, THE PRELATE

With the coronation of Elizabeth I in 1558, the spiritual and religious situation in England was mottled. Because of the increased circulation of the Bible and *The Book of Common Prayer,* there was a vast increase of scriptural knowledge. Yet there was confusion and consternation in the churches. The nation teetered on the brink of civil war; the Counter-Reformation was in full force; many foreign states were hostile; and the queen's claim to the throne was somewhat sullied.[1] Elizabeth and her men were determined to steer a middle course between Rome and Geneva. Parliament opened with a sermon by Dr. Cox, who was a moderate Protestant.

A pressing priority was the appointment of a new archbishop of Canterbury— the reluctant **Matthew Parker** (1504–1575), who was from Norwich and who took his degree at Cambridge in 1525. He had been a Master at Cambridge and Dean of Lincoln. He had lost his preferments during Mary Tudor's reign but did not lose his life even though his convictions were with the German Reformers and his associations were with Bilney and Latimer. He was consecrated at Lambeth in 1559.[2] Other new appointments to the episcopal bench at this time were Grindal for London, Cox for Ely, and Jewel for Salisbury.

Parker was a thoughtful and scholarly leader, not a great preacher but always well heard. He set himself to a recasting of the Articles and their revision out of which emerged the Thirty-nine Articles, the release of another *Book of Homilies,* the publication of The Bishops' Bible, and the collection of 6,700 other manuscripts still to be found at Cambridge. All of this was critical to build up the churches and to increase the number of available preachers. The complaint was lodged, "There is hardly one in a hundred who is both able and willing to preach the Word of God."[3] To these gaping needs Matthew Parker gave himself and the resources of his office.[4]

1. James Atkinson, *The Great Light: Luther and the Reformation* (Grand Rapids: Eerdmans, 1968), 236ff.
2. L. Elliott-Binns, *The Reformation in England* (London: Duckworth, 1937), 153.
3. F. R. Webber, *A History of Preaching in Britain and America* (Milwaukee: Northwestern, 1952), 1:185.
4. Rich research has been uncovered in recent years on the state of local church life in A. Tindal Hart, *The Country Clergy in Elizabethan and Stuart Times* (London: John Baker, 1958) and *The Man in the Pew: 1558–1660* (London: John Baker, 1966). Also Alan Fager Herr, *The Elizabethan Sermon: A Survey and a Bibliography* (New York: Octagon, 1969).

5.5.10 EDMUND GRINDAL, THE PERSISTENT

When the archbishop of Canterbury, Matthew Parker, died in 1575, Queen Elizabeth appointed **Edmund Grindal** (1519–1583) as new titular head of the Church of England. Grindal hailed from Cumberland and was trained at Cambridge, where he became proctor of the University in 1548 and Lady Margaret Preacher in 1549.[1] Later he was chaplain to Ridley and to Edward VI, and then prebendary at Westminster. When Mary Tudor came to power he fled to the Continent, where he lived first at Strasbourg. After Elizabeth's accession, Grindal served as bishop of London, bishop of York, and then as the archbishop of Canterbury. Manifestly he was not political enough for the delicate balancing act required for his job. Perhaps Elizabeth appointed him because he was unmarried. Why else we cannot see.

The situation for preaching was erratic. There were not many effective preachers to begin with, and Elizabeth clamped down on what she felt were the "impertinent babblings" of both Catholics and Protestants.[2] Court sermons continued, and more than one preacher discoursing before the queen was told to "stick to the text!"[3] The Act of Uniformity was further constrictive in effect. Some services were held in secret. After so much exposure to the Continental Reformers, Grindal was quite Puritan in his leanings. He refused to dampen the meetings for "prophesying," so popular among those inclined to Puritanism. When the queen asked Archbishop Grindal to subdue these "subversive" gatherings, he refused and was suspended for five years of disgrace, finally to be restored shortly before his death.

Grindal was himself well received as a Reformation preacher of grace and gave special attention to the pulpit at St. Paul's Cross where up to six thousand people would convene in the churchyard.[4] In his own preaching he used a modification of the classical sermon with careful divisions of the sermon and evidence of the Puritan adjustment. We shall analyze this development at greater length in our attention to Hyperius in the next chapter.[5] Upon Grindal's death, he was succeeded by **John Whitgift,** an ultra-Calvinist to the point of being supralapsarian (believing that the decree for damnation was from all eternity) but who believed in "the supreme importance of the episcopacy."[6] Whitgift was hard on the Puritans, as was Elizabeth, who did not care for them. He served until after the queen's death.

1. F. R. Webber, *A History of Preaching in Britain and America* (Milwaukee: North-western, 1952), 1:207.
2. Alan Fager Herr, *The Elizabethan Sermon: A Survey and a Bibliography* (New York: Octagon, 1969), 12.
3. Ibid., 38.
4. Ibid., 23–25.
5. J. W. Blench, *Preaching in England in the Late Fifteenth and Sixteenth Centuries* (New York: Barnes and Noble, 1964), 100ff.
6. L. Elliott-Binns, *The Reformation in England* (London: Duckworth, 1937), 167.

5.5.11 JOHN JEWELL, THE PROTECTOR

The most polished preacher in the Elizabethan era was **John Jewel** (1522–1571), who came from Devonshire and did his academics with great acclaim at Oxford. There he was particularly impressed by the new Regius Professor of Divinity, **Peter Martyr Vermigli,** the close associate of Bucer, who was at Cambridge. On Mary's coming to the throne, Jewel fled to the Continent. After hearing John Knox, Jewel became convinced of the merit of the Reformation. In 1559 he returned to England and preached in London, often at St. Paul's Cross. The following year he was made bishop of Salisbury.[1]

Jewel was an ardent controversialist who did not shrink from the burning issues. He was displeased when he learned that the queen had a crucifix, candles, and clergy with vestments in her royal chapel. He preached his famous "challenge sermon," first at St. Paul's Cross, later before royalty, and then made a direct assault on Romish practices. He promised that if anyone could prove Catholic practices by Scripture or by any teacher of the church for the first six hundred years after Christ, he would personally adhere to the Roman Catholic Church again. He then wrote his classic *Apology for the Church of England,* which goes right to the jugular of the issue of authority for the church in all ages.[2]

Jewel was a servant of Christ who had immense intellect and learning and who consecrated these gifts to his Lord. His sermons were meticulously crafted and full of Scripture. He preached in cadences similar to those of the Prayer Book and the King James Version which was yet forty years in the future. Like Grindal, Jewel often used the modified version of the modern style, "Short but elegant," as Blench summarized it.[3] Sensitivity to climax is evidenced in his emotional outline. He maintained extensive correspondence for many years with Bullinger and others. Early in his life he preached a sermon on 1 Peter 4:11. The subject: preaching. His divisions were simple but profound: (1) that the preacher should preach; (2) what he should preach; (3) how he should preach.[4] That was his life and ministry. His health finally broke, and he passed on in 1571.

---

1. F. R. Webber, *A History of Preaching in Britain and America* (Milwaukee: North-western, 1952), 1:208.

2. W. M. Southgate, *John Jewel and the Problem of Doctrinal Authority* (Cambridge, Mass.: Harvard University Press, 1962), 49ff., 146ff.

3. J. W. Blench, *Preaching in England in the Late Fifteenth and Sixteenth Centuries* (New York: Barnes and Noble, 1964), 102ff.

4. E. C. Dargan, *A History of Preaching* (New York: Hodder and Stoughton, 1905), 1:509.

5.5.12 RICHARD HOOKER, THE PURIST

The strains between the more episcopal and the more Puritan in the Church of England were intensifying. In the last several decades of the sixteenth century, no one better epitomized the Episcopalian than **Richard Hooker** (1553–1600). He was born in Exeter in Devonshire, and with Bishop Jewel as his patron he went to Oxford to study. Ordained in 1581, he served a parish in Lincolnshire and was made a Master of the Temple in 1585. His counterpart there was a stolid Puritan, Walter Travers. Out of their ongoing debates Hooker wrote several volumes in defense of the Elizabethan settlement and the Church of England.

On of his works is the famous *Laws of Ecclesiastical Polity.* In opposition to Travers and **Thomas Cartright** (1535–1603), who was called "the earliest complete incarnation of Puritanism on its controversial and theological side," Hooker argued for the episcopacy. Whether one agrees with him or not, one is forced to recognize that no one has ever stated the position more skillfully.[1] The tone of his polemic was reasonable.[2] He argued that the forms of worship are not stipulated in Scripture and pleaded for liberty of conscience.

Richard Hooker was considered one of the foremost preachers of the end of the sixteenth century. His sermons were replete with Scriptures usually taken in the literal sense. He denied that Paul and James contradict each other,[3] and used the modification of the modern form described briefly in Grindal and Jewel. His sermons are the most ornate that we have considered thus far. He reproduced the Ciceronian period more aptly than any other preacher of note. He was poetic and classic but with evidence of the Anglican maturity we have felt missing early on in this turbulent history.[4] Blench speaks of "a new wholesomeness of tone" and a "fragrant spirituality" in his pulpit discourse. Hooker would say:

> I am not in ignorance whose precious blood hath been shed for me; I have a Shepherd full of kindness, full of care, and full of power: unto him I commit myself; his own finger hath engraven this sentence in the tables of my heart, "Satan hath desired to winnow thee as wheat, but I have prayed that thy faith fail not": therefore the assurance of my hope I will labor to keep as a jewel unto the end; and by labor, through the gracious mediation of his prayer, I shall keep it.[5]

Blench asserts that the Anglican piety of Hooker and Andrewes is the fountain from which flowed the stream so vital for George Herbert and T. S. Eliot.

1. L. S. Thornton, *Richard Hooker: A Study of His Theology* (London: SPCK, 1924); Robert K. Faulkner, *Richard Hooker and the Politics of a Christian England* (Berkeley: University of California, 1981). Thornton is a good interaction with the man and his message, and Faulkner probes the *Zeitgeist.*

2. F. R. Webber, *A History of Preaching in Britain and America* (Milwaukee: Northwestern, 1952), 1:218.

3. J. W. Blench, *Preaching in England in the Late Sixteenth and Seventeenth Centuries* (New York: Barnes and Noble, 1964), 64.

4. Ibid., 228.

5. Ibid., 320.

5.5.13 Bernard Gilpin, the Protestant

Renowned in the north country as the apostle of the north, **Bernard Gilpin** (1517–1583) is recorded in the annals of preaching as a powerful preacher of the gospel of grace. Nurtured in a well-to-do home in Westmoreland, Gilpin studied at Oxford, graduated in 1540, and was ordained in 1549. His discussions with Peter Martyr at Oxford rattled his Roman Catholic foundations. Deeply disquieted by the state of the church, he went abroad to study at Louvain and Antwerp. Here he came to a deeply Protestant persuasion.[1] When he returned to England in 1556, his uncle Bishop Tunstall secured several parishes for him where he preached with extraordinary fervor and was known as a gifted preacher and tender shepherd.

The cross of Christ was one of Gilpin's favorite themes, but his preaching incurred the displeasure of the establishment and he was summoned to appear before Queen Mary. In an accident en route to London he broke his leg. While he recuperated, the queen died. He was never tried. Thereafter several offers of episcopal preferment came to him, but he always declined them because of his sense of call to preach and his reservations about the episcopacy.

Gilpin's sermons were simply constructed. He made use of classical quotations and went right to the heart of "popery," which he felt should be sent packing to Rome. He was deeply concerned about social injustice and the lack of schools for children, and he built schools in his parishes.[2] The countryside was rough, but he did not hesitate to enter situations of great peril. His eloquence, piety, and "the graces of his character" cause him to loom large in this cadre of preachers, truly a Westminster Abbey of the heroes of faith from a tumultuous time.[3]

1. F. R. Webber, *A History of Preaching in Britain and America* (Milwaukee: Northwestern, 1952), 1:193–94.

2. J. W. Blench, *Preaching in England in the Late Fifteenth and Sixteenth Centuries* (New York: Barnes and Noble, 1964), 271.

3. E. C. Dargan, *A History of Preaching* (New York: Hodder and Stoughton, 1905), 1:504.

5.6 THE SUSTAINED EXPRESSION OF REFORMATION PREACHING

God was reconciling the world to himself in Christ, not counting men's sins against them. And he has committed to us the message of reconciliation. We are therefore Christ's ambassadors, as though God were making his appeal through us. We implore you on Christ's behalf: Be reconciled to God.

—Paul in 2 Corinthians 5:19–20

Finally, brothers, pray for us that the message of the Lord may spread rapidly and be honored.

—2 Thessalonians 3:1

What began incipiently as a hole in the dike rapidly became a tidal wave which threatened to inundate the whole of Europe. In a sense, many readers of this chronicle are part of a ripple effect of the Reformation and its exaltation of the Scripture and the preaching of the Scripture. Each of the Reformers had a drove of followers who walked in his footsteps. Dargan describes **Heinrich Bullinger** (1504–1517), who succeeded Zwingli in Zurich, as "tall of form, with a flowing beard, a benevolent and intelligent expression, a pleasing voice, a dignified yet animated bearing." He reports that between 1549 and 1567 Bullinger preached 100 sermons on Revelation, 66 on Daniel, 170 on Jeremiah, and 190 on Isaiah.[1]

Names on the honor roll must also include the Petri brothers in Sweden, Hans Tausen in Denmark, Myconius and Oecolampadius in Switzerland, Augustino Cazalla and Juan Gil in Spain, Bernardino Ochino of Italy, and on and on. Three particular personalities command our attention before we leave the sixteenth century.

---

1. E. C. Dargan, *A History of Preaching* (New York: Hodder and Stoughton, 1905), 1:414.

5.6.1 THE DYNAMIC JOHN KNOX OF SCOTLAND

Give me Scotland or I die.

I would most gladly pass through the course that God hath appointed to my labors . . . giving thanks to His Holy Name; for that it hath pleased His mercy to make me not a Lord-like Bishop, but a painful preacher of His blessed Evangel.

—John Knox

Now we turn to Scotland to pick up the thread of the Reformation and its preaching in the tapestry of this rugged and vital land. The story of this people and their "intense individualism, fierce stubbornness, prickly pride and suspicion of each other's motives," along with their fondness for "religious and metaphysical argument" spring naturally from their true Celtic origin and their ancient Celtic religious tradition.[1] The Roman Catholic Church made slow headway, especially in the Highlands, but when it was established, Scottish Catholicism was highly reactionary and impervious to challenge. In the sixteenth century Scotland was four centuries behind the rest of Europe.[2]

Except for a handful of preaching friars, preaching was almost nonexistent. Nary a bishop could preach, except Bishop James Kennedy of St. Andrews, who died in 1465, and at Ayr, the bishop of Glasgow attempted to do so:

> It proved a fiasco, for he had uttered only a few sentences when he had to apologize to his audience saying, "They say we should preach: why not? Better late thrive than never thrive. Have us still for your bishop, and we shall provide better for the next time." The bishop had desired to counter the preaching of George Wishart in Ayr. Instead he hastily left the town, and did not attempt to preach there again.[3]

So the inert clergy, "dumb dogs," and "idle bellies" as they were termed, were no positive factor, but some Lollards and students from Wittenberg along with writings of the Reformers began to seep in. Tyndale's Bibles also began to infiltrate. The "evangelical themes of sin and salvation began to stir men's hearts."[4]

The first of the Scottish martyrs was **Patrick Hamilton**. He was born to a noble family, and studied at Paris and the Louvain. Soon he came under the influence of John Major and Erasmus. His ideas were not well received at St. Andrews, where he was on faculty, and he took refuge at Marburg University, an important evangelical center. He returned to Scotland to preach, was tricked by Archbishop Beaton, and burned at the stake, February 27, 1528. He carried his beloved Bible in his hand to his death.

Likewise **George Wishart,** a highly focused preacher who introduced systematic Bible exposition to Scotland and translated Bullinger's Helvetic Confession, ran afoul of now Cardinal Beaton and was consigned to the stake March 1, 1546. These unpopular executions were a crossing of the Rubicon for the Roman Catholics.

Young **John Knox** (1505 or 1513–1572) was born near Haddington and matriculated at St. Andrews in 1529, the year after Patrick Hamilton's martyrdom. He also heard George Wishart's last sermon before his arrest in 1546. Knox defended Wishart and began to receive what he called some "lively impressions of the heart." Ordained in 1540, he began to share expositions from John's gospel in the Castle Chapel at St. Andrews and introduced the public celebration of the sacrament according to the Reformed ritual. For nineteen months he was consigned to galley service as a punishment, but was released to spend time in England (1549–1554) as a minister at Berwick-on-Tweed (where kneeling for communion was discontinued) and as chaplain for Edward VI. He was especially enamored with the high-priestly prayer of Jesus in John 17 and considered John 17:3 as his anchorage even to the time of his death.[5]

From 1554 to 1559 Knox was in France, Switzerland, and Germany. He came back to Scotland briefly but then spent another year in Geneva where John Calvin was his mentor and model.

The Scottish Parliament established the Reformed Church by law during Knox's absence, and structures emerged "to maintain the Word of God and His Church and to seek ministers of Christ's gospel and sacraments to serve His people."[6] House churches proliferated. The appeal went forth to Knox to return and take leadership, which he did in 1559 after writing his celebrated "First Blast of the Trumpet Against the Monstrous Regiment of Women" (1558). The diatribe had been aimed at Mary Tudor, but Elizabeth Tudor took umbrage.

Upon his return to Scotland, Knox expounded Scripture daily in St. Giles, Edinburgh, where he had been appointed pastor. He preached a vehement sermon in Perth against idolatry and again in St. Andrews on "Cleansing the Temple." In the years 1561 to 1563 he had five recorded interviews with Queen Mary, a dedicated Roman Catholic. The intrigues and tangles of the politics and Scottish nationalism of the time are stranger than fiction.[7] Mary, queen of Scotland (and now also queen of France as wife of Francis II) used French troops to subjugate the Protestants. Queen Elizabeth, because of no liking for Knox but out of detestation of the French, gave her full backing to the Protestant cause. The courage of Knox and his strong preaching were critical during this time.

The Scots Confession (1560) was largely the work of Knox and anticipated in many ways the Westminster Confession of 1647. In 1560, the first General Assembly of the Church of Scotland was convened. Despite the great shortage of good preachers, the Church of Scotland always insisted on "a high standard of preaching."[8] Knox measured up.

The preaching of John Knox was incredibly stirring. When he preached Moray's funeral at St. Giles, he moved the entire company to tears. A marked apocalyptic and eschatological edge to Knox's preaching was clear.[9] James Melville, who heard Knox preach in 1571, a year before his death, testified:

> Of all the benefits I had that year was the coming of that most notable prophet and apostle of our nation, John Knox, at St. Andrews. I heard him teach the prophecies of Daniel that summer and the winter following. In the opening of his text he was moderate the space of a half an hour, but when he reached the application he made me tremble so much that I could not hold the pen to write. He wielded this power when in bodily weakness, for he had to be helped into the church and lifted into the pulpit where he had to lean on his first entry. But when he came to his sermon he was so active and vigorous that he was like to beat the pulpit into pieces and fly out of it.[10]

One thoughtful student of the preaching of Knox identifies six features to be emulated:

1. True preaching must be doctrinal. Knox always preached within a clear sense of theological structure.

2. True preaching must be empathetic. He knew where his people were and utilized gripping illustrations of truth.
3. True preaching must be pointed. He was not afraid to confront the issues of the times and in human life.
4. True preaching must ring with urgency. "Knowing therefore the terror of the Lord . . ." (1 Cor. 5:11).
5. True preaching must be realistic. He was not in denial in relation to the dangers and heartaches faced.
6. True preaching must be victorious. He kept focusing on the God of Scripture who maintains his cause on earth.[11]

The English ambassador Randolph wrote William Cecil after hearing Knox preach: "The voice of one man is able in one hour to put more life in us than five hundred trumpets continually blustering in our ears."[12] In 1570 Knox suffered a stroke which hindered his speech. He moved to St. Andrews, where he appeared in the pulpit for the last time on November 9, 1572. He died November 24, 1572. The Regent Morton said at his grave, "Here lyeth a man who in his life never feared the face of man."

---

1. For a helpful survey of the Scottish background to the Reformation, see Nigel Tranter, *Robert Bruce: The Steps to the Empty Throne* (London: Hodder and Stoughton, 1969); *The Stewart Trilogy* (London: Hodder and Stoughton, 1976); also *Unicorn Rampant* (London: Hodder and Stoughton, 1984), this being a study of James Stuart, who became James VI of Scotland and James I of England. Recent cinema such as *Braveheart* (on William Wallace) and *Rob Roy* afford marvelous scenery and superb historical representation.
2. James Atkinson, *The Great Light: Luther and Reformation* (Grand Rapids: Eerdmans, 1968), 222.
3. A. M. Renwick, *The Story of the Scottish Reformation* (Grand Rapids: Eerdmans, 1960), 17.
4. Atkinson, *The Great Light*, 223.
5. F. W. Boreham, "John Knox's Text," in *A Bunch of Everlastings* (Nashville: Abingdon, 1920), 110ff.
6. Atkinson, *The Great Light*, 226.
7. For solid biographies of John Knox, see Henry Cowan, *John Knox: The Hero of the Scottish Reformation* (New York: Knickerbocker, 1905); W. Stanford Reid, *Trumpeter of God* (New York: Scribner's, 1974).
8. Richard G. Kyle, *The Mind of John Knox* (Lawrence, Kans.: Coronado, 1984), 215ff. This book is flawed in its understanding of the relationship between the Word of God and the words of Scripture, which are the same.
9. Quoted in John Bishop, "John Knox: The Thundering Scot," *Preaching* (September–October 1992), 74.
10. Renwick, *Story of the Scottish Reformation*, 110.
11. Kevin Reed, "John Knox and Faithful Preaching," *Banner of Truth* (November 1984): 5–7.
12. Quoted in Renwick, *Story of the Scottish Reformation*, 83.

5.6.2   THE DOCTRINALLY SENSITIVE JACOB ARMINIUS OF THE NETHERLANDS

> We declare, therefore, and we continue to repeat the declaration till the gates of hell re-echo the sound, that the Holy Spirit, by whose inspiration holy men of God have spoken this word, and by whose guidance they have as his amanuenses consigned it to writing—that this Holy Spirit is the author of that light by the aid of which we obtain a perception and an understanding of the divine means of the word and is the effector of that certainty by which we believe those meanings to be truly divine, and that he is the necessary Author, the all-sufficient Effector.

> There are two stumbling-blocks against which I am solicitously on my guard—not to make God the author of sin, and not to do away with the freedom inherent in the human will.
>
> —Jacob Arminius

Three systems of theology spring from the Reformation: the Reformed, the Lutheran, and the Arminian. The latter has had extensive impact upon parts of Evangelical Anglicanism (John Jewel, Lancelot Andrewes), the Wesleyan movement (Wesley's periodical was called *The Arminian Magazine*), and many other still viable and vital parts of Christ's church to this very day. The spur to the formulation of the Arminian system came out of discussions and controversies over how to understand what the Bible says about predestination. These topics had long been discussed and debated—even Dante has a lively discussion on free will in Canto XVI of *Purgatorio*.

Jacob Arminius (1559–1609) was born in Oudewater on the Ijseel River in South Holland. His father died when he was an infant, and his mother and siblings were slaughtered by the Spanish Papists when Oudewater was destroyed in 1575. The tyranny of the duke of Alva is a sad and melancholy tale. Young Arminius was studying in Marburg and had come under the spell of the logic of Peter Ramus. Ramus challenged the rigidities of Aristotle and exerted a profound influence on many of the Puritans, particularly on William Perkins, as we shall see in the next chapter.[1] Arminius was a brilliant and retentive student. He studied at the New Free University in Leiden, established by King William, prince of Orange, and graduated in 1581 at the age of twenty-two. One of his teachers there was the uncle of Hugo Grotius, the noted jurist who had reservations about Calvin's teachings.

Through the patronage of friends, Arminius was able to study for six years in Geneva, Padua, and Basel. The rector at Geneva was **Theodore Beza,** Calvin's successor. Beza was a linguist and controversialist who had come to hold a "derivative Calvinism," that is, something beyond that held by the master himself. Beza was an unabashed *supralapsarian:* he believed that God made the decree to elect some to heaven and damn some to hell even before the decree to create. Arminius did not challenge the sovereignty of God but held that his was a sovereignty of moral supremacy.[2] He felt that Beza's view in effect made God the author of sin and made God's love and mercy problematic. Beza's extreme view (which is sometimes called "hard Calvinism") was not in the Belgic Confession of 1561 or the Heidelberg Catechism of 1563, but it did surface at the Synod of Dort in 1618–19. Many of the subsequent controversies had to do with the effort to require Arminius to subscribe to a view not even in the earlier symbols. He stoutly resisted the whole idea of making any creedal statement as of the same level as Holy Scripture itself.

When Arminius returned to Holland in 1587 it was to begin fifteen years of pastoral ministry in Amsterdam. The preachers in Amsterdam circulated among the churches and generally preached consecutive book studies. The sermons were about half an hour long. Arminius was warmly pastoral and much appreciated, especially by the Amsterdam merchants. He began conducting evening services in the Old Church where he was ordained in 1588. His preaching became very popular, as one listener described him:

> This flattering reception ought to excite no wonder; for—I speak before those who knew him well—there was in him a certain incredible gravity softened down by a cheerful amenity; his voice was rather weak, yet sweet, harmonious, and piercing. . . . He disdained to employ any rhetorical flourishes, and made no use of the honeyed sweets collected for this purpose from the Greeks.[3]

After an extended series on Jonah, we have record of a series of sixty-nine sermons on Malachi. Arminius married Lijsbet in 1590. He was a good family man and upright citizen. In 1603 he was appointed to a professorship in Leiden, and in 1605 he was made rector of the University. The controversies that arose in the Reformed Church that gave birth to the Remonstrants were questions about predestination and the order of decrees, free will, and the nature of original sin. Beyond question, Arminius stood in the mainstream of the Reformation on Scripture, *sola gratia,* justification, and the propitiatory nature of Christ's atonement.[4] He stood with Melancthon for a more moderate understanding of predestination based on foreknowledge. He did not believe that knowledge is causal. One of his staunch allies was Professor Hemmingsen, a student of Melancthon at the University of Copenhagen. A series of vicious colds wasted him away, and he died of consumption in 1609.

The ideal situation for Arminius was Free Churches based only on the Holy Scriptures.[5] The independent Robert Browne group that lived in Holland in the 1590s did not much care for Arminius and his sense of order in the church. The collected works of Arminius show him to be an erudite student of Scripture (as per his superb study of Romans 9). He was a godly man, a gifted teacher, and an able preacher. In his message on the occasion of receiving his doctorate, he prayed: "Sprinkle thou our spirits, souls and bodies, with the most gracious dew of thy immeasurable holiness."[6] His exposition that day on "The Priesthood of Christ" is chock full of Scripture. His treatment divides into three logical parts. His discourse is full of Christ and the blood atonement of Christ.[7] "He being dead yet speaks."

1. We have a choice biography, Carl Bangs, *Arminius: A Study in the Dutch Reformation* (Grand Rapids: Francis Asbury/Zondervan, 1971).
2. A. Skevington Wood, "Understanding Arminius: Origins of His Theology," in *Life of Faith* (July 8, 1972), 9–11.
3. Bangs, *Arminius,* 114.
4. Richard A. Muller, *God, Creation, and Providence in the Thought of Jacob Arminius* (Grand Rapids: Baker, 1991).
5. Gerald O. McCulloh, ed., *Man's Faith and Freedom* (Nashville: Abingdon, 1961), 15.
6. Jacob Arminius, *The Writings of Arminius* (Grand Rapids: Baker, 1956), 19.
7. Ibid., 2ff.

5.6.3 THE DARINGLY ASSERTIVE MENNO SIMONS OF THE NETHERLANDS

Faith firmly believes and lays hold upon and acknowledges every word of God, the threatening Law as well as the comforting Gospel, to be dependable and true. Whereby in turn the heart is pierced and moved through the Holy Ghost with an unusual regenerating, renewing, vivifying power, which produces first of all the fear of God.

And we, before God and His angels, seek nothing on this earth but that we may obey the clear and printed Word of the Lord, His Spirit, His example, His command, prohibition, usage, and ordinance (by which everything in Christ's kingdom and church must be regulated if it is to please Him) according to our weakness in all subjection and obedience.

The Word of Christ remains and is the word of the cross; all who accept it in power and truth must be prepared for the cross. This both the Scriptures and experience teach abundantly.

—Menno Simons

The Anabaptists are another important wellspring of Reformation vitality. The movement abounded with laypersons and was reordinationist, that is, it did not accept the validity of any other ordination. Strong opposition surfaced against absolute predestination and the notion of the invisible church. The emphasis was on believers' baptism, the gifts of the Spirit, regeneration, sanctification, and the believers' church. Professor George Williams in his irreplaceable work on "the radical Reformation" characterizes their preachers as "literalistic preachers of repentance."[1] Luther was unnerved by the Zwickau Prophets and the unstable Thomas Muntzer and his experiment in Munster (his millennialism fueled by Joachim of Fiora's earlier teaching).

In the mainstream, however, the Anabaptists stressed the preaching of the Word. **Casper Schwenckfeld** (1489–1561) and **Balthaser Hubmeier** (1485–1528) both preached in fields and anywhere available. The latter would hold eight-day meetings with preaching every evening. His messages were full of stories. The fiery **John Hut** preached the imminence of Christ's return,[2] and **Clement Ziegler** in the Alsace had a great burden for the Jews in the latter days, as per Malachi 4:5. Ziegler preached his message mainly in churchyards.

Although he was not the first Mennonite as such (the Swiss Brethren in Zwingli's domain antedated him), the primary light of the regrouping after the Munster debacle was **Menno Simons** (1496–1561). Simons was born in West Frisia in the Netherlands. He studied for the priesthood in the Franciscan Monastery in Bolsward and was ordained in 1524. He was not overly serious in his priestly duties, indulging freely in "card playing, drinking and all manner of frivolous diversions."[3]

One day while officiating at Mass, he was overcome with doubts about Transubstantiation. For an extended period of time he agonized, and finally was rebaptized by Obbe Philips of the evangelical Anabaptist Brotherhood. He actually lived a double life for some time, preaching evangelical truth from a Roman Catholic pulpit. He finally made the break and was reordained as an elder in 1537. Wenger says, "His great work was the proclamation of the gospel of Christ," through which many souls were saved.[4] Simons felt his earlier preaching was not sufficiently loving, but was redirected to the Word and Christ, who transforms from within. He wrote twenty-four books and pamphlets, the chief of which was his influential *The Foundation Book,* written in 1540, of which Loeschen says sixty percent is Scripture itself.[5]

Menno Simons, after whom part of the movement was named, held a high view of the preaching office. He believed that the preacher must be called and ordained. The conduct and uprightness of the preacher are indispensable. "It is not enough that in appearance a man speaks much of the Word of the Lord. It must also be verified by devout and unblamable conduct, as the Scriptures teach."[6] The preaching is to be without "perverting glosses, without the admixture of leaven," for the Word of God "preached without admixture in the power of the Spirit is the only right and proper Seed from which truly believing and obedient children of God are born."[7]

Menno Simons was ultimately called as Shepherd of the Brotherhood and preached throughout Holland, northwest Germany, and Holstein in Denmark. One biographer says of his preaching: "Menno's greatness lay not so much in his eloquence, although he was a good preacher, nor in his literary craftsmanship, although he could write well for the common man. He was no great theologian, although he knew how to present the plain teachings of the Bible with force and clarity. He was not even a great organizer, although he rendered a real service in the guidance which he gave to the bishops and ministers of the growing church." His greatness is to be seen in his character, his writings, and his message. "He merely caught a clear vision of two fundamental Biblical ideals: the ideal of practical holiness, and the ideal of the high place of the church in the life of the believer and in the cause of Christ."[8]

Simons and his wife and family were mercilessly hunted. In 1542 the Emperor Charles V issued an edict against him. Even the Reformers were harsh and cruel. Calvin said of him: "Nothing could be more arrogant and more impudent than this donkey."[9] At last he died, broken in body but not in spirit.

Anabaptism as a movement sprang from a return to the Scripture and a concern for a more thorough reformation of the church. Simons claimed he had never read the Bible until two years after his ordination as a priest. Then he read with a passion and preached the Scriptures. He had problems with infant baptism because he did not see it in the Bible. He constantly stressed the new birth. Simons believed that "while all persons inherited a corrupt nature which inevitably leads to actual sins, the death of Christ on the cross removed the guilt of original sin for everyone!"[10] Like all the Anabaptists, Simons had "a stiff aversion to the twin doctrines of predestination and the bondage of the will."[11] But "God's infallible Word" was his firm foundation, and on the Word and its careful exegesis all of the Reformers stood united and, thus, their collective emphasis on the essentiality of biblical preaching.

1. George Huntston Williams, *The Radical Reformation* (Philadelphia: Westminster, 1962), 124.
2. Ibid., 163.
3. John Horsch, *Mennonites in Europe* (Scottsdale, Pa.: Herald Press, 1942), 185.
4. J. C. Wenger, *Glimpses of Mennonite History and Doctrine* (Scottsdale, Pa.: Herald Press, 1947), 78.
5. John R. Loeschen, *The Divine Community: Trinity, Church and Ethics in Reformation Theologies* (Kirksville, Mo.: The Sixteenth Century Journal Publishers, 1981), 68.
6. Menno Simons, *The Complete Writings of Menno Simons* (Scottsdale, Pa.: Herald Press, 1956), 169.
7. Ibid., 164.
8. Ibid., 28–29.
9. Wenger, *Glimpses of Mennonite History and Doctrine*, 80.
10. Timothy George, *Theology of the Reformers* (Nashville: Broadman, 1988), 268. This application of Romans 5:12–21 is the basis of the approach Menno Simons and the Wesleys took to the vexed issue of infant salvation.
11. Ibid., 271.

CHAPTER SIX

The Ripening Maturity of Biblical Preaching in the Seventeenth Century

... who have tasted the goodness of the Word of God. ...

—Hebrews 6:5

It is not as though God's word had failed.

—Romans 9:6

As for God, his way is perfect; the word of the LORD is flawless.

—2 Samuel 22:31

The Spirit of the LORD spoke through me; his word was on my tongue.

—2 Samuel 23:2

Indeed, to them you are nothing more than one who sings love songs with a beautiful voice and plays an instrument well, for they hear your words but do not put them into practice.

—Ezekiel 33:32

Let the word of Christ dwell in you richly as you teach and admonish one another with all wisdom. ...

—Colossians 3:16

This hearing of the Word of God, hearing what the Lord of the Church wants to say to His Church in its actual situation, is the primary task of the church, the basic human action in worship.

—C. E. B. Cranfield

The translation of the Bible and "the living preaching of the Word of God" (to use the rich expression from the Heidelberg Catechism) are logically and properly complementary and intertwined. In his massive work, *The English Bible and the Seventeenth-Century Revolution,* Christopher Hill documents the explosive results of letting the Word loose.[1] In previous centuries translators had been martyred for their labors. Even prelates had warned that the Word of God "causeth insurrection and teacheth the people to disobey . . . and moveth them to rise against their princes, and to make all common, and to make havoc of other men's goods." One observer commented, "The Bible in English under every weaver's and chambermaid's arm hath done much harm." In this sense the Scripture was a dangerous dynamic unleashing societal change and challenge.

The English language was at the peak of its utility for prose and poetry. "Those Elizabethans had a sense of diction," Matthew Arnold commented.[2] This was amply demonstrated by Shakespeare, Spenser, Sydney, Raleigh, and Bacon. At the Hampton Court Conference convened by James I in 1604, the Puritan leader Dr. John Reynolds proposed a new translation of the Bible without notes. The king was taken with the project and promoted it. The result was the so-called Authorized Version of 1611, whose stately cadences and rhythms have been such a blessing down to the present.[3] The history of the English Bible with its parallels in other languages through the centuries is a narrative of romance and risk. The Bible is a miracle book, and its extraordinary power and vitality can be chronicled from the turbulent seventeenth century or any other century to the praise of God.[4]

---

1. Christopher Hill, *The English Bible and the Seventeenth-Century Revolution* (New York: Penguin, 1994).
2. T. Harwood Pattison, *The History of Christian Preaching* (Philadelphia: American Baptist Publication Society, 1903), 163.
3. F. F. Bruce, *The Books and the Parchments: Some Chapters on the Transmission of the Bible* (London: Pickering and Inglis, 1950), 217ff.
4. Gwynn McLendon Day, *The Wonder of the Word* (Chicago: Moody, 1957); Lawrence E. Nelson, *Our Roving Bible: Tracking its Influence Through English and American Life* (Nashville: Abingdon, 1945). Nelson quotes the great Yale scholar William Lyon Phelps: "The Bible has been a greater influence on the course of English literature than all other forces put together" (9).

6.1 GROWING IN MATURE REFLECTION ON THE PREACHING CRAFT

Let a lawful and a godly seigniory look that they preach, not quarterly or monthly, but continually.

—Thomas Cartright

A veritable torrent of biblical preaching was unleashed in the Reformation. In form the Reformers reverted to the ancient Augustinian pattern of the personal, conversational homily. They seemed weary of the traditional restraints and gave little attention to structure. They were medieval in agreeing with **Robert of Basevorn** (1322) that preaching is the second act of God after creation (i.e., after creating man, God preached) and with **Humbert of Romanis** (d. 1277) that preaching carries on the discourse of heaven.[1] English preachers like John Colet, John Fisher, and Bishop Tunstall tended to use the ancient form which had no particular scheme.

The other option for them would have been the university sermon with its divisions and subdivisions as described in our treatment of Alan of Lille. While *divisio* was overdone by some, as in **Jean Raulin** (b. Toulouse 1443), whose sermons were clogged with divisions and subdivisions, the dividing of the sermon and the text does promote unity. The process of principalization and contemporization present some risk, but are effective with the use of divisions.[2] The use of a protheme (introduction) and theme are aids to understanding and recollection. Amplification of this form was further supplied by **William of Auvergne** (bishop of Paris, 1228–1249) and by English writers and preachers such as **Thomas Waleys** (c. 1349) from Oxford and **Ranulph Higden** of Chester (d. 1364). Most noteworthy is **Simon Alcock** (d. 1459), whose work *On the Mode of Dividing a Theme for Dilating Sermon Material* was exceedingly influential.[3] Preachers like Tauler, Erasmus, Hugh Latimer, John Bradford, John Jewel, Richard Hooker, and Stephen Baron used this form.

The revival of preaching inevitably fostered reflection and experimentation on form and structure. Two new forms came into existence at this time. What Professor Blench calls "the modified modern style" soon became popular. This bridging form employed divisions but with considerably greater freedom. This form was used by Grindal, often by Jewel, and by its chief exemplar, the silver-tongued **Henry Smith,** who will be considered shortly. A key advocate of this modification, one whom we will analyze in our next section, was **Andrew Hyperius** of Marburg.

The argument for the use of divisions arises out of the tendency for a homily to be a rambling cluster of sermonettes, much like unwinding a ball of twine. John Oman flinched from the sermon whose divisions were only pauses. He advocated a plot and a plan, a sequencing, the artful interruption and sustaining of discourse without slavish adherence to a skeletal structure.[4]

Yet another form was emerging, which was really a subdivision of the basic modification referred to by Blench above. We have already observed it in John Hooper, and it became dominant in Puritan preaching. Its chief theoretician was **William Perkins,** and it proved to be a major formative influence in the logic of **Peter Ramus.** Clearly, the seventeenth century was a time of unusual fecundity and homiletical formulation.

---

1. James J. Murphy, *Rhetoric in the Middle Ages: A History of Rhetorical Theory from St. Augustine to the Renaissance* (Berkeley: University of California Press, 1974), 270.
2. For an illuminating probing of this issue, see Ramesh Richard, *Scripture Sculpture* (Grand Rapids: Baker, 1995), 163.
3. Murphy, *Rhetoric in the Middle Ages,* 339.

4. John Oman, *Concerning the Ministry* (Richmond: John Knox, 1936), 209–13. Trenchant discussion of *lucidus ordo* can also be found in M. Reu, *Homiletics* (Grand Rapids: Baker, 1924, 1967), 456–85; R. L. Dabney, *On Preaching* (Edinburgh: Banner of Truth, 1870, 1979), 214–32.

6.1.1 ANDREW HYPERIUS—THE THINKER

How he stampt and took on I cannot tell, but crash quoth the pulpit, and there lay Hubberd in the middest of his audience.
—John Foxe, the martyrologist

As Augustine's work dominated for a thousand years, so now we detect new hands and minds shaping the preaching. **Andreas Gerard** (1511–1564), or as he was more widely known, **Andrew Hyperius,** has been called "the father of the later Reformation preaching."[1] He was born in Ypres in Flanders, hence his more common name. His father, who died when Andrew was yet a boy, had been a prominent lawyer. His father had laid out a program for his son's education which led him to the University of Paris and on to England, where he was much influenced by Reformed ideas. In 1542, he was made a professor in Marburg in Germany. He was widely respected for his theological acumen.

Hyperius authored two books on preaching, the first of which, *Topica Theologica,* was a survey of preaching themes and how they could be handled. The more homiletically significant work was *De Formandis Concionibus Sacris (On the Making of Sacred Discourses).* No less than von Harnack called this piece "the first really scientific treatise on the theory of preaching."[2] It was titled *The Practice of Preaching* when it was "Englished" by John Ludham in 1577. Since neither Luther nor Calvin bequeathed their followers any systematic statement of principles for preaching, this volume loomed large as an influence both on the Continent and in Britain.

Bridging between the ancient homily and the university sermon of Thomistic order and structure, Hyperius adapted the latter for more common and general use. He was not indifferent to matters of form, but was freer and more direct in his approach. Hyperius typically began with the reading of the Scripture lesson, gave an invocatory prayer, introduced his theme, developed the proposition with possible divisions, and moved to the conclusion. Traditional sections of confirmation and confutation were frequently omitted.[3] There is increased flexibility and adaptability in this modified form. Interestingly, in Dietrich Bonhoeffer's lectures on preaching at the Confessing Church Seminary at Finkenwalde in the 1930s, he stresses the importance of Hyperius and his modification of Augustine.

Hyperius also stipulated some general axioms for preaching the Word:

1. the sermon is to be adapted to the capacity of the hearers;
2. theological questions which excite curiosity rather than edification are to be avoided;
3. the doctrines to be taught are to be confirmed from the prophetic and apostolic writings;

4. time, place, and audience are to be considered in developing the doctrinal explanation;
5. only the canonical writings are to be used in confirming what is taught;
6. the proofs used are to be simple and direct;
7. preference is to be given to the simple sense;
8. figurative language is to be used sparingly, types and allegories seldom, and neither are to be used for proof;
9. the mode of expression should not provoke contradiction;
10. when a doctrine is taught, it should be practically applied both in regard to the church and the individual.[4]

The relevancy and applicability of these axioms for preaching in an age of great controversy are evident. The strong emphasis on audience is an obvious effort to overcome the excessively scholarly preaching of the *oratio* and the emphasis on doctrine a clear foreshadowing of the great Reformed and Puritan emphasis on doctrine with its possible perils. We now want to see how this translates in parish preaching.

---

1. John Ker, *Lectures on the History of Preaching* (New York: Armstrong, 1889), 174.
2. Warren W. Wiersbe and Lloyd M. Perry, *The Wycliffe Handbook of Preaching and Preachers* (Chicago: Moody, 1984), 50.
3. J. W. Blench, *Preaching in England in the Late Fifteenth and Sixteenth Centuries* (New York: Barnes and Noble, 1964), 102.
4. Hering's *Lehrbuch der Homiletik* as quoted in A. E. Garvie, *The Christian Preacher* (New York: Scribner's, 1923), 142.

6.1.2   HENRY SMITH—THE PRACTITIONER

None ought to take upon them the function of preaching in the church, unless they have their warrant or authority from God, as Aaron had, Heb. 5:4. And although they have not their authority in that form and manner as Jonah had his, namely, as it were, by word of mouth even from God himself, "Arise, and go to Nineveh," yet they must have their warrant from him, else their calling is unlawful.
—Henry Smith in the sermon "The Calling of Jonah"

Called "the most popular Puritan preacher of the Elizabethan era,"[1] **Henry Smith** (1560–1609 or 1613) was born to a wealthy family in Leicestershire. Smith illustrates and embodies choice aspects of strong biblical preaching. He took his M.A. in 1583 at Oxford, where he was esteemed "for his prodigious memory and for his fluent, eloquent and practical way of preaching."[2] Drawn to Puritan ways and tending to be anti-episcopal, he declined to take a benefice, choosing preaching over patrimony. One of his early sermons preached in 1582, "The Lost Sheep Found," is a model of direct and clear statement.

In 1587 Smith was appointed lecturer at St. Clement Danes in London. We shall describe later the critical function of the Puritan lectureships of the day, but suffice it to say that they were a means for bypassing certain ecclesiastical strictures unfavorable to the Puritan wing in the Church of England. Archbishop Whitgift dismissed him from his post after one year, but he was soon reinstated and continued for an extended period of time. The church was always full when he preached, with people standing in the alleyways outside to hear. J. B. Marsden said that Smith was "probably the most eloquent preacher in Europe."[3] Many regarded him as "the first preacher of the nation."[4] Quaint Thomas Fuller, who wrote his biographical memoir, spoke of him as "the silver-tongued preacher," one metal below Chrysostom.[5] His sermons were so sought after that they were widely pirated. Smith finally collected fifty-six of them in an edition we possess today.

Plagued with ill health, Smith always considered himself a moderate in the Church of England and eschewed separatists like the Brownists and the Barrowists. He exemplified what he called "living sermons." For Smith, the sermon was central to worship. Those who read homilies he termed "dumb dogges." He fretted over the tendency for preachers to turn from the grand themes of Scripture to ecclesiastical politics and sensational antics. He would concur with Archbishop Sandy's diagnosis of the situation:

> The preacher is gladly heard of the people, that can carp the magistrates, cut up the ministers, cry out against all order and set all at liberty. But if he shall reprove their insolency, pride and vanity, their monstrous apparel, their excessive feasting, their greedy covetousness, their biting usury, their halting hearts, their muttering minds, their friendly words and malicious deeds, they will fall from him then. He is a railer, he doteth, he wanteth discretion.[6]

Henry Smith proved that faithful biblical preaching will draw the audiences. Key to Smith's listenability was his use of variety. Occasionally he used the ancient homily form. He avoided the developing New Puritan Form as we have described it. Chiefly he used the modified modern form as espoused by Andrew Hyperius. In terms of his style, he preferred the plain but most often blended it with an ornate style even within the same sermon. Blench includes him in a quartet of preachers "whose richly colored style reaches out towards the fully ornate mode, forming a bridge between it and the plain style."[7] Here is an example:

> There is no salt but may lose his saltnesse, no wine but may lose his strength, no flower but may lose his scent, no light but may be eclipsed, no beauty but may be stained, no fruit but may be blasted, nor soule but may be corrupted, we stand all in a slippery place, where it is easie to slide, and hard to get up, like little children which overthrow themselves with their cloaths, now up, now downe at a straw, so soone we fall from God, and slide from his word and forget our resolutions, as though we had never resolved.[8]

The richness of his imagery, his masterful use of homely similes, his occasional employment of classical reference bespeak his ability to utilize effective variation. His most famous sermon, "Dialogue Between Paul and King Agrippa," climaxes in a powerful exposé of "the almost Christian." Other examples of his hardy and sturdy preaching include such titles as "The Trumpet of the Soul Sounding to Judgment," "The Sinful Man's Search," "The Sweet Song of Old Father Simeon," "The True Trial of the Spirits," and "The Art of Hearing." Of ill-trained preachers Smith inveighed:

> None should meddle with the word (which is the law of God) but they which are fit, lest they make it despised. Hannah said, "I will not offer the child to God before he be weaned," 1 Samuel 1:22, that is, before he be taken from the dug; but now they offer their children to God before they are weaned, before they can go, before they can speak; and send them to fight the Lord's battles before they have one stone in their hand to sling at Goliath, that is, one scripture to resist the tempter.[9]

In Henry Smith we see giftedness and spiritual endowment. But an undoubted aspect of his strength and appeal is seen in his sensitive adaptation of form and the utilization of variety in setting forth and framing the scriptural text to which he had great devotion. In this he models wisdom and exemplary vision.

---

1. R. B. Jenkins, *Henry Smith: England's Silver-Tongued Preacher* (Macon, Ga.: Mercer University Press, 1983), 1.
2. Ibid., 11.
3. Ibid., 16.
4. Ibid., 20.
5. F. R. Webber, *A History of Preaching in Britain and America* (Milwaukee: Northwestern, 1952), 1:215.
6. Jenkins, *Henry Smith,* 45.
7. J. W. Blench, *Preaching in England in the Late Fifteenth and Sixteenth Centuries* (New York: Barnes and Noble, 1964), 182.
8. Ibid., 184–85.
9. Jenkins, *Henry Smith,* 77–78.

6.1.3   William Perkins—The Prospector

> When being young, I heard worthy Master Perkins, so preach in a great assembly of students, that he instructed them soundly in the truth, stirred them up effectually to seek after godliness, made them fit for the kingdom of God; and by his example showed them what things they should chiefly intend, that they might promote true religion, in the power of it, unto God's glory, and other's salvation.
> —William Ames, student and admirer of William Perkins

For to leave the right handling of scripture is the way to bring in all error
and barbarism in religion.

—William Perkins

In turning to **William Perkins** (1558–1602) we are looking at a pivotal figure
in both theology and homiletics. He is often called the greatest of the sixteenth-
century Puritan theologians or the prince of the Puritan theologians. Ian Breward
described him as "the most widely known theologian of the Elizabethan church."[1]
He had international standing rivaling that of Luther and Calvin. Samuel Morison
maintained that the "typical Plymouth Colony library comprised a large and small
Bible, Ainsworth's translation of the Psalms, and the works of William ('Painful') Perkins, a favorite theologian." For our purposes, not at all incidentally, he
authored what may be the first homiletics book in English and a volume that
exerted tremendous influence, *The Art of Prophesying*.

William Perkins was born in Warwickshire and attended Cambridge, where
he earned his M.A. in 1584. In his early years he was given to drunkeness and
astrology but was converted after overhearing a father point him out to his child
as "that drunken Perkins."[2] He later served as a jail chaplain with such effectiveness that townspeople would come up to the prison to hear him preach. Greatly
touched by Puritan influences at Cambridge, he was, like Henry Smith, a moderate who would not himself be called a "Puritan."[3] Although much dissatisfied
with church government and worship in the Church of England generally, he refused to separate. He was heavily burdened by the slowness of the Reformation
and the shortage of Bible preachers in the established church. In 1603 there were
9,244 parishes but only 4,830 preachers licensed to preach. Perkins' inner life of
devotion was exceedingly rich (in fact it was his felicitous fusion of theology
and piety which really made him) and evinces affinity for the much earlier Walter
Hilton and his widely read *The Ladder of Perfection*.

Influencing Perkins' homiletical persuasion were Augustine, Erasmus, and
Hyperius. But we cannot understand Perkins or the Puritan mode of preaching
without first examining **Peter Ramus** (1515–1572). Ramus was born in northern France in a family of modest means but achieved a fine education where he
became professor of dialectic. He wrote sixty books on logic and philosophy and
coauthored thirteen with his colleague Taleus.[4] Ramus protested against Aristotelian scholasticism's domination in the sixteenth century and opted for Platonism
instead. He inclined to deductive approaches to reality and posited a universe of
order, "a copy of an ordered hierarchy of ideas existing in the mind of God."[5] He
made charts and diagrams setting forth the logical pairings found everywhere in
reality. While arrangement was important to Ramus, the subject matter reigned
supreme. (The Puritans generally and William Perkins specifically downplayed
rhetoric.) In 1562 Ramus converted to Protestantism, and in 1572 he was killed
in the massacre of St. Bartholomew's Day in France, when up to fifty thousand
Huguenots (French Protestants) were slain.

Ramian logic and rhetoric triumphed throughout England, especially at Cambridge and most particularly through the increasingly influential William Perkins.
There were many translations of Ramus into English, including one by John

Milton. The dialectic of dichotomies and their harmonization is seen in Perkins'
approach to preaching, which began with the reading of the text and comments on
the background and exegesis of the passage, then doctrinal propositions followed
by "uses" or application. Like Ramus, Perkins loved charts and diagrams.[6] The
weaknesses in the Ramean formulation are seen in the Puritans' overemphasis on
introspection and the tendency to an extreme authoritarianism in which certain
select minds will decide.

The last commentary Perkins wrote was his great masterpiece on Galatians.
This is the material he preached at Great St. Andrew's Church in Cambridge and
was refined in its final form by Perkins' good friend, Ralph Cudworth, the well-
known Cambridge Platonist, after Perkins' death. In his discussion of Galatians
3:1 and "plain style preaching," Perkins lays out not only his approach to the
commentary but to all preaching:

> The first is, true and proper interpretation of the Scripture, and that by it
> selfe: for Scripture, is both the glosse, and the text. The second is, savorie
> and wholesome doctrine, gathered out of the Scriptures truly expounded.
> The third is, the Application of the said doctrine, either to the informa-
> tion of the judgement, or to the reformation of the life.[7]

On Scripture Perkins stood stalwartly for the authority of the literal sense of
the Bible. He saw preaching as central in God's plan, for "in the preaching of the
Word and in the administration of the sacraments men could see."

> The great and glorious account which God makes of the word of his
> ministers, by them truly taught and rightly applied; namely that he, as it
> were, tieth his blessing to it: for ordinarily till a man know his righteous-
> ness by the means of an interpreter, God hath not mercy on him.[8]

Perkins's *The Art of Prophesying* is well worth reading. Chapter 3 is on the
Word and the Christocentricity of true preaching. He analyzes the nature of authentic persuasion. Preparation of preaching involves two processes:

1. interpretation of the Scripture
2. the right cutting or dividing of the Scripture (2 Timothy 2:15)

He speaks magnificently of the kinds of application and the spiritual life of
prayer and worship necessary for the communication God owns.[9] The sermon is
not a parade of the preacher's learning, and indeed Perkins is responsible for the
wise counsel, "It is also a point of art to conceal art."

All Puritans in a sense follow Perkins, although he had special influence on
William Ames, Thomas Goodwin, George Herbert (not a Puritan), John Robinson,
Richard Baxter, and Bishops Joseph Hall and James Ussher. Although Perkins
was a staunch Calvinist and crossed polemical swords with Arminius himself,
he wavered on some of Beza's extreme ideas (as did Peter Baro, Samuel Barsnet,
Richard Hooker, and John Cotton).[10] From many vantage points, William Perkins

is a seminal figure, not least in his laying of the foundations for so much of the Puritan preaching of all time.

---

1. Ian Breward, ed., *The Works of William Perkins* (Berkshire: Sutton Courtenay Press, 1970), xi.
2. F. R. Webber, *A History of Preaching in Britain and America* (Milwaukee: Northwestern, 1952), 1:220.
3. Breward, ed., *The Works of William Perkins,* 22.
4. William H. Kooienga, *Elements of Style for Preaching* (Grand Rapids: Zondervan, 1989), 37. Perry Miller in *The New England Mind: The Seventeenth Century* (Cambridge, Mass.: Harvard University Press, 1939), 338–39, argues that the Puritan sermon is *de novo* the product of Peter Ramus, but there is evidence of antecedents for this form from much earlier. Perkins and the Puritans are also indebted here to the Latin commentaries of Musculus (Wolfgang Muesslin, 1497–1563); see J. W. Blench, *Preaching in England in the Late Fifteenth and Sixteenth Centuries* (New York: Barnes and Noble, 1964), 101; see Walter J. Ong, *Ramus: Method, and the Decay of Dialogue* (Cambridge, Mass.: Harvard University Press, 1958). A solid study.
5. Ibid., 37.
6. Breward, ed., *The Works of William Perkins,* for example the elaborate chart on "A Golden Chain," 168.
7. William Perkins, *A Commentary on Galatians* (New York: Pilgrim, 1989). Cf. for instance, Galatians 3:13.
8. Breward, ed., *The Works of William Perkins,* 41.
9. Ibid., 323–49.
10. R. T. Kendall, *Calvin and English Calvinism to 1649* (Oxford: Oxford University Press, 1982). An instructive study of Beza, the first to make predestination central, Amyraut's position (1596–1644), and Perkins' vacillation.

6.1.4   JEAN CLAUDE—THE FORMULATOR

> When too little text is taken, you must digress from the subject to find something to say; flourishes of wit and imagination must be displayed, which are not of the genius of the pulpit: and in one word, it will make the hearers think, that self is more preached than Jesus Christ; and that the preacher aims rather at appearing a wit, than at instructing and edifying his people.
>
> —Jean Claude

A significant conduit of mature reflection on preaching is the Frenchman **Jean Claude** (1619–1687). Here is a parish pastor who developed great strength in preaching and left a rich legacy of homiletical instruction for subsequent generations in a series of remarkable divine providences. Part of the severely decimated French Protestant remnant, Claude was born in a small village in southern France, the son of a pastor who was dedicated to the spiritual and pastoral education of his son. Claude may have had some theological training at Montauban[1] and served congregations at St. Afrique, Nimes, and Charenton. He became embroiled in controversies with the Roman Catholics, wrote a powerful tome titled *Defense of the Reformation,* and debated the eminent Bossuet publicly. When the Edict of Nantes was revoked in 1685, he was forced to leave the country within twenty-four hours and spent his last several years working and preaching among the refugees in the Hague. Even his opponents called him "ce fameux M. Claude."

While his early preaching tended to be like the ancient homilies, Claude made the transition to what we have called the modified modern approach in which principalization and division of the text convey what the text says with appropriate application. Claude's own powerful preaching exerted an influence on even the great court preachers in France. What can be called the French model usually had two or three main points with relaxed development and emphasis on subpoints. Peter Bayley's classic study identifies Claude as a model of this tradition.[2]

The most conspicuous contribution of Claude has been his *Essay on the Composition of a Sermon.* This skillful work was translated into English by the eminent Cambridge preacher Robert Robinson and has continued to wield its effect to this day in several respects. It shaped **Charles Simeon,** one of the great fathers of the evangelical wing of the Church of England. We shall note Simeon's immense contribution later, but here we want to register the influence of Claude on his thinking.

Simeon's multiple-volumed expository sermons, *Horae Homileticae,* still in print, contains Claude's piece which Simeon himself indexed.[3] Here Claude explored the choice of a text and warned against selecting one too short or too long. He pled for serious exegesis and explication of the whole text, that is, in its context. He urged "perpetual application" of the text.[4] Claude dwelt on the divisions of the text and in the sermon, urging consideration of the genre or character of the passage as a whole. He dealt with the elucidation or amplification of the text, with the exordium and introduction, and commended conclusions which are "lively and animating, full of great and beautiful figures, aiming to move the Christian affections."[5]

When we read Simeon's admonition in relation to the proposition, we hear echoes of Jean Claude. Listen:

> Reduce your text to a simple proposition, and lay that down as the warp; and then make use of the text itself as the woof; illustrating the main idea by the various terms in which it is contained. Screw the word into the minds of your hearers. A screw is the strongest of all mechanical powers . . . when it has turned a few times, scarcely any power can pull it out.[6]

As we revel in the preaching of the seventeenth century, we must be mindful of this serious reflective work on preaching and its formulation, so basic to what was happening at the time.

---

1. E. C. Dargan, *A History of Preaching* (New York: Hodder and Stoughton, 1912), 2:124ff.

2. Peter Bayley, *French Pulpit Oratory: 1598–1650* (Cambridge, Mass.: Cambridge University Press, 1980), 110.
3. Charles Simeon, *Horae Homileticae* (Grand Rapids: Zondervan, 1955), 22:291ff.
4. Ibid., 297.
5. Ibid., 408.
6. As quoted in John R. W. Stott, *I Believe in Preaching* (London: Hodder and Stoughton, 1952), 226.

6.2 THE TUDOR AND CAROLINE DIVINES AND THE RISE OF THE CRAFT

Beware, beware, ye diminish not this [preaching] office; for if ye do, ye decay God's power to all that do believe. We must be ready to hear God's holy word; we must have good affections to hear God's holy word; and we must be ready to make provision for the furtherance of the preaching of God's holy word, as far forth as we be able to do.

—Hugh Latimer

The preaching of the seventeenth century in England arose out of the turbulence and tumult of the previous century. The legacy of biblical preaching had instilled a great hunger for the Word of God. Latimer and all the cohorts of the Reformation left a testimony and testament to the Word of God. How much it would be needed!

The first Stuart king, **James I,** was in many ways a despicable human being. Those in the stream of the Reformation were hopeful because the king had been raised a Scot, but he was "physically repellent . . . a pedant . . . [with] a crude, boyish humor . . . a drunkard and a sex pervert"[1] and yet cunningly able to ingratiate himself. The temptation for ecclesiastics was to fawn and flatter the royal presence, and into this trap Bishop Bancroft and Bishop Whitgift and even John Donne fell.[2]

James professed love for the sermon, and whenever he entered the chapel the preacher went into the pulpit, thus interrupting the flow of worship. Archbishop **William Laud** was the sycophantic advisor and confidante of James's son, **Charles I,** and continued to press the insane efforts for religious uniformity and to persecute and hound all nonconformists. The ultimate beheading of the king in 1649[3] and the years of the Puritan Commonwealth under Oliver Cromwell were the unfamiliar terrain over which England and her preachers traversed. Four years earlier Laud had been executed for "high treason."[4] Still, the restoration of the monarchy did not seem to resolve the religious tensions and strains of the period.

Yet for all this there was much preaching and avid attention to preaching in many quarters. Caroline Richardson has given us a splendid study of the preparation of clergy for preaching.[5] All classes went to church, and personal diaries show considerable interaction and comment with the sermon. Samuel Pepys, the most eminent of all the diarists, was an inveterate churchgoer, sometimes attending two or three different churches on a Sunday. Preaching was in vogue. He was well disposed toward the Puritans and comfortable in the Church of England. It is now to some more focused attention on preachers of this period that we turn.

---

1. Sidney Dark, *Seven Archbishops* (London: Eyre and Spottiswoode, 1944), 121.
2. T. Harwood Pattison, *The History of Christian Preaching* (Philadelphia: American Baptist Publication Society, 1903), 170.
3. C. V. Wedgewood's trilogy on *The Great Rebellion* is classic. These volumes are *The King's Peace, The King's War,* and especially *A Coffin for King Charles* (New York: Macmillan, 1964). A particularly helpful study of the Civil War of recent vintage is Christopher Hibbert, *Cavaliers and Roundheads: The English Civil War, 1642–1649* (New York: Scribner's, 1993).
4. Dark, *Seven Archbishops,* 141.
5. Caroline Francis Richardson, *English Preachers and Preaching 1640–1670* (New York: Macmillan, 1928).

6.2.1 THE POINTMAN OF THE PREACHERS—LANCELOT ANDREWES

I need more grief, I plainly need more of it. I am far from that which I ought to have. I can sin much! I cannot repent much. My dryness! My dryness! Woe unto me! Would that I had such grief, or even more! But of myself I cannot obtain it. I am parched, I am parched like a spotsherd. Woe is me! Thou, O Lord, O Lord, a fountain of tears. Give me a molten heart.

—Lancelot Andrewes in his classic
Preces Privatae (Private Devotions)

Lancelot Andrewes (1555–1626) was the primary court preacher in the time of James I *stella praedicantium,* a brilliant star in a lustrous firmament. He was born in London, the oldest of fourteen children born to a merchant family. From the beginning, he was precocious. Throughout his life he rose at 4 A.M. to study. He knew fifteen languages and could write better in Greek and Latin than in English.[1] He studied at Cambridge, where he was exposed to Puritan influence, and at Oxford. He was lecturer at Pembroke College, Cambridge, and served as one of the translators of the King James Version of the Bible. Andrewes was among the group translating the Pentateuch and Joshua through 2 Chronicles. He was successively prebend of St. Paul's, Dean of Westminster (he shared in the funeral of Queen Elizabeth I and the coronation of James I), and then bishop of Chichester, Ely, and Winchester.

T. S. Eliot, who acknowledged a great debt to both Lancelot Andrewes and John Donne, said of Andrewes' sermons, they "rank with the finest English prose of their time, any time."[2] Critics like Canon Wellsby allege undue servility to King James I. Eminence poses its own perils. He was a close friend of Francis Bacon. Charged to refute the errors of Cardinal Bellarmine in debate, he acquitted himself splendidly. His preaching always seemed to have a lifting effect upon the king. "The atmosphere changed when Lancelot Andrewes appeared."[3] *Lex ordandi, lex credendi* (how we pray is what we really believe) is borne out in Andrewes because his life was prayer and his theology flourished through it. His classic devotions and prayers continue to be widely used, and indeed Charles I used them just before his death.

Andrewes was a "preacher's preacher, very theological and very dependent on the Scripture." Mueller says that Andrewes tended to underplay and Donne to over-play.[4] Donne used a more varied rhythm while Andrewes had a staccato, elliptical quality in his preaching. Examination of his sermons shows "the profoundly liturgical character of his preaching."[5] F. E. Brightman has shown the vital linkage of prayer and celebrative worship in the preaching of Andrewes. As one of the evangelical Arminians, he was critical of strict Calvinism's denial of free will[6] and stressed the work of the Holy Spirit in preaching. This emphasis on the Holy Spirit is not all that common in the history of preaching.[7] He was strongly Trinitarian and Christocentric in his pulpit discourse. Lossky's priceless study leads us through the Christmas sermons of Andrewes on through Lent to Easter and then to Whitsuntide (or Pentecost, the greatly neglected festival of the church). His fifteen sermons on the Holy Spirit are doctrinally rich, as when he says:

> "Another Comforter" . . . "Another;" which word presupposes one besides, so that two there be. One they have already; and now another shall have, which is no evil news. For thus instead of a single, they find a double comfort. But they both are needed . . . Christ was one; was, and is still. Christ had been their comforter . . . but expedient it was He should go, for expedient it was they had one in Heaven; and expedient withal, they had one in earth, and so another in his stand.[8]

Andrewes still clung to allegorization, and he could moralize with the best of them. But he divided the text and the sermon very much in the modified modern style, with three main points and ordered subdivisions. He tended to be more chaste in his ornamentation than many, although he did use patristic citation. He loved to recreate the Christmas and Easter scenes.[9] He possessed a good sense of humor and enjoyed puns.

Eliot's essays on Lancelot Andrewes indicate the nature of the moral and spiritual impact Andrewes made on his life. His poem "The Journey of the Magi" was inspired by a sermon of Andrewes preached in Whitehall in 1622.[10] The wholesome spirituality and intensity in the inner spiritual life of Andrewes is impressive. Ophelia's complaint to Laertes in *Hamlet* has often been reiterated, but it has no application to Lancelot Andrewes:

> Do not, as some ungracious pastors do,
> Show me the steep and thorny way to heaven:
> Whilst like a puff'd and reckless libertine
> Himself the primrose path of dalliance treads,
> And recks not his own rede.
>
> —Shakespeare's *Hamlet,*
> first performed in London in 1603

1. Thomas S. Kepler, ed., *The Private Devotions of Lancelot Andrewes* (New York: World, 1956), xvii.
2. Nicholas Lossky, *Lancelot Andrewes: The Preacher (1555–1626)* (Oxford: Clarendon, 1991), 1.
3. Ibid., 24.
4. William R. Mueller, *John Donne: Preacher* (New York: Octagon, 1977), 235.
5. Lossky, *Lancelot Andrewes,* 28. One of his choice Christmas sermons, "The Sign to the Shepherds," is included in Wilbur M. Smith, *Great Sermons on the Birth of Christ* (Natick, Mass.: W. A. Wilde, 1963), 132–55.
6. Ibid., 332.
7. Ibid., 331, 333. Several more recent volumes have spoken to this lucuna: Dennis F. Kinlaw, *Preaching in the Spirit* (Grand Rapids: Frances Asbury/Zondervan, 1985); James Forbes, *The Holy Spirit and Preaching* (Nashville: Abingdon, 1989); Tony Sargent, *The Sacred Anointing: The Preaching of Dr. Martyn Lloyd-Jones* (Wheaton, Ill.: Crossway, 1994).
8. Ibid., 214.
9. J. W. Blench, *Preaching in England in the Late Fifteenth and Sixteenth Centuries* (New York: Barnes and Noble, 1964), 205ff.
10. Russell Kirk, *Eliot and His Age* (LaSalle, Ill.: Sherwood Sugen and Co., 1971), 136.

6.2.2   THE WORDMAN OF THE PREACHERS—JOHN DONNE

> Batter my heart, three-personed God, for you
> As yet but knock, breathe, shine and seek to mend;
> That I may rise and stand, o'erthrow me, and bend
> Your force to break, blow, burn and make me new. . . .
> Take me to you, imprison me, for I
> Except you enthrall me, never shall be free,
> Nor ever chaste, except you ravish me.

These moving lines reflect a deep spirituality, and are the work of **John Donne** (1572–1631). Donne was one of the noted "metaphysical poets" of this time and an English writer who has been rediscovered and celebrated in this century as few others. T. S. Eliot, while preferring "the cool, cultivated medieval temper" of Lancelot Andrewes, was yet taken with Donne's "flashing brilliance" and gave himself to reading his sermons.[1] For indeed as Frank Warnke describes him, Donne was "the greatest preacher of the greatest age of English pulpit oratory." Ten volumes of his sermons have been published by the University of California Press at Berkeley.[2]

John Donne was born to a distinguished Roman Catholic family in London which traced its lineage back to Sir Thomas More. Privately tutored at Oxford starting in 1584 but debarred from any degree because of his religious affiliation, he was much influenced in his early years by St. Teresa of Avila and St. John of the Cross. This was not an easy time to be a Roman Catholic in England, and Donne was witness to the execution of the brilliant young Edmund Campion in 1581 (memorialized in the book by Evelyn Waugh in 1935). He studied further at Cambridge and for the law at the Inns of Court and traveled abroad. He was restless, and his early poetry was quite erotic. In 1596 he was part of a military expedition with Essex and Raleigh to Cadiz in Spain. He was feeling among other things the dissolution of the medieval synthesis. To use his own words, "'Tis all in peeces, all cohaerence gone."[3]

Clearly in much stress and strain, Donne was in process of passage to Protestantism. He became secretary to Sir Thomas Edgerton, Keeper of the Seal, and secretly married his niece in 1601. Consequently he was in everyone's disfavor and soon unemployed. During this time he wrote his *Biathanatos,* which sought to rationalize suicide. At some point he was converted to Christ, and ultimately, at age forty-three, he took holy orders and was ordained in 1615.

A current Roman Catholic critic, John Carey of Oxford, disparages him and impugns his motives by alleging that Donne really wanted to be ambassador to Venice. For Carey, Donne was "self-advancing . . . pitiless . . . egotistical . . . with an urge to dominate women . . . [and] relishes dwelling on God's destructive purposes."[4] But this preacher-poet began to find a wide hearing for his rich biblical discourse. He preached at Paul's Cross in 1617, and in 1621 was appointed dean of St. Paul's in London, where he remained until his death.

Both his preaching and his poetry show his deeply-fixed theological roots. Donne was a follower of Augustine in many respects. Potter and Simpson mark a curve of positive and striking sermonic development.[5] Izaak Walton, one of his parishioners, called him "another Ambrose." Walton's description is telling:

> Preaching the Word so, as shewed his own heart was possest with those very thoughts and joys that he laboured to distill into others. A Preacher in earnest; weeping sometimes for his Auditory, sometimes with them: always preaching to himself like an Angel from a cloud, but in none; carrying some, as St. Paul was, to Heaven in holy raptures, and inticing others by a sacred Art and Courtship to amend their lives; here picturing a vice so as to make it ugly to those that practised it; and a virtue so as to make it beloved even by those that lov'd it not; and all this with a most particular grace and an unexpressible addition of comeliness.[6]

Donne saw himself as a trumpeter of the Word. He was a strong advocate of careful preparation, insisting on careful reading of the original text of Scripture. He used irony, satire, wit, and macabre images.[7] He employed diminuendo and crescendo. He spoke of "The Book of the World," "The Seal of the Sacrament," and "The Eyes of the Soul." Such epigrammatic language as endures can be seen in his phrases, "For whom the bell tolls," "No man is an island," or "Go and catch a falling star." Torrential eloquence can be marked along with a sense of dramatic immediacy and great personal intensity. He had a profound sense of calling to preach, a *vocatio radicalis,* in terms of which he stated: "It becometh me to make my selfe as acceptable a messenger as I can, and to infuse the Word of God into you, as powerfully from the Word of God it selfe, quickened by his Spirit."[8] Donne's unshakable persuasion was that the center of all preaching is "Christ Jesus and him crucified; and whosoever preaches any other Gospell, or any other things for Gospell, let him be accursed" (4.231).

Donne saw preaching as art and drama as well as exposition. The Puritans would have none of this. Much later Archbishop Davidson remarked that "sermons are often without real substance, deficient in intellectual quality, and unable to arouse interest or response in their hearers."[9] It is in the address to the latter of these challenges that the Donnean sermon is so instructive. His sermons were dramatic and dialogic. He used powerful metaphors and linguistic elevation. His hands and his voice were important for him. He used rhetorical device as did the prophets, Christ, and the apostles. The suspicion always is in some circles that anything too well ordered must be insincere. How does this follow?

Of the plain, middle, and ornate styles, Donne is actually quite middle. Certainly sermons in this era tended to be florid. But the danger of the plain style is that the sermon becomes a lecture without undulation or hills and valleys at all. The problem for the preacher is suggested in what Chips writes about her church in a recent Robertson Davies novel:

> What gets my goat is the sermon. . . . Then you come down with a bang from all the splendor of the Prayer Book and the really super prose of Cranmer to hear what some chap thinks it would be good for you to hear.[10]

John Donne addressed that issue in one way. We shall now inspect others. Donne's preaching and poetry show an obsession with death. Quite early on his young wife died, as did six of their twelve children. While he was at St. Paul's three waves of the Black Death swept over London with forty-thousand people dying in the last. Thirty-two of his fifty-four songs and sonnets are about death. His great sermon "Death's Duell" is a classic. Donne himself died after a long, lingering illness. He had hoped to die in the pulpit, yet he found Christ sufficient in his extremity. His personal experience validates his preaching.[11] In his last sermon he brought his hearers to Calvary:

> We leave you in that blessed dependency, to hang upon Him that hung upon the cross. There bathe in his tears, there suck of his wounds, and lie down in peace in his grave, till he vouchsafes you a resurrection and an ascension into that kingdom which he hath purchased for you with the inestimable price of his incorruptible blood.[12]

---

1. Alzina Stone Dale, *T. S. Eliot: The Philosopher Poet* (Wheaton, Ill.: Shaw, 1988), 90, 72.

2. George R. Potter and Evelyn M. Simpson, eds., *The Sermons of John Donne*, 10 vols. (Berkeley: University of California Press, 1953–1962). A top selection is also in the Modern Library's *The Complete Poetry and Selected Prose of John Donne* (New York: Modern Library/Random House, 1952). A sampling is in Erwin Paul Rudolph, ed., *The John Donne Treasury* (Wheaton, Ill.: Victor, 1978).

3. Michael Francis Moloney, *John Donne: His Flight from Medievalism* (Urbana: University of Illinois, 1944), 109.

4. John Carey, *John Donne: Life, Mind and Art* (New York: Oxford University Press, 1981), 95, 123.

5. Gale H. Carrithers Jr., *Donne at Sermons* (Albany: State University of New York Press, 1972), 78.

6. William R. Mueller, "The Sermons of John Donne," *Christianity Today* (September 28, 1962): 1203. Mueller also is the author of a fine study, *John Donne: Preacher* (New York: Octagon, 1977).

7. Winfreid Schleiner, *The Imagery of John Donne's Sermons* (Providence, R.I.: Brown University Press, 1970).

8. Robert B. Shaw, *The Call of God: The Theme of Vocation in the Poetry of Donne and Herbert* (Cambridge, Mass.: Cowley, 1981).

9. Quoted in Charles Smyth, *The Art of Preaching: A Practical Survey of Preaching in the Church of England* (London: SPCK, 1940), 1.

10. Robertson Davies, *The Cunning Man* (New York: Viking, 1994), 316.

11. Philip Yancey, "A Wrestling Match with the Almighty," *Christianity Today* (September 8, 1989): 22ff.

12. T. Harwood Pattison, *The History of Christian Preaching* (Philadelphia: American Baptist Publication Society, 1903), 176f.

6.2.3   The Pictureman of the Preachers—George Herbert

> Lord, how can man preach Thy eternall word?
> He is a brittle crazie glasse:
> Yet in Thy temple Thou dost him afford
> This glorious and transcendent place,
> To be a window, through Thy grace.

In these lines of the parson-poet we meet **George Herbert** (1593–1633), a skilled artisan of the craft. Born into a wealthy and titled family, Herbert studied at Cambridge, where in 1619 he was made orator of the university. He developed high tastes and obtained the notice of even James I, whose court he often attended. Disappointed in politics, he sensed God's call to preach and took a small congregation at Bemerton near Salisbury. Notwithstanding what might seem to be a meager opportunity, Herbert was determined:

> And though the iniquity of the late times have made clergymen meanly valued, and the sacred name of priest contemptible; yet I will labor to make it honorable, by consecrating all my learning, and all my poor abilities to advance the glory of that God who gave them; knowing that I never can do too much for him, that hath done so much for me as to make me a Christian. And I will labor to be like my Saviour, by making humility lovely in the eyes of all men.[1]

Consumed by ill health, he did not have long to serve. In contrast to Donne's fire and complexity, we cannot but be impressed by Herbert's gentleness and simplicity.

Described as "not witty or learned or eloquent but holy," George Herbert preached the Word. He also wrote 169 poems collected in *The Temple,* using many verse forms and ranging over many Christian doctrines, including election and eschatology. He reflected on affliction and his sense of vocation. He wanted to be fruitful "like the orenge tree" for his Lord.[2] His is a highly sacramental theology, but he chose the plain style for his discourses, worrying that "overheated imagination can obscure the heavenly glory."[3] He did not disdain the ministrations of the country parson who

> holds the Rule, that Nothing is little in God's service: If it once have the honour of that Name, it grows great instantly. Wherefore neither disdaineth he to enter into the poorest cottage, though he even creep into it, and though it smell never so lothsomely. For both God is there also, and those for whom God dyed . . .[4]

Preaching that is "speech alone" is bereft of blessing, and as he insisted on his deathbed, all "must be sprinkled with the blood of Christ."

While much of his poetry was written in Latin and Greek, Herbert divulged some of the richness of his inner life and communication in his extended series of verses in reply to the Scot Andrew Melville's *Accusations.* This is also evident in some of his charming and moving poems on Christ's passion.[5]

The Carolingian preachers give us a heightened appreciation for their diversity and the beauty and symmetry possible in the craft of preaching.

---

1. M. C. Allen, "George Herbert: Poet to the Clergy," *The Pulpit* (September 1964): 7–10.
2. Robert B. Shaw, *The Call of God: The Theme of Vocation in the Poetry of Donne and Herbert* (Cambridge, Mass.: Cowley, 1981), 78.
3. Ibid., 98.
4. Ibid., 90. Two other poet-preachers of note are Robert Herrick and Richard Crashaw.
5. Also note Mark McCloskey and Paul R. Murphy, trans., *The Latin Poems of George Herbert* (Athens: Ohio University Press, 1965).

6.2.4   THE MARKSMAN OF THE PREACHERS—JEREMY TAYLOR

> If homilies or sermons be made upon the words of Scripture, you are to consider whether all that be spoken be conformable to the Scriptures; for, although you may practice for human reasons, and human arguments, ministered from the preacher's art, yet you must practice nothing but the command of God, nothing but the doctrine of Scripture; that is, the text.
>
> Let not the humours and inclinations of the people be the measures of your doctrines, but let your doctrines be the measure of their persuasions.
>
> —Jeremy Taylor

Sometimes called the poet of the preachers, **Jeremy Taylor's** (1613–1667) sermons stand as great English literature. He was called the English Chrysostom. One pulpit observer commented, "We have no modern sermons in the English language that can be considered as very eloquent . . . for eloquence we must ascend as high as the days of Jeremy Taylor."[1] Coleridge called him "the most eloquent of divines." Similar accolades have come from Ralph Waldo Emerson and James Russell Lowell. His critic Robert Southey described him: "From whose mind of its treasures redundant streams of eloquence flowed, like an inexhaustible foundation."[2] Was he too grandiose? Too ornate? The more florid and oratorical among us must constantly ask ourselves, Am I becoming too convoluted and turgid?

Taylor was born the son of a barber and baptized in Holy Trinity Church in Cambridge. In 1626 he entered Cambridge, taking orders in 1629. He lectured at St. Paul's in London, where he was an instant favorite, for "no one had preached in St. Paul's with such impassioned eloquence since the great Dean [John Donne] who had been dead three years."[3] Here he caught the attention and favor of Archbishop Laud, whose protégé he became along with George Herbert. **William Laud** (1573–1645), successively bishop of London and archbishop of Canterbury as well as key advisor to King Charles I, sponsored Taylor on a fellowship at Oxford and then saw him placed at age twenty-five in Uppingham, a small country church. Laud, a high churchman, Arminian but a strong Anselmian, pressed for Scottish uniformity. As a result, Parliament effectively abolished the episcopacy and Laud was accused of "high treason" in 1640. Some of the Puritan complaints were laughable, such as Laud's positive attitude toward plays which were "accompanied by lust-provoking music and profuse exorbitant laughter."[4] He was beheaded in 1645.

Taylor survived the civil war in Golden Grove, where he wrote and preached, steadfast in his loyalty to the crown and the Church of England. He was imprisoned a number of times. In the Restoration he was consecrated as a bishop in the Church of Ireland at St. Patrick's Cathedral in Dublin, where he also served as vice chancellor of the University of Dublin. These were ecclesiastically stormy and personally sorrowful years for Taylor, who died in 1667.

Taylor was a controversialist but wisely counseled preachers, when preaching "do not trouble your people with controversies."[5] As one who shrank from hyper-Calvinistic ideas, particularly the doctrine of reprobation as preached by some Puritans, he was called Arminian Taylor. His treatise *The Liberty of Prophesying* was to freedom of speech and tolerance what Milton's *Areopagetica* was to freedom of the press. Taylor was best known for his great personal piety and his devotional writings, such as *The Rule and Exercises of Holy Living* (1650) and *The Rule and Exercises of Holy Dying* (1651), are still circulated. These are actually portions of his preaching.

A master of English prose, Taylor was known above all for his great integrity and character. He pled for "an upright and holy life." His influence on John Wesley was profound, and Wesley acknowledged that his acquaintance with Taylor when he was in his twenty-third year was defining for him.[6]

Taylor's preaching utilized long sentences. He loved homely illustrations. He preached vividly on heaven and hell, death and judgment, God's mercy and

God's severity. He warned of relying on deathbed repentance, and abhorred the doctrines of extreme unction and prayers for the dead. Sixty-four of his sermons have been preserved, including a most striking series on "Christ's Advent to Judgment," which graphically depicts the wicked in their confusion and believers in the house of feasting. Allusions, metaphors, and similes abounded in his preaching. Horton Davies, speaking of Puritan preaching, lamented that "the wit of South, the brilliant and quaint imagination of Donne, the sustained metaphors of Jeremy Taylor or the racy language of Latimer are not to be found there."[7]

While we have two distinct styles here, is it entirely fair to say of Taylor that "he delights but does not move"?[8] He was a child of his age and effective in his setting, as were the Puritans. Webber decries Taylor's description of the fallen angels which he contrasts with the simplicity of the biblical statement, but is not Taylor's treatment defensible? Taylor's own words are: "The angels themselves, because their light reflected home to their orbs, and they understood all the secrets of their own perfection, they grew vertiginous, and fell from the battlements of heaven."[9] Perhaps he overused quotations as in his declamation, "Aelian tells of the geese flying over the mountain Taurus; that for fear of eagles, nature hath taught them to carry stones in their mouths, till they be past their danger."[10] In a funeral sermon for the archbishop of Armaugh, he waxed eloquent in his tribute. "For in him were visible the great lines of Hooker's judiciousness, of Jewel's learning, of the acuteness of Bishop Andrewes."[11] Overdone? Possibly, but memorable. Jeremy Taylor remains an uncommon preacher still read in our times.

---

1. Thomas S. Kepler, ed., *Jeremy Taylor's The Rules and Exercises of Holy Living* (New York: World, 1956), xx.
2. Ibid., xxii.
3. W. J. Brown, *Jeremy Taylor* (London: SPCK, 1925), 10.
4. Sidney Dark, *Seven Archbishops* (London: Eyre and Spottiswood, 1944), 134.
5. Frank Livingstone Huntley, *Jeremy Taylor and the Great Rebellion* (Ann Arbor: University of Michigan, 1970), 6.
6. H. Trevor Hughes, *The Piety of Jeremy Taylor* (London: Macmillan, 1960), 175.
7. Ibid., 116.
8. F. R. Webber, *A History of Preaching in Britain and America* (Milwaukee: Northwestern, 1952), 1:246.
9. Ibid., 247.
10. Caroline Francis Richardson, *English Preachers and Preaching 1640–1670* (New York: Macmillan, 1928), 84.
11. Ibid., 103.

6.2.5   The Crossman of the Preachers—Joseph Hall

He [Bishop Hall] never durst climb up into the pulpit to preach any Sermon, whereof he had not penned every word in the same order, wherein

he hoped to deliver it: although in his expressions he was no slave to syllables, neither made use of his notes.
—John Lightfoot at Bishop Hall's funeral

We are surveying what are sometimes called the metaphysical preachers, so-called because of their classical learning and the wit, imagination, and learning characterizing their sermons.[1] In these preachers the extravagance of the age is clearly reflected (in general contrast to the Puritans). Classical rhetoric was still the basis of the educational system, and even the Puritans had rhetorical leanings,[2] although their interest in rhetoric was more for the explication of the scriptural text than the composition of the sermon. We have been looking at "the luscious style" of Jeremy Taylor and his "witty preaching," which caused Coleridge to place him with Shakespeare, Milton, and Bacon. As we shall see, Richard Baxter, the Puritan yet within the Church of England, chose the plain style of preaching. But several of the Caroline divines cut a unique swath. We turn to them now.

Joseph Hall (1574–1656) was born in Leicestershire, graduated from Cambridge in 1592, and taught rhetoric there for two years. He was ordained in 1601 and began his parish ministry in Halsted, Suffolk.[3] In his storied career he was successively chaplain to the Prince of Wales, chaplain in France to the British ambassador, in the retinue of James I in his ill-conceived visit to Scotland to impose the English liturgy on the Scottish people, rector at Waltham for twenty-two years, a Royal Commissioner to the Synod of Dort, and bishop of Exeter and bishop of Norwich. Hall was of the Calvinistic persuasion but was also disliked by Laud for his views on the toleration of the Puritans. Finally he was deprived of his bishopric by the Long Parliament, imprisoned in the Tower of London, and stripped of all his possessions. His final days were lived in poverty but in peace.[4]

Hall was renowned as a preacher of the Word. Twelve volumes remain of his collected works, which include much preaching and his poetry. He preached three times a week and loved to preach biblical characters and biographical sermons. He did careful work out of the original languages, loved proverbs and quotations, and used wit in a way that the Puritans did not. In arguing against veneration of relics, he said:

But to dig up their holy bones, that I may borrow Luther's word, out of their quiet graves and to fall down before these worm-eaten monuments of the Saints, to expect from them a divine power, whether of cure or of sanctification, equally to respect Francis's cowl, Anna's comb, Joseph's breeches, Thomas's shoe, as Erasmus complains, with the Sone of God Himself, can seem no better to us than a horrible impiety.[5]

Hall advocated thoughtful use of the church year as an instructive device. He did research on the history of heraldry to illustrate aspects of truth in an outstanding sermon. He had a great love for Scripture, and one of his enduring memorials is his book of sermonic material titled *Contemplations Upon the*

Principal Passages in the Holy Story. He was called the English Seneca for his eloquence.

Hall's reputation as a gifted and effective preacher focused on his preaching of Christ and his Cross. His preaching on the seven last words of Christ is monumental. Hall stands in an enviable succession of preachers who concentrated their best work on the sufferings of our Lord and the meaning of his atonement. One such sermon at Paul's Cross on Good Friday, April 14, 1609, was on John 19:30 and includes the following meditation on the anguish of the suffering Savior:

> That head, which is adored and trembled at by the angelical spirits, is all raked and harrowed with thorns; that face of whom it is said, Thou art fairer than the children of men, is all besmeared with filthy spittle. . . . and furrowed with his tears; those eyes, clearer than the sun, are darkened with the shadow of death; those ears, that hear the heavenly concerts of angels, now are filled with the cursed speakings and scoffs of wretched men; those lips, that spake as never man spake, that command the spirits both of light and darkness, are scornfully wet with vinegar and gall; those feet, that trample on all the powers of hell (his enemies are made his footstool) are now nailed to the footstool of the cross; those hands, that freely sway the sceptre of the heavens, now carry the reed of reproach, and are nailed to the tree of reproach; that whole body, which was conceived by the Holy Ghost, was all scourged, wounded, mangled: this is the outside of his sufferings.[6]

---

1. Horton Davies, *Like Angels from a Cloud: The English Metaphysical Preachers 1588–1645* (San Marino, Calif.: Huntington Library, 1986), 49. A joyous piece of careful research!
2. W. Fraser Mitchell, *English Pulpit Oratory from Andrewes to Tillotson: A Study of its Literary Aspects* (London: SPCK, 1932), 69, 95.
3. F. R. Webber, *A History of Preaching in Britain and America* (Milwaukee: Northwestern, 1952), 1:229.
4. E. C. Dargan, *A History of Preaching* (New York: Hodder and Stoughton, 1912), 2:153.
5. Davies, *Like Angels from a Cloud,* 318.
6. Ibid., 374–75.

6.2.6 The Spokesman Among the Preachers—Thomas Fuller

In explaining why he concluded a sermon somewhat abruptly: "These things deserve larger Prosecution; but this is none of Joshua's day, wherein the Sunne standeth still; and therefore I must conclude the time."

About the Puritans: "I never knew nor heard of an Army all of Saints, save the Holy Army of Martyrs; and those, you know, were dead first."

> Defending wit in sermons providing: "The sweetnesse of the sauce spoile not the savourinesse of the meat."
>
> —Thomas Fuller

One of the most extraordinarily popular preachers in this golden age of preaching was **Thomas Fuller** (1608–1661), who when preaching at the Savoy in the Strand attracted so many outside visitors that his own people had difficulty finding seating. It was said that he always preached to two congregations—one in the sanctuary and the other outside the windows of the church. His father was rector at St. Peter's, Aldwincle, and he was educated at Cambridge, where he graduated in 1624. He served a succession of posts, including Inns of Court and the Savoy. As all of these preachers now before us, he was a staunch loyalist and royalist and in the difficult years he was at Oxford and Exeter. After the Restoration, Fuller was appointed chaplain to King Charles II.

Two volumes of his printed sermons remain, and his influential books, *Church History of Britain* and *History of the Worthies of England,* were widely circulated in his time and subsequently. He was known as a jovial Calvinist who used humor, puns, and playful banter with his congregation—a tactic that is usually difficult and sometimes dangerous.[1]

Charles Lamb called him a great storyteller, and his very appearance, "corpulent, ruddy, cheerful and head adorned with a comely light-colored haire which was so by nature exactly curled,"[2] made him like a big teddy bear to his adoring listeners. Gifted with an amazing memory, he stressed literal exegesis over allegorization, but pooh-poohed rigid literality.

> Besides, Christ at his death spake no other language than what his tongue and his Disciples were used to in his life time: I am the Vine, I am the Way, I am the Doore. Hee who is so sottish as to conceive that Christ was a materiall Doore shoeweth himself to be a post indeed.[3]

Earlier on he delighted in consecutive book exposition in his preaching. His sermons were more like the Puritan style of selecting a thematic doctrine from the text and tracing its uses. Some of his unforgettable epigrams linger with us, such as "You cannot repent too soon because you do not know how soon it will be too late" or "God's children are immortal while their Father hath anything for them to do on earth" (possibly the source for Mark Twain's famous quote).

Fuller was a man of quirks and quaintness; hence, we are not surprised to find these qualities in his preaching. His wit sprang from "that genuine observance of similitudes,"[4] which informed his notion of amplification in the sermon; he sought out "the untold wonders of association, which a phrase or often a single word suggested to him, and which he immediately shared with his hearers."[5] The grave peril which Fuller faced and of which all preachers must beware is any ostentatious effect which draws attention to itself and away from the compelling biblical subject. His sermons were heard well and they read well. These qualities are commendable, but cause us to walk a fine line.

1. John W. Drakeford, *Humor in Preaching* (Grand Rapids: Zondervan, 1986).
2. Horton Davies, *Like Angels from a Cloud: The English Metaphysical Preachers 1588–1645* (San Marino, Calif.: Huntington Library, 1986), 172.
3. Ibid., 118.
4. W. Fraser Mitchell, *English Pulpit Oratory from Andrewes to Tillotson* (London: SPCK, 1932), 233.
5. Ibid., 236.

6.2.7 THE OARSMAN AMONG THE PREACHERS—JOHN TILLOTSON

Of Tillotson's preaching it was said: "He was not only the best preacher of the age, but seemed to have brought preaching to perfection; his sermons were so well liked that all the nation proposed him as a pattern and studied to copy after him."

—Bishop Burnet

The firmament was bright with preachers in seventeenth-century England. We have yet to consider the Puritan school with its immense contribution. Worthies mentioned in this galaxy must include **Edmund Calamy** (1600–1666), known for his careful craftsmanship in preaching. Calamy opposed the execution of Charles I but did adopt nonconformist views and spent time in prison after the Restoration. **Herbert Palmer** (1601–1647) could read the Bible at age four. He was fluent in French, a member of the Westminster Assembly of Divines, and wrote much of the Shorter Catechism. Palmer burned himself out in his preaching. **William Chillingworth** (1602–1644), famous for his words, "The Bible, I say the Bible only is the religion of Protestants," was a strong expositor of Scripture and highly intellectual. **Isaac Ambrose** (1604–1663) suffered much for his Puritan views but is most remembered for his beautiful study, *Looking unto Jesus*.[1] Archbishop **James Ussher** (1581–1656) was primate of the Church of Ireland (Protestant). He was a learned and tolerant Calvinist, and author of the famous Ussher's chronology which put the creation at 4004 B.C. Ussher was opposed to florid preaching, and introduced plain style preaching at Oxford and Westminster. He used poignant imagery and metaphor, and was especially gifted in his preaching on the cross.[2] Bishop **John Pearson** was an effective court chaplain in the Restoration. Pearson was a linguist, and a friend of Baxter at the Savoy Conference. He is remembered for his classic work on the Apostles' Creed. **William Gurnall,** who gave us his sermonic work on *The Christian in Complete Armour,* was reordained in the Church of England.

Amid the ecclesiastical complexity of this age, a key figure is **John Tillotson** (1630–1694), a popular preacher in London. Fourteen volumes of his sermons are extant. Admired by Addison and praised by Doddridge for his clarity, Tillotson became archbishop of Canterbury in 1690, and for a few short years exerted immense influence on church life and preaching. His style was persuasive, not polemic.[3] His sermons were logical and intellectual but memorable, as was his famous sermon on "The Reasonableness of the Resurrection." He was such a smooth stylist that the poet Dryden said of him, "if he had any talent for English prose it was owing to his having often read the writings of the great Archbishop Tillotson."[4] Tillotson's sermons were like literary essays, in which each word was carefully considered, with a general sense of the text neglected and no division of the text.[5]

This was the age of the reaction of the Cambridge Platonists against the Puritans on the one hand and the extreme embellishment of the metaphysical preachers and the high churchmanship of Laud on the other. Such luminaries as Benjamin Whichcote, Ralph Cudworth, Henry More, and Nathaniel Culverwell were all effective preachers but veered toward a sterile, rationalistic preaching. Meanwhile, Robert South lurched toward clever political preaching. South was more courtier than preacher. The two sermons for which he is remembered were one preached against extemporaneous prayer and another in memory of Charles I.[6]

The result of these developments was decline in the English pulpit to the end of the century.

Archbishop Tillotson bears some of the culpability for the diminution of biblical preaching, despite his love for the Scripture and his Puritan upbringing. Tillotson admirably appealed to reason and common sense, but the great danger was that his sermons became highly polished moral essays. His sermons took on a read rather than a spoken quality, and no longer plumbed the biblical text.

The essay sermon is still with us today, particularly in mainline and liturgical circles. Such sermons are smooth and controlled, never succumbing to panting passion or the rarified air of the mountain peak. Thus preaching lost momentum by the end of the century. As Smyth argues, it would be the evangelists of the next century who restored the powerful preaching of the Cross of Christ.[7]

---

1. Helpful sketches of these preachers will be found in F. R. Webber, *A History of Preaching in Britain and America,* vol. 1 (Milwaukee: Northwestern, 1952).
2. Horton Davies, *Like Angels from a Cloud: The English Metaphysical Preachers 1588–1645* (San Marino, Calif.: Huntington Library, 1986), 164–68.
3. Webber, *A History of Preaching,* 1:267.
4. Ibid., 208. For a good sampling, see James Moffat, *The Golden Book of Tillotson* (London: Hodder and Stoughton, 1926). Note particularly "The Bible a Plain Book," 67–68. Striking and appropriate literary quotations.
5. Charles Smyth, *The Art of Preaching: A Practical Survey of Preaching in the Church of England 747–1939* (London: SPCK, 1940), 99, 106.
6. T. Harwood Pattison, *The History of Christian Preaching* (Philadelphia: American Baptist Publication Society, 1903), 208ff.
7. Smyth, *The Art of Preaching,* 173.

6.3 FRENCH PULPIT ORATORY AND THE REFINEMENT OF THE CRAFT

To preach is the publication and declaration of God's will, made to men by one lawfully commissioned to that task, to the end of instructing and moving them to serve his divine Majesty in this world so as to be saved in the next.

—Francis of Sales

With the waning of Spanish and Portuguese power, especially after the defeat of the Spanish Armada in 1588, England and France come increasingly to the fore, and their very position and power in the seventeenth century mean inevitable clash between them. It was a time of greatness for France. Henry of Navarre (Henry IV) with the aid of the Duke of Sully reduced taxes and oversaw impressive economic growth. He also signed the Edict of Nantes in 1598, giving a degree of freedom of worship to the persecuted Protestants, the Huguenots. Henry was himself a Huguenot but became a Roman Catholic to achieve peace in 1593.

Louis XIII, his son, became king on his father's assassination in 1610, and, under the dominant leadership of Cardinal Richelieu, saw the establishment of an absolute monarchy. All Huguenot political power was destroyed as power centralized in the hands of the king. Thousands of Huguenots fled. When Louis XIII died in 1642, he was succeeded by his five-year-old son, Louis XIV, who ruled for seventy-two years. He was known as Louis the Great or the Grand Monarch. His chief minister was Cardinal Mazarin. Louis XIV fought four major wars. The final conflict, the War of the Spanish Succession, was lost largely through the English and left France prostrate just before his death. Through the malignant influence of his chief mistress, Madame de Maintenon, Louis XIV revoked the Edict of Nantes in 1685 and fiercely persecuted the Huguenots. Even though France bled seriously through the flight of so many prosperous and upstanding citizens, the king remained unbearably headstrong, declaring, "I am the state!" France's strength and leadership were visibly reduced. At the time of Louis XIV's death, France was a shadow of what she had been before. Yet even in such stressful times, God and His Word were not silent.

6.3.1 THE SHAPING INFLUENCES ON FRENCH PREACHING

We must preach the Word of God. . . . Preach the Gospel says the Master. . . . St. Francis explains this when he commands frairs to preach on virtues and vices and on hell and paradise. There is sufficient matter in Sacred Scripture for all of that; nothing further is needed.

—Francis of Sales

Pattison asserts that "the pulpit eloquence of France in the seventeenth century was distinguished by extraordinary richness of thought and splendor of diction . . . to the present hour the great sermons of that era remain the classics of the language."[1] Dargan called it "the classic age" or "the golden age" of the French pulpit. We know that Tillotson studied the court preachers of France, but it is of interest that we find such striking parallels between England and France.

For a sense of the often tense environment for preaching at this time, we may peruse the biography of **René Descartes**. Born in 1596 near Tours, Descartes was trained in a Jesuit college where the need for reform was obvious.[2] The essential purpose of education was to "pour [persons] forth to preach and teach the Word of God to the masses" to counteract increasing Protestant influence.[3] Using his notion of "clear and distinct ideas," Descartes developed a psychological theory of cognitive grasp which eventuated in his famous *Cogito, ergo sum* (I think, therefore I am).

While in contact with Cardinal Berulle, who championed a revival of Augustinianism emphasizing a radical dependence on God (which Descartes could never accept), he relished the freedom of Protestant Amsterdam. He was especially stung by the condemnation of Galileo in 1633[4] and turned from his brilliant and productive labors in physics to metaphysics. He met the sixteen-year-old genius Pascal at this time, but troubled in his own personal affairs and in conflict with Protestant theologians like Voetius at Utrecht, he finally took the patronage of Queen Christina of Sweden, moving there in his midfifties. Descartes died in Stockholm in February of 1650. His biographer calls him "a zealous Roman Catholic who feared the displeasure of the Church above all else."[5]

The flurry of interest in preaching theory from the time of Alan of Lille in the twelfth century stands in contrast to the paucity of biblical preaching at this time. Yet there were those who strove to uphold solid preaching. One of the princely figures of the time was **Francis of Sales** (1567–1622), who went to Geneva to attempt to convert Beza. He served as prince bishop of Geneva in exile at Annecy. He authored several widely influential works on Christian spirituality, including *The Introduction to the Devout Life* and *Treatise on the Love of God*, and preached powerfully. His great burden was "a call to universal holiness."[6] His work was read by Jeremy Taylor and John Henry Newman. He attempted to fuse the Tridentine decrees on preaching (which affirmed the classical canons) with his personal affection for the instructional emphasis of **Charles Borromeo** of Italy.

Borromeo's book, which recommends elucidation of the Scripture and simple rhetorical devices, was approved by the Council of Bordeaux in 1624.[7] Also influential was the book written for the new diocesan seminaries by the bishop of Verona, **Agostino Valiero**. His work appeared in 1574 and argued the difference between the homily and the classical oration.[8] Spanish and Jesuit theorists were also at work. And De Sales himself wrote a famous letter to Andre Fremiot, bishop-designate of Bourges, addressing the craft of preaching.[9] We quote from this letter at the beginning of each of these sections.

Other spiritual movements beyond the French School of Cardinal Berulle contributed to the spiritual venue of preaching. Above all was **Cornelius Jansen** (d. 1638), a convinced Augustinian, who settled around Port Royal des Champs, which would become a stronghold of Scripture and gospel purity. Port Royal des Champs was the chief influence shaping **Blaise Pascal** (1623–1662), the brilliant apologist for the Christian faith. Calvary was the great divide in Pascal's search for truth. Pascal was a Christian layman imbued with a supernaturalistic worldview which was bibliocentric. Cailliet says, "At the heart of Christianity he saw Christ Himself . . . . All our virtue and felicity."[10]

The crushing of Port Royal and the condemnation of Antoine Arnauld, who was head of the Jansenists, were ominous signs. They foreshadowed the fact that "spiritual life in France was threatened by authoritarian proceedings copied from the Inquisition, and all morality was threatened at the same time."[11] Yet this would provide the spiritual milieu for an astounding outburst of preaching in the most unlikely places. God was yet at work, and He would bless his holy Word.

---

1. T. Harwood Pattison, *The History of Christian Preaching* (Philadelphia: American Baptist Publication Society, 1903), 214.
2. Stephen Gaukroger, *Descartes: An Intellectual Biography* (Oxford: Clarendon, 1995), 27.
3. Ibid., 39.
4. For important studies of the bearing of Galileo's controversy with the church at Rome, see Giorgio De Santillana, *The Crime of Galileo* (Chicago: University of Chicago, 1955); James Reston Jr., *Galileo: A Life* (New York: HarperCollins, 1994). Touching description of visits to the dying old man by Thomas Hobbes and John Milton.
5. Gaukroger, *Descartes*, 291.
6. Cheslyn Jones, Geoffrey Wainwright, Edward Yarnold, *The Study of Spirituality* (New York: Oxford, 1986), 381.
7. Peter Bayley, *French Pulpit Oratory* (London: Cambridge University Press, 1980), 45.
8. Ibid., 48.
9. Francis of Sales, *On the Preacher and Preaching* (Chicago: Henry Regnery, 1964).
10. Emile Cailliet, *Pascal: The Emergence of Genius* (New York: Harper Torchbooks, 1945, 1961).
11. Ibid., 201.

6.3.2 THE SHINING INSTANCES OF FRENCH PREACHING

Preaching must be spontaneous, dignified, courageous, natural, sturdy, devout, serious, and a little slow. But to make it such what must be done? In a word, it means to speak with affection and devotion, with simplicity and candor, and with confidence, and to be convinced of the doctrine we teach of what we persuade. The supreme art is to have no art. Our words must be set aflame, not by shouts and unrestrained gestures, but by inward affection.

—Francis of Sales

Francis always insisted that the test of a sermon was not whether a congregation responded, "What a beautiful sermon," but whether they departed saying "I will do something." We shall soon see some extraordinary preaching, but to preach on parade is perilous. Eloquence can never be a goal in itself, but we must never forget, as John Donne observed, "There are not so eloquent books in the world, as the Scriptures."[1]

King Louis XIV led an especially strong Counter-Reformation, not only against the Huguenots but also against Jansenism within the church. The stamping out of these renewal movements led to moral laxity in the nation, which ultimately brought France to the French Revolution and the Enlightenment. There were no

Pietists to ameliorate the radicality of the Enlightenment in France.[2] Of course the French church always had a unique relationship to the Roman pontiff (Gaullicanism). We will scrutinize the spheres and subjects of French preaching in this period, for as Huizinga maintained, preaching can show us the "structure of feeling" of a whole civilization.

---

1. Peter Bayley, *French Pulpit Oratory 1598–1650* (Cambridge, Mass.: Cambridge University Press, 1980), 3.
2. Kurt Aland, *A History of Christianity* (Philadelphia: Fortress, 1986), 2:267.

6.3.2.1 Roman Catholic Preaching by Parish Priests and Primates

What soul is so unfeeling that it does not take very great pleasure from learning the path to heaven in so good and holy a way, and does not feel the greatest consolation in love of God? There is another kind of delight . . . this is a sort of tickling of ears, which derives from a certain secular, worldly and profane elegance and from various affectations and arrangements of ideas, words and phrases . . . it depends wholly on artifice . . . they do not preach "Jesus Christ crucified"; they preach themselves.
—Francis of Sales

The contemporary Cambridge scholar Peter Bayley has given us an invaluable study of the preaching of fifty or sixty preachers in this period.[1] Some preachers made minimal comments in conjunction with the Mass, but there was some significant preaching on the part of some in the Roman Catholic Church. Then there were the Protestant preachers for whom preaching was at the core of the worship experience. The earlier preaching in this period was more in the plain style. **Jean Bertraut** of Caen (1552–1611), the well-known poet, was one such preacher. Another was the Franciscan **Jean Boucher** of Poitiers (1560–1631). Their style reflected the influence of the essays of Montaigne. Their sermons possessed some decorative features, but were nothing to compare with the "thesaurus sermons" which came into vogue, packed with "anecdotes, illustrations and analogies."[2]

Reacting against the tendency to monotony and flabbiness in this style was **Jean-Pierre Camus** (1584–1652), bishop of Belley and friend of Francis of Sales. He developed what Bayley calls "catenary prose," the use of long examples, "breathless, inchoate," with little regard for elocution.[3] Predictably, a rhetorical reaction set in, as is seen in the preaching of Etienne Molinier of Toulouse (d. 1647). He moved back into more traditional rhetoric. The emphasis on *le naturel,* and more "orchestrated prose" will be seen more prominently among the Protestant preachers surveyed in the next section.

But the master preacher who emerged out of this flux was doubtless **Jacques Benigne Bossuet** of Dijon (1627–1704). Reared in a large, middle-class family, he had a transforming experience early in his life when he discovered the Book of Isaiah in his uncle's study. It was the first time he had read the Scripture, and it began a lifelong journey of study in the Word. Bossuet received his doctorate and was ordained in 1652. Very much drawn to Augustine (whose commentaries he always carried with him), he was also greatly influenced by the gracious and gentle **Vincent de Paul,** with whom he held a memorable retreat after his ordination.[4]

Serving at first in Paris and then as dean in Metz, Bossuet was soon marked as a powerful preacher. His first major visibility came in a Lenten course of sermons at the Louvre in 1662. Over his lifetime, he delivered five courses of Lenten sermons and three courses of Advent sermons in Paris, although the state of his surviving sermons is not good. He loved the work of Pascal, and observed that if he could write anything that would last, he would wish to write the *Pensees.*

Elevated to the episcopacy, Bossuet was appointed bishop of Condom before serving as the bishop of Meaux with 230 parishes. Bossuet was a champion of the Gallican insistence on the uniqueness of the French church in Catholicism. He preached a famous sermon to the Assembly of the French Clergy in 1681 on the subject of Christian unity and service. He was uneasy about papal power. He pursued dialogue with leading Protestants like Paul Ferry and Jean Claude and kept abreast of trends in the Church of England.[5] He was critical of Richard Simon, early pioneer of biblical criticism, and battled with Fénelon over Madame Guyon and Quietism (the unacknowledged "offspring" of St. Teresa of Avila), which he adamantly opposed.

Bossuet was invited to preach in the royal court because of his friendship with Queen Anne, but he was quite bold before the king and his invitations to preach decreased. He gave the funeral oration of Queen Anne as well as that of the widow of the English King Charles I. He anguished over the profligacy of the French court and pleaded with the king to repent of his backsliding. He served as tutor to the Dauphin of France, and became known as "The Eagle of Meaux" for his great ministry. The following observations can be made about his preaching:

1. He studied constantly, keeping the light on in his room all night and arising to study often.
2. He quoted much Scripture in his sermons.
3. The sermons were elaborately written and outlined.
4. His preaching was highly theological.
5. He loved to preach on John the Baptist and particularly the humility of the Forerunner.
6. He preached often on the Cross and the believer's death with Jesus. Typical is an outline on "Today you will be with me in paradise": (1) Today—what swiftness; (2) with me—what companionship; (3) in paradise—what rest![6]
7. Bossuet was strong on the relationship of the Word and the eucharist.
8. He was known for his funeral orations, "in a class by themselves."[7]

There was something collegial about Bossuet, as we mark in his extensive contacts with the German Protestant philosopher Leibniz. At the same time there was a regrettable narrowness, as when he welcomed troops into his diocese to root out the Huguenots. On balance, however, he was a positive influence on preaching because of his conviction to "speak the Scripture."

1. Peter Bayley, *French Pulpit Oratory 1598–1650* (Cambridge, Mass.: Cambridge University Press, 1980).
2. Ibid., 77.
3. Ibid., 88.
4. H. L. Sidney Lear, *Bossuet and His Companions* (London: Rivertons, 1876), 42.
5. W. J. Sparrow Simpson, *A Study of Bossuet* (London: SPCK, 1937), 115.
6. Ibid., 135.
7. Ibid., 145.

6.3.2.2 Preaching Among the Protestants

> I say the same thing about language. It must be clear, simple and natural, without display of Greek, Hebrew, novel or fancy words. The structure must be natural, and without prefatory and ornamental phrases. I approve of saying "firstly," "on the first point," and "secondly," "on the second point," so that the people may see the order followed. . . . We must be on guard against introducing conversations between characters in the episodes unless they are in words taken from Scripture or very probable.
>
> —Francis of Sales

Reference has already been made to the anguish and persecution of the French Protestants, the Huguenots. By mid-sixteenth century they were a numerically and politically potent force. Kings, nobles, and military (Admiral de Coligny) were staunch Huguenots. Caught in the coils of domestic intrigue between the Medicis and the Guisess, thousands were slain in the massacre of 1572. They enjoyed some reprieve in the Edict of Nantes in 1598 but again felt persecution in the seventeenth century. Although they dominated in seventy-five cities of France, they were forced to flee, and many took refuge in England. Here they were instrumental in building the English textile industry. Toleration was not achieved until Napoleon's concordat with the pope in 1801.

We have already noted the significant homiletical contribution of **Jean Claude** (1619–1687), who was forced to flee to the Netherlands. Bossuet was wary of Claude, because, as he put it, "I feared for those who heard him." The Huguenot preachers "drew their inspiration largely from the expositions of Scripture which form the greater part of the Reformers' writings."[1] They followed Hyperius, who insisted a sermon be based on a scriptural text. Like Keckerman, they believed in strong persuasion but essentially preached biblical commentary with application.

While an earlier preacher like **Charles de Beauvais** (c. 1636) used three main headings with thirty-two sections in a sermon, Claude advocated a less cumbersome form with great care for thematic clarity and unity. Eloquence was always a watermark of French preaching, as was the case in the popular preaching of **Pierre du Moulin** (1568–1658). **Moses Amyraut** (1596–1664) impressed even Richelieu and Mazarin,[2] and the widely heard controversialist and stylist, **Jean D'Ailly** (1619–1687), has been considered the greatest leader in the French church since John Calvin.

Professor Vinet, who wrote two centuries later, asserted that there were at this time "great theologians, great controversialists, great diplomats, and above all, great Christians."[3] Yet this strong, vital church was to be decimated and nearly destroyed, leaving a negligible remnant which over the years became for the most part theologically concessive and liberal.

Bayley in his invaluable study uses **Jean D'Ailly** (1594–1670), pastor in Saumur and Charenton and later moderator of the Synod of Loudun, as a good example of the Protestant preaching of the day. Daille balanced careful use of the scriptural text with rhetorically sensitive discourse.[4] For Roman Catholic preachers, the text was merely a starting point "or even a purely decorative element, stripped of any analytic function."[5] But for Protestant preachers, a close inspection and analysis of the text was mandatory. Another greatly used preacher was **Pierre Du Bosc** (1623–1692) from Normandy, who served his entire ministry in Caen. Du Bosc was respected by friend and foe alike. After he had appealed to King Louis XIV on a matter related to Protestant persecution, the king remarked to the queen, "Madam, I have just heard the best speaker in my kingdom." Broadus cautions us to remember that he had not yet heard Bourdaloue or Massillon. Du Bosc was highly educated and an avid student. He surpassed even Claude in the forcefulness and power of his discourse. He fled to Rotterdam just prior to the revocation of the Edict of Nantes, where he ministered to the refugees.

Counted among the giants of French Protestant preachers was **Jacques Saurin** (1677–1730), who was reared in Nimes, where his father was a Protestant minister. He fled with his family to Geneva at the revocation. After a stint in the English military fighting against France, Saurin was educated under the great Turretin at Geneva. For five years he served a refugee congregation in London, where he had an unhappy marriage. He served in the Hague in the Netherlands, and always seemed to be in the center of some turbulence. His preaching was less formal and more soaring than Claude's, but not as textually rooted and grounded. As a preacher he was sometimes tedious and onerous, at other times like a bird in flight.[6] Yet Robinson, who has translated Saurin, pays glowing tribute to his subject:

> In the introduction of his sermon, he used to deliver himself in a tone modest and low; in the body of the sermon, which was adapted to the understanding, he was plain, clear and argumentative; pausing at the close of each period, that he might discover by the countenances and motions of his hearers whether they were convinced by his reasoning. In his addresses to the wicked, Saurin was often sonorous, but oftener a weeping suppliant at their feet. In the one he sustained the authoritative dignity of his office; in the other he expressed his Master's and his own benevolence to bad men, "praying them in Christ's stead to be reconciled to God." In general, his preaching resembled a plentiful shower of dew, softly and imperceptibly insinuating itself into the minds of his numerous hearers, as the dew into the pores of plants, till all the church was dissolved, and all in tears under his sermons.[7]

It would yet be one hundred years before there is much stirring among French-speaking Protestants. Then we shall have Caesar Malan, L. Gaussen, d'Aubigne and Alexandre Vinet as well as the Swiss Monods. Yet in the darkest and most difficult days, God is never without his witness.

---

1. Peter Bayley, *French Pulpit Oratory 1598–1650* (Cambridge, Mass.: Cambridge University Press, 1980), 61.
2. B. G. Armstrong, *Calvinism and the Amyraut Heresy* (Madison: University of Wisconsin, 1969). The great preponderance of Baptists are not five-point Calvinists but rather Amyrauldian, holding perhaps two or three of the five points. This explains the importance of Amyraut, who deserves much more study than is ordinarily given him.
3. E. C. Dargan, *A History of Preaching* (New York: Hodder and Stoughton, 1912), 2:118.
4. Bayley, *French Pulpit Oratory 1598–1650*, 117.
5. Ibid., 102–3.
6. A. E. Garvie, *The Christian Preacher* (New York: Scribner's, 1923), 173.
7. T. Harwood Pattison, *The History of Christian Preaching* (Philadelphia: American Baptist Publication Society, 1903), 219.

6.3.2.3 Preaching in the Royal Court Before the Potentates

I said that our preaching must be a spontaneous action, in contrast to the constrained and studied action of the pedants. I said dignified, in contrast to the rustic ways of some preachers who make a show of striking their fists, feet, and stomach against the pulpit, shout and utter howls that are strange and often improper. I said courageous in contrast to those who have a certain fearful way of acting as if they were speaking to their fathers and not to their pupils and children. I said natural, in contrast to all artificiality and affectation. I said sturdy, in contrast to a kind of dead, soft, ineffectual action. I said devout, to avoid obsequious and worldly acts of flattery. I said serious, in contrast to those who doff their caps so many times to the audience, make so many signs of respect, and perform so many little tricks by showing their hands or surplices, and aming other such indecorous movements. I said a little slow, to avoid a kind of curt and brusque way that diverts the eyes rather than pierces the heart.

—Francis of Sales

Throughout history, God's spokesmen have addressed a royal court, including Joseph before Pharaoh, Daniel before Nebuchadnezzar, prophets like Micaiah the son of Imlah before Ahab and Jehosophat, and the apostle Paul before King Agrippa. Those who preached before Henry VIII or Elizabeth I did not have an easy road, nor did the court preachers in Germany such as Father Abraham of Vienna or Krummacher, whom we shall consider subsequently. No situation, however, lent itself less to flattery or ease than did the royal court of Louis XIV of France. Yet the Lord raised up one of the brightest and most brilliant array of preachers to articulate his truth for this very opportunity. No doubt rhetorically overwrought at times, this preaching was often ornate, and is frequently called French lacquer style because of its elegance.

The history of preaching shows many curious venues for the proclamation of the truth of God. We return to Bossuet, who did preach at court but was not one of the favorites. Bossuet first came to the attention of high society through an impromptu sermon preached to nobility in the salon of Rambouillet.[1] We now move on to consider the court preachers who emerged in the strategy of divine providence.

None was more lustrous than **Louis Bourdaloue** (1632–1704), a Jesuit born in Bourges, the son of a lawyer. Early on he earned a reputation as one whose preaching missions swayed throngs of hearers. When Bossuet retired from court preaching, Bourdaloue was selected to take his place. For thirty-four years he filled the post as the prime preacher of France and was known as "king of preachers and preacher to kings." Louis XIV loved to hear preaching, and told Bourdaloue that he would rather hear him repeat his sermons every two years than to hear someone else preach new ones.[2]

Bourdaloue did not have the poetic flair of Bossuet, but he had strong personal appeal and impeccable personal integrity. As a teacher first of all, his appeal was to reason. "My design is to convince your reason," he would say. He exhibited strong biblical preaching. The Jesuit John Reville depicts him as logic—force—fire! His messages were "masterpieces of anatomical dissection." He used two or three mains with subs and then a closing peroration for the final assault. His was a manliness of expression, a clarity and earnestness which rushed on "like a swollen stream."

Feugere said of him that he was "as the royal serpent which with velvet coils slowly surrounds the object of its prey, softly, indeed, but in such a way that the captured animal cannot escape."[3] Like Nathan to King David, Bourdaloue preached against the vices of the court specifically. Often he preached with his eyes closed so that he would not be distracted and would open them to powerful effect. On one occasion the king stated after the sermon, "The preacher has done his duty; it is for us to do ours." In a personal interview after an especially probing sermon on sin, Bourdaloue urged the king, "May God in his infinite mercy grant me to see the day when the greatest of monarchs shall be the holiest of kings."[4]

Bourdaloue preached mightily on the passion of Christ. Twin addresses titled "Christ Judged by the World" and "The World Judged by Christ" are particularly incisive. In preaching on impurity and reprobation, he emphasized that the reprobate soul after death faces darkness, disorder, slavery, and remorse.[5] He also preached on Christ's words to the women of Jerusalem who witnessed his crucifixion. Here is his outline:

   I. Sin caused the passion;
  II. Sin renews the passion, "crucifying Christ afresh";
 III. Sin defeats the passion; it breaks the heart of Jesus.

One can only marvel in reading a sermon like "Perverted Conscience" at how apropos his messages were for his audience and how fearless he was. His prayer to the Holy Spirit was: "O Spirit of my God, fountain of all grace, author of all holiness, come! Enlighten and strengthen us. Come! Sanctify this house, which is devoted to you, and which would not be governed but by you, because any other spirit but you would not keep up the regularity, harmony and perfect charity, which have always maintained the peace of God in it."[6]

Another singularly used instrument of righteousness was **Francois de Fénelon** (1651–1715). Fénelon was from a noble family in the south of France. Louis XIV called him "the finest and most visionary thinker in the kingdom." He was trained at Cahors and Paris and served in parish ministry in St. Sulpice in Paris. From early on he had something of Port Royal's "obstinate rationality." He was more tolerant of Protestants than any of the others and known for his cultivation of the interior life. His treatise on *Christian Perfection* is a classic and reflects his drastic theocentricity.[7]

Fénelon taught how to live Christianly in a licentious setting like the royal court. He was noted as an educator of young women and as preceptor of the king's grandson, the Duke of Burgundy. He was deeply infused with Quietistic views and the inspiration of Molinos, the controversial Spanish thinker.

In 1695 Fénelon was named archbishop of Cambray. He and Bossuet tangled over the teachings of Madame Guyon, which according to Fénelon was like all the artillery of heaven firing against a little fly. Consequently Fénelon was banished from court. He retired to his diocese, where he preached and served the poor until his death.

His sermons were carefully written and then delivered from the heart without notes. He wrote a significant work on preaching titled *Dialogues on Eloquence* in which he opts for a simpler, more direct style. He was described as "a tall, thin man of a goodly shape with a large nose, eyes through which the mind poured like a torrent, and a countenance of which I never saw the like, and which, once seen, was never forgotten. It blended every quality, even the most opposite. It had gravity and gallantry, seriousness and gaity; in it you were aware of doctor, bishop and fine gentleman at once: what was most conspicuous in it, as in his whole person, was thought, wit, and graces, decorum, and above all, nobility. It required an effort to cease looking at him."[8]

Called by Saintsbury "the greatest preacher of France," **Jean Baptiste Massilon** (1663–1742) was known as the great searcher of hearts. He hailed from a humble background but became a teacher at both college and seminary levels. In 1693 he was appointed as the head of the seminary at Magloire. Massilon was the Advent preacher at Versailles in 1699 and deeply impressed the king, who said of him, "When I hear most preachers, I am contented with them; when I hear Massilon I am discontented with myself." Even Voltaire praised him for his daring. He preached with a gentle persuasiveness and "spoke to the heart in language always understood." But the domineering mistress of the king was offended by Massilon's preaching, and he did not sustain favor.

Massilon was appointed bishop of Clermont in 1717. His sermon on "The Woman That Was a Sinner" (Luke 7:37ff.) shows clearly why he made some at the court uncomfortable. Yet it was he who preached the funeral of Louis XIV. When he stood in the pulpit at Notre Dame, he paused emphatically and then spoke his first words, "Only God is great!"

Although conscious of Bourdaloue's influence, Massilon was determined to stake out his own turf. Sometimes he would breathe an audible prayer right in the middle of a sermon. Analysis of his sermons is rewarding.[9] Sermon 16 on "The Word of God" (based in Matthew 4:4) is characteristically broken down into mains and subs and colorfully develops the potency of the Word of God. Sermon 17 on "The Delay of Conversion" (based on John 1:23) is overtly evangelistic. Unfortunately neither the king nor his heirs really responded to these watchmen on the walls, and the next centuries were blood-soaked.

Only one preacher of this stature ever emerged in France, and he lived in a later era. Yet we refer now to **Henri Lacordaire** (1802–1861) because he stands squarely in this succession. A Burgundian with great reserve, he testified, "It was in my weary state of isolation and mental sadness that God came to seek me." Lacordaire became conscious of his call to preach but utterly failed in his first attempts. He lamented, "It is evident that I have neither the physical power, nor the mental flexibility, nor the knowledge of a world in which I have lived and always shall live apart; in short, I have nothing to the degree required to be a preacher in the full sense of the word."[10]

Yet Lacordaire stood on the shoulders of the giants, and discovered the reality: "The orator is like the rock of Horeb—until touched of God, it is a barren stone, but once let His finger be laid upon it, and it becomes a fertilizing spring."[11] He occupied the pulpit at Notre Dame in Paris (1843–1851) and was widely known for his conferences on chastity and humility of soul. He was frequently in tears at the cross, "frightened of all this success."[12] He was a member of the French National Assembly and knew de Tocqueville. His preaching conferences in Toulouse in 1854 were epochal. Some marked similarities with the earlier preachers set him apart from his compatriots.

---

1. E. Paxton Hood, *The Throne of Eloquence: Great Preachers, Ancient and Modern* (New York: Funk and Wagnalls, 1888), 9ff.

2. E. C. Dargan, *A History of Preaching* (New York: Hodder and Stoughton, 1912), 2:101.

3. A. E. Garvie, *The Christian Preacher* (New York: Scribner's, 1923), 178.

4. T. Harwood Pattison, *The History of Christian Preaching* (Philadelphia: American Baptist Publication Society, 1903), 230.

5. Dargan, *A History of Preaching,* 105.

6. Pattison, *The History of Christian Preaching,* 226.

7. Francois de Fénelon, *Christian Perfection,* ed. Charles F. Whiston (New York: Harper, 1947); and James Mudge, *Fénelon: The Mystic* (Cincinnati: Jennings and Graham, 1906).

8. Pattison, *The History of Christian Preaching,* 233.

9. *Sermons by John-Baptist Massilon* (Edinburgh: Archibald Allardice, 1824).

10. H. L. Sidney Lear, *Henri Dominique Lacordaire* (London: Rivingtons, 1882), 97.

11. Ibid., 100–101.

12. Ibid., 204.

6.4 GERMAN PREACHERS AND THE RESILIENCY AND RENEWAL OF THE CRAFT

The reformation work of Luther's was to be continued and the church which had become paralyzed in forms of dead doctrinal conformity was to be brought back to the living source of God's Word.
—Joachim Justus Breithaupt, one of Francke's close associates

The Teutonic and Germanic people have been front and center for many centuries. Yet they did not achieve national unity until well into the nineteenth century. Until then they were largely a collection of highly competitive nobles and various smaller states. After the religious Peace of Augsburg (1555), which essentially endeavored to balance a status quo between Roman Catholics and Protestants, there continued to be intense debate as to its implementation.

The abdication of **Charles the Great** of the Holy Roman Empire in the same year concluded an era.[1] The fierce moves of the Roman Catholic Counter-Reformation complicated a fragile situation. Particularly vexed conflict led to the Thirty Years' War, which began in 1618 and finally ended with the Treaty of Westphalia in 1648. The second phase of this bloody conflict saw the victories of **Gustavus Adolphus** of Sweden, whose father, **Charles IX,** had finally established Protestantism in Sweden by shaking Sweden loose from Polish Catholic control.[2] In an unimaginable ordeal, over half the population of Germany perished in the war itself or through starvation. All of the powers of Europe used Germany as a battleground for vicious internecine slaughter.

---

1. Kurt Aland, *A History of Christianity* (Philadelphia: Fortress, 1986), 2:152ff.
2. Ibid., 213.

6.4.1   THE POST-REFORMATION MOOD IN THE GERMAN CHURCH

Pietism is undoubtedly the most significant movement which has happened within Protestantism since the Reformation.
—Kurt Aland

Spener was the reformer of the life of the German church (*reformatio vitae*), as Luther was the reformer of its doctrine (*reformatio doctrinae*).
—John Ker

The effect of the Thirty Years' War on the churches was numbing. Yet additional factors led to the decline of preaching in Germany from Luther's death until Philipp Spener. Germany was virtually a desert after this fratricidal futility. Controversy between Roman Catholics and Protestants and controversies between factions among the Protestants quenched vitality. Calixtus of Helmstadt was at the throat of Calovius of Koenigsberg in the so-called syncretism debate.[1] What is more, orthodoxy shriveled in arid speculation and a constrictive hardening of the categories. Doctrine and rigid confessionalization supplanted Scripture as the prime focus. The sermons dried up. Aristotelianism reappeared. Baptismal regeneration was central. Stoeffer in his classic analysis shows that *fiducia* became *assenus* and there was general ethical insensitivity.[2] One observer offered the comment: "Churchly oratory discards Scripture; this logic and polemic can not minister to edification."[3]

Garvie describes a volume of sermons from **Jacob Andrea** preached in 1658 in Esslingen: one quarter consists of sermons against the Papists; one quarter against the Zwinglians; one quarter against the Schwenkfeldians, the mystics and perfectionists of the times; and one quarter against the Anabaptists.[4] This is surely a stack of straw for hungry hearts!

Of course there were substantive issues often discussed as when **Andrew Osiander,** one of the pioneers in the Reformation, argued that justification was not forensic, nor was it imputed but infused (he confused justification with sanctification).[5] In all of this there was an unabated hunger for the Word of God. Forgetting the legacy of Hyperius, preachers turned to **Andreas Pancratius,** who advocated synthetic or topical preaching. He dismissed analytic preaching or the division of a text.

The answer to the extended spiritual drought came in the spiritual renewal called Pietism, which corresponded in some significant ways with Jansenism in France and Puritanism in England.

One who embodied the longing for spiritual life and who is often called father of German Pietism is **Johann Arndt** (1555–1621). This second phase of the Protestant Reformation has important linkage to English Puritans and to Jeremy Taylor. It also draws heavily on the mystical and relational emphases in Luther, who like Arndt loved Tauler, and *Theologia Germanica,* which emphasized the life of self-denial. Some have too strongly stated the roots of Pietism in medieval mysticism[6] and nudged Pietism too close to Boehme's pantheistic and Rosicrucian ties. There are tinges of Theosophy and Christadelphianism here.

Arndt avoided the exaggerated subjectivism of mysticism with a virile "Christ-mysticism" (to use Deissman's good phrase). He was a pastor's son but was orphaned early and reared by friends. While studying medicine, he was converted and felt God's call to ministry. His concern was with the practical Christian life. Arndt was a staunch advocate of daily Bible reading and devotions. He was troubled by what seemed to be a contradiction in Luther between "justification by faith alone" and baptismal regeneration. He strongly preached conversion in the churches he served. He stressed union with Christ. An overlay of amorous language from the Song of Solomon is perceptible in his style.

The most powerful of his written works, *True Christianity,* is an exposition of *unio mystica.*[7] Arndt at this point was influential in the thinking of Albert Schweitzer, who testified, "In my youth I gained from my mother a love for Arndt; he was a prophet of interior Protestantism."[8] Arndt's writings and sermons also helped mold Spener and others. He was firmly anchored in Scripture, as we note in "God's Word Must Demonstrate Its Power in Man through Faith and Become Living."[9] Arndt's thrust is plain: "God gave the whole of the Holy Scriptures in spirit and in faith and everything in them must happen in you spiritually."

Others who followed Arndt were the cousins **John Gerhard** (1582–1637), whose sermons were heavy yet warming, and **Paul Gerhard** (1607–1676), the great hymnwriter whose hymns are still sung, such as "O Jesus, Thy Boundless Love to Me."[10]

The glaciers were receding in this spiritual ice age. A thawing was taking place. It would soon be spring.

---

1. John Ker, *Lectures on the History of Preaching* (New York: Armstrong, 1889), 171. Ker is especially helpful on the German picture while totally neglectful of almost all else.
2. F. Ernest Stoeffer, *The Rise of Evangelical Pietism* (Leiden, Netherlands: E. J. Brill, 1965). A masterpiece!
3. E. C. Dargan, *A History of Preaching* (New York: Hodder and Stoughton, 1912), 2:64.
4. A. E. Garvie, *The Christian Preacher* (New York: Scribner's, 1923), 143–44.
5. Reinhold Seeberg, *Textbook of the History of Doctrines* (Grand Rapids: Baker, 1952, reprint), 2:369ff.
6. As Emil Brunner's statement, "Squeezed in between rationalism and orthodoxy, and mediating between them at the same time as it was marked off from both, a place was found for Pietism, a mode of understanding faith, the deepest roots must be sought in medieval mysticism," as given in Peter C. Erb, *Pietists, Protestants and Mysticism* (Metuchen, N.J.: Scarecrow, 1989), 1.
7. Peter Erb, trans., Johan Arndt's *True Christianity* (New York: Paulist, 1979).
8. Ibid., 1.
9. Ibid., 49ff.
10. The whole matter of artistic expression in relation to preaching is beyond our scope, but suffice it to say that paintings by Dürer and Grunewald and Rembrandt's magnificent "Christ Preaching" rendered in 1650 are significant ancillary considerations for our study as well as the hymns and oratorios. Note Jane Dillenberger, *Style and Content in Christian Art* (New York: Crossroad, 1986), 181ff.

6.4.2 THE POST-REFORMATION MOVEMENT OF SPIRITUAL AWAKENING IN THE GERMAN CHURCH

German Pietism was essentially a preaching movement.

—Martin Schmidt

With the Pietists everything began at the very beginning with the Exposition of Scripture.

—Kurt Aland

Of the Pietistic movement and the quickening it brought to Germany and Scandinavia and beyond,[1] John Ker writes:

For a whole century after the death of the leaders of the Reformation, Germany was in a state of spiritual hardness and coldness of the most distressing kind. The warmth and life were chiefly in polemical passion. Witnesses for the better kind of Christianity were rare, and they were subjected to bitter attacks as enthusiasts. Yet a genuine revival came in the course of the seventeen century, and we shall hope that another and a more lasting one will dispel the rationalism of the present day.[2]

The church was in large part "a magnificent neological ice palace," when the mighty breath of the Spirit arrived. Peter Erb calls it, "The most important development in Protestant spirituality."[3] The summons was to new life in Christ, to regeneration of the sinner, and the nurture of the spiritually newborn. As Van Oosterzee insisted:

> Spener did succeed in recalling to life the spirit of Luther and Arndt in many a pulpit, and in making the preaching a powerful embodiment of the theologia regenitorum.[4]

The result was a reshaping of theological education (and the establishment of Halle University). Preaching was stimulated, hymnody revitalized, the growth of family worship appeared, charitable institutions were built, and a whole new missionary impetus began. John Wesley was heir to the best in Pietism in his insistence: "Let us unite the two so long divided—knowledge and vital piety." There is much here in emphasis on personal relationship to Christ that replicates the English Puritans such as William Perkins, Henry Smith, Richard Sibbes, and Bishop Joseph Hall. Echoes of the same are seen on the Continent in Reformed circles represented by William Teelinck, William Ames (who fled to Holland), Jean de Labadie, and the hymnwriters and poets, Joachim Neander and Tersteegen. The focus was on meeting and knowing the living Christ through the Spirit by the Word.

Yet the word "Pietism" is virtually pejorative in many circles. Dale Brown calls Pietism "one of the least understood movements in Judeo-Christian history."[5] Barth had a strong aversion to it. Martin Marty argued that "Pietism was one of the major strides of Christian retreat from responsibility." Albrecht Ritschl in three volumes lobbed the charge that Pietism was too individualistic, too separatistic, and too anti-intellectual (despite the fact that Spener's M.A. was on Thomas Hobbes, and Francke was in much dialogue with the philosopher Leibniz). Troeltsch terms it a sect.

Pietists were immediately embroiled in dispute and controversy. Francke and friends were expelled from Leipzig and Erfurt. Aland concedes a kind of "narrowness" in early Pietism (one might add that this is found in any reforming wedge such as Puritanism or Jansenism),[6] but Francke and his cohorts were protesting against the absence of any lectures or studies on the exposition of Scripture. This was a Bible movement tingling with eschatological urgency. No wonder Cotton Mather in correspondence with Francke in 1715 fairly chortled:

> The world begins to feel a warmth from the fire of God which thus flames in the heart of Germany, beginning to extend into many regions; the whole world will ere long be sensible of it.[7]

But there was danger here. Webber worries about confessional erosion, about the replacement of justification by sanctification. The strong emphasis on holiness makes any good Lutheran skittish (remember Luther's problem with "good works" and the Book of James), but he overstates a bit when he says that "in its final stages Pietism degenerated into salvation by good works rather than by the grace of God in Christ."[8]

We cannot totally dismiss the concern. Immanuel Kant was raised a Pietist. Schleiermacher, "the father of German liberalism," who exchanged theology for psychology, along with his father was trained at Herrnhut and studied and taught at Halle (1787–1789), although he was much influenced by romanticism also.[9] Johan Semler, the rationalist and early higher critic, was an ardent Pietist who conducted family devotions with fervor.

The University of Halle was the first to succumb to rationalism. The peril in protesting against dead orthodoxy and emblazoning the appeal for new life is ultimately to exalt the ethical and demote the doctrinal. John Baillie argues that Kant's dictum "I must therefore abolish knowledge to make room for faith" betrays his Pietistic proclivity.[10] Neve concedes that "the pietistic way of life and theological liberalism may go a long way together." Paul Fuhrman's trenchant descriptive refers to "liberalism's insistence on the primacy of life over doctrine."[11] Neve well demonstrated that Baxterianism (Richard Baxter, to whom we shall refer at length in the next chapter) was "a theology which furnished doctrinal foundations for his type of ardent Pietism, but which after him contributed to breaking down the forms of doctrine and polity and conservative theology in England." Numbers of his followers became Arians and anti-Trinitarian.[12] Zinzendorf also veered toward some odd views on the Trinity, but J. A. Bengel corrected him. When under the influence of Pietism a brother pleads: "No creed, no loyalty oaths, no worship forms, no hierarchical traditions, no dogmatics," we know the fox is in the henhouse.[13]

Thus Ritschl's criticism of "separatism" and undue individualism is belied with but few early exceptions by subsequent history.[14] Pietists tended to become experience-oriented in their quest for ecumenism, and hence are quite broad. Pietistically based fellowships were not the only ones to be infected by liberalism and rationalism, but they were among the first to go. The achievement of balance between doctrine and life is not easy, but it is imperative. As R. V. G. Tasker says so well: "The appeal to live a Christian life must always be based upon Christian doctrine. . . . If Christian ethical standards are being abandoned, it must always be because Christian faith is weak."[15]

---

1. Valdis Mezezers, *The Herrnhuterian Pietism in the Baltic and Its Outreach into America and Elsewhere in the World* (North Quincy, Mass.: Christopher, 1975). In 1736 Zinzendorf went to Riga in Latvia; a great revival broke out in 1739, out of which hundreds of missionaries went forth.

2. John Ker, *Lectures on the History of Preaching* (New York: Armstrong, 1889), 180.

3. F. Ernest Stoeffler, *Classics of Western Spirituality: Pietists—Selected Writings* (New York: Paulist, 1983), ix.

4. Quoted in A. E. Garvie, *The Christian Preacher* (New York: Scribner's, 1923), 187.
5. Dale Brown, *Understanding Pietism* (Grand Rapids: Eerdmans, 1978). The thesis of this book goes to the point of "The Problem of Subjectivism in Pietism."
6. Kurt Aland, *A History of Christianity* (Philadelphia: Fortress, 1986), 2:226–245. An important discussion.
7. John T. McNeil, *Modern Christian Movements* (Philadelphia: Westminster, 1954), 74.
8. F. R. Webber, *A History of British and American Preaching* (Milwaukee: Northwestern, 1952), 2:281.
9. J. L. Neve, *A History of Christian Thought* (Philadelphia: Muhlenberg, 1946), 2:104.
10. John Baillie, *The Idea of Revelation in Recent Thought* (New York: Columbia University Press, 1956), 10.
11. Paul Fuhrman, *God-Centered Religion* (Grand Rapids: Zondervan, 1942), 21.
12. Neve, *A History of Christian Thought,* 31.
13. David L. Larsen, "The Perils of Pietism," a lecture to the Southern California Covenant Ministers, December 28, 1959, published in the *California Covenanter,* July 27, 1961, 4ff. John Sailhamer points out that Professor Sigmund Baumgarten of the University of Halle provided the "decisive turning point from a view of Scripture as revelation to a view of Scripture as a record of revelation in events"; see *The Pentateuch as Narrative* (Grand Rapids: Zondervan, 1992), 28 n. 32. This is a tragically significant paradigm shift.
14. Koppel S. Pinson, *Pietism as a Factor in the Rise of German Nationalism* (New York: Octagon, 1968).
15. R. V. G. Tasker, *The Gospel in the Epistle to the Hebrews* (London: Tyndale, 1950), 51.

6.4.3 THE POST-REFORMATION MESSENGERS OF THE WORD IN THE GERMAN CHURCH

> While the older preachers made the teaching of orthodoxy and the refutation of gainsayers their principal end and aim, from Pietist pulpits there was heard little besides the sinfulness of man, the need of repentance, and the merits of Christ. That tares were mingled with the wheat in the field of Pietism, that some Pietists held extravagant opinions and that others were little better than hypocrites, seems to admit no doubt; but also it cannot be doubted that they infused a new life into the Lutheran community at a time when the lamp of Christian life burned very low.
>
> —S. Cheetham, *A History of the Christian Church,* London, 1907

Having looked at certain of the proto-Pietists, we now turn to the patriarch of the Pietists, called by some the second Luther. **Philipp Jacob Spener** (1635–1705) was born in the Alsace into a godly and devout home. He was educated in Strasbourg, where among other studies he learned Hebrew from an erudite Jew. (Spener always had a great love for the Jews and believed in a great day of conversion and glory for the Jewish people.) He was by temperament a gentle man who spoke softly. He studied a year in Geneva and came to know **Jean Labadie** (1610–1674), who in quest of a pure church left the Reformed church.

Labadie's emphasis on small groups and his fiery preaching left a deep mark on Spener. He also had some contact with Geger the Waldensian in Geneva.

Some are very nervous about admitting Reformed influence on Spener and any kind of cross-fertilization at this time, but the lines do cross. No one has demonstrated this more adeptly than W. R. Ward, who points out that Francke and all the Protestants read Molinos. Puritan works flooded into Germany. John Bunyan was read at the Halle orphanage when no actual preacher was present.[1]

Spener subscribed to Lutheran orthodoxy, but he felt the Reformation was not finished. He stood unequivocally for "the absolute authority of Scripture" (F. E. Stoeffer) and "verbal inspiration" (Dale Brown). He promoted the exaltation of Scripture and encouraged a renewed interest in the biblical languages. Spener emphasized the necessity of a personal relationship with the Lord. Rebirth (or *wiedergeburt*) was the subject for one collection of sixty-six sermons.[2]

Spener commends the sentiments of the Lutheran theologian **David Chytraeus** (1531–1600), who was a professor at Rostock and whose important and thoroughly Anselmian work *On Sacrifice* has now been translated.[3] While Luther held to the imminency of Christ's second coming, it was Spener who introduced chiliasm, or the belief in the one thousand year millennial reign of Christ, into Lutheranism.[4] His doctoral dissertation was on Revelation 9:13–21 and shows his belief in the imminent wrap-up of human history. He was also a student of Joachim of Fiore.[5]

In 1666, Spener took a call to be senior minister in Frankfurt-am-Main. Here he developed his conventical groups and pushed confirmation as a requirement for the training of youth. He edged away from the preaching of the pericope toward something more solidly expository. Lutheran orthodoxy used several approaches in preaching but was greatly influenced by English preaching. Spener felt a keen affinity for the Epistles of Paul and preached them most frequently; for this he was faulted. From 1686 to 1691 he was Saxon court preacher in Dresden, where he had his first contacts with Francke. From 1691 to 1705 he was first minister at the St. Nicholas Church in Berlin, from which vantage point he shaped the new university in Halle. Sometime after blessing his godchild, Nicholas von Zinzendorf, he died at the age of seventy and was buried in the St. Nicholas Church, where his wife is also interred.

In his *Pia Desideria* (holy longings), an introduction he wrote for Arndt's *True Christianity,* he encapsulated the essential thrusts of Pietism:

1. spread the Word of God
2. emphasize the priesthood of all believers
3. cultivate the inner spiritual life
4. remember that truth can be lost in disputes
5. candidates for the ministry should be true Christians
6. sermons should edify the hearers

These symbolic points were augmented by detailed instructions against dancing and the like.[6] The ascetic strain in Spener also came to the fore in his lengthy statement on drinking in *Pia Desideria.*

Spener's own preaching tended to be lengthy. His exegesis was solid but he used no illustration to speak of. Contrary to prevailing practice, he did omit extensive Greek and Latin quotations. Clearly, he is not the colorful character that Luther was. His personal reserve is reflected in his sermons, but he made a positive impression:

> Not exceeding medium height, his physical form slim and yet equal to the task of the office, his pale face which created a sense of strength of judgment and a deep sense of contemplation, his very prominent brow with eyes clear and piercing, but moderated with a sweet modesty, his nose inclined somewhat to aquiline form, his mouth a little drawn apart, with the whole face reflecting a serene tranquillity with kindness.[7]

The golden age of Pietism was entrusted to **August Hermann Francke** (1663–1727), who was born in Lubeck and who found Arndt's *True Christianity* his companion through youth. He was converted in 1687 and drawn into the Spenerian circle. He stayed for awhile with the Speners and then moved to Halle. He "conserved and compacted Spener's insights," holding steadily the "Lutheran regard for the objective authority of Scripture."[8] Like Spener, he loved Hebrew and Greek, and one year read the Hebrew Old Testament through seven times under the guidance of a Jewish rabbi. In 1691 he became professor of Hebrew and Greek at Halle and pastor of St. George's Church in Glaucha to ensure adequate income.

Francke was a model pastor, enjoying pastoral calls and personal contact with his congregants (something quite innovative), and loving to preach three times a week. He was outstanding as an educator of children, and founded orphanages. He was a visionary for missions and corresponded with Leibniz about China. He influenced the schools of Russia through his contacts with Peter the Great, whose wife once visited the Halle institutions incognito.[9] Francke also sent quantities of Bibles to Swedish prisoners in Siberia (which was a factor in the spread of Pietism to Sweden).

In 1716, Francke was named vice-chancellor of the university and faced the massive incursions of the Enlightenment upon the simple faith of Halle Pietism. An activist in every respect and well designated the Melancthon of Pietism, Francke worked himself to exhaustion and died at the age of fifty-four.

Francke may have been a more effective preacher than Spener. His delivery was livelier, and he gave more thought to rhetorical aspects of communication. Like Spener, his sermons were long to the point of prolixity. His mighty message on "The Doctrine of Our Lord Jesus Christ Concerning Rebirth" (based on John 3:1–16) had a double introduction and five parts. His sermon on the rich man and Lazarus did not fixate on aspects of the afterlife but properly on Jesus' point, "Our Duty to the Poor."[10]

The contacts and outreach of Pietistic life and "the simple Halle Gospel" were astounding. The bottom line for Francke was conversion as an object: "Gospel preachers should constantly make it their aim and direction of their preaching to lead their hearers to Christ and to His grace."[11]

There were also radical Pietists, like **Gottfried Arnold** (1666–1714) from Saxony, who was influenced by Spener to enter pastoral ministry. Both Spener and Francke made immense spiritual impact on Arnold. Laxity among believers led Arnold into the radical camp. Ironically this movement veered toward separatism and indifference to basic theological formulation in matters touching universalism, Arianism, the church, and even a negative view toward Scripture.[12] As time passed, Arnold's pastoral instincts brought him back toward the center. However, with **Johan Dippel** (who substituted "Christ in us" for "Christ for us") and **Gerhard Tersteegen** (1697–1769, "the poet-laureate of the interior life" but termed "pagan mystic" by Ritschl), he remained on the fringes of Pietism.

Pietism in Wurtenberg centered at the University of Tubingen and flourished between 1680 and 1775. Spener visited often. Reuchlin (1660–1707) held a conventicle in his home.[13] Here **Johan Albrecht Bengel** (1687–1752) also held forth. His eschatologically oriented theology was shaped by the influences of Cocceius, Vitringa, and Lampe of Halle. John Wesley called him "the great light of the Christian world." He set the date of 1836 for the Second Advent of Christ.

Nicholas von Zinzendorf (1700–1760) was born in Dresden and reared by his maternal grandmother, who knew Spener. A brilliant student at Halle, Zinzendorf settled Moravian emigres at his ancestral estate, where he founded Herrnhut. He made many evangelistic tours, including a visit to America. Although his "blood and wounds cult" was extreme, we treasure his hymn "Jesus Thy Blood and Righteousness."

Revivals soon swept through central Europe and involved many children. The people were being "converted by revival preaching."[14] What was transpiring in Europe had effect elsewhere. Muhlenberg, the Lutheran leader in America, used so many Hallesian preachers that some of his followers went West to produce a pure church (the origins of the Missouri Synod). Doddridge's grandfather was from Bohemia. John Wesley, who visited Herrnhut and Halle, married a Huguenot widow. George I of England had a chaplain who was in close contact with Francke, as was George Whitefield. Trevacca, the training school of the Countess of Huntingdon, was derived from the Halle pattern, and John Fletcher, its great leader, was from Switzerland. Ward, who traces all of these cross-connections, reminds us that there was no insularity in what the Spirit of God was doing in this powerful time of preaching.

---

1. W. R. Ward, *The Protestant Evangelical Awakening* (Cambridge, Mass.: Cambridge University Press, 1992). A helpful note on Jean Labadie is found in John Ker, *Lectures on the History of Preaching* (New York: Armstrong, 1889), 199.
2. Manfred Waldemar Kohl, "Wiedergeburt as the Central Theme in Pietism," *Covenant Quarterly* (November 1974): 15ff.
3. John Warwick Montgomery, *Chartraeus on Sacrifice* (St. Louis: Concordia, 1962).
4. Ward, *The Protestant Evangelical Awakening*, 51.
5. K. James Stein, *Philipp Jakob Spener: Pietist Patriarch* (Chicago: Covenant, 1986), 67.
6. F. Ernest Stouffer, *The Rise of Evangelical Pietism* (Leiden, Netherlands: E. J. Brill, 1965). A brilliant study.

7. Stein, *Philipp Jakob Spener,* 268. It is significant that Richard Lischer in *Theories of Preaching: Selected Readings in the Homiletical Tradition* (Durham, N.C.: Labyrinth Press, 1987), 60ff. includes Philip Jacob Spener under the heading, "The Reform of Preaching," stressing the inner transformation of the preacher and his hearers.
8. F. Ernest Stouffer, *German Pietism During the Eighteenth Century* (Leiden, Netherlands: E. J. Brill, 1973). Invaluable.
9. Gary R. Sattler, *God's Glory, Neighbor's Good: A Brief Introduction to the Life and Writings of August Hermann Francke* (Chicago: Covenant, 1982), 77.
10. Ibid., for a choice collection of Francke's sermons, 113ff.
11. For analysis of this line of influence, particularly in the Danish mission to India, see Kenneth Scott Latourette, *A History of the Expansion of Christianity: Three Centuries of Advance* (Grand Rapids: Zondervan, 1970), 3:277–81; *The Great Century: Europe and the United States* (Grand Rapids: Zondervan, 1970), 4:90, 92. In thinking of the Danish-Halle mission, we must remember the Danish royal court was the most Pietistic at this time.
12. Peter C. Erb, *Pietists, Protestants, and Mysticism: The Use of Late Medieval Spiritual Texts in the Work of Gottfried Arnold* (Metuchen, N.J.: Scarecrow, 1989), 38.
13. F. Ernest Stouffer, *German Pietism during the Eighteenth Century* (Leiden, Netherlands: E. J. Brill, 1973).
14. Ward, *The Protestant Evangelical Awakening,* 112. This volume is a masterpiece of erudition and inspiration.

6.5 THE COUNTER-REFORMATION AND THE RIVALS IN THE CRAFT

> It is the office of the ecclesiastical orator to open up for the people the truth and the secrets of God, to teach men and women how to live piously and innocently, to abolish those most repulsive errors, destructive superstitions, depraved customs, and compel men and women to the pious, true, and divine wisdom and to the Christian religion; to nourish the souls of their listeners with a knowledge of the truth (than which there is no more pleasant food). For the preacher, this is the proposed end: by persuading to increase the kingdom of God, to acquire souls for Christ, to adorn the holy Church, to lessen the tyranny of the devil, excite souls redeemed by the precious blood of Christ to eternal life and beatitude.
>
> —Agostino Valiero, bishop of Verona (1531–1606)

After the Council of Trent (1545–1563), the Roman Catholic Church gave itself to the improvement of preaching, As in England, France, and Germany the seventeenth century, a "golden age of preaching," can be seen in Roman Catholic countries like Spain and Italy.[1] It was an age of eloquence throughout the West.

Even in staunchly Roman Catholic Italy, there were voices raised for the gospel of the grace of God, although any idea of justification by faith alone was quickly quashed. **Cardinal Contarini** (d. 1542), who was papal representative at the Colloquy of Ratisbon, agreed with the Reformers on justification.

Some in this circle fled, like **Peter Martyr,** and many were killed. **Juan de Valdes** (d. 1541), of Spanish nobility, fled from the Spanish Inquisition to Italy.

Ministering in Naples, Valdes wrote many books, including a solid commentary on Matthew and *The Spiritual Alphabet* (c. 1536), which trumpeted the doctrine of justification.[2] At the heart of his ministry was the cross of Christ and the doctrine of satisfaction.

A Benedictine monk and friend of Valdes, **Don Benedetto** (d. 1544) wrote *Benefit of Christ,* which was translated into French, German, English, and Croatian. These works are now available in English editions. The latter, as Leon Morris observes in an introduction to the treatise, majors in the finished work of Jesus Christ on the cross.[3] In Benedetto we also sense a radiant joy in Christ. But the momentum of the Counter-Reformation did not leave many vestiges of the gospel of grace in southern Europe.

In the current popularity of historical rhetoric we are seeing some remarkable studies, among which is certainly McGinness's thorough piece on the revival of sacred oratory in Rome. The success of Protestant preaching obviously spurred Roman Catholics to new emphasis on preaching. The Council of Trent specifically addressed its importance. The Fifth Lateran Council's concern about "the ills of preaching" had not made much difference.[4] Preaching was one of the keys of Protestant appeal, and efforts were now joined to rally Catholicism's dormant pulpits. The Council of Trent called on preachers above all "to concern themselves with the Gospel of Jesus Christ . . . that sermons be scriptural, and that preachers take up the Gospel everyday and 'never omit mentioning what occurred in that passage of the Gospel.'"[5]

Older medieval homiletical patterns were discarded, although there was still a considerable appeal to St. Francis and the resuscitation of preaching under his auspices. Preachers were urged to avoid scholastic debate and nit-picking in favor of "the matter necessary for salvation." Even preaching on the Second Coming of Christ was common in this eschatologically charged time. The object of preaching was to move the will, not simply to inform the mind and titillate the emotions. Persuasion was seen as essential to the process.[6]

Changing tastes in the Sistine Chapel indicate a preaching revival subsequent to the Council of Trent. The Catechism of the Council of Trent was published in 1566, and stressed doctrine and oratorical skills. All over Rome, preaching gained in popularity and in quality. But the message, while ostensibly concerning Christ, was highly synergistic as a whole, semi-Pelagian at best, and heavily moralistic.[7] Unmerited favor was in evidence in baptismal regeneration, but in so-called second justification human works and deeds were necessary to sustain a right relationship to God. The intrusion of the treasury of merit, Mariolatry, saints, and relics all conspired to dim any perception of the true nature of saving and sustaining grace.

Seventeenth-century preaching in Rome saw considerable refinement in the art of amplification in the sermon.[8] The technique of outdistancing in preaching, that is, having each point exceed the previous point in scope and size, was widely utilized. Of course some invective against the heretics flavored Catholic communication, and an increasingly triumphalistic tone put forth the pope as the only reliable guide. His dignity and jurisdiction were seen as undeniably *de iure divino*. Panegyrics for the bishop of Rome were common. Preaching emphasized classical rhetoric and humanistic pursuits. The flurry of interest in the pulpit began to subside before the century was over.

The thrust of the Counter-Reformation was felt worldwide. Its chief architect, the Basque **Ignatius Loyola** (1491–1556), became a soldier for Christ in the Society of Jesus, which he founded after a cannonball fractured his right leg in battle in 1521. His *Spiritual Exercises* are still classic and record the single-mindedness of a man who dedicated himself to exterminating Protestants. The growth of his movement was phenomenal. Notwithstanding his fanaticism, Ignatius had a deep spiritual commitment, considering himself and his compatriots as "the companions of Jesus," although he maintained a special devotion to the Queen of Heaven.

Ignatius personally commissioned young **Francis Xavier** (1506–1552), who was born in Pamplona, Spain, of aristocratic parents. Trained at the University of Paris, Francis was ordained by Ignatius to propagate the gospel. Sponsored by the Portuguese, at thirty-five he went to India. Troubled that the Portuguese seemed to be in India only for pepper and pearls, he gave himself to preaching. Subsequently he went to Malacca in the East Indies, to Japan (where he was struck by the magnificent squalor of Kyoto), and close to China.

Preaching was primary for Francis, and he was unusually gifted at it.[9] De Wohl says of him, "Francis preached either in good French or in bad Italian. He had no inhibitions about speaking in a language of which he knew only a couple of thousand words, if that many. Somehow they understood him, he knew that."[10] What gripped Francis throughout was the Lord's question: "What shall it profit a man if he gain the whole world and lose his soul?" But as his mission work unfolded, "There was no time for preaching," and the abuses of mass baptisms took place.[11] Francis died at forty-five, exhausted and emaciated. If only his great gifts had focused on the "riches of God's grace" and "the riches of God's glory."

The danger in the preaching of this century was that of pulpit pretension and false finery, what Paxton Hood termed "pulpit pedantry." At what point do style and form distract from the biblical message? When does the packaging conceal the truth?

---

1. A probing study is Hilary Dansey Smith, *Preaching in the Spanish Golden Age* (Oxford: Oxford University Press, 1978). J. M. Neale mentions Antonio Vieyra (1608–1697), a Jesuit, who preached in the royal chapel in Lisbon and who ministered between Portugal and Brazil, where he died. His sermons were eminently biblical and occasionally tinged with great irony. In Spain, Paravicino, Francesco Blamas, and Francesco Labata are mentioned by Dargan.

2. James M. Houston, Juan de Valdes and Don Benedetto, *The Benefit of Christ,* in the Classics of Faith and Devotion Series (Portland, Oreg.: Multnomah, 1984).

3. Ibid., xiii.

4. Frederick J. McGinness, *Right Thinking and Sacred Oratory in Counter-Reformation Rome* (Princeton, N.J.: Princeton University Press, 1995), 34.

5. Ibid., 45.

6. Ibid., 56.

7. Ibid., 99.
8. Ibid., 105. Paul Scott Wilson introduces us to Alphonsus Liguori (1696–1787), a lawyer who became a gifted preacher and founded a preaching order, the Redemptorists. He wrote one hundred books and prescribed two- or three-week preaching missions. He also practiced street preaching. He used "the great sermon" for adults and "the small sermon" for children in another place so as not to strip the sermon of its substance. See Paul Scott Wilson, *A Concise History of Preaching* (Nashville: Abingdon, 1992), 115–22. His critics complained his results were short-lived.
9. Louis de Wohl, *Set All Afire (Ignatius)* (San Francisco: Ignatius, 1953), 29, 39. A novel.
10. Ibid., 56. John W. O'Malley in his *The First Jesuits* (Cambridge, Mass.: Harvard University Press, 1993) shows how "itinerant preachers . . . engaged in a holiness ministry" made immense impact. Cf. also W. W. Meissner, *Ignatius of Loyola* (New Haven, Conn.: Yale University Press, 1992).
11. Jonathan D. Spence, *The Memory Palace of Matteo Ricci* (New York: Penguin, 1983). This is the skillful portrait of a Jesuit who went to China to minister to the Ming Dynasty. Since the Madonna and child were more appealing to the Chinese than the crucified Christ (even though Loyola's exercises called for the Jesuits to live as if Jesus Christ were being crucified before their eyes), they redrafted the gospel message to appeal to the refined tastes of the Chinese literati and omitted significant emphasis on the cross. Professor Hugh Trevor-Roper of Oxford observed that what was left was "an unobjectionable residue, with no divine power to win converts." How much better to share "Christ and him crucified" which is "the wisdom and power of God."

CHAPTER SEVEN

The Robust Days of the Puritan Pulpit

A man finds joy in giving an apt reply—and how good is a timely word!
—Proverbs 15:23

Jesus answered, "It is written: 'Man does not live on bread alone, but on every word that comes from the mouth of God.'"
—Matthew 4:4

It has always been my ambition to preach the gospel where Christ was not known. . . . Now to him who is able to establish you by my gospel and the proclamation of Jesus Christ, according to the revelation of the mystery hidden for long ages past, but now revealed and made known through the prophetic writings by the command of the eternal God, so that all nations might believe and obey him—to the only wise God be glory forever through Jesus Christ! Amen.
—Romans 15:20; 16:25–27

But as surely as God is faithful, our message to you is not "Yes" and "No." For the Son of God, Jesus Christ, who was preached among you by me and Silas and Timothy, was not "Yes" and "No," but in him it has always been "Yes."
—2 Corinthians 1:18–19

Now when I went to Troas to preach the gospel of Christ and found that the Lord had opened a door for me. . . . Unlike so many, we do not peddle the word of God for profit. On the contrary, in Christ we speak before God with sincerity, like men sent from God.
—2 Corinthians 2:12, 17

> What they wanted in strength, they supplied in activity; but what won them repute was their ministers' painful preaching in populous places; it being observed in England that those who hold the helm of the pulpit always steer people's hearts as they please.
>
> —Thomas Fuller, speaking of the Puritans

We have already noted the vital spiritual movements of the seventeenth century such as the Jansenists in France and the Pietists of Central Europe and surges of biblical preaching in England, France, Germany, and even Spain and Italy. Yet we have now before us one of the most extraordinary developments in the history of preaching, special in the depth of its biblicality, the scope of its address to the times, the sweep of its influence in Europe, and its spread with such vitality to the New World.

Puritanism has frequently been vilified as a failure of ideas, a fallback to reactionism, and a fiasco in society and culture. As we shall see, this is not an adequate representation. Puritanism was a reform movement in the Church of England, beginning in the sixteenth century and flourishing in the seventeenth, but still reverberating in our own time. Puritanism had theological, political, ecclesiastical, and polemical aspects. Puritans were not all cut from the same piece of cloth. There were Anglican and separatist Puritans; there were hyper-Calvinistic and Arminian Puritans; there were moderates and radicals. Puritanism was a revival movement, and it stirred generations for God. At its core was the preaching of the Word of God.

There are those who virtually beatify Puritanism. There are indeed happily many lines of interrelationship between Continental Pietism and Puritanism. Yet there are also blemishes and blight in Puritanism that we must face as we consider its preaching. We must also beware of the impossible and less than prudent dedication to recreating Puritanism in our own time. We can learn many lessons from our earlier brothers and sisters in all movements of God in the church, but the replication of any era (even the apostolic age in its fine-lined detail) is neither possible nor desirable.

7.1 THE GENEALOGY OF THE PURITANS

> Promote preaching of the word of faith which is so powerful . . . for faith comes by the word preached.
>
> —Thomas Watson

> What power and efficacy the word hath . . . it is a word that changeth and altereth the whole man.
>
> —Richard Sibbes

The roots of Puritanism trace back to John Wycliffe and the Lollards through the Reformers, via the theological insights of Cranmer and the preaching of Latimer. The Elizabethan Settlement in 1558–59 brought back Protestantism, but it was a compromise that did not please all. Those who wanted a cleaner sweep of Romish vestigial remains were first called Puritans in 1566, or precisions by some. Theirs was a simple biblical faith, a strong preference for low church and even free liturgy, and a nonhierarchical mode of church governance. It should not be supposed that Puritanism was a monolith since there was great divergence on many issues, but the unifying thread was the desire for the purification of the church and an abiding dissatisfaction with the Tudor modus operandi.

The initial issues were trivial: the use of the sign of the cross in baptism, the ring in marriage ceremonies, and the wearing of the surplice during the services (the Vestiarian controversy).[1] Differences in theology (Calvinism versus Arminianism); differences in polity (conflicts over the episcopacy versus Presbyterianism); and differences in practice (the Sabbatarian issue for instance) all became part of the simmering broth. Some plainly and simply opted for total separation, such as **Robert Browne** (1550–1633), whose Brownists cut loose completely and whose heirs included the Pilgrim Fathers. They went from Scrooby in England to Leiden in Holland under the leadership of William Brewster. They then went on to establish Plymouth Colony in the New World in 1620.[2]

Stoeffer sees Puritanism and Pietism as "the second phase of the Reformation," as experiential Protestantism.[3] Puritanism was a total worldview with implications for all of life and existence: a new piety, a new politics, a new person, the "citizen activist."[4] As those who had taken refuge on the Continent returned to England, their ideas seemed threatening to the queen and to the ecclesiarchs generally. When James I was crowned, he convened the Hampton Court Conference in 1604 to resolve the tensions between the Puritans and the High Church party entrenched in the Church of England. A few minuscule changes were made in the ritual, but apart from the authorization of the King James Version of the Bible the positions of the respective parties only hardened. M. Lloyd-Jones emphasizes Tyndale and his bibliocentrism and John Knox and his vehement preaching as profoundly formative in their influence (agreeing with Thomas Carlyle that Knox is "the founder of Puritanism").[5]

What Lloyd-Jones termed "a continuous and persistent sense of dissatisfaction"[6] led to endless conflict and ultimately to the civil war and the Puritan Commonwealth. Because of the unique centrality of the sermon in Puritanism, and because even though they were not a majority, the Puritan pulpit outdrew such pastimes as bearbaiting, Shakespeare, and Jonson.[7]

A fascinating ad hoc institutional structure was set up to enlarge preaching opportunity and exposure. These were the preaching lectureships. Lectureships were like sustained special meetings outside of a liturgical context. They were funded by the laity and allowed for "an extra clergyman to be attached to a parish for preaching purposes alone." There were cathedral lectureships, local parish lectureships, and borough corporation lectureships for which Puritans were often hired.

In the first generation, Thomas Cartwright, William Ames, and William Perkins all lectured. Before he became a bishop John Hooper lectured and wrote his old mentor Henry Bullinger in Zurich about his experience.

> Great, great, I say, my beloved master and gossip, is the harvest, but the laborers are few . . . Such is the maliciousness and wickedness of the bishops that the godly and learned men who would willingly labor in the Lord's harvest are hindered by them; and they neither preach themselves, nor allow the liberty of preaching to others. For this reason there are some persons here who read and expound the holy scriptures at a public lecture, two of whom read in St. Paul's cathedral four times a week. I myself, too, as my slender abilities will allow me, having compassion upon the ignorance of my brethren, read a public lecture twice in the day to so numerous an audience that the church cannot contain them.[8]

The lectures were about an hour long and quite exegetical. Often the preacher would give a series on related texts, although there were instances where the preacher "followed never a whit of the text."[9] The Laudians fought the lectureships, but the Puritans obviously triumphed. The lectureships were the Puritan answer to the demand for a godly preaching ministry. By 1664, twenty-six or twenty-seven remained in London. Three hundred years later, a few still survive.

For years leading up to the Long Parliament of 1640, there flourished what was called the Puritan or Carolinian underground. A network of organized conventicles distributed literature in the interest of the promulgation of the Word and its exposition. Archbishop Laud tended not to differentiate among the Puritanically inclined, so he and his henchmen went after the leaders, such as the "Presbyterian man of war," Dr. Alexander Leighton. A Scot who was both a medical doctor and a preacher, Leighton was fearless and unflinching. He was apocalyptic in his message and wrote a treatise against high Calvinism. He was arrested in 1630 and appeared before the Star Chamber. He was mutilated and imprisoned for ten years for treason and sedition.

The story of the Puritan Triumvirate, William Prynne, John Bastwick, and Henry Burton, epitomizes the Puritan struggle.[10] Prynne's massive *Histriomastix,* a book against stage plays, seemed necessarily seditious to Laud, so he ordered Prynne's ears cut off and his confinement in the Tower. Burton was a master in the composition and circulation of anti-episcopal tracts (using Dutch printers). Henry Burton "preached a seditious sermon at his private church" and had the temerity to repeat it on a lecture day in Colchester. The trials were farcical, and the three were confined in their respective fortresses because of their opposition to growing ritualism and *jure divino* episcopal claims.[11]

Still another opportunity to inspect Puritan preaching is afforded us in the sermons preached to the Long Parliament and in London at a time when tensions were building toward civil war. In his original and creative study, Professor Stephen Baskerville shows us that the very act of preaching was of the essence in the Puritan movement toward freedom.[12] The famous Puritan plain style was an important aspect to the vehicle of massive societal and personal change. Baskerville quotes Samuel Hieron: "The exercise of preaching ought to receive from us all esteem . . . the preaching of God's holy word, though it be meanly esteemed by the world, it is the ministry of the Spirit."[13] Baskerville traces the pervasive themes in this preaching: divine providence, sin, covenant, faith, and the church.

Finally the gathering storm burst over England. It started with a riot at St. Giles in Edinburgh in Scotland against Laud himself when he was seeking to enforce uniformity. Extended military action, with plundering and abuse on both sides, saw the defeat of the Royalists and the institution of the rule of Colonel Cromwell and Parliament. Neither they nor England would be the same again. The Barebones Parliament of 1653, which yielded power to Cromwell, was named for one of its members, an Anabaptist preacher from London whose name was Praisegod Barebones (his two brothers were named Christ-came-into-the-world-to-save Barebones and If-Christ-had-not-died-thou-wouldst-be-damned Barebones, sometimes called Damned Barebones for short).

1. Paul S. Seaver, *The Puritan Lectureships* (Palo Alto, Calif.: Stanford University Press, 1970), 4.
2. The best study is that of George F. Willison, *Saints and Strangers* (New York: Time Reading Program, 1945, 1964).
3. F. Ernest Stoeffer, *The Rise of Evangelical Pietism* (Leiden, Netherlands: E. J. Brill, 1965).
4. Stephen Baskerville, *Not Peace But a Sword: The Political Theology of the English Revolution* (London: Routledge, 1993), 8.
5. M. Lloyd-Jones, *The Puritans: Their Origins and Successors* (Edinburgh: Banner of Truth, 1987).
6. Ibid., 56.
7. Seaver, *The Puritan Lectureships,* 5.
8. Ibid., 78.
9. Ibid., 144.
10. Stephen Foster, *Notes from the Caroline Underground: Alexander Leighton, the Puritan Triumvirate and the Laudian Reaction to Non-Conformity* (Hamden, Conn.: Archon, 1978).
11. Ibid., 47.
12. Baskerville, *Not Peace But a Sword,* 8.
13. Ibid., 47.

7.2 THE GENIUS OF PURITANISM

The minister may, yea and must privately use at his liberty the arts, philosophy, and variety of reading, whilst he is in framing his sermon, but he ought in public to conceal all these from the people and not to make the least ostentation. It is also a point of art to conceal art.

—William Perkins

Embrace every occasion which the Lord offereth in the public ministry of his word . . . get something from every sermon, from this which you have this day heard.

—John Brinsley

Probably no religious entity has ever been so grossly maligned and misunderstood as have the Puritans. To be puritanical in our culture is to be overly prudish, unbearably rigid, and spiritually snobbish. Undeniably there was an underside to Puritanism, but in the history of preaching we do have what is an almost unprecedented prominence of biblical preaching affecting an entire culture. Daniel J. Boorstin observed of Puritan New England, for instance, that "there was hardly a public event of which the most memorable feature was not the sermon."[1] In understanding this unparalleled phenomenon, we must inquire into those factors comprising the Puritan genius.

---

1. Quoted in Ralph G. Turnbull, *The Preacher's Heritage, Task and Resources* (Grand Rapids: Baker, 1968), 115.

7.2.1   THE PURITANS—THE ABSOLUTE INFALLIBILITY OF THE SCRIPTURE

Protestants suppose the Scripture to be given forth by God to be . . . a complete rule of . . . faith.

—John Owen

For over a millennium and a half, the church's view of the Scriptures was that the Bible is the authoritative Word of God. This is where the Puritans stood. John Eliot from Roxbury in Massachusetts assured his listeners that "the writings of the Bible are the very words of God."[1] Carden lists the designations of the Bible in Puritan sermons: "word of truth," "great store-house of truth," "Scriptures of truth," "ye eternal word," "the Holy Scriptures," "the Sacred Word," "the infallible Oracles," "his [God's] revealed will," "the Rule," "the purest spiritual milk," "a treasure."[2] The use of both Old and New Testaments in Puritan preaching corroborate their theological formulation—they loved and believed in the Bible!

The Puritans encouraged Bible translation and distribution. Laypeople were to study and know their Bibles. The family altar and reading of the Bible in the home were encouraged. Puritans were aware of the original autographs and their importance. The Scriptures as given were without error.[3]

Counseled Thomas Watson: "Think in every line you read that God is speaking to you."[4] This conviction is reflected in The Westminster Confession of Faith (1643), which speaks of the Holy Scripture and "our full persuasion and assurance of the infallible truth and divine authority thereof is from the inward work of the Holy Spirit, bearing witness, by and with the Word, in our hearts. . . . Nothing is at any time to be added—whether by new revelations of the Spirit or traditions of men." This firm grounding in the Scripture was the foundation and basis of everything Puritan. They were truly a people of the Book.

It follows from this view of Scripture that the exposition of the Word, the public gathering "to hear God speak," was the central focus of Puritan life. Professor Stout has shown us that the average colonial Puritan heard more than seven thousand sermons requiring some fifteen thousand hours of concentrated attention in a lifetime. Based on his study of sermon manuscripts, Stout has authentically grasped the heart of Puritanism. Wrote Stout:

> The ministers enjoyed awesome powers in New England society; they alone could speak for God in public assembles of the entire congregation. Their sermons were the only voice of authority that congregations were pledged to obey unconditionally. Yet because sermons had to be based on *Sola Scriptura,* even the ministers' authority was limited. Their authority was by virtue of their specialized knowledge of the Scriptures and their ordination, not through any special perfections or infallible inspiration.[5]

Preaching was pervasive in Puritan culture because of and through the Bible. Although the premise is an extension of the Reformation presupposition about the centrality of the Word and its proclamation, the permeation of a society by Scripture among the Puritans rarely if ever has been equaled in history.

----

1. Allen Carden, *Puritan Christianity in America* (Grand Rapids: Baker, 1990), 36.
2. Ibid., 36.
3. Leland Ryken, *Worldly Saints: The Puritans As They Were* (Grand Rapids: Zondervan, 1986), 142.
4. J. I. Packer, *A Quest for Godliness: The Puritan Vision of the Christian Life* (Wheaton, Ill.: Crossway, 1990), 99.
5. Harry S. Stout, *The New England Soul: Preaching and Religious Culture in Colonial New England* (New York: Oxford University Press, 1986), 19.

7.2.2 THE PURITANS—THE ESSENTIAL PRIMACY OF PREACHING THE SCRIPTURE

> What strong castles have been demolished by preaching, how many thousand enemies have been made friends by preaching, how many kingdoms have been subdued by preaching, how . . . the preaching of the word had gone into all the earth and unto the ends of the world and rent in pieces the kingdom of the devil. . . . In a word, preaching is that whereby Christ destroys the very kingdom of Antichrist. Though it is the devil's masterpiece laid the deepest in policy and founded not only states but in men's consciences, yet Christ destroys it by the "word of his mouth"—that is, the preaching of the gospel in the mouths of his ministers.
> —Stephen Marshall, "trumpet" of St. Margaret's Church, 1646

Whether ensconced in the Church of England or of Baptist, Congregational, Presbyterian, or Independent persuasion, for Puritans the pulpit and preaching were paramount. In building their own edifices, particularly in New England, the pulpit was physically front and center. The aim of preaching was the transformation of the individual and the reorganization of society. In what was called "the rhetoric of the Spirit," the objective of spiritual preaching was to "catch the conscience of the common man."[1] The Puritans were logicians and believed that reason was part of the *imago dei*. Their indebtedness to Peter Ramus and his emphasis on disjunction and careful use of hypothesis meant their preaching sought simplification, clarity, precision, and conciseness.[2]

Nearly all of the Puritan preachers were trained at Cambridge or Oxford. They were conversant with Hebrew, Greek, and Latin, and were often quite literary. Puritan culture flowered in writers like John Milton, John Bunyan, and Daniel Defoe. Harvard and Yale were established in New England for the primary purpose of training preachers. The Puritan sermon was a work of art, "a way of conceiving the inconceivable," to use Perry Miller's apt phrase.

The aura of the Word was over the culture. Literacy was widespread. Books were considered cordials like fasting and prayer. Some knew the Bible almost by heart.[3] Emory Elliott's analysis is that "the power of the Puritan sermon was in its symbolic and metaphorical meaning, which resulted from a dynamic interaction between the clergy and their people."[4]

In the new rhetoric of the Puritans there was a move away from reading the sermon in the interest of this "dynamic interaction" with the listeners.

Solomon Stoddard cautioned, "Sermons when read are not delivered with authority in an affecting way."[5] We shall see how Jonathan Edwards, who once read his sermons, endeavored to be delivered from his "paper." The Puritan sermon was really a subgenre of the so-called university sermon we have previously analyzed and of the Hyperian modified modern type (see 6.1.1, 6.1.2, 6.1.3 n. 5). All of the Puritans used divisions and subdivisions in the sermon. Their sermons began with exegetical observations, then the body was shaped in relation to a chief doctrinal subject or theme and applied in a series of uses. This is not classical exposition, in which the sermon is shaped by the very development within the text itself. F. R. Webber understood this:

> This method of homiletics led to a diffused sermon structure instead of unity and progress. Instead of constructing a sermon on the plan of several rivers, which unite and form one great stream that moves forward steadily toward a definite goal, the sermons of Puritan times were constructed on the plan of a tree. A general theme was stated, and then each one of its details was traced out in turn, as one might trace each limb and each branch of a tree. It was a mixed style. Some of the preachers of those days derived their divisions and subdivisions from the text, but more often than not, the divisions and subdivisions were based partly on the thoughts of the text and partly upon ideas suggested by the general nature of the subject. Often there was little actual advancement of thought, leading the hearers onward, and culminating in a powerful impression. Rather were the sermons of those days a number of minor truths tied together by the text. If as Dr. John Watson says, three detached sermonettes do not make done sermon, how can thirty or forty ideas result in unity?[6]

The subordination of the text to the doctrinal theme suggested within it is seen in a series of fifty-eight sermons Thomas Brooks preached on the theme, "The

Necessity, Excellency, Rarity and Beauty of Holiness." The thrust was powerful and the truth was stated, but the text of Scripture is minimized when so little text is exposed. We must prefer the Hyperian modification, which like the homily follows the order of the text but divides the text for exposition.

The Puritan sermon tended to be long and heavy, but it had the great advantage of being theological and doctrinal. Puritan preachers ranged over the theological encyclopedia. Our generation of preachers could profit from their example They preached from within a sense of doctrinal construct. We read their sermons to learn doctrine on sin, for instance. We see what every student of Puritan preaching notes as the persistent millennial or chiliastic strain, even in Jonathan Edwards, for whom the postmillennialist figure is the controlling metaphor in his epochal *Magnalia Christi Americana.*

Most of the Puritans were futurists and of a millennialist school that anticipated a great movement among the Jews to Christ. Indeed Oliver Cromwell invited the Jews to return to England, from which they had long been banned. This tradition was sustained down to Spurgeon himself, who affirmed, "Our hope is the personal, premillennial return of the Lord Jesus Christ in glory."[7] This is just a sample of the doctrinally rich and substantial issues addressed from the Puritan pulpits on both continents. But the text was not king!

1. William Haller, *The Rise of Puritanism* (Philadelphia: University of Pennsylvania Press, 1938), 19, 30.

2. Perry Miller and Thomas H. Johnson, eds., *The Puritans* (New York: Harper Torchbooks, 1938), 1:24, 29.

3. David L. Hall, *Worlds of Wonder, Days of Judgment: Popular Religious Belief in Early New England* (New York: Knopf, 1989), 219.

4. Emory Elliott, *Power and the Pulpit in Puritan New England* (Princeton, N.J.: Princeton University Press, 1975), 204. A delightful panegyric for Puritan preaching is by Peter Lewis, *The Genius of Puritanism* (Haywards Heath, England: Carey Publications, 1979), 19–52.

5. Donald Weber, *Rhetoric and History in Revolutionary New England* (Oxford: Oxford University Press, 1988), 26.

6. F. R. Webber, *A History of Preaching in Britain and America* (Milwaukee: Northwestern, 1952), 1:202–3.

7. Charles H. Spurgeon, *The Sword and Trowel* (London: The Preacher's College, 1891), 446. Solid studies of this theme are Iain Murray, *The Puritan Hope* (London: Banner of Truth, 1971); Peter Toon, ed., *Puritans, the Millennium and the Future of Israel: Puritan Eschatology* (Cambridge, Mass.: James Clarke, 1970). On the Jews more particularly, see my study, *Jews, Gentiles and the Church* (Grand Rapids: Discovery House, 1995). Perry Miller advanced the bizarre idea that Cocceius projected federal theology to blunt the pain of predestination. Federal theology, important to the Puritans, would seem to rise quite clearly from the biblical text as in Romans 5:12–21. Note also Charles S. McCoy and J. Wayne Baker, *Fountainhead of Federalism: Heinrich Bullinger and the Covenantal Tradition* (Louisville: Westminster/John Knox, 1991). This book has a helpful treatment of Johannes Cocceius as well as Bullinger.

7.2.3 THE PURITANS—THE INESCAPABLE APPLICABILITY OF THE SCRIPTURE

> God never proposed to leave his holy word to be no more but read, either privately in men's houses or publicly in our churches, but appointed there should be men ordained to expand the same by voice and apply it to the occasions and necessities of the people.
>
> This is the soul of prophesying and the very life of preaching. It openeth the scripture to show what it meaneth; it fits to the particular uses and necessities of the people.
>
> —Samuel Hieron

The practicality and profitability of the Scriptures have been an emphasis from the beginning of biblical preaching (cf. 2 Timothy 3:16–17), but few eras have been as plush and prolific in application as the Puritans. With much doctrinal exposition, the Puritans always concluded their sermons with an extensive section of "uses" which sought to bridge from the "then" to the "now." Since this has not been strong in the preaching of more recent years, we do well to analyze this aspect of Puritan preaching with some care. John Brown in his Beecher Lectures relates of one William Bourne, who

> seldom varied the manner of his preaching, which after explication of the text, was doctrine proof of it from Scripture, by reasoning and answering more and more objections; and then the uses, first, of information, secondly, of confutation of popery, thirdly of reprehension, fourthly of examination, fifthly, of exhortation, and lastly of consolation.[1]

All of this can add up to considerable complexity. John Owen is a case in point. His sermon on Habakkuk 3 had a fourfold division subdivided into "almost 150 observations, reasons, uses, particulars, etc."[2]

In an extensive analysis of Jonathan Edwards' sermons, Ralph Turnbull demonstrates the emphasis on application in Edwards' sermons.

1. "The Sovereignty of God": twelve pages of exposition, three pages of application;
2. "Sinners in the Hands of an Angry God": four pages exposition, five pages application;
3. "The Excellency of Christ": thirteen pages of exposition, nine pages of application;
4. "A Warning to Professors": five pages of exposition, five pages of application;
5. "True Saints, when absent from the body are present with the Lord": thirteen pages of exposition, three pages of application;
6. "The True Excellency of a Gospel Minister": nine pages of exposition, four of application;
7. "A Farewell Sermon": nine pages of exposition, ten pages of application.[3]

In *The Westminster Directory for the Publick Worship of God (Of the Preaching of the Word)*, issued by the Westminster Assembly, great emphasis is placed on not resting "in general doctrine" but in moving the truth of the Word to the hearers, some of whom are asleep, some seekers, some young, some old, some fallen, some sad. A specific appeal was to be made to the mind, the affections, and the will in self-examination and encouragement.[4]

Such audience analysis in the interest of direct application must be distinguished from audience-centered preaching as it has arisen in our time. The compact application of the Puritans has given way to continuous application today.

Further evidence for the Puritan penchant for application can be seen in the widely acclaimed development of the Puritan work ethic. This was a consequence of the preaching of the Puritan doctrines of grace and godly living. In his recent masterful study, *Trust: The Social Virtues and the Creation of Prosperity*, the noted social theorist Francis Fukuyama leans on Max Weber's *The Protestant Ethic and the Spirit of Capitalism* to show that "the early Puritans, seeking to glorify God alone, and renouncing the acquisition of material goods as an end in itself, developed certain virtues like honesty and thrift that were extremely helpful to the accumulation of capital."[5] Fukuyama shows how these Puritan traits were replicated in Protestant converts in the Methodist revivals in the eighteenth and nineteenth centuries and among Protestant converts in Latin America in our time.[6] Not only Weber but also R. H. Tawney in his memorable *Holland Lectures* in 1922 mulls over the extraordinary impact of Puritan preaching and values in the shaping of an economic and political system. Observed Tawney:

> The growth, triumph and transformation of the Puritan spirit was the most fundamental movement of the seventeenth century . . . Puritanism was the schoolmaster of the English middle classes . . . a godly discipline was, indeed, the very ark of the Puritan covenant. . . . What is required of the Puritan is not individual meritorious acts, but a holy life—a system in which every element if grouped round a central idea, the service of God, from which all disturbing irrelevancies have been pruned, and to which all minor interests are subordinated.[7]

The great stress then on the practical application of the preaching of the Word can be seen as it translates so vividly and strikingly in the sinews of a society in its day-by-day experience.

---

1. John Brown, *Puritan Preaching in England* (New York: Scribner's, 1900), 60.
2. F. R. Webber, *A History of Preaching in Britain and America* (Milwaukee: Northwestern, 1952), 1:202.
3. Ralph G. Turnbull, *Jonathan Edwards the Preacher* (Grand Rapids: Baker, 1958), 168ff.
4. For further discussion of this, see David L. Larsen, *The Anatomy of Preaching* (Grand Rapids: Baker, 1989), 95ff.
5. Francis Fukuyama, *Trust: The Social Virtues and the Creation of Prosperity* (New York: Free Press, 1995), 37.

6. Ibid., 45. Fukuyama quotes David Martin's significant study, *Tongues of Fire: The Explosion of Protestantism in Latin America* (Oxford: Blackwood, 1990).

7. R. H. Tawney, *Religion and the Rise of Capitalism* (New York: Mentor, 1926), 164ff.

7.2.4 THE RADICAL INTERIORITY OF THE CHRISTIAN LIFE

> Make my every sermon a means of grace to myself,
> and help me to experience the power of thy dying love,
> for thy blood is balm, thy presence bliss, thy smile heaven,
> thy cross the place where truth and mercy meet.
> When I preach to others let not my words be merely elegant and masterly,
> my reasoning polished and refined,
> my performance powerless and tasteless,
> but may I exalt thee and humble sinners.
> O Lord of power and grace,
> all hearts are in thy hands, all events at thy disposal,
> set the seal of thy almighty will upon my ministry.[1]

While the Puritans were devotees of one authoritative Book and set on preaching it and the doctrines it delineated, Puritanism was a movement of revival and the cultivation of the inner affections. Packer calls them "restless experientialists."[2] Stoeffer, in his classic study, roots the "rise of evangelical pietism" in the Puritan camp, with its quest for personal piety even stronger than its pursuit of institutional purity.[3] The genius of the Puritan pulpit was its balance, however precarious at times, between the propositional and the personal, the outer and the inner, the Spirit and the Word. When Puritanism began to flag, it was because this delicate balance was lost in favor of an ossified externalism which was devoid of life.

We can see this balance in **William Perkins** (cf. 6.1.3), who stressed the propriety of human learning, and then the acquisition of divine knowledge (revealed truth), and subsequently "that inward learning taught by the Spirit of God."[4] This emphasis is seen in the Westminster Shorter Catechism:

> The Spirit of God maketh the reading, but especially the preaching of the Word, an effectual means of convincing and converting sinners, and of building them up in holiness and comfort, through faith, unto salvation (89).

G. F. Nuttall in his definitive study on the Holy Spirit in Puritan thought argues that the Puritans were not primarily dogmatic but experiential (compared to Calvin, who saw the Holy Spirit as a necessity of thought but not known overtly in experience).[5] For Richard Sibbes, the Spirit was in the Scripture inspiring it, but the Spirit was also in the believing reader and preacher of Scripture enlightening it. Thus it is that John Robinson, in his farewell to the Pilgrim Fathers, was reported to have said, "The Lord hath more truth and light yet to break forth out of his holy word."

The first to upset this equilibrium were the Quakers, who stressed the inner light of the Spirit in every person, including the unregenerate. Neither Baxter nor Owen would recognize infallible revelation apart from Scripture, while George Fox contended that he had independent revelation.[6] The hazard of this Spirit without the Word approach can be seen in the fact that Quakers frequently did not preach from a text at all.[7] This was also displayed in certain radical Puritans, the Ranters and the Shakers.

The Puritans believed in "immediacy in relation to God." Their illustrious political leader **Oliver Cromwell** (1599–1658) testified to "the full assurance of the Spirit's nearness," and stressed the inner transformation of the Spirit. "His presence hath been amongst us, and by the light of His countenance we have prevailed."[8] Both Richard Sibbes and Thomas Goodwin returned again and again to the grave danger of grieving the Holy Spirit. The Puritans were deeply into the life of prayer and communion with God, privately, in the family circle at home, and in public gatherings and worship. Their theology of the gifts of the Spirit and the Spirit's manifestation in prayer set them at odds with the Anglican habit of "set prayers." Worship and preaching directed by Scripture are enlivened by the Spirit.[9]

Puritan spirituality focused on conversion, cherished the Word and personal and corporate worship (with a strong emphasis on baptism and the Lord's Supper), and maintained high reverence for the Lord's Day.

Similar to the Caroline divines, the Puritans stressed "the mystical union" with Christ and loved to preach from the Song of Solomon. Wakefield cites **John Preston** (1587–1628), "Prince Charles' Puritan Chaplain," who composed a piece titled "The Soliloquy of the Devout Soul Panting after the Love of the Lord Jesus."[10] Apart from this arduous cultivation of the inner spiritual life there would never have been what we call Puritanism. Their preaching would have been sucked into the hot sands of secularism—as would ours as well.

---

1. From Arthur Bennett, *The Valley of Vision: A Collection of Puritan Prayers and Devotions* (Edinburgh: Banner of Truth Trust, 1975), 186.
2. J. I. Packer, *A Quest for Godliness: The Puritan Vision of the Christian Life* (Wheaton, Ill.: Crossway, 1990), 30.
3. F. Ernest Stoeffer, *The Rise of Evangelical Pietism* (Leiden, Netheralnds: E. J. Brill, 1965).
4. John Brown, *Puritan Preaching in England* (New York: Scribner's, 1900), 74.
5. Geoffrey F. Nuttall, *The Holy Spirit in Puritan Faith and Experience* (Oxford: Blackwell, 1946), 6.
6. Ibid., 54.
7. Ibid., 153. For an important study of the intellectual leader of early Quakers, see D. Elton Trueblood, *Robert Barclay* (New York: Harper and Row, 1968). Barclay (1648–1690) also confronted the celebrated lunatic **Lodowick Muggleton,** whose followers were called "Friends" and who bombastically castigated preaching, worship, and churches. The last of his followers died about midway in our century. William Blake's mother was a follower of Muggleton.
8. Ibid., 136. Still my favorite biography of Cromwell is by Antonia Fraser, *Cromwell: The Lord Protector* (New York: Knopf, 1973).

9. A magnificent study is Roy Walter Williams, *The Puritan Concept and Practice of Prayer* (Unpublished Ph.D. dissertation, University of London, 1982). A copy is in the library of Trinity Evangelical Divinity School, Deerfield, Illinois.

10. Gordon S. Wakefield, "The Puritans," in *The Study of Spirituality,* ed. Cheslyn Jones, Geoffrey Wainwright, Edward Yarnold (Oxford: Oxford University Press, 1986), 444. See also the choice study, Ted A. Campbell, *The Religion of the Heart* (Columbia: University of South Carolina, 1991).

7.3 THE GLORIES OF THE PURITAN PULPIT

Preaching of the Word, being the power of God unto salvation, and one of the greatest and most excellent works belonging to the ministry of the Gospel, should be so performed that the workman need not be ashamed, but may save himself and those that hear him.

—*The Westminster Directory for the Publick Worship of God*

The Bible, I say the Bible only.

—William Chillingworth

Puritanism was, as Perry Miller argued, a kind of "Augustinian piety." It was a deep-seated dissatisfaction with the terms of the Reformation embodied in the Elizabethan settlement. Puritanism's insistence on a conversion experience for every believer set Puritans against the sacerdotal. As Brauer said of the Puritan understanding of conversion, "They preached for it, sought it and testified of it."[1]

Within and against governmental restrictions and ecclesiastical controls, the Puritans forged their alliance. Laypersons were thrust to the fore. Puritans such as Thomas Adams and John White opposed the deposition of King Charles I (John Preston, the future Master of Emmanuel College, had been his chaplain while he was growing up), but the nation plunged into a bloody civil war in which one hundred thousand people were killed.

In the widening conflict, the Puritans became increasingly powerful. Preaching remained at the center of their worship.[2] They viewed preaching as the antidote to social and political disorder. Preaching was effective, from the Puritan perspective, in that "Growing awareness of the importance of consent in establishing social order underlay Puritan emphasis on the efficacy of preaching as a means of social control."[3] But many in the Establishment saw Puritans as the cause of insurrection and destablization.[4]

During the civil war (1642–1649), Puritan preachers saw the destiny of their nation in the drama of Scripture. They sponsored a series of "Humiliations and Thanksgivings" (1641–1642) to summon the nation to God. Throughout the Long Parliament, many of the outstanding Puritan preachers opened Scripture and preached to the members. Stephen Marshall brought an extended series on Psalm 102. In the parliamentary year 1648–1649, 125 different preachers addressed Parliament. Most of them belonged to the Westminster Assembly.[5] John Owen, though not in the Assembly, was extremely influential and preached the sermon in Parliament on the day following King Charles' death.

Analysis of these sermons yields invaluable insight into effective biblical communication.[6] However, Richard Baxter, "the loquacious Presbyterian" and an army chaplain himself, indicated that he was personally appalled by the language of some of the "hot-blooded sectaries." Still, preaching was unquestionably ascendant once again.

---

1. Jerald C. Brauer, "Conversion: From Puritanism to Revivalism," *Journal of Religion* (1958): 227–43.
2. David Zaret, *The Heavenly Contract: Ideology and Organization in Pre-Revolutionary Puritanism* (Chicago: University of Chicago Press, 1985), 62; for a full treatment of this, see Horton Davies, *The Worship of the English Puritans* (Westminster, London, England: Dacre, 1948), 182–202.
3. Zaret, *The Heavenly Contract*, 87.
4. Ibid., 75.
5. John F. Wilson, *Pulpit in Parliament: Puritanism During the English Civil Wars 1640–1648* (Princeton, N.J.: Princeton University Press, 1969), 108.
6. Ibid., 137ff.

7.3.1   GOSPEL TRAILBLAZERS—EARLIER PURITAN PREACHERS

They hould that the highest and supreame office and authoritie of the Pastor, is to preach the gospell solemnly and publickly to the Congregation, by interpreting the written word of God, and applying the same by exhortation and reproof unto them. They hould that this was the greatest worke that Christ and his Apostles did.

—William Bradshaw

The makers of Puritanism were almost all university men. Although a few came from Oxford, the great majority came from Cambridge, where early on Christ College and then Emmanuel College were great centers of Puritan activity. The latter was even known as "the nursery of Puritanism."

Even Oliver Cromwell put his son Henry at Emmanuel. **Laurence Chaderton** (1536–1640), from an old Roman Catholic family, went up to Cambridge in 1564 and met Christ there. For over fifty years he was afternoon lecturer at St. Clement's, where he consistently drew enormous crowds. He was deep into the Scriptures, and used the plain style with "the eloquence of the body." Chaderton exerted a seminal influence on his own brother-in-law, **Ezekiel Culverwell,** in whose congregation at Sudbury was the young **John Winthrop,** later the governor of Massachusetts Bay Colony. Chaderton also shaped **William Perkins,** who touched **John Cotton** and **John Robinson,** whose ministries would be in the New World.[1] Chaderton was also one of the translators of the King James Version and faithfully preached the Word into an advanced age.

We have already identified early Puritan trailblazers such as John Hooper (cf. 5.5.6), who visited and studied in Geneva, and **Archbishop Edmund Grindal** (cf. 5.5.9), whose exile in Germany reconfigured his views and ministry. Grindal much preferred the sermon to the homily, and sharpened the contrast in a famous letter:

> The Godly preacher is termed in the Gospel, a Faithful Servant, who knoweth how to give his Lord's family their apportioned food in season; who can apply his speech according to the diversity of times, places and hearers; which cannot be done in the Homilies: exhortations, reprehensions, and persuasions, are uttered with more affection, to the moving of the Hearers, in Sermons than in Homilies. Besides, Homilies were devised by the Godly Bishops in your Brother's time, only to supply necessity, for want of Preachers; and are by Statute not to be preferred, but to give place to Sermons, whensoever they may be had.[2]

Grindal undoubtedly brought the shape of the Puritan sermon back to England from Germany (cf. 6.1 n.5).

Other worthies in this early succession are **Thomas Cartright** (cf. 5.5.11 in relation to Richard Hooker), **Henry Smith** (cf. 6.1.2), so well and so widely heard, and of course the inimitable **William Perkins,** who instructed lucidly on the preaching craft (cf. 6.1.3).[3] Following this noble band were Bishop **Joseph Hall** (cf. 6.2.5) and **Richard Clifton** (1545–1616), who after serving as rector in Nottinghamshire joined the Puritans at Scrooby and succeeded John Robinson. Clifton ultimately fled to Amsterdam, where he had a noteworthy ministry. **John White** (1570–1615) came out of Cambridge and served in Manchester, where his reputation as a vehement preacher ripened. He was generally polemical, and espoused an extreme Calvinism and defended the monarchy.[4]

In this line of distinguished Puritan forefathers we must certainly see the eloquent **Thomas Adams** (1580–1653?), often called the Shakespeare of the Puritans. Solid in his conviction, he was immensely creative, and bore similarity to some of the more ornate Caroline divines. He argued, "It was not one for one that Christ died, not one for many: but one for all . . . and this one must needs be of infinite price."[5] Like the Caroline preachers, he was stoutly loyal to the monarchy.

The poetic Adams added to the Puritan homiletical legacy. When preaching out of the text, "Their poison is like the poison of a serpent, like the deaf adder that stops her ear," Adams used eleven characters to convey his point—among them salamanders, crocodiles, caterpillars, and lizards. His apt aphorisms flavored his messages:

> There be pirates in the sea, alas! but a handful to that huge army of them in the world. Take a short view of them, borrowed of a divine traveler. Fury fights against us like a mad Turk; fornication, like a treacherous Joab, in kisses it kills us; drunkeness is the master gunner that gives fire to all the rest; gluttony may stand for a corporal; avarice for a pioneer; idleness for a gentleman of the company; pride must be the captain. But the arch-pirate of all is the devil, that huge leviathan

that takes his pastime in the sea. And his pastime is to sink merchants' freight that are laden with holy traffic for heaven. Historians speak of a fish that is a special and oft-prevailing enemy of the whale, called the sword-fish. The most powerful thing to overcome this leviathan is the sword of the Spirit.[6]

Adams also preached on "The Three Divine Sisters—Faith, Hope and Charity," and published an expository commentary on 2 Peter which echoes his preaching on that Epistle. His published *Sermons and Expositions* (1630) are appreciated.

Stephen Marshall (1594–1655) often preached at St. Margaret's (the parish church at Westminster). He was one of the prime movers in the Westminster Assembly. Marshall was sent to Scotland to bridge the gap with the Scots, and was one of the authors of *Smectymnuus,* an important tract outlining the vision of nonconformity.[7] He attended Archbishop Laud before Laud's execution in 1645.

Marshall's preaching was powerful and effective. He loved to preach from both Testaments. Wilson adjudges him to be "without peer as preacher to the Long Parliament" and effective as a broker both before and behind the scenes.[8] Something of a clerical politician, he was more importantly a biblical preacher whose preaching made a vast difference. He was buried in Westminster and disinterred upon the Restoration.

As we turn to the more typical Puritan preachers, we shall adopt Professor Knight's bifurcation—two main categories in England that were then transferred to New England: (1) Perkins and Ames, those who stress cultivating true piety through spiritual discipline within a sense of covenantal obligation; and (2) Sibbes and those who emphasize the experience of the Spirit's indwelling and the "joys of Christian fellowship."[9] In the wake of certain tensions that arose on both continents, the Amesians were accused of legalism and the Sibbesians charged with of antinomianism. We shall now trace this important succession.

---

1. John Brown, *Puritan Preaching in England* (New York: Scribner's, 1900), 67ff.
2. Horton Davies, *The Worship of the English Puritans* (Westminster, London, England: Dacre, 1948), 187.
3. Brown, *Puritan Preaching in England,* 75.
4. F. R. Webber, *A History of Preaching in Britain and America* (Milwaukee: Northwestern, 1952), 1:222.
5. Brown, *Puritan Preaching in England,* 91ff.
6. T. Harwood Pattison, *The History of Christian Preaching* (Philadelphia: American Baptist Publication Society, 1903), 182.
7. Webber, *A History of Preaching,* 1:235.
8. John F. Wilson, *Pulpit in Parliament: Puritanism During the English Civil Wars* (Princeton, N.J.: Princeton University Press, 1969), 109.
9. Janice Knight, *Orthodoxies in Massachusetts: Rereading American Puritanism* (Cambridge, Mass.: Harvard University Press, 1994).

7.3.2   GOSPEL TRUMPETERS—ADVOCATES OF COVENANT AND DISCIPLINE

> The preaching of the Word is that lattice where Christ looks forth and
> shows himself to his saints.
>
> —Thomas Watson

The drumbeat of the more traditional Puritans emphasized strenuous preparation of the heart for reception of divine grace. It accented power and sovereignty
as the essential divine attributes, and was furnished by the germinal thinker
William Ames (1576–1633), student and follower of the great William Perkins.
A graduate of Christ's College, Cambridge, Ames emigrated to Holland, where
he attended the Synod of Dort. He became a professor at Friesland and died in
Rotterdam. His famous *Marrow of Sacred Divinity* was a Puritan staple and exerted a profound influence on Puritan thinking. It was considered fundamental
at Harvard and Yale in the seventeenth century. Ames shaped so much of the
tone and texture of Puritan preaching. He saw theology as "the science of living
to God," and stressed the nurture of a clear conscience in all details of life (especially in his *Cases of Conscience*). He wrote:

> But although divers parts of the Scriptures were written, upon some
> speciall occasion, and were directed to some certaine men, or asemblies:
> yet in God's intention, they doe as well pertaine to the instructing of all
> the faithfull thorough all ages, as if they had been specially directed to
> them.[1]

Thus sanction for morning and afternoon services was to be found in the double
burnt offering of Numbers 28:9, etc. With this approach, Ames disparaged topical preaching:

> Ministers impose upon their hearers and altogether forget themselves
> when they propound a certain text in the beginning as the start of the
> sermon and then speak many things about or simply by occasion of the
> text but for the most part draw nothing out of the text itself.[2]

Not only in his fidelity to the text but also in his broad address in applying
Scripture to every aspect of human life, Ames sets landmarks long observed.
Sermon outlines must facilitate remembrance of the sermon. His famous epigram
encapsulates the serious approach of the Puritan to Scripture: "The receiving of
the word consists of two parts: attention of mind and intention of will." Ames is
one of the formative pillars of Puritan orthodoxy.

---

1. Horton Davies, *The Worship of the English Puritans* (Westminster, London, England:
   Dacre, 1948), 5.
2. Leland Ryken, *Worldly Saints: The Puritans As They Really Were* (Grand Rapids:
   Zondervan, 1986), 98.

7.3.2.1 John Robinson—Pastor of the Pilgrims

> I charge you before God and his blessed angels to follow me no further
> than I follow Christ.
>
> —Pastor John Robinson in his farewell sermon
to the Pilgrims, from Ezra 8:21

Another young Cambridge graduate, **John Robinson** (1575–1625), was apparently born near Lincoln and served several curacies but was expelled because of his separatistic bent. He became associated with the Scrooby separatists who met in William Brewster's house and fled to Amsterdam in 1608. From there he moved to Leyden, where he became pastor of a Puritan congregation that grew to three hundred constituents.[1]

The influence of William Perkins was evident in Robinson's doctrinal and homiletical views. The émigrés purchased a house which was remodeled to serve as a meeting house and parsonage and had a number of small cottages behind it for poor members of the congregation. Robinson preached to the appreciative congregants twice on Sunday and on Thursday evening and was considered a "commone father unto them."[2]

While properly labeled a separatist among the Puritans,[3] Robinson exemplifies the strong Puritan commitment to an emphasis on covenant, the preaching of the Word, and the prime requisite of conversion. The three volumes of his sermons demonstrate his high view of the preached Word. As Maclure states in his masterful study:

> For the Puritans, the sermon is not just hinged to Scripture; it quite literally exists inside the Word of God; the text is not in the sermon, but the sermon is in the text. . . . Put summarily, listening to a sermon is being in the Bible.[4]

The clear focus of Puritan preaching was salvation by grace alone (although this was later compromised in some quarters by a moralistic tendency).[5]

Members of the assembly took their places by 8 A.M. on the Lord's Day under the strict scrutiny of the deacon. Men, women, and children sat apart, thus "dignifying the meeting,"[6] and began the worship service with prayer. Pastor Robinson read from the Geneva Bible with expository comments (not mere "dumb reading"). After the singing of a psalm came a two-hour sermon, an exposition of the text "with a quiet and moving eloquence, a deep human understanding, and a wealth of apt illustration that held his brethren spellbound."[7] The singing of another psalm followed and the sacraments were administered when appropriate. The service closed about noon with the benediction. The afternoon service was less formal and featured "prophesying" by the pastor or ruling elder Brewster, likewise from a text.

Under continued pressure because of his publishing activities, William Brewster and others explored the possibility of a concession in Virginia by way of refuge. Because they further wanted to farm and did not want their children to grow up Dutch, they finally negotiated with some English merchants who agreed to sail them to the New World, where they arrived in Provincetown harbor on November 21, 1620. Pastor Robinson planned to join this segment of his flock but bade them farewell in a memorable address. He was never to see the 104 again. He wrote moving letters to encourage them in their dark hours. When he became ill in 1625, he insisted on preaching his customary two sermons on Sunday. He died a week later on March 1.[8]

1. F. R. Webber, *A History of Preaching in Britain and America* (Milwaukee: Northwestern, 1952), 1:232.
2. George F. Willison, *Saints and Strangers* (New York: Time Reading Program, 1945, 1964), 91.
3. Timothy George, *John Robinson and the English Separatist Tradition* (Macon, Ga.: Mercer University Press, 1982).
4. Millar Maclure, *The Paul's Cross Sermons, 1534–1642* (Toronto: University of Toronto Press, 1958).
5. C. F. Allison, *The Rise of Moralism: The Proclamation of the Gospel from Hooker to Baxter* (London: SPCK, 1966).
6. Willison, *Saints and Strangers,* 92.
7. Ibid., 93.
8. Ibid., 279.

7.3.2.2 Richard Mather—Founder of a Dynasty

The word of God is very plaine . . . [God] will give grace to whoever will receive it and come for it . . . it is a great encouragement and comfort that the righteousness of our God will move him and prevail with him, to pereform what he hath promised and so to give unto his the grace of faith.

There is an inseparable connection of the gifts and graces of Christ, so that if he give conversion and justification, he will sanctification also.
—Richard Mather

Of note both as a preacher and as a father of preachers, **Richard Mather** (1596–1669) was born in the village of Lowton near Liverpool. He became a teacher at a grammar school in Toxteth Park and eventually became master there. While there, he heard the preaching of the Word through Mr. Harrison of Hyton. Along with reading William Perkins, he came under deep conviction after one of Harrison's sermons on the new birth (from John 3:3, 5) and beside a Lancashire hedge he came to the assurance of salvation in 1614.[1] He had no particular ecstasy, but as Perkins stipulated, he should expect none.[2] Mather did matriculate briefly at Oxford but in 1619 took holy orders and returned to become the minister at Toxteth Park.

Already suspect for nascent Puritanism, Mather gave himself to preaching twice each Sabbath to his own charge and in surrounding churches during the week. He married, and in the next fifteen years had six sons. For the next fifty years, he never missed preaching on the Sabbath. His preaching drew heavily on the books of Samuel and Isaiah and the Epistles of Paul, with considerable reinforcement of the analogy between God's ancient chosen people and his faithful in the seventeenth century.[3]

Mather became increasingly convinced that congregationalism was correct, and predictably came into serious tensions with his bishop, who expelled him. He endured a period of much soul-searching and pondering of "England's apostasy," and reflected on the martyrdom of John Bradford. Mather soon moved with his family to New England, where he took up pastoral responsibilities in the Dorchester church in Massachusetts Bay Colony. Eventually he became president of Harvard. Yet in all his years in New England, Mather was a nostalgic exile.

As did all the Puritans, Mather preached with a sense of the impending end and Christ's soon appearing. He used Perkins' *The Art of Prophesying* as his model. Mather wrote books, such as his reply to Samuel Rutherford and the Scots who criticized New England congregationalism, and he made efforts to translate Psalms from the Hebrew. His many sermons and regular lectures display no "literary virtuosity,"[4] but he faithfully held forth "the undisputed word of Christ" in Puritan plain style. While typically given to much introspection and self-examination, the Puritan "frames," he took a staunch stand with Ames and Perkins and "the preparationists" who stressed God's work of preparing the elect for salvation through common grace. He opposed such notions as "the indwelling of the Holy Spirit"[5] and worried about the mystic manifestations of the antinomians.

Still, his ministry of fifty-two years was always with a thrust to heighten the awareness of the line between the saved and the unsaved. At times he seemed like a Calvinist in his study but an Arminian in his pulpit, and he came close to Richard Sibbes in subscribing to the validity of the universal call.[6]

When Mather's wife eventually died, he married the widow of the Reverend John Cotton. In his later years, he increasingly sounded the jeremiad from his pulpit as he witnessed a decline in faith and piety. His farewell exhortation was delivered from the observation of forty years of spiritual ebbs and flows and had the ring of authenticity in its depiction of the fall of nations and the hope of redemption.[7]

One of Mather's great legacies was his sons—two of whom returned to England and Ireland to minister, and Increase, who took his M.A. at Trinity College in Dublin after graduating from Harvard. In four generations this family had eleven well-known preachers who published five hundred books. Richard Mather is representative of Puritan preachers who combined intellectual and affective elements in a striking and stirring fashion.

---

1. B. R. Burg, *Richard Mather of Dorchester* (Lexington: University Press of Kentucky, 1976), 9.
2. Robert Middlekauff, *The Mathers: Three Generations of Puritan Intellectuals* (New York: Oxford University Press, 1971), 14.

3. Ibid., 16.
4. Burg, *Richard Mather of Dorchester,* 69.
5. Ibid., 41.
6. Norman Pettit, *The Heart Prepared: Grace and Conversion in Puritan Spiritual Life* (New Haven, Conn.: Yale University Press, 1966); John von Rohr, *The Covenant of Grace in Puritan Thought* (Atlanta: Scholars Press, 1986).
7. Burg, *Richard Mather of Dorchester,* 161.

7.3.2.3 Thomas Goodwin—Exemplar of Wholeness

> Whereas some men are for preaching only extempore, and without study, Paul bids Timothy meditate and study, and give his mind wholly to these things.

> The same Spirit that guided the holy apostles and prophets to write it must guide the people of God to know the meaning of it; and as he first delivered it, so must he help men to understand it.
>
> —Thomas Goodwin

On every short list of the most admired and respected Puritan pastor-theologians is the name **Thomas Goodwin** (1600–1680). He was born in Norfolk and educated at Cambridge. Although dedicated by his parents to Christian ministry, he did not care for preaching until he came under conviction while attending a funeral and was converted. He describes his experience:

> I observed of this work of God on my soul that there was nothing of constraint or force in it, but I was carried on with the most ready and willing mind, and what I did was what I chose to do. With the greatest freedom I parted with my sins, formerly as dear to me as the apple of my eye, yea, as my life, and resolved never to return to them more. And what I did was from deliberate choice; I considered what I was doing, and reckoned with myself what it would cost me to make this great alteration. What the world thought of these things hindered me not at all. The weeds that entangled me in those waters, I swam and broke through with as much ease as Samson did with his withes; for I was made a vassal and a captive to another binding, such as Paul speaks of.[1]

Goodwin served churches in Cambridge and London, but under the influence of John Cotton he became a Congregationalist, or Independent. When Laud made things too hot in England, he ministered to an English congregation at Arnheim in Holland for a brief while, returning to England in the Puritan ascendancy. Goodwin was a key member of the Westminster Assembly and exerted a prevailing influence on The Directory for Public Worship in Three Kingdoms.[2] In 1647 he accepted an invitation from John Cotton to come to minister in New England, and was about to sail when the pleas of his own dear congregation in

London dissuaded him and he remained as their pastor.[3] Cromwell appointed Goodwin as President of Magdalen College, Oxford, where he also preached in St. Mary's Church.

In sermonic form, Goodwin was among the best. John Brown advances the thesis that John Owen preached primarily to the mind, Richard Baxter to the conscience, and Thomas Goodwin to the spiritual affections. Goodwin was a traditional Calvinist, though not "exaggerated" in his beliefs.[4] In fact, he nearly became an Arminian because of acute depression stemming from uncertainty over his election.

Goodwin was influenced by Richard Sibbes, who once told him, "Young man, if you ever would do good, you must preach the Gospel and the free grace of God in Jesus Christ" (c. 1625). He was to Alexander Whyte, "The greatest pulpit exegete of Paul that has ever lived." His massive works, *The Objects and Acts of Justifying Faith* and *The Work of the Holy Spirit in Our Salvation,* are still in circulation by Banner of Truth Trust.

Though early on exposed to more elegant form at Cambridge and endowed with great gifts of natural eloquence, Goodwin had to fight a great battle against what he called his "master lust," the desire to impress. Sermons with "literary distinction" may be, to use his own words, "distinguished rather for ostentatious display of rhetoric than for clear statement of evangelical truth."[5] When once preparing to preach a university sermon at Cambridge, he had to excise the "purple patches" and preach a sermon which was "simple, earnest and faithful."

In his noted sermon on April 27, 1642, to the Commons Fast on "Zerubbabel's Encouragement to Finish the Temple" (from Zechariah 4:6–9), Goodwin saw the overarching apocalyptic implication for England of the analogy with Israel.[6] His great sermon on "The Heart of Christ in Heaven to Sinners on Earth" had the basic proposition "The living Christ is the same in character and purpose as the historical Jesus; and what He is in heaven that as universally present He also is to us on earth."[7] Goodwin was also a strong premillennialist, *a la* Joseph Mede, the "father of English premillennialism."[8]

---

1. John Brown, *Puritan Preaching in England* (New York: Scribner's, 1900), 102.
2. Horton Davies, *The Worship of the English Puritans* (Westminster, London, England: Dacre, 1948), 127.
3. F. R. Webber, *A History of Preaching in Britain and America* (Milwaukee: Northwestern, 1952), 1:237.
4. Brown, *Puritan Preaching in England,* 101.
5. D. Martyn Lloyd-Jones, *The Puritans: Their Origins and Successors* (Edinburgh: Banner of Truth, 1987), 384.
6. John F. Wilson, *Pulpit in Parliament* (Princeton, N.J.: Princeton University Press, 1969), 208–9.
7. A. E. Garvie, *The Christian Preacher* (New York: Scribner's, 1923), 157–58.
8. Mal Couch, ed., *Dictionary of Premillennial Theology* (Grand Rapids: Kregel, 1996), 250.

7.3.2.4 John Owen—Pillar of Orthodoxy

> Protestants suppose the Scripture to be given forth by God to be . . . a perfect complete rule of faith.

> The first and principal duty of a pastor is to feed the flock by diligent preaching of the word.

> Scripture contains all things necessary to be . . . practiced in the worship of God.
>
> —John Owen

Called the systematic theologian of Puritanism and the Calvin of England, **John Owen** (1616–1683) must be viewed as one of the heavyweights in the pulpit during this renaissance of preaching. He was the son of a clergyman, born in Oxfordshire of Welsh ancestry. He earned his M.A. at Oxford when he was only nineteen and preached before Parliament in 1649. J. I. Packer pays singular tribute to Owen by acknowledging him as the most formative influence in shaping his Christian life and theology.[1] D. Martyn Lloyd-Jones in both his style and emphasis is much like John Owen. In Owen we find one of the defining mentors for "the Doctor."[2]

"To scorn delights and live laborious days" had been the watchword for John Milton, who served the Commonwealth as a translator of Latin and Italian documents. Milton became a chief Puritan pamphleteer, not returning to his poetry until after the Restoration.

We see the same intense productivity in Owen, who shocked the sensibilities of some with his "powdered hair and cocked hat." When the civil war hit, Owen did not care to go into battle, serving instead as the reluctant chaplain to Cromwell. Later he became dean of Christ Church College, where he was called "the greatest of all the Deans of Christ Church College" by Professor Benjamin Jowett. Owen eventually served as chancellor of Oxford in 1651.

Among Owen's students were John Locke, Philip Henry, and William Penn. He was offered the presidency of Harvard and invited to First Church, Boston, but declined. As an Independent, he was deposed after the collapse of the Commonwealth in 1660. He served as *de facto* leader of the Independents after the Restoration, and was pastor of an independent church in London from 1673 until his death.[3]

John Owen's preaching style was "elaborate and exhaustive." We see in him the prolixity and pedantry that sometimes marred Puritan preaching. In his address to Parliament on the day after the decapitation of Charles I, Owen took Jeremiah 15:19d–20 as his text. His theme: "Treacherous Contrivances against the God of Heaven." In typical Puritan fashion, Owen did exhaustive work in excavating the text within its setting. He then developed a series of ten "propositions allegedly in the text," one of which he pressed more generally.[4]

His monumental seven volumes of exposition on Hebrews[5] is his magnum opus. His study of the Holy Spirit[6] and of *Apostasy from the Gospel*[7] are still available and widely read, though they are often tough slogging. In length and treatment he tended to be tedious. As Dargan observes, Owen had neither "the logical coherence" of Barrow and Howe, nor the popular tone of Baxter or the beauties of Jeremy Taylor.[8] Yet Alexander Whyte called Owen, "The most massive of the Puritans." Spurgeon labeled him "the prince of the Puritans," and advised, "To master his works is to be a profound theologian."

Like many of the Puritan preachers, when Owen was barred from his pulpit he wrote voluminously. A learned man, he laced his works with Latin and Greek quotations. He and Goodwin were contemporaries at Oxford and Baxter, Thomas Manton and John Bunyan were his friends. Allegedly he said of Bunyan, "Had I the tinker's abilities, I would gladly relinquish my learning." Like all Puritans he was dedicated to the practical application of the truth he preached.[9] When he died in 1683, he was buried in Bunhill Fields, London, the Westminster Abbey of nonconformity.

---

1. J. I. Packer in his introduction to John Owen, *Sin and Temptation* (Portland, Oreg.: Multnomah, 1983), xvii–xxx.
2. D. Martyn Lloyd-Jones, *The Puritans: Their Origins and Successors* (Edinburgh: Banner of Truth, 1987), 73–100.
3. Peter Toon, *God's Statesman: The Life and Work of John Owen, Pastor, Educator and Theologian* (Grand Rapids: Zondervan, 1973).
4. John F. Wilson, *Pulpit in Parliament* (Princeton, N.J.: Princeton University Press, 1969), 163.
5. John Owen, *The Epistle to the Hebrews*, 7 vols. (Edinburgh: Banner of Truth, 1992). A one-volume abridgment is *Hebrews: The Epistle of Warning* (Grand Rapids: Kregel, 1985).
6. John Owen, *The Holy Spirit: His Gifts and Power* (Grand Rapids: Kregel, 1954).
7. John Owen, *Apostasy from the Gospel* (Edinburgh: Banner of Truth, 1992).
8. E. C. Dargan, *A History of Preaching* (New York: Hodder and Stoughton, 1912), 2:179.
9. Sinclair B. Ferguson, *John Owen on the Christian Life* (Edinburgh: Banner of Truth, 1987). See also, David J. McKinley, "John Owen's View of Illumination: An Alternative to the Fuller-Erickson dialogue" in *Bibliotheca Sacra* 154 (January–March 1997): 93–104.

7.3.2.5 John Bunyan—The Storyteller of the Ages

I preached what I smartingly felt.

I never endeavored to, nor durst make use of other men's lines (although I do not condemn all that do), for I verily thought and found by experience that what was taught me by the Word and Spirit of Christ could be spoken, maintained and stood to by the soundest and best established conscience.

—John Bunyan

Justly renowned for his vastly popular *Pilgrim's Progress* and *The Holy War,* **John Bunyan** (1628–1688) was not only a noteworthy figure in the history of English literature but also was a preacher of no small accomplishment. Born in Elstow near Bedford, Bunyan followed his father's trade as a tinker, making and repairing pots and pans. He served in the Parliamentary army, closely escaping death on several occasions.

Known as something of a rake, he was influenced toward the things of the Lord by his first wife, who read to him from Arthur Dent's *The Plain Man's Path to Heaven* and Lewis Bayly's *The Practice of Piety,* popular books among the Puritans. He was further nudged toward the kingdom through Luther's commentary on Galatians ("most fit for a wounded conscience") and the ministry of John Gifford, pastor in Bedford.[1] After hearing three women talking about the joys of the Christian life, Bunyan sought the new birth. His protracted introspection and depression at this time are typically Puritan. At the time of his conversion he could not read or write.

Finally, like Christian at Mt. Calvary, the chains fell off. In 1653 Bunyan joined St. John's Church, a nonconformist fellowship in Bedford pastored by Gifford. Two years later he was called to be the pastor-preacher of the assembly, but "His call to be their preacher aroused the opposition of many who denied that he had a right to preach, since he had practically no education, no theological training, and of course, was never able to read any of the original languages."[2]

Yet his fame as a preacher grew and with the Restoration so did his problems with the Act of Uniformity. As a result, he was imprisoned for twelve years. This was a fruitful time of literary production. He was also permitted to preach in the jail and toward the end of his sentence even preached outside. To help his family, who visited him faithfully, he made lace while in prison. He said that his beloved blind daughter "lay nearer my heart than all I had beside."

Again in 1672 Bunyan assumed pastoral office in Bedford. In a second imprisonment he wrote *Pilgrim's Progress.* Professor Trevelyan writes of the leading character:

> That lonely figure with the Bible and the burden of sin is not only John Bunyan himself. It is the representative Puritan of the English Puritan epoch. The poor man seeking salvation with tears, with no guide save the Bible in his hands, that man, multipled, congregated, regimented, was a force by which Oliver Cromwell and George Fox and John Wesley wrought their wonders, being men of a like experience themselves.[3]

Soon his preaching was heard by throngs in London and elsewhere.

The helpful study by Professor Tindall of Columbia University has shown that while many of the Puritan preachers were university men, there were those like Bunyan who came from humble backgrounds.[4] On occasion Bunyan would boast that he was not like Pontius Pilate, who could speak Hebrew, Greek, and Latin. Yet Bunyan was steeped in Scripture, and once indicated that his library was only the Bible and a concordance.

Not only was his the plain style of the Puritans, but he was "folksy and colloquial . . . he had the gift of filling out the brief stories and sparse records of the Scripture with human detail."[5] He had an active imagination and sometimes over-allegorized Scripture.[6] An early sermon from 1658 opened up Luke 16:19–31, the story of the rich man and Lazarus. He titled the sermon "A Few Sighs from Hell; or, The Groans of a Damned Soul." He followed the order of the verses, made his argument, and gave five uses. We do not see homely language here, and the sermon may well have been edited by an admirer in order to make him seem more standard in his preaching.[7] In a later sermon (1678), "Come and Welcome to Jesus," Bunyan took the text "All that the Father giveth me shall come to me; and him that cometh to me I will in no wise cast out" (John 6:37) and made the words "shall come" into a character by that name. Wakefield points out the tender evangelical "warmth and emotion" that swept over the listeners as he expounded the last clause.[8]

Although he stands in the wake of Ames, Perkins, and Owen, as he grew older Bunyan became burdened about legalism and the excesses of some Sabbatarians. Some call the later Bunyan a Pietistic Puritan. Considered a Baptist, he still did not insist on immersion for church membership, rather respecting conscience in the matter of mode of baptism. Richard Muller argues that Bunyan (not unlike Richard Baxter at this point) "reformulated federalism" in a reaction against legalistic covenant theology, hoping to avoid the opposite danger of antinomianism.[9]

As a preacher, Bunyan stands (as does his statue in Bedford) with his eyes to heaven, the Book in his hand. His characters Evangelist, Watchful the porter who speaks the kindly word, and Greatheart, the servant of Interpreter, set forth his perception of the preacher's role.[10]

Bunyan wrote one hundred books and preached whenever and wherever possible.[11] He died in his fifty-ninth year, his life cut short by pneumonia contracted while on a mission of mercy. He was buried at Bunhill Fields, the dissenters' graveyard.

In a fitting epitaph, Froude says that for two centuries John Bunyan "affected the spiritual opinions of the English race in every part of the world more powerfully than any book or books except the Bible."[12]

---

1. John Bunyan, *Grace Abounding to the Chief of Sinners* (Grand Rapids: Baker, 1978).

2. Wilbur M. Smith in his introduction to *John Bunyan, The Holy War* (Chicago: Moody, 1948), 19.

3. Ibid., 28.

4. William York Tindall, *John Bunyan Mechanick Preacher* (New York: Columbia University Press, 1934).

5. Gordon Wakefield, *Bunyan the Christian* (London: Harper/Collins Religious, 1992), 38.

6. Ibid., 36ff.

7. Caroline Francis Richardson, *English Preachers and Preaching 1640–1670* (New York: Macmillan, 1928), 74.

8. Wakefield, *Bunyan the Christian,* 39.

9. Richard A. Muller, "Covenant and Conscience in English Reformed Theology: Three

Variations on a Seventeenth Century Theme," *Westminster Theological Journal* 42 (1980): 318, 321.

10. John Brown, *Puritan Preaching in England* (New York: Scribner's, 1900), 139.

11. John Bunyan, *The Works of John Bunyan,* ed. George Offor, 3 vols. (Edinburgh: Banner of Truth, 1853, 1862).

12. Smith, in *John Bunyan,* 33.

7.3.2.6 John Howe—Thinker Par Excellence

> But what I sensibly felt through the admirable bounty of my God and the most pleasant, comforting influences of His Spirit on October 22, 1704, far surpassed the most expressive words my thoughts can suggest. I then experienced an inexpressibly pleasant melting of heart, tears gushing out of mine eyes for joy that God had shed abroad His love abundantly through the hearts of men; and that, for this purpose, mine own heart should be so signally possessed of and by His blessed Spirit.
> —John Howe (comment inscribed on a blank page in his Bible and found at his death)

Standing as an able representative of the more conservative Puritans is **John Howe** (1630–1705), who was born in Leicestershire, the son of a clergyman who was ejected from the Church of England for his nonconformity. A brilliant thinker, Howe was trained at Cambridge and Oxford. He was a close friend of Henry More and Ralph Cudworth, of the Cambridge Platonists. His pastoral tenure at Great Torrington in Devon was a model in effective preaching and impact. He corresponded weekly with his father-in-law in Latin. He was called the Platonic Puritan. Tall and dignified in appearance,[1] Howe was summoned to be the chaplain for Oliver Cromwell and subsequently for Cromwell's son Richard. He was not happy to leave his parish for these duties, but report has it that Cromwell went to hear him at Whitehall Chapel and sent him a request for the treatment of a certain text. Howe then expounded upon it in a manner so appealing that Cromwell would not be denied in his desire for Howe as his chaplain.

On a typical fast day, Howe deported himself in this manner:

> It was his common way to begin about nine in the morning with a prayer for about a quarter of an hour, in which he begged a blessing on the work of the day and afterward read or expounded a chapter or psalm, in which he spent about three-quarters of an hour; then prayed an hour, preached another hour, and prayed again for half an hour. After this he retired and took a little refreshment for a quarter of an hour or more, the people singing all the while. He then returned to the pulpit, prayed for another hour, gave them another sermon of about an hour's length, and so concluded the service of the day, about four o'clock in the evening, with half an hour or more of prayer.[2]

After his service as chaplain, he returned to Great Torrington but was silenced by the Act of Uniformity. Destitute, in 1671 he went to Ireland where he was chaplain to Lord Masarene at Antrim Castle. He preached the funeral sermon for Richard Baxter in 1681. He emigrated to Utrecht in the Netherlands in another wave of persecution, but returned to finish out his days in an independent church in London after the Declaration of Indulgence in 1687. His purpose in ministry was ever "the promotion of practical godliness, and of Christian liberty and love, irrespective of all sectarian considerations."[3]

Howe always preached without notes and could be exceedingly lengthy. He preached five sermons weekly. His gesture was vehement and voice and diction somewhat affected. He preached fourteen sermons on "we are saved by hope" from Romans 8; seventeen sermons on 1 John 4:20; and eighteen on John 3:6. He tended to launch strongly, wane and ramble somewhat, and then end strongly. One parishioner commented that Howe spent so much time setting the table in his introduction that the audience fairly lost its appetite for dinner.

His admirable treatise on "Delighting in God" embodies all of these strengths and weaknesses. Especially striking are his sermons "Vanity of Man as Mortal" and "The Redeemer's Tears over Lost Souls." His collected works contain much of his pulpit utterance, and his sermon "Yield Yourselves to God" from Romans 6:13 is typical. Laced with Scripture and divided into mains, subs, and sub-subs, the sermon is heavy but vibrant. One of his best-remembered messages was his famous sermon on "Carnality of Religious Contention."

Robert Hall called him "the greatest of the Puritan divines" and said of him, "I have learned far more from John Howe than from any other author I have ever read . . . there is an astounding magnificence in his conceptions."[4]

---

1. E. C. Dargan, *A History of Preaching* (New York: Hodder and Stoughton, 1912), 2:180.
2. T. Harwood Pattison, *The History of Christian Preaching* (Philadelphia: American Baptist Publication Society, 1903), 200.
3. J. P. Hewlett, "A Life of the Author," in *The Works of Rev. John Howe* (Ligonier, Pa.: Soli Deo Gloria, 1990), 1:xix. This fine set is published in three volumes.
4. F. R. Webber, *A History of Preaching in Britain and America* (Milwaukee: Northwestern, 1952), 1:266.

7.3.2.7 Philip Henry—Contender for the Faith

Let your preaching be plain. Painted glass is most curious; plain glass is most perspicuous. Preach a crucified Saviour in a crucified style. Be a good crucifix to your people. Let your matter be substantial; wholesome food; God and Christ, and the gospel, faith, repentance, regeneration. Aim purely at God's glory and the salvation of souls. Study, as if there were no Christ; preach as if there had been no study. To this end get your sermon into your own souls. It is best, from the heart, to the heart. Get your sermons memoriter. How can you expect your people should remember, and repeat, if you read?

—Philip Henry

Taking his place in this lustrous succession is **Philip Henry** (1631–1696), whose son Matthew Henry has given us the story of his father's life. The Henry family had roots in Wales. Philip Henry was born in Whitehall, London, and knew Prince Charles and Prince James as "boyhood companions." He early listened to preaching. "He used to sit always upon the pulpit stairs, and it was his constant practice from eleven or twelve years old, to write, as he could, all the sermons he heard, which he kept very carefully, transcribed."[1]

Henry graduated from Christ Church, Oxford, in 1647. He served as tutor and preacher until he ran afoul of the authorities and was imprisoned on several occasions, preaching intermittently in Flintshire. Of his first parish it was said, "Here by his close and practical preaching he was made exceedingly useful, and wrought under God a wonderful change in the parish, which before was esteemed one of the most loose and profane places in all that county."[2]

Philip Henry was an avid student of Scripture and published a commentary on Genesis, as well as numerous sermons. Because of his limited opportunities under the Five-Mile Act, he frequently preached *gratis*. He tended to preach in a series *(lectio continua),* carefully aiming his discourse at his hearers and their situation, "fetching his similitudes for illustration from those things which were familiar to them. He did not shoot the arrow of the word over their heads in high notions or under their feet by blunt and homely expressions, but to their hearts, in close and lively applications."[3]

In his introduction he sought to make a point of contemporary contact, as when preaching on the conversion of Paul from Galatians 1:16, "He began his sermon with this remark, to raise attention: 'Much is said in story concerning the seven wonders of the world (and he named them); but I have been sometimes thinking, whether I could not name seven things which I would call the seven wonders of the church. And what do you think of these seven? (and he names seven, the last of which is the conversion of the Apostle Paul).'"[4]

Henry produced splendid sermon series on the Ten Commandments, the Lord's Prayer, types of Christ in the Old Testament, and forty sermons on the prodigal son from Luke 15 in 1673. He had his Bible re-bound with blank pages alternating with Scripture pages, and transcribed exegetical notes on them as an aid to sermon preparation. So rich were messages that he was known as "heavenly Henry."[5] Once he spent two months preaching the doctrine of the Lord's Supper and half a year preaching on the living Christ's letter to the Laodicean church.

The Puritan dedication to exegetical preaching within a strong sense of doctrinal construct is clearly seen in Philip Henry's pulpit labors. Concerning repentance he would often say, "If I were to die in the pulpit, I would desire to die preaching repentance; as if I die out of the pulpit, I would desire to die practicing repentance."[6] One Scripture verse which was particularly meaningful to him as a preacher was Isaiah 50:4, "The Sovereign LORD has given me an instructed tongue, to know the word that sustains the weary. He wakens me morning by morning, wakens my ear to listen like one being taught." This was the influence which touched so many and shaped his illustrious son Matthew.

1. Matthew Henry, *The Life of Rev. Philip Henry* (Edinburgh: Banner of Truth, 1974), 6.
2. F. R. Webber, *A History of Preaching in Britain and America* (Milwaukee: Northwestern, 1952), 1:270–71.
3. Henry, *The Life of Rev. Philip Henry,* 59ff.
4. Ibid., 241.
5. Webber, *A History of Preaching,* 1:271.
6. Henry, *The Life of Rev. Philip Henry,* 141.

7.3.3   GOSPEL TORCHBEARERS—ADVOCATES OF PROMISE

The preaching of God's holy word is the ministry of the Holy Spirit.

Preaching is the ordinance of God, sanctified for the begetting of faith, for the opening of the understanding, for the drawing of the will and affections to Christ.

—Richard Sibbes

We come now to the second grouping in Professor Knight's taxonomy: "The Sibbesians who set their clocks not on preparative disciplines but on the direct experience of the Spirit's indwelling, the joys of Christian fellowship and the divine attribute of overflowing love."[1] The Amesians and the Sibbesians clashed in the 1630s and later—the former being accused of legalism and the latter being accused of antinomianism. The tension was especially marked in New England.

This entire century in England was one of endless disruption and religious turmoil. Yet this is when preaching flourished in the culture as at perhaps no other time. We must take into account not only all of the acrimony leading up to the civil war and the subsequent emergence of the Puritan Commonwealth but also the fact that the Restoration picked up where events had been before.

Again the nation was plunged into chaos as the Stuarts persisted in their Romish-tilted policies, to the consternation of most of their subjects. The Cavalier Parliament (1661–1679) passed laws aimed directly at the Puritans: the celebrated Corporation Act (no Roman Catholic or Puritan could be a member of a municipal body); the Act of Uniformity (all clergy were to accept *The Book of Common Prayer*); the Five-Mile Act (two thousand clergy who refused to obey the Act of Uniformity were prohibited from coming within five miles of their former dwellings); and the Conventicle Act (all non-Anglican religious meetings were forbidden.).[2] Charles II prescribed listening to sermons as the remedy for insomnia, thus showing the general royal attitude toward the craft. Not until the Glorious Revolution and the enthronement of William and Mary in 1688 was any relief to be experienced.

Until the Revolution, any ministry outside the bounds of the established church was severely interrupted. Even those within the Church of England who were of Puritan bent were sent packing. An especially egregious case was the noted Puritan centrist **Thomas Watson** (1620–1686), whose preaching was among the most eagerly received in London.[3] Watson served St. Stephen's, Walbrook, for fifteen years with distinction before his ejection, when he experienced unspeakable hardship and privation.

But this was not uncommon and helps explain why many chose to move on to the New World. Our problem here is the ample supply of preachers who call for our attention. The level of sermonic discourse was amazingly high, even among the rank-and-file clergy.[4] Of course, there were the more eccentric preachers, some of whom were extraordinarily gifted. John Stoughton was given to bizarre sermon titles like "Baruch's Sore Gently Opened, and the Salve Skillfully Applied," or "The Church's Bowel Complaint." Then there was the "Spiritual Mustard Pot to Make the Soul Sneeze with Devotion," "The Snuffers of Divine Love," and "A Pack of Cards to Win Christ."[5] Nor are we particularly drawn to the book titled *Sermons to Asses, to Doctors of Divinity, to Lord's Spiritual and to Ministers of State,* or to John Haslebach, who expounded on a single chapter in Isaiah for twenty-one years. Another preacher served up an entire sermon on the letter O. These colorful characters aside, we now turn to one of the venerable patriarchs of the Puritans.

---

1. Janice Knight, *Orthodoxies in Massachusetts: Rereading American Puritanism* (Cambridge, Mass.: Harvard University Press, 1994).
2. David Green, *History of England* (Ames: Littlefield, Adams and Co., 1958), 128–29.
3. See Thomas Watson, *The Sermons of Thomas Watson* (Ligonier, Pa.: Soli Deo Gloria, 1990); *The Doctrine of Repentance* (Edinburgh: Banner of Truth, 1987). Curiously neither Dargan nor Webber mention Thomas Watson or Richard Sibbes.
4. John Chandos, ed., *In God's Name: Examples of Preaching in England 1534–1662* (London: Hutchinson, 1971). A splendid sampling of some of the lesser lights.
5. Paxton Hood, *The Throne of Eloquence* (New York: Funk and Wagnalls, 1888), 276.

7.3.3.1 Richard Sibbes—Teacher of Spirituality

Of this blest man, let this just praise be given, Heaven was in him, before he was in heaven.

—Izaak Walton of Richard Sibbes

The eminent Thomas Manton called him "the heavenly Doctor Sibbes"; Spurgeon said that "Sibbes never wastes the students' time; he scatters pearls and diamonds with both hands." Lloyd-Jones intones, "There are Puritans and there are Puritans . . . I shall never cease to be grateful to one of them called Richard Sibbes who was a balm to my soul at a period in my life when I was overworked and badly overtired, and therefore subject in an unusual manner to the onslaughts of the devil."[1]

Richard Sibbes (1577–1635) was born in Tostock, Suffolk, and matriculated at Cambridge at the same time as Jeremy Taylor. There he took successively his B.A., M.A., B.D., and D.D. degrees. He was named college preacher in 1609.

Peter Bayne (Perkins' successor) had led Sibbes to Christ at Cambridge, giving us an interesting succession in the Cambridge Lectureship: Perkins, then Bayne, then Sibbes, then John Preston, who was led to Christ by John Cotton, who was led to Christ by Richard Sibbes! And Richard Baxter came to Christ through a book of sermons by Sibbes purchased by his father.

Sibbes was lecturer at Cambridge until 1615, when Laud ousted him. He was then appointed preacher at Gray's Inn while Francis Bacon lived there. Bacon's famous "I am a bruised reed" undoubtedly was derived from Sibbes' sermon on that topic. Through Archbishop Ussher, Sibbes simultaneously served as provost at Trinity College, Dublin, and as Master of Catharine Hall, Cambridge (where John Milton was writing his sonnets on Sibbes' themes).

Thomas Manton spoke of Sibbes "sweet-dropping voice," and, in some respects, he was "sweet-natured to a fault."[2] He stammered noticeably when speaking, and shrank from separatism. Despite his timid nonconformist views, he never left the Church of England. Neither did he marry.

Sibbes is a seminal thinker for those holding that reason must be in subjection to the authority of the Spirit by the Word. Sibbes was influenced by mysticism of a healthy sort, as we see in his works *Bowels Opened* and *A Breathing after God*. He did not go as far as **Frances Rous** (1579–1659), who spoke of climbing the mystical ladder and who in his *Mystical Marriage* was much like St. Bernard of Clairvaux. Several have commented that only his Puritan biblicism saved him from extremes.[3] Yet Izaak Walton valued his books so highly, he left several marked volumes for his children to read.

Sibbes is the primary figure in Nuttall's study on *The Holy Spirit in Puritan Faith and Experience*. Sibbes insisted:

> There must be an infused establishing by the Spirit to settle the heart in this first principle . . . that the Scriptures are the word of God. . . . There must be a double light: so there must a Spirit in me, as there is a Spirit in the Scripture before I can see anything. . . . The breath of the Spirit in us is suitable to the Spirit's breathing in the Scriptures; the same Spirit doth not breathe contrary motions . . . as the spirits in the arteries quicken the blood in the veins, so the Spirit of God goes along with the word and makes it work.[4]

Though staunchly Calvinistic, Sibbes led those who were of a freer spirit and had a balanced view of experience and feeling.[5] His delivery was the plain style common among the Puritans. As one observer said, "Great affectation and good affections seldom go together."[6] Sibbes argued in his classic *The Bruised Reed*:

> The church of Christ is a common hospital, wherein all are in some measure sick of some spiritual disease or other; that we should all have ground of exercising mutually the spirit of wisdom and meekness.

Sibbes' memorable sermons on "The Sword of the Wicked" from Psalm 42:10 and "The Saint's Safety in Evil Times" (one sermon from Psalm 7:14 and another from 2 Timothy 4:16–17) are moving and enlightening. Although there were many divisions, he used the question/answer and the objection/answer technique as an aid to understanding and concluded with an impressive array of "uses."[7] All of his sermons blended short sentences with fairly complex structure and excellent devotional application.

Sibbes followed Thomas Goodwin as vicar of Trinity in Cambridge. He died on July 5, 1635, in his fifty-eighth year.

---

1. Alexander B. Grosart, "Memoir," in *Works of Richard Sibbes* (Edinburgh: Banner of Truth, 1973), xv–xvi.
2. Ibid., xi.
3. F. Ernest Stoeffer, *The Rise of Evangelical Pietism* (Leiden, Netherlands: E. J. Brill, 1965).
4. Geoffrey F. Nuttall, *The Holy Spirit in Puritan Faith and Experience* (Oxford: Blackwell, 1946), 23.
5. For significant studies, see Bert Affleck, "The Theology of Richard Sibbes" (Ph.D. dissertation, Drew University, 1968); Harold Palton Shelly, "Richard Sibbes: Early Stuart Preacher of Piety" (Ph.D. dissertation, Temple University, 1972). Both are available in the University of Michigan Microfilm 85–10.
6. W. Fraser Mitchell, *English Pulpit Oratory from Andrewes to Tillotson* (London: SPCK, 1932), 117.
7. Richard Sibbes, *Works of Richard Sibbes* (Edinburgh: Banner of Truth, 1973), 108ff., 119ff., 295ff., 314ff.

7.3.3.2 Richard Baxter—Master of the Puritan Pulpit

I preach as never sure to preach again, and as a dying man to dying men.

The Holy Spirit, by immediate inspiration, revealed unto the apostles the doctrine of Christ, and caused them infallibly to indite [compose] the Scriptures. But this is not that way of ordinary illumination now.

This trying the Spirit by the Scriptures, is not a setting of the Scriptures above the Spirit itself; but is only a trying of the Spirit by the Spirit; that is, the Spirit's operations in ourselves and his revelations to any pretenders now, by the Spirit's operations in the apostles, and by their revelations recorded for our use. For they and not we are called foundations of the church. We may be sure the inward testimony of the Spirit never is opposite to the outward testimony of his gospel which is the Spirit's testimony also.

—Richard Baxter

Perhaps the best-known of all the Puritan preachers is **Richard Baxter** (1615–1691), called by some "the most successful preacher and winner of souls and nurturer of won souls that England has ever had." Edmund Calamy spoke of him as "The most voluminous theological writer in the English language." Baxter wrote 160 works. Spurgeon highly regarded him as the tonic for his own sluggishness.[1]

Born in Shropshire in modest circumstances, Richard Baxter was largely self-educated. The young Baxter was not altogether sure when he was converted, but he sensed God's call to holy orders and was ordained by the bishop of Worcester. He did some teaching and preaching around Dudley, and in 1641 was made lecturer and curate at Kidderminster near Birmingham.

Kidderminster was a town of about four thousand souls. The area was desperately depraved and engulfed in an abysmal ignorance of spiritual truth. The resident vicar preached only quarterly and was known as a heavy drinker. Kidderminster's inhabitants were primarily weavers, and virtually none of them knew the Lord. Except for a brief stint with Cromwell's army, Baxter ministered faithfully from 1647 to 1660. He visited and catechized eight hundred families every year. He put forth the principle in his famous *The Reformed Pastor:* "The first and main point, which I submit to you is that it is an unquestionable duty of all ministers of the church to catechize and teach personally all who are submitted to their care."[2] Dean Stanley said of Baxter's "awakening ministry" in Kidderminster:

> There have been three or four parishes in England which have been raised by their pastors to a national, almost a world-wide fame. Of these the most conspicuous is Kidderminster: for Baxter without Kidderminster would have been but half of himself; and Kidderminster without Baxter would have had nothing but carpets.[3]

Although Baxter had opposed the deposition of the king, he could not adhere to the Act of Uniformity and was put out of Kidderminster. He was even offered a bishopric, but chose imprisonment rather than compromise. He was brought to trial before the infamous Judge Jeffreys and spent a year and a half in the Tower. Matthew Henry was among the many friends who visited him during his incarceration.

In appearance Baxter was tall and slender with "long tapering fingers," high forehead, and Roman nose. His eyes were described as "piercing."[4] His health was poor, and he was "seldom an hour without pain." But his consuming passion was to preach. Although he preached in Westminster Abbey and before the king and Parliament, his favorite venue was Kidderminster, where his preaching greatly moved his congregation. He returned most of his salary to the poor and never lived in the vicarage, allowing the aging incumbent to occupy it to his last days.

The outstanding characteristic of Baxter's preaching was his remarkable earnestness.[5] He often felt the lack of formal education and did not labor long on his manuscripts. Yet in one sermon he advanced sixty-six main points. The "uses" in another sermon filled thirteen pages.

Baxter often progressed through the presentation of competing ideas.[6] He tended to do his writing when in a state of physical collapse. His *A Call to the Unconverted* sold twenty-thousand copies in the first year. His classic *The Saints' Everlasting Rest* was equally popular. In all of his output he reflected his conviction that preachers need "the skill necessary to make plain the truth, to convince the hearers, to let in the irresistible light into their consciences, and to keep it there and drive all home; to screw the truth into their minds and work Christ into their affections . . ."

Although a controversialist by nature, Baxter was burdened for Christian concord.[7] He was bitterly disappointed when the Savoy Conference following the Restoration did not unite Anglicans and nonconformists. He was moderate in his own thinking, with "no Calvinist axe to grind,"[8] and rejected rigid Calvinistic extremism. This led some to describe him as fickle. His greatest strengths were his pastoral theology, his imagery in preaching, and his skill in application.[9] But some of his followers overemphasized these aspects, and Baxterism had some regrettable manifestations (cf. 6.4.2). The Kidderminster church is today a Unitarian assembly.

In his later years, Baxter developed considerable interest in the apocalyptic, and argued that Protestants need to take more interest in Bible prophecy.[10] He veered toward historicism in his prophetic hermeneutic. He wrestled much with the role of the Christian prince, and was crushed by the collapse of the Commonwealth. Baxter sought to reverse the Calvinist tide, advocated "free-will"[11] with Ussher on his side,[12] and fought the particular Baptists. (He denounced Bunyan as an "unlearned antinomian.") Baxter's was a middle way, and he craved consensus on what he called "mere Christianity," from whence C. S. Lewis obtained his famous title.

In all of this, the overmastering passion of Baxter's persuasive preaching was the conversion of the lost. His *A Call to the Unconverted* is a scalding meditation on Ezekiel 33:11 and well represents the communication which made Baxter so effective in the pulpit.[13] Closely reasoned and logical, it is studded with Scripture. In Richard Baxter we have a pastor whose influence moved Wesley, Doddridge, Spurgeon, Isaac Watts, Wilberforce, Whitefield, and ministers in our own day.[14]

---

1. Timothy Beougher and J. I. Packer, "Go Fetch Baxter," in *Christianity Today* (December 19, 1991): 26ff. Both of these scholars wrote most helpful doctoral dissertations on Baxter; cf. J. I. Packer, "The Redemption and Restoration of Man in the Thought of Richard Baxter: A Study in Puritan Theology" (D.Phil., Oxford University, 1954); Timothy K. Beougher, "Conversion: the Teaching and Practice of the Puritan Pastor with Regard to Becoming a 'True Christian'" (Ph.D. dissertation, Trinity Evangelical Divinity School, 1990).

2. Richard Baxter, *The Reformed Pastor* (Portland, Oreg.: Multnomah, 1982), 5.

3. John Brown, *Puritan Preaching in England* (New York: Scribner's, 1900), 169.

4. Charles F. Kemp, *A Pastoral Triumph: The Story of Richard Baxter and His Ministry at Kidderminster* (New York: Macmillan, 1948), 6.

5. Ibid., 23.

6. Caroline Francis Richardson, *English Preachers and Preaching 1640–1670* (New York: Macmillan, 1928), 73.

7. *Autobiography of Richard Baxter* (London: Dent, 1974 ed.).

8. Geoffrey F. Nuttall, *The Holy Spirit in Puritan Faith and Experience* (Oxford: Blackwell, 1946), 163.

9. N. H. Keeble, *Richard Baxter: Puritan Man of Letters* (Oxford: Clarendon, 1982).
10. William M. Lamont, *Richard Baxter and the Millennium* (London: Croom Helm, 1979), 51.
11. Ibid., 141. See also Peter Toon, *Puritans and Calvinism* (Swengel, Pa.: Bible Truth Depot, 1973), 83, 86, 89.
12. Ibid., 153.
13. Richard Baxter, *A Call to the Unconverted* (Grand Rapids: Baker, 1976).
14. Lamont, *Richard Baxter and the Millennium,* 286.

7.3.3.3 Thomas Manton—Anchor of Stability

> That knowledge is best which endeth in practice. . . . The hearer's life is the preacher's best commendation.
>
> —Thomas Manton

The Puritan penchant for practical application for daily life along with a bracing sense of doctrinal construct is seen vividly in one of the eminent Puritan preachers, **Thomas Manton** (1620–1677). Manton is a superb example of that fusion of warm piety and massive knowledge which characterized the Puritans.[1] He was born in Somerset, the son and grandson of ministers. Educated at Oxford, he served parishes at Stoke-Newington in Middlesex and Covent Garden in London. Functioning as chaplain and as examiner for the Protector, he was nonetheless uneasy about regicide, and urged the restoration of Charles II. He preached often to Parliament. His early preaching tended to be over the heads of his hearers. One poor man told him after a sermon:

> "Sir, I came with ernest desires after the word of God, and hopes of getting some good to my soul, but I was greatly disappointed; for I could not understand a great deal of what you said; you were quite above me."
> It is then reported that Manton replied: "Friend, if I did not give you a sermon, you have given me one; and by the grace of God I will never preach before my Lord Mayor in such a manner again."[2]

Although favored by the court in the Restoration, he refused to take the oath and was ejected in 1662. Imprisoned after preaching an illegal sermon, he continued to preach in the prison itself. Baxter, Charnock, and Ussher were his close friends. He died in 1677, with Dr. Bates preaching a memorable funeral sermon. One who attended his funeral spoke of him as "deservedly styled the King of Preachers." Appropriately his funeral was "attended with the vastest number of ministers of all persuasion that ever I saw together in my life. And the ministers walked in pairs, a Conformist and a Nonconformist."[3]

Manton's depth in exegetical work is seen in his still popular commentaries on James and Jude. He was well read in ancient and modern history. His pulpit expression was "natural and free, clear and eloquent, quick and powerful . . . inflamed by holy zeal."[4] Much of his preaching was published posthumously.

Manton was in the habit of repeating his main headings in his closing prayer and "was noted for his lively and affectionate administration of the Lord's Supper." Charnock paid tribute to him "the best collector of sense of the age." Barstow called him "one of the most elaborate and ingenious of all the Puritan preachers."

Manton's exposition of Psalm 119 is classic and ran to 190 sermons. Typical of his preaching are the exceedingly rich studies in John 17. Sermon 3 follows the standard Puritan pattern, beginning with exegetical highlights, proceeding to doctrinal affirmations, and concluding with the customary uses. A number of ancillary Scriptures were woven into the sermon's fabric. Manton's messages were high-density content with little *lucido ordo,* but they were forceful and full of Christ and the gospel.[5] His fluid prose style is evident here:

> The sum of the gospel is this, that all who, by true repentance and faith, do forsake the flesh, the world and the devil, and give themselves up to the Father, Son and Holy Spirit, as their creator, redeemer and sanctifier, shall find God as a father, taking them for his reconciled children, and for Christ's sake pardoning their sin, and by his Spirit giving them his grace; and, if they persevere in this course, will finally glorify them, and bestow upon them everlasting happiness; but will condemn the unbelievers, impenitent, and ungodly to everlasting punishment.[6]

---

1. Thomas Manton was at the forefront of the emphasis on personal piety, as noted by Dewey D. Wallace Jr., *The Spirituality of the Later Puritans* (Macon, Ga.: Mercer University Press, 1987), 2–3; for further substantive insights, see Greg K. Daniel, "The Puritan Ladder of Meditation: An Explication of Puritan Meditation and its Compatibility with Catholic Meditation" (M.A. thesis, Trinity Evangelical Divinity School, 1993). An important resource is Patrick Collinson, *The Elizabethan Puritan Movement* (Berkeley: University of California Press, 1983).
2. William Harris, "Memoir," in *The Complete Works of Thomas Manton* (London: James Nisbet, 1870), 1:xiii.
3. Caroline Francis Richardson, *English Preachers and Preaching 1640–1670* (New York: Macmillan, 1928), 31.
4. Harris, "Memoir," 1:xxii.
5. Thomas Manton, *An Exposition of John 17* (Evansville, Ind.: Sovereign Grace Book Club, 1958), 39ff.
6. Manton, *The Complete Works,* 2:102ff.

7.3.3.4 Stephen Charnock—Revitalizer of the Church

A spiritual worshipper actually aspires in every duty to know God. . . . To desire worship as an end, is carnal; to desire it as a means for communion with God is spiritual, and the fruit of a spiritual life. . . . Evangelical worship is a spiritual worship, and praise, joy and delight are prophesied of as great ingredients in attendance on gospel ordinances, Isaiah 12:3–5 . . . Delight in God in a gospel frame, therefore the more joyful, the more spiritual.

—Stephen Charnock

Stephen Charnock (1628–1680) was a rare and vital spirit among the Puritans. He was born in London, where his father was a solicitor in Chancery. While studying at Emmanuel College, Cambridge, he was powerfully converted. At first he became a preceptor with a wealthy family but then began his work as a parish minister in Southwark, where he saw many come to Christ. He went on to Oxford for an M.A. His unusual intellectual gifts were soon recognized, and he became a senior proctor in 1652.

Charnock served briefly as an assistant to John Owen before going to Ireland. There he served as chaplain to the governor, Henry Cromwell, son of the Protector. He preached every Lord's Day there and was given an honorary B.D. by Trinity College. With the collapse of the Protectorate, he lacked opportunity for some time, but in 1675 he joined Thomas Watson in a Presbyterian ministry in Crosby Square. It was here that he delivered his justly famous messages on "The Existence and Attributes of God." He died in his fifty-third year.

Charnock possessed an extraordinary mastery of the Greek and Hebrew originals. He always carried a book with him and wrote down any profitable thought that came to mind.[1] He was respected for his keen judgment and vivid imagination, and was capable of remarkable concentration.[2] His "reasonings and applications" were renowned. In 1666 he lost all of his books in the great fire of London, a deprivation he felt sharply. Through it all, "He excelled as a preacher."[3]

Initially Charnock preached without notes, but his eyes began to fail him and he had to read his sermons with a magnifying glass. He loved to preach on the cross of Christ and pleaded with sinners to "turn" to the crucified Savior. "Perspicuous plainness, convincing cogency, great wisdom, fearless honesty and affectionate earnestness are the chief characteristics of his sermons,"[4] Symington writes. Webber cites one of the most widely disseminated works of Charnock, *Discourses on Christ Crucified*, which was reprinted in America. In a notable sermon based on 1 Corinthians 2:2, his third main division was "The Fruits of His Death."

1. The death of Christ appeases the wrath of God for us;
2. The death of Christ satisfies the demands of the Law;
3. The death of Christ removes the guilt of sin;
4. The death of Christ conquers the power of Satan;
5. The death of Christ brings us sanctification;
6. The death of Christ opens the kingdom of heaven for us.[5]

This richly woven tapestry of biblical and theological truth was massive but magnificent. The republished sermons of Charnock are as fine an array of Puritan preaching as is available today.[6]

1. F. R. Webber, *A History of Preaching in Britain and America* (Milwaukee: Northwestern, 1952), 1:259.
2. William Symington, "The Life and Character of Stephen Charnock," in *Discourses upon the Existence and Attributes of God* (Grand Rapids: Baker, 1979), 1:11.
3. Ibid., 15.
4. Ibid.
5. Stephen Charnock, *Discourses on the Knowledge of God* (Edinburgh: Banner of Truth, 1985).
6. Webber, *A History of Preaching,* 1:261.

7.3.3.5 John Flavel—Model of Holiness

> The preaching of the gospel by Christ's ambassadors is the principal means appointed for reconciling and bringing home sinners to Christ. . . . A crucified style best suits the preachers of a crucified Christ. . . . Prudence will choose words that are solid, rather than florid. . . . Words are but servants to matter. An iron key, fitted to the wards of the lock, is more useful than a golden one that will open the door to the treasures. Prudence will cast away a thousand fine words for one that is apt to penetrate the conscience and reach the heart.
>
> —John Flavel

One of the godliest and most fragrant testimonies among the Puritan pastor-theologians was **John Flavel** (1630–1691), whose lineage traces back to forebears who came to England with William the Conqueror in the eleventh century. He was the son of Richard Flavel, a minister in Devon, who was roughly treated in the Restoration. Richard's two sons were both ministers of the gospel. John graduated from Oxford and in 1650 was made a probationer and assistant to a very ill clergyman in Diptford in Devon. In that same year he was ordained and became rector upon the death of the incumbent. Not long after, he went to Dartmouth, with which he was associated off and on through the Restoration period until his death in 1691. Here is one tribute to him:

> I could say much, though not enough, of the excellence of his preaching; of his seasonable, suitable and spiritual manner; of his plain expositions of Scripture, his talking method, his genuine and natural deductions, his convincing arguments, his clear and powerful demonstrations, his heart-searching applications and his comfortable supports to those that were afflicted in conscience. In short that person must have a very soft head, or a very hard heart, or both, that could sit under his ministry unaffected.[1]

John Flavel was "full and copious in prayer" and an ardent soulwinner. The dangerous times in which he ministered seemed only to burn off the dross in his life. While Flavel was preaching in the woods near Exeter, the constabulary came suddenly, and in the great confusion Flavel escaped.

He wrote extensively, the six volumes of his works often being reprinted. Among those who drank deeply of this spring are Jonathan Edwards and George Whitefield (who ranked him with John Bunyan and Matthew Henry), and later in Scotland, R. M. McCheyne and Andrew Bonar.[2] Other favorites are *Pneumatologia (Treatise on the Soul of Man)* and *The Method of Grace (How the Holy Spirit Works)*.

D. Martyn Lloyd-Jones types him as a "Christ-Mystic" who accented the objective bases of Christian experience. "He wrought it, though we wear it," Flavel liked to say. Yet he affirmed the subjective reality as well. Isaac Watts shares an anecdote from Flavel's life:

> There going on his way his thoughts began to swell and rise higher and higher like the waters in Ezekiel's vision, til at last they became an overwhelming flood. Such was the intention of his mind, such the ravishing tastes of heavenly joys, and such the full assurance of his interest therein, that he utterly lost all sight and sense of the world and all of the concerns thereof, and for some hours he knew no more where he was than if he had been in a deep sleep upon his bed. Arriving in great exhaustion at a certain spring, he sat down and washed, earnestly desiring, if it was God's good pleasure, that this might be his parting place from the world. Death had the most amiable face in his eye that ever he beheld, except the face of Jesus Christ which made it so, and he does not remember, though he believed himself dying, that he even thought of his dear wife and children or any earthly concernment. On reaching his inn the influence still continued, banishing sleep—still, still the joy of the Lord overflowed him and he seemed to be an inhabitant of the other world. He many years after called that day one of the days of heaven, and professed that he understood more of the life of heaven by it than by all the books he ever read or discourses he ever entertained about it.[3]

In his sermon "Crucifying the Flesh, or the Mortification of Sin," Flavel saw the text as the center of gravity in the sermon. He began with exegetical observations, identified and expounded the doctrine under five mains, and then inferentially draws out appropriate "uses" (i.e., motives, rules, and meditations which follow upon the truth). The last sermon he delivered in Dartmouth was from 1 Corinthians 10:12, "Wherefore let him that standeth take heed lest he fall." It was characteristically deeply moving, "tending to awaken careless professors, and to stir them up to be solicitous about their souls."[4]

---

1. "The Life of John Flavel" in *The Works of John Flavel* (Edinburgh: Banner of Truth, 1968), 1:vi.

2. Ibid.

3. Ibid., 1:xv.

4. John Flavel, *The Method of Grace* (Grand Rapids: Baker, 1977), 436ff.

7.3.3.6 Isaac Barrow—Watcher on the Wall

The insatiable appetite for laughter keeps itself within no bounds. Have you crowded to this place for the purpose of listening and studying and making progress, or only for the sake of laughing at this thing and making a jest of that other? There is nothing so remote from levity which you do not instantly transmute into mirth and absurdity, and let a discourse be such as to move no laughter, nothing else will pleasure, neither dignity, nor gravity, nor solidity, neither strength, nor point, nor polish.

—Isaac Barrow

Reinforcing the impression of the diversity among the Puritans is the singular ministry of **Isaac Barrow** (1630–1677). Barrow was not a pastor but a professor of Greek and mathematics. Yet he had a reputation as an Arminian preacher, albeit a long-winded one. He was born in London and reared in a merchant's home, often the despair of his father. He began to shine as a student at Cambridge and studied in Europe, particularly in Constantinople, "where he devoted a full year to the reading of Chrysostom in the original."[1] A loyalist to Charles I, he was successively professor of geometry and Lucasian Professor of Mathematics at Cambridge. Eventually he would yield that prestigious chair to his student and friend, Isaac Newton. Appointed chaplain to Charles II in the Restoration, Barrow was at the time of his passing the vice-chancellor of the university.

In appearance, Barrow was utterly unimpressive. As one witness to a sermon reported: "A pale, meagre, unpromising-looking man . . . dressed in a slovenly manner with his collar unbuttoned and his hair uncombed. It so happened that an alarm of fire was raised and most of the congregation went away. The preacher, unmoved by the commotion, gave out his text and went through his sermon to the two or three people present. Richard Baxter was one of those who remained . . . who declared that he had never heard a better discourse."[2]

Like Howe, Barrow could preach for an hour, give his congregation a break, and preach another hour. When preaching at Westminster one Lord's Day, the dean asked him to give only the first half of his sermon, which he did—and preached for almost two hours. On another occasion, a listener came to hear him and asked if the afternoon service had started. He was told that Barrow had not yet finished his morning sermon. Yet another account has the bellringers ringing the bells to stop him. King Charles II considered Barrow to be the best scholar in England but unfair as a preacher because he left nothing for others to say.

Barrow loved the church fathers, and occasionally quoted pagan moralists, but was most concerned with the Scripture. His sermons were not flowery, but were exhaustive in attention to the text. There was an attractiveness in his prose style,[3] and his strong personal devotion to Christ was his hallmark. He shared the Puritan view on the "naturalness and plainness" which should accompany preaching, and yet he was oratorically moving.[4]

Some called him the English Bossuet. Not unlike Chrysostom, Barrow had a remarkable ability to "reanimate attention while considering a topic from as large a number of angles as possible."[5] He knew how to use "lively and apt images."

Mitchell calls him "the one great orator produced by England before Burke."[6] Tillotson has considerably revised many of his published sermons.

Broadus considers Barrow an example of intellectual richness. Many identify his great sermon on "The Crucifixion of Christ" as praiseworthy. It had five main divisions and twelve full applications after the Puritan manner. He argued that "this way of suffering had in it some particular advantages conducing to the accomplishment of our Lord's principal design." He preached movingly about the passion of our Lord and its place in the redemptive plan of God.

Barrow is properly remembered as an Anglican with a strong Puritan bent. A bust of him remains in Westminster Abbey.

---

1. F. R. Webber, *A History of Preaching in Britain and America* (Milwaukee: North-western, 1952), 1:262.
2. T. Harwood Pattison, *The History of Christian Preaching* (Philadelphia: American Baptist Publication Society, 1903), 202.
3. W. Fraser Mitchell, *English Pulpit Oratory from Andrewes to Tillotson* (London: SPCK, 1932), 323.
4. Ibid., 323.
5. Ibid., 326.
6. Ibid., 400.

7.3.3.7 Joseph Alleine—Martyr in the Cause

> The distinctive principle of a true Puritan was reverence for the strict letter of Holy Scripture, as God's direct message to each individual man, and as forming our final and absolute authority in religion.
> —Charles Stanford

The last notable Puritan of the Sibbesian style is **Joseph Alleine** (1634–1668). He portrayed the turbulence and unsettledness of the Restoration. Before the Puritan Revolution, ecclesiastical pressures and political machinations led some to say:

> Men must content themselves and think it well
> If once a month they hear the sermon bell.

The rise of the Puritan lectureships and Puritan preaching began to redress that grievous situation. Joseph Alleine was born in Divizes in Wiltshire, where his father had been mayor. He entered "the so-called Puritan University" at Oxford in 1649 when Cromwell was chancellor and John Owen was dean of Christ College. Thomas Goodwin was the principal of the college. (Though a Puritan, Goodwin still used the magnificent organ in the chapel.) Alleine left before obtaining his degree to assist George Newton at St. Mary Magdalen Church in Taunton, Somerset. With his Bible in his hand, "His very appearance was a sermon," it was said. He defended illegal preaching. He was ordained a Presbyterian in 1655 and in that same year married Theodosia.[1]

Alleine dearly loved the flock at Taunton, urging that "If I should die 50 miles away, let me be buried at Taunton." His preaching had a "piercing directness, a powerful and charming eloquence." He was "insatiably greedy for souls"[2] and had as his compelling central theme "Jesus Christ and him crucified." Although he was a Calvinist, he "proclaimed a completed and gratuitous salvation to all who were willing to accept it."[3] He rose daily at 4 A.M. to spend time with God and then catechize the flock. He "had a poet's enjoyment of nature, but with a Puritan's love for the Bible."[4]

Alleine was among those who were unwilling to subscribe to the Act of Uniformity, and he was arrested and imprisoned. Taunton was singled out because of the sieges in the 1640s and Newton and Alleine were flung down. Presiding Judge Foster wanted to exterminate nonconformity. In his trial, Alleine was accused of preaching.[5] Of that much he was certainly guilty. When the jailer was late, he preached while waiting to be incarcerated. Through a series of imprisonments, he preached in the jail and from the jail window. Even though frail, he would preach up to fourteen times in a week. Finally his health broke. Even his wife and aged father were imprisoned. His last incarceration destroyed him, yet he continued to preach and fast.

Alleine's most powerful books were *An Alarm to Unconverted Sinners or The Sure Guide to Heaven* and his *Christian Letters,* in which he variously addresses his wife and the congregation at Taunton and expounds on the gracious love of God for sinners.[6] As his wife made clear, "He was very urgent with those who were unconverted."[7] He died at the age of thirty-four as a true martyr, and though he left no children, Alleine left a legacy of many spiritual sons and daughters.

---

1. Rich resources on Alleine's life are Richard Baxter, *The Life and Death of Joseph Alleine* (New York: Robert Carter, 1840) and the memorial volume written largely by his wife, *The Life and Death of that Excellent Minister of Christ Mr. Joseph Alleine* (London, 1671).
2. Charles Stanford, *Joseph Alleine: His Companions and Times* (Mobile, Ala.: R E Publications, 1861), 140.
3. Ibid., 143.
4. Ibid., 156.
5. Ibid., 227.
6. For excerpts from the letters, see Dewey D. Wallace Jr., ed., *The Spirituality of the Later English Puritans* (Macon, Ga.: Mercer University Press, 1987), 179–93.
7. Ibid., 56. He was such a kindly, gentle soul and sustained a cheerful disposition even under constant duress; see Caroline Francis Richardson, *English Preachers and Preaching 1640–1670* (New York: Macmillan, 1928), 285.

7.4 GEYSERS OF PURITAN PREACHING IN AMERICA

Mr. Cotton preaches with such authority, demonstration, and life that, methinks, when he preaches out of any Prophet or Apostle I hear not him; I hear that Prophet and Apostle; yea, I hear the Lord Jesus Christ speaking in my heart.

—observation by a listener

The work of the Spirit doth always go with the Word.

—Thomas Hooker

The experience of Puritan emigration in the seventeenth century must be understood in light of the persecutions and turbulences in England at that time.[1] In their courageous move from England to New England, the Puritans brought the centrality of the preached Word with them, but the ordeal was indescribable.[2] We now trace the contours of biblical preaching in the New England experience of the "come-outers" who settled those shores and aspired to be a "city set on a hill."

The tension between the Amesian piety and the Sibbesian piety as set forth by Professor Knight is transplanted directly to New England, where the embroiling conflict became more pronounced. The Ames/Perkins axis was represented in New England by Thomas Hooker, Thomas Shepard, and Peter Bulkeley, while John Cotton, John Davenport, and John Wheelwright comprised the Sibbesians.[3] We shall examine several of these leaders and through them pinpoint the centrality of biblical preaching in the New England experience.

1. John Brown, *The Pilgrim Fathers of New England and their Puritan Successors* (London: Religious Tract Society, 1895). Brown gave the Beecher Lectures at Yale on Puritan Preaching and served a church in Bedford.
2. Andrew Delbanco, *The Puritan Ordeal* (Cambridge, Mass.: Harvard University Press, 1989).
3. Janice Knight, *Orthodoxies in Massachusetts: Rereading American Puritanism* (Cambridge, Mass.: Harvard University Press, 1994).

3.4.1 JOHN COTTON—LEADER IN OLD BOSTON

I never yet observed any part of a Scripture . . . but without carnal affectation or straining of wit, it might holily be applyed both with power and profit and delight to an honest heart.

Knowledge is no knowledge without zeal.

Yet there is also an essential wisdom in us, namely, our Reason, which is not natural.

—John Cotton

Conspicuous in the pantheon of the early founders is **John Cotton** (1585–1652). He was a significant link between England and the new experiment in New England, and had "an early and clear prominence" in the affairs of

Massachusetts Bay. Perry Miller spoke of him as "the mouthpiece of the ruling oligarchy." He was above all things a preacher who has left us nineteen volumes of sermons and who epitomized what William Haller described as "English Puritanism, denied opportunity to reform the established church, wreaking its energy during a half century and more upon preaching."[1]

Born in Derby, Cotton went to Cambridge at age thirteen and studied at Emmanuel College, where he made his mark as "a witty, elegant preacher."[2] Here he was converted through the preaching of Richard Sibbes and adopted the plain style of Puritan preaching. Through his ministry, John Preston was converted, the later distinguished master of Emmanuel. Cotton himself served as dean and catechist at Emmanuel and then served twenty-one years as vicar of famous St. Botolph's in Boston, Lincolnshire. Though more and more a Puritan, he continued to use *The Book of Common Prayer* all of his life.

Cotton preached in his English days on Sundays and on Thursday and Friday mornings early and on Saturday afternoon. He loved to preach expository series through a book in the Bible. He studied and prepared twelve hours a day.[3] He loved Scripture and laced his sermons with verses ancillary to his text. In his children's catechism of sixty-two questions, he used sixty-six Old Testament citations and 106 from the New Testament. In a twelve-page treatment of the church, he used more than four hundred scriptural references. He was known for his evangelistic preaching. Although later he embraced a stricter Calvinism, earlier on he held to a kind of voluntarism in which the hearers of the gospel could either receive or reject it. John Preston would follow him in these views.

At age fifty, Cotton moved to Boston, where he commenced a twenty-year ministry at First Church. Cotton spoke out for the new form of church government emerging in New England. His commitment was to the gathered church, and yet he feared the separatism of Roger Williams and Williams' rejection of communion with English churches.[4] Anne Hutchinson, who had been one of his members in Lincolnshire in England, followed her pastor to New England and found early support from him. But in her drift to extreme views on private special revelation and her antinomian bent, Cotton and Hutchinson parted ways.

Cotton Mather, John's grandson, assessed his distinguished grandfather:

A man of might, at heavenly eloquence, To fix the ear and charm the conscience, As if Apollos were reviv'd in him, Or he had learned of a seraphim
(from *Magnalia Christi Americana*).

John Cotton was not as lively as Shepard and Hooker nor as severe. His style was only occasionally gripping. He was not an original thinker, yet he utilized much variety in his work. We discern a distinct eschatological tone in his preaching. He had interest in poetry and music. Governor John Winthrop, with whom Cotton worked closely, paid him tribute: In 1633 "more were converted and added to that church [Cotton's] than to all the other churches in the Bay . . . Divers profane and notorious evil persons came and confessed their sins, and were comfortably received into the bosom of the church."[5]

Interestingly, Cotton's Pauline sermons on the gospel and salvation became popular in New England. His emphasis may well have been pushed by Mrs. Hutchinson to deal with the antinomian extremism of freedom from all law.[6] In his widely read writings such as *The Way of Life, Christ the Fountaine,* and *God's Mercie Mixed with His Justice,* Cotton sets forth his convictions on conversion. His intriguing *An Exposition Upon the Thirteenth Chapter of the Revelation* speaks of the Book of Life:

> When the Lord wrote down thy name, or mine, or any man's name, who stood by His elbow (if I may so speak) to put Him in mind of my name or thine? He thought of us, if our names be there, and He set us down, and He delivered us to Christ Jesus by name. Whatever thy name is, He took notice of thy name. Such a man in such a place, he will live in this or that country. He is one; take notice of him; lay down a price for him. In fulness of time send a spirit into his heart. If he live in a popish country, save him from popery. If in a worldly country, save him from the world. Wherever he lives, save him from himself and bring him to my heavenly kingdom.[7]

John Cotton is a significant first-generational sample of Puritan biblical preaching.

---

1. William Haller, *The Rise of Puritanism* (Philadelphia: University of Pennsylvania Press, 1938), 15.
2. Everett H. Emerson, *John Cotton* (New York: Twayne, 1965), 33.
3. Ibid., 35.
4. Edwin S. Gaustad, *Liberty of Conscience: Roger Williams in America* (Grand Rapids: Eerdmans, 1991), 38–43, 72–85, 98–103. Gaustad also shows Williams' great love for the Jews and his intensified millennialism.
5. Emerson, *John Cotton,* 104.
6. Well analyzed in Emory Eliott, *Power and the Pulpit in Puritan New England* (Princeton, N.J.: Princeton University Press, 1975). See also Donald R. Come, "John Cotton: Guide of the Chosen People" (Ph.D. dissertation, Princeton University, 1948); Stephen K. Cottingham, "An Analysis and Evaluation of John Cotton's Apologetic against Seventeenth-Century Antinomianism" (Th.M. thesis, Dallas Theological Seminary, 1984). For background, see Gertrude Huehns, *Antinomianism in English History* (London: Cresset Press, 1951).
7. Emerson, *John Cotton,* 98.

7.4.2 INCREASE MATHER—SECOND GENERATION CONSERVATOR

Yea it is a sad truth, that religion hath seldom been upheld in the power of it, for above one or two generations together.

—Increase Mather

The power of the Puritan sermon was in its symbolic and metaphorical meaning, which resulted from a dynamic interaction between the clergy and their people.

—Emory Elliott

The most striking representative of the second-generation New England Puritans is **Increase Mather** (1639–1723). His father Richard was one of the founders who came from England (cf. 7.3.2.2) and served the Dorchester church near Boston. Here Increase was born, the youngest of six sons. Richard taught Increase to read as well as to handle Greek and Latin, so he was ready to enter Harvard at age twelve. He also studied at Trinity College, Dublin, and he served as a military chaplain on the island of Guernsey.

Increase Mather was precocious and always interested in scientific investigation. In 1693 he wrote a book about comets. He energetically supported inoculations for smallpox but was conservative theologically and politically. The Salem witchcraft trials troubled him and he put an end to them. He served as rector at Harvard (1685–1701) and spent four years in England (1688–1692) pleading with King William III for a new charter. He was instrumental in obtaining one, and effectively merged Massachusetts and Plymouth colonies in 1691.

Increase Mather preached his first sermon in his father's church in Dorchester in 1657. He had been converted two years earlier in a pattern not uncommon:

> About which time the Lord broke in upon my conscience with very terrible convictions and awakenings. In the months of March, April, and till the latter end of May, 1655, I was in extremity of anguish and horror in my soul. Once at Dorchester when my Father was gone abroad on a public occasion and not to return for a day or two, I shut myself up in his study, and there wrote down all the sins which I could remember I had been guilty of, that lay as a heavy burden on my conscience. I brought them before God, and cried to him for pardoning mercy; and at night burnt the paper which in way of confession I had sorrowfully spread before the Lord.[1]

He went on to serve Second Church in Boston, usually called North Church, from 1664 until his death in 1723. His widowed father married John Cotton's widow, and Increase married Maria, daughter of the John Cottons and his stepsister. Desiring continuity with the vision of the founders, Increase and his generation lamented the spiritual drift in New England. He lambasted backsliding at Harvard, becoming somewhat bitter over trends and asserted that "Philistines had captured the ark." In one of his jeremiads, a style which he developed into a form, he preached on "Ichabod," from Ezekiel 9:3, "And the Glory of the God of Israel was gone up from the Cherub whereupon he was, to the Threshold of the House."[2]

The 1670s were the high point of Puritanism, and Increase Mather's sermons were widely heard (the parish had fifteen hundred souls) and widely published. He memorized all of his sermons and delivered them without notes. Mather had a good-sized library and read broadly. His theme increasingly became "the great radical apostasy of New England." One of his trademark jeremiads was his fast-day sermon in 1671, "The Day of Trouble Is Near," in which he argued that God "doth sometimes bring times of great trouble upon his people."[3] He felt the wars with the Indians, the outbreak of smallpox, and the scourge of fires were all chastening blows from God upon New England because of spiritual declension.

His were "muscular sermons" preached to issues like drinking and dancing. He preached three sermons on murder on the occasion of the execution of James Morgan. Mather also preached series on "practical truths" and on "The Duty of Parents to Pray for Their Children." He wrote a small book on witches and another on angels. In 1674 he preached a memorable series on "Some Important Truths about Conversion."[4] He saw the "storms of God's wrath" on the horizon and in a typical sermon, "The Times of Men," gave these directions to his flock:

1. Take notice of the hand of God in this that is come to pass.
2. Lay it to heart.
3. Let us adore the hand of God.
4. Let us labor to understand the Lord's mind and meaning in this awful Providence.
5. Let us repent of past and present iniquities.
6. Be prepared for a change of times.[5]

Not known for high commitment to pastoral ministry, Increase Mather gave himself to sixteen hours of study daily and to preaching, disregarding chronic health problems and periodic bouts of depression. He took his stand with Charles Chancey and John Davenport against the "Half-way Covenant," which was a relaxation of the requirement that both parents needed to be in the faith for a child to be baptized, adopted in 1662.[6] Increase broke with his own father over this but ultimately changed his own position years later and came to favor it.

Mather was a preacher of hellfire in a way revived in the next century by Jonathan Edwards. Mather would say:

Thy soul is hanging over the mouth of hell by the rotten thread of a frail life: if that breaks, the devouring Gulf will swallow thee up forever.[7]

He embraced the plain style and shrank from the kind of elegance his son Cotton found appealing, but beyond doubt Increase Mather was a preacher of considerable oratorical effect. One of his chief biographers calls him "The Last Puritan" because of his staunch adherence to the vision of the founders.

Not surprisingly his "rhetoric of wrath" caused him to move deeply into eschatology and apocalypticism (not unlike the later Richard Baxter). His rhetoric reverberated with eschatological urgency. When there was a stirring among the Jews in the Levant because of a false messiah, Mather saw this as a possible sign of the Second Coming. He wrote a tome titled *The Mysteries of Israel's Salvation* in which he argued that the Jews would miraculously return to Palestine at the end of the age. In this he was influenced by the thinking of Voetius,

Brightman, John Cotton, and Joseph Mede, who also influenced Thomas Goodwin. While Mather was in England, he visited with Richard Baxter over the millennial issues and the conversion of the Jews.[8]

Daniel and Revelation became important sources for the messages of judgment and impending doom as well as hope. The use of typology would become universal in the second and third generation, as the parallels between the Puritans in New England and ancient Israel were a fertile field for endless analogy. Yet all of this did not divert Increase Mather's longing to see "the pangs of the new birth," nor did he ever desist from his conviction that "Faith and repentance are the great duties required in the New Testament." For Mather, "This was the scope and sum of all the Apostle's preaching."

1. Mason I. Lowance, *Increase Mather* (New York: Twayne, 1974), 27.
2. Ibid., 140.
3. Everett Emerson, *Puritanism in America 1620–1750* (Boston: Twayne, 1977), 92.
4. Michael G. Hall, *The Last Puritan: The Life of Increase Mather* (Middletown, Conn.: Wesleyan University Press, 1988), 91.
5. Emory Elliott, *Power and the Pulpit in Puritan New England* (Princeton, N.J.: Princeton University Press, 1975), 116.
6. Peter Y. DeJong, *The Covenant Idea in New England Theology* (Grand Rapids: Eerdmans, 1945).
7. Robert Middlekauff, *The Mathers: Three Generations of Puritan Intellectuals 1596–1728* (New York: Oxford University Press, 1971), 91.
8. Hall, *The Last Puritan,* 274.

7.4.3 COTTON MATHER—MOVER AND SHAKER IN NEW ENGLAND

This day I likewise obtained of God that he would make use of me as of a John to be herald of the Lord's kingdom now approaching, a voice crying in the wilderness for preparation thereunto.

A great and general assembly was now called . . . By the providence of God it then fell unto me to preach . . . I ran the hazard of much reproach by testifying in that sermon against the persecution of erroneous and conscientious dissenters by the civil magistrate.

Should I tell, in how many forms the Devil has assaulted me, and with what subtilty and energy his assaults have been carried on, it would strike my friends with horror.

—Cotton Mather's diary

Clearly the leading scholar in Puritan New England was **Cotton Mather** (1663–1728). Described as "the real virtuoso of the new themes and language of the sermons of the last decades of the century," Cotton may have been the brightest star in the Mather galaxy. He was the most brilliant and prolific thinker of his times. His life motto was *fructuosus* (i.e., being fruitful). Never traveling very far from his birthplace in Boston, Mather entered Harvard at eleven years of age and began preaching soon after. He could give orations in Latin and wrote his M.A. thesis on the possibility of the divine origin of the Hebrew vowel pointings. Ultimately he would grow disappointed in Harvard and, along with Elihu Yale, became one of the founders of Yale College.

At eighteen, Cotton became his father's associate at North Church. Something of a stutterer as a young person, he overcame the problem. He preached two or three times a week, both at North Church and elsewhere. One month he spoke seventy-two times. We have seven thousand pages of his early sermon notes. Exegesis was not his forte, but his content was rich, theological, and well applied. He had an unusually effective ministry among the young people of Boston. While the quality of Puritan preaching was uneven and "the hourglass was often turned with resignation," even in printed form Mather's sermons have life.[1] His literary output was massive, running to 388 titles. He had a personal library of eight thousand volumes and read in many fields.

Cotton Mather came to the assurance of personal faith only with great struggle, seeing himself as "one of the filthiest creatures on earth."[2] He was a man of extraordinary personal devotion and prayerfulness. In a sense he was a kind of John the Baptist for the fourth-generation preacher Jonathan Edwards, who would so shake New England and rekindle the "preaching of intense zeal" after Mather's death.[3] Looking at Mather's huge *Magnalia Christi Americana* (with its controlling millennial metaphor), one is impressed with the contrast between the Virginia settlers who took such delight in high culture but were essentially receptors, and the Puritan mind which was so dedicated to expression and creation of thoughts and beliefs.[4] In Mather we see what the prominent Puritan scholar Barrett Wendell called "the passionate enthusiasm of their faith." He foresaw a brighter day ushered in ultimately by the return of the Lord Jesus Christ to set up his kingdom.[5]

Mather was much more attuned to pastoral ministry than was his father and advocated visitation and catechizing of families. His personal life was filled with much tragedy, including the deaths of two wives, the severe mental illness of his third wife and the deaths of thirteen of his fifteen children. His involvement in the Salem witchcraft debacle was not his greatest hour.[6] He wrote a manual for the preparation of pastors titled *Manductio ad Ministerium,* widely influential in his time. Like his father, he had scientific inclination, supported inoculation against smallpox, and was elected a member of the Royal Society in London.

Cotton Mather shows the complex interrelationship between Continental pietism and Puritanism. He stands with Richard Baxter and August Hermann Franke as the embodiment of cross-fertilization. Although he was a devout Calvinist, he was a preparationist who expected and called for conversions (cf. Thomas Shepard who believed the odds were 1,000 to 1 against a given conversion). Mather carried on an extensive correspondence with Franke.[7] This relationship began when the SPCK in London sent a copy of the *Magnalia* to Franke in Halle and Franke wrote a seventy-page letter to Mather in return. Professor Richard

Lovelace has shown the mutual enrichment which this relationship produced in terms of a sound balance between right theology and genuine experience. This did involve some move away from hyper-Calvinism on his part[8] and a healthy "Christ-mysticism."[9] Lovelace calls this "an eclectic spirituality" and cites Ritschl's phrase "the unitive tendency of Pietism" to describe the concern for Christian unity which captured Mather.

Other benefits we see in Mather are his emphasis on lay ministry (uncommon in Puritanism), his love for distribution of tracts and his "collects" of prayer for persons whom he saw on the street, his use of collegia, or small groups, after the manner of the pietistic conventicles,[10] his sensitivity to social issues and his "revivalistic expectation" in which he cites the Halle model. His prayer was

> Wherefore under a terror of God, it becomes us to labour fervently in our prayer that the glorious God of our Life would revive decayed piety . . . and that His quickening Spirit would not withdraw any further . . . Lord, revive thy work in the midst of the nations.[11]

Illustrative of this was his growing burden for missions and for outreach to the Indians (in view of the fact that Puritans did not ordinarily have missionary zeal) and his correspondence with Bartholomew Ziegenbalg, the Pietistic missionary to Malabar.[12]

The preaching of Cotton Mather always had a pronounced Christocentric thrust. He had a great love for Bible prophecy but guarded against date-setting. His appetite for scholarship dove into the deeper veins of Scripture. The ministry of the Word was for him "the principal agent in spiritual nourishment and awakening . . . and thus he still used long bouts of preaching and teaching as the basic protein of his ministry."[13]

Mather would preach for at least an hour, often an hour and three quarters. Once his pastoral prayer went for two hours, and he had to apologize. He did his exegesis and outlining in the typical Puritan form and valued illustrative anecdotes to help his audience get the picture. He spent considerable time internalizing his message because he neither read from a manuscript nor memorized his sermon. He typically took about seven hours for preparation. He spoke in free style, extempore. He attempted to begin slowly and quietly, using short sentences and emphasizing key words. He loved the use of exclamation marks in his writing, which tells us something about his flow.[14] If his goal was to use short sentences, he did not always succeed—the first sentence in his life of Governor Phips ran 254 words.

Benjamin Coleman described Mather's preaching:

> Here he excelled, here he shone; being exceeding communicative, and bringing out of his treasury things new and old, without measure. Here it was seen how his wit, and fancy, his invention, his quickness of thought and ready apprehension were all consecrated to God, as well as his heart, will and affections.[15]

Cotton Mather did depart from the plain style of the Puritans into what Professor Lovelace describes as "an opulent and humorous floridity—its puns, tropes, allusions, and encrustations of literary jewelry—Mather's style is constantly in danger of sounding ridiculous, whenever his taste, or ear, fails."[16] Yet notwithstanding, Lovelace quotes Sidney Mead, the Unitarian church historian, as saying that Mather's work "unknowingly was fanning the spark that eight years later would burst into flame in Jonathan Edwards' Northampton church."[17]

---

1. Thomas Jefferson Wertenbaker, *The Puritan Oligarchy: The Founding of American Civilization* (New York: Grosset and Dunlap, 1947), 79.

2. Kenneth Silverman, *The Life and Times of Cotton Mather* (New York: Columbia University Press, 1985), 29. This is the Pulitzer Prize-winning biography for 1985. Copious and clear, the study has spiritual limitations.

3. Wertenbaker, *The Puritan Oligarchy,* 82.

4. Ibid., 104.

5. Barrett Wendell, *Cotton Mather: The Puritan Priest* (New York: Harcourt and Brace, 1963). See the new introduction and evaluation of Wendell by Alkan Heimert, xxi.

6. Ibid., 65. The classic study here is Marion L. Starkey, *The Devil in Massachusetts* (New York: Time Reading Program, 1963).

7. Robert Middlekauff, *The Mathers: Three Generations of Puritan Intellectuals 1596–1728* (New York: Oxford University Press, 1971), 305.

8. Richard F. Lovelace, *The American Pietism of Cotton Mather: Origins of American Evangelicalism* (Grand Rapids: Christian University Press, 1979), 6.

9. Ibid., 181, 187.

10. Ibid., 220.

11. Ibid., 248.

12. Ibid., 34.

13. Ibid., 203.

14. Emory Elliott, *Power and the Pulpit in Puritan New England* (Princeton, N.J.: Princeton University Press, 1975), 188.

15. Lovelace, *The American Pietism of Cotton Mather,* 26.

16. Ibid., 288.

17. Ibid., 283.

7.4.4   THOMAS SHEPARD—SOLDIER OF CHRIST

Saints have an experimental knowledge of the work of grace, by virtue of which they come to know it as certainly . . . as by feeling heat, we know that fire is hot; by tasting honey, we know it is sweet.

As it is with conduit pipes, so here. . . . Let the pipes be laid ever so well, and laid ever so far up, yet if they are not laid wholly and all the way up to the conduit head, no water will ever come down to that family.

—Thomas Shepard

When he was heard by Edward Johnson, the author of *Wonder-Working Providence of Zion's Saviour in New England,* **Thomas Shepard** (1605–1649) was totally convincing: "All doubts and fears were swept away."[1] Jonathan Edwards was much influenced by Shepard, and quoted him often. He had a unique niche as pastor of the Cambridge church and as one of the founders of Harvard. Shepard came from Essex, as did John Eliot, the noted missionary to the Indians. He matriculated brilliantly at Emmanuel College, Cambridge, where John Preston had great influence on him. While at Cambridge, Shepard heard Thomas Goodwin preach on conversion and the ministry in a powerful way, but he castigated himself incessantly for his hesitation in taking action.

Shepard was such a staunch Calvinist that he urged those who were not of the elect to praise God for their damnation. Only on the matter of an incipient preparationism (the idea of steps and stages leading to conversion) did he deviate from the old Amesian line, as he spoke of "conviction, compunction and humiliation" as preliminary stages in the *ordo salutis* followed by "justification, reconciliation, adoption, sanctification and glorification."[2]

Shepard got himself into ecclesiastical troubles, and Laud called him "a prating coxcomb." On the eve of his departure for New England, he solemnly intoned, "It shall not be with us there as it is with the wicked Israelites who when they came into the good land of rest, they then forgot the Lord and all his works past."[3] But it was not long before he was denouncing "that inundation of abominable filthinesses breaking in upon us."[4]

The glass was always half-empty for Thomas Shepard. If there is truth in the characterization of Puritan society in New England in the seventeenth century as "harsh," we sense something in Shepard that was excessive. Giles Fermin termed him a "gloomy exclusionist," and he in fact denounced all toleration and debated endlessly with the Baptists (and just about anyone else). The more recent publication of his diary shows him as a man in great internal turmoil. His "tortured self-examination leads to no conviction, no real certainty."[5]

Shepard writhed with jealously when his wife reported the good sermon of a colleague.[6] He preached exclusively on prayer for such a long time and scolded his people so vehemently on their prayerlessness that some of his most prayerful saints left him.[7] He lamented his faults at great length, which were chiefly his too great love for his books, neglect of family worship, his failure to speak to his children about their spiritual life as he should have (although all three sons went into the ministry and called him blessed), and his natural gloom.

Yet despite his many flaws and his "raw-headed preaching," Shepard's sermons were monumental. Although severe, he was more vivid and lively than even John Cotton. He is not easy to read because of his "ragged style," but he was forceful. He expected results in his preaching and used analogy to great effect.[8] He testified, "I learned from Paul what it was to be spiritually-minded, and I learned from him also how to compare spiritual things with spiritual."[9] Samuel Blair demonstrated that in the Great Awakening the writings of "those old pious and experimental writers" like Thomas Shepard were revisited.[10]

In one of the most widely published sermons in New England history, "The

Sincere Convert," Shepard traced the path from remorse to repentance to saving faith, and spoke passionately about the issues:

> That God the Father of our Lord Jesus Christ may be honored by the performance of these duties, therefore use them. Christ shed his blood that he might purchase unto himself a people zealous of good works, (Titus 2:14), not to save our souls by them, but to honor him. O, let not the blood of Christ be shed in vain! Grace and good duties are a Christian's crown; it is sin only makes a man base. Now, shall a king cast away his crown, because he brought not his kingdom by it? No; because it is his ornament and glory to wear it when he is made a king. So I say unto thee, It is better that Christ should be honored than thy soul saved; and therefore, perform duties because they honor the Lord Jesus Christ.[11]

In this sermon he also trumpeted his confidence in the return of the Lord Jesus for his own. In his "Parable of the Ten Virgins" (from which he had preached for four years), he spoke of two future comings of the Lord.[12]

His own last words encapsulate the man: "O my sinful heart! O my often-crucified and never wholly mortified sinfulness! O my life-long damage and my daily shame. O my indwelling and so besetting sins, your evil dominion is over now! It is within an hour or two of my final and everlasting release! For I am authoritatively assured that by tomorrow morning I shall have entered into my eternal rest! And then, O my ransomed soul, one hour in heaven will make me forget all my hell on earth!"[13]

---

1. Thomas Jefferson Wertenbaker, *The Puritan Oligarchy: The Founding of American Civilization* (New York: Grosset and Dunlap, 1947), 209.
2. Andrew Delbanco, *The Puritan Ordeal* (Cambridge, Mass.: Harvard University Press, 1989), 49.
3. Ibid., 103.
4. Ibid., 206.
5. Everett Emerson, *Puritanism in America 1620–1750* (Boston: Twayne, 1977), 125.
6. Alexander Whyte, *Thomas Shepard: Pilgrim Father and Founder of Harvard, His Spiritual Experience and Experimental Preaching* (Edinburgh: Oliphant Anderson and Ferrier, 1909), 280.
7. Ibid., 228.
8. Harry S. Stout, *The New England Soul: Preaching and Religious Culture in Colonial New England* (New York: Oxford University Press, 1986), 43.
9. Whyte, *Thomas Shepard,* 94.
10. Iain H. Murray, *Jonathan Edwards: A New Biography* (Edinburgh: Banner of Truth, 1987), 214.
11. Stout, *The New England Soul,* 42.
12. Thomas Shepard, "The Parable of the Ten Virgins" (Ligonier, Pa.: Soli Deo Gloria, 1994), 24–25.
13. Whyte, *Thomas Shepard,* 144.

7.4.5 THOMAS HOOKER—ORATOR OF NEW ENGLAND

When there is a kind of spiritual heat in the heart, when there are holy affections, and the heart of the minister is answerable to that, he communicates and delivers to the people.

My brethren, it is all one, if hearing the Minister speak unto you the word of God, and bring home to you the reproofs and admonitions and counsels thereof, you kick his Word from you, and happily take up arms against him; it is all one (I say) as if you take up arms against God and despised him.

That rhetoric which we find in Scripture to be used by the Prophets and Apostles, hath great use in preaching if it be used with the like prudence . . . narratives, examples, precepts . . . because that manner doth make most for the common use of all kinds of men, and also most to affect the will and stir up godly motions, which is the chief scope of Divinity.

—Thomas Hooker

More than ninety Oxbridge graduates built and enriched the spiritual and intellectual life of New England. Among the most distinguished and influential of them was **Thomas Hooker** (1586–1647). Born into a middle-class family in the tiny hamlet of Marfield in Leiscestershire, he studied at Emmanuel College, Cambridge, where he received his B.A. in 1608 and his M.A. in 1611. More importantly, it is where he was converted. After serving in a fellowship at the university, he took a living in the Esher parish in rural Surrey, where he served with distinction and where also he married. His pastoral skills were sharpened especially through his dealings with an oppressed soul known as Mrs. Drake, of whose trials he wrote in *Poor Doubting Christian,* a book which brought him dramatically into the limelight. He began to be in demand as an occasional preacher in London and at this time assisted his friend Thomas Shepard in finding his first pulpit. In 1626 he was called as lecturer to St. Mary's, Chelmsford, where his reputation as a preacher of ability was greatly enhanced.

A man of choleric temperament, Hooker used the Ames and Perkins model for his preaching with exegetical comments followed by doctrine, reasons, and uses. He strongly emphasized headings and the "firstly" and "secondly" in his preaching to safeguard against wandering from the text and theme.[1] Recognizing the gifts and effectiveness of Hooker's preaching, Cotton Mather wrote:

Hereby there was a great reformation wrought, not only in the town, but in the adjacent country, from all parts whereof they came to "hear the wisdom of the Lord Jesus Christ," in his gospel, by this worthy man dispensed; and some of great quality among the rest, would often resort from far to his assembly; particularly the truly noble Earl of Warwick.[2]

Hooker was known for fire and lightning in the pulpit and was seen by many as a demanding if not a harsh preacher. Yet he gave assiduous attention to the overlapping roles of prophet and shepherd, seeing himself often as "an evangelizing prophet." He loved to be in his pulpit above all else.

In 1629 he was called to appear before Archbishop Laud's High Commission and was removed from pulpit ministry. He kept a small grammar school at Little Baddow, where John Eliot was his assistant. Continuing to preach illegally in homes, Hooker was once again summoned. He fled to the Netherlands with his family in 1631.

Living in Delft, Hooker found the climate neither physically nor ecclesiastically tolerable, and he migrated to New England. He settled in Newtown, where a covenant was established in 1633, but the community never became a commercial center. In 1636 he led about one hundred members and 160 head of cattle one hundred miles westward to settle in the beautiful Connecticut Valley. We know the settlement as Hartford.[3] He preached at the first session of the General Court in 1638 and was instrumental in shaping the first written constitution in the thirteen original colonies. The document is considered a milestone in the history of constitutional government in the United States.[4] Yet Perry Miller is right in his epochal work that Thomas Hooker is to be seen first and foremost as a preacher, not a founder.

Hooker was always in the eye of some storm, but was known as a steady and consistent Bible preacher. One observer described his pulpit presence:

> When he spoke his entire person was fired with enthusiasm, his eyes shone, his gestures were animated. He seemed to be inspired by the "divine relish" he had of his subject, "the sacred panting of his holy soul after the glorious objects of the invisible world" . . . "The distinct images of things would come so nimbly, and so fitly into his mind, that he could utter them with fluent expressions."[5]

Numerous instances are reported of those who came to hear "that bawling Hooker" in order to mock him but who remained afterward to pray. In Leicester the burgesses hired some fiddlers to play outside the church in order to drown out the preacher, "but the sound of his pleadings and warnings floated out of the door above the scrapings of the fiddlers." The chief burgess leaned forward to listen and became sincerely penitent.

Hooker was known for his "verbal wit and his ear for neatly balanced sentences."[6] He spoke often of the terrors of heaven and hell, and his preaching made use of narrative in a way not common at this time. Hooker used the journey of the sinner/saint resourcefully, with considerable typology and metaphor. His dramatization and skill in interrogative dialogue[7] were striking; his narrative was termed "epic-scale."[8] True, his inaccessible "language of Canaan" needed to be translated for subsequent generations, but it was effective for the times. He was a traditional Calvinist except for his strong insistence on the soul's preparation for the Spirit's work, and he developed a theology of preparation.[9]

Hooker's preaching was characterized by stupendous energy. He spent nearly a year in Acts 2:37. He was also known for his powerful and efficacious prayers.[10] Hooker warned against too much reliance on emotion, and urged: "Therefore away with your sense and feeling, and go to the promise." While preaching on the Holy Spirit, he would wait for the Spirit's working.[11] He periodically experienced "particular faith," or the settled assurance that this prayer would be specifically answered.[12] He did on occasion exercise the gift of prophecy.

Hooker's sermons were widely published and circulated. In a great sermon on Romans 4:12 titled "The Activity of Faith," he urged his hearers along this line:

> But look to it, wheresoever faith is, it is fruitful. If thou art fruitless, say what thou wilt, thou hast no faith at all. Alas, these idle drones, these idle Christians, the Church is too full of them. Men are continually hearing and yet remain fruitless and unprofitable; whereas if there were more faith in the world, we should have more work done in the world; faith would set feet and hands, and eyes, and all on work. Men go under the name of professors, but alas, they are but pictures; they stir not a whit; mark, where you find them in the beginning of the year, there you will find them in the end of the year, as profane, as worldly, as loose in their conversations, as formal in duty as ever. And is this faith? Oh, faith would work other matters, and provoke a soul to other passages than these.[13]

1. Frank Shuffelton, *Thomas Hooker 1586–1647* (Princeton, N.J.: Princeton University Press, 1977), 106.
2. Ibid., 75.
3. John Brown, *The Pilgrim Fathers of New England and Their Puritan Successors* (London: Religious Tract Society, 1895), 319ff. For a disclosure of the current spiritual state of the church in Hartford, see Gary Dorsey, *Congregation: The Journey Back to Church* (New York: Viking, 1995).
4. For a good selection of election sermons from this period, see A. W. Plumstead, ed., *The Wall and the Garden: Selected Massachusetts Election Sermons* (Minneapolis: University of Minnesota Press, 1968).
5. Thomas Jefferson Wertenbaker, *The Puritan Oligarchy: The Founding of American Civilization* (New York: Grosset and Dunlap, 1947), 81.
6. Sargent Bush Jr., *The Writings of Thomas Hooker: Spiritual Adventure in Two Worlds* (Madison: University of Wisconsin Press, 1980), 13.
7. Shuffelton, *Thomas Hooker 1586–1647*, 67.
8. Bush, *The Writings of Thomas Hooker*, 343.
9. Ibid., 154, 159.
10. Mason L. Lowance, *Increase Mather* (New York: Twayne, 1974), 56.
11. David L. Hall, *Worlds of Wonder, Days of Judgment* (New York: Knopf, 1989), 28.
12. Richard F. Lovelace, *The American Pietism of Cotton Mather: Origins of American Evangelicalism* (Grand Rapids: Christian University Press, 1979), 181.
13. F. R. Webber, *A History of Preaching in Britain and America* (Milwaukee: Northwestern, 1957), 3:38.

7.4.6 PETER BULKELEY—COVENANTER OF THE PURITANS

> If God be God over us, we must yield him universal obedience in all
> things. He must not be over us in one thing, and under us in another, but
> he must be over us in everything.

> The Lord looks for more from thee then from other people; more zeal
> for God, more love to his truth, more justice, and equality in thy ways;
> thou shouldst be a special people, an only people, none like thee in all
> the earth. Oh be so, in loving the Gospel and the Ministers of it . . . take
> heed lest for neglect of either, God remove thy Candlestick out of the
> midst of thee; lest being now as a city upon an hill, which many seek
> unto, thou be like a Beacon upon the top of a mountain, desolate and
> forsaken.

> —Peter Bulkeley

Daniel Boorstin rightly claims that preaching is "the characteristic Puritan
institution." One of the eminent Puritan fathers who deserves notice in this history is **Peter Bulkeley** (1582–1646), the founder and first pastor of the congregation in Concord. Bulkeley hailed from Bedfordshire, where he followed his
father as rector of Odell on the Ouse River. His was a strong family; his brother-
in-law had been Cromwell's attorney general.[1] With a Cambridge M.A. (1608),
Bulkeley was a person of broad reading and much learning. His interest in chem-
istry is reflected in the thirty-five volumes of notes, now found in the Walter R.
Steiner Medical Library at Hartford, written largely by Bulkeley and his sons.[2]

In the face of mounting ecclesiastical pressure, Bulkeley emigrated to New
England at the relatively advanced age of fifty-two. Purchasing land from the
Indians, he led in the building of the famous colony on the banks of the Merrimac
River. Known for his able preaching, Bulkeley was frequently cast into roles of
significant leadership. He and Thomas Hooker jointly presided over the three-
week inquiry into antinomian dissent in 1637. The concerns were John Cotton,
Anne Hutchinson, and John Davenport (John Cotton had refused to attend
Bulkeley's installation in Concord).[3] Bulkeley also played a prominent part in
elections for Massachusetts political office.

Bulkeley was an outspoken preparationist. Hooker and he argued that the unconverted must make some significant response to the overtures and initiatives
of grace, that the soul is not entirely passive, and that good works are a test of
true salvation and sanctification. In advancing this argument, Bulkeley had to be
careful that he did not move onto the ground of meritorious works. He clearly
moved away from the doctrine of irresistible grace when he insisted that men
"make the covenant of grace void unto themselves by neglecting and slighting
the offers and tenders of grace which are made unto them."[4] Under Hooker and
Bulkeley, the New England ministers gave definition to these concerns. As a result, they excluded Anne Hutchinson and came to terms with John Cotton, but
utterly failed with John Wheelwright, who was also banished.

In distinction to John Cotton, Hooker and Bulkeley maintained that faith precedes justification. Bulkeley steadfastly followed John Preston in arguing that the process of preconversion work does not involve meritorious works. Cotton finally came to oppose Anne Hutchinson.

The most significant contribution of Bulkeley, however, is his sermons collected under the title *The Gospel-Covenant or The Covenant of Grace Opened* (although it was not published until 1641). In the judgment of Perry Miller, this is "the outstanding work" on this central doctrine from the Puritan founders. The idea of covenant is clearly a defining doctrine in both Old and New Testaments. Bulkeley insists there are three covenants: (1) the covenant between the Father and the Son; (2) the covenant of works with our first parents in innocence; and (3) the covenant of grace proffered because of the broken covenant of works. The idea of covenant and compact suffuses all of Puritan life. Undergirding the whole projection is the character of God, of whom Bulkeley said, "God cannot be a covenant-breaker." Both individual and corporate covenants (the latter included with so-called federal theology) "are proclaimed through the same medium—the sermon."[5]

The so-called covenant of grace is not without a condition, Bulkeley said. One's "calling and election" are made sure by evidence in the life (which is what the antinomians most dangerously denied). The sermon is critical because it is through the sermon that the terms of obedience are articulated. There is an element of voluntarism here, which comes close to a denial of the strictures of the Synod of Dort to the effect that grace is irresistible. Bulkeley insisted, "There is danger in sinning against the covenant of works, but it is more dangerous to sin against grace. For there is help for such as break the covenant of works, but no help for such as make void the covenant of grace in themselves."[6] The practical implications of the Puritan view of covenant extend to marriage and the rearing of children.[7]

Bulkeley's influence is seen especially in the life of Samuel Willard, who worked closely with Increase Mather and followed him to the presidency of Harvard. Willard's *Systematical Divinity* was one of the great Puritan landmarks. He sat under the ministry of Bulkeley in Concord, and prepared for entrance into Harvard while there.[8]

Once again, we see the centrality of the sermon in Puritan society.

1. John Brown, *The Pilgrim Fathers of New England and Their Puritan Successors* (London: Religious Tract Society, 1895), 314.
2. Thomas Jefferson Wertenbaker, *The Puritan Oligarchy: The Founding of American Civilization* (New York: Grosset and Dunlap, 1947), 262.
3. Andrew Delbanco, *The Puritan Ordeal* (Cambridge, Mass.: Harvard University Press, 1989), 118.
4. Everett Emerson, *Puritanism in America 1620–1750* (Boston: Twayne, 1977), 60.
5. Harry S. Stout, *The New England Soul: Preaching and Religious Culture in Colonial New England* (New York: Oxford University Press, 1986), 27.
6. Emerson, *Puritanism in America 1620–1750,* 60.
7. Edmund S. Morgan, *The Puritan Family: Religion and Domestic Relations in Seventeenth-Century New England* (New York: Harper Torchbooks, 1944, 1966), 91, 97, 161–62.

8. Ernest Benson Lowrie, *The Shape of the Puritan Mind: The Thought of Samuel Willard* (New Haven, Conn.: Yale University Press, 1974), 10–11.

7.4.7   JOHN DAVENPORT—ELDER AMONG THE PURITANS

That practice that exposeth the blood of Christ to contempt and baptism to profanation, the Church to pollution and the Commonwealth to confusion is to be admitted.

The porter looks well unto the doors of the Lord's House.

—John Davenport

Emblematic of the older generation of the founders who detected ominous spiritual slippage and who eloquently cried out against it is **John Davenport** (1597–1670). Born in Coventry, the son of the mayor, he was a graduate of Magdalen College, Oxford. Davenport began to preach at the age of nineteen in a noted ministry at St. Stephen's, Coleman Street, London. During this time he hid John Cotton. Davenport himself had to flee the pincers of Laud, and became copastor of the English church in Amsterdam. There he became embroiled in a fierce dispute when he opposed the baptism of children whose parents were not Christians.[1]

Davenport was dogged in his insistence on biblical authority: "The whole Scripture is breathed of God, and therefore infallible, and stamped with God's own authority in every sentence of it, 2 Timothy 3:16." He returned to England briefly and then migrated to New England, where he led a group of colonists to Quinnipiac in Connecticut. There he founded New Haven. He was elected pastor and served with powerful impact for thirty years. With John Cotton and Thomas Hooker, Davenport was invited back to England to be part of the Westminster Assembly, but none were able to go. He was one of the most well-heard ministers in New England and advanced with the understanding that "God's usual way which he will bless for the converting or turning of elect sinners to himself, is by sending his Ministers with a Message from himself to them, in their preaching God's Word unto them" (from *God's Call*).

In the antinomian controversy, Davenport argued for greater pastoral understanding of Anne Hutchinson. He desired to correct rather than condemn.[2] So recently arrived from England, Davenport stood more with the preaching of Sibbes and Cotton than with Hooker and Bulkeley. He preached the last sermon at the synod called to inquire into the problem, and issued a strong call to unity based on Philippians 3:16.

Twenty-five years later, however, in the divisive conflict over the Half-way Covenant, Davenport led the forces opposing Solomon Stoddard's crusade to relax baptismal requirements. Davenport was successful in enlisting the support of Increase Mather for the cause, though Mather later switched positions and identified with his own father's thinking. This shift was possibly more a function of broadening church control over more persons than it was the result of a theological stance. Davenport manifested the longing for a pure church, a desire that was common among the fathers.[3]

This issue divided First Church when Davenport was called to succeed the revered John Norton in 1668. Believing that his opposition to the Half-way Covenant made Davenport unsuitable, a strong minority opposed him. But Davenport desired the call to Boston, and once in place gave no ground to the dissenters. Richard Mather was chosen as mediator in the dispute but was not admitted by Davenport. The elder Mather soon died, possibly influencing Increase Mather in his change of heart on the issue.[4] Many problems now confronted Davenport. Ultimately, he planted another congregation.

The year before he died, he preached an election sermon and verbalized the burden of the founders:

> I shall conclude with a brief reminding you of the first beginning of this Colony . . . Churches were gathered in a Congregational way, and walked therein, according to the Rules of the Gospel . . . Now therefore take heed and beware, that the Lord may not have just cause to complain of us . . . lest you lose by God's punishing justice what you received from his free mercy . . . take heed and beware lest he remove the golden candlesticks, and the burning and shining lights in them, as he hath already done to many eminent lights; and woe to them for whom the Gospel is spurned, for their abusing it, and the messengers of it . . . And see that your fruitfulness is good, answereth the cost and pains that God hath been at with you in his Vineyard, lest the Lord be provoked to deal with us as he did with his ancient Vineyard (1669).

---

1. F. R. Webber, *A History of Preaching in Britain and America* (Milwaukee: Northwestern, 1957), 3:42.
2. Andrew Delbanco, *The Puritan Ordeal* (Cambridge, Mass.: Harvard University Press, 1989), 157.
3. Robert Middlekauff, *The Mathers: Three Generations of Puritan Intellectuals 1596–1728* (London: Oxford University Press, 1971), 56–57.
4. Michael G. Hall, *The Last Puritan: The Life of Increase Mather* (Middletown, Conn.: Wesleyan University Press, 1988), 78ff.

7.5 THE SCOTTISH PULPIT IN THE SEVENTEENTH CENTURY

To the Presbyterians of the seventeenth century the Bible, as interpreted by them, was an absolutely infallible guide of religion and moral conduct.

—Duncan Anderson

It is only with the realization of his implicit faith in the Bible as the infallible law in human conduct, so infallible that "if an angel from heaven should reveal anything contrary to the Scriptures, or offer to add anything to that perfect rule of faith and manners, he ought to be accursed, that

understanding comes of the motives which made fervent royalists take
up arms against their king.

—Duncan Anderson

He chose to give us birth through the word of truth. . . . Therefore, get
rid of all moral filth and the evil that is so prevalent and humbly accept
the word planted in you, which can save you.

—James 1:18, 21

The startling prominence and power of the Scottish pulpit in the eighteenth
and nineteenth centuries can be understood only in light of the legacy of biblical
preaching that **John Knox** (cf. 5.6.1) and **Andrew Melville** (1545–1622) bequeathed to their spiritual heirs. Holy Scripture was at the center of Scottish life
as even Robert Burns much later reflects in "The Cotter's Saturday Night." It
was Melville who took the king by the sleeve in 1596 and told him: "There is
twa Kings and twa Kingdoms in Scotland; there is King James, the head of this
commonwealth; and there is Christ Jesus the King and His Kingdom the Kirk,
whose subject King James the Sixth is."

The Scots Confession of 1560 came from the Reformation Parliament and was
foundational for the reconstituted Church of Scotland.[1] The confession "professed
and believed as wholesome, sound doctrine, grounded upon the infallible truth
of God's Word" was the platform from which "the true church is discerned from
the false by the true preaching of the Word of God, the right administration of
the sacraments, and ecclesiastical discipline uprightly ministered."[2] Later, Principal Rainy held, "Surely it is a striking thing that what so united the nation was
a resolution that God's authority, discerned by themselves in His Word, that and
nothing else, should set up institutions in their Church. That principle was written then on the fibre of the Scottish people in a manner that is legible yet."[3]

The biblical idea of covenant (three hundred times in the Old Testament alone),
flowered in covenant theology and its close cousin, federal theology, was developed by **Johannes Cocceius** on the Continent, (1603–1669).[4] The National Covenant of 1638 and the Solemn League and Covenant of 1643, along with the
Westminster Confession of 1647, solidified the theological stance of the Scottish Covenanters. After the fall of the Cromwellian commonwealth, virtually the
whole of Scotland united against the reestablishment of the episcopacy in 1661
under Charles II.

Many Scotsmen gave their lives in defiance when the Westminster Confession
was abolished and English troops were sent in 1666 to force people to go to the
established church. An uprising followed when an old man was roasted alive for
not paying his fine for nonattendance at church. Although conciliation was
attempted by Bishop Leighton, what was known as the "killing times" followed
and the Scottish people endured incredible oppression. Upwards of eighteen
thousand were martyred in a country with less than two million people. The
persecution ended in late 1688 when **William of Orange** took the throne in the
Glorious Revolution. William's trusted Scottish chaplain was the greatly loved
William Carstares, a Church of Scotland minister and son of a Church of

Scotland minister. At long last in 1689 came the Act Abolishing Prelacy in Scotland, and in the following year Presbyterian government was established in the Church of Scotland. Soon the Treaty of Union between England and Scotland was enacted, joining the two countries.

Throughout the trial, even while devout Scots met secretly in house churches, preaching was prominent.[5] The Bible was deeply interwoven with every facet of daily life, as Duncan Anderson has so well shown.[6] Family worship was deep-dyed in the customs of the time.[7]

Scottish sermons were generally given from memory, and delivered after considerable reading of Scripture "without any other colours than those that are peculiar to Faith and Reason." The objective was to evoke "a responsive thrill to the stimulus of the Scriptures."[8]

Great throngs came to hear preachers like **John Welsh** (1624–1681) of Irongay, the Covenanting field preacher and great-grandson of John Knox. Then there was the extraordinary preacher **Robert Bruce** (1554–1631), sometime minister in Inverness. He rebuked King James for talking during the service in St. Giles and was expelled from his pulpit by the king.

We now examine some sterling examples of Scottish preaching.

---

1. As a fantastic resource for every aspect of Scottish church history and practice, see Nigel M. de S. Cameron, ed., *Dictionary of Scottish Church History and Theology* (Downers Grove, Ill.: InterVarsity Press, 1993).
2. Ninian Hill, *The Story of the Scottish Church* (Glasgow: James Maclehose, 1919), 117.
3. Ibid., 164.
4. G. D. Henderson, *The Burning Bush: Studies in Scottish Church History* (Edinburgh: St. Andrew Press, 1957), 71. See C. S. McCoy, *The Covenant Theology of Johannes Cocceius* (New Haven, Conn.: Yale, 1957).
5. Hector Macpherson, *Scotland's Battles for Spiritual Independence* (London: Hodder and Stoughton, 1905).
6. Duncan Anderson, *The Bible in Seventeenth Century Scottish Life and Literature* (London: Allenson, 1936).
7. Ibid., 104.
8. Ibid., 94ff.

7.5.1 ALEXANDER HENDERSON—DESIGNER OF THE NATIONAL COVENANT

The badge of the Church of Scotland, a bush burning but not consumed, was as true a type of Scotland's inexpugnable defense of her ancient liberties, as it was of the Jewish people in their emergence from Egyptian bondage. And so the early history of the Presbyterian Church had been one long struggle of dogged resistance to superior power.

—Dean Stanley in 1872

You will know the truth, and the truth will set you free.

—John 8:32

Your word is truth.

—John 17:17b

There are divers among us that have had no such warrant for our entry to the ministry as were to be wished. Alas, how many of us have rather sought the kirk than the kirk sought us!

—Alexander Henderson

Third only in influence to John Knox and Andrew Melville was **Alexander Henderson** (1583–1646), "The scholarly and statesmanlike" leader in the stand against the episcopacy.[1] Often called the Second Reformer, Henderson was born in Fifshire and in 1603 graduated with honors from St. Andrews, where he became a regent and a teacher of philosophy and rhetoric. Up to this point he supported the episcopacy, the system of church government by bishops. He was made pastor of the country church at Leuchars, but the members locked the doors on him when he arrived. Sometime soon after he went secretly to hear Robert Bruce, the avid follower of Andrew Melville, preach at Forgan church. The text was John 10:1, and Henderson was converted not only to Christ, but as reported, "He worshipped God and going away, reported that God was of a truth in whose ways were so opposite his own."[2] He was soon in the forefront of those who challenged the king.

Alexander Henderson is considered the chief architect of the National Covenant, the Magna Carta of Presbyterianism in Scotland. This battle cry of resistance and conviction was provoked by a series of riots caused by the forceful imposition of Laud's Liturgy. It all climaxed on Sunday, July 23, 1637, when the two archbishops and all of their retinue made their way in their robes to St. Giles Cathedral in Edinburgh. Then it was that Jenny Geddes, a poor woman who kept an herb stall, "flung her stool with a curse at the head of the Dean."[3] An uproar ensued.

The next year the National Covenant was presented and in the churchyard at Gray Friars sixty-thousand Scots gathered. Henderson prayed fervently and read the covenant, and it was subscribed with many tears and great resolve.[4] Subsequently elected moderator of the Church of Scotland, Henderson continued in his country parish until he was fifty-four. He then successively served Gray Friars Church and Great St. Giles.

Henderson led the Scottish delegation to the Westminster Assembly and drafted the Solemn League and Covenant. Never married, he was small of stature, had dark hair with a pointed beard, and was never robust in health.[5] Yet he was a stately soul of great personal piety. One convert from Leuchars said to him: "I love you, Sir, because I think you are a man in whom I see much of the image of Christ."[6]

His courage did not falter even in the face of the direst dangers. In 1638 he preached to the assembly in Glasgow from Psalm 110:1, a solemn sermon called "The Bishops' Doom," followed by the intonation of their excommunication. He dissolved the historic assembly with the words: "We have now cast down the walls of Jericho; let him that rebuildeth them beware of the curse of Hiel the Bethelite."[7] At this same assembly, as part of many nights in prayer, Henderson led the great duke of Argyll to Christ. The duke was Scotland's first citizen and never wavered in his support of the Covenanters.[8]

Henderson's preaching was clear and expository. Only three sermons were printed in his lifetime, but posthumously many sermons were published. Webber confirms that Henderson's sermons were in the style of the day and were clearly divided with subdivisions and sub-subs. Especially to be noted are his series from Hebrews 11 and on the different pieces of the whole armor of God.[9] That the infallible Scriptures had the defining word to speak is demonstrated in the skillful use of the applied texts, as when Henderson preached before the Lord General at Berwick on the Lord's Day, May 26, 1639. He used as his text Exodus 17, the fight of the Israelites with "Amalek's ungracious progeny." His courageous ministry in the Word assured him a niche in the annals of great biblical preaching in Scotland.

1. J. H. S. Burleigh, *A Church History of Scotland* (Oxford: Oxford University Press, 1960), 215.
2. Marcus L. Loane, *Makers of Religious Freedom in the Seventeenth Century* (Grand Rapids: Eerdmans, 1961), 21.
3. Ibid., 27.
4. Alexander Smellie, *Men of the Covenant* (London: Andrew Melrose, 1905). An exquisite volume of the most spiritually radiant and provocative vignettes.
5. Loane, *Makers of Religious Freedom in the Seventeenth Century*, 49.
6. Ibid., 50.
7. Ibid., 39.
8. Smellie, *Men of the Covenant*, 63.
9. F. R. Webber, *A History of Preaching in Britain and America* (Milwaukee: Northwestern, 1955), 2:79.

7.5.2 DAVID DICKSON—THE DEFENDER OF PRESBYTERIANISM

The Covenant of Grace. . . "a contract between God and men, procured by Christ upon these terms, that whosoever in the sense of their own sinfulness shall receive Christ Jesus offered in the Gospel shall have Him." . . . Grace is ordinarily bestowed by God by the preaching of the gospel, which is offered "indifferently to all hearers, that they may be tried, whether they pleased to receive the offer or not" . . . Grace is justly withheld from those who do not receive the offer, but is given by means of the condition of faith to the elect.

—David Dickson, *Therapeutica Sacra*

Standing squarely in the front ranks of post-Reformation leadership with Alexander Henderson is the redoubtable **David Dickson** (1583–1663). He was born in a wealthy merchant's family in Glasgow and took his M.A. at the University of Glasgow in 1610. Thereafter he served as a professor of philosophy in his alma mater. He was ordained and took the pastorate in Irvine in Ayrshire, where he served for twenty-three years and was affectionately known as Dickson of Irvine. Like Henderson, he drew from a wide geographic area, and "Yea, not a few came from distant places and settled at Irvine that they might be under the drop of his ministry."[1]

As early as 1622 Dickson was in the vanguard of those protesting oppression and served as a chaplain for the Covenanters' military. Ultimately he was summoned to be professor of theology at Glasgow for a decade and for another ten years at the University of Edinburgh in a similar capacity during difficult years of sharp confrontation. Intermittently suspended from his charge because of his stand, he did not give way, although he and Rutherford broke over strategization in the fray.

Dickson was moderator of the church the year following the great Glasgow Assembly (1638), which was held in Edinburgh. He kept company with the duke of Argyll on his last two nights before his execution. He was a gifted exegete and wrote commentaries on Hebrews, Matthew, the Psalms, and all of Paul's Epistles. He also coauthored with his student James Durham the noted *Sum of Sacred Knowledge,* and translated the beloved hymn "O Mother Dear, Jerusalem."

But it was as a preacher that Dickson was most remembered. An English merchant related that he had heard Robert Blair preach in Fife, and Rutherford and then Dickson in Irvine. He reported that Blair "showed me the majesty of God," and "a little fair man [Rutherford] showed me the loveliness of Christ. Then I came and heard at Irvine a well-favored proper old man, with a long beard, and that man showed me all my heart."[2]

Unlike most preachers of his day, who preached four or five sermons from a single verse, Dickson would take three or four verses in a sermon, saying that "God's bairns [children] should get a good portion of His own bread."[3] He discouraged the use of Greek and Hebrew words in sermons and opposed the affectation of spending the first half of the sermon demolishing false and fanciful interpretations.

Dickson preached to the conscience, and there was revival in power at Irvine and Stewarton under his ministry. Indeed, G. D. Henderson remarks that "the emotional revivalist of Stewarton is not utterly lost in the exegete of the Gospel according to Matthew."[4] To him there was no nobler calling than that of preaching. When he was elected to the chair of theology at Edinburgh, he commented, "The professor of divinity at Edinburgh is truly a great man, the professor of divinity at Glasgow is a still greater man, but the minister of Irvine was the greatest man of all."[5]

---

1. Duncan Anderson, *The Bible in Seventeenth Century Scottish Life and Literature* (London: Allenson, 1936), 95.

2. Alexander Smellie, *Men of the Covenant* (London: Andrew Melrose, 1905), 192.

3. F. R. Webber, *A History of Preaching in Britain and America* (Milwaukee: Northwestern, 1955), 2:83.

4. G. D. Henderson, *The Burning Bush: Studies in Scottish Church History* (Edinburgh: St. Andrew Press, 1957), 106.

5. T. Harwood Pattison, *The History of Christian Preaching* (Philadelphia: American Baptist Publication Society, 1903), 185.

7.5.3 Samuel Rutherford—Lover of Christ and Holiness

Fair Anwoth by the Solway,
To me thou art still dear!
E'en from the verge of Heaven
I drop for thee a tear.

Oh, if one soul from Anwoth
Meet me at God's right hand,
My Heaven will be two Heavens,
In Immanuel's land.

—Mrs. A. R. Cousin

Oh, if I might but speak to three or four herd-boys of my Master, I would be satisfied to be the meanest and most obscure of all the pastors this land, to live in any place, in any of Christ's outhouses.

—Samuel Rutherford

One of the most inspiring preachers in Scottish history is known to us through many biographers and through his amazing letters. We refer to **Samuel Rutherford** (1600–1661), born a gentleman's son near Nisbet in Roxburghshire. He was educated at Edinburgh, where he served as a tutor in Latin before being called as pastor in Anwoth, a small village in southwestern Scotland. John Welsh, son-in-law to John Knox, was an earlier incumbent in this parish. Here Rutherford preached and taught and visited and loved his people. He knew great personal sorrow at Anwoth in the death of his wife and two children.[1]

His publication of *Exercitationes Apologeticae pro Divina Gratia (An Apology for Divine Grace)* brought him censure and suspension. He did not return to Anwoth but moved on to a professorial chair at St. Andrews and then to be a main participant in the Westminster Assembly. He was a controversialist and polemicist of the first order. His antiroyalist *Rex Lex* was a bombshell that strained all of his relationships and got him into deep trouble. Even those who stood with him on most things rebuked him (including Oliver Cromwell and John Milton, the latter rebuking Rutherford in one of his sonnets).[2] In his last imprisonment after the Restoration, he repeated over and over the text, "Thy Word was found, and I did eat it, and it was to me the joy and rejoicing of my heart." He was martyred March 29, 1661.[3] His last words were reportedly, "Glory, glory, dwelleth in Immanuel's land."[4]

Through the Lowlands, Anwoth became the spiritual center for the whole of southwestern Scotland. The work started slowly for Rutherford; the sanctuary sat but 250 people. His beginning sermon was from John 9:39, "Jesus said, 'For judgment I have come into this world, so that the blind will see and those who see will become blind.'" Here Archbishop James Ussher visited him incognito, asking him how many Commandments there were. Discovering who his distinguished guest was, Rutherford asked him to preach on the Lord's Day, and he took as his text: "A new commandment I give to you, that you love one another."[5]

The glory of Rutherford's life and ministry must be seen as his constant "absorption in Christ," whom he worshiped as "the outset, the master-flower, the uncreated garland of heaven, the love and joy of men and angels."[6]

Alexander Whyte saw Rutherford as inspiring Scotland's best preaching for generations. His published *Quaint Sermons,* and his *Communion Sermons* (edited by A. A. Bonar) are passionate and poignant. "He hath neither brim nor bottom," Rutherford exclaimed of Christ. "Get love and no burden Christ will lay on you will be heavy."[7]

He could have had prestigious chairs in Dutch universities, but Rutherford felt the call in his homeland despite constant jeopardy. He saw himself as a Joshua sent ahead to spy the riches of the land and bring the news back to his persecuted brothers and sisters.

Rutherford was the spiritual father to Covenanters such as James Guthrie and his cousin William Guthrie. He was a staunch advocate of conventicles, "private men's liberty in public praying and expounding of Scripture."[8] Hungry saints would travel vast distances to a communion service where it was reported Rutherford would preach.[9]

His famous series of sermons on the names of Jesus Christ is especially memorable. "With a high-pitched voice, called in Scotland pulpit-skriech, and trembling with emotion, he would picture the beauties of the Rose of Sharon, the life-giving properties of the Bread of Life, the glory of the Bright and Morning Star, the fruitfulness of the Branch of Righteousness and the Root of Jesse, the invincibleness of the Lord of Hosts and the majesty of the King of Kings and the Lord of Lords."[10]

---

1. Warren W. Wiersbe, *Living with the Giants* (Grand Rapids: Baker, 1993), 13.
2. T. Harwood Pattison, *The History of Christian Preaching* (Philadelphia: American Baptist Publication Society, 1903), 185.
3. Alexander Smellie, *Men of the Covenant* (London: Andrew Melrose, 1905), 58.
4. Wiersbe, *Living with the Giants,* 17.
5. Marcus L. Loane, *Makers of Religious Liberty in the Seventeenth Century* (Grand Rapids: Eerdmans, 1961), 67.
6. Smellie, *Men of the Covenant,* 56. See Andrew A. Bonar, ed., *The Letters of Samuel Rutherford* (Edinburgh: Oliphant, Anderson, 1891).
7. Loane, *Makers of Religious Liberty in the Seventeenth Century,* 96.
8. G. D. Henderson, *The Burning Bush: Studies in Scottish Church History* (Edinburgh: St. Andrew, 1957), 58.
9. Duncan Anderson, *The Bible in Seventeenth Century Scottish Life and Literature* (London: Allenson, 1936), 91.
10. F. R. Webber, *A History of Preaching in Britain and America* (Milwaukee: Northwestern, 1955), 2:91.

7.5.4   John Livingstone—Seeker of the Lost

> I found that much study did not so much help me in preaching as getting
> my heart brought to a right disposition; yea, sometimes I thought that
> the hunger of the hearers helped more than my own preparation.
>
> —John Livingstone

> As I began to speak, the Holy Spirit came on them.
>
> —Acts 11:15a

The storms of persecution raged over the Scottish church during the seventeenth century. In many cases, "The flower of the clergy were driven from their charges."[1] The unremitting focus of preaching, however, remained "the great saving truths of the gospel."[2] Later critics faulted the lack of polish and ornament in this biblical preaching. They lambasted **James Renwick** (1662–1688) and other evangelicals for their fervor, their multiplied headings and involved subdivisions, their word pictures, and their allegorical biases.[3] But Renwick steadfastly preached the Word. He was executed in the Grassmarket in 1688.

Another firebrand was **John Livingstone** (1603–1672). Born in a minister's family in Stirlingshire, he was well-trained at Glasgow and St. Andrews. Although he was licensed to preach, he found it difficult to procure a charge of his own and went to Ireland, where he served briefly until his nonconformist views inclined him to go to America. Stormy seas caused the ship to return to port, and he served in Stranraer until called to Ancrum.[4]

Periodic revivals graced Livingstone's ministry. One particular sermon catapulted him to national prominence when at the age of twenty-seven he was asked to preach at Shotts. Young and unsure, he wandered in the fields until he "got good assistance." Braced with Ezekiel 36:25–26, he rose to preach to an immense throng.[5] His words "had the flame of the Holy Ghost glowing in them, and they conquered and captivated the souls of men."[6] After preaching for an hour and a half he was led to give an additional hour of tender exhortation and warning. The result was not fewer than five hundred men and women who "traced the dawn of their undying life," pressing forward to confess their sins and seek the Lord.

John Livingstone was a humble man whose spirit did not always please either his friends or his foes. Yet he appealed both to the upper class and the lower class. Deposed in the Restoration, he took exile in Rotterdam, where he developed his Orientalist gifts. Livingstone was skilled in Hebrew, Chaldee, Syriac, and Arabic, to say nothing of his abilities in French, Spanish, and Italian.[7] On his deathbed, his last words were, "I cannot say much of great services; yet if ever my heart was lifted up, it was in preaching of Jesus Christ."[8] He kept his charge and satisfied his God.

---

1. W. G. Blaikie, *The Preachers of Scotland: From the Sixth to the Nineteenth Century (The Cunningham Lectures)* (Edinburgh: T & T Clark, 1888), 155.

2. Ibid., 158.
3. Ann Matheson, *Theories of Rhetoric in the Eighteenth-Century Scottish Sermon* (Lewiston, N.Y.: Edward Mellon Press, 1995), 14.
4. F. R. Webber, *A History of Preaching in Britain and America* (Milwaukee: Northwestern, 1955), 2:92–93.
5. Ibid., 93.
6. Alexander Smellie, *Men of the Covenant* (London: Andrew Melrose, 1905), 99.
7. Webber, *A History of Preaching*, 2:94.
8. Smellie, *Men of the Covenant*, 104.

7.5.5 JAMES FRASER OF BRAE—UPHOLDER OF THE FREE GOSPEL

> The great object of all their sermons was the presentation of Jesus Christ and Him crucified. Nothing can exceed the pathos with which they besought their hearers to be reconciled to God and to endure patiently His cause . . .We do not claim for them the highest scholarship, the profoundest thought, the most polished style, or the finest eloquence, but we do claim for them that they preached Christ most effectively, and that they drew for themselves, and exhorted all their hearers to draw, their motives for their daily conduct from the cross of their Redeemer.
>
> —William M. Taylor in *The Scottish Pulpit*

James Fraser of Brae (1639–1699) stands among the field preachers, so-called because of their disenfranchisement amid the religious oppression. From a noble family and heir to vast estates, young Fraser studied law at Edinburgh before coming into a profound encounter with the Lord. His experience turned him to ministry. He began to expound the Scriptures but was condemned for it and imprisoned at Bass Rock. Described as "a huge mass of conglomerate rock rising from the waters of the North Sea," Bass Rock was a place of unbelievable misery.[1] In the winters the cells were filled with suffocating smoke. Yet Fraser continued to study Scripture and to teach from the black hole in which he was incarcerated. He also studied Greek and Hebrew, and wrote his famous *A Treatise on Justifying or Saving Faith*.

Thomas Hog (1628–1692), who had served near Dingwall, also languished at Bass Rock. He was a gifted preacher who spoke "with an unusual measure of life and power."[2] Hog spent his last years as pastor in Culross.

Alexander Whyte delivered twenty-eight lectures on Fraser, and termed his treatment of justification an evangelical classic. Fraser had access to an old book titled *Marrow of Modern Divinity*, which along with the writings of Samuel Rutherford and Thomas Shepard of New England markedly shaped his thinking. Fraser harked back to earlier Reformed views, and held that the assurance of salvation is inherent in saving faith. He believed that the gospel invitation could be given to all and that the unregenerate sinner has "a particular right to the promises of the gospel before closing with Christ."[3]

This stands in contrast to **Thomas Halyburton** (1674–1712), who did not feel any assurance could be held out to the sinner if he came.[4] Fraser was an advocate of the position we have previously described as preparation for grace, which holds that the preparatory work cannot be meritorious, since justification is by faith alone. His discussions anticipated the very important "Marrow controversy," which we shall consider in reviewing the next century. With only his Bible in his dungeon, Fraser concluded that the offer of grace is given to all persons impartially.

1. Alexander Smellie, *Men of the Covenant* (New York: Andrew Melrose, 1905), 390.
2. F. R. Webber, *A History of Preaching in Britain and America* (Milwaukee: Northwestern, 1955), 2:127.
3. David C. Lachman, *The Marrow Controversy 1718–1723* (Edinburgh: Rutherford House, 1988), 92. This is a Ph.D. dissertation done at St. Andrews University in Scotland.
4. Ibid., 121.

7.5.6 WILLIAM GUTHRIE—PREACHER IN THE FIELDS

In days of struggle a free pulpit was contended for as for dear life . . . a ministry free to utter the message of Christ was indispensable, and if it could not be enjoyed under the arches of the cathedral or the roof of the parish church, it must be sought in conventicles and chapels, or even among the mountains and moorlands, with sentinels all round to give warning of the dragoons.

—W. G. Blaikie

This is what we preach, and this is what you believed.

—1 Corinthians 15:11b

In the wake of the Restoration, the Glasgow Act of 1662 imposed the episcopacy upon Scotland and required all clergy to submit to bishops. Though they were ejected from their pulpits, more than four hundred clergy would not keep silent.[1] In some cases huge congregations would meet outdoors—in Fife on one day sixteen thousand people met for services.

Many preachers and laypersons were executed or sold as slaves. Among the field preachers and their honor roll of faith are such names as James Guthrie, Donald Cargill, Alexander Peden, and Richard Cameron (1648–1680). Out of the field preaching of Cargill and Cameron came the United Societies, or "the Cameronians," who, while never having many adherents, exerted an influence far greater than their numbers. By 1988 only five Cameronian congregations remain in Scotland (with about 150 members), but ties are maintained with the Reformed Presbyterian Church in Northern Ireland.

One of the inspirational founts of influence on the field preachers was the cousin of James Guthrie. "The little man who never bowed," **William Guthrie** (1620–1665), was the first pastor at Fenwick in Kilmarnock. The oldest son of landed gentry, he lived for a brief while in the ancestral castle but felt God's call and settled the estate on another brother in order that he might preach. He studied under Samuel Rutherford at St. Andrews and soon became a pacesetter in gospel causes, serving as moderator of the Protesting Synod of Glasgow and Ayr in 1654. Coming into a newly formed parish in which the people were steeped in ignorance and superstition, he saw literally thousands converted and confirmed. He was known as a man of extraordinary prayer and "the greatest practical preacher in Scotland."[2] He loved to fish and hunt and often turned these jaunts into innovative occasions of gospel proclamation. Though somewhat melancholy and sickly throughout his life, Guthrie would come in disguise to homes resistant to the gospel and spend the night. Once he stayed with a poacher who bragged he could earn half a crown on Sunday mornings when his neighbors were in church. Guthrie offered a half a crown if he would come to church. When he did, Guthrie led him to Christ. Crowds came to Fenwick, and of his ministry there it was said, "He had a strange way of persuading sinners to close with Christ, and answering all objections that might be proposed."[3]

His preaching was scriptural, delivered with great enthusiasm and vigor, and encased within a deeply satisfying sense of theological construct.[4] His well-known little book *The Christian's Great Interest* was prized by John Owen, who called it his *"vade mecum"* (a book carried as a constant companion). What Guthrie called "imperfect notes" of sermons were also sent forth under the title *A Clear Attractive Warning Beam of Light*. Blaikie quotes Kirkton's contemporary assessment of the church then:

> Every parish had a minister, every village had a school, every family almost had a Bible; yea, in most of the country, all the children at school could read the Scriptures, and were provided with Bibles either by their parents or ministers. Every minister was a very full professor of the Reformed religion, according to the large Confession of Faith framed at Westminster. None of them might be scandalous in their conversation, or negligent in their office, so long as a presbytery stood. I have lived many years in a parish where I never heard an oath; and you might have ridden many miles before you heard any. Also you could not, for a great part of the country have lodged in a family where the Lord was not worshipped by reading, singing and public prayer. Nobody complained more of our church-government than our taverners, whose ordinary lamentation was, that their trade was broke, people were too sober.[5]

When twelve soldiers came to depose him from his office, Guthrie's people were filled with sorrow and anger. He had preached the previous Wednesday after a great fast out of Hosea's mournful cry, "O Israel, thou hast destroyed thyself," but on the Lord's Day he took the softer word: "But in me is thine help."[6] Deprived of his parish pulpit, he preached on the grasses. Though he was not bitter, he was called from this life soon after at the age of forty-five.

---

1. F. R. Webber, *A History of Preaching in Britain and America* (Milwaukee: Northwestern, 1955), 2:107ff.

2. W. G. Blaikie, *The Preachers of Scotland from the Sixth to the Nineteenth Century* (Edinburgh: T & T Clark, 1888), 123.
3. Alexander Smellie, *Men of the Covenant* (London: Andrew Melrose, 1905), 123.
4. Blaikie, *The Preachers of Scotland,* 126.
5. Ibid.
6. Smellie, *Men of the Covenant,* 125.

7.5.7   ROBERT LEIGHTON—PEACEMAKER IN TURMOIL

Beautiful spirit! fallen alas!
On times when little beauty was;
Still seeking peace amidst the strife,
Still working, weary of thy life;
Toiling in holy love,
Panting for heaven above.

—Walter Smith

Amid the debilitating dissensions which tore the fabric of Scotland in the seventeenth century, there were godly men and women who retained loyalty to the episcopacy. The most striking of these was **Bishop Robert Leighton** (1611–1684). Among his circle of influence was the remarkable **Henry Scougal** (1650–1678), the son of a minister who became bishop of Aberdeen, and himself a close friend of Leighton. Young Henry entered Aberdeen at age fifteen and graduated to serve a church and return to Aberdeen as a professor. Scougal wrote *The Life of God in the Soul of Man.* This remarkable volume stressed union with Christ and greatly shaped the Wesleys and led Whitefield to Christ. Scougal died of consumption at the age of twenty-eight.[1]

Leighton, who was known as the "sweetest and saintliest of the Puritans," was born in a minister's home. His father had suffered greatly—his ears had been cropped, his nose had been slit, he had stood in the pillory, and he had been in jail.[2] The younger Leighton matriculated at Edinburgh, though he spent some time studying abroad where he was influenced by the Jansenists in France. He was irenic in temperament. After serving a large parish, he became principal at the University of Edinburgh and preached often in English and Latin to large and appreciative congregations. After the Restoration, he took a bishopric in hopes of effecting unity and understanding in his homeland, though he insisted on the smallest and most insignificant of the bishoprics. Ultimately he became the arch-bishop of Glasgow.

Leighton made a strong impression in the pulpit with his deeply spiritual pres-ence and his simple and direct preaching style. His magisterial commentary on 1 Peter is still used today. Bishop Burnett praised Leighton:

He had the great elevation of soul, the largest compass of knowledge, the most mortified and heavenly disposition I ever yet saw in a mortal; he had the greatest parts as well as virtue, with the most perfect humility that I ever saw in a man; and had a sublime strain in preaching, with so grave a gesture, and such a majesty both of thought, of language, and of pronunciation, that I never once saw a wandering eye when he preached, and have seen whole assemblies often melt into tears before him.[3]

Leighton opposed all persecution, yet he was seen as a wobbler by the Covenanters. Not all faithful preachers of the Word will see ecclesiastical issues exactly the same. Most rejected Leighton's efforts at accommodation. Perhaps he hated strife too much and too quickly sought to escape the cross of controversy. He found himself more and more at odds with several of his fellow bishops. When he retired, he spent the last decade of his life disengaged from the ecclesiastical scene. Even those who disagreed sharply with his position paid tribute to him as "attired in brightness like a man inspired" and a man "who seemed to be in a perpetual meditation."[4]

---

1. G. D. Henderson, *The Burning Bush: Studies in Scottish Church History* (Edinburgh: St. Andrew Press, 1957), 94ff.
2. T. Harwood Pattison, *A History of Christian Preaching* (Philadelphia: American Baptist Publication Society, 1903), 186.
3. Ibid., 187.
4. Alexander Smellie, *Men of the Covenant* (London: Andrew Melrose, 1905), 191.

7.6 THE DECLINE OF PURITANISM AND PURITAN PREACHING

The fatal error was that the "moderate" pulpit sought to accomplish these ends apart from the life-doctrine of Christianity—apart from its doctrine of salvation. The world was to be taken as it was, and made a friend of—it did not need to be first conquered to Christ. The Church was to bestow her blessing on all the forces and forms of culture around her, whatever might be the spirit in which they were carried on, and the objects at which they aimed.

—W. G. Blaikie

An indispensable aspect of the Puritan genius was the priority and quality of its biblical preaching. Few if any times in church history have exceeded it in terms of the impact and influence of its preaching. Yet undeniably Puritanism, though it leaves us with an impressive legacy, began to flag in the seventeenth century and with it the luster of its pulpit. While in the next century a new upsurge of preaching rolled over the British Isles and New England with ripple effects even in our own time, the Puritan hegemony would not be and could not be replicated.

What happened to weaken and waste Puritanism and the Puritan pulpit? We have no part with those who disparage Puritanism and its failures or give themselves to the endless vilification of Puritan ways, but in an age where we see the decline of preaching a careful analysis of the phenomenon of the Puritan decline is imperative.

1. *External and ideological factors.* The major paradigm shift in worldview called the Enlightenment beat heavily on theological orthodoxy as received down through the centuries. Orthodoxy was the apostolic core of doctrine transmitted across the centuries. Whatever ecclesiological differences may have existed, the supernatural gospel was recognized all but universally as true Christianity. Archbishop Leighton took a different trail in regard to the church but stood with orthodoxy in maintaining that justification means, "The sinner stands guiltless of any breach, yea, as having fulfilled the whole law."[1]

But now building on the humanistic impulses of the Renaissance and the "new science" of Copernicus and Isaac Newton, the Enlightenment is humankind's declaration of independence from God and the authority of His Word. Beginning in Britain with John Locke's attempt to bring all of Scripture within the bounds of human reason and with David Hume's empiricism, or the French "encyclopedists" and Voltaire and Rousseau, and on through Germany's Lessing and Herder and ultimately Immanuel Kant, this is to be the Age of Reason, secular life and existence and autonomous man.[2] Dogma and theology were undercut, and while in its earlier expressions Enlightenment thinking coexisted with religion, the later experience became bitter and acrimonious. The bottom line here is the systematic elimination of God from all of life. The Puritans ran head-on into this juggernaut.

We shall delve further into the effect of the Enlightenment and modernity upon preaching in the next chapter. Here we must cite an example of the deleterious effect of the rebellion against all authority—**Ralph Waldo Emerson** (1803–1882), the New England preacher, poet, and thinker. Not much is left of Emerson's Puritanism in the wake of his "modern disintegrative studies of the Bible."[3] Like Hawthorne, Melville, and Emily Dickinson, he broke with his past and Scottish common sense Realism and ultimately left the Unitarian ministry. Emerson built on the Schleiermachian legacy in which humanity is the starting point.[4] His second wife was a descendant of John Cotton, but that was about all that was left. His sermons were anthropological.[5] Puritanism and all of Christendom would never be the same.

2. *Historical and political factors.* The virtual identity of the medieval papacy as both spiritual and temporal ruler was on balance a negative. We can never underestimate the effects of human depravity. Both in England in Cromwell's Protectorate and in New England, church and state were hard to differentiate. The church is to be salt and light that infuses every sector of culture with spiritual tinge, but when the church becomes the government we lose the essential focus. The collapse of the Commonwealth, abruptly in England and gradually in New England, tended to have similar and extensive negative effect on both the ministry and the preaching of the Puritans. We are not Israel, as the Puritans sometimes forgot and as Dominion theologians and Reconstructionists also seem to forget in our time.

3. *Internal and spiritual factors.* Spiritual movements tend to expire because of their own excesses, as we shall be reminded again when we consider the great awakenings of the next century. The perpetuation of sound vitalities tends to be undermined by internal more often than external forces. Those Puritans we have called Sibbesian were accused of antinomianism but tended to emphasize the life

of the Spirit and tilted toward grace as over against law or works. Amesians like Bulkeley and Shepard triumphed in the antinomian controversy, and they tended to legalism. The result was a marked tendency toward moralism, and this is always a vapid futility for preaching.[6] The fixation on the Fourth Commandment and Sabbatarianism is proof of this. Nathaniel Mather came under the "great reproach of God" for whittling on a Sunday afternoon at the age of sixteen. Bunyan felt he could never be forgiven for playing "cat" after a Sabbath service.[7]

A further area of "hardening of the categories" is seen in the growing intolerance for any variation in views. We do not need to sacrifice an iota of conviction to allow for difference of opinion. The persecuted so soon become the persecutors. The whole Roger Williams episode is a case in point. Williams was banished from Massachusetts and founded Rhode Island where church and state were separate. He was the champion of the Indians as well as of freedom for Jews and Quakers. The Salem witchcraft trials are symptomatic of an unhealthy rigidity and turning inward. Missions seldom flourished in Puritanism (Alexander Duff who was born in 1806 was the first missionary sent out by the Church of Scotland), and evangelism waned.

Elliott-Binns argues that Puritanism was hard hit by "the loose morals which followed the Restoration" and the subsequent reaction against the Puritans, as well as by the "over-intellectualization which robbed Christianity of its life."[8] The Age of Reason found the Puritans exceedingly cerebral and rationalistic. The more whole-souled response to God is the best defense against massive intellectual assault by unbelief and skepticism. In this maelstrom of change and transition, not only Puritanism but also the preaching of Puritanism began a downward slide on the slippery slope. The next century would bring both solace and despair.

1. Happily quoted by D. Martyn Lloyd-Jones, *The Life of Peace: An Exposition of Philippians 3 and 4* (Grand Rapids: Baker, 1992). The Doctor did not often have good things to say about bishops.
2. Wilhelm Windelband, *A History of Philosophy* (New York: Harper Torchbooks, 1901, 1958), 2:437ff.
3. Robert D. Richardson Jr., *Emerson: The Mind on Fire* (Berkeley: University of California Press, 1995), 13–14.
4. Ibid., 98.
5. Wesley T. Mott, *The Strains of Eloquence: Emerson and His Sermons* (State College: Pennsylvania State University Press, 1990). This study documents Emerson's change in theology.
6. C. F. Allison, *The Rise of Moralism: The Proclamation of the Gospel from Hooker to Baxter* (London: SPCK, 1966).
7. Leland Ryken, *Worldly Saints: The Puritans as They Really Were* (Grand Rapids: Zondervan, 1986), 192.
8. L. E. Elliott-Binns, *The Early Evangelicals: A Religious and Social Study* (London: Lutterworth, 1953), 56.

CHAPTER EIGHT

Malaise and Revival: Preaching in the Eighteenth Century

Although I am less than the least of all God's people, this grace was given me: to preach to the Gentiles the unsearchable riches of Christ.

—Ephesians 3:8

Pray also for me, that whenever I open my mouth, words may be given me so that I will fearlessly make known the mystery of the gospel, for which I am an ambassador in chains. Pray that I may declare it fearlessly, as I should.

—Ephesians 6:19–20

And that you have already heard about in the word of truth, the gospel that has come to you. All over the world this gospel is bearing fruit and growing, just as it has been doing among you since the day you heard it and understood God's grace in all its truth.

—Colossians 1:5b–6

This is the gospel that you heard and that has been proclaimed to every creature under heaven, and of which I, Paul, have become a servant.

—Colossians 1:23b

And pray for us, too, that God may open a door for our message, so that we may proclaim the mystery of Christ, for which I am in chains. Pray that I may proclaim it clearly, as I should.

—Colossians 4:3–4

> Beware, beware, ye diminish not this office; for if ye do, ye decay God's power to all that do believe . . . we must be ready to hear God's holy word; we must have good affections to hear God's word; and we must be ready to make provision for the furtherance of the preaching of God's holy word, as far as we be able to do.
>
> —Hugh Latimer

> To preach is to open up the inspired text with such fruitfulness and sensitivity that God's voice is heard and God's people obey Him.
>
> —John R. W. Stott

For over a millennium and a half the absolute and infallible authority of the Bible was virtually uncontested in the church or in society. What Principal Rainy said of the Scottish church was true elsewhere: "Surely it is a striking thing that what so united the nation was a resolution that God's authority, discerned by themselves in His Word, that and nothing else, should set up institutions in their Church. That principle was written then on the fibre of the Scottish people in a manner that is legible yet."[1] Indeed both Protestants and Roman Catholics were in basic agreement on the inspiration of Scripture, as Professor Burtchaell observes:

> Despite a radical disagreement on these issues (i.e. the relationship of Scripture and tradition, etc.) both groups persevered in receiving the Bible as a compendium of inerrant oracles dictated by the Spirit. Only in the 19th century did a succession of empirical disciplines newly come of age begin to put a succession of inconvenient queries to the exegetes.[2]

Catholicism effectively lost her Bible as the uniquely inspired revelation from God when in the wake of the Council of Trent tradition assumed greater and greater significance. Protestantism began to lose her infallible Scripture in the face of the massive assault of unbelief and skepticism we speak of as "the Enlightenment" (or as the Germans call it, *Aufklarung*). This movement had its roots in Renaissance humanism and the stirrings of modern science. At first the challenge to authority was essentially philosophical. Sir Isaac Newton was a convinced theist who believed that God is the master mechanic of the universe.[3] Then the Scottish empiricist David Hume challenged the idea of first cause, and ultimately Immanuel Kant took God out of the sphere of knowledge as such.

What began in the British Isles became more radical in France and moved on to Germany, where Lessing argued that "accidental truths of history can never become the proof of necessary truths of reason." This is the "great broad ditch" which can never be transversed. The assertion of the primacy of human reason, the ultimacy of nature, and the relativity of all ethical premises soon confronted the church. If indeed "reason is the judge of all truth, even revelation,"[4] then we perceive a direct challenge to orthodox Christianity and all of her institutions, including preaching. The sixteenth century may have been "the century of genius," as Alfred North Whitehead insisted, but it spawned a corrosion of authority in the next century which we still feel.

The Enlightenment was hostile to Christian doctrine and authority.[5] The failures of the church along with Enlightenment preaching from the pulpit led to moral and ethical chaos. Hume's attack on miracles set up a life-and-death struggle for the church.

Discerning clergy and laity such as Edmund Burke fought against these poisonous philosophies.[6] Leibniz in Germany sought to save orthodoxy, but his Christianity was a modified one. For Leibniz, Christ's redemption had no real significance, and he totally lacked a doctrine of the Holy Spirit.[7] Enlightenment preaching took over in Germany,[8] going so far that one Christmas sermon was about stall feeding. "Christianity was watered down into nothing but ethics, instruction about how to lead an upstanding bourgeois life."[9]

In France the nucleus of the revolution was formed in Enlightenment thinking and the negation of the supernatural by intellectuals such as Voltaire. Principal **William Robertson** of Edinburgh (1721–1793) led the moderates' charge in Scotland and was supported by noted preachers such as **Hugh Blair** (1718–1800), whose elegant sermons were pure moralism. His platform was clear: "The end of all preaching is, to persuade men to be good."[10] It is a rhetoric of optimism:

> Of old, it was customary to preach upon controverted and mysterious points of divinity, but it is now hoped that the generality of the Clergy confine the subject of their preaching to what has a tendency to promote virtue and good morals, and to make a people peaceable and useful members of society.[11]

In England the preaching of **Archbishop Tillotson** (cf. 6.2.7) set the pace for neoclassical preaching and a glacial epoch which impeded dissent as well as the established church. The Arian blight, crass materialism, and moral decay were confronted by an impotent church whose preachers "let alone the mysterious points of religion, and preached to the people only good, plain, practical morality."[12] Paul Johnson shows how "the decline of clerical power in the eighteenth century" created a vacuum into which the secular intellectual stepped who really had nothing to say to the crying need of the hour.[13] Our task in this chapter is to show the faithfulness of a godly remnant in the time of a great malaise and the glorious visits of the Holy Spirit in revival preaching that reshaped history before the end of the century.

In a curious argument, David Bebbington asserts that the Enlightenment as such really started evangelicalism.[14] Doubtless it had both a positive and negative influence. But on balance the Enlightenment brought heavy losses to Christianity.

E. W. Hengstenberg (1802–1869) of Bonn became a rationalist under the impact of the Enlightenment. In fact he set forth the principles of rationalism for his university. The Lord touched his heart in a Moravian service through a simple Bible study, and he became a true follower of Christ. In his inaugural lecture as professor of Oriental languages at Berlin he stated:

It matters not whether we make a god out of stone or out of our own understanding, it is still a false god; there is but one living God, the God of the Bible.[15]

His last audible words were: "That is the nothingness of rationalism: the fundamental thing is Christ. . . . " And that is indeed the issue, the hinge of all history in time and in eternity.

---

1. Ninian Hill, *The Story of the Scottish Church from the Earliest Times* (Glasgow: James Maclehose, 1919), 164.
2. James Burtchaell, *Catholic Theories of Biblical Inspiration Since 1810: A Review and Critique* (Cambridge, Mass.: Cambridge University Press, 1969), 1–2.
3. Richard S. Westfall, *Never at Rest: A Biography of Isaac Newton* (Cambridge, Mass.: Cambridge University Press, 1980). This treatment is especially good on his religious crisis in 1662 and his Puritan cast. See also E. A. Burtt, *The Metaphysical Foundations of Modern Science* (Garden City, N.Y.: Doubleday/Anchor, 1954).
4. Kurt Aland, *A History of Christianity* (Philadelphia: Fortress, 1986), 2:272.
5. Crane Brinton, *Ideas and Men* (New York: Prentice-Hall, 1950). Brinton defines the Enlightenment as a cosmology which is "the belief that all human beings can attain here on this earth a state of perfection hitherto in the West thought to be only for Christians in a state of grace, and for them only after death" (2:113).
6. Russell Kirk, *The Conservative Mind from Burke to Santayana* (Chicago: Regnery, 1986); Russell Kirk, *Edmund Burke: A Genius Reconsidered* (Peru, Ill.: Sherwood Sugden, 1967, 1988), 128–91.
7. Aland, *A History of Christianity,* 2:283.
8. John Ker, *Lectures on the History of Preaching* (New York: Armstrong, 1889). Interestingly, Ker moves from the ossification of preaching in Protestant Scholasticism directly to the Enlightenment and "Illuminism," which he treats quite fully, lamenting its largely negative and destructive influence on German preaching.
9. Aland, *A History of Christianity,* 2:283, 291.
10. Ann Matheson, *Theories of Rhetoric in the Eighteenth-Century Scottish Sermon* (Lewiston, N.Y.: Edwin Mellen Press, 1995), 120.
11. Ibid., 143.
12. A. Skevington Wood, *The Inextinguishable Blaze: Spiritual Renewal and Advance in the Eighteenth Century* (Grand Rapids: Eerdmans, 1960), 7–25. For a similar sketch of the decomposition of morality and society in Hannoverian England, see L. E. Elliott-Binns, *The Early Evangelicals: A Religious and Social Study* (London: Lutterworth, 1953). He characterizes what passed for religion as "a savourless conception of religion." The debility of the Church of England was due to the death of Queen Anne—"a disaster"; the deistic controversy; the loss of the Puritans; the withdrawal of the nonjurors upon the accession of William and Mary; the decline and silencing of Convocation which hamstrung any response to the Methodists; more and more aristocratic bishops; the degenerate state of many local clergy-nonresident benefices.
13. Paul Johnson, *The Intellectuals* (New York: Harper and Row, 1988) quoted in E. Michael Jones, *Degenerate Moderns* (San Francisco: Ignatius, 1993), 14–15.

14. D. W. Bebbington, "Evangelical Christianity and the Enlightenment" in *Crux* (December 1989): 29ff. Bebbington, who is so insightful on many matters evangelical, disappoints on this and always in his lower view of inspiration and his bizarre notion that the Second Coming of Christ is no part of accepted doctrine; see his *Evangelicalism in Modern Britain* (London: Unwin Hyman, 1989), 87, 83.
15. Quoted in William Childs Robinson, "The Inspiration of Holy Scripture," *Christianity Today* (October 11, 1968): 6.

8.1 STANDING IN THE GAP

Why, Sir, you are to consider, that sermons make a considerable branch of English literature; so that a library must be very imperfect if it has not a numerous collection of sermons.

—Samuel Johnson

I read that Lady Yarmouth sold a bishopric to a clergyman for 5000 pounds. She betted him that he would be made a bishop and he lost, and paid her. As I peep into George II's St. James, I see crowds of cassocks rustling up the back stairs of the ladies of the court; stealthy clergy slipping purses into their laps; that godless old king yawning under his canopy in the chapel royal as the chaplain before him is discoursing. Whilst the chaplain is preaching the king is chattering in German almost as loud as the preacher; so loud that the clergyman actually burst out crying in his pulpit because the defender of the faith and dispenser of bishoprics wouldn't listen to him. No wonder that skeptics multiplied. No wonder that clergy were corrupt . . . No wonder that Whitefield cried out in the wilderness, that Wesley quitted the insulted temple to pray on the hillside.

—William Makepeace Thackeray

Preach the Word; be prepared in season and out of season.

—2 Timothy 4:2a

Pithy in utterance, eloquent in style, **Robert South** was an English preacher who represented conformity to rather than correction of the dangerous drift to *latitudinarianism*—the broad church commitment to pluriformity and, most often, doctrinal indifference. **Bishop Joseph Butler** of Durham (1692–1752), on the other hand, took up the cudgel against deism and unbelief with a vengeance. Born into a merchant's Presbyterian home, Butler chose the established church while in a brilliant academic career at Oxford. In the solitude of Stanhope, an isolated country parish, he wrote his famous *Analogy of Natural and Revealed Religion* and his *Fifteen Discourses*.[1]

Joseph Addison wrote of the English spirituality of the time that there was "less appearance of religion than in any neighboring state or kingdom whether it be Protestant or Catholic." Montesquieu said of France that "the subject of religion if mentioned in society excited nothing but laughter."[2] John Caird described the Georgian sermon as "having been constructed almost expressly to steer clear of all possible ways of getting human beings to listen to it."[3] Samuel Wesley's curate at Epworth had an absorbing theme in his preaching—the necessity of making a will. Moralism and politics dominated preaching as the Word of God slipped from prominence. Only a little flock treasured the spiritual patrimony. We want to look at them quite closely, particularly in England and Scotland.

---

1. Even William E. H. Lecky pays tribute to Bishop Butler for his analysis of moral judgments and his definition of conscience; see *History of European Morals* (New York: D. Appleton, 1877, 1913), 1:20–21, 32, 76, 83.
2. T. Harwood Pattison, *The History of Christian Preaching* (Philadelphia: American Baptist Publication Society, 1903), 247.
3. Ibid., 248.

8.1.1 PHILIP DODDRIDGE—PREACHING WITH CONVICTION

Some sense of sin, and some serious and humbling apprehension of our danger and misery in consequence of it, must need be necessary to dispose us to receive the grace of the Gospel, and the Saviour who is there exhibited to our faith.

What then is to be done? Is the convinced sinner to lie down in despair? to say, "I am a helpless captive, and by exerting myself with violence, may break my limbs sooner than my bonds, and increase the evil I would remove." God forbid! You cannot, I am persuaded, be so little acquainted with Christianity, as not to know, that the doctrine of divine assistance bears a considerable part in it . . . you have heard of "doing all things through Christ who strengtheneth us," (Philippians 4:15) whose grace "is sufficient for us," and "whose strength is made perfect in weakness" (2 Corinthians 12:9). Permit me, therefore, now to call your attention to this, as a truth of the clearest evidence, and of the utmost importance.
　　　　　　　　　　　　　　　　　　　　　　　　　　　—Philip Doddridge

Indeed we have come to days "when Puritanism walked in shadows, spoke in whispers." Horton has drilled to the core when he observes: "Puritans began to lose their central focus—the gospel of grace—and allowed their reformist impulse to create a salvation by personal and social improvement, Christianity became the social glue: urbane, civil and less concerned with theology."[1] Yet some stood firm and valiantly.

One such champion was from among the independents (the Congregational-Presbyterian), **Philip Doddridge** (1702–1751). Born in London the youngest of twenty children, he was actually laid aside as stillborn. Only he and one sister survived, and they were orphaned when he was thirteen. The Duchess of Bedford offered to send him to Oxford or Cambridge if he would stay in the Church of England, but he declined. Friends helped him to enter a Dissenters' Academy at

Kibworth near Leicester, where he taught as well. He began to preach at twenty, and at twenty-seven he was called to the important Congregational church in Northampton, where he ministered for twenty-two years. Although he had met the Lord at sixteen it was only under the stirring appeals of Baxter that bona fide communion with God became a reality.[2] He transferred the academy to Northampton, where over the years he trained more than two hundred young preachers. We still have his "Lectures on Preaching" from these early years.

His biographers generally concede that while of ready and fervent speech, he did not "climb the Alps" in his preaching. He did have an eminent gift of prayer.[3] Moderately Calvinistic, he stressed the urgent necessity of preaching Christ. His best-known book, *The Rise and Progress of Religion in the Soul,* is an earnest outpouring to sinners with the grand object of getting them to the cross of Christ. One sensed in his preaching "quite a rush of love toward God and Christ." He longed for revival and quickening and believed that it would come.

Doddridge was deeply committed to the mastery of Latin, Hebrew, and Greek (and a knowledge of shorthand) for all ministers. One of his contemporaries described him as "not handsome in person; very thin and slender, in stature somewhat above the middle size, with a stoop in his shoulders; but when engaged in conversation or employed in the pulpit, there was a remarkable sprightliness in his countenance and manner, which commanded general attention." One of his students said of his preaching:

> His favorite topics of public discourse were the distinguishing doctrines of Christianity. He considered himself as a minister of the Gospel, and therefore could not satisfy himself without preaching Christ and Him crucified. He never puzzled his hearers with dry criticisms and abstruse disquisitions; nor contented himself with moral essays and philosophical harangues. He thought it cruelty to God's children to give them stones when they came for bread.[4]

He wrote many hymns, of which we have 374, most of them as conclusions to sermons he preached. Such rich favorites persist among us as "Awake, My Soul, Stretch Every Nerve," "O Happy Day that Fixed My Choice," "See Israel's Gentle Shepherd Stand," "Great God We Sing that Mighty Hand," and "My God and Is Thy Table Spread." He also published *Family Expositor,* a paraphrase and commentary on the New Testament which was widely used. Never strong in body, Doddridge began to fail and sought rest and recovery in Lisbon, where he died at the age of forty-nine. Doddridge's faithful heralding of Christ and the Cross in his methodical and orderly style touched many in his own lifetime and down to our own.[5]

---

1. Michael Scott Horton, *Made in America* (Grand Rapids: Baker, 1991), 20.

2. T. Harwood Pattison, *The History of Christian Preaching* (Philadelphia: American Baptist Publication Society, 1903), 254.

3. John Stoughton, *Life of Philip Doddridge* (London: Jackson and Walford, 1851).

4. F. R. Webber, *A History of Preaching in Britain and America* (Milwaukee: Northwestern, 1952), 1:315.
5. Philip Doddridge, *The Rise and Progress of Religion in the Soul* (Grand Rapids: Baker, 1977), 72. Here is the "gospel which I preach and proclaim." He brings his hearers right to the crucified One.

8.1.2   MATTHEW HENRY—PREACHING WITH CONTENT

> Though the people at Chester are a most loving people, and many of them have had and have an exceeding value for me and my ministry, yet I have not been without discouragements there and those such as have tempted me to think my work in that place has been in large done. Many that have been catechized with us and many that have been long communicants with us have left us and very few have been added to us.
>
> —Matthew Henry

The terrain was rough and the grade steep even for such a gifted preacher as **Matthew Henry** (1662–1714). Born into a godly minister's home (cf. 7.3.2.6), he was inclined toward the ministry and Zion's way from an early age. He was converted under the preaching of his father before his eleventh year[1] and began to imitate preaching. He was well into Latin and Greek verses even earlier and studied at Dr. Doolittle's Academy in Islington. Nonconformists (those who communed outside of the established church, the Church of England) were not admitted to Oxford or Cambridge at this time. He heard **Edward Stillingfleet** and **Tillotson** preach but was not drawn to the established church. He studied for the law at Gray's Inn but was not diverted from his call "to make known the mystery of Christ."[2]

["Mercies received" was his testimony] Henry was ordained a nonconformist and shared his dedication as he commenced his ministry in the independent church in the charming, old walled city of Chester in the west of England near Wales:

> I purpose and resolve that, by the grace of God, I will abound more than ever in all manner of gospel obedience; that I will strive to be more humble, serious and watchful and self-denying, and live more above the world and the things of it; that I will pray with more life, and read the scriptures with more care, and not be slothful in business, but fervent in spirit, serving the Lord; that I will abound in good discourse, as I have ability and opportunity with prudence; endeavoring as much as I can "to adorn the doctrine of God my Saviour in all things."[3]

Matthew Henry knew much personal sorrow and ill-health, losing his first wife and several children in death. He was known for his unremitting preparation for preaching (in his study at 4 or 5 A.M. each day) and for his fervency in the pulpit. He was influenced early on by contacts both with Baxter in prison and by hearing John Howe (cf. 7.3.2.6). He usually preached seven times a week. His Sabbath (Sunday) morning service began at 9 A.M. with the singing of Psalm 100, brief prayer, exegetical findings from an Old Testament passage, singing another psalm, and praying for half an hour. Then came the one hour sermon from the text, followed by more prayer and then singing and the benediction. An afternoon and evening service followed. On Thursday there was always a Bible lecture. Known among his flock of about 350 for his frequent pastoral calls, he nonetheless studied deeply and thoroughly. As his biographer comments, "He then invariably conducted them to Calvary."[4]

Beyond his own congregation, Henry ministered regularly in the jails and in villages around Chester. Unlike some, such as **William Greenhill** (1571–1677), who spent almost a lifetime of preaching in Ezekiel, Henry took a variety of texts from all parts of the Bible. He would stick assiduously with the announced text and masterfully use biblical allusions to great effect.[5] He would spend Saturday afternoons catechizing in the manner of Richard Baxter. A new meeting house was built on Crook Lane in the course of the twenty-five years he ministered in Chester. Out of this rigorous study and the hundreds of sermons he preached has come of course his justly renowned devotional commentary, which he finished through Acts (and which various associates completed after his passing).

Still in print and influential, Matthew Henry's commentary is a good sample of his preaching and lecturing ministry. Spurgeon used to read it through regularly on his knees. His "expositions" were endorsed by Doddridge and Watts in his lifetime, by William Romaine and George Whitefield and by **Dr. Adam Clark,** who attributes his own commentary to the stimulus of Matthew Henry. His object in the "expositions" was "to give the sense, and cause men to understand the reading."[6] His is a more mild Calvinism, insisting on "faith" as a condition[7] (although not a meritorious work) and strong for inviting "all people to him."[8] Perhaps alliteration was overdone and there is some "quaintness" in application occasionally, but this is exceedingly rich fare. The subjects and series he preached during his time in Chester provided nourishment for his people and pointed to the way of salvation for the unsaved.[9]

At last he left Chester and took the call to serve a congregation of about one hundred people at Hackney. By this time he was showing severe symptoms of diabetes (frequent nephritical attacks). On his return to Hackney from a taxing ministry, he was thrown from his horse. He tried to preach once more but died a day later on June 22, 1714, at the age of fifty-two, leaving his second wife and seven children. What a beautiful ministry in a dry and difficult time! I never fail to be blessed by something in Matthew Henry. Recently in preaching from John 14:27 on Jesus' last will and testament, I began with Henry's description: When Jesus died he left his spirit with the Father, his body with Joseph of Arimathea, his garments with the soldiers, his mother with the apostle John—and he left us peace, his peace!

---

1. J. B. Williams, *Memoirs of the Life, Character and Writings of the Rev. Matthew Henry* (Edinburgh: Banner of Truth, 1828, 1974), 5.

2. Ibid., 31.

3. Ibid., 42.

4. Ibid., 121.
5. Ibid., 123.
6. Ibid., 251.
7. Ibid., 241.
8. Ibid., 244.
9. Ibid., 274.

8.1.3 ISAAC WATTS—PREACHING WITH CLARITY

> In Bach's sacred music . . . he wanted others to praise God with him . . .
> if so, he was to that extent a preacher as well as an artist.
> —Professor Garry Wills in *Certain Trumpets*

> To the law and to the testimony! If they do not speak according to this
> word, they have no light of dawn.
> —Isaiah 8:20

While **Isaac Watts** (1674–1748) can properly be called "the inventor of hymns in the English language" and "the father of the English hymn," he was also a preacher of distinctive gifts and influence. Up to this time mainly psalms were sung (and among Puritans, *only* psalms were sung—no organs, choirs, or stained glass). Watts was born in Southampton to a staunchly nonconformist family. His father was a schoolmaster and a deacon in Above Bar Congregational Church and knew time in prison because of his religious stand.

The oldest of eight children, Watts began to learn Latin at the age of four, Greek at nine, French at ten, and Hebrew at thirteen.[1] He enrolled at Thomas Rowe's Academy near London, a one-man institution of higher learning led by a minister ejected for his nonconformity. Watts was a genius with a flair for organizing and condensing vast amounts of learning.

He wrote his first hymn, "Behold the Glories of the Lamb," when his father urged him to do something positive rather than find fault with the "lifeless psalm-singing" of his day. His Scripture-based hymns were the substance of his *Horae Lyricae* and other collections of his work. While tutoring, he wrote many hymns including such classics as "O God Our Help in Ages Past," "Joy to the World," "Come Holy Spirit, Heavenly Dove," "Alas! and Did My Savior Bleed," "Jesus Shall Reign," "Am I a Soldier of the Cross," and "When I Survey the Wondrous Cross," which some call the most perfect hymn ever written in the English language. He also wrote books on logic which attracted the attention of Dr. Samuel Johnson. In 1702 he became pastor of Mark Lane Congregation in London where John Owen had once served. Never married and only five feet tall, Watts was never very well, yet God blessed the ministry of the Word at Mark Lane, and the congregation increased from sixty to four hundred. Watts believed the preacher should make his message clear to the simple as well as convincing to the learned. Above all, the preacher should never forget the essential question for his hearers: "What must I do to be saved?"

Struck by a terrible fever in 1712, Isaac Watts took four years to make a partial recovery. During that time he was offered hospitality by the former Lord Mayor of London, Sir Thomas Abner. He stayed there for thirty-six years, continuing as pastor of Mark Lane until his death at the age of seventy-five. His reputation grew during these years, and he became "London's most important nonconformist minister."[3] Two Scottish universities gave Watts honorary doctorates; he handled his finances well; he enjoyed close correspondence with Zinzendorf, Cotton Mather, and Jonathan Edwards. He wrote *Divine Songs for Children* in 1715. In all he published fifty-five books and wrote more than six hundred hymns.

Watts' preaching was intense but not florid. One delightful collection of his sermons, *The World to Come,* treats "the glories of the resurrection for the saved and the sorrows of eternity without Christ for the lost." Discourse 12 on "The Nature of the Punishments of Hell" is indeed somber. Discourse 13 on "The Eternal Duration of the Punishments of Hell" is solidly scriptural in its argument. Discourse 4 is an especially charming message based on 2 Thessalonians 1:10, "Christ Admired and Glorified in His Saints." His main points are to show the reasons for the admiration and glorification of Christ in his saints.

    I. That persons of all characters should have been united in one, and persuaded to believe in the same Savior and embrace the same salvation.
    II. That so many wicked obstinate wills of men and so many perverse affections should bow down and submit themselves to the holy rules of the gospel.
    III. That so many thousand guilty wretches should be made righteous by one righteousness, cleansed in one laver from all their iniquities, and sprinkled unto pardon and sanctification, with the blood of one man, Jesus Christ.
    IV. That a company of such feeble Christians should maintain their course to heaven, through so many thousand obstacles.
    V. That so many dark and dreadful providences were working together in mercy, for the good of all the saints.
    VI. That heaven should be so well filled out of such a hell of sin and misery as this world is.
    VII. That so many vigorous, beautiful and immortal bodies should be raised at once out of the dust, with their old infirmities left behind them.
    VIII. That the saints shall all appear in that day, as so many images of his person and as so many monuments of the success of his office.

Then, as per the custom of the Puritan preachers, he follows the basic thought development with an impressive series of uses which he divides under five heads.[4] This is more like the inverted pyramid style of Donald Grey Barnhouse and D. Martyn Lloyd-Jones in our time, with the preacher using a small piece of text to supply the theme and then drawing upon the full range of scriptural revelation for the construction of the body of the sermon. Watts' preaching and correspondence suggest how he decried the decay of nonconformity in England and how he longed for a quickening. It was he and **John Guyse** of Hertford who first published Jonathan Edwards' narrative of revival in Northampton.[5] In the meantime, from his deathbed Samuel Wesley laid his hands on Charles and said that God would again visit the land. "I shall not see it, my son," said the elder Wesley, "but you will."[6]

---

1. S. Maxwell Coder, "Biographical Sketch of Dr. Isaac Watts," in Isaac Watts, *The World to Come* (Chicago: Moody, 1954), 18.
2. Ibid., 24.
3. Ibid., 26.
4. Ibid., "Christ Admired and Glorified in His Saints," 160–85.
5. A. Skevington Wood, *The Inextinguishable Blaze: Spiritual Renewal and Advance in the Eighteenth Century* (Grand Rapids: Eerdmans, 1960), 61–62.
6. T. Harwood Pattison, *The History of Christian Preaching* (Philadelphia: American Baptist Publication Society, 1903), 255.

8.1.4 JOHN NEWTON—PREACHING FOR CONVERSION

I am ashamed that I have done and suffered so little for Him that hath done and suffered so much for ill and hell-deserving me.

The more I looked at what Jesus had done on the cross, the more He met my case exactly. I needed someone or something to stand between a righteous God and my sinful self: between a God who must punish sins and blasphemies and myself, who had wallowed in both to the neck. I needed an Almighty Saviour who should step in and take my sins away, and I found such a one in the New Testament . . . I saw that because of the obedience and sufferings of Jesus, God might declare His justice, in punishing my sin, and declare His mercy also, in taking that punishment on Himself on the Cross, so that I might be pardoned.

—John Newton

So spiritually bleak were the times that the famous jurist Blackstone reported that he had visited church after church in London and "did not hear a single discourse which had more Christianity in it than the writing of Cicero." William Jay of Bath observed that "The Establishment was asleep in the dark and the Dissenters were asleep in the light." William Cowper depicted "the fashionable preacher of a city congregation" thusly:

> Behold the picture! Is it like? Like whom?
> The things that mount the rostrum with a skip
> And then skip down again, pronounce a text,
> Cry "Hem!" and reading what they never wrote
> Just fifteen minutes, huddle up their work,
> And with a well-bred whisper close the scene.[1]

"Holding forth the Word of Life" for twenty-eight years in London in this stygian darkness was **John Newton** (1725–1807), who like Doddridge and Watts before him was an accomplished hymnwriter as well as a preacher. His father was a Jesuit-trained seaman and his mother a dissenter. He was reared on Scripture, the catechism, the hymns of Isaac Watts, and the preaching of Dr. David Jennings of the Congregational church at New Stairs, Wapping. He learned from his dear mother that "the third mark of profaneness is to make jest of the Word of God, or preaching or prayer, or any part of true religion."[2] With his mother dead, he spent ten years at sea, enduring flogging and imprisonment before he took up slave trading.[3] Yet during this time he read the Scriptures and Thomas à Kempis. The Book of Proverbs particularly reproved him for his ungodly and wicked lifestyle.

During a fierce storm he yielded to Christ,[4] but still he plied the slave trade and was ultimately made surveyor of tides in Liverpool. Here he came under the influence of both Wesley and Whitefield as well as William Grimshaw, and married his beloved Mary while preparing for the ministry. Through the influence of the evangelical Lord Dartmouth, he was ordained and appointed to his first parish charge in Olney where he labored for sixteen years. Here he preached, wrote hymns, and collected the famous Olney Hymns, among them his own "Amazing Grace," "Glorious Things of Thee Are Spoken," "How Sweet the Name of Jesus Sounds," and "Safely Through Another Week." Here also he developed his friendship with that most peculiar curious Christian brother, **William Cowper** (1731–1800). Tillotson's moralistic preaching could not help Cowper, but Newton's plainer and more direct Christ-centered discourse deeply touched him. He wrote:

> The Spirit breathes upon the Word, and brings the truth to sight;
> Precepts and promises afford a sanctifying light.
> A glory gilds the sacred page, majestic like the sun;
> It gives a light to ev'ry page, It gives, but borrows none.

Cowper's bouts with mental illness and his relationship with Mrs. Unwin are long stories in themselves.[5]

Newton's first preaching was done shyly, as he quickly read his sermon manuscripts. Then he learned the value of eye contact. He was a small, quiet-voiced man, yet with a delightful sense of humor. He offered Sunday dinner to those who had come more than six miles to church. His warm and caring sermons were characterized by a clear organizational principle and were filled Scripture-filled.[6] His most famous preaching was a series of fifty sermons on the Scripture texts that were the basis of Handel's *Messiah*. Complementing his ministry was his extraordinary dedication to letterwriting.[7]

An avowed Calvinist, Newton nonetheless eschewed high Calvinism. Having become the real leader of evangelical forces in England, he was invited to become the pastor of St. Mary Woolnoth, where he served for twenty-seven years.

Newton built St. Mary Woolnoth to be the most significant ministry in London at the time. His preaching attracted the Lord Mayor of London. He preached an evangelistic crusade in Portsmouth every year for his holiday and helped establish the London Missionary Society. He and Mary had a beautiful marriage. His broad friendships and influence extended to young William Wilberforce, Hannah More, Charles Simeon, and to dissenters like William Jay, who visited often. Jay reports in his memoirs that Newton's study was in the attic of his home. Written above it were these words: "Remember that thou wast a bondman in the land of Egypt."[8]

Wilberforce records his impressions of the old man:

> Called upon Old Newton—was much affected in conversing with him— something very pleasing and unaffected in him . . . on the whole he en- couraged me—though got nothing new from him, as how could I, except a good hint. That he never found it answer to dispute . . . when I came away I found my mind in a calm, tranquil state, more humbled, and look- ing more devoutly to God.[9]

In advanced age, Newton became deaf and almost blind. In his last sermon he forgot where he was, and a curate had to come up and tell him. He said, "My memory is almost gone; but I remember two things: that I am a great sinner and that Christ is a great Saviour." His authentic experience of God's saving grace gave his preaching and his ministry an intrinsic credibility under God. The heart of it is clear by his own words:

> The union of a believer with Christ is so intimate, so unalterable, so rich in privilege, so powerful in influence that it cannot be fully represented by any earthly simile. The Lord, by His Spirit, showed and confirmed His love and made Himself known as He met me at the throne of Grace . . . . Wonderful are the effects when a crucified, glorious Saviour is pre- sented by the power of the Spirit, in the light of the Word, to the eye of faith.

---

1. Quoted from T. Harwood Pattison, *History of Christian Preaching* (Philadelphia: American Baptist Publication Society, 1903), 247–48.
2. Bernard Martin, *An Ancient Mariner: A Biography of John Newton* (New York: Abingdon, 1950), 11.
3. John Pollock, *Amazing Grace: The Dramatic Life Story of John Newton* (San Fran- cisco: Harper, 1981), 63.
4. Martin, *An Ancient Mariner,* 52.
5. For a magnificent new study, see George M. Ella, *William Cowper: Poet of Paradise* (Durham, N.C.: Evangelical Press, 1993); also Hugh l'Anson Fausett, *William Cowper* (New York: Harcourt, Brace, n.d.).
6. David Lyle Jeffrey, ed., *A Burning and Shining Light: English Spirituality in the Age of Wesley* (Grand Rapids: Eerdmans, 1987), 393ff.
7. See his famous *Cardiphonia* (1787).
8. *The Autobiography of William Jay* (Edinburgh: Banner of Truth, 1854, 1974), 237.
9. Martin, *An Ancient Mariner,* 205.

8.1.5 THOMAS BOSTON—PREACHING WITH COURAGE

> But yet seeing I am called out to preach this everlasting gospel, it is my duty to endeavor, and it is my desire to be (Lord, thou knowest) a fisher of men. But, alas! I may come in with my complaints to my Lord, that I have toiled in some measure, but caught nothing, for anything I know, as to the conversion of any one soul. I fear I may say, I have almost spent my strength in vain, and my labor for nought, for Israel is not gathered. O my soul, what may be the cause of this, why does my preaching so little good? No doubt part of the blame lies on myself, and a great part of it too. But who can give help and in this case but the Lord himself? and how can I expect it from him but by prayer and faith in the promises and by consulting his word where I may by his Spirit shining on my heart (shine, O Sun of righteousness), learn how to carry, and what to do, to the end the gospel preached by me may not be unsuccessful?
>
> —Thomas Boston

The developing theological polarity in the Scottish church began with the decline of spiritual life, moved on to loose theology and conformity to the world, and then inevitably to "cold, passionless preaching."[1] At first evangelical truth was more ignored than opposed, as Blaikie shows in his classic analysis. The old supernatural gospel passed away in many stylish circles in which Thomas Boston's book *Human Nature in Its Fourfold State* (1720) was pilloried as "severe and reactive dogmatism."[2] The increasingly secular sermons of the moderates did nothing to dent the growing strength of deism; indeed, "moderate preaching did not arrest its spread even among the clergy."[3] One of Blair's staunch defenders says of his approach, "Blair made little use of supporting biblical evidence. He derived his proofs from the common experience of man, and the Bible provided a secondary source by which to confirm them."[4]

At the forefront of "the twelve apostles" who led the biblical cause and who were all ostracized by the General Assembly was **Thomas Boston** (1676–1732). He was born in Berwickshire. As a boy, he often sat outside the prison where his nonconformist father was incarcerated. He was converted under the preaching of the godly **Henry Erskine** (1624–1696), whose texts on that occasion were John 1:29 and Matthew 3:7. Boston recalled them: "By these, I judge, God spoke to me. My lost state by nature and my absolute need of Christ, being thus discovered to me, I was set to pray in earnest."[5] He was "touched quickly" by this preaching and at great sacrifice studied at Edinburgh. After a brief stint as a tutor, he took the pastoral charge at Simprin, where he stayed for eight years, and then on to Ettrick in Selkirkshire, where he ministered with great distinction until his death. He was "staked at Ettrick," as he put it, even though he might well have moved to something far more prestigious.

While ministering to the ninety souls at Simprin, he discovered the old English Puritan work, *Marrow of Modern Divinity,* in the home of one of his members. Flying in the face of official opposition, Boston and his circle began to preach universal grace.

Believing the Gospel offer was for all, that to mankind as sinners the call and overture of divine are to be addressed, the moderate Calvinists of the eighteenth century were animated and dominated by the missionary spirit of Christianity.[6]

The "Marrow-men," as they were called, used Preston's phrase as their watchword, "Go and tell every Man without exception, that there's good news for him, Christ is dead for him."[7] This is what Boston called "the authentick gospel offer."[8]

Boston was a gifted linguist and expert on Hebrew accents, but not a particularly skilled orator. His illustrations were homely, his sermons richly theological, thoroughly biblical, and sensitive. His *Soliloquy on the Art of Man-Fishing* was a masterpiece of passionate discourse.[9] He was a master of variety and the vivid. John "Rabbi" Duncan called him "a genius of the commonplace." When he preached on vital union with Christ, his outline was (1) a spiritual union; (2) a real union; (3) a close and intimate union; (4) though not merely a legal union, it is yet a union supported by law; (5) an indissoluble union; (6) a mysterious union.[10] Davidson of Braintree said of his preaching, "He was indeed one of the most powerful preachers of the Gospel I ever heard open a mouth."

---

1. W. G. Blaikie, *The Preachers of Scotland from the Sixth to the Nineteenth Century* (Edinburgh: T & T Clark, 1888), 216.
2. Ibid., 222.
3. Ibid., 240.
4. F. R. Webber, *A History of Preaching in Britain and America* (Milwaukee: Northwestern, 1955), 2:124.
5. Ibid.
6. A. E. Garvie, *The Christian Preacher* (New York: Scribner's, 1923), 168.
7. David C. Lachman, *The Marrow Controversy 1718–1723* (Edinburgh: Rutherford House, 1988), 204.
8. Ibid., 448.
9. Thomas Boston, *The Art of Man-Fishing* (Grand Rapids: Baker, 1977).
10. Blaikie, *The Preachers of Scotland,* 202.

8.1.6   EBENEZER AND RALPH ERSKINE—PREACHING WITHOUT COMPROMISE

An age of cold and feeble rationality, when evangelism was derided as fanatical and its very phraseology was deemed an ignoble and vulgar thing in the upper classes of society. A morality without goodness, a certain prettiness of sentiment, served up in tasteful and well-turned periods of composition, the ethics of philosophy or the academic chair rather than the ethics of the Gospel—the speculations of natural theology and perhaps an ingenious and scholar-like exposition of the credentials rather than a faithful exposition of the contents of the New Testament—these for a time dispossessed the topics of other days, and occupied that room in our pulpits which had formerly been given to the demonstrations of sin and the Saviour.

—Thomas Chalmers

The Marrow Controversy over the gospel (particularly as it focused on the heresy charges against Professor Simson) had its ecclesiological implications. Two gifted brothers were in the vanguard in the forming of the secession church, or the first Associate Reformed Presbytery, the sons of Henry Erskine, **Ebenezer Erskine** (1680–1754) and **Ralph Erskine** (1685–1752). Both were educated at Edinburgh with Ebenezer serving at Portmoak in Fife and then at Stirling, while Ralph spent his entire ministry in Dumfermline. Ralph came first into vital experience with Christ and Ebenezer later after he overheard a conversation between his brother and his wife about a firm ground on which to rest. His life was changed.[1] Ebenezer was one of the original twelve Marrow-men and led out in the formation of the secession church, to be followed in a few years by his younger brother. Both were gifted and able preachers in a time of theological confusion. Yet they drew back from association with George Whitefield because of Whitefield's fellowship with the established church. The evangelical wing of the Church of Scotland thus espoused Whitefield's cause and ministry while the moderates like Robertson and Blair scorned him.

Ebenezer has been described as "the more stately and dignified" preacher of the two and was widely heard, especially in Communion seasons when people would journey considerable distances to listen to the Word as he preached it. These were twice-yearly occasions of great solemnity and often great power.[2] A bit more joyous than Thomas Boston, Ebenezer was clear exposition of grace. Often he spoke from the Old Testament (thirty of fifty-one texts, particularly messianic portions) and with a tendency to stray from the text. He traveled extensively in the interests of the secession and preached throughout Scotland. Here are his main divisions in a sermon on Psalm 89:14 (we have excluded an amplitude of subs and sub-subs):

I. A view of the throne of grace
II. Its basis or foundation
III. The pillars supporting and surrounding it
IV. Why justice and judgment are its foundations
V. The application of the whole.[3]

Ralph's preaching was more fervent and passionately eloquent and was noted for its effective conclusion and final appeal. His critics then and now fault him for his verbosity and overwrought language and for his "uncomplicated system of eternal reward and punishment."[4] But while his sermons may have been overly enthusiastic, they remained faithful to the gospel. Ralph's preaching must be seen in the context of a large parish of five thousand souls. He maintained fellowship meetings throughout the parish and was a poet and master violinist.[5]

The Erskines thrived on the great fundamental doctrines of Scripture and Christian faith. John Brown of Haddington reported: "I can never forget those days when I traveled over the hills of Cleish to hear that great man of God [Ralph Erskine], whose sermons I thought were brought home by the Spirit of God to my heart. At those times I thought I met with the God of Israel, and saw Him face to face."[6]

1. W. G. Blaikie, *The Preachers of Scotland from the Sixth to Nineteenth Century* (Edinburgh: T & T Clark, 1888), 204. On the controversy involving Professor Simson, who argued from the goodness of God rather than the Bible that God would save the heathen without the knowledge of Christ, see Henry F. Henderson, *The Religious Controversies of Scotland* (Edinburgh: T & T Clark, 1905).
2. Nigel M. de S. Cameron, ed., *Dictionary of Scottish Church History and Theology* (Downers Grove, Ill.: InterVarsity Press, 1993), 200.
3. F. R. Webber, *A History of Preaching in Britain and America* (Milwaukee: Northwestern, 1955), 2:171.
4. Ann Matheson, *Theories of Rhetoric in the Eighteenth-Century Scottish Sermon* (Lewiston, N.Y.: Edwin Mellen Press, 1995), 274.
5. Cameron, *Dictionary of Scottish Church History and Theology*, 301–2.
6. Webber, *A History of Preaching*, 2:174.

8.1.7 JOHN BROWN OF HADDINGTON—PREACHING TO A COMMUNITY

To the Marrow men and those who lighted their torches at the same altar fire we owe the maintenance in Scotland of the evangelistic and evangelical succession at a time when the dominant party in the Church of Scotland, becoming heartless in a high and dry hyper-Calvinism, abandoned theology for morality, and so drifted into moderatism.

Of *The Marrow of Modern Divinity:* The design of the treatise is to elucidate and establish the perfect freeness of the Gospel salvation; to throw open wide the gates of righteousness; to lead the sinner straight to the Savior; to introduce him as guilty, impotent and undone; and to persuade him to grasp, without a moment's hesitation, the outstretched hand of God's mercy.

—A. E. Garvie

At a time when, as Cowper put it, "preaching and pranks share the motley scene," there were those who swam against the prevailing currents. One such preacher was **John Brown of Haddington** (1722–1787). Brown was born in Carpow in Perthshire in meager circumstances. Orphaned at eleven, Brown had only a few months of schooling, spending his early years tending sheep in the hills of Abernethy.

Despite his lack of formal training, Brown read Alleine (cf. 7.3.7), and William Guthrie (7.5.6), and the Bible in a little lodge he and another shepherd had built to protect themselves from the sharp winds. He taught himself Greek and Latin. His great longing was for a copy of the Greek New Testament. He walked twenty-four miles to St. Andrews to a bookstore where Professor Pringle listened to him read and gave him a copy.[1]

Brown's idiosyncratic ways brought him suspicion, false charges, and much misunderstanding in his home parish. He traveled as a peddler for five years and fought against the Pretender ("Bonnie" Prince Charlie of the Stuarts who drew some Scots to challenge the Hannoverians) in 1745. He listened to Ebenezer Erskine, whose emphasis on "God in Christ, a God of love," deeply moved him. He joined with the Erskines, studied briefly with Ebenezer, and finally took the call to Haddington church in 1751, serving there for thirty-seven years. Thomas Carlyle liked to remark that John Knox had been born at Haddington.

In the winter months, Brown preached morning and evening; the rest of the year he preached morning, afternoon, and evening. He visited every family annually and examined adults and children in the catechism.[2] For nineteen of his years in Haddington he did professorial work for the Burgher section of the secession church and wrote a two-volume Bible dictionary and his scholarly *Self-Interpreting Bible*. But it was his biblical preaching that made his mark. His preaching was characterized by "great plainness, faithfulness, seriousness and earnestness."[3] One professor who heard him reported:

> I well remember a searching sermon he preached from the Word, "What went ye out for to see? A reed shaken with the wind." Although at that time I had no experimental acquaintance with the truth as it is in Jesus, yet his grave appearance in the pulpit, his solemn, weighty and majestic manner of speaking, used to affect me very much. Certainly his preaching was close, and his address to the conscience pungent. Like his Lord and Master, he spoke with authority and hallowed pathos, having tasted the sweetness and felt the power of what he believed.[4]

Even David Hume enjoyed hearing him. When Hume was asked to explain, he replied that he liked to hear Brown because he preached as if Jesus Christ were at his elbow. Brown strongly opposed "the light sermonizing of the moderates." While their home was often full of visiting students, six of their eight children died young, and Mrs. Brown died also in 1771 at the age of thirty-eight. Both of his surviving sons became preachers of distinction. He maintained personal ties with Whitefield and the Wesleys through a long correspondence with Lady Huntingdon.[5] He was thus clearly not a scholastic Calvinist but an evangelical Calvinist. He had pronounced millenarian views and expected the conversion of the Jews after their reinstatement in their own land.[6] "Oh, to hate sin and the cause of it!" was his watchword. Ultimately the anti-burgher group of the secession and other seceders joined with the relief church founded by Thomas Gillespie and Thomas Boston (the younger) to form the United Presbyterian Church in 1847. The foundation of all of these movements is the unfettered Word in all of its pristine beauty and power.[7]

---

1. Robert Mackenzie, *John Brown of Haddington* (Edinburgh: Banner of Truth, 1918), 34.
2. F. R. Webber, *A History of Preaching in Britain and America* (Milwaukee: Northwestern, 1955), 2:185.
3. Mackenzie, *John Brown of Haddington,* 106.
4. Ibid., 106.

5. Ibid., 158.
6. Ibid., 206.
7. In a moving appeal for expository preaching based on sound exegesis, W. G. Blaikie draws the chief lesson from three hundred years of Scottish preaching, "that notion of sin which reaches deepest into the human conscience . . . which is taught at the cross of Christ . . . no sprinkling of rose-water on the surface . . . preaching which ignores the work of Christ as an atonement ignores the central truth of Christianity." See *The Preachers of Scotland from the Sixth to the Nineteenth Century* (Edinburgh: T & T Clark, 1888), 303–5. These are the Cunningham Lectures, 12th series.

8.2 SINKING INTO THE GLOOM

In the leading Protestant countries—Germany and England—and from them elsewhere, there was a cold wave of skeptical recoil from the religious enthusiasm of earlier times. Deism and latitudinarianism in England, philosophic skepticism (partly due to English Deism and partly to French infidelity) and rationalistic criticism in Germany, combined to make the eighteenth century the "dark age of Protestantism."

—E. C. Dargan

For Christ did not send me to baptize, but to preach the gospel—not with words of human wisdom, lest the cross of Christ be emptied of its power.

—1 Corinthians 1:17

The same harsh winds of unbelief that led moderates to deny the gospel in Scotland hit France and Germany with galelike velocity. The radicalism of the French Enlightenment was marked, and the drastic consequences of the celebration of autonomous man are seen nowhere more pathetically than in Germany, with a ripple effect in all of the surrounding countries. **Immanuel Kant** of Prussia (1724–1804) is rightly called the watershed thinker of the Enlightenment, because he worked on the basis of reason alone and was agnostic regarding ultimate reality. Remembering his Pietistic roots, we perceive how quickly theistic defenses were demolished and the tidal waves of unbelief and nihilism swept over Europe. The darkness which ultimately fell over Europe resulted in Nietzsche, world wars, the Holocaust, and deconstructionism.[1] A case study in the devastation wrought by Enlightenment antisupernaturalism can be traced in the Tubingen School of the atheistically inclined **F. C. Baur** and his student, **David Strauss,** who denied the historicity of Jesus.[2] Baur remained active in church until his death. **J. S. Semler** continued to have morning devotions with his family, but the supernatural gospel was gone. The fallout for pulpits throughout Germany is unimaginable.

Using an identical epistemology, some protested the sterility of rationalism and developed the imaginative, and the poetic, but even the romanticists had no more to offer than did the rationalists. Exalting feeling above thought was **Jean-Jacques Rousseau** (1712–1756), who was born in Geneva, the grandson of a Calvinistic minister. He argued that man is naturally good, yet he fathered five children out of wedlock. His "I feel, therefore I am" was as much under the tyranny of self-autonomy as the earlier "I think, therefore I am."[3]

In England the romantic **Samuel Taylor Coleridge** (1772–1834) was also the son of a clergyman. Apart from his gross plagiarism, he had "a profoundly religious impulse." While he was ultimately victimized by his opium addiction, he often preached in dissenting chapels, his voice "rising like a steam of rich, distilled perfume." Influenced by Eichorn at Gottingen in Germany, he was very close to **William Wordsworth**. Oddly enough, he had millennial overtones and cherished a great love for the Jewish people.[4] He ardently disliked the Enlightenment, remarking that "the Enlightenment was full of enlighteners but lacking in light." Some have called him the Schleiermacher of Anglican theology. This is all part of the avalanche that threatened to bury biblical faith and biblical preaching in the eighteenth century.

---

1. For a good analysis of these issues, see Ravi Zacharias, *Can Man Live Without God?* (Dallas: Word, 1994), 35ff. Zacharias vigorously argues that "Apart from God, chaos is the norm."
2. Horton Harris, *The Tubingen School: A Historical and Theological Investigation of the School of F. C. Baur* (Grand Rapids: Baker, 1975, 1990). He concludes that "biblical exegesis and interpretation without conscious or unconscious dogmatic presuppositions is impossible," 262.
3. Will and Ariel Durant, *Rousseau and Revolution* (New York: Simon and Schuster, 1967), 10:31ff.
4. Richard Holmes, *Coleridge* (New York: Viking, 1989), 219. Keats said it best for the romantics when he wrote: "O for a life of sensations, rather than of thoughts." See Daniel Hoffman, "S. T. Coleridge and the Attack on Inerrancy," *Trinity Journal* 7 n.s. (1986): 55–68.

8.2.1 JOHANN LORENZ MOSHEIM—THE MENACE OF MEDIATION

A sermon is a discourse in which, following the guidance of a portion of Scripture, an assembly of Christians, already instructed in the elements of religion, is confirmed in knowledge or aroused to zeal in godliness.

It should be in keeping with the dignity and importance of the subject; it should be lively and have as much ornament as does not interfere with clearness; and the language should as far as possible be that which is used in ordinary life among cultivated people.
—Johann Lorenz Mosheim

In the clash between historic Christian orthodoxy and Enlightenment rationalism or romanticism, some opt for a diluted supernaturalism and an appropriate communicational form. Mediating views of scriptural authority represent a desperate effort to salvage something of the Christian gospel, but inevitably satisfy neither side. Compromise on truth issues is always unsatisfactory; compromise on taste issues is necessary.

We have already seen Principal Robertson in Scotland and Archbishop Tillotson making an earnest but futile effort to stake out a middle ground. Now in Germany we see the brilliant and able **Johann Lorenz Mosheim** (1693–1755) make the same commitment. Born in Lubeck and serving as professor of history and chancellor at Gottingen, he was an exceedingly popular preacher.[1] Beamed to the more sophisticated classes, Garvie says that Mosheim "was too fluent; and so his sermons assumed an inordinate length, e.g. his funeral sermon for Frederick II fills eighty-three printed pages."[2] On occasion his audiences were so large that soldiers would be called to keep order. But Garvie observes: "He was lucid, but superficial; he was eloquent, but not fervent; his reasonableness and seriousness did not sound the depths of God or man."[3] His instincts were still orthodox, but Ker must say: "He tones down its strong features, and presents it in such a way that it awakens a sense of chill."[4] This is the bane of the mediating.

Mosheim was so congenial and collegial that he avoided confrontation. Analysis of his sermons shows that he was guided more "by the usefulness of religion" than by penetrating to "the marrow of the text—the excellency of the knowledge that I may win Christ and be found in Him."[5] The trend was to be selective in Scripture, accommodating interpretation to the antisupernaturalistic biases in vogue. "Most of this school took to 'moral preaching.' Sometimes they changed the language of the Bible in order to make it more rational. For conversion or regeneration they spoke of amendment of life; for justification of forgiveness on condition of repentance; for the Holy Spirit, of the exercise of the higher reason; for the atonement of Christ of the spirit of sacrifice which He has taught us by His example, and so on."[6] Such wholesale concessions to unbelief and infidelity please no one. This strategization did nothing to alleviate the increasingly raw situation. Evangelistic vision and passion were lacking. The cupboard was becoming bare.

---

1. Robert Browning in his marvelous "Christmas Eve" depicts the lecture hall at Gottingen, where the discussion is as to the derivation of the Christ myth, not at all concealing "the exhausted air-bell of the critic." See W. E. Williams, ed., *Browning*, (New York: Penguin, 1954), 161ff.
2. A. E. Garvie, *The Christian Preacher* (New York: Scribner's, 1923), 199.
3. Ibid.
4. John Ker, *Lectures on the History of Preaching* (New York: Armstrong, 1889), 242.
5. Ibid., 262.
6. Ibid., 247.

8.2.2 JOHANN ALBRECHT BENGEL—THE MEANING OF THE MESSAGE

Eat simply the bread of the Scriptures as it presents itself to thee; and do not distress thyself at finding here and there a small particle of sand which the millstone may have left in it. Thou mayest, then, dismiss all those doubts which at one time so horribly tormented myself. If the Holy Scriptures—which have been so often copied, and which have passed so often through the faulty hands of ever fallible men—were absolutely without variations, the miracle would be so great, that faith in them would no longer be faith. I am astonished, on the contrary, that the result of all those transcriptions has not been a much greater number of different readings.

Scripture is the foundation of the Church: the Church is the guardian of Scripture. When the Church is in strong health, the light of Scripture shines bright; when the Church is sick, Scripture is corroded by neglect; and thus it happens, that the outward form of Scripture and that of the Church, usually seem to exhibit simultaneously either health or else sickness; and as a rule the way in which Scripture is being treated is in exact correspondence with the condition of the Church.

Apply yourself wholly to the text and apply the text wholly to yourself.
—Johann Albrecht Bengel

Among those who stood valiantly for the faith was the heir of true Spenerian and Franckian Pietism, **Johann Albrecht Bengel** (1687–1752). Pietism, with its light touch on doctrine, was vulnerable to Enlightenment sorties, and indeed the notorious rationalist Semler was appointed to Halle in 1751. Not a glimmer of Pietism was seen at Halle by the end of the century save for "the venerable Georg Knapp, who remained faithful among the faithless."[1]

Bengel was born near Stuttgart and studied there and in Halle. He was an avid student of Scripture, and his magnum opus was his five-volume *Gnomon of the New Testament* (i.e., index finger), a Latin commentary on the text with a wide sphere of influence, including John Wesley, whose *Notes on the New Testament* are based on this work by Bengel.[2] Kaiser has shown how Bengel was the first to classify New Testament texts into families and how he explored biblical figures of speech (of which he identified one hundred in an epochal index).[3] His preaching was richly expository. He was greatly influenced by Vitringa on the Apocalypse and sadly veered toward date-setting (he set 1836 as the year of the "end"), but he lived with eschatological awareness.[4] He wrote:

My greatest burden is not my weak physical frame, or my relative afflictions, or the attacks made on me, though from all these I have suffered. It has been hidden in the heart, the burden of eternity. Eternity itself in its infinite moment has pressed upon me, and sometimes entered my soul like a sword.[5]

A whole school of preachers emanated from his wake, including Georg Conrad Rieger. He predicted increasing skepticism and unbelief as attacks on the supernatural became bolder with preaching becoming "bare morality." He saw a mounting desire for "the kernel without the husk" (i.e., Christianity without the Bible) and the introduction of "attractive tales" rather than Scripture. Bengel's own grandson, **Ernst Gottlieb Bengel,** who served at Tubingen, taught that Jesus was essentially an ethical teacher. The younger Bengel was the mentor who most shaped F. C. Baur.[6] Yet Johann Bengel expected a renewal and revival, and correctly assessed his own legacy: "I shall be forgotten at first, but I shall be remembered again."[7]

1. John Ker, *Lectures on the History of Preaching* (New York: Armstrong, 1889), 224.
2. Interestingly, Emil Brunner asserts that "Quite apart from its rejuvenation of the dried-up Protestant Church, what Pietism accomplished in the sphere of social ameliora-tion and foreign missions is at the least the token of that Spirit which is promised in the Bible to those who truly believe, and is among the most splendid records of achieve-ment to be found in Church history," in *The Divine-Human Encounter,* (Philadelphia: Westminster, 1943), 23.
3. Walter C. Kaiser Jr., *Toward an Exegetical Theology: Biblical Exegesis for Preach-ing and Teaching* (Grand Rapids: Baker, 1981), 62, 124.
4. C. John Weborg, "The Eschatological Ethics of Johann Albrecht Bengel," *Covenant Quarterly* (May 1978): 31ff. We sense the great influence of Johannes Cocceius in Bengel; see C. S. McCoy, *The Covenant Theology of Johannes Cocceius* (New Haven, Conn.: Yale University Press, 1957). G. Schrenk says: "Bengel without Cocceius is unimaginable."
5. Ker, *Lectures on the History of Preaching,* 228. Bengel's influence on Zinzendorf is addressed in Gottfried Malzer, *Bengel und Zinzendorf* (Witten, Germany: Luther-Verlag, 1968). For treatment of Zinzendorf, see 6.4.3.
6. Horton Harris, *The Tubingen School: A Historical and Theological Investigation of the School of F. C. Baur* (Grand Rapids: Baker, 1975, 1990), 1, 16, 139.
7. Ker, *Lectures on the History of Preaching,* 237.

8.2.3 FRANZ VOLKMAR REINHARD—THE MOUTHPIECE TO THE MONARCHY

> If anyone is ashamed of me and my words, the Son of Man will be ashamed of him when he comes in his glory and in the glory of the Fa-ther and of the holy angels.
>
> —Luke 9:26

> I tell you, whoever acknowledges me before men, the Son of Man will also acknowledge him before the angels of God. But he who disowns me before men will be disowned before the angels of God.
>
> —Luke 12:8

One of the ablest and most articulate preachers of this time, **Franz Volkmar Reinhard** (1753–1812), took his stand on the issues of his day:

> I became a preacher at the time when our Illuminist theologians had suc-ceeded in making the Christian doctrine so clear and intelligible that nothing remained but pure rationalism . . . I felt I must be either an out-and-out rationalist or a supernaturalist . . . if there was no consistent

middle path, and if I had to choose between rationalism and supernaturalism, I was obliged to hold by the Bible, and to accept what could be proved from it. I honour all conscientious inquiry, I am open to all light, but my rule of judgment, my guide in perplexity, is the Gospel of Christ.[1]

Called by Dargan "the leading preacher in Germany at the end of the eighteenth century," Reinhard was born into a devout Lutheran pastor's home in the Duchy of Sulzbach. His father was a faithful preacher of the Word and taught his son Scripture and Latin. He loved clear outlines and was able to reproduce his father's sermons ten years after they were preached.[2] He studied at Regensburg and was a bibliophile of the first order. He was drawn to the clarity and eloquence of Demosthenes. He studied further at Wittenberg (a great center of the Bible movement), where he became a professor and preacher to the university. In 1792 he was called to be court preacher at Dresden, where he attained great distinction as a powerful preacher and as a disseminator of the historic gospel.

The doctrine of the free grace of God was his absorbing theme. As he put it:

There are moments when the awakened conscience speaks with a remorseless claim; when it shows us our sins in all their magnitude; when it makes us feel with deep conviction and with humbling power the want of any good in us; when our guilt before God, and the punishment we deserve, are set before us in a light that strikes us to the ground and leaves us in a condition the most helpless. Woe then to the sinner who feels himself so convicted, so condemned, so agonized, if he does not know the hope of the Gospel, if it has not been proclaimed to him that we are justified freely by His grace through the redemption that is in Christ Jesus! Happy then all who know this Gospel and hope in it![3]

Ker wonders if Reinhard preached Christ "in us" as well as "for us,"[4] but the evidence is that he was a faithful, balanced preacher on the whole. Still, Ker shows the tension of his encounter with the influence of illuminism in his time.

With respect to the process of developing the trajectory of the sermon, Ker remarks:

He worked out each sermon with the greatest care. First he sketched a scheme in which the chief thoughts were outlined in logical order and on this he set great value, both for its own sake and as an aid to his memory. The sermon, in his view, is a piece of art, to which, as to its outer form, both logic and rhetoric must contribute, but logic is the most important. Its thoughts must come up in regular order, group themselves in proportion, and lead to proper conclusions. The language should be suited to this, simple, clear, pointed. The preacher must never forget that he is above all a teacher; he who makes it his chief aim to awaken and move robs his office of much of its value, for if we are to reach the heart, it must be through the understanding.[5]

John Ker's lectures on the history of preaching seem top-heavy with analysis of German preaching but reflect the deep concern of this esteemed preacher and scholar about trends he saw in his own beloved Scotland.

---

1. John Ker, *Lectures on the History of Preaching* (New York: Armstrong, 1889), 286f.
2. E. C. Dargan, *A History of Preaching* (New York: Hodder and Stoughton, 1912), 2:228.
3. Ker, *Lectures on the History of Preaching*, 254–55.
4. Ibid., 256.
5. Ibid., 267–68.

8.2.4 FRIEDRICH SCHLEIERMACHER—THE MIASMA OF MODERNISM

[Speaking of the Moravian Brethren] There is no other place which could call forth such lively reminiscences of the entire onward movement of my mind, from its first awakening to a higher life, up to the point which I have at present attained. Here it was that, for the first time, I awoke to the consciousness of a higher world . . . Here it was that mystic tendency developed itself which has been of so much importance to me, and has supported me and carried me through all the storm of skepticism. Then it was germinating, now it has attained its full development; and I may say that, after all I have passed through, I have become a Herrnhuter again, only of a higher order.

—Friedrich Schleiermacher

It may be possible that erroneous conceptions of the significance of the baptismal estate may in part account for the perpetuation of this conception of preaching in Germany. A baptized congregation is assumed to be a Christian congregation and should be addressed as such. Perhaps this may in part explain the relative ineffectiveness of German preaching.

—Lewis O. Brastow

Nowhere do we see the disaster of the opening of the spiritual sinkhole we have been describing any more vividly or drastically than in the life and teaching of **Friedrich Schleiermacher** (1768–1834). He was born into the devoutly Pietistic home of a cavalry chaplain of the Reformed church in Breslau. Educated in Moravian Brethren schools, he ultimately went to Halle over the objection of his father and studied under Semler and other old rationalists. He jettisoned belief in everlasting punishment, Christ's deity and atonement, and the supernatural character of Christian faith. After much study in Kant, he turned toward this mystical modification we can call "the new rationalism."[1]

Schleiermacher served several pastoral charges and became widely known as a powerful communicator, setting as his model the Scottish moderate, Hugh Blair.[2] While serving as chaplain at the Charity Hospital in Berlin he issued a translation of the sermons of Blair. He added a romantic overlay to his Kantian thought (very much a la Goethe) and spent several years teaching at Halle. The fallout of the Napoleonic Wars necessitated Schleiermacher's relocation to Berlin, where he was a court preacher, professor, and pastor.

People would begin to gather at 7 A.M. to hear his Sunday sermon. He had a great disdain for the Old Testament generally and his ten-volume collection of sermons use only twenty Old Testament texts, chiefly from the wisdom literature and prophets. Imbibing Spinozistic pantheism, Schleiermacher had no supernatural revelation (for him, revelation was only "another name for human discovery"),[3] nor did he have a transcendent God.[4] Such a view of Scripture, as we have maintained, has a profound influence on preaching. Denying that the doctrine of the Trinity has any significance, and without any objective truth, Christianity becomes feeling. Preaching becomes a horizontal endeavor to sound a cheerful note.

Truly the father of modern liberalism, Schleiermacher never came to grips with the message of the Reformation. He had a "constant hankering after the pulpit"[5] and was very much like Beecher and Brooks in his preaching.[6] He was vague on Jesus but preached him warmly and greatly touched the great Neander's heart.[7] His appearance in the pulpit was arresting—"short of stature, and as to his shoulders slightly deformed; but he had a broad forehead, firm-set lips, strong Roman nose, a keen eye, and an altogether serious and vigorous countenance and a penetrating voice."[8] His oft-quoted sermon on "The Dying Saviour Our Example" is typical. The sermon is striking but based on the premise that dogma should not be allowed to obtrude "in the Good Friday service."[9] Schleiermacher correctly saw that preaching and theology are inseparably intertwined, but his theology with its egregiously deficient Christology is too thin.[10] For him Christmas meant "the feeling of immediacy in one's life."[11] The influence of these theological denials of the supernatural, and the strong emphasis on religion as feeling has resurfaced explosively in our times in an increasingly common approach to preaching. Is the purpose of preaching to make us feel good about God? And in such an anthropocentric approach, is this God really anyone other than ourselves?

---

1. The legacy of the Kantian bifurcation in epistemology is so foundational for understanding modern thought and preaching. Hence I recommend a work like S. Korner, *Kant* (New York: Penguin, 1955). The influence of Heidegger, the modern existentialist philosopher, cannot be followed apart from realizing he was trained in Marburg Kantianism; see Thomas Langan, *The Meaning of Heidegger* (New York: Columbia University Press, 1960).

2. Lewis O. Brastow, *Representative Modern Preachers* (New York: Macmillan, 1904), 11.

3. H. R. Mackintosh, *Types of Modern Theology* (New York: Scribner's, 1937), 71.

4. Karl Barth, *Protestant Theology from Rousseau to Ritschl* (New York: Harper, 1959); Karl Barth, *The Theology of Schleiermacher* (Grand Rapids: Eerdmans, 1983). This is based in large part on a study of Schleiermacher's sermons.

5. Mackintosh, *Types of Modern Theology,* 39.

6. Brastow, *Representative Modern Preachers,* 42–43.

7. Mackintosh, *Types of Modern Theology,* 54.

8. Brastow, *Representative Modern Preachers,* 43.

9. Ibid., 34.

10. Richard R. Niebuhr, *Schleiermacher on Christ and Religion* (New York: Scribner's, 1964), 14.

11. William Alexander Johnson, *On Religion: A Study of Theological Method in Schleiermacher and Nygren* (Leiden, Netherlands: E. J. Brill, 1964), 54.

8.2.5 CLAUS HARMS—THE MODUS OPERANDI OF THE MIDDLE

In those days the word of the Lord was rare; there were not many visions.

—1 Samuel 3:1b

We must pay more careful attention, therefore, to what we have heard, so that we do not drift away.

—Hebrews 2:1

I had to write and urge you to contend for the faith that was once for all entrusted to the saints.

—Jude 3b

Even in the face of such widespread and pervasive theological declension, there were voices crying in the wilderness. Among them were **Claus Harms** (1778–1855), born in the well-to-do home of a miller in the province of Holstein. The young Harms was inclined to spiritual things and made his way through the University of Kiel. At this time he tended toward the prevailing rationalistic ideas, but within that arid desert he thirsted for the reality of the Lord. His first step was Schleiermacher's *Discourses on Religion,* which he read ravenously and which with its discussion of Jesus led him to Christ. Now awakened, he began to dig into Luther and the Reformers and became a preacher of considerable conviction and forcefulness.

Preaching first as a student and then as a visiting pastor, he was well heard in a widening circle from the pulpit of St. Nicholas Church in Kiel, where he began as an archdeacon in 1816. The university snubbed him as "an obscurantist, a darkener of the light of reason, a retailer of old, worn-out ideas, he and his Bible and Luther!"[1] He was given the preaching time during the dinner hour, but gradually spiritually hungry people revised their dining time and even Professor Eckermann, "father of Kiel rationalism, never missed an afternoon service."[2] He won the war of the pamphlets and was even invited by the king of Denmark to preach in Copenhagen and by the emperor of Russia to come and settle in St. Petersburg. Most curious of all, he was invited by the king of Prussia to succeed Schleiermacher in Trinity Church, Berlin.[3] But he was determined to labor in the vineyard in Kiel.

Harms led a revival in confessionalism which shook all of Northern Germany. He attacked rationalism and set forth a new set of ninety-five theses in favor of the evangelical faith. He greatly stressed biblical preaching. His divisions of the text were clear. Dargan says of his ministry: "During his whole career he was the most powerful preacher in Northern Germany."[4] Harms wrote on the importance of a right spirit in the preacher nurtured by the Holy Spirit's power and the results of seasons of retreat and refreshing and waiting before God. He quoted Hamann, "The nearer the Scripture, the nearer the skies." (cf. 1.1 n. 1). A sample of his style as translated is striking:

> Who are the careless? We cannot seek them out or count them; but let each man step forward to the word with his heart. Who is the careless? The man who has behind him a youth full of sins, his riper years guilty without repentance, and who, because in old age he has been forced to give up some sins, is confident that all is right. Man! thou hast built their house upon a fire-vomiting hill, and thou dost not know it. Before thou art aware, in "a little while," it will burst out and hurl thee into an abyss where thou shalt no longer stand erect. Thou dost not fear this? Even that is thy carelessness—thy sinful carelessness—from a sermon on John 16:19, on "a little while."[5]

---

1. John Ker, *Lectures on the History of Preaching* (New York: Armstrong, 1889), 340.
2. Ibid., 340.
3. Ibid., 341.
4. E. C. Dargan, *History of Preaching* (New York: Hodder and Stoughton, 1912), 407.
5. Ker, *Lectures on the History of Preaching,* 347.

8.2.6 FRIEDRICH AUGUST THOLUCK—THE MAGNIFICENT MOLLIFIER

> The Church theology and Christian life have had their progress and regress, counting back from the days of the Reformation to the days of their origin, from our times back to the sixteenth century; nor will it be otherwise with regard to the future development of the Church of Christ. Our understanding and our moral state will ever alternately move on and turn back, and, opposed to the Kingdom of the Lord, a realm of Antichrist will remain, and will continue to grow, until it be destroyed by the last victory. May the Lord give us clear eyes and warm hearts, in order that, from all the aberrations that His Church has undergone till now, there may redound to us an everlasting gain.

> Every sermon should have heaven for its father and earth for its mother.
> —Friedrich August Tholuck

Given the intensity and strain of the theological tug-of-war, it is not surprising to find a mediating school that would attempt a fence-straddling position. But is that really possible when the issue is the supernaturalism of biblical faith? Nonetheless, such well-known names as Neander, Dorner, Olshausen, and

Tholuck are in this group. We shall look at Tholuck because of his eminent preaching.

Friedrich August Tholuck (1799–1877) was born in Breslau, the son of a goldsmith. He studied at Berlin with particular interest in things oriental but turned to theology under the influence of Count Ernst von Kottwitz of the Moravian Brethren in Silesia. This mentor led him into the study of the Pauline Epistles, and "through the great mercy of God he found wisdom and life in Christ crucified."[1] Tholuck read about the life of Henry Martyn and dedicated his life to missions in the East. He intended to take a position with the British and Foreign Bible Society in Malta, but his health collapsed. He followed De Wette at Berlin, and in 1826 he took the place of the venerable Dr. Knapp at Halle. This fulfilled a great longing for Tholuck, since he had become much enamored by August Francke's example. The Halle faculty, led by the great Hebraist Gesenius, strongly opposed his coming—the school had become a "hot-bed of rationalism," with only five students out of nine hundred professing belief in the deity of Christ.[2]

Not only did Tholuck produce a substantial body of scriptural commentary (with noteworthy volumes on Romans, Hebrews, John, the Sermon on the Mount, and the Psalms) but also he won the hearts of the students. He "was an evangelist as well as an evangelical,"[3] and was considered the best preacher in all of Germany. Conspicuous for his conversational tone, Tholuck artfully flouted homiletical convention and made effective use of his vivid imagination. As chaplain to the university he drew not only students but also townspeople to his sermons. He truly preached the gospel message. One of his five volumes of university sermons has been translated under the title *Light from the Cross.* It is a choice treasure and must be considered one of the ten best collections of sermons on the cross of Christ ever published.[4] It is divided into two parts:

I. The Cross as a Revealer of the Hearts of Men. A series based on Luke 2:34–35 and probing into the lives and experiences of various personalities in relation to Calvary. Strong preaching on sin. His models were Luther, Hamann, and Bunyan.
II. The Sufferings and Death of Christ. Sermon 7 is especially outstanding on Luke 23:26–31, "Weep not for me but for yourselves." His messages on the seven last words of Christ are among the first of its kind.

Beyond question Tholuck was a true believer, and at the end of his life was in great peace, saying, "I fear not for myself; the death of Christ avails for me."[5] But there is something missing in the man and in his messages. He brings us to the Cross, but he does not share doctrine. He is theologically inarticulate. How can we preach the death of Jesus without theological construct? "Christ died for our sins" is heavily freighted with Anselmian and transactional implication. Is this the price middle-grounders must pay? Tholuck was neutered doctrinally.[6] In order to mollify his critics and take advantage of opportunities for ministry, he skimmed along the surface of a text with his eyes closed to theology. As a consequence, he left his heirs penniless.

1. John Ker, *Lectures on the History of Preaching* (New York: Armstrong, 1889), 318.
2. J. C. Macaulay, "Biographical Introduction," F. A. Tholuck, *Light from the Cross* (Chicago: Moody, 1952), 12.
3. Ibid., 13.
4. Ibid.
5. E. C. Dargan, *A History of Preaching* (New York: Hodder and Stoughton, 1912), 410.
6. The dilemma of the "mediating" is seen recurring through history. In the reorganization of Princeton Seminary in 1929 such basically conservative professors as Charles Erdman and others sought to avoid alignment but paid an immense price for their attempted neutrality. We can easily lose our influence and the respect of both sides.

8.2.7   HENRIC SCHARTAU—MESSENGER IN THE LAND OF THE MIDNIGHT SUN

We had poor preachers, poor in preaching or in life, but the great Shepherd of souls kept His promise, which in like cases He has given to His dearly bought sheep, even to those that have drifted away, "I shall shepherd them according to their need." During a wretched and careless altar address He gave me grace so that, while reading the confession, I had a living insight and conviction, especially at the words, "I therefore know that I am worthy of hell and eternal condemnation." I clearly understood . . . I would certainly be lost . . . but I also received grace to accept the words of absolution unto forgiveness . . . based on His bloody atonement. Since that day I have, by the power of God, and in spite of errors and much wavering, been preserved unto salvation.

When the Holy Scriptures are left to occupy the seat of honor and other writings are used as their footstool, then scriptural learning will be dominating in one's preaching without debasing one to copy the methods or idiosyncrasies of any particular school. One may then emulate the gifts of others without deviating from one's own high pattern.

—Henric Schartau

An influential preacher in southern and western Sweden in this time of enveloping shadows was **Henric Schartau** (1757–1825). Born in Malmo in Skåne, the son of a city clerk and councilman, Schartau grew up in a family where Scripture was highly valued. At fourteen, he enrolled in the University at Lund, where "fighting, drinking and gambling were very general."[1] But, to use his own words, "The wise hand which had grasped my heart led me likewise imperceptibly into the Word of God."[2] Schartau was led captive not only to the Word but also to Scrivner's *Treasury* (**Christian Scrivner,** 1629–1693, a widely-read German Pietist). He was also shaped by J. A. Bengel's works but was cool toward the accompanying Moravian Brethren emotionalism (although he was a great admirer of the Norwegian lay reformer, Hauge). At the core Schartau was a follower of Luther with a tinge of John Arndt. "Schartau indeed went deep into the mine of Holy Scripture . . . he brought out great treasures and thus built up his discourses."[3]

Like Luther, he preached law before he preached grace. His outlines were famous, and he worked hard at delineating the steps to salvation by grace, the *ordo salutis*. Sometimes under his intense preaching listeners would become so aware of the danger of hell and future judgment that they would cry out for everyone to repent.

Karl Olsson sees Schartau's "orders of blessedness" as a counteraction against "the non-confessional and unscriptural mood of the Enlightenment."[4] In all of this, Schartau was much maligned and vilified. Yet he urged that there be no quarreling in the pulpit. His style was rugged and perhaps legalistic, but we must remember he lived in an antinomian time. He was the quintessential Swede:

> His was an art, known by but few,
> Of being strong and gentle too.

In retrospect, this able preacher has risen in esteem. The Swedish Academy coined a memorial to him with the inscription: "He was a faithful shepherd of his flock and a true teacher."[5] His collected sermons show the function of a clear proposition, great dedication to the text, and a concern for clear and practical application.

---

1. Henrik Hagglund, *Henric Schartau and the Order of Grace* (Rock Island, Illinois: Augustana, 1928), 13.
2. Ibid., 14.
3. Ibid., 18.
4. Karl Olsson, *By One Spirit* (Chicago: Covenant, 1962), 664 n. 2.
5. Hagglund, *Henric Schartau and the Order of Grace*, 36. A fine collection of fifteen sermons is appended.

8.3 STIRRING UP THE GIFT

Quicken me, O LORD, according unto thy word.
—Psalm 119:107b (KJV)

Will you not revive us again, that your people may rejoice in you?
—Psalm 85:6

LORD, I have heard of your fame; I stand in awe of your deeds, O LORD. Renew them in our day, in our time make them known; in wrath remember mercy.
—Habakkuk 3:1

Although some held forth the word of life "in a crooked and depraved generation," shining "like stars in the universe" (Phil. 2:15), the eighteenth-century spiritual landscape was generally bleak. Times were reminiscent of the grim days of the Old Testament judges, but a sovereign God deigned to visit his people and stirred among them.

One of the most glorious visits of God to his people in all of history took place in the eighteenth century. It was the Great Awakening. At a time when a deistic poet like **Alexander Pope** was pushing the notion that "the proper study of mankind is man" and when the jurist **Blackstone** observed that it was impossible to tell from the sermons preached in English churches whether the preacher was Muslim, Confucian, or Christian, God came in mighty revival.

At the epicenter of any spiritual detonation is the recovery of the preaching of the Word of God. Revival, according to C. E. Autrey, is "the reanimation of God's people."[1] The people of God "felt a divine vibration."[2] The message was not new; the preachers were "enthusiastically orthodox,"[3] illustrating again the principle that the preaching of the Scriptures became central.[4] It was a revival of the Reformation in a real sense. As Skevington Wood argues, the irresistible authority of the Word under the unction of the Holy Spirit swept through in cyclonic force. "The note of authority returned to the pulpit: an authority springing from the Word and finding its corroboration in the heart of man."[5] He then quotes J. C. Ryle:

> The spiritual reformers of the last century taught constantly the sufficiency and supremacy of the Holy Scripture. The Bible, whole and unmutilated, was their sole rule of faith and practice. They accepted all its statements without question or dispute. They knew nothing of any part of Scripture being uninspired. They never allowed that man has any "verifying faculty" within him by which Scripture statements may be weighed, rejected or received. They never flinched from asserting that there can be no error in the Word of God; and that when we cannot understand or reconcile some parts of its contents, the fault is in the interpreter and not in the text. In all their preaching they were eminently men of one book. To that book they were content to pin their faith, and by it to stand or fall.

Antecedents and catalysts of various kinds were used of God to prepare the way:

1. Many faithful servants of Christ remained true to the gospel, often at great price.
2. Gifted apologists like Butler and exegetes like Bengel held the field for historic orthodoxy even under the withering fusillade of enemy fire.
3. The revival really began with the Pietists on the Continent; Spener and Francke helped "restore biblical preaching and Bible study."[6] W. R. Ward traces the awakening to Silesia and the children's prayer meetings. The revival of 1727 began with the conversion of an eleven-year-old girl. Much opposition was encountered, for only in New England "did the establishment take up with the revival."[7] Wesley visited Herrnhut and Halle and fellowshiped with Francke; Whitefield was also in touch with young Francke. Trevecca was derived from Halle as a model. Wesley's wife was a Huguenot. Bengel's

eldest daughter married a fervent Herrnhuter. Doddridge's grandfather was from Bohemia. All this shows that the revival was, as Ward contends, a pan-Protestant phenomenon.

4. Gifted devotional writers like **William Law** (1686–1761) addressed the needs of the heart and most significantly dealt with the root causes of widespread unbelief. His *A Serious Call to a Devout and Holy Life* had an immense effect on John Wesley, for instance. He has been called "a herald of the Evangelical Revival."[8]

5. Revival fires were kindled in the religious societies springing up everywhere by a series of awakening sermons, such as those delivered in the Savoy Chapel in London by **Dr. Antony Horneck.** Horneck came from the Rhineland, studied at Oxford, and was much used in societies dedicated to the promotion of scriptural holiness. Samuel Wesley had one of the most vigorous societies in his parish at Epworth.[9]

Yet, as Elliott-Binns insists, "[The revival] came without organization and almost without expectation." And really, after Continental Pietism and its relatives, the dawn first began to glimmer in beautiful and rugged Wales.

---

1. Earle E. Cairns, *An Endless Line of Splendor: Revivals and Their Leaders from the Great Awakening to the Present* (Wheaton, Ill.: Tyndale House, 1986), 54–55. Another key study is James Burns, *Revivals: Their Laws and Leaders* (Grand Rapids: Baker, 1909, 1960). See also my "The Corollary of Revival—Evangelism," *The Evangelism Mandate* (Wheaton, Ill.: Crossway, 1992), 164–174.

2. A. Skevington Wood, *The Inextinguishable Blaze: Spiritual Renewal and Advance in the Eighteenth Century* (Grand Rapids: Eerdmans, 1960), 236.

3. L. E. Elliott-Binns, *The Early Evangelicals* (London: Lutterworth, 1953), 91.

4. Wilbur M. Smith, *The Glorious Revival under King Hezekiah* (Grand Rapids: Zondervan, 1937), 23ff.

5. Wood, *The Inextinguishable Blaze,* 227.

6. Cairns, *An Endless Line of Splendor.*

7. Wood, *The Inextinguishable Blaze,* 112.

8. William Law, *A Serious Call to a Devout and Holy Life* (New York: E. P. Dutton, Everyman's Library, 1955).

9. Wood, *The Inextinguishable Blaze,* 30ff.

8.3.1 GRIFFITH JONES—THE DAYSTAR OF THE AWAKENING

Nothing was to be seen in almost every parish but young men and young women flocking together into the churches and churchyards and engaging in different gambols and pastimes such as ball playing, football, leaping, fighting and such like frolics. . . . Common preaching will not do to rouse sluggish districts from the heavy slumbers into which they are sunk. Indeed, formal prayers and lifeless sermons have also entered the Principality under the pretence of order. Five or six stanzas will be sung as dry as Gilboa, instead of one or two verses like a new song, full of God, of Christ, of the Spirit of grace, until the heart is attuned to worship . . . you are content with a preacher speaking so lifelessly and so low that you can hardly understand the third part of what he says; and you will call this decency in the sanctuary.

—Christmas Evans

Through the lovely valleys of Wales, where once the gospel message had reverberated with rejoicing, now the lassitudes prevailed. **William Wroth, Rees Prichard, Walter Cradock,** and the eloquent **Vavasor Powell** (1617–1670), who was imprisoned thirteen times for his field preaching, were the bright stars in the darkness. But the first preacher of the dawn was the venerable **Griffith Jones** (1683–1761) of Llanddowror. He was a shepherd boy who was called to preach in a dream. Born into "a religious and respectable family," he had the rare opportunity of education while many were illiterate. Jones was ordained in 1709 and served out his life preaching in the Vale of Taf.

The revival message he preached was not pleasing to all. He was accused of preaching outside the walls of a church (when the church could not hold the congregations in excess of four thousand). He saw the signs of spiritual starvation. He organized not only catechetical classes but schools to teach reading until over 215 such schools existed in South Wales. He sponsored the publication and distribution of more than thirty thousand Bibles in the Welsh language. He was responsible for a great effort of charity for the poor and dispossessed.[1] But gospel preaching was always his forte. He divided his sermons carefully, explicated the text with thoroughness, and "as he advanced, his subject fired him more and more."[2] Said one analyst of his style:

When he came to the application, he entered upon it with a solemn pause. He seemed to summon up all his remaining force; he gave way to a superior burst of religious vehemence and, like a flaming meteor, did bear down all before him. His voice broke silence and proceeded with a sort of dignified pomp. Every word was like a fresh attack, and carried with it a sort of triumphant accent. By his preaching the drunkards became sober; the sabbath-breakers were reformed; the prayerless cried for mercy and forgiveness; and the ignorant were solicitously concerned for an interest in the Divine Redeemer.[3]

Before the conclusion of his ministry he had met with both Wesley (he heard him preach outdoors at Bath) and Whitefield, and had forged a bond with the ministry and outreach of the Countess of Huntingdon. Not the least of his spiritual productivity can be seen in the lives of preachers he led to Christ and influenced. An arrogant young curate was soundly converted in one of his meetings in 1735 and became one of the flaming preachers of the Welsh awakening: **Daniel Rowland** (1713–1790). He was known for the great centrality to which he gave Christ in every sermon—his blood, his sacrifice, his righteousness.

Others influenced by Griffith Jones during this unparalleled time of great preaching in Wales was the lay preacher **Howell Harris** (1714–1773), who was converted in the same year as Rowland. At the advice of Jones, Harris gave himself to establishing societies in the Church of England. These became the nucleus of the Calvinistic Methodist Church of Wales. When he was denied ordination, Harris became an itinerant evangelist. His greatest years of fruitfulness were from 1735 to 1750. In his prime it was said that he preached on hell as if he had been there. Toughs would seek to rough him up, and on one occasion a musket was fired at him and narrowly missed.

Harris was one of Whitefield's closest friends and actually gave Whitefield the woman he loved rather than be tempted by her affection.[4] Yet he entered a period of dryness and broke with Whitefield when the latter would not tolerate the moral indiscretion of Harris. Harris also strayed in doctrine (1751–1753), going too deeply into "the felt Christ" of the Moravians and veering toward patripassionism.[5] These bypaths also strained his long relationship with Rowland. To the praise of God, Harris repented but never totally mended his ties with Whitefield. He was still mightily used as a preacher, and when he died at age fifty-nine, twenty thousand people attended his funeral.

Like many Welsh preachers, Harris's discourses erupted like molten lava. Here is how Whitefield described him:

> A burning and shining light has been in those parts; a barrier against profaneness and immorality, and an indefatigable promoter of the true Gospel of Jesus Christ . . . He is of a most catholic spirit, loves all that love our Lord Jesus Christ, and therefore, he is slighted by bigots and dissenters. He is condemned by all that are lovers of pleasure rather than lovers of God: but God has greatly blessed his pious endeavors. Many call him as their spiritual father; and I believe, would lay down their lives for his sake. He discourses generally in a field, from a wall, a table, or anything else, but at other times in a house. He has established near thirty societies in South Wales, and still his sphere of action is enlarged daily. He is full of faith and the Holy Ghost . . . Blessed be God, there seems to be a noble spirit gone out into Wales, and I believe ere long there will be more visible fruits of it.[6]

Still another in this sterling succession of revival preachers in Wales must be noted in the person of **William Williams** of Pant-y-celyn (1717–1791). Williams has been called the Charles Wesley of Wales. He began studying for medicine, but was converted after hearing Howel Harris preach in 1738. Soon Williams felt the call to preach himself. He traveled three thousand miles a year in revival ministry and wrote more than eight hundred hymns, including "Guide Me, O Thou Great Jehovah" and "O'er the Gloomy Hills of Darkness."[7] In Williams and his contemporaries, God's Spirit was clearly on the move.

---

1. A. Skevington Wood, *The Inextinguishable Blaze: Spiritual Renewal and Advance in the Eighteenth Century* (Grand Rapids: Eerdmans, 1960), 43.

2. F. R. Webber, *A History of Preaching in Britain and America* (Milwaukee: North-western, 1955), 2:560.

3. Wood, *The Inextinguishable Blaze,* 42.

4. Harry S. Stout, *The Divine Dramatist: George Whitefield and the Rise of Modern Evangelicalism* (Grand Rapids: Eerdmans, 1991), 157. This is the only treatment I can find of the moral wobbling of Howell Harris.

5. Robert Bennett, *The Early Life of Howell Harris* (Edinburgh: Banner of Truth, 1909, 1962).

6. Wood, *The Inextinguishable Blaze,* 51.

7. D. Martyn Lloyd-Jones, "William Williams and Welsh Calvinistic Methodism," in *The Puritans and Their Successors* (Edinburgh: Banner of Truth, 1987), 191ff.

8.3.2 JOHN WESLEY—THE DYNAMO OF THE AWAKENING

Let me be *homo unius libri.* (Let me be a man of one book.)

The Bible must be the invention of either good men or angels, bad men or devils, or of God. (1) It could not be the invention of good men or angels, for they neither would nor could make a book, and tell lies all the time they were writing it, saying "Thus saith the Lord," when it was their own invention. (2) It could not be the invention of bad men or devils, for they would not make a book which commands all duty, forbids all sin, and condemns their souls to hell to all eternity. (3) Therefore I draw this conclusion that the Bible must be given by divine inspiration.

I look on all the world as my parish. . . . God buries the workmen, but continues His work.

—John Wesley

The true end of preaching is to amend men's lives, not fill their heads with unprofitable speculation.

—Susanna Wesley

The human workhorse in the Great Awakening was **John Wesley** (1703–1791), who ministered tirelessly for sixty-six years. At his energetic peak, Wesley traveled five thousand miles per year, averaging three sermons a day. He published a four-volume commentary on all of Scripture, a dictionary of the English language, a five-volume work on natural philosophy, grammars on the Hebrew, Latin, French, and English languages, three books on medicine, six on church music, seven volumes of sermons, edited *The Arminian Magazine* and a library of fifty volumes of the classics called The Christian Library. He rose at 4 A.M. and worked until 10 P.M. In his eighty-sixth year he still rode thirty to fifty miles a day. "I know my commission," he said. "Courage mounteth with occasion."

The principal personalities of the Awakening differed on certain theological issues. (For instance, Wesley's Arminianism led to a break with the Calvinistic

Whitefield. Fortunately this wound was largely healed, and Wesley ultimately preached Whitefield's funeral.) But the basis of doctrinal agreement is impressive, particularly with reference to the authority of Scripture, the sinfulness of man, the absolute centrality of Christ's atonement, the necessity for the new birth, and so forth.[1] Whitefield was undoubtedly the more eloquent preacher and Wesley the more brilliant organizer, but both were evangelists who communicated with indisputable results.

John Wesley—the Believer

John Wesley was the fifteenth child of Samuel and Susanna Wesley. His father was a high church evangelical whose father and grandfather had been clergymen, while his mother was reared in Puritan nonconformity. Susanna's marriage to Samuel deeply alienated her nonconformist parents. Samuel was impulsive and imperious and dedicated twenty-five years to writing a Latin commentary on the Book of Job. Susanna gave herself with an identical pertinacity to the raising of her nineteen children (she was one of twenty-five children herself). She personally instructed her children in the Scriptures and with regard to their personal relationship to Christ. Susanna home-schooled her children and taught them Greek by their eighth year.

Samuel Wesley served the Epworth parish in Lincolnshire. Many in his congregation hated him, and he spent time in debtor's prison. To his chagrin, his wife conducted preaching services in the rectory during his incarceration. In John's sixth year, enemies burned the rectory down, and the lad was miraculously spared as "a brand from the burning."[2] John grew to believe God had something special for him.

Matriculating at Charterhouse School in London, John went to Oxford. Shocked by the profligacy of so many students, he gave himself to a hard regimen. He was made a don at Oxford and received ordination in 1725. With his brother Charles and others he founded the famous Holy Club. Wesley said of this time, "I preached much but saw no fruit of my labor." He was still struggling for spiritual light and in considerable bondage to the law. Discouraged, he went to Georgia in "the hope of saving my own soul."[3] His brief stint in America was not successful. He observed the inner peace of Moravian believers during a fierce storm on the sea, and upon returning to London sought out a Moravian chapel where he heard Luther's preface to his commentary on Galatians being read. Wesley entered into faith and assurance of salvation. Only three days earlier, Charles had been saved. This "strange warming of his heart" at Aldersgate was the turning point of his life and ministry. Of this Pentecost Sunday he told the archbishop:

> It is true that from May 24, 1738, whenever I was desired to preach, salvation by faith was my only theme . . . And it is equally true that it was for preaching the love of God and man that several of the clergy forbade me their pulpits.

John Wesley—the Preacher

Wesley loved to share his own personal testimony as he preached. "As soon as I saw clearly the nature of saving faith and made it the standing topic of my preaching, God then began to work by my ministry as He had never done before."[4] His friend from the Holy Club, George Whitefield, taught him to do field preaching. On Monday, April 2, 1739, he preached to three thousand people outdoors at Kingswood near Bristol, and it became his modus operandi. He loved to preach at 5 A.M. before the men went to work. Only five feet seven inches tall and weighing 122 pounds, the slender white-wigged preacher had a strong voice and never failed to be understood, even when in his eighties he spoke to thirty-three thousand people.

His style was calm and reasoned. Without humor or pathos, there was yet a moral earnestness about his preaching, a subdued intensity that gave him intrinsic credibility. His journal is fascinating, as he often records, "I gave them Christ!" He felt reservations about Whitefield's bombastic style and flamboyant gestures. He said Whitefield was too much like a Frenchman in a box. Wesley's own delivery was not dramatic but was "a combination of terror and tenderness." "But for an occasional lifting of his right hand, he might have been a speaking statue." As one interpreter puts it: the message was carried by what he said rather than how he said it.[5] He used the pause to good effect. He personified piety. Of course he preached "Christian perfection," which to him was having the mind of Christ, walking as he walked, nothing more and nothing less. Yet he never claimed to have reached it himself.[6]

Wesley was more textual than expository, demonstrated in his famous sermon on "The Great Assize" from Romans 14:10, preached at the time of assizes. The sermon was bare of illustration but rich with Scripture and metaphor.[7] Wesley was lucid and logical and never failed to give a clear proposition. In his sermon from 1 Corinthians 14:20, "The Poverty of Reason," he states: "Reason, however cultivated and improved, cannot produce the love of God . . . it cannot produce either faith or hope, from which alone this love can flow." He pleaded for a religion of the heart and conversion. His magnificent sermon on "The Scripture Way of Salvation" from Ephesians 2:8 is clear:

I. What is salvation?
II. What is that faith by which we are saved?
III. How are we saved by it?

While the interrogative outline is notoriously wooden and lacking in assertiveness, clearly Wesley is at the aorta of this great text. He urged his preachers:

Preach our doctrine, inculcate experience, urge practice, enforce discipline. If you preach doctrine only, the people will be antinomians; if you preach experience only, they will become enthusiasts; if you preach practice only, they will become pharisees; and if you preach all of these and do not enforce discipline, Methodism will be like a highly cultivated garden without a fence, exposed to the ravages of the wild boar of the forest.[8]

John Wesley—the Organizer

Whether the Great Awakening in England averted a bloodbath like that of the French Revolution is a matter of debate and scholarly discussion, but even the skeptical Lecky observed:

> Although the career of the elder Pitt, and the splendid victories by land and sea that were won during his ministry, form unquestionably the most dazzling episodes in the reign of George II, they must yield, I think, in real importance to that religious revolution which shortly before had begun in England by the preaching of the Wesleys and Whitefield.[9]

Along with his preaching, Wesley brought what has been rightly called an organizing flair to the ministry. In 1739 he preached for the first time on "Free Grace" at the Foundry in London, which became the headquarters for Methodism (a name first used of the Holy Club at Oxford). In 1740 the first of the societies was founded, and the first Annual Conference was held in 1744. The Wesleys never intended to leave the Church of England and remained officially within its ranks until their deaths. Wesley adapted from the Moravian bands (the Pietistic conventicles) his lay-led class meetings. Twenty percent also belonged to a band, committed to the fervent pursuit of holiness. In the whole structure lay pastors were working side by side with clergy.[10]

Wesley was quite high church throughout his long life, taking the Lord's Supper weekly.[11] He had a keen sense of the body of Christ and was burdened also for the abolition of slavery and the amelioration of bad conditions in prisons. His commitment to an itinerant ministry harks back to his own evangelistic experience, and while he never traveled to America again, he commissioned Thomas Coke and Francis Asbury to be superintendents in America. Asbury was the only one to stay in America during the revolution. He called himself a bishop with much disapproval of Wesley. Yet the sense of esprit and élan constantly comes through, as in a journal entry for Christmas Day, 1747:

> We met at four and solemnly rejoiced in God our Saviour. I found much revival in my own soul this day. . . . Both this and the following days I strongly urged the wholly giving up ourselves to God, and renewing in every point our covenant that the Lord should be our God.

In two areas Wesley never found satisfaction. His own marriage was desperately unhappy, ending when his shrewish wife left him. Neither was he able to plant Methodism in Scotland. Whitefield himself had his problems there, but Wesley's experience was especially sour.[12]

Still "the grand itinerant" persisted. How many heard him in church yards, fields, in the collieries! As John Nelson wrote when hearing him for the first time:

It made my heart beat like the pendulum of a clock and when he did speak, I thought his whole discourse was aimed at me. When he had done, I said, "This man can tell the secrets of my heart."[13]

1. Timothy L. Smith, *Whitefield and Wesley on the New Birth* (Grand Rapids: Frances Asbury/Zondervan, 1986).
2. A Methodist Preacher, *John Wesley the Methodist* (New York: Eaton and Mains, 1903), 3. A veritable gold mine is to be found in W. L. Doughty, *John Wesley Preacher* (London: Epworth, 1955). "Monotony is a great fault," he said.
3. F. R. Webber, *A History of Preaching in Britain and America* (Milwaukee: Northwestern, 1952), 1:337.
4. A. Skevington Wood, *The Inextinguishable Blaze: Spiritual Renewal and Advance in the Eighteenth Century* (Grand Rapids: Eerdmans, 1960), 113.
5. Richard P. Heitzenrater, *The Elusive Mr. Wesley* (Nashville: Abingdon, 1984), 2:83.
6. Harald Lindstrom, *Wesley and Sanctification* (Nashville: Abingdon, 1946). This study clearly shows Wesley's commitment to humanity's moral inability, to salvation by grace and to the gospel of ruin by the fall, redemption by the Cross, and regeneration by the Holy Spirit. See also George A. Turner, "John Wesley as an Interpreter of Scripture," in *Inspiration and Interpretation,* ed. John Walvoord (Grand Rapids: Eerdmans, 1957), 156–78.
7. Edward H. Sugden, ed., *John Wesley's Fifty-Three Sermons* (Nashville: Abingdon, 1983), Sermon 48.
8. P. Boyd Mather, "John Wesley and Aldersgate 1963," *The Christian Century* (December 18, 1963): 1581ff.
9. Quoted in T. Harwood Pattison, *The History of Christian Preaching* (Philadelphia: American Baptist Publication Society, 1903), 255.
10. Howard Snyder, *The Radical Wesley and Patterns for Church Renewal* (Downers Grove, Ill.: InterVarsity Press, 1980).
11. Ole E. Borgen, *John Wesley on the Sacraments* (Grand Rapids: Frances Asbury/Zondervan, 1972). A Swedish bishop's definitive study.
12. Samuel J. Rogal, "John Wesley at Edinburgh: 1751–1790," *Trinity Journal* 4 n.s. (1983): 18–34.
13. Quoted in Bill J. Leonard, "Preaching in Historical Perspective," in *Handbook of Contemporary Preaching,* ed. Michael Duduit (Nashville: Broadman, 1992), 31.

8.3.3 CHARLES WESLEY—THE DREAMER OF THE AWAKENING

I am not afraid that the people called Methodists should ever cease to exist, either in Europe or America. But I am afraid, lest they should only exist as a dead sect, having the form of religion without the power. And this undoubtedly will be the case unless they hold fast both the doctrine, spirit and discipline with which they first set out.

—John Wesley

> My gracious Master, and my God, Assist me to proclaim, "To spread through all the earth abroad The honours of thy name."
>
> —Charles Wesley (c. 1740)

Much of the vitality of the Great Awakening was certainly due to the giftedness of John Wesley and George Whitefield, but an indispensable factor was the preaching, praying, and praising of **Charles Wesley** (1707–1788). Charles was the eighteenth child of Samuel and Susanna Wesley, born in the Epworth rectory in Lincolnshire. At the age of eight he was sent to the Westminster School (by Westminster Abbey), where his older brother Samuel attended, and in due time went on to Christ Church, Oxford.

Like his older brother John, Charles (who was more mercurial in temperament) was not truly converted until after a frustrating experience in Georgia. Upon returning to England, Charles met the Lord, largely through the influence of his good friend from Oxford, George Whitefield, and through the insights of the Moravian Peter Bohler. Although previously he had been overcome by strong drink and fits of temper, his life changed dramatically.

> He breaks the power of canceled sin, He sets the prisoner free;
> His blood can make the vilest clean, His blood availed for me.

Though not yet understanding justification by faith alone, Charles Wesley was ordained in the Church of England.[1] He began to preach to the prisoners in Newgate and elsewhere. For the next sixteen years he traveled in itinerant ministry preaching the gospel of the grace of God. He ministered both in Wales and Ireland.

Charles' preaching was always with many tears, and his words came "in sentences which had the rush and impact of bullets."[2] Happily married, he preached even on his honeymoon. The great sorrow of his life was that his three children did not become Christians. These strenuous exertions were draining on his poetic nature, but as many have observed, he was overshadowed by his illustrious colleagues apart from whom he would have been better known as a mighty preacher of the Word of God. After he preached for two hours on John 3, many conversions were reported, including one notorious drunkard.[3]

Charles made Bristol his headquarters; John was centered at the Foundry in London. Charles often served as a liaison between his brother John and George Whitefield. Some strains developed as Whitefield moved more and more toward Calvinism.

Throughout these busy years he wrote nine thousand poems, many of which were set to music. He penned hymns such as "Hark, the Herald Angels Sing!" "Rejoice, the Lord Is King," "Jesus, Lover of My Soul" and "Christ the Lord Is Risen Today." The theological richness of these hymns is striking. Largely through Methodist influence, hymn-singing became an accepted part of worship. Other Methodist hymnwriters at this time included Oliver the converted shoemaker who wrote "The God of Abraham Praise," and Edward Perronent, who composed "All Hail the Power of Jesus' Name."[4]

A particularly close associate of both the Wesleys was **John William de la Flechere** or **Fletcher** (1729–1781), born in Nyon in Switzerland. Steeped in Holy Scripture, he served in Madeley, a mining village in Shropshire. He was an exceptionally gifted preacher who spoke with "great freedom of speech and enlargement of heart." He traveled often with the Wesleys and served as principal of the Countess of Huntingdon's school at Trevecca until they parted company over limited atonement. The students said that to have breakfast with Fletcher was like having the holy Communion, he was so full of the love of Christ. Long a consumptive, he poured out his limited energy in ministry. His famous *Checks to Antinomianism* needs a contemporary reissue.[5]

We sense that we are in the company of a select cadre of individuals who preached and lived in a most extraordinary time. "Lord, do it again" should be our earnest prayer.

Charles Wesley captured the sense of the Great Awakening in his lines:

> A charge to keep have I—a God to glorify,
> A never-dying soul to save and fit it for the sky.
> To serve the present age, my calling to fulfill—
> O may it all my powers engage, to do my Master's will!
> Arm me with jealous care, as in Thy sight to live,
> And O, Thy servant, Lord, prepare, a strict account to give.

---

1. Arnold A. Dallimore, *A Heart Set Free: The Life of Charles Wesley* (Wheaton, Ill.: Crossway, 1988), 45.
2. F. R. Webber, *A History of Preaching in Britain and America* (Milwaukee: Northwestern, 1952), 1:350.
3. Dallimore, *A Heart Set Free,* 86.
4. L. E. Elliott-Binns, *The Early Evangelicals* (London: Lutterworth, 1953), 416.
5. Joseph Benson, *The Life of the Rev. John de la Flechere* (New York: Methodist Book Concern, 1904); J. Marrat, *The Vicar of Madeley: John Fletcher* (London: Charles H. Kelly, 1902) shows how Charles Simeon desired to catch the glow of Fletcher's fire, 128.

8.3.4 GEORGE WHITEFIELD—THE DRAMATIST OF THE AWAKENING

I love those who thunder out the Word!

If thou canst prove, thou unbeliever, that the book which we call the Bible, does not contain the lively oracles of God; if thou canst shew that holy men of old did not write this book as they were inwardly moved by the Holy Ghost, then we must give up the doctrine . . . but unless thou canst do this, we must insist upon it . . . if for no other, yet for this one reason, because that God, who cannot lie, has told us so.

—George Whitefield

Great, warming currents were melting huge chunks of spiritual glaciation. The revival breezes came from Continental Pietism, touching Lutherans, the Reformed, and Anabaptists alike with Puritan flavor and revivalistic fervor. It was the time of "the religion of the heart."[1]

Invariably, spiritual awakening is intertwined with the recovery of the Word of God and its preaching. Edwards, in documenting his contention that "true revival is a revival of gospel preaching," cites many examples like that of Asahel Nettleton in America. His preaching was "vigorous and bold . . . warm, pungent and awakening."[2]

We now consider that great era of powerful preaching, full of Christ and his blood atonement. George Whitefield was at the vortex of it all.

George Whitefield—the Character

He has been called the Demosthenes of the pulpit. "He preached like a lion." He was the major influence on the Awakening in New England. Some have termed him the greatest evangelist since the apostle Paul. Lloyd-Jones called him "the greatest preacher England ever produced." **George Whitefield** (1714–1770) was born in Gloucester in the Bell Inn, a tavern owned by his father, to a family of six boys and one girl. His father died when he was two, and he suffered much in his mother's unhappy second marriage. When he was four he had measles. This resulted in permanent damage to his eyes for which he was often called Dr. Squintus. At fifteen he was taken out of school and tended bar, but all through this time Whitefield sought time to read the Bible. In 1732 he went to Oxford and served for three years as a servitor in Pembroke College (from which Samuel Johnson had just come). There he became acquainted with the Wesleys and joined the Holy Club.

Although Whitefield had a reputation as a drunkard and a thief, he seemed penitent. At Oxford, after reading William Law, August Francke, and Henry Scougal, and through the friendship of Charles Wesley, he was converted.[3] "God was pleased to remove the heavy load," he recalled. Later he went to Georgia, as did the Wesleys, and wherever he went, his ministry could be called "preaching that startled a nation." In all he made thirteen trips to America.

His preaching was powerful and dramatic. Reportedly, after his first sermon fifteen people went mad. C. S. Horne said of him, "We may accept the almost universal verdict that for dramatic and declamatory power he had no rival in his own age, and no superior in any age."[4]

Dallimore's two volumes convey the spiritual warmth and great godliness of Whitefield.[5] A typical exclamation: "Oh that we were all a flame of fire!" He was first and always a soulwinner, saying, "Oh, that I might catch them with a holy guile." Reading more and more of the old Calvinists, he drew away from the Wesleys but always insisted "we are ready to give a universal offer to all poor sinners."[6]

Whitefield's marriage was not fulfilling, and his only son died at four months. He himself was afflicted with frequent illness and always got sick just before he preached. At the age of fifty-six, George Whitefield died of asthmatic complications after preaching in Massachusetts. Wesley gave the funeral address in England. One of the mighty giants had fallen.

George Whitefield—the Communicator

A more striking contrast cannot be drawn than that between the calm dignity of John Wesley and the emotional and sprightly preaching of George Whitefield. He preached with great pathos, weeping in every sermon. He had a great faculty for description; his preaching abounded with anecdotes. Dallimore characterizes his preaching as biblical, doctrinal, and simple. Gillies, his first biographer, reports just some of the astonishing numbers:

1. The incredible extent of his preaching: forty to sixty hours a week
2. The number of times he preached: one thousand times a year for thirty years
3. The immensity of his audiences: Benjamin Franklin heard him preach to thirty thousand
4. The breadth of his appeal—peer and peasant alike loved him

Dallimore observes, "He had a most peculiar art of speaking personally to you in a congregation of four thousand people."[7] Another observer remarks: "He made them laugh, he made them moan, he swayed them like reeds in the wind. A surly old general who despised preachers followed the crowd, listened as the young preacher described a blind man stumbling nearer and nearer to the edge of a precipice, forgot himself and preacher-hate and shouted right out in the meeting, 'Good God, he's over!'"[8]

Whitefield used the three-point homiletic and spoke in an amazing voice. It was reported that a man leaning on a gate a mile away could hear enough and was saved. David Garrick, the actor, panted, "I'd give one hundred guineas to be able to say 'oh' like George Whitefield." With his interest in narrative and in portraying Christ and biblical characters (his Zacchaeus rendition was especially famous), Whitefield anticipated emphases which were uncommon in his day.

Some hagiographers of Whitefield have been uneasy over Harry Stout's recent *The Divine Dramatist,* which presents the great revivalist as a "born actor," as one who read plays as a youth but who turned on the worldliness of the theater later in life.[9] Stout points to the "dramaturgy" in the Church of England service which Whitefield never left (he always wore the gown in preaching, even in the fields).

Whitefield utilized imaginative flight, as in the frequent use of the metaphor of an ocean voyage,[10] and not always wisely, as when he purported to impersonate the marriage agent for Christ or when he hid a trumpeter to peal forth suddenly after a sermon on the Second Coming—and precipitated a panic and hysteria.[11] Whitefield did adapt to the fields and the marketplace in his time. And he did make use of his wealthy friend and his ornate carriage to drive through the town and invite people to the service.[12]

Stout is sadly out of balance in some of his criticisms, but we can hardly fault him for bringing us real aspects of Whitefield's preaching. Were we to fuse the hagiographic Dallimore with the realistic Stout we would have an effective blend.[13]

Whitefield cried out, "I'll preach Christ till I do to pieces fall!" This is almost literally what happened—he preached himself to death. Even here he was the actor, for he used his own physical maladies and miseries to portray the agonies of the damned.[14]

In terms of structure, Whitefield followed a modified Puritan pattern. Like the Wesleys, he broke away from reading manuscripts and especially loved free prayer. He wrote, "I find I gain greater light and knowledge by preaching extempore, so that I fear I should quench the Spirit did I not go on to speak as He gives me utterance."[15]

George Whitefield—the Intercontinental Commuter

Whitefield reminds us of the old adage: If we take care of the depth of our ministry, God will take care of the breadth. The Lord enlarged the scope of Whitefield's ministry geographically, ecclesiastically, and socially.

Though self-conscious of his meager origins in a society of great social stratification, Whitefield got along with almost everyone. His remarkable friendship with Benjamin Franklin, who became his American agent, is most telling. Franklin eulogizes Whitefield in his *Autobiography*.[16] Whitefield never stopped seeking to win Franklin to Christ. David Hume was reportedly so taken with Whitefield's message that "he forgot to sneer." Bolingbroke admitted, "He has the most commanding eloquence I have ever heard in any person." Whitefield's close ties with Jonathan Edwards were typical, and his ability to steer a middle course between the moderates and the separatists in Scotland extended his sphere of influence.

Whitefield's relationship to **Selina, Countess of Huntingdon** (1707–1791), bears out the point. Converted as a girl of nine when she saw a corpse her own age, she married the wealthy Theophilus Huntingdon and heard the Wesleys, Whitefield, Romaine, and Fletcher in her private chapel. She was well read in Scripture and theology and helped Charles Wesley see the error of excessive Moravian quietism. Her two sons died of smallpox in 1744, and her husband died in 1746. She lent support and encouragement to her friends, as well as to Watts and Doddridge and John Newton. She knew and influenced Georg Handel. It was her conviction that "on the character of ministers the prosperity of the churches will at all times greatly depend."[17] She sold all her jewels to sponsor Trevecca College and her spiritual enterprises, and was drawn more and more to Whitefield's theological slant. He was one of her chaplains and she helped build his London headquarters, the Chapel at Tottenham Court Road.

Whitefield was a true Puritan in some ways, but was his own man. He loved Christmas and preached a great sermon on "The Observation of the birth of Christ, the Duty of All Christians; Or, the True Way of Keeping Christmas." The argument is so biblical, so practical, so winsome, even to the appeal not to overindulge during the holy season and thus to "forget the Lord of Glory."[18] John Greenleaf Whittier commemorates Whitefield in these lines:

Lo! by the Merrimac Whitefield stands
In the temple that was never made with hands—
Curtains of azure and crystal wall,
And dome of the sunshine over all!
A homeless pilgrim, with dubious name
Blown about on the wings of fame;

Now as an angel of blessing classed,
And now as a mad enthusiast.
Possessed by the one dread thought that lent
Its goad to his fiery temperament,
Up and down in the world he went,
A John the Baptist crying—Repent!

---

1. Ted A. Campbell, *The Religion of the Heart* (Columbia: University of South Carolina Press, 1991). A rich study.
2. Brian H. Edwards, *Revival: A People Saturated with God* (Durham, N.C.: Evangelical Press, 1990), 102.
3. Timothy L. Smith, *Whitefield and Wesley on the New Birth* (Grand Rapids: Francis Asbury/Zondervan, 1986), 39ff.
4. A. E. Garvie, *The Christian Preacher* (New York: Scribner's, 1923), 217.
5. Arnold A. Dallimore, *George Whitefield: The Life and Times of the Great Evangelist of the Eighteenth-Century Revival*, 2 vols. (Wheaton, Ill.: Crossway, 1970, 1979). Stout calls this a "filiopietist" biography.
6. Dallimore, *George Whitefield*, 2:239.
7. Ibid., 2:482.
8. Frank S. Mead, "The Story of George Whitefield," *The Sword of the Lord* (January 31, 1992): 3–4.
9. Harry S. Stout, *The Divine Dramatist: George Whitefield and the Rise of Modern Evangelicalism* (Grand Rapids: Eerdmans, 1991), 7.
10. Ibid., 47.
11. R. T. Kendall, *Stand Up and Be Counted* (Grand Rapids: Zondervan, 1984), 87ff.
12. Stout, *The Divine Dramatist*, 72.
13. It is curious that Stout does not once mention Whitefield's conversion. Does he not understand the criticality of conversion? His stress on the effeminacy of Whitefield (24) is bizarre, and he certainly overstresses "marketing." How much of this was part of a conscious strategy in Whitefield? (cf. Frank Lambert, *"Pedlar in Divinity": George Whitefield and the Transatlantic Revivals, 1737–1770* (Princeton, N.J.: Princeton University Press, 1994). He gives heavy fire to Whitefield's "genius for self-promotion" and his "shameless ego-centricity."
14. George Marsden's review of Stout in *Christianity Today* (April 27, 1992): 60 is choice, and the review by William L. Sachs in *The Christian Century* (January 29, 1992): 104–5 is also full of good questions.
15. Jay E. Adams, *Sermon Analysis* (Denver: Accent, 1986), 118ff.
16. Stout, *The Divine Dramatist*, 222.

17. William Edward Painter, *Life and Times of Selina, Countess of Huntingdon* (London: Shirley, 1844).
18. *Whitefield's Sermons,* vol. 1 (London: Banner and Truth, 1959).

8.3.5 *JONATHAN EDWARDS—DEEP THINKER OF THE AWAKENING*

Sinners should be earnestly invited to come and accept the Saviour—with all of the winning, encouraging arguments that the Gospel affords.

Yet if in these sermons he shall find the most important truths exhibited and pressed home on the conscience with that pungency which tends to awaken, convince, humble and edify; if he shall find that serious strain of piety which, in spite of himself, forces upon him a serious frame of mind; if in the perusal, he cannot but be ashamed and alarmed at himself, and in some measure feel the reality and weight of eternal things; if, at least he, like Agrippa, shall be almost persuaded to be a Christian; I presume he will not grudge the time required to peruse what is now offered him. These, if I mistake not, are the great ends to be aimed at in all sermons, whether preached or printed, and are ends which can never be accomplished by those modern fashionable discourses which are delivered under the name of sermons.

—Jonathan Edwards

For generations the words "Puritan" and "Puritanism" were pejorative terms, and no one was more anathemic than **Jonathan Edwards.** Oliver Wendell Holmes described Edwards' basic convictions as "barbaric . . . not only false but absurd." Mark Twain spoke of Edwards as a "drunken lunatic . . . a resplendent genius gone mad. . . . I was ashamed to be in such company."[1] Edwards' sermon "Sinners in the Hands of an Angry God" was to many a symbol of religious reaction, and even James Houston, a sympathetic friend and editor, speaks of it as a *faux pas,* excusing it as only one out of twelve hundred extant sermons.[2]

Yet in recent years there has come a tremendous renascence of interest in the Puritans and Edwards, starting with Perry Miller's work at Harvard on *The Puritan Mind.* Miller overplayed the influence of John Locke and Sir Isaac Newton in the shaping of Edwards and really did not understand evangelical conversion and revival in any biblical sense, but he was a sparkplug in Puritan studies. Academic dissertations on Edwards have exponentially increased in recent times. Noll points out that the three-volume *Encyclopedia of the American Religious Experience* has more references to Edwards than to any other person. The magnificent Yale edition of Edwards' complete works stands as a monument to this resurgence of interest.[3]

Now it is generally recognized that Jonathan Edwards was the most powerful and effective preacher ever heard in America. Many concede Edwards to be America's prime theologian and one of her most distinguished philosophers. His influence on other molders of thought is mind-boggling: Thomas Chalmers of Scotland in the next century spent a year in rapture over Edwards' concept of the magnificence of the Godhead, and James Orr of Scotland praised Edwards' "exalted vision of God."[4] Noll speaks of Edwards as "besotted with God." Others of his admirers, like D. Martyn Lloyd-Jones, contend that "Puritanism reached its fullest bloom in the life and ministry of Jonathan Edwards."[5] What mattered most to Lloyd-Jones was that "[Edwards] preached sermons . . . he did not deliver lectures."[6] Richard Lovelace speaks of him as "the greatest mind produced in America" as well as the theologian of revival.[7] Even Roman Catholic theologians have boarded the bandwagon, conveniently ignoring the antipathy Edwards felt for Roman Catholic doctrine and practice.[8] But what does this towering figure in biblical preaching mean to us?

Jonathan Edwards—the Man

Jonathan Edwards (1703–1758) was born to the manse, the son of Timothy and Esther Edwards, who were serving the Congregational church in East Windsor, Connecticut. The only son of eleven children, he was early marked as precocious, learning Greek, Latin, and Hebrew from his father beginning at age five. He wrote a treatise on flying spiders at age eleven. At thirteen, he entered Yale and graduated four years later as valedictorian.

In reaction to his father's high Calvinism,[9] Edwards read Locke's "Essay Concerning the Human Understanding" when he was fourteen. He came to "sweet delight in God" at Yale in 1721 while reading 1 Timothy 1:17.[10] He was commanded by "vehement longings for God" and set himself to read the Scriptures "steadily, constantly and frequently." He made a series of resolutions for his new walk in Christ and had a great interest in millennial ideas and unfulfilled prophecy.

After taking his M.A. at Yale, Edwards briefly pastored a small Scottish Presbyterian church in New York City, on Wall Street near Broadway, and a congregation in Bolton, Connecticut. He then returned to serve as a tutor at Yale. In 1727 he was ordained, and in July of that year married Sarah Pierrepont. His marriage always greatly strengthened him, and he and Sarah were parents of twelve children.

Although John Locke's influence over Edwards has been overstated, Locke's emphasis on a knowledge based on sensation and experience rather than innate ideas was important for him. Puritan preaching was often unemotional, but Edwards' "heightened imagination" rekindled "a warmer, more emotional preaching," even with a rather dull delivery.[11]

Edwards served as an assistant pastor to his maternal grandfather, Solomon Stoddard, who at eighty-three was winding up a sixty-year pastorate at Northampton, Massachusetts. Edwards' preaching was especially appreciated when the longtime pastor died. A vigorous twenty-three-year ministry ensued during which successive waves of revival and awakening swept over the Northampton church. It was to become the eye of a spiritual storm that reached to the ends of the earth.

Jonathan Edwards—the Mind

New England was on the way from *The Scarlet Letter* to *Peyton Place*. Its trademark Puritanism was in serious decline. The Half-way Covenant (an issue surveyed in 7.4.2), supported by Solomon Stoddard but opposed by Edwards (an issue which would ultimately cost him dearly), was intended to prop up a shaky church. In fact, it poisoned the church with unbelief and carnality.

Edwards did not embrace everything Calvinistic.[12] He advocated experiential religion. The sermon was to be the agent of conversion, which in turn served as the doorway into the experience.

> An increase in speculative knowledge in divinity is not what is so much needed by our people as something else. Men may abound in this sort of light and have no heat. . . . Our people do not so much need to have their heads turned as to have their hearts touched; and they stand in the greatest need of that sort of preaching which has the greatest tendency to do this.[13]

Harold Simonson argued that in *Religious Affections: How a Man's Will Affects His Character Before God* the more dominant influences on Edwards "were Augustine, Calvin, and the Scriptures."[14] Simonson's contention is that "true religion is a fixed engagement of the heart."

Although the Northampton church had experienced five revivals during Stoddard's time, it seemed to Edwards that the people heard the gospel preached as if they had never heard it before. In the spring of 1735, Edwards preached a series of sermons on "Justification by Faith," and there came a moving of the Spirit, stirring up the believers and bringing the unconverted to Christ. "There scarcely was a single person in the town, young or old, left unconcerned about the great things of the eternal world."[15]

Case histories of these conversions are deeply moving. Edwards' descriptions in *The Narrative* had immense impact on both sides of the Atlantic. Edwards, Whitefield, and the Tennents reported great "effusions" of the Spirit as the revivals spread. When Edwards preached "Sinners in the Hands of an Angry God" in Enfield on July 8, 1741, the people cried out so loudly that the sermon could scarcely be heard. In terrible agony, some chewed on carpet. Others tried to cling to the pillars of the church lest they slip into hell. Blacks and Indians alike were touched by the revivals. All told, there were four hundred converts.[16]

Jonathan Edwards—the Message

Picture the six-foot one-inch, emaciated figure standing in the pulpit, sermon notes held close to his eye because of his shortsightedness. In his other hand, he held a candle. His voice was weak and monotone. It could only be the Holy Spirit who energized such preaching.

Edwards used the typically Puritan plain style, simple and direct. He referred often to Scripture. In one set of fifteen sermons, he used 374 biblical quotations, an average of twenty-five per sermon.[17] Eighty-two percent of his words were fewer than five letters. He used *you* with great effect and artfully employed illustration and anecdote. Turnbull has helpfully categorized Edwards' sermons for us.[18] We appreciate the evangelist's adroit versatility as we consider his series of thirty sermons on Isaiah 51:7, "A History of the Work of Redemption." Listen as he preaches on God's wrath and judgment:

> The bow of God's wrath is bent, and the arrow made ready on the string, and justice bends the arrow at your heart, and strains the bow; and it is nothing but the mere pleasure of God—and that of an angry God, without any promise or obligation at all—that keeps the arrow one moment from being made drunk with your blood. Thus all of you that never passed under a great change of heart by the mighty power of the Spirit of God upon your souls; all of you that were never born again, and made new creatures, and raised from dead in sin to a state of new and before unexperienced light and life, are in the hands of an angry God. However you may have had religious affections, and may keep up a form of religion in your families and closets and in the house of God, it is nothing but his mere pleasure that keeps you from being this moment swallowed up in everlasting destruction.

But the revival began to wane, and the years 1743 to 1748 were years of conflict for Edwards. In 1750 he was overwhelmingly voted out of his church. His farewell sermon is a model of Christian love and charity, and he was willing to stay on for six additional months because the church had no supply. He then went to Stockbridge as a missionary to the Indians for seven years. While he was there he wrote several of his most piercing works. His scholarship was widely respected, and he was called to succeed his deceased son-in-law, Aaron Burr (father of the infamous statesman), as president of the College of New Jersey (later Princeton University). Soon after arriving in New Jersey he was inoculated for smallpox and died, being less than six months in his position. His last words to his loved ones were, "Trust in God and ye need not fear." What a preacher of grace indeed. The message may seem heavy to us and not always balanced, but we need to be reminded of his demeanor as he preached the message:

> A preacher of a low and moderate voice, a natural way of delivery; and without any agitation of body, or anything else in the manner to excite attention; except his habitual and great solemnity, looking and speaking as in the presence of God.[19]

The lingering lessons from the vital pulpit ministry and life of Jonathan Edwards are many. As one contemporary writer explained it: "While others preached self-reliance and sang the song of the self, Edwards drew nearer the truth—that nothing can be saved without confronting its own damnation, that the way to gain one's life is to lose it."

---

1. Mark Noll, "God at the Center: Jonathan Edwards on True Virtue," in *The Christian Century* (September 8–15, 1993): 856. Some scholars try to argue that the Great Awakening was the result of the last gasp of the "traditional, premodern, anti-capitalistic

values" of rural New England; see James German, "The Social Utility of Wicked Self-Love: Calvinism, Capitalism, and Public Policy in Revolutionary New England," *Journal of American History* (December 1995): 965ff.

2. James Houston, ed., *Religious Affections* (Portland, Oreg.: Multnomah, 1984), xv.

3. Noll, "God at the Center," 857.

4. Ibid., 858.

5. D. Martyn Lloyd-Jones, *The Puritans: Their Origins and Successors* (Edinburgh: Banner of Truth, 1987), 351.

6. Ibid., 359.

7. Richard F. Lovelace, "The Surprising Works of God," *Christianity Today* (September 11, 1995): 29ff.

8. Anri Morimoto, *Jonathan Edwards and the Catholic Vision of Salvation* (University Park: Penn State University Press, 1995). While helpfully pointing out that while Edwards was a theologian of the heart but not a "theologian of subjectivity," Morimoto fails to grasp the importance of forensic justification, which is both real and legal. This is a major sticking point between Roman Catholics with their "double justification" and historic Protestants. Morimoto gives in to "salvation for non-Christians," which is universes away from Edwards.

9. Ralph Turnbull, *Jonathan Edwards the Preacher* (Grand Rapids: Baker, 1958), 16.

10. Iain H. Murray, *Jonathan Edwards: A New Biography* (Edinburgh: Banner of Truth, 1987), 34ff. The best yet.

11. Turnbull, *Jonathan Edwards the Preacher*. Murray (ibid.) shows that Edwards ceased preparation of and use of a manuscript in preaching after 1741 (189).

12. John H. Gerstner, *Steps to Salvation: The Evangelistic Message of Jonathan Edwards* (Philadelphia: Westminster, 1960). Even Gerstner must concede that for Edwards people can seek after God, and he is "most optimistic about the outcome of genuine seeking," 96.

13. Houston, *Religious Affections,* xvi. In the Classics of Faith and Devotion series. A "must" to understand Edwards.

14. Harold Simonson, *Jonathan Edwards: Theologian of the Heart* (Grand Rapids: Eerdmans, 1974).

15. James A. Stewart, ed., *Jonathan Edwards—The Narrative* (Grand Rapids: Kregel, 1957), 25.

16. Professor Alan F. Segal, a Jewish scholar, has argued that Paul's conversion is the New Testament paradigm for revolutionary change. See his *Paul the Convert* (New Haven, Conn.: Yale University Press, 1990).

17. Jay E. Adams, *Sermon Analysis* (Denver: Accent, 1986), 107.

18. Turnbull, *Jonathan Edwards the Preacher,* 168ff.

19. Thomas Prince in John Piper, *The Supremacy of God in Preaching* (Grand Rapids: Baker, 1990), 102. Piper's lectures on the God-centered preaching of Edwards are luminous and exciting.

8.3.6 · Gilbert Tennent—The Developer of the Awakening

In arguing for preaching terrors first and comforts second, Tennent pictures a neighbor who was sleeping securely and dreaming pleasantly while his house was afire.

You would not surely go to whisper in [your neighbor's] ear some soft round-about discourse, that his house was you feared not in the best condition possible; it might perhaps take damage if suitable care were not taken to prevent it. I say would I go thus about the bush with a poor man in a time of such danger? No, I believe not: I fancy you would take a rough method, without ceremony or grimace.

—Gilbert Tennent

Spiritual tides were at low ebb in the eighteenth century in the mid-Atlantic states as well as New England. Jonathan Dickenson concluded that in New Jersey "religion was in a decline, with most church members moribund and the body of the people careless and carnal."[1] Vital Christianity seemed to be in the death throes in Pennsylvania as well.

In the year 1720 a Dutch Reformed minister, **Theodore Freylinghuysen** (1691–1748), born in Germany near the Dutch border, began a revival ministry in the Raritan Valley of New Jersey. He preached with evangelical fervor and insisted on conversion and a changed life. The strategy of "the new lights" (or those in favor of revivals) was always more aggressive and confrontational than some of the old diehards could handle. In general the newer rhetoric of the Awakening sermons of this century involved moving away from reading manuscripts to a "more fragmentary mode of sermonic discourse."[2]

On occasion Freylinghuysen exchanged pulpits with members of the Tennent family, who served Presbyterian churches in New Jersey. **William Tennent Sr.** (1673–1746) was born in Northern Ireland, graduated from the University of Edinburgh, and was ordained in the Church of Ireland (Episcopal). In 1718 he came to the United States and was accepted by the Presbyterian synod, serving in Neshaminy, Pennsylvania, until his death. In 1726 he established a training school for ministers in his manse, called the Log College, where he trained his four sons and many others for the ministry.

Again we see the influence of Continental Pietism on the revivalists in this region. It was their aim "to rejuvenate sincere practical piety among the colonial laity."[3] William Tennent's message was directed against rebels who "resisted the Divine Sovereign by corrupting the Scriptures, by forsaking God's Word, or by refusing to 'improve' themselves after experiencing providential afflictions . . . still others revolted by relishing every sort of iniquity or by simply offering empty ecclesiastical performances."[4]

One of his sons, **Gilbert Tennent** (1703–1764), was born in Ireland, trained at the Log College, and received an honorary M.A. from Yale. After teaching at the Log College for a year, he took a Presbyterian charge in New Brunswick, New Jersey. Here in 1739 he welcomed Whitefield, and they became fast friends and travel companions. His brothers **John Tennent** and **William Tennent Jr.** had an unusual ministry at Freehold, New Jersey, where many were "taken in the gospel net." After strong biblical preaching, "the terror of God fell generally upon the inhabitants of this place; so that wickedness, as ashamed in a great measure, hid itself."[5] Gilbert's ministry was even more extensive. In one series in Boston, more than six hundred were converted. In 1743 he took the pastorate of the Second Presbyterian Church in Philadelphia, where he served until his death.

Between 1753 and 1755, he ministered in England and Scotland with Samuel Davies in the interest of raising funds for the College of New Jersey; he did raise a subscription from Lady Huntingdon, George Whitefield, and others. Davies, "an astonishing preacher" himself, has given us one of the most realistic descriptions of Whitefield's ministry in Moorfields.[6] Davies had the opportunity to preach before young George III and his queen, who expressed themselves as being enchanted but were rude and audible in their interruptions of the service. Samuel Davis fixed his eyes on the royal pair and boldly intoned the text: "When the lion roars, the beasts of the field tremble; when Jehovah speaks, let the Kings of the earth keep silence before him."

The die was cast in Gilbert Tennent's ministry as early as 1740, when he preached his famous sermon on "The Danger of an Unconverted Ministry" from Mark 6:34. Whitefield paid tribute to Tennent's preaching:

> I never before heard such a searching sermon. He [Gilbert Tennent] convinced me more and more that we can preach the Gospel of Christ no further than we have experienced the power of it in our own hearts. Being deeply convicted of sin, by God's Holy Spirit, at this first conversion, he has learned experimentally to dissect the heart of a natural man. Hypocrites must either soon be converted or enraged at this preaching. He is a son of thunder, and does not fear the faces of men.[7]

Tennent had also visited with Zinzendorf during the latter's one visit to America in the winter of 1741 to 1742. Tennent was troubled by Zinzendorf's perfectionistic tendencies and his tilt toward universal redemption, but he was especially concerned over Zinzendorf's depreciation of the role of the law and conviction for sin. Tennent also questioned Whitefield's participation with the Moravians.[8] He and Whitefield broke on this issue. Again we see that revivals tend to falter because of their own excesses. After lightning hit his house, threw him down, and scorched his feet, Tennent's adversaries saw God's hand of warning against their inveterate foe. He preached a memorable sermon in reply titled "All Things Come Alike to All."[9] The tensions with Whitefield exacerbated. At this time he led in the building of a new church (Arch Street Presbyterian Church). He continued to aid in the development of the College of New Jersey where he preached a notable revival. He died in 1764 and was buried in the center aisle of the church he had so long and ably served. he preached fire and judgment, but he could apply the "gospel balsam" with great skill and positive effect.

---

1. A. Skevington Wood, *The Inextinguishable Blaze: Spiritual Renewal and Advance in the Eighteenth Century* (Grand Rapids: Eerdmans, 1960), 54.

2. Donald Weber, *Rhetoric and History in Revolutionary New England* (Oxford: Oxford University Press, 1988), 150. Further relevant reading can be found in Leonard I. Sweet, ed., *Communication and Change in American Religious History* (Grand

Rapids: Eerdmans, 1993); Paul K. Conkin, *The Uneasy Center: Reformed Christianity in Ante-Bellum America* (Chapel Hill: University of North Carolina Press, 1995); Max Stackhouse, *Creeds, Society and Human Rights* (Grand Rapids: Eerdmans, 1984). Particularly suggestive on "Free Church Calvinists" or the Puritans (55–57).

3. Milton J. Coalter Jr., *Gilbert Tennent, Son of Thunder: A Case Study of Continental Pietism's Impact on the First Great Awakening in the Middle Colonies* (New York: Greenwood, 1986), xviii.
4. Ibid., 7.
5. Wood, *The Inextinguishable Blaze,* 58–59.
6. D. Martyn Lloyd-Jones, *The Puritans: Their Origins and Successors* (Edinburgh: Banner of Truth, 1987), 123ff.
7. Coalter, *Gilbert Tennent,* frontispiece.
8. Coalter, *Gilbert Tennent,* 108ff.
9. Ibid., 126.

8.3.7 WILLIAM MCCULLOCH—THE DEFINER OF THE AWAKENING

The yearning for salvation and the sense of God's nearness break forth at certain epochs simultaneously with over-mastering power and with effects that are felt centuries and millennia later.
—Archbishop Nathan Soderblom of Sweden
in the Gifford Lectures of 1931

For the Scots, the Bible had been front and center from the days of the Scottish Reformation and John Knox. But the emerging spirit of great toleration gave rise to "lapse and languor." The Marrow-men and the seceders struck a blow for true faith, but a significant defining experience for biblical faith and preaching came in the controversial "Cambuslang Work" of 1742.[1]

Cambuslang was a village of six hundred near Glasgow. **William McCulloch** (1691–1771), the son of a schoolmaster in Whithorn, studied at Edinburgh and Glasgow universities and was ordained in 1731, when he assumed pastoral ministry in Cambuslang. Not noted for his preaching endowments, it was joked that McCulloch sent the men of the community to the alehouses when he preached. Yet he was learned in several languages and an authority in mathematics and astronomy.[2]

While his first years were uneventful, McCulloch sought to establish prayer societies in which intercession for awakening took place. "He spent much time in secret prayer, waiting with humble patience for a favourable return. He greatly encouraged private Christians to meet for social prayer, and particularly that God would revive His work everywhere."[3] Whitefield's first visit to Scotland had highlighted a style of preaching "that commanded and compelled attention."[4] McCulloch picked up the torch and soon began to preach law and grace with a rich sense of doctrinal construct. People began to crowd out the church.

All of this was in a context of deep internal problems for the parishioners—a terrible storm and a period of famine. Many were critical of the new style of preaching, but fifteen people found salvation.[5]

The people wanted more Bible lectures and more prayer meetings. Soon two hundred converts were listed. Sermons were preached every day, at 2, 6, and 9 P.M. with widespread symptoms of "uncontrolled distress." There were the phenomena of revival, including convulsions, prophecies, and tongues. Seekers were carried into the manse like wounded soldiers.[6] McCulloch sent for Whitefield, who made fourteen trips to Scotland in all.

Whitefield soon left the Tabernacle in the charge of his associate, John Cennick, and went straight to Glasgow, where he addressed twenty-thousand people. He then went to Cambuslang. On July 9, 1742, he preached to thirty-thousand. The sacrament was celebrated in the fields until 2 A.M. Old John Bonar, ancestor of the Bonar brothers, was one of those fired up for Christ. Communion tables were set up in the preaching tents. After one of these powerful communion services, Whitefield preached his famous sermon on "being married to Christ."[7]

News of the revival began to spread. Its effects were soon felt in Kilsyth under the ministry of Pastor **James Robe** (1688–1753), who endured a wicked and licentious community. Robe also began preaching on the doctrine of regeneration, and many were awakened and converted. Public worship sometimes began at 8:30 A.M. and continued for up to twelve hours.

The Erskines were critical of both McCulloch and Robe for remaining in the national church. In fact, the revivals arrested the drift toward secession. The Erskines spoke of Whitefield himself as "a limb of the anti-Christ" and said that he "trimmed and temporized" the message. Nonetheless "the fruits of it remain."[8] In 1751 McCulloch could still count four hundred in his parish who had been converted in the revival. The revival had a great influence on Thomas Chalmers and others who led "the great disruption" in 1843, upon English Anglicans, and on the work of foreign missions.

McCulloch corresponded extensively with Jonathan Edwards. Here we appreciate the networking of God's quickening Spirit through so many different cultures and personalities.

Yet another heroic champion of biblical preaching at this time was **John Erskine** (1721–1803), the long-time pastor of Grayfriars Church. Not related to the seceder Erskine brothers, he led evangelicals in the Church of Scotland and was a great friend of Whitefield's. Erskine wrote often to Jonathan Edwards, and like McCulloch was an ardent proponent of missionary outreach. The parents of Sir Walter Scott were members of his congregation. While Scott leaned toward the moderates, he gave a sympathetic portrayal of Erskine in chapter 37 of his novel *Guy Mannering*.

---

1. Arthur Fawcett, *The Cambuslang Revival* (Edinburgh: Banner of Truth, 1771). This very searching account needs to be set over against the contemporary drift in the Church of Scotland, which has fewer than eight hundred thousand members and loses some twenty thousand every year. Ian Bradley in *Marching to the Promised Land: Has the Church a Future?* points out that at this rate of decline the Church of Scotland will cease to exist in 2047.

2. F. R. Webber, *A History of Preaching in Britain and America* (Milwaukee: North-western, 1955), 2:220.
3. A. Skevington Wood, *The Inextinguishable Blaze: Spiritual Renewal and Advance in the Eighteenth Century* (Grand Rapids: Eerdmans, 1960), 120.
4. Ibid., 119.
5. Fawcett, *The Cambuslang Revival,* 100, 106ff.
6. Ibid., 114.
7. Harry S. Stout, *The Divine Dramatist* (Grand Rapids: Eerdmans, 1991), 149.
8. Fawcett, *The Cambuslang Revival,* 166ff.

8.4 SENT WITH THE GOSPEL

He who goes out weeping, carrying seed to sow, will return with songs of joy, carrying sheaves with him.

—Psalm 126:6

The seed is the word of God.

—Luke 8:11b

As the rain and the snow come down from heaven, and do not return to it without watering the earth and making it bud and flourish, so that it yields seed for the sower and bread for the eater, so is my word that goes out from my mouth: It will not return to me empty, but will accomplish what I desire and achieve the purpose for which I sent it.

—Isaiah 55:10–11

Where were Protestant missions during this time? The surging missionary passion of the early church and the throbbing courage of gospel emissaries during the Middle Ages do not find replication in the Reformers or the Puritans. Yet incubated in the bosom of Continental Pietism and ignited by the Great Awakening, missions were poised on the brink of a glorious explosion.

A return to the Lord always requires a new seriousness about what is on God's heart and what obedience to God entails. The Great Commission (in its five forms) mandates making disciples, preaching the gospel to every creature, preaching repentance and forgiveness of sins in Christ's name to all nations, being sent as Christ was sent, and being Spirit-empowered as witnesses in Jerusalem, Judea, Samaria, and to the ends of the earth. Preaching is an integral part of the Lord's plan for the expansion of the church. It is now our joy to pursue the action which came out of the mighty spiritual revival we call the Great Awakening.

8.4.1 BARTHOLOMEW ZIEGENBALG—GOING AFAR

We missionaries on our own part are endeavoring, according to the Measure of Grace God Almighty has imparted to us, plentifully to spread abroad the Seed of the Word of God among the Heathen in their own language, there being no other means for touching the hearts of the heathen in order to their conversion.

—Bartholomew Ziegenbalg

I am sending you to them to open their eyes and turn them from darkness to light, and from the power of Satan to God, so that they may receive forgiveness of sins and a place among those who are sanctified by faith in me.

—Acts 26:17b–18

We have seen that early Protestants had little sense of the world task of the church. Luther himself taught that the Great Commission was for the apostles alone. The Puritans with few exceptions did not evince any strong missionary impulse.

With Dutch independence and the advance of the Dutch East India Company, a training school for missionaries was set up in Leyden under the aegis of **Hugo Grotius,** whose *De Veritate Religionis Christianae (The Truth of Christianity)* spurred missionary enterprise. **George Candidius** went to Formosa to evangelize, as did others to Ceylon and India.

A new impetus to the world task arose out of Pietism and the Moravians from Herrnhut. Herrnhut, through Zinzendorf's efforts, became what Latourette calls "the center of a missionary enterprise which extended over much of the world."[1] Here was "an emphasis upon the conversion of individual non-Christians and a distrust of mass movements of whole communities."[2] Pivotal was the Danish outreach through the Halle Pietists and A. H. Francke with encouragement from the newly formed Society for the Propagation of Christian Knowledge (SPCK, founded in 1698).

King Frederick IV of Denmark was moved by the missionary passion of his court preacher, a German named **Franz Julius Lutkens,** and desired to send out missionaries. Francke was asked to recommend candidates since none could be found in Denmark. He nominated two godly students from Halle, **Bartholomew Ziegenbalg** (1683–1719) and **Henry Plutschau** (1677–1747). The two were ordained in Denmark and posted to the Danish colony at Tranquebar southwest of Madras in 1706.

In the face of stiff opposition, Ziegenbalg learned the Tamil language and with the help of a new recruit from Halle, **Johan Grundler** (Plutschau's failing health necessitated his return home), built a chapel, preached the Word, baptized converts, and translated the Scriptures into Tamil.[3] Assistance for the project came from the SPCK under the auspices of **Anton Wilhelm Boehm,** the German chaplain to Prince George, Danish consort to Queen Anne. Letters from India and Ziegenbalg came to Boehm in London onboard vessels of the East India Company. These were read in sessions of the SPCK in London and forwarded to royalty in Copenhagen. Francke and Cotton Mather shared much about this work, impressing us with the providential interconnectedness of gospel witness.[4]

Ziegenbalg died at thirty-six and endured unspeakable misunderstanding. Yet in his brief life, he oversaw a printer's ministry in the publication of Scriptures, catechisms, hymnals, and other works.[5] He left 350 native converts and many catechumens. He departed from this life singing "Jesus My Redeemer Lives."

The challenge of preaching cross-culturally is one we all face, but learning to preach in a second or third language poses unusual difficulty. The company of those who have surmounted the obstacles is great and noble.[6] We salute these spiritual pioneers and groundbreakers!

---

1. Kenneth Scott Latourette, *Three Centuries of Advance* (Grand Rapids: Eerdmans, 1939, 1967), 3:47.
2. Ibid., 51.
3. V. Raymond Edman, *The Light in Dark Ages* (Wheaton, Ill.: Van Kampen, 1949), 353.
4. Ernst Benz, "Pietist and Puritan Sources of Early Protestant Missions," *Church History* (June 20, 1951): 28–55.
5. T. J. Bach, *Vision and Valor* (Grand Rapids: Baker, 1963), 31.
6. Admirably and ably treated in David J. Hesselgrave, *Communicating Christ Cross-Culturally: An Introduction to Missionary Communication,* 2d ed. (Grand Rapids: Zondervan, 1991). A wealth of data for all communicators.

8.4.2   DAVID BRAINERD—GETTING DOWN

> I prayed privately with a dear Christian friend or two; and I think I scarce ever launched so far out on the broad ocean that my soul with joy triumphed over all the evils on the shores of immortality. I think that time and all its gay amusements and cruel disappointments never appeared so inconsiderable to me before.
>
> —David Brainerd

Another brilliant star flamed across the mission horizon. **David Brainerd** (1718–1747) enjoyed only four years of ministry, yet he bequeathed a magnificent legacy to Native Americans and to missions.

Brainerd was born on a farm in Haddam, Connecticut. His father died when he was nine, and his mother died five years later. He stayed with his pastor for a time and was converted in 1738. Beginning at Yale the next year, he heard Ebenezer Pemberton preach on missions and the love of Christ. Brainerd resolved "to be wholly the Lord's, to be forever dedicated to his service."[1]

As a New Light and in favor of the revivals that visited Yale, Brainerd commented about a tutor that "he had no more grace than a chair." Expulsion followed, but he sought further study in theology, was licensed by the Congregationalists, and was sent by the Scottish Society for the Propagation of the Gospel to work with the Indians in Stockbridge. Here he preached to the Indians with great passion. Turning down a large and wealthy church on Long Island, he went on to minister to the Delaware Indians north of Philadelphia. He soon burned himself out for the Lord.[2]

Brainerd did live to see revival come to the Indians. Forty-three adults and forty-two children were converted. When his health broke down in 1746, he went to the Jonathan Edwards' home, where Edwards' daughter Jerusha, his fiancée, cared for him until his death at the age of twenty-nine. David's brother John took over his work. Jonathan Edwards wrote a famous account of his ministry. He preached with great power and said of his preaching,

> I have frequently been enabled to represent the divine glory, the infinite preciousness of the great Redeemer, the suitableness of His Person and purchase to supply the wants and answer the utmost desires of immortal souls; to open the infinite riches of His grace and the wonderful encouragement proposed in the Gospel to unworthy, helpless sinners; to call, invite and beseech them to come and give themselves to Him and be reconciled to God through Him; to expostulate with them respecting their neglect of One so infinitely love and freely offered; and this in such a manner, with such freedom, pertinency, pathos, and application to the conscience as I am sure I never could have made myself master of by the most assiduous application of mind.[3]

Brainerd was consumed with missions. Listen as he pours out his heart in prayer: "All things here below vanished and there appeared to be nothing of any importance to me but holiness of heart and conversion of the heathen to God."

The legacy of this incendiary can be traced to the impact his life made on Henry Martyn, William Carey, Adoniram Judson, Robert Murray McCheyne, Thomas Coke, Samuel Marsden, and many others.

Jonathan Edwards preached Brainerd's funeral sermon:

> How much is there, in particular, in the things that have been observed of this eminent minister of Christ, to excite us, who are called to the same great work of the gospel-ministry, to earnest care and endeavors, that we may be in like manner faithful in our work, that we may be filled with the same spirit, animated with the like pure and fervent flame of love to God, and the like earnest concern to advance the kingdom and glory of our Lord and Master, and the prosperity of Zion! Oh that the things that were seen and heard in this extraordinary person, his holiness, heavenliness, labour and self-denial in his life, his so remarkably devoting himself and his all, in heart and practice to the glory of God, and the wonderful frame of mind manifested in so stedfast a manner, under the expectation of death, and the pains and agonies that brought it on, may excite in us all, both ministers and people, a due sense of the greatness of the work we have to do in the world, the excellency and amiableness of thorough religion in experience and practice, and the blessedness of the end of such a life, and the infinite value of their eternal reward, when absent from the body and present with the Lord; and effectually stir us up to endeavors that, in the way of such a holy life, we may at last come to so blessed an end.[4]

---

1. Earle E. Cairns, *An Endless Line of Splendor* (Wheaton, Ill.: Tyndale, 1986), 245.
2. T. J. Bach, *Vision and Valor* (Grand Rapids: Baker, 1963), 34ff. See Philip E. Howard

Jr., ed., *Jonathan Edwards, The Life and Diary of David Brainerd* (Chicago: Moody, 1949).

3. F. R. Webber, *A History of Preaching in Britain and America* (Milwaukee: North-western, 1952), 3:109f.

4. D. Martyn Lloyd-Jones, *The Puritans: Their Origins and Successors* (Edinburgh: Banner of Truth, 1987), 370–71.

8.4.3 WILLIAM CAREY—GLOBALIZING MISSION

Neglecting my business! My business, sir, is to extend the kingdom of Christ. I only make and mend shoes to help pay expenses.

I would rather win to Christ the poorest scavengers in Leicester than draw off to Harvey Lane the richest members of your flock.

Having so little acquaintance with ministers, I was obliged to draw all from the Bible.

Preach the never-failing word of the cross. Do not be above sitting down to the patient instruction even of one solitary native.

—William Carey

William Carey (1761–1834) was the father of modern missions. Spending more than forty years in pioneer work in India, Carey inaugurated a whole new era.

He was heir to an evangelical ecumenism. Hailing from a schoolmaster/weaver's home in Northampton, he was "born on the tidal wave of the Wesleys and Whitefield."[1] He became a Baptist but sought the blessing of the Anglican John Newton before he sailed for Bengal.

From early on he had a hunger for spiritual reality.[2] But he had also read about Captain Cook's voyages in the South Pacific and always felt the "lure of the South Seas."[3] He cobbled and studied Greek with a map of the world before him. Carey's studies were ultimately included in his significant work, *An Enquiry into the Obligations of Christians, to Use Means for the Conversion of the Heathens.*

Carey married Dorothy Plackett and served village chapels, where he preached with much verve. He avidly read about Moravian missions in "the Pietist advance," but Eliot and Brainerd ignited the torch for missions within him. Edwards' works he could hardly lay down. John Erskine's concerts of prayer in Scotland touched him.

The ultra-Calvinist John Ryland Sr. rebuked him with the words, "Young man, sit down. When God pleases to convert the heathen, He will do it without your aid or mine."[4] But Carey chose to follow Andrew Fuller and Robert Hall. Fuller believed in the offer of grace to all through his study of the Scriptures, the examples of Eliot and Brainerd, and a study of Edwards. Hall's sermon, "Help to Zion's Travellers," made a deep impression on Carey. Hall argued, "The way to Jesus is graciously open for everyone who chooses to come to him."[5]

Carey's sermon to the Association at Nottingham on May 31, 1792, is one of the great sermons of history. Taking as his text Isaiah 54:2–3, Carey poured eight years of vision and passion into the message. Carey pressed God's appeal: "Get up, find larger canvas, stouter and taller poles, stronger tent-pegs. Catch wider visions. Dare bolder programs. Dwell in an ampler world." His application: "Expect great things from God. Attempt great things for God."[6] Out of this gathering came the commission and the call to India. Soon Carey and John Thomas were off, never intending to return.[7]

The platform for Carey's ministry was clear: "I have God and His Word is true!"[8] He supported his family by raising indigo, and he quickly mastered languages that made possible the translation of the Bible into six tongues, parts of the Bible into twenty-nine more, and the development of seven grammars and three dictionaries. Yet he testified, "Preaching the gospel is the very element of my soul."[9]

Carey preached half-hour sermons in two hundred villages, traveling about twenty miles a day during one stretch. He struggled with the Home Board for years, especially after Fuller's death. He also taught languages at Fort William College and combated infanticide and suttee (the practice of burning the widow of a deceased man on his funeral pyre).

The three thrusts of his ministry were to preach the gospel, translate the Bible, and establish schools.[10] Amid much personal anguish and suffering, Carey was steady and unflinching in his determination to see the vision through.

---

1. S. Pearce Carey, *William Carey, Fellow of Linnaean Society* (London: Hodder and Stoughton, 1923), 9. This standard biography is written by his great-grandson.
2. Ibid., 10.
3. Timothy George, *Faithful Witness: The Life and Mission of William Carey* (Birmingham, Ala.: New Hope, 1991), 20.
4. Ibid., 53.
5. Ibid., 57.
6. Carey, *William Carey,* 83.
7. Ibid., 139.
8. Ibid., 154.
9. Ibid., 165.
10. George, *Faithful Witness,* 173.

8.4.4   HENRY MARTYN—GIVING ALL

I prayed both before and after, that the Word might be for the conversion of souls, and that I might feel indifferent, except on this score.

O what a snare the public ministrations are to me.

—Henry Martyn

Out of the ferment and fire of the Great Awakening came the modern missionary enterprise. One of its great champions was the physically frail but spiritually hardy missionary to India and Persia, **Henry Martyn** (1781–1812).

Born in rugged Cornwall at Truro in the home of a former tin miner, Martyn was able to attend "the Eton of Cornwall" and went to St. John's College, Cambridge. There he took his B.A. and M.A. with highest honors, coming out as senior wrangler and first prizeman and earning a fellowship. While at Cambridge he came under the ministry of **Charles Simeon** and went on to be his curate. Simeon's parish, Holy Trinity Church, Cambridge, became a springboard for overseas missions.

Martyn helped found the Church Missionary Society, to whom he gave the challenge, "What can we do? When shall we do it? How shall we do it?" Martyn took his own challenge seriously, obtaining a position as chaplain for the East India Company. Ordained in 1803 in Ely, he left behind his lovely Lydia Grenfell, who stayed home when her mother refused to give her consent.[1] Martyn sailed for India in 1805.

First stationed at Dinapur, he gave himself to preaching to the English and mastering Hindustani. Webber observes, "His sermons attracted great attention and it was not uncommon for him to have eight hundred English people in his congregation."[2] Soon he was preaching to the nationals in their language.

Martyn became a close friend of William Carey. Upon his transfer to Cawnpur, he extended his ministry and translated the New Testament and *The Book of Common Prayer* into Hindi. One man who came to Christ under his preaching was to be the first Indian clergyman of the Church of England in India. Martyn soon translated the Scripture into Arabic and Persian, resolving to present a copy to the ruler of Persia.

In his diary, Martyn had exclaimed, "Now let me burn out for God." He undertook a journey by horseback to Persia and—he hoped—on to Constantinople. But his health was ravaged and his strength left him. He sent a message home urging, "Tell them to live more with Christ; to preach Christ; to catch His spirit, for the spirit of Christ is the spirit of missions. The nearer we get to Him, the more intensely missionary do we become." At the age of thirty-one, Henry Martyn died at Tokat in Persia.

---

1. George Smith, *Henry Martyn* (London: Religious Tract Society, 1892).
2. F. R. Webber, *A History of Preaching in Britain and America* (Milwaukee: Northwestern, 1952), 1:724–25.

8.4.5 ALEXANDER DUFF–GLORIFYING GOD

> We must pay more careful attention, therefore, to what we have heard, so that we do not drift away.
>
> —Hebrews 2:1

> For we also have had the gospel preached to us, just as they did; but the message they heard was of no value to them, because those who heard did not combine it with faith.
>
> —Hebrews 4:2

> Humbly accept the word planted in you, which can save you.
>
> —James 1:21b

Even in a time of doctrinal muddle and tension in the Scottish church, he was recognized not only as Scotland's first missionary but also as one of her greatest statesmen. **Alexander Duff** (1806–1878) was "one of the most convincing pulpit orators" of his age, a child of the revivals in "the finest flowering of missionary zeal in Scottish history." **Robert Murray McCheyne** said of him, "He kindles as he goes."

Duff was born in Moulin in the highlands of Perthshire. His father James, a farmer, was converted under the preaching of **Charles Simeon**. After nearly drowning in a swollen stream, Alexander came to trust in Christ's atoning blood and went on to St. Andrews to study in 1821. Here he came under the spell of **Thomas Chalmers** (cf. 9.1.3), whose lectures on moral philosophy were so enthralling that many students were too transfixed to take notes. Duff imbibed the story of Henry Martyn and consequently helped lead in the formation of a Missionary Society at St. Andrews.

As late as 1796, the Church of Scotland had turned down a proposal for a general collection for missions, but Chalmers and his student cohorts ignited a movement that led to an opening in India. The polarizing issue was the evangelical contention that "the preaching of morality without doctrine was insufficient."[1]

Chalmers' lectures instilled a deep conviction of God's love for those afar off. Chalmers conducted what amounted to an evangelistic laboratory for his students in which he led them in home visitation. "This is what I call preaching the gospel to every creature," he maintained.[2]

Duff and his fellows learned to give Bible expositions. In action, "six feet tall, ruddy of countenance, with a decided Scottish brogue," Duff preached the Word with great enthusiasm and excitement, his earnestness described as "apoplectic."[3] One of his most memorable addresses was as a young man of twenty-eight speaking to the General Assembly of the Church of Scotland—for three hours.

The death of a college friend, Urquhart, melted Duff. He surrendered to go to India. Ordained in 1829 at St. George's in Edinburgh, he sailed for Calcutta almost immediately. Latourette pays high tribute to the diverse missionary enterprises initiated by Duff.[4] The college he founded became the largest in India. Duff's mission strategy to win Hindu intellectuals was highly successful, and many high-caste Hindus came to Christ.

In 1843, the religious rift known as the disruption took place. It involved several issues, including patronage, but at its heart was the outgrowth of two entirely different theological tracks. The disruption forced the hand of Duff and the other missionaries, and they followed Chalmers to establish another college. By 1862, it boasted 1,723 students.

Duff's able preaching made his furloughs great times of rallying missionary motivation in the homeland. His best known sermon, "Missions the Chief End of the Christian Church," was widely heard and distributed. He addressed Parliament, and his visit to the U.S. in 1854 made an impact unlike any since

Whitefield's visits. When ill health required him to leave India permanently, Duff returned home to head up the missionary work of the Free Church and to become the first professor of missions at New College. Duff stands tall in the company of preachers.

---

1. Stuart Piggin and John Roxborough, *The St. Andrews Seven* (Edinburgh: Banner of Truth, 1985).
2. Ibid., 79.
3. F. R. Webber, *A History of Preaching in Britain and America* (Milwaukee: Northwestern, 1955), 2:364.
4. Kenneth Scott Latourette, *A History of the Expansion of Christianity: The Great Century, North Africa and Asia* (Grand Rapids: Zondervan, 1944, 1970), 6:116.

8.4.6 ROBERT MORRISON—GLOWING IN THE GLOOM

What peculiar fitness for the pulpit, qualifying me to commend myself to every man's conscience in the sight of God? With what stock of self-experienced texts and principles of inspiration am I entering this tremendous office? Has my soul ever tasted of the wormwood and the gall? What cords of infinite love have caught and held my heart? What oracles of heaven have I found and treasured up? Of what tests and truths could I now say, "I believe and therefore speak"? Say then, my conscience, as thou shalt answer at the judgment-seat of God; am I taking this honour to myself, or am I called of God as was Aaron? Is Christ sending me, and laying a necessity upon me to preach the Gospel? Am I thrusting myself into the office? Is He breathing on my soul, and causing me to receive the Holy Ghost? Is He enduing me with deep compassion to the souls of men and with a deep sense of my own unfitness?

I pant so much for the liberty to declare freely the unsearchable riches of Christ, and to teach fully the doctrines of the Christian religion, that I have often felt a wish to quit my present station and seek one less restricted.

—Robert Morrison

The father of Protestant missions to China, **Robert Morrison** (1782–1834), stood in the succession of Scots who were the heirs of the Great Awakening. He was born in humble circumstances; his family lived in one side of the house and the cow in the other. Ultimately the family, in which Robert was the youngest of eight, moved on to Newcastle in England.

The home was devout, and Robert's father became an elder in the High Bridge Presbyterian Church. Young Robert loved to study and knew Psalm 119 by memory at age twelve. As a boy, he played with George Stephenson of locomotive fame. Robert was converted at the age of fifteen, in a vivid, life-changing fashion.

The fear of death compassed me about, and I was led to cry mightily to God that He would pardon my sin, that He would renew me in the spirit of my mind. Sin became a burden. It was then that I experienced a change of life, and I trust a change of heart too. I broke off with my careless companions and gave myself to reading, to meditation, and to prayer. It pleased God to reveal His Son in me, and at that time I experienced much of "the kindness of youth and the love of espousals."

Young Morrison joined a prayer society. He mastered shorthand, which would be invaluable to him in future ministry, and learned Latin from the Rev. Adam Laidlaw. He attended Hoxton Academy and opened himself to the call of the London Missionary Society, either to Timbuktu or China.[1] He had a notable preaching mission in Newcastle in 1806, and set sail for China the next year.

Morrison translated for the East India Company but was restricted in his ministry. His duties placed him between Macao, where his family lived, and Canton, the great gateway city to China. Morrison turned down the opportunity to be a chaplain for the East India Company because it "would not afford him the opportunity of preaching the Gospel of Christ."[2] He carried on extensive correspondence with Carey and his coworkers at Serampore, all the while carrying on his translation work bolstered by the presence of a dear colleague, **William Milne,** who with his family joined the Morrisons in 1813.

Morrison initiated the Ultra-Ganges Mission, which did effective work in Malaya. In 1815 his family returned to England without him. He would not see them for six years.

Although Morrison shrank from publicity, he was increasingly known as the first China-scholar in Europe. In 1819 and the next year he completed the Old and New Testaments as well as a dictionary and catechism. But tragedies began to hound him, and Morrison took a furlough. He had never wavered from his commitment that "the end designed by the Missionary Society is to preach the Gospel to the heathen and convert the natives from Satan to God . . . to effect this end a knowledge of languages is an indispensable means."[3]

During his furlough, Morrison had contact with Edward Irving, Sir Walter Scott, and Dr. Adam Clarke as well as receiving the D.D. from Glasgow University. But his heart was in China, and he returned to Macao in 1826. White ants destroyed his library, yet he gave himself to preaching to Caucasians and Chinese and to the preparation of a Bible commentary in Chinese.

Though much maligned, Morrison gave himself unwaveringly to the task for twenty-five years, dying at his post. His life ended in his early fifties. Latourette observes, his body "had long been showing the effects of the adverse conditions but which the resolute will of its master had kept going until almost the very last."[4]

---

1. Marshall Broomhall, *Robert Morrison: A Master-Builder* (New York: George Doran, 1924); a fine sketch is also in J. Theodore Mueller, *Great Missionaries to China* (Grand Rapids: Zondervan, 1947), 39ff.

2. Broomhall, *Robert Morrison*, 68.

3. Ibid., 152.

4. Kenneth Scott Latourette, *A History of the Expansion of Christianity: The Great Century* (Grand Rapids: Zondervan, 1944, 1970), 6:299.

8.4.7   ROBERT MOFFAT—GROWING THE CHURCH

> I have tried to look upon those hands and those feet streaming with blood. I have tried to look on that thorny crown that encircled the sacred head of the Son of God. I have tried to hear his voice; I have read in the words of eternal truth what he said, and I believed that he was the Son of God, and the Saviour of the world. I believed that what he said was true when, as he left the sacred mount of Olives to ascend his mediatorial throne, he said: "Go ye into all the world, and preach the Gospel to every creature."
>
> —Robert Moffat in York Street Chapel, Walworth

Another case linking the preaching of the Great Awakening and the great century of missionary advance is the herculean career of **Robert Moffat** (1817–1870). Although one of his more modern biographers faults him for rigid theology and vanity, even he must concede that Moffat was the great pioneer missionary of southern Africa and that his many years of preaching, translating, and printing were signal years of gospel advance.[1]

Moffat was born in Ormiston, 26 miles from Edinburgh. His father was a ploughman and a member of the United Presbyterian Church. His mother read to him about Moravian missionaries in Greenland and Labrador. When he left home to take a position as a gardener in Cheshire in England, his mother admonished him to read his Bible twice daily. To the consternation of his parents he found great inspiration in a Methodist hall, and there was converted:

> One evening while poring over the Epistle to the Romans, I could not help wondering over a number of passages which I had read many times before . . . turning from one passage to another, each sending a renovation of light into my darkened soul. The Book of God, the precious undying Bible, seemed to be laid open, and I saw what God had done for the sinner . . . I felt that, being justified by faith, I had peace with God through the Lord Jesus Christ.[2]

He was particularly moved by the ministry of **William Roby**, pastor of Grosvenor Chapel, Manchester (Congregational), and a member of the board of the London Missionary Society. Lapping up Roby's formally Calvinistic lectures on theology (his only formal education), he felt the call to missionary service. Roby spoke from the premise of "the divine authority of Scripture," which became Moffat's watchword for a lifetime. His theory of preaching mirrored Roby's: the sermon and its "ideas, words, phrases and sentences" should be "simple" and in the language of the people.[3]

Moffat was commissioned at a service in Surrey Chapel on August 31, 1816, and then sailed for Capetown, Africa.[4] He was married in Africa to his sweetheart, Mary Smith, in 1819; she was his faithful wife and partner in ministry for fifty-three years.

Moffat was known as a peacemaker among warring tribes and found himself in the middle of the great Boer trek northward. He gave immense investment to the translation of Scripture into Bechuana, the first draft of which was finished in 1838. The gospel stories were easier than the Epistles. When Moffat introduced the word *epistole,* the native preachers confused it with the much more familiar *pistols.*

Preaching almost continuously, Moffat one evening found himself as the guest of a wealthy farmer who asked him to conduct a service of divine worship. Moffat asked where the servants were, to which the old man said:

> Hottentots! Do you mean that, then! Let me go to the mountain and call the baboons, if you want a congregation of that sort. Or stop, I have it: my sons, call the dogs that lie in front of the door, that will do.

Moffat then preached from the gospel text, "Truth, Lord, but even the dogs eat of the crumbs that fall from the Master's table." The landowner interrupted him after a few minutes and announced, "He shall have the Hottentots." In came the slaves, who had never been in the master's house or heard a preacher. Moffat continued preaching. When all had left, the old man said to Moffat, "My friend, you took a hard hammer and you have broken a hard head."[5]

Moffat did pioneer work in Great Namaqualand and saw revival come to Kuruman, where he headquartered for forty years and initiated a ministry among the Matabele, south of the Zambesi. He led several great chiefs to Christ, most prominent of whom was the great Moselekatse. A picture of Moffat preaching from a wagon to the chief's people is powerful.[6]

On one foray, a chief and his retinue confronted the Moffats with an ultimatum to leave the area. Moffat pulled his tall frame even taller and, with Mrs. Moffat standing in the doorway with her baby in her arms, spoke in ringing tones:

> If you are resolved to rid yourselves of us, you must resort to stronger measures, for our hearts are with you. You may shed blood or burn us out. We know you will never touch our wives and children. Then shall they who sent us know, and God, who now sees and hears what we do, shall know that we have been persecuted indeed.[7]

The chief before dispersing is reported to have said: "These men must have ten lives, since they are so fearless of death; there must be something in immortality."

At age seventy-four, Moffat retired to England. The following year his wife died. He continued to speak and shape thinking on missions.[8] When he died in 1883, *The Times* of London spoke of his ministry: "The Bechuanas became new men . . . a proof that the ground was not barren and that even in South Africa the good seed might be trusted to spring up and to bring forth abundant fruit. The progress of South Africa has been mainly due to men of Moffat's stamp."[9] Such is another validation of the power of biblical preaching.

---

1. Cecil Northcott, *Robert Moffat: Pioneer in Africa* (New York: Harpers, 1961); also see the tribute in Kenneth Scott Latourette, *A History of the Expansion of Christianity: The Great Century* (Grand Rapids: Zondervan, 1970), 5:345.
2. Ibid., 20.
3. John S. Moffat, *The Lives of Robert and Mary Moffat* (London: Unwin, n.d.), 18–19.
4. Northcott, *Robert Moffatt*, 34.
5. Moffat, *The Lives of Robert and Mary Moffatt*, 23–24.
6. Northcott, *Robert Moffatt*, 233.
7. Ethel Daniels Hubbard, *The Moffats* (New York: Friendship, 1917, 1944), 91.
8. Moffat, *The Lives of Robert and Mary Moffatt*, 156.
9. Northcott, *Robert Moffatt*, 329.

8.5 SOWING IN GRACE

The fires of the Revival had been kindled from heaven, and before the accession of George III the Congregational churches had caught the flame. Their ministers were beginning to preach with a new fervour, and their preaching was followed with a new success. The religious life of their people was becoming more intense. A passion for evangelistic work was taking possession of church after church, and by the end of the century the old meeting-houses were crowded; many of them had to be enlarged, and new meeting-houses were being erected in town after town, and village after village, in every part of the kingdom.

—Dr. R. W. Dale

Not only a resurgence of missionary outreach but many positive developments emerged from the Great Awakening (1726–1756) and the Second Evangelical Awakening (1776–1810). We shall trace the rise of the evangelical wing in the Church of England, to which the history of preaching has such indebtedness, and the revitalization of nonconformity.

A new freedom in ministry found expression[1] and a new concept of the Christian minister came into focus. The doctrines of sin[2] and of the Holy Spirit were treated biblically. Hymns and liturgy became part of the changing landscape in a new way. Bible societies were founded. Social sensitivity and concerns for justice were seen in the Clapham Sect. **Robert Raikes** (1735–1811) popularized the Sunday school. Training schools for ministry flourished. In the Baptist tradition, the heirs of **Benjamin Keach** (1640–1704) and **John Gill** (1697–1771) the commentator, or the young and controversial **Augustus M. Toplady** (1740–1778), who was converted listening to a Methodist preaching in a barn, display the scope and sweep of this mighty series of movings of the Spirit. We shall proceed now to examine some of these pulpit princes.

1. John S. Simon, *The Revival of Religion in England in the Eighteenth Century* (London: Robert Culley, n.d.), 288.

2. Ibid., 275. The duchess of Buckingham wrote to the Countess of Huntingdon: "I thank your Ladyship for the information concerning the Methodist preaching; these doctrines are most repulsive and strongly tinctured with impertinence and disrespect toward their superiors in perpetually endeavoring to level all ranks and do away with all distinction, as it is monstrous to be told that you have a heart as sinful as the common wretches that crawl on the earth. This is highly offensive and insulting, and I cannot but wonder that your Ladyship should relish any sentiments so much at variance with high rank and good breeding."

8.5.1 William Romaine—The Seed Which Is Sound

When I was about sixteen years of age, I heard Mr. Romaine preach a sermon in the city of Oxford, in which he advanced with great earnestness most of the principal gospel-doctrines. I was so completely exasperated at this mode of preaching, that I could have found it in my heart to have torn him to pieces. About ten days after under a sermon delivered by Dr. Hawes, my views of divine things, my sensations, the objects of my love and hatred, were all totally changed; and I cordially embraced and relished those very doctrines which before I detested and abhorred.

—Rev. Thomas Bliss, son of the professor of astronomy at Oxford

My Jesus hath contrived so much work for me in these parts, and he is so evidently and powerfully with us, that I cannot leave my neighbors, who crowd to hear far more than ever, and they are to me as my own soul. We are beyond all description happy in our lovely Lord. Such meetings I never knew—and twice a day—and many churches open. Oh! that I could but stay—I am so knit in heart to my neighbors and the most of them come and sit quietly to hear, that I know not how to leave them. But it must be.

—William Romaine of a visit to Hartlepool

At the heart of the revival was a proper view of Scripture and the gospel. As Bishop Ryle contends, "The instrumentality by which the spiritual reformers of the eighteenth century carried on their operations was of the simplest description . . . it was neither more nor less than the old apostolic weapon of preaching."[1]

They preached everywhere, they preached simply, they preached fervently and devoutly. A key figure in the movement was **William Romaine** (1714–1795). Born in Hartlepool in Durham of French Huguenot stock, he studied at a school founded by Bernard Gilpin (cf. 5.5.12) and then at Christ Church, Oxford. Romaine mastered the biblical languages, particularly Hebrew and the Hebrew Psalter, and sought to develop as a public speaker, even attending a performance of David Garrick "to improve himself in the graces of oratory."[2]

Early on, Romaine was high church and a Hutchinsonian (an obsessive fixation on Hebrew roots). All through his life he preached through the whole Bible with a particular love for the charms of the Old Testament. In dress he tended to be rough and careless, in habits fastidious and rigid, in temperament a Boanerges (like James and John, "sons of thunder"), controversial, aloof, lacking in personal warmth and friendliness. Yet he was an enormously effective preacher.[3]

Romaine experienced a spiritual crisis in which he was stripped of all of his familiar dependencies. He became more expository and devotional in his preaching and moved into the orbit of the Wesleys, Whitefield, the Countess of Huntingdon, and Henry Venn. Romaine married Mary Price in 1755; one son died in the military in Ceylon and another became a well-known preacher. Over a period of forty-five years of ministry, he was in and out of many London churches as a lecturer, becoming one of the most popular preachers in London. He even did a stint as a professor of astronomy.

Londoners were apprehensive about a possible French invasion and by the news of thirty-thousand fatalities in the Lisbon tidal wave. Romaine addressed their fears by preaching from Amos 4:12 on "Prepare to Meet Thy God," "An Alarm to a Careless World" and "The Parable of the Dry Bones" from Ezekiel 37. He understood the latter to speak primarily of the restoration of the Jews at the end of the age but secondarily as a figure of the need for revival in the church. In 1757 he issued his famous "An Earnest Invitation to the Friends of the Established Church for Setting Aside One Hour a Week for Prayer and Supplication During the Present Troublesome Times."

After Romaine preached in the Oxford University pulpit on "imputed righteousness," he was prohibited from preaching there again.[4] But his plain manners, coarse haberdashery, and introversion could not obscure his rich ministry in the Word nor deny him the post as "the leading pioneer Evangelical clergyman in the Church of England." He served as a chaplain for the Countess of Huntingdon and took many evangelistic tours. He deplored the increasing controversies between the Arminians of Wesley and the Calvinists of Whitefield, although he tilted toward the latter and as well to Sandeman's intellectual assent. Rowland Hill went to hear him preach and reported he had been fed "with the fat of the land."[5] The placid Newton felt Romaine veered close to antinomianism, but it was a time of polarization and extremes (among the worst of which was Madan's advocacy of polygamy).

Declining a call to Philadelphia, Romaine was appointed to St. Anne's, Blackfriars, where he labored for twenty-nine years. For a long time he was the only evangelical with a benefice in London. As Ryle asserts, in his ministry there he became "the rallying point for all in London who loved evangelical truth in the Church of England."[6] Within sight of St. Paul's and Westminster, he did not hesitate to take controverted stands, not always correctly, as on the Jewish Naturalization Act, or in the Gordon Riots where he and the Wesleys took opposite sides. Then there was his ill-advised "An Essay on Psalmody" (1775), in which he calls for the singing of the psalms only (something Romaine did not practice himself). John Newton expressed the wistful regret that the work had ever been published. Newton's coming to St. Mary Woolnoth greatly strengthened Romaine's ministry since this was a second pulpit for an evangelical in London.

Romaine enjoyed immense stature among conservative spiritual leaders in a mightily energized Church of England. So loyal was he to the established church that he would not preach in a dissenting setting. Davis claims that a chief asset of Romaine was his ability to preach doctrine interestingly and understandably. "To the amazement of the laity and the consternation of the clergy, he did not take it for granted that all who had been baptized in the Church of England were regenerated people."[7]

Not outward form but inward change was his insistence, with Christ crucified ever as his message. His delivered and printed sermons brought a great harvest of conversions. Such sermons as "A Method for Preventing the Frequency of Robberies and Murders," "A Discourse on the Self-Existence of Jesus Christ," and "The Duty of Watchfulness Enforced" suggest the burden of his heart. Romaine continued preaching four or five times a week until his death at eighty. He was greatly mourned in his passing. He is an important pillar in a growing edifice of vitality.

---

1. J. C. Ryle, *Five Christian Leaders* (London: Banner of Truth, 1960), 19.
2. Donald Gordon Davis, "The Evangelical Revival in Eighteenth Century England as Reflected in the Life and Work of William Romaine" (Ph.D. dissertation, University of Edinburgh, 1949), 19.
3. Ibid., 51.
4. Ibid., 105.
5. Ibid., 168.
6. Ryle, *Five Christian Leaders*, 76.
7. Davis, "The Evangelical Revival," 304.

8.5.2 WILLIAM JAY—THE SEED WHICH IS SPIRITUAL

The glorious Gospel of the blessed God our Saviour is the great object of our attention as minister and people; this only am I allowed to preach, this only are you allowed to hear. If you "hold the Head" you will not be "carried about by strange doctrines." A disposition for novelty in religious truth is the spring of error running through the flowery field of speculation into the gulf of apostasy. No system of doctrine will serve in the stead of that grace by which the heart is to be renewed and the life sanctified.

—William Jay

Some, like Romaine, were dedicated to seek renewal within the Church of England. Others, like the Wesleys, Whitefield, and the Countess of Huntingdon were determined to make every effort for such a rekindling but failed. Still others took the course of independency or dissent. Either their temperament or circumstances forced them to choose a separation. **William Jay** (1769–1853) exemplifies this course of action. For sixty-two years Jay served as pastor of the Argyle Chapel in Bath and was widely known as an expert exegete and expositor. He was born in a stonecutter's home in Salisbury and nurtured in a modest but pious context. Drawn by curiosity to Methodist preaching in his village and the announcement that "Christ Jesus came into the world to save sinners," he was wonderfully converted. He served as his father's apprentice for two years and then went on to study at an academy in Marlborough operated by a nonconformist minister. Soon after commencing study, he preached his first sermon at age sixteen at Ablington near Stonehenge from 1 Peter 2:3, "If so be ye have tasted that the Lord is gracious." His outline was simple but direct:

I. The Lord is gracious;
II. The best way to know this is to taste Him;
III. Such knowledge will have an influence.

He preached one thousand times before reaching the age of eighteen.[1] At nineteen he preached for Rowland Hill at Surrey Chapel in London and did so annually thereafter for fifty years. Throughout his life he was a relentless campaigner for total abstinence from alcohol.

Jay preached at several places until 1791, when he was ordained at Argyle Chapel in beautiful Bath. The chapel was twice enlarged to accommodate the audiences that wanted to hear the Word.[2] At Argyle, "the dipped and the sprinkled have dwelt in peace." Jay, although not physically robust, rose at 5 A.M. daily to study and pray and would seek before preaching to exercise out his nervous trepidations.[3] His desire was to come to the pulpit "anointed as with fresh oil."

He read widely with special interest in John Owen, Leighton, Newton, and Flavel. He was much involved in the outreach of the London Missionary Society and preached its annual sermon five times. In his preaching he confessed, "I always loved arrangement and division," and he dedicated himself to never preaching more than forty-five minutes.[4] He loved to preach and his audiences knew it. "Preaching has been the element of my heart and my head," he testified. In recognition of his solid ministry, Princeton bestowed an honorary degree on him in 1810. He was a textual preacher, not taking a long portion but staying within the parameters of that text. He was a moderate Calvinist and cherished fellowship in a wide circle of Bible-believing Christians.

Jay was especially close to Newton and Wilberforce, and his personal recollections of these worthies are a delight. He dined with and heard John Wesley. Joseph Parker paid him the tribute of saying that Jay "first and last kept to the Bible. He seemed to penetrate into its eternal meaning, and to apply that meaning to the immediate wants of the age."[5] His sermons were full of scriptural quotation and allusion. Sheridan spoke of his "manly oratory." Rowland Hill avowed that in preaching William Jay "blows the silver trumpet." One visitor from America claimed, "He seemed to chain each heart to his own and to draw the whole to the Saviour's feet."

1. William Jay, *The Autobiography of William Jay* (Edinburgh: Banner of Truth, 1854, 1974), 44.
2. F. R. Webber, *A History of Preaching in Britain and America* (Milwaukee: Northwestern, 1952), 1:451.
3. Jay, *Autobiography of William Jay,* 107. The collected works of William Jay run to fourteen volumes.
4. Ibid., 146.
5. Webber, *A History of Preaching,* 1:451.

8.5.3 ROWLAND HILL—THE SEED WHICH IS SCRIPTURAL

Preaching was indeed his element; it was an exercise necessary to the health and vigour of his mind, so that Mrs. Hill used frequently to say, in his declining years, "What I dread is, lest he should ever be so feeble as not to be able to preach—in that case, what would become of him I cannot tell."

—Edwin Sidney

If I may be permitted to drop one tear, as I enter the portals of the city of my God, it will be at taking an eternal leave of that beloved and profitable companion, repentance.

Of a preacher who knew the truth but hesitated to preach it fully: "He preaches the gospel as a donkey mumbles a thistle . . . very cautiously."

—Rowland Hill

We are looking at preachers whose preaching changed the course of a nation's history. As Wesley said of Grimshaw, we are looking at preachers whose lives made a nation tremble.[1] The same surely could be said of the saintly **Rowland Hill** (1744–1833). His father, Sir Rowland Hill, baronet of Hawkstone near Wales, was sheriff of Shropshire and a member of Parliament, as were two of Rowland Hill's brothers. The older Hill was a "zealous advocate of religious causes" and sent his son to Eton. The younger Hill was influenced by John Fletcher and William Romaine, and read Archbishop Leighton.[2] In fact, he was converted at Eton after reading a sermon by Bishop Beveridge. When Hill went up to Cambridge in 1764 he immediately began to preach and was zealous in ministry to the sick and imprisoned. He corresponded with Whitefield and loved John Berridge.

Because of his irregular preaching commitments, six bishops refused to ordain him as deacon. His father had grave reservations about his preaching to the colliers, as did John Wesley. Whitefield told him that "preaching should be part of the education of a student in divinity."[3] His style was "to present simple and forcible treatment of a scriptural text . . . lucid views of the doctrines of the gospel, mingled with sudden bursts of vivid, sublime and sometimes singular illustrations."[4]

After obtaining both his B.A. and M.A., Hill married. Soon he was ordained a deacon "without any promise or condition" by the bishop of Bath and Wells but was not allowed to proceed farther. He did take a curacy, but his preaching was more and more out of the loop of the established church. He "revived Whitefield's cause at the Tabernacle in Moorfields,"[5] and became known as an inspirational preacher who had a particular love for preaching to children and writings children's hymns.

In 1779 Hill founded the Surrey Chapel in St. George's Fields, a depraved neighborhood. Although open to ministers of all denominations, worship was conducted according to the ritual of the Church of England. Both organ and choir at Surry Chapel were outstanding. Hill fostered prodigious Sunday schools and pushed missionary concern, standing with the plate after a missionary day at the Surry Chapel. He was one of the first directors of the London Missionary Society, assisted in founding the Religious Tract Society, and was one of the anchors of the British and Foreign Bible Society. He preached for seventy years and was known for his powerful illustrations, his sublime images from nature, his high energy, and his powerful voice. He was generally opposed to long addresses but invariably gave vent to "bursts of eloquence" of an unusual quality.[6]

Rowland Hill had a propensity for humor. His *Village Dialogues* (chats on various practical issues) show him at his innovative best. As a moderate Calvinist, he was a great winner of souls, and had a spotless reputation for integrity and uprightness. Hill remained a thoroughly evangelical Anglican but was too broad in his churchmanship to be confined within the ecclesiastical straitjacket. He wanted his successor to be from the Church of England, but the search was difficult because Hill's solution to the ecclesiastical riddle did not fit any true loyalty to the established church. He died in his eighty-ninth year. His friend William Jay preached the funeral sermon out of Zechariah 11:2, "Howl, fir-tree, for the cedar is fallen." Jay had heard the old pilgrim singing as he walked through the chapel shortly before his passing:

> And when I die . . . receive me, I'll cry,
> For Jesus has loved me, I cannot tell why;
> But this I can find, We two are so joined,
> He'll not be in heaven and leave me behind.

Hill was a master craftsman, always drawing "his sermon fresh from a prayerful reading of the Bible."[7] A partisan of the view that "the fall must be preached as an introduction to the Gospel,"[8] Hill was heard in a variety of circles. Richard Sheridan said he went to hear Hill "because his ideas come hot from the heart."

Hill was an admirer of Thomas Chalmers and invited him to preach in his church. The Dean of Carlisle, **Isaac Milner,** went to Hill after a service to tell him: "Mr. Hill, Mr. Hill, I *felt* it today—'tis this slap-dash preaching, say what they will, that does all the good."

Once Lady Ann Erskine saw a crowd and hearing that Rowland Hill was preaching asked that the coachman drive near. Hill saw her and stopped in his discourse to deliver a quintessential Rowland Hill appeal.

"I have something for sale." The astonished listeners wondered of what he was speaking. "Yes, I have something for sale . . . it is the soul of Lady Ann Erskine. Is there anyone here that will bid for her soul? Ah, do I hear a bid? Who bids? Satan bids. Satan, what will you give for her soul? 'I will give riches, honor and pleasure.' But stop, do I hear another bid? Yes, Jesus Christ bids. Jesus, what will you give for her soul? 'I will give eternal life.' Lady Ann Erskine, you have heard the two bids—which will you take?" Lady Ann Erskine fell down on her knees and cried out, "I will have Jesus."

---

1. J. C. Ryle, *Five Christian Leaders* (London: Banner of Truth, 1960), 5.
2. Edwin Sidney, *The Life of the Rev. Rowland Hill* (London: Baldwin and Craddock, 1835), 14.
3. Ibid., 33.
4. Ibid., 74.
5. Ibid., 71.
6. Ibid., 205.
7. Ibid., 422.
8. Ibid., 443. We have only several complete sermons of Rowland Hill.

8.5.4 CHARLES SIMEON—THE SEED WHICH IS SPLENDID IN HARVEST

My endeavor is to bring out of the Scriptures what is true and not to trust in what I think may be there. I have a great jealousy on this head, never to speak more or less than I believe to the mind of the Spirit in the passage which I am expounding . . . I love the simplicity of the Scriptures and I seek to receive and inculcate every truth precisely in the way it is set forth in the sacred volume. . . . Reading one's own ideas into Scripture is not preaching God's truth.

I am willing that every part of God's Word should speak exactly what it was intended to speak . . . give every text its just meaning, its natural bearing and its legitimate use. . . . A screw is the most powerful of mechanical forces. The screw as it turns round again and again is forced deeper and deeper and gains such a hold that it is impossible to withdraw it. In my sermons the application is always another turn of the screw.

—Charles Simeon

While Romaine and Newton established an evangelical foothold in London and others sought to enhance evangelical strength in outlying areas, the most unexpected and far-reaching beachhead for evangelical advance was established and flourished in Cambridge under **Charles Simeon** (1789–1836). In fifty-four years of ministry at Holy Trinity Church in Cambridge, Simeon inaugurated what has been called "the Simeonite era of the Evangelical party."[1] The evangelical wing owed much to the Great Awakening (some have said "Methodism is the

Church of England felt"), for Methodists and Evangelicals shared the conviction that "the Bible is the supreme test of any doctrine."[2] Elliott-Binns assays the strength of evangelicals in every corner of England and sees them as those who hold to verbal inspiration, the centrality of conversion, the reality of heaven and hell, an understanding of satisfaction in the atonement, and the Reformation article of justification by faith alone.

Born in Reading, Charles Simeon was the fourth and youngest son of Richard Simeon, a prosperous attorney. At seven Charles Simeon went on to Eton, where there were some spiritual stirrings, and then on to King's College, Cambridge, at nineteen. Required to take communion, he read Bishop Wilson on the Lord's Supper, and concluded, "The Jews knew what they did when they transferred their sin to the head of their offering. . . . Accordingly I sought to lay my sins on the sacred head of Jesus."[3]

Simeon began instructing his father's servants when he was home, as he did the servants at King's College. He was ordained by the bishop of Ely in 1782 and served at St. Edwards, but longed for Holy Trinity Church. Through his father's influence, he obtained the appointment against the majority wishes at Holy Trinity. The parishioners locked their pews and the churchwardens locked the doors. For five years Simeon had very limited preaching. "I preached to bare walls," he said, and though the situation began to ease he had another five years of strenuous opposition. Believing that "the servant of the Lord must not strive," he gave himself to the improvement of his preaching and met in hired rooms for instruction classes.

In this time he discovered the French Huguenot Jean Claude (cf. 6.1.4), who convinced him to make his sermons more clear and to be more in illustration. "Write your own before you consult commentaries," Simeon would urge later.[4] In all of this, Simeon was, as Henry Venn observed, "exceedingly esteemed, exceedingly despised." As Charles Smyth remarked, "Simeon was almost the first man in the history of the English pulpit since the Middle Ages to appreciate that it is perfectly possible to teach men how to preach and to discover how to do so."[5] He had sermon parties every other Friday night and worked with students "to let the sermon come naturally from the text," he himself having "uncommon skill in arrangement."

While most Anglican preachers were Tillotsonian, Simeon gave thrust to biblical exposition. In the 2,537 sermon skeletons in *Horae Homileticae,* which is still in print, he attached Claude's lectures on preaching. His strategy was to avoid grammatical observations, critical observations, and historical and philosophical observations, and to advance discussion of the text through explication, observation, propositions, and perpetual application. His philosophy was to advocate unity in design, perspicuity in arrangement, and simplicity in diction. "The leading point of the passage is to be mainly regarded and subordinate parts only so far noticed as to throw additional light on the thought."[6] He put in on an average twelve hours per sermon.

Simeon regularly preached at the university in Great St. Mary's and began drawing large attendance at Holy Trinity. He instituted an evening service which was derided but quickly filled to overflowing. He was known for the discipline of his quiet time in which he found "marrow and fatness" for his own soul and the energy to preach. He practiced free style (extempore), believing that "there is a medium between such extemporaneous effusions and a servile adherence to what is written."[7] He preached with considerable zeal and fervor, "pounding the Scripture," as was said. He affirmed, "It is for the want of a good and impressive delivery that destroys the usefulness of a great proportion of pious ministers."[8]

Simeon's throbbing missionary passion was reflected in his curate, Henry Martyn. Simeon himself was one of the founders of the Church Missionary Society. He traveled hundreds of miles annually visiting pastors and preaching. He sought to preserve the established church. "Stay in the church," he counseled. There were secessions, but there would have been many more if Simeon had not been at Cambridge. Yet he would preach in Presbyterian churches or fill in for his friend John Fletcher of Madeley. He was also a friend of John Wesley, and felt there were extremes in both Calvinism and Armininism. A trenchant quote opens his view:

> The author is disposed to think that the Scripture system is of a broader and more comprehensive character than some very dogmatical theologians are inclined to allow; and that, as wheels in a complicated machine may move in opposite directions and yet subserve one common end, so may truths apparently opposite be perfectly reconcilable with each other and equally subserve the purposes of God in the accomplishment of man's salvation. The author feels it impossible to avow too distinctly that it is an invariable rule with him to endeavor to give to every portion of the Word of God its full and proper force, without considering what scheme it favours, or whose system it is likely to advance. Of this he is sure that there is not a decided Calvinist or Arminian in the world who equally approves of the whole of Scripture . . . who, if he had been in the company of St. Paul whilst he was writing his Epistles, would not have recommended him to alter one or other of his expressions.[9]

Simeon had a genius for problem-solving.[10] While there was a certain irritability in him, and he occasionally had great passions about small things, he was called the apostle by a great throng of admirers. He established a manufactory for the plaiting of straw as employment for the poor at Stapleford. He also had a great burden for the Jews, and spoke of "the absurd position of the non-restoration of the Jews."[11] Despite vacationing each summer in Scotland, he wore himself down by his pace. He preached his last Sunday morning sermon in his seventy-eighth year. Greatly weakened by a chill, Charles Simeon entered his rest on November 13, 1836. "Through evil report and good report he ceased not to preach Thy saving Word," as says the prayer quoted in King's College Chapel on the anniversary of his death. Simeon can rightly be called the father of modern evangelical homiletics.

---

1. L. E. Elliott-Binns, *The Early Evangelicals: A Religious and Social Study* (London: Lutterworth, 1953), 365.

2. Ibid., 385.

3. William Carus, ed., *Memoirs of the Life of the Rev. Charles Simeon* (London: J. Hatchard, 1847), 9. More recent and invaluable studies are H. C. G. Moule, *Life of Charles Simeon* (Chicago: InterVarsity Press, 1892), and Hugh Evan Hopkins, *Charles Simeon of Cambridge* (London: Hodder and Stoughton, 1977).

4. Ibid., 143. To this day Cambridge has lively churches (still including Holy Trinity) which feature expository preaching, N. B. Robert Benne, "Cambridge Evangelicals," in *Christian Century*, (October 27, 1933): 1036ff.

5. Charles Smyth, *The Art of Preaching: A Practical Survey of Preaching in the Church of England 747–1939* (London: SPCK, 1940), 175.

6. Carus, *Memoirs*, 532.

7. Ibid., 146.

8. Ibid., 685.

9. Quoted in A. M. Stibbs, *Understanding God's Word* (Chicago: InterVarsity Press, 1950), 36. Note also D. N. Samuel, ed., *The Evangelical Succession* (Cambridge, Mass.: James Clarke, 1979), 70ff.

10. Charles Smyth, *Simeon and Church Order: A Study of the Origins of the Evangelical Revival in Cambridge in the Eighteenth Century, The Birkbeck Lectures 1937–38* (Cambridge, Mass.: Cambridge University Press, 1940). Smyth also quotes Macaulay (1844): "If you knew what his authority and influence were, and how they extended from Cambridge to the most remote corners of England, you would allow that his real sway in the church was far greater than that of any primate," 7.

11. Carus, *Memoirs*, 635.

8.5.5 *THE TRIUMVIRATE: GRIMSHAW, BERRIDGE AND VENN—THE SEED WHICH IS STRONG*

They [the great evangelicals of the eighteenth century] gradually changed the whole spirit of the English Church. They infused into it a new fire and passion of devotion, kindled a spirit of fervent philanthropy, raised the standard of clerical duty and completely altered the whole tone and tendency of the preaching of the Ministers.

—William Lecky

Significant strides in evangelical advance were also made out on the hustings, as the case of **William Grimshaw** (1708–1763) clearly indicates. He was born in Brindle, Lancashire, attended Christ College, Cambridge on a scholarship because of his poor background, and served St. Mary's Chapel in Todmorden until 1742. There he drank too much and cursed in his reading for orders at Cambridge. The death of his wife and the suicide of a member sobered him with guilt, and he began to read the Bible and Owen on justification. This was his conversion. The clouds began to lift and the Bible became a new book to him. To Henry Venn he wrote:

I was now willing to renounce myself: every degree of fancied merit and ability: and to embrace Christ for my all in all. O, what light and comfort did I now enjoy in my soul, and what a taste of the pardoning love of God.[1]

In 1742 he was appointed to Haworth, a center of the combing industry in Yorkshire. (Haworth was where Rev. Patrick Bronte began his ministry in 1820 and where his daughter Charlotte wrote *Jane Eyre*.)[2] The powerfully built and colorful Grimshaw used marketplace language in reaching the uncouth and unpromising parish. The Haworth ministry was virtually defunct when he started with twelve communicants, but soon his effective pastoral skills and his powerful preaching were having effect. He wrote a friend about his launch in the primitive place:

> In that year our dear Lord was pleased to visit my parish. A few souls were affected under the Word, brought to see their lost estate by nature and to experience peace through faith in the blood of Jesus. My church began to be crowded, insomuch that many were obliged to stand out of doors. Here as in other places, it was amazing to see what weeping, roaring and agonies my people were seized with at their apprehension of the sinful state and the wrath of God.[3]

Grimshaw had a love for souls and was a giant in prayer. He had four special prayer times every day. It was said of him that he was a Calvinist on his knees and an Arminian on his feet. In doctrine "he was not numbered among the Calvinists" but held adamantly to a juridical view of the atonement.[4] In his powerful extempore prayers he took hold of the horns on the altar. He preached twenty to thirty times weekly. The fact that his parsonage was filled with Methodist preachers and that he sent his daughter to the Methodist School at Kingswood demonstrates the linkage between the Awakening and the evangelicals in the Church of England. Both Whitefield and John Wesley held meetings with him. Their strong desire was that the Methodists should not leave the church.

Grimshaw's preaching was legendary, though we do not possess any of his sermons. He was careful in dividing the text, and "He had a happy skill in teaching those around him spiritual lessons from the incidents of daily occurrence and the objects which were before their eyes."[5] He rebuked vice, and went into ale houses to haul people to the services. Little wonder that he was called Mad Grimshaw. Many of his "Timothys" became noncomformists, like John Fawcett who wrote "Blessed Be the Tie That Binds." Although he never preached in London, Grimshaw had Romaine as his dear friend and frequent pulpit supply. Fittingly, a Methodist minister preached Grimshaw's funeral service.

Another eccentric but vital part of this evangelical circle was **John Berridge** (1716–1793), who was so inept on his father's Nottinghamshire farm that his father threatened to send him to Cambridge to become "a light to the Gentiles." That is exactly what happened. If Berridge was a hapless farmer, he was a brilliant student, reading fifteen hours a day and using Greek and Latin like his mother tongue.[6] But through his first curacy and on into his thirty-eight-year ministry at Everton in Bedfordshire, he was not converted.

At the age of forty-two this all changed. Formerly his wit and cleverness carried him, but now he ceased reading manuscript sermons and began to preach Christ and justification. One thousand people with deep spiritual concerns visited him in his first year after conversion. Never married, he itinerated one hundred miles and preached a dozen times a week. He worked closely with Whitefield and the Wesleys. His message of justification by faith alone was so flaming that his bishop reprimanded him and threatened to imprison him, and would have except for the intervention of William Pitt. The "phenomena" were present in the great revival which came to Everton.[7]

John Berridge had immense influence on Rowland Hill. When Berridge had exhausted his resources in ministry, William Romaine "begged on his behalf."[8] His preaching had a "rustic homeliness." His main points were boldly underlined. Tall and thin in appearance, he had an iron constitution, but at the end he was alone, blind, and deaf. Yet Berridge testified, "Lord, if I have thy presence and love, that sufficeth."[9]

Simeon preached Berridge's funeral sermon and six clergy, including the Venns, carried the casket. We again witness quite an unusual confraternity of preachers of the gospel! All of the movers in the revival came to visit Everton, including John Wesley and the Countess of Huntingdon. On Berridge's grave were words of characteristic testimony:

> Here lie the earthly remains of John Berridge: Late Vicar of Everton, and an itinerant servant of Jesus Christ, who loved his Master and His work, and after running on his errands many years was called to wait on Him above.
> Reader: Art thou born again? No Salvation without New Birth![10]

Still another figure in this firmament was **Henry Venn** (1724–1797), who came from seven generations and 230 years of evangelical clergy testimony. Webber insists he must be included in a list of the ten greatest English preachers of the eighteenth century.[11] Venn had an excellent academic career at Cambridge, where he was known for his prowess at cricket. He was much taken with William Law but in danger of a fixation on works righteousness. Thus the Countess of Huntingdon wrote him:

> Oh my friend, we can make no atonement to a violated law; we have no inward holiness of our own; the Lord Jesus Christ is "the Lord our righteousness." Cling not to such beggarly elements, such filthy rags, mere cobwebs of Pharisaical pride; but look to him who hath wrought out a perfect righteousness for his people . . . now, my dear friend, no longer let false doctrine disgrace your pulpit. Preach Christ crucified as the only foundation of the sinner's hope. Preach him as the Author and Finisher as well as the sole Object of faith, that faith which is the gift of God. Exhort Christless sinners to fly to the City of Refuge.[12]

God used this correspondence to change Venn's preaching. He served in Clapham (1754–1759), and then up in Huddersfield for twelve years, where he preached

6,250 sermons to "the rough and ignorant weavers of Yorkshire."[13] Whitefield said of his preaching, "The worthy Venn is valiant for the truth, a son of thunder." So many came to hear Venn that he had to preach outdoors. He sent twenty-two men into the ministry. He had a dynamic impact on the whole community, like McCheyne's in Dundee. Marcus Loane observed, "Few parish ministers in English history have so moved and shaken town and county by the simple act of preaching."[14] In preaching, Venn often looked as if he were about to jump out of the pulpit. Ryle asks rhetorically, "Who can deny the immense effect of good delivery?"[15]

Venn's health finally broke at Huddersfield, and he took the charge at Yelling near Cambridge in 1771. Here he finished out his active ministry. Every Tuesday, he and Simeon would dine at Berridge's. His devotional writings and his preaching made a memorable mark. Venn felt he had "always been too much on the side of free grace for many Arminians and too much on the side of experimental religion for many Calvinists." At the suggestion of Charles Simeon, Venn organized the Church Missionary Society in 1799.

Henry Venn's son, John, was rector of Clapham (1759–1813). In turn, John's son, Henry, was a gifted and powerful preacher who served parishes with distinction, counted Thomas Chalmers as one of his closest friends, and who in 1846 became the CEO of the society.[16] He was a visionary and eminent missions statesman, and lived with his son, John, who was rector at Mortlake, in his last year. To his great anguish, he saw his son become doubtful about the supernatural and in 1864 break with the evangelicals. His father, Henry, had keen interest in the revival of 1859 and died in 1873. Much earlier when Cowper heard that old Henry Venn was very ill, he wrote Newton in 1791, "I am sorry that Mr. Venn's labors below are so near to a conclusion . . . I should envy him and Mr. Berridge and yourself, who have spent, and while they last, will continue to spend your lives in the service of the only Master worth serving. Labouring always for the souls of men, and not to tickle their ears as I do."[17] What a succession of preachers! The fruit of it all will be seen in the next century and in our own.

---

1. George G. Cragg, *Grimshaw of Haworth: A Study in Eighteenth-Century Evangelicalism* (London: Canterbury, 1947), 15.
2. For recent treatments of Rev. Patrick Bronte and his family, see Juliet Barker, *The Brontes* (New York: St. Martin's, 1994), a comprehensive work; Lyndall Gordon, *Charlotte Bronte: A Passionate Life* (New York: Norton, 1995). Bronte adapted to the church where the pulpit dominated the altar. Although "a little peculiar in his manner," Bronte developed "the assurance to preach without notes."
3. Cragg, *Grimshaw of Haworth*, 22.
4. Ibid., 70.
5. Ibid., 59.
6. J. C. Ryle, *Five Christian Leaders* (London: Banner of Truth, 1960), 120.
7. For a balanced and open address to the issue of the phenomena, see D. Martyn Lloyd-Jones, *The Sovereign Spirit: Discerning His Gifts* (Wheaton, Ill.: Harold Shaw, 1985).
8. Edwin Sidney, *The Life of the Rev. Rowland Hill* (London: Baldwin and Cradock, 1835), 56.

9. Ryle, *Five Christian Leaders,* 130.

10. Ibid., 132.

11. F. R. Webber, *A History of Preaching in Britain and America* (Milwaukee: Northwestern, 1952), 1:401.

12. Ryle, *Five Christian Leaders,* 158–59.

13. Earle E. Cairns, *An Endless Line of Splendor: Revivals and their Leaders from the Great Awakening to the Present* (Wheaton, Ill.: Tyndale, 1986), 64.

14. Marcus L. Loane, *Cambridge and the Evangelical Succession* (London: Lutterworth, 1951), 134.

15. Ryle, *Five Christian Leaders,* 177.

16. Wilbert R. Shenk, *Henry Venn: Missionary Statesman* (Maryknoll, N.Y.: Orbis, 1983).

17. George Melvyn Ella, *William Cowper: Poet of Paradise* (Durham, N.C.: Evangelical Press, 1993), 428.

8.5.6 ANDREW FULLER—THE SEED WHICH IS SPREAD

Carey, as it were said, "Well, I will go down if you will hold the rope."

One thing in particular I would pray for; namely, that I may not only be kept from erroneous principles, but may so love the truth as never to keep it back. O Lord, never let me, under the specious pretence of preaching holiness, neglect to promulgate the truths of Thy Word; for this day I see, and have all along found, that holy practice has a necessary dependence on sacred principle. O Lord, if Thou wilt open mine eyes to behold the wonders of Thy Word, and give me to feel their transforming tendency, then shall the Lord be my God. Then let my tongue cleave to the roof of my mouth, if I shun to declare, to the best of my knowledge, the whole counsel of God.

I preached a sermon to the youth last Lord's Day: For what is our hope, or joy, or crown of rejoicing? Are not even ye in the presence of our Lord Jesus Christ at His coming? For ye are our glory and our joy. I think I must have had nearly a thousand. They came from all quarters. My heart's desire and prayer for them is that they might be saved.

—Andrew Fuller

"The pulpit is an awful place; we preach for eternity." So wrote **Andrew Fuller** (1754–1815) in his diary. Raised and ministering his whole life among the Strict or Particular Baptists, Fuller was a great soul with a large vision. He was reared among the fens in a rural setting but early discovered and loved books. Highly athletic, he wrestled and skated with the best of them. Converted at fifteen, he was early embroiled in controversies generated by the hyper-Calvinism in his home church of Soham near Ely. At twenty-one he began to serve the church, and souls were saved. The shackles of hyper-Calvinism undercut the validity of the universal call. The issue was: can the preacher appeal to people to come to Christ? The old diehards denied that souls should be called to repentance and faith.[1]

Called and ordained in 1775, Fuller preached to his small congregation of about forty with great faithfulness. The disunity in the church discouraged him, and he became sick and almost died.[2] He studied the Scriptures to gain a proper theology. His motto was "Never be an imitator." Out of his agonies came his widely-read book, *The Gospel Worthy of All Acceptation,* in which he argues that it is not a matter of cannot but a matter of will not.[3] After two years of struggling with the call to move to Kettering in 1782 he took the charge in there, where he ministered for thirty-three years. He gained a wide reputation as a preacher-theologian, often being called the apostle Fuller.

Although a constant visitor among his people, Fuller was best-known for his Sunday morning expository preaching. He covered most of the Bible in his ministry. Sunday evenings and on special occasions he preached topically or textually. Pattison adjudges, "He had not the finish of Foster nor the splendour of Hall, but his simple and vigorous style expressed simple and vigorous thought."[4] Thomas Chalmers came to hear him, and, after sensing Fuller's freedom, resolved never again to preach from notes.

Fuller became a founder of the Baptist Missionary Society (cf. 8.4.3), and was the prime mover behind William Carey and the India Mission. Carey's crucial *Enquiry* really rose out of Fuller's *The Gospel Worthy.* Even with the death of his wife and many of his children, Fuller traveled widely for the mission, making five trips to Scotland, where he met and enjoyed the largess of the wealthy Haldane brothers.

Like many others, such as Charles Simeon, the Haldanes, Thomas Chalmers, and Rab Duncan, Fuller had a special love for the Jewish people and saw spiritual significance for them in the future.[5] He wrote a weighty challenge to deism and rationalism titled *The Gospel Its Own Witness.* This was the volume Wilberforce had on his table when William Pitt came to visit him.[6] Virtually unschooled, Fuller received honorary doctorates from Yale and Princeton. When Fuller passed on, Robert Hall the younger preached the funeral service. Augustus Hopkins Strong's *Systematic Theology* makes thirteen references to Andrew Fuller. Spurgeon, who himself was accused of Fullerism, called him "the greatest theologian of the century."[7]

---

1. Gilbert Laws, *Andrew Fuller: Pastor, Theologian, Ropeholder* (London: The Carey Press, 1942), 20.

2. Ibid., 34.

3. William Rushton, *A Defense of Particular Redemption: Wherein the Doctrine of Andrew Fuller Relative to the Atonement of Christ Is Tried by the Word of God* (Elom College, N.C.: Primitive Publications, 1831). The fact that the Primitive Baptists are still publishing this work indicates that the issue is far from settled for some.

4. T. Harwood Pattison, *The History of Christian Preaching* (Philadelphia: American Baptist Publication Society, 1903), 287.

5. Iain Murray, *The Puritan Hope* (London: Banner of Truth, 1971), 154ff.

6. Laws, *Andrew Fuller,* 94.

7. Ibid., 127. For a bit of a personal sense, see "Andrew Fuller's Text" in F. W. Boreham,

A Bunch of Everlastings (New York: Abingdon, 1920), 235ff. We shall meet Boreham as a preacher in his own right, but his sketches on the great texts of servants of Christ are outstanding, as are all of his essays which had amazing circulation and are now being reprinted by Kregel Publications in Grand Rapids.

8.5.7 ROBERT HALL—THE SEED WHICH IS SUFFICIENT

He always began with a prayer (sometimes of considerable length) uttered with great earnestness and simplicity, but injured in effective power from an apparent asthmatical difficulty of articulation. There was the same constitutional or organic difficulty in the commencement of his sermons. But the breathing of his sentences became more easy as he advanced, and before long there was a moral grandeur in his delivery which triumphed over all organic defect or physical weakness. While he rolled out his beautiful and purely constructed sentences one felt as if under the training of a higher nature. In occasional flights of imagination, in discussion of metaphysical subtlety, we were for a while amazed and almost in fear for the preacher. And then he would come down, with an eagle's swoop, upon the matter he had in hand, and enforce it with a power of eloquence such as I never felt or witnessed in the speaking of any other man. Such is my feeling now. Many a long year has passed away since I last heard Robert Hall. I have listened with admiration to many orators in the two Houses of Parliament, and to many good and heart-moving preachers, but I never heard one who was in my mind on the same level with Robert Hall.

—Prof. Adam Sedgewick

Robert Hall (1764–1831) was a most unusual preacher. Born into a minister's family in Arnesby, Leicestershire, his godly father, the elder Robert Hall, authored the well-known *Help to Zion's Travelers*. An inveterate reader from very early, he had read Edwards *On the Will* and Butler's *Analogy* by age nine. He attended Rylands' School in Northampton and there was exposed to massive doses of Latin, Greek, and rhetoric.

But Robert was virtually an invalid from childhood, which did not allow him to sit while studying, so he lay on the floor for hours. His breathing was often irregular. Despite his health problems, he preached an ordination sermon when he was sixteen, duly impressing the many ministers present.[1]

Hall studied at King's College, Aberdeen, taking his degree in 1784. Following that he assisted Dr. Evans at the Broadmead Church (Strict Baptist) in Bristol. He was much taken with the preaching of **Robert Robinson** (1735–1790), a young barber who had been converted under the preaching of Whitefield. Robinson had gone on to become pastor of a small Baptist church in Cambridge which grew exponentially. We know Robinson as the translator of Jean Claude's *Essay on the Composition of the Sermon* and the author of the hymn "Come Thou Fount of Every Blessing." Robinson followed his mentor **Joseph Priestly** into heterodox views on inspiration, the atonement, and the Trinity. Young Hall took Robinson's place in 1790, and endeavored to imitate the somewhat stilted form. The death of his own father sobered him,[2] and he left this bondage and also his addiction to the model of Dr. Samuel Johnson's "tea-table talk."

Hall began to preach the Bible and the historic faith with confidence. His sermons started slowly but built momentum. He elucidated profound truths simply and clearly. Hall would sometimes stop for a brief time of prayer before launching into the application of the sermon.[3] **John Foster** (1770–1843), who was himself a gifted preacher, evaluated the preaching of his good friend Robert Hall as being unusually imaginative and carefully prepared.[4]

Exhausted by his regimen, the frail Hall suffered a total physical and emotional collapse in 1805 and had to leave Cambridge. He drew closer to the Lord during this trying time, and soon articulated his famous "An Act of Solemn Dedication of Myself to God." He regained his strength and took the call to Harvey Lane, Leicester, in 1807 and then in 1826 the charge at Broadmead in Bristol.

Hall was a moderate Calvinist who believed in general redemption. He called Gill's formulations "a continent of mud" (Gill was a strict Baptist of great rigidity). His sermons were long, but he carried his audience with him through the sheer attraction of truth powerfully stated through the Spirit. The two most-remembered of his sermons were topical (a testimony to the power of relentless unity): "Modern Infidelity Considered" and "The Death of Princess Charlotte," from Jeremiah 15:9, "She hath given up the ghost; her sun has gone down while it is yet day."[5]

His sermon in the *Collected Works* on "The Lamb of God—His Character—His Sacrifice—and His Claim to Universal Attention" from John 1:35, 39 is Christocentric and evangelistic, taking as its central idea, "The justice of the Deity, not to be propitiated by any other means, pursues the transgressor on earth and in hell; nothing in the universe can arrest it in its awful career, until it stops in reverence at the cross of Christ!"[6] Likewise his messages on "The Joy of Angels over a Repenting Sinner," from Luke 15:7, and "The Glory of Christ's Kingdom" from Psalm 145:11 are ripe and rich discourse.[7] Professor Bebbington calls Hall "the most powerful of early nineteenth-century English preachers" and cites his greatest sermon as evidence, which was "a defence of the principle of the substitution of the innocent for the guilty."[8]

How do we correlate the uniqueness of this able preacher with his life experience and the power of God along the journey? What varied instruments God uses in all ages!

---

1. Olinthus Gregory, ed., *The Works of Robert Hall* (London: Henry C. Bohn, 1841), 6:8.

2. Ibid., 6:30.

3. Ibid., 6:56.

4. Ibid., 6:144, 150, 156.

5. E. C. Dargan, *A History of Preaching* (New York: George H. Doran, 1912), 2:502.

6. Gregory, *The Works of Robert Hall,* 6:300.

7. Ibid., 6:356ff., 123ff.
8. D. W. Bebbington, "Evangelical Christianity and the Enlightenment," in *Crux* 25:4 (December 1989): 30.

Printed in the United States
63910LVS00002B/103

9 780825 430855